Loving Sex
A Lifetime Guide

Loving Sex

A Lifetime Guide

Dr. Philip Cauthery and
Doctors Andrew and Penny Stanway

STEIN AND DAY/*Publishers*/New York

First published in the United States of America in 1984

Copyright © 1983, 1984, by Dr. Philip Cauthery and
Doctors Andrew and Penny Stanway

All rights reserved, Stein and Day, Incorporated

Designed by Mushroom Production London
Illustrations by Barrie Thorpe, Lydia Malim, Ann Savage

STEIN AND DAY/*Publishers*
Scarborough House
Briarcliff Manor, N.Y. 10510

Library of Congress Cataloging in Publication Data

Cauthery, Philip.
  Loving sex.

  Includes index.
  1. Sex. I. Stanway, Andrew. II. Stanway, Penny.
III. Title.
HQ21.C443   1984   306.7   83-40582
ISBN 0-8128-2968-9

Acknowledgements.

We are grateful to the following people for permission to use the photographs in this book: Vision International (page 169). Multimedia/Vision International (page 62). Anthea Sieveking. Vision International (pages 9, 16, 18, 23, 34, 173, 174-5, 204, 263, 285, 298-299, 302, 309, 313, 314, 404, 420). R. Sidney, Vision International (pages 412-413). M. Koren, Multimedia/Vision International (page 25). Paolo Koch/Vision International (page 315). A Orbach, Multimedia/Vision International (1 jacket photo, page 146). Fiévet, Vision International (page 348 top left). Joffre, Vision International (page 348 top right). Clement, Vision International (page 349 top). P Ribieras, Vision International (pages 348-9 bottom). Mushroom Production London (page 58). Popperfoto (pages 10, 13, 53, 89, 100-1, 356-7, 428-9). Family Planning Association (page 251). Gay News Ltd (pages 364, 365). Professor Tanner (page 39). Pictor (page 422). Rex Features Ltd (pages 42, 376, 391). Stockphotos International (2 jacket photos, title page, pages 46-7, 55, 66, 424-5). Syndication International Ltd (pages 63, 360-1). Tony Stone Associates London (page 103). David Bradfield (pages 114, 115, 116, 117, 118, 195, 224, 225, 226). D Anthony (pages 156, 158 top right and bottom). Dr Shettles (page 266).

Contents

INTRODUCTION 8

1 BABY AND CHILDHOOD SEXUALITY 15

2 EARLY ADOLESCENCE 30

3 MID- AND LATE ADOLESCENCE 41

4 SEXUAL ATTRACTION 49

5 SEXUAL ENCOUNTERS 60

6 WHO'S BEST? 71

7 COURTSHIP 79

8 ENGAGEMENT 87

9 ROMANCE 98

10 MARRIAGE AS A RELATIONSHIP 106

11 MARRIAGE AS A WAY OF LIFE 121

12 MARRIAGE, DIVORCE AND SOCIETY 136

13 SOME SEXUAL ANATOMY 150

14 SEX DIFFERENCES 166

15 COPULATION 177

16 FOREPLAY (LOVEPLAY) 186

17 INTERCOURSE 201

18 LOVING BEHAVIOUR 221

19 SEXUAL DIFFICULTIES 229

20 CONTRACEPTION AND PLANNING A FAMILY 247

21 CONCEPTION AND INFERTILITY 265

22 ABORTION 280

23 PREGNANCY AND CHILDBIRTH 284

24 OTHER PEOPLE'S CHILDREN 308

25 TEACHING CHILDREN ABOUT SEX 312

26 MASTURBATION 329

27 SEXUAL MORALS 339

28 MATURITY 351

29 HOMOSEXUALITY 359

30 SEX-RELATED DISEASES 367

31 PROSTITUTION 374

32 AM I ODD? 380

33 SEX AND HEALTH 397

34 SEX IN OLD AGE 409

35 LOVE 418

INDEX 435

Loving Sex A Lifetime Guide

Introduction

Sexuality is a vast subject covering many fields of study. Genitality, with which it is usually confused, is only a small part of it, yet sex books and sex education tend to deal almost entirely with genitality.

This is understandable because the anatomical differences between the sexes, and especially the genital differences, are the subject of endless fascination and interest from childhood onwards. In our western culture we put so many prohibitions on interest in our genitals and genitality that there is a danger of becoming absorbed with the topic to the exclusion of the more important aspects of sexuality in our relationships and lives.

Men and women are highly complex physical, emotional and psychological beings and to ignore the love, the feelings and the relationships that go hand in hand with genitality is like driving a car with only one wheel. The result is the same—a dangerous imbalance. For many people the sexual aspects of their lives are less fulfilling than they should or could be and they end up passing on their hang-ups, wrong perceptions and misunderstandings about sex and sexuality to their children.

As a culture we try to overcome our natural interest in but unnatural emphasis on the genitals by talking a lot about love, and most readers would agree that if men and women could love each other perfectly the world would be a very different place. In a sense if we can love another human being perfectly we are half-way towards loving everyone, and the world needs love more than ever before. The sort of love we need is not the vague love that teenagers feel for all mankind but rather a mature, practical and real love for one another.

Real love is in short supply and many people, because of their upbringing, do not love themselves enough to be able to love another person. Yet others love themselves so much that they are unable to allow another person to intrude in any significant way. Men and women in all kinds of relationships often feel they do not love each other very much and some even hate each other. Some men dislike all women and some women, all men. What a terrible state of affairs to have got ourselves into in a society that should be based on love.

Unfortunately, the man-woman relationship has many enemies. To the extent that the state or religions demand that their interests be given prior consideration, and that the man–woman relationship itself should be governed by them, they intrude on and

Being loved: To be born welcome and wanted is the greatest gift any child can have.

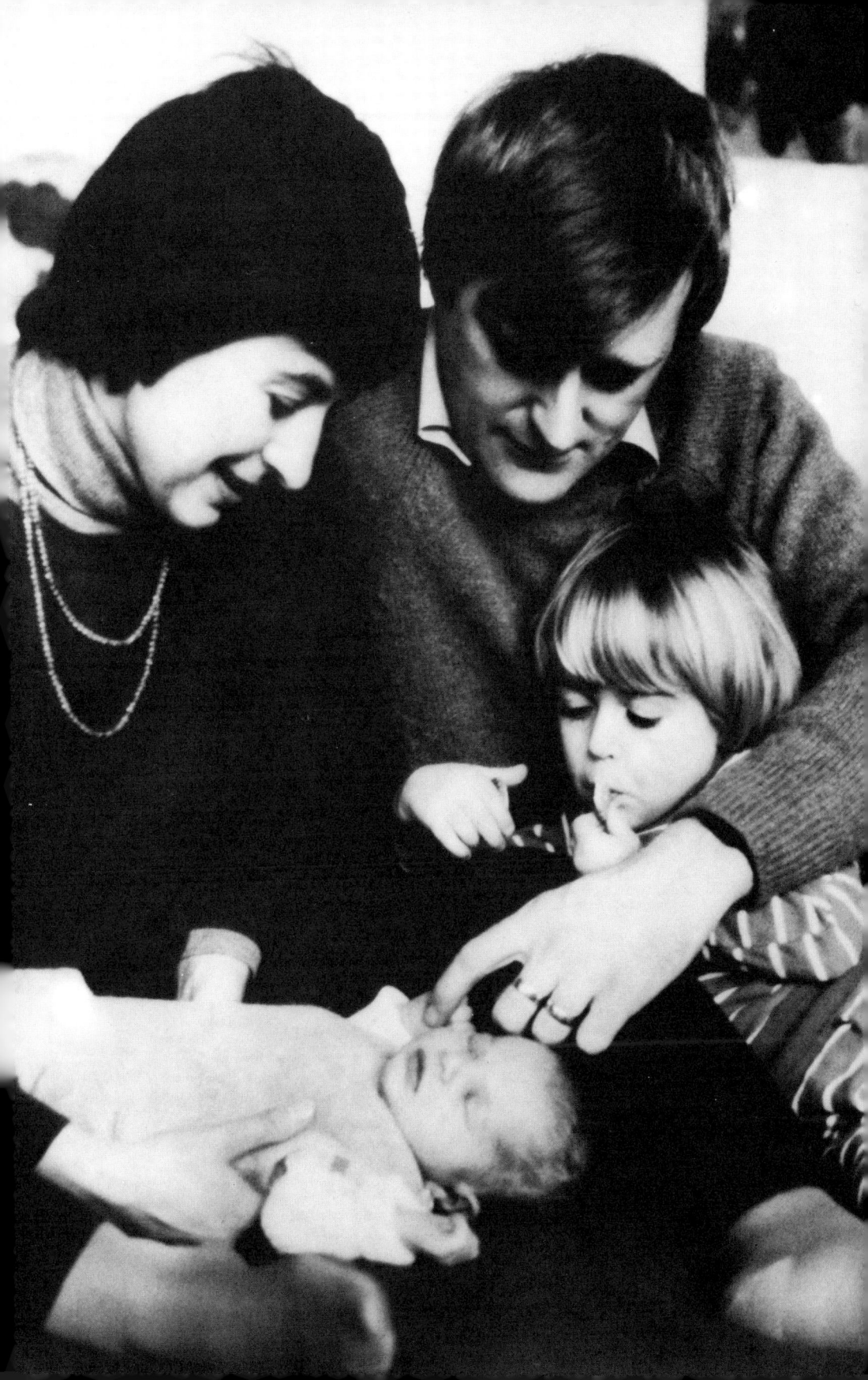

may even damage the relationship. Both, of course, do so 'accidentally' under the guise of trying to further the relationship.

In fact, for a supposedly caring society based on Judaeo-Christian morals, we seem to be doing rather badly in this area. Premarital pregnancies and VD are on the increase in spite of efforts to curb them; over a third of marriages end in divorce; more than a tenth of all children live in one-parent families; most parents have problems in dealing with their teenagers' emerging sexuality; and depression, the most widespread psychological illness of our society, is not only commoner than ever but often has a psychosexual basis. There is certainly no room for complacency. But what can the average family hope to do to redress the balance?

Obviously the only way to change things is to shield our children from the negative cultural influences that we suffered, but this is not easy because we as parents are steeped in them.

What we shall do in this book is look at love and sex from the cradle to the grave and, with the benefit of knowledge of both family and psychosexual medicine, weaving a picture of interlinking complexity that shows how a child grows up to become a sexual person. We then follow this person through life and look at other major milestones along the way. The subject is enormous and we have drawn on research from all over the world to add to our own clinical experience. After all, no one person can have seen it all and, in the final analysis, everyone is different.

We have tried to make the book comprehensive rather than encyclopaedic and each chapter could easily have been extended to a book in its own right. Because we have had to be brief on very important subjects we have tried to concentrate on what families most want to know and have tried to be as practical as possible. After all unless you have had a wide experience of teenagers and talked to them about their intimate fears, problems, loves, hates and aspirations you can't really know how your own child fits into the picture of 'normality'. Many parents end up feeling hopelessly confused, especially in our fast-changing world.

Being a parent is probably more difficult today than ever before because the conflicts within society are so great, and the last thing that most parents need is yet another sex manual to tell them and their family how to behave genitally. We have tried to cover the subject of love and sex in the widest possible way, based on our (and others') clinical experience, which repeatedly confirms that although sex *can* help cement a relationship in troubled times the reverse—that genital sex looks after itself in a good relationship—seems to be even more true. Many people with so-called sex problems have personality or interrelationship problems deep down—the sex problem is simply the obvious symptom of which they complain.

When we announced our intention of writing a book in this area we were inundated with questions from all kinds of people about the need for, scope of and even the wisdom of a book about sex and love aimed directly at the family. Perhaps the best way of tackling some of these questions, which may even be of concern to you the reader, would be to answer them here.

'Yes, I love you more than ever. With effort and a little luck, love can increase year by year.

Why another sex book?

Because many sex books concentrate on people as if all that mattered were their genitals. This is ill-advised. Physical sex has been greatly over-emphasised in modern Western society. The mood is now right for a book that looks at sex and sexuality in a wider context and this involves concepts of reason, loving, caring and togetherness. Far too many books have emphasised the 'I'm the most important person in the world' approach to the subject. Love and sex in reality involve other people's lives and do so very intimately.

Why a family book of love and sex?

Because our individual sexuality starts to express itself the day we are born. We need to understand the sexual components of life from birth to old age so that we can be more effective, happy and fulfilled human beings and parents and prevent our children from suffering from many of the problems we have as adults. We all want what is best for our children yet which of us is equipped to provide it in today's changing and complex society?

Surely there's enough talk about sex already?

Yes, there is but there is far too little talk about the way the modern family can cope with its sexuality in a genitally-obsessed society and how parents can stop *talking* and get on with *doing* when it comes to steering their children's sexuality. We hope that this book will not simply change the way parents think but will also change the way they act—both between themselves and towards the rest of the family. Actions are what really matter. We are judged in this world more by our behaviour than our thoughts.

Is this another book telling me how to bring up my children?

No. It's a book that, by increasing your insight and understanding of the whole subject of sexuality and love, should help you understand your and your children's complex emotions and feelings in situations as different as birth and breastfeeding; dealing with your pubertal daughter; influencing your teenage son; wondering what to do about your children living with their boyfriend or girlfriend; reassessing marriage in general and your own in particular; sex problems within your marriage; worries about old age; and much, much more.

No one has the right to tell people what to do when it comes to bringing up their children *but* there are many errors that people make in this area – errors that they later wish they had known about and often bitterly regret. Clinical experience of dealing with these problems enables us to help the reader because he or she can learn from thousands of other people's mistakes—hopefully before they make them themselves. It's easy to say that there are no absolute rights or wrongs about family sexuality and that whatever you do your children will turn out all right but this simply isn't true. None of

Learning to love: Will you love me for ever?

us can hope to bring up perfect human beings but we can do our very best to reduce negative influences by a little informed thought-and care. Whatever happens in the formal world of sex education the majority of influences on a child (and therefore on that person as an adult) come from his or her parents. Because of this we owe it not only to our children but also to *their* future spouses and children to get things as right as we can in the first twenty years or so of their lives.

Why on earth should I read about all this? Surely sex is natural, healthy, fun and normal?

Unfortunately sex is none of these things for a lot of people at some stage of their lives. We all have a sex drive of some kind, whether it's weak or strong, indulged or ignored and our perceptions of ourselves as sexual beings vary enormously according to our upbringing. To copulate then is natural—it can be undertaken with anyone and not in the context of an interpersonal relationship. However we can do a lot better than simply copulate because we are highly elaborate verbal and emotional creatures and even genital sexual expression is a very complex business.

One of the greatest and most harmful aspects of modern views on sex and sexuality is that most people imagine that everyone is having a better sex life than their own. For most people it is just something they do as a part of their everyday lives and if they love each other it can be a beautiful expression of that love. Many couples have sex in much the same way as they satisfy the other main appetite in their lives—that for food. On the majority of occasions it is not a world-shattering event. On other occasions it is a more exciting and even a wonderful experience. Just as we don't eat out at top restaurants all the time (and if we did we would soon become jaded) so most people don't have stunning sex lives all the time. Unfortunately, too many couples throw out the 'good' in striving for the 'excellent' and this is a shame, for them and their families.

Does anything go then?

That's entirely up to you. As doctors seeing people with real problems we don't condemn anyone for what they are or what they do but you will have to decide how you interpret and react to the book for yourself and your family. The book is totally non-judgemental and we have tried very hard not to let our personal preferences and prejudices come across. Each family will apply the contents of this book differently according to its race, religion, economic state, level of education, level of expectation, personalities, their care for each other and their family and so on. For this reason we have included chapters on homosexuality, prostitution and several other areas not immediately and obviously to do with the family. However, the majority of parents worry about homosexual influences on their young teenagers at some stage; and the majority of the clients of prostitutes are married men, so an understanding of even these subjects is of considerable importance to family love and sex.

We have written a book with no clear beginning and no end because *sexuality* has no beginning and no end. The baby who has just been born is at one and the same time at a starting point (for him) but an end point for his recently pregnant mother. One's first love-affair is a vital milestone along the path of life yet will, however important it seems at the time, fade away and be displaced by more mature love. Our life experiences in love and sex form an endless continuum that does not even go with us to the grave—it lives on in our children and their children.

The way to get the best out of this book is to start reading it wherever you like, read on from wherever you start and then restart at the beginning. We say this because we have planned the book to follow the life cycle, with many of the chapters following on one from another. It can be confusing and even difficult to read the odd chapter because a lot of the basic 'homework' will have been done in previous chapters and until you have read them it may not make the sense it should.

So, in conclusion, what we hope will come out of this book is a better future based on improved man–woman relationships. This comes down to real, live individuals relating to and understanding each other, and not to religious, political or medical theories and rules. The world is in a rather troubled state but there is hope for the future if only the basic unit of society, the family, can be made to work better. This it can only do if its members understand each other better and live in this increased knowledge and understanding.

Having said this, there is no such thing as perfection and few people's lives are 'ideal' in this or any other area. But this does not mean that we should not or cannot have some notion of what is worth striving for.

Chapter 1

Baby and childhood sexuality

To many people in our culture any concept of childhood sexuality seems totally unwholesome and unattractive, and many find it impossible to think of children as sexual beings at all. This is because most people think of sexuality as being inextricably linked to genitality. This is not true of adult sexuality and is even less so when it comes to children.

Babies and children *are* sexual creatures and it is only in a sex-repressed culture such as ours that credence would be given to any alternative suggestion. In the vast majority of cultures in the world children witness adult sexuality (and in a few cultures even intercourse) as part of their everyday life experience. Things are different in our culture which puts pressure on children to be 'innocent' and sees them as empty slates on which anything can be written, so that they are in need of protection. Of course children do need protecting, but to protect them against sex—one of our basic appetites and means of expression—is strange, to say the least.

If it could be proved that, by allowing children to gain a knowledge of sexuality naturally as they grow up, we would be harming or damaging them in any way, we would, of course, be against it—but there is no such proof. On the contrary, work done by Margaret Mead, the well-known anthropologist, suggests that in societies in which children are not repressed sexually, as happens in the West, the children show no preoccupation with sex and grow up far better balanced on the subject than ours do. In such cultures, perversions and deviations are rare and the sexes get on well together as adults.

The problems when discussing baby and childhood sexuality come about because for adults—as we have said—sexuality is often wrongly equated with genitality. There is evidence that the two are not so closely linked in babies and young children, who get just as much enjoyable and intense physical pleasure from other pursuits and experiences as we adults do from intercourse and other types of genitality.

At the risk of putting readers off it is probably useful to consider what Freud said about sexuality at this stage, if only because his theories have not been improved on in nearly a century. The Freudians suggest that a child goes through several well-defined stages of sexual, or, more correctly, psychosexual development from the cradle to sexual maturity in the teens. The first stage is the *oral* one

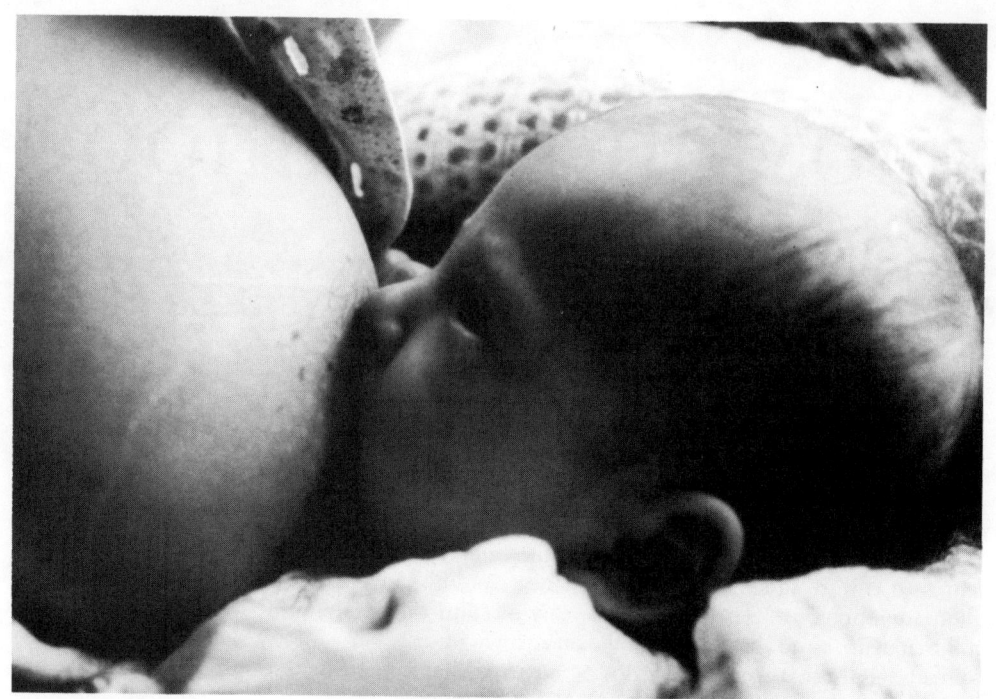

Loving through the mouth: Whether it is breast or bottle, a mother and her baby of this age are learning to love each other.

in which most pleasure is centred around the baby's mouth; the second is the *anal* one in which pleasure mostly comes from excreting (urinating and opening the bowels); the third stage is the *phallic* one during which the child discovers his penis or her clitoris as the best source of pleasure; the fourth is a period of *latency* during which psychosexual development more or less marks time; and lastly, with puberty, the child becomes *genital* and obtains the majority of his or her sexual and sensual pleasures from genital sensations. Most children progress from one stage to the next at a fairly predictable pace but can, because of bad rearing, stop at a particular stage, go awry, or go back a stage or two after having successfully negotiated one stage. It is clearly seen in clinical practice that adults can move up and down the scale from a major preoccupation with the adult (genital) stage. At any one stage in a person's life one of these phases is dominant in his or her sexuality but regression is possible to any of the previous stages. We shall look at all of these stages in more detail as the chapter progresses.

Although Freud was by no means the first person to discuss infant sexuality he was blamed for opening up the subject by people who preferred to talk of the innocence of childhood. Such people believe in the sinfulness of adults, that sex is sin, and therefore that children should be protected from it.

As we have seen, a capacity for adult sexual behaviour is inherent in every baby. Just as the genetic 'blueprint' for the physical, emotional, intellectual and personality development of the child gradually unfolds in a sequence, so does its sexuality. The 'blueprint', though, is only half the story because external circumstances also have an effect. For example, a boy may be born with the genetic potential to grow to 6 feet in height but nutritional and emotional deprivation may result in his only reaching a height of 5 feet 9 inches before the growth centres in his bones cease to function at a certain age, again determined by his blueprint, after which time no further growth is possible. In our culture, the different stages of sexual interest and behaviour which emerge according to the blueprint tend to produce a negative or hostile response, if not from the child's parents then from others. Although the basic pattern of the sexual blueprint is the same in both sexes, it is somewhat different in detail and there is a great difference in the way our culture treats the emergent sex drive in girls compared with that in boys.

The Stage of the Mouth (*The oral stage*)

Once it is realised that sexuality and genitality are not the same thing it becomes possible to discuss infant sexuality without impugning a baby's 'innocence'. The notion that a baby's lips and mouth are sources of intense pleasure is acceptable to almost everyone, especially anyone who has watched a baby feed at the breast. Later, following the blueprint, other areas become the focal point of peak pleasure, the mouth remaining pleasurable but not primarily so as in a baby.

The phase of development when the mouth is the primary source of pleasure is called the *oral* stage. The oral stage starts before birth because a foetus has been seen on X-rays to suck its thumb *in utero*. The bliss and contentment a baby displays on sucking after birth, if all goes well, is very plain to see. Mothers usually hug their babies to their bodies, talk soothingly and rock them. In doing so they are giving the child much more than milk. They are building up a sense of trust and confidence and are laying the foundations for the child to see itself as a person who is loved and valued. Provided the baby is not allowed to cry too much and so become frustrated when he or she needs food or maternal attention, he or she will slowly begin to experience feelings which eventually lead to a sense of optimism, self-assurance and perhaps self-esteem. If the mother leaves the baby to scream untended she will lay the foundations for self-doubt, depression and distrust of the world. It is quite possible to see that repeated and severe frustrations of the baby's oral drives and needs, even at this early stage, could result in their excessive persistence in later life. They may not remain primary but they may remain so strong that they influence both sexuality and other behaviour. It is certainly widely held that babies that do not enjoy and fulfil this oral stage as they should are more likely to want 'oral' gratification in adulthood. This can manifest itself in cigarette smoking, in certain cases in alcoholism, in persistent eating (especially under stress), or even in an unusually high level of interest in oral sex.

Although sucking at the breast or bottle relieves a baby's hunger it is also pleasurable in its own right and children, when they can control the movement of their muscles effectively, suck their thumbs if

The mouth gives most pleasure.

no other source of oral pleasure is available. Later still the child learns to suck, or at least to put in his or her mouth almost anything appealing in the environment. These are self-pleasuring or auto-erotic activities and may, without stretching the imagination too far, be seen as a forerunner of masturbation. The opposition that thumb sucking, especially in older children, often encounters from parents, presumably recognises this fact, no matter how unconsciously. Of course at the conscious level the parents' fear is that their child's teeth could be damaged or that others will think the child is babyish or unloved.

This can be used to illustrate a point of general importance. Although we all want pleasurable experiences, the ways in which we obtain them most naturally may not necessarily be socially acceptable. Because of this, restraint is taught in childhood. For example, an adult man sucking his thumb would be considered very odd but sucking a pipe is quite acceptable.

To generalise further, many of our pleasure drives are opposed, at least in part, by cultural conditioning and are, as a result, displaced on to other activities which gratify a particular need in a way that is, perhaps, less satisfactory but more socially acceptable, thereby possibly leading to a mild degree of frustration. These displacements are taken to be the mark of civilisation and the process is thought to account for many great achievements in the areas of creative thinking, writing, painting, music, sculpture and so on. In a humbler form the displacements probably enrich our lives and comfort in every way. For example, a woman's displacement of pleasure drives to her home, social life and children usually improves life for all concerned. Men, or some men, may, perhaps for a genetic reason, be capable of more distant displacements and this may account for male supremacy in areas of achievement. This is not to deny that women are capable of more distant displacements or men of displacements closer to the family and home; it is simply to say that the main focal points for such displacements may be slightly different for the two sexes, so enabling each to contribute slightly differently to civilisation. Men, on balance, tend to push society forwards and women to maintain the status quo.

To return to the oral stage, parents, of course, make use of the oral drive to pacify their baby in the early stages of life. This is why breastfeeding is so successful a way of feeding a baby—it does so much more than nourish the child. A tired, unhappy or ill baby can be pacified by putting him or her to the breast.

Two further points should be made. Presumably the infant is, at first, incapable of realising that it is the mother who relieves the tension of hunger or who provides the comfort of cuddling and rocking. At first the baby must think that it is the breast that does these things. Eventually, he or she realises that the breast is part of his mother and, if all is well, the baby starts to develop the capacity to love. A newborn baby expresses love through the mouth, and attachments between the mother and child develop which build up a capacity to form stable, affectionate relationships later in life. If this stage is not happily achieved the child's later relationships may be less than full. Sexual and emotional development are first linked in this way. Through constant contact with the mother's body and her

The age of self-discovery: Although he is still at the potty stage, he is progressing satisfactorily to the next.

various attentions to his or her needs, a baby becomes aware of his or her own body and its pleasures. Self-exploration of the body follows and much later the exploration of other people's bodies.

When an infant boy is at the breast he may have an erection. He may also have one during urination, nappy changing, bowel emptying, or as a result of any excitement. Similarly, girls may roll their thighs and, according to some mothers, even lubricate vaginally. Children learn to touch their genitals fairly early and babies have been observed to stimulate themselves to orgasm. At this stage, however, the genitals are not the baby's primary source of pleasure. The mouth ensures survival and is still the main source of pleasure.

The Potty Training stage *(The anal stage)*

Provided all goes reasonably well with the oral stage, the child progresses to the next phase at around the middle of the second year. This is the *anal* (excretory) phase, in which the body's excretory functions become the primary source of interest and pleasure. As bowel and urinary control become possible, usually in the second or third year, the child experiences pleasure in expelling and retaining faeces and urine. The child's mother is involved because of starting some form of toilet training. Boys are taught to hold their penis and to direct the stream whereas girls are expected to remove clothing and to crouch or sit down.

In ancient Egypt, where the sexes were treated equally, the reverse was the case and the women often urinated standing and men crouching. Some experts in this field believe that female feelings of inferiority start at this point of child development because of the urination postures taught to girls. Certainly, for many adult women who are otherwise totally open about their sexual behaviour, urination can be a source of considerable embarrassment. Urination, too, seems to have an erotic significance for at least some women, some of whom can masturbate to orgasm by stimulating their urethral opening or with the muscular efforts required to hold back their urine. Emotional upsets in later life can also be psychosomatically expressed as disorders of urination by women, in whom urinary problems are vastly more common than in men.

It has been observed that little girls of about a year often laugh as they urinate and this has been attributed to the tickling sensation that urine causes in the vulva. If this is true, urination will serve further to draw a girl's attention to the pleasurable sensations she can get from her vulva, whereas a boy is impressed more with his urinary stream and the actual performance of the act.

Either because they develop sooner than boys or because they are intrinsically more affection-dependent and want to please, or both, girls learn to control their bladders earlier than boys and are also less prone to bed-wetting. The ability to feel shame develops around the age of one and a half years and many mothers use this to help their children gain control over their bowels and bladder. Moral development starts with toilet training as it is the first time a baby's parents control his or her bodily desires and pleasures to bring them into line with society's accepted norms.

Once children have learned to control their bowel movements they have some power over their mothers, depending on whether they choose to perform or not, and many children use this power over their mothers very effectively. The child's stools thus become the first gift he or she has to give or withhold. His or her stools, including their smell and appearance, can fascinate and excite the child.

Although a mother expresses delight as her child performs on the potty she nevertheless controls his or her interest in the result by saying it is 'dirty' or has 'germs' and flushes it away. Later, when the child is in full control of his or her bowels, he or she may play with or collect the stools and hide them away. Old people whose interest in sex has waned often return to this anal stage and become preoccupied with their bowel functions, just like a developing child.

If the anal stage progresses well it is an impetus towards creativity and productivity but frustrations can, it is thought, lead to the character traits of obstinacy, compulsiveness and over-orderliness. These are seen as a defence against a desire to return to the pleasures of the anal stage. Obsessionalism may be a more extreme defence. On the other hand frustrations may be expressed later as untidiness, disorderliness and even destructiveness. Anal pleasures may continue to be over-represented, relative to other pleasures, later in life, and some individuals require additional anal stimulation during masturbation or intercourse to get their best orgasms. Many prostitutes tell of how they are asked to insert a finger into the anus of a client experiencing ejaculatory difficulties. Some women claim to have orgasms only from anal intercourse and a persistence of anal eroticism is obviously a possible basis for some cases of passive homosexuality.

Interest in the anus and anal area extends to the buttocks at this stage. Both sexes later say they notice the buttocks of members of the opposite sex. Fantasies about beating or being beaten on the buttocks may start here and may be reinforced by parents actually or playfully smacking or threatening to smack their child's bottom. Prostitutes say many men like to be beaten before intercourse or even that being beaten is enough in itself to produce an orgasm and ejaculation. Some women, too, say they enjoy being smacked on the bottom prior to intercourse. Here the psychological mechanism may be different. **Some women have been reared to think that sex is so naughty that they can only get pleasure from it if they are punished first for their naughtiness.**

The anal stage, then, has a lot of implications and probably the best advice to parents is to take potty training very gently, consistently and slowly, and to stop the potty training for a while if the child doesn't seem ready.

The Clitoris/Penis stage (*The phallic stage*)

If all goes well with the anal stage the anal interests and pleasures slowly become secondary to phallic pleasures, around the age of three years. This is the *phallic* stage. In this stage the clitoris or penis increasingly becomes the predominant source of body pleasure. More or less deliberate masturbation usually starts about now. Most parents say either that their child did not masturbate or, if the child did so, that they accepted it. Clinical evidence suggests that this is usually not true.

The phallic stage is, in one sense, an early childhood step towards independence from the parents but it is nearly always suppressed, if not by direct prohibition and punishment then by disapproval and distraction. Very few parents are sufficiently at ease with their own sexuality to be able to watch their young child play with his or her genitals. In some families the genitals are never mentioned or even acknowledged as existing. Anything without a name probably does not exist for a child of this age, so simply by not talking about a child's genitals as you would about any other part of the body you are expressing a negative attitude which undoubtedly influences the child's future feelings and behaviour.

This is *unmentionable sex*. Girls particularly suffer in this way, while most boys are given a word for the penis. In most families the genitals are given names—often of a comic type. Playing with the genitals can be condemned in the same way as was the interest in stools and sex then becomes *dirty sex*. Religiously inclined families may suggest that God does not like genital play and sex becomes *sinful sex*. Direct punishment can associate the phallic stage with fear and so sex becomes *fearful sex*. Some children are still warned of ill effects from genital touching and so sex can become *unhealthy sex*. Girls especially are rebuked on the basis that such practices are not 'nice' in girls and so sex becomes *nasty sex*.

Similar techniques are sometimes used to turn sex into a matter of shame, extreme privacy and embarrassment. This is *shameful sex*. To a greater or lesser extent everyone in our culture encounters all these reactions, if not from parents then from other sources, and if not in the phallic stage, then later. These attitudes are continuously reinforced throughout childhood and adolescence in most families.

Somewhat surprisingly, clinical evidence strongly suggests that most of these suppressions are put over to the child in unconscious ways by the parents, who are therefore not being consciously untruthful when they say they did not suppress their child's sexuality. What was taught to *them*, the parents, in this way in childhood they in turn pass on to the next generation. The child stores the information away, mainly in the unconscious mind, so the transaction is between the unconscious of the parents and the unconscious of the child. This accounts for the extreme cultural conservatism over sexual matters.

The results of sexual suppression in the phallic stage seem to be more serious for girls. This may be because they are more severely suppressed. Mothers are generally much more indulgent towards genitality in boys than in girls. This subject is considered in more detail in chapter 2. Here it suffices to say that clinical experience seems to prove that the difficulties of a wide section of the adult female population in experiencing full sexual pleasure originate at this stage.

Before the phallic stage is reached a child has learned to distinguish between mummy and daddy and later between women

The age of 'innocence: For many of us this is the last time in our lives that we are at ease with nudity in front of the opposite sex.

and men. When very young he or she will have seen both parents and any brothers or sisters naked because few adults think such matters register to a young child. The young child may even have been present in the room when his or her parents were having intercourse and if so, according to some people, his or her behaviour over the next few days may show signs of disturbance. Later, witnessing or hearing intercourse can lead to the notion that sex is an aggressive and sadistic act and many children fear that their father is hurting their mother, especially if she is noisy when she has an orgasm. This is why it is probably best in our culture not to let children of any age see their parents having intercourse. Some phobias are thought to be triggered off in susceptible children who repeatedly witness parental sexual acts after the age of about two or three.

Parental nudity, which has always been commoner amongst the better educated, is of much less significance, especially if the child's friends are being reared in the same sort of way. Although we ourselves doubt it, it is thought by some psychosexual experts that it is best for a boy not to see his mother naked after the age of four or so and for a girl not to see her father naked from about a year. Children whose friends are used to seeing their parents naked will probably be unaffected but children can be very cruel, even this young, and will tease children who seem to be brought up in ways that are contrary to the way they know. As children discuss this sort of thing at school it is probably best not to subject your children to experiences at home that will make them feel odd among their friends. They may believe that they have odd parents if their friends say so and this could be harmful to them.

A special aspect of this stage in relation to boys is that only about 4 per cent of boys have a fully retractable foreskin at birth and 50 per cent by one year. Forcible attempts at retraction by some mothers, to clean the underneath, to see whether circumcision is necessary or just to stretch it, may account for some late-adolescent boys and men with tight foreskins who react with great alarm at any attempt at retraction. Their reluctance leads them to masturbate with the foreskin in the forward position and its development does not keep pace with the increase in size of the penis at puberty.

Little boys' penises need nothing done to them at all. If the foreskin will not pull back completely by the age of five, see your doctor for advice.

As children begin to look at the genitals of children (and adults) of the opposite sex, boys may come to see girls as being boys who have had their genitals removed, perhaps as a punishment for touching them. Some fear a similar punishment themselves. Girls sometimes conjure up the idea that they really have a secret penis or seem, perhaps, to blame their mothers because they have not got one. The difficulty in such speculation is that children rarely say how they feel and their reactions can only be guessed at from their behaviour.

The age of mutual discovery: The fascination of the girl contrasts with the bafflement of the boy.

Gender identity

The processes by which a child eventually comes to feel with certainty

that he or she is a boy or a girl—so-called gender identity—proceed slowly and with confusion. One process which affects the issue is the one of identification with the same-sex parent. Whether it is instinctive or whether they are identifying with and copying their mothers, many very young girls display marked femininity in their behaviour. Many are like miniature women and by three or so have developed social skills which many a young man would like to have.

Girls also seem to be able to discern the sex of another individual earlier and more reliably than can boys. When a girl discovers the genital differences between the sexes, or even before, she pays more attention to her father than before, and where her relationship with both her parents is good the change is marked. She wants to attract her father's attention and to involve him in her affairs. In an elementary way she may compete with her mother to take trouble on his behalf and be of service to him. She may want to get into his bed and drive her mother from it. Later she may say she is going to grow up and marry her father. Clearly her father is her first heterosexual love and in some way she is involved with him physically. She wants him to kiss and cuddle her and may show signs of jealousy at any attention her mother receives. Many a little girl uses her feminine skills effectively to get her own way with her father. If he is really cross with her it can emotionally disturb her for hours or days, but maternal displeasure has much less effect. Obviously, if she learns from him that she is attractive, lovable and valuable she will, other things being equal, have confidence in herself as a woman later

Confidence in later life.

in life. Nevertheless, if the father is over-close, as some are, perhaps out of a latent fear of adult women, she can later have difficulty in leaving him psychosexually for another man. The balance, as in so many cases of sexuality, is a fine one.

A part of a girl's mind may in one sense hate and fear her mother, because she thinks that her mother realises that she wishes her mother would go so that she could have an exclusive relationship with her father. She fears her mother will retaliate. However, she also loves her mother and realises that her mother is her care-taker. As a result she remains attentive to her mother, to see if her secret has been discovered. It is thought that the greater empathy that women have compared with men comes from this developmental stage, as does a woman's skill at concealing her true feelings.

A boy does not have to make the same switch from his mother, but his feelings about her and his father are similar to, but the reverse of, those of a girl. The intensity of such feelings tends to increase during the phallic stage. Physical contact with his mother may lead to an erection and his interest in her body may intensify. Many men who say they find partially dressed women more arousing than naked ones may have started this notion at this stage because they are more likely to have seen their mother partially rather than wholly undressed. A mother may be seductive to her son of around the age of five but at the same time sharply rebuke him for his sexual interest in her. Simultaneously his increasing fear of retaliation by his father, from whom he may fear removal of his penis—as has happened to girls, he thinks—leads to this so-called *Oedipal* interest in his mother being controlled rather than given free rein.

From clinical work with adult men it seems that two important consequences follow from this. The first is the establishment of a notion of female sexlessness. This view of women is, of course, reinforced by our culture which declares that girls are 'sugar and spice and all things nice'. The second consequence is that the boy enters the world of men. Females and their interests are spurned as inconsequential. The view develops that girls are best avoided and they are often banned, to the chagrin of many of them, from boys' games. Identification with the father, or another suitable male person, proceeds more rapidly and the boy strives for mastery over male pursuits. One reason why boys identify with their fathers later than girls do with their mothers is that mothers are more continuously available as models for girls than are fathers for boys. In any case a boy probably first identifies with the mother and it is she, rather than his father, who first outlines the conventional male role for a boy. Women teachers may later continue the process which rewards boys for masculine behaviour and disparages them for feminine interests.

Are girls really sexless?

Most boys stop masturbating as the phallic stage ends and gives way to the stage of latency which roughly corresponds with the grade and junior-school years. Curiously, adult men seem to have no conscious recollection of childhood masturbation and its later rediscovery at puberty is regarded as a new acquisition. This is in contrast with women, about a third of whom say they cannot remember a time when they did not masturbate.

Girls do not resolve the problems of the Oedipal stage in the same brisk fashion in which most boys do. Their interest in their father often continues although perhaps in a weakened form. Often it is later displaced on to horses, which may symbolise masculine power, although, no doubt, there are other reasons for a girl's love of her horse.

The Quiescent stage *(The latency stage)*

During the latency stage of sexual development, a child's early interest in his or her parents widens out to other adults such as teachers, and interest in the mysteries of sex enlarges into interest in other mysteries and learning generally. Curiosity about sex may lead to the use of dictionaries, other available books and newspapers to learn about sexual matters. In this way general curiosity and learning can be promoted. Investigations of the genitals of friends of the opposite sex, which may have started as early as three or so, may continue until seven or eight. Children who have seen their parents having intercourse may pretend to do it with others, girls sometimes undertaking the male role, but it has no sexual significance in adult terms. Sex play between brothers and sisters up to and including the latency stage of psychosexual development (which ends at puberty) is innocuous, as is any other heterosexual play, but if continued it can fix the children on each other in such a way that their subsequent ability to relate effectively to members of the opposite sex is impaired.

The pre-adolescent stage

Hormonal changes occur as puberty approaches. Girls who stopped masturbating at the end of the phallic stage often start again around the age of nine or ten. It is still an 'innocent' activity which the girl may feel little guilt about unless she was heavily suppressed for earlier masturbation or sex games. This increase in eroticism may be reflected in an increasing interest in portrayals of nude adult females and the father who was previously welcome in the bathroom is now banned. Dreams or fantasies of appearing partially or wholly nude occur and are exciting. Sex games are undertaken now only with other girls and under the guise of dressing-up games or sexual enactment games such as kiss-me-like-a-boy-would, and mutual genital inspection and bottom smacking may occur. The phase is a sort of 'homosexual' one and is perfectly normal. Girls rarely teach each other to masturbate—unlike boys. The reason may be that sexual skills are more innate in girls whereas in boys, as in primate males generally, there is a larger learned component to sex. Girls can seem to be very mature just before puberty and often take a special interest in relationships between the sexes, both human and animal.

Boys tend to gang together even more strongly in pre-adolescence and although there may be mutual showing of genitals it is not really a homosexual stage. They tend at this stage to denigrate women, presumably because of residual fears of them from earlier childhood arising from encounters with them in the form of mothers and teachers, and they also tend to regress towards the anal stage. Talk about excretion, and breaking wind, making noises, eating crudely and failing to wash adequately are signs of this regression.

At this point, the end of latency, the first half of childhood is complete. The child has largely been reared within the small world of his or her own family with its particular combination of advantages and disadvantages. Any harm done in the process of psychosexual, and other, development will from now on become increasingly evident. It is this long incubation period between cause and effect which makes it so difficult to be sure about the significance of earlier events. The distortion of memory, the inaccessibility of the unconscious, the repression of painful thoughts and family myths make it hard to disentangle the facts. The most important lessons in life, the very early ones, do not even register in the conscious memory. And yet, in spite of the problems, it is possible to use the information given briefly in this chapter to understand what lies behind the difficulties experienced by adolescents and adults in their relationships with others and themselves. From what they say and avoid saying, from the way they say it and their associated emotional changes, from their dreams and fantasies, from their preferences and practices, and in other ways, it becomes possible to know what happened to them and how they felt, even unconsciously, during childhood. Sometimes repressed material is retrieved from the unconscious and the person then relives it as vividly as if it had occurred only an instant before, and all the emotions originally associated with it return.

Of course everyone is different, but three patterns constantly recur in clinical practice though they appear in many guises. The first is a poor relationship with the self, involving excessive self-criticism, excessive self-consciousness, self-detestation or depression and excessive self-blame. The two main causes are disturbed parental relationships, the child perhaps having been at least partly unwanted or believing himself or herself to be, and poor child spacing. The second is the suppression of sexuality, resulting in the child being frozen at some particular stage, perhaps making him or her regress to an earlier stage or deviating him or her from 'normal' development. The third is a persistent attachment to the opposite-sex parent which can arise, amongst other reasons, if that parent was over-close or over-rejecting. The consequences can be profound not only for the individual's future sexuality but for his or her emotions, personality and inter-personal relationships.

Summary

Although this brief account of baby and childhood sexuality can be verified by the average observant parent, it is still not universally accepted. Some people find it hard to believe that events in childhood can exert such a profound effect on such matters as the ability to enjoy intercourse later in life. If it is accepted that infant and childhood sexuality and the way it is handled are the foundation for what comes in adulthood, then its enormous importance can be readily appreciated. To argue that childhood experiences have no bearing on events in later life is contrary to all the available evidence and to common sense. After all, we happily accept such reasoning on non-sexual matters.

> Some do not accept childhood sexuality.

A more subtle and difficult criticism arises in the question of why children who are treated in virtually the same way with regard to sexual and emotional matters display totally different sexualities and sexual problems in adulthood. The answer probably lies in the fact that no two people can really be subject to exactly the same influences, and therefore any two people will respond differently to similar experiences. How secure children feel in their place in the family also affects their vulnerability to experiences. Also, the child's own perceptions of what is happening may be different from those of a brother or sister who is going through the same experience. For these and no doubt other reasons, the long-term consequences of a similar upbringing can vary enormously. Parents too are not static personalities—they change as the years pass and react differently to, and therefore have a different influence on, each of their children.

All of this makes the study of childhood sexuality a minefield, but an understanding of the processes outlined in this chapter can put problems into perspective. We are a product of our yesterdays as well as of our genetic blueprint.

Chapter 2

Early adolescence

Early adolescence starts with puberty in both sexes. Why puberty starts when it does is uncertain but obviously its onset and progress are mainly governed by the genetic blueprint of an individual. Adverse physical and emotional environments can undoubtedly also affect it.

Hormonal changes begin to occur a year or two before the start of puberty and there is evidence that these affect behaviour. In consequence pre-adolescence, puberty itself and early adolescence are sometimes thought of as a single phase which has been labelled *young adolescence*.

Puberty is often thought of as starting at the same age in both sexes, but this is contrary to the widely accepted view that girls develop faster and over a shorter period of time than boys. There is little doubt that the associated behavioural and growth changes occur earlier in girls. A boy's adolescent spurt in height occurs, on average, two years after that of a girl, so for a time girls are on average taller than boys and may even be stronger. This may partly contribute to the avoidance of girls by boys which characterises this stage. The early onset of puberty is much commoner in girls than in boys and, when it occurs in boys, unlike girls, the cause is usually a disease or disorder. The late onset of puberty, in contrast, is of less medical concern in boys because perfectly normal boys may be late just as perfectly normal girls may be early.

The early-adolescent girl

The first sign of puberty is nearly always the development of the breasts, often one, the left, before the other. Mounds appear and the pigmented area around the nipple, the areola, enlarges. Up to this time the sensitivity of the area is roughly equal in boys and girls but in girls it now begins to increase. The breast 'buds' appear at around the age of eleven but can form as early as eight or as late as thirteen. Full breast development takes about two and a half years. Depending on her personal and family attitudes and those of her friends, a girl will either welcome or conceal these breast changes.

Pubic hair development normally starts a few months after the breasts begin to develop but can start before. Some girls, perhaps because of guilt about masturbation, lack of information or mis-information, believe that hair growth is a sign of abnormality or even a sign of changing sex and so may cut it or shave it off. Around this time the vagina starts to produce an increased amount of whitish fluid.

Coinciding with, or just before, these changes, the girl experiences a physical growth spurt. This reaches a peak soon after the pubic hair begins to appear, and then the rate of growth begins to slacken. About two and a half years after the first signs of breast development, menstruation first occurs. The biological term for the time of the first period is the menarche. Many women say they were never warned in advance about their periods starting, but most mothers say they prepared their daughters. This apparent contradiction can easily be explained. Because the subject concerns sex and because the mother has unwittingly inspired anxiety in relation to sex over the childhood years, her daughter does not want to know and banishes the information from her consciousness even though she has in fact been given it. Whatever the explanation, a girl's first period can be a shock which leads to fears of injury (possibly, in her mind, from masturbation) or illness. Depending again upon her mother's attitudes and those of the other girls at school, some girls welcome their first period while others are ashamed and secretive. All girls probably worry to some degree about their lack of control over the event. Earlier, hard-won mastery over other body functions in childhood now seems to be partly lost, and many worry about the shame they might feel if they ever leaked blood, making their period obvious to others.

The average age at which a girl's first period occurs is probably one measure of the affluence of a society, and in the West it has been falling for centuries. The decline has reached its lowest limit so far in the generation of girls born in the years immediately after the Second World War. The first period now usually occurs at about thirteen years, but may be as early as eleven or as late as fifteen and still be quite normal. A first period before eleven years or periods failing to appear by fifteen years may need investigation but usually such girls turn out to be just beyond one end of the age range but still perfectly normal. Various factors affect the age at which the menarche occurs. For example, blind girls tend to start early, whereas girls living at a high altitude or those who have younger brothers usually start late. It is not known why this should be.

A girl can become pregnant before her first period but most girls are infertile for the first year or so of having periods because they are not yet ovulating (producing eggs). After this there is a slow build-up towards maximum fertility in the early twenties.

Early periods may be prolonged, heavy or irregular. Signs that a girl is becoming fertile are regular and predictable periods, especially if they are accompanied by premenstrual symptoms such as breast tenderness or pain and painful periods. Girls who have intercourse in early adolescence usually do so without precautions. When they do not get pregnant some wrongly assume they are infertile and, as a result of desperately trying to prove to themselves that they are fertile, eventually become pregnant.

Hair usually begins to appear in the armpits at about the time of the first period. The onset of all these changes of puberty varies from girl to girl and any one girl may not follow the usual sequence. The whole process can take from one to five years to complete.

Along with these specific sexual changes, fat is deposited under the skin, making a girl's contours more plump and rounded. This makes her body sexually attractive to men. At this stage many girls are confused by their feelings. They have impulses both to show and to conceal their bodies, but by the end of early adolescence they have usually come to terms with their emerging sexuality. Under hormonal influences their interest in sex heightens but it is restrained if they have been conditioned early on to think that sex is wrong, sinful or dirty and by any already entrenched ideas about how 'nice' girls should behave. A girl's desire to grow up and be treated as a woman is exciting to her but also fear-inspiring, giving her a simultaneous desire to remain in, or regress to, childhood as a form of escape from the realities of impending womanhood. Other contradictions arise from the fact that she has a need to be seen by men as desirable whilst at the same time fearing she might not be acceptable to them or that she may appear brazen or cheap.

As a result of these feelings early adolescence is often stressful for a girl. She is trying to adjust to the changes in her body, to menstruation, to her enhanced sexual interest and, to a greater or lesser extent, to her wish to be found desirable by men. Unlike the early-adolescent boy, her entry into the sexual arena is dramatic and swift. Because her biological drives are so strong, her parents are often concerned and anxious and this can lead to family conflict towards the end of early adolescence. Her earlier good relationship with her father may worsen as he tries to control her comings and goings but the cruellest battle is often fought with her mother. In some families these rows can become very bitter with the father physically punishing the girl and the mother accusing her of being a whore.

Many, perhaps most, girls openly rebel at some stage and tell their mother that they hate her. If the parents 'win', the girl's subsequent development may be impaired, but the greater danger is that the girl may feel she can win by running away or having early intercourse simply to spite her parents. Many experts in this field believe that girls who behave like this are simply seeking love from a man to replace the parental love they have lost, but others believe that much more often it comes about because a girl unconsciously wants to punish her mother. Sometimes a girl goes to great lengths to let her parents know that she is no longer a virgin, but more often this rebellious act is kept quiet.

So the answer for parents of early-adolescent girls is to try to understand their desires and fears and to do all they can to cope with the situation without reaching a stage of open warfare with her. It is obviously best if a girl can start out on her adolescent life with the backing of a family she can trust to love her and whom she in turn can love and trust. Few girls really want to annoy or upset their parents.

With her many conflicts and bodily changes it is easy to see why the early-adolescent girl can be so moody and changeable. It is also fairly obvious why many girls fail in the tasks of early adolescence.

EARLY ADOLESCENCE 33

The making of a woman: Pre-pubescent girl (left) and fully mature woman (right).

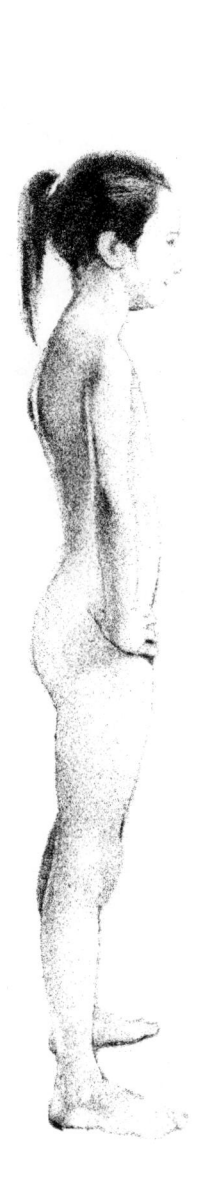

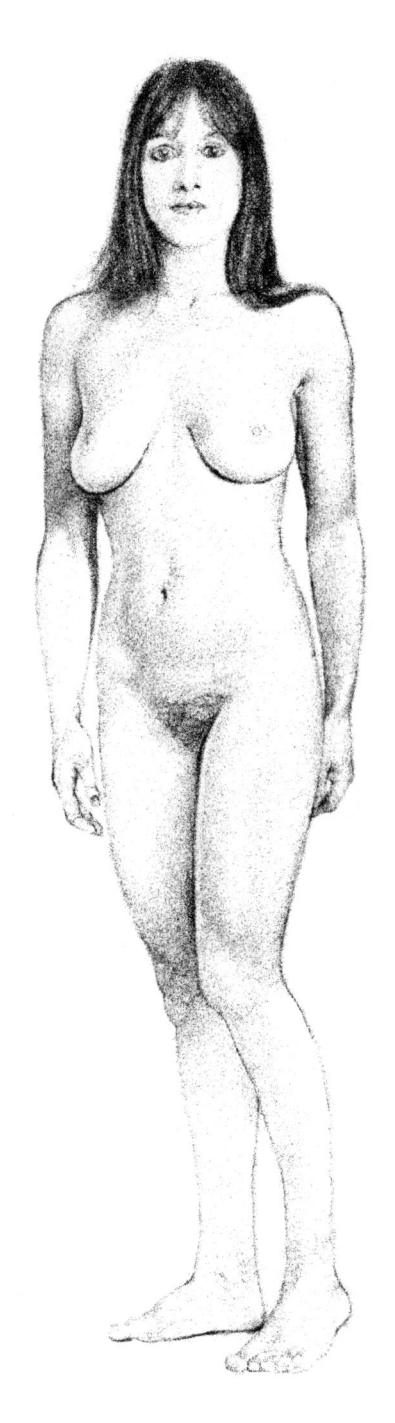

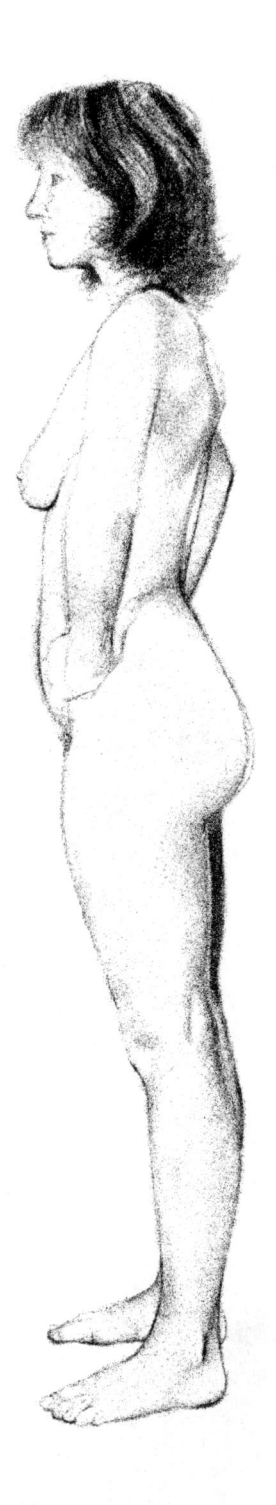

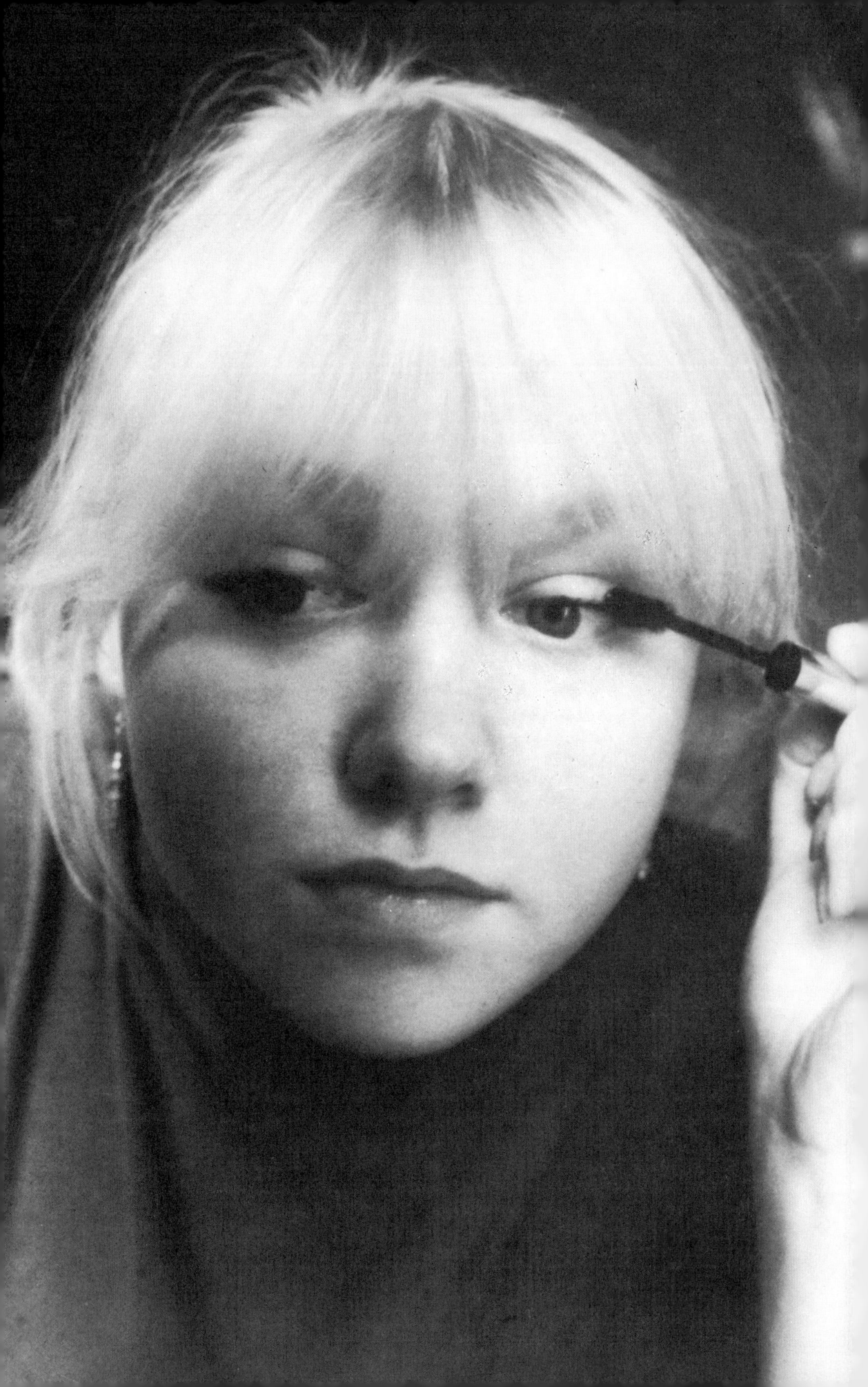

The origins of a lot of mental ill health in women can be traced back to early adolescence as can an inability to cope with the female role. As in boys, frank psychiatric illness such as neurosis, depression or schizophrenia may be precipitated by puberty. Some girls opt out by becoming fat or by developing anorexia nervosa, thus regressing, Peter Pan-like, to childhood, ceasing to menstruate and losing their breasts. Others become over-devoted to academic work, to religion or to animals. Some girls act out their distress and become sexually delinquent and others try to seduce an older man who is sometimes the exact opposite of their father. Others, especially those who had a poor relationship with their mothers in early childhood, may secretly wish to return to childhood and 'solve' the problem but over-react in the opposite direction and rush into 'adult' pursuits such as sex and drink.

The most important thing about early adolescence is that a girl should come to accept the new role her hormones and body changes have imposed on her. These are paralleled by changes in her mind and emotions which can be contradictory and difficult to cope with, as we have seen. Most of her problems do not arise because of these changes as such (although all change is unsettling to some extent because you cannot see the end-point), but rather from the conflicts produced by the changes and from the consequences they imply. At the centre of it all is the change in her sexuality. Early adolescence is the time when she accepts, or fails to accept, that she is a sexual being. This involves much more than simply realising that she will eventually have intercourse and possibly produce babies. She has to accept that she has sexual interests, wishes, desires and pleasures and that her life will never be the same again. She has now entered the sexual arena and has to take her chances with the rest of us.

Emerging sexuality.

Her sexual fantasies change during early adolescence from being relatively impersonal to being more explicit and more excitingly personal. Usually the fantasies of early-adolescent girls are of a fairly vague and crude nature, frequently involving situations such as stripping, prostitution and rape. Some girls of this age go out of their way to find newspaper items and books about these things which then arouse them. Many, but not all, girls discuss their findings with their friends at school in the hope of understanding what they are about. It is a strange paradox that a girl of this age is likely to assume that she is a sex expert and many reject sexual information from her parents and teachers. This is a perfectly normal stage.

Fantasies may be suppressed because they are seen as disgusting and any that involve her father or father-like figures are nearly always severely suppressed. Many a girl's behaviour may be the exact opposite of what she really wants because of her attempts to control and over-control her desires. For example, it is common for girls who really want to be close and loving to their fathers to avoid all contact with them at this stage.

Am I attractive? Girls usually take an emphatic turn towards heterosexuality at puberty.

During early adolescence masturbation usually increases in intensity and frequency but does not change much in form. Any bad masturbation habits a girl has already acquired tend to become further entrenched and fixed at this stage. Girls who rub their vulvas to have an orgasm usually further refine their own particular pattern of stimulation but new features often emerge. One technique, for example, is to clasp the whole vulva when arousal has reached a certain stage and then to count to ten before resuming stimulation. Very guilty girls who want to get it over with as quickly as possible do not use delaying tactics such as these, often to the detriment of their ultimate enjoyment of sex.

Shame and masturbation.
The other change that occurs is a considerable increase in shame as the full sexual significance of masturbation dawns on a girl. This comes about because her sexual experience seems to contradict all that she has previously supposed to be 'nice' in a girl. Some girls accept the situation easily but others have more difficulty. Some repress their sexuality so completely that they actually give up masturbation in early adolescence. Others struggle against it and try to keep it under strict control. For example, some girls promise God they will never do it again. Some reinforce their control by telling themselves that they are doing themselves harm or that they will change sex as a result. This last fear arises from the fact that until recently masturbation was spoken of as being essentially a thing boys did. Many a girl therefore used to believe (and some still do) that she was the only girl who did it, and even if she asked her friends (which was rare), to try to get reassurance, they too denied masturbating because they had been made to feel guilty about it.

This rise in shame about masturbation can, unfortunately, lead to changes in behaviour, and some of these can be annoying for the girl and her family. Common examples are frequent hand-washing for fear—among other things—that others may be able to detect that she has been masturbating, and a neurotic over-concern about spots. A girl may become even more secretive about her sexual interests and is often easily embarrassed when sex is mentioned by adults. Her mother's sexuality can also lead to embarrassment and even frank hostility. If her mother becomes pregnant, for example, she can feel compromised and ashamed. Now she really understands what her mother must have felt for her father and what must have happened to her to get pregnant, she feels even more ambivalent towards her mother and may even resent her father's having sex with her at all.

All of this is fairly normal in our culture and is not greatly affected by sex education. Those of us who are parents can, given the knowledge, go some way towards understanding the problems a girl has at this difficult time of her life.

Of much more concern though are those early-adolescent girls who in a sense dissociate themselves from their sexuality and try to find ways to indulge it whilst denying to themselves that they are doing so. The deception does not take the form of straightforward lying—it is rather an internal self-deception based upon a psychological trick. Examples are endless. One is to separate fantasy from its associated masturbatory activity—in this way it is possible to deny, to oneself, the sexual nature of the act. On the other hand, fantasy alone may be used as a masturbatory act or the fantasy may be highly symbolic and apparently non-sexual. Another way is either to deny that an orgasm has occurred or to experience it only after the physical act is complete. Yet another is to displace the orgasm from the genitals to some other part of the body, especially to the oesophagus or the stomach. Some incidental activity such as rope climbing or cycle riding may be utilised to produce an orgasm. These and many other ways may be used, both at the time and in adulthood, to deny that there is (or was) a sexual content to the early-adolescent stage. Unfortunately, this denial has poor implications for the girl's future as we shall see in chapter 3.

Although early-adolescent girls talk about sex to each other, it is usually in a non-personal way. It is rare for girls, unlike boys, at this stage to involve their own sex physically in their sexual activities, although they often develop emotional crushes on admired older girls or schoolmistresses. A helpful way of thinking of this is to understand that the girl usually thinks of the older person as being successful in an area of concern to her. This is often in sophistication and attractiveness to men. The girl wants closeness, partly to learn the secret of success and partly to be held in esteem, almost as a friend, by someone she considers likable and successful. True lesbian activity at this age is very rare indeed and parents need have no fear that crushes will mean that their daughter will become a lesbian.

The majority of girls are keen to test out the effectiveness of their changing bodies in attracting male attention. Most girls first experience kissing and perhaps breast fondling during this stage. Some relate wildly exaggerated stories to their friends with the unconscious aim of emphasising their desirability. Although boys are her principal interest, the early-adolescent girl rarely commits herself but rather conducts her sexual experiments from the security of a group of girlfriends.

Although some girls display little or no open interest in boys at this stage, for a variety of reasons, most of which need cause no concern, others become over-involved. Apart from rebellion, other motives for early intercourse include the inability to face up to masturbation. Unless she renounces sex altogether and regresses to childhood, the only other course is to seek sexual stimulation from others, usually boys. Such a girl may well intend to go no further than allowing the boy to masturbate her but since these girls usually go for considerably older, more experienced boys, intercourse is likely to result.

However, very few girls of this age experience intercourse in any adult way, and the danger is that this pattern of inadequate and unsatisfactory response in intercourse becomes fixed. Girls should be advised, not warned, against too early intercourse for this reason. Experience shows that the vast majority of girls are not ready for intercourse at this stage of their development but keeping them away from it can be a difficult problem for many parents. Most girls do not even consider intercourse at this age, but those that do need help to protect them from the emotional and psychological traumas that can easily follow.

The early-adolescent boy

The first sign of puberty, occurring somewhere between the ages of ten and fourteen, is in the scrotum, which enlarges and becomes reddened. At around the same time there is an increase in the size of the testes (balls). This latter change is under the immediate control of a pituitary hormone called the luteinizing hormone, but the testosterone production by the testes thereafter is also under the control of a pituitary hormone called the follicle-stimulating hormone. The secondary sexual characteristics that then develop, such as the increase in the size of the penis, beard and body-hair growth, the voice breaking, muscle development and so on are brought about by the testosterone produced by the enlarging and functioning testes.

Largely under the influence of testosterone, erections increase in frequency, as do sexual fantasies and eventually, at around the age of twelve to fourteen, most boys start to masturbate. The starting point is often hearing about masturbation from slightly older boys or seeing someone else masturbating. Most normal boys promptly turn into ardent practitioners. For many boys, the start of their interest in masturbation occurs slightly before ejaculation is possible and their orgasms are of the so-called 'dry run' variety. Friendships with other boys usually intensify and mutual genital display, comparison and masturbation are fairly common. This reduces the sense of guilt boys feel, because they know other boys are doing it as well. They also realise that they are like other boys and that the practice is widespread. Although this developmental phase is frequently homosexual in this way, it is completely normal and should not really be called homosexual at all.

Although a few boys may be seduced by older girls or women at this stage, most are unable to handle heterosexual advances even from girls of about their own age.

Old erotic interests in his mother (from the Oedipal stage of development) re-emerge and the process of final growing away from her begins, so eventually freeing the boy to love and to make love to a woman outside the family. His father and 'extensions' of his father in other admired men are usually idealised and used as models. They usually inspire his day-dreams of achievement. In some cases old rivalries and fears of his father may surface again, sometimes leading to depression and, rarely, to suicide.

The reawakening of his attraction to his mother is the starting point of the boy's interest in heterosexuality. Although his outward attitudes may not show it, his notions about girls begin to change sharply. Girls become increasingly desirable and of fascinating interest. This can lead to blushing and social unease when he is in contact with them. He very often uses 'girlie' or naturist magazines, although guiltily, to stimulate his sexual fantasies. Discussions about, and definitions of, pornography are endless but a practical way of looking at the subject is to distinguish it from erotica on the basis that pornography promotes incorrect sexual learning. Obviously adolescents, and particularly early-adolescent boys who are in a stage of rapid sexual learning, need to be shielded from pornography.

EARLY ADOLESCENCE

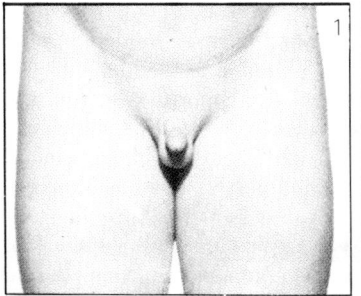

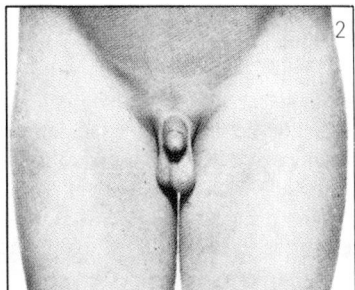

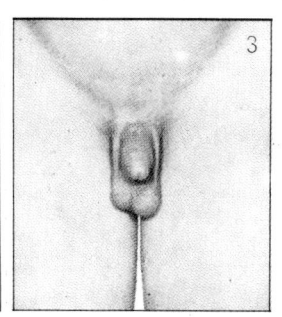

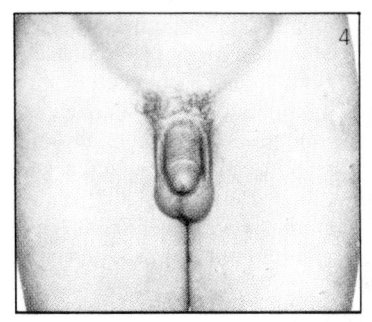

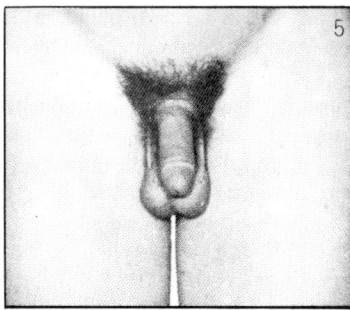

Genital development in boys

1. Pre-puberty. Genitals are about the same size as in earlier childhood.

2. Scrotum and testes enlarge, mainly in length. Skin of scrotum becomes redder.

3. Penis begins to enlarge, mainly in length. Testes and scrotum also enlarge.

4. Penis continues to enlarge, with growth in breadth. Testes and scrotum further enlarge. Scrotal skin becomes darker.

5. Fully developed adult.

Whether 'girlie' magazines are erotica or pornography is debatable. If they teach boys that all the girls they are likely to meet will have bodies like those of the models or would automatically behave sexually as they do, then they may promote incorrect sexual learning. But in that they encourage an admiration for the female body and an interest in heterosexuality, they are undoubtedly helpful.

On average, boys begin to understand the mechanics of intercourse two or three years later than girls and are frequently well advanced into early adolescence before they get a grasp of the subject. As a result their sexual fantasies are vague and voyeuristic. Permitting them to see photographs or films of 'normal' intercourse helps healthy learning and can only be regarded as harmful if it can be proved that it encourages them to have intercourse too early and before they would otherwise have done.

Early adolescence is the time of the dirty joke. Although these may be entertaining, they inspire performance fears because they usually involve accounts of a huge penis or prodigious sexual feats on the part of the man in the story. Misinformation about women, their functions and their fatal powers is rife.

In all this, the standards and attitudes of a boy's group of friends—for which the psychological jargon term is 'peer group'—exert a powerful influence on his own. In the main this is superficial because his basic standards were set years before by his parents. Matters as unimportant as hairstyle and style of dress are common causes of conflicts with parents, but all that is happening is that the boy is conforming to the requirements of his peer group. Most boys are not overtly rebellious, unlike many girls, probably because they are given more freedom anyway. In many families a form of amused and mutual tolerance becomes established between a mother and her son from early adolescence onwards, and she exerts influence by persuasion rather than by any direct attempt to impose her authority.

Early adolescence is the stage at which teenagers start to take the initiative in forming relationships with others outside the family. If they have not got the social skills necessary to form friendships they become increasingly isolated. Where such skills are lacking, they can be taught. Usually, with boys, the friendships are with members of their own sex. Boys of this age have more friends than do girls, and confide in them less but worry more about their ability to make friends. They tend to be more concerned with competitive striving and with establishing themselves in the eyes of other boys, whereas girls are more concerned about feelings of jealousy in connection with their best friends. For adolescents of both sexes people in the peer group function as testers, models and mirrors outside the family.

Genital anomalies, delayed puberty, delays in one aspect of development (such as the voice breaking) or a display of feminine interest or traits can lead to teasing from the peer group, which is not unfriendly if the boy is likable but can result in self-imposed isolation if he reacts badly.

Many early-adolescent boys are concerned about nocturnal emissions (wet dreams) and also about breast development. The first nocturnal emission usually occurs between the ages of thirteen and fifteen and in some families the subject is totally ignored. Some boys become very concerned about the reactions of their mothers. A few boys not only display no concern about it but also leave evidence of masturbation for their mothers to find. Such boys are thought by experts to have difficulty in breaking away from their mothers.

The breasts (or just one) enlarge in around a third of all boys during early adolescence and this can produce embarrassment if it is conspicuous. It certainly produces plenty of teasing in school changing rooms. The vast majority regress spontaneously but if the growth is large and persistent, surgery may be necessary.

Summary

Early adolescence, then, is the stage at which girls and boys learn to accept their body changes and emerging sexuality as the start of their progress from childhood to adulthood. Although it is a time of considerable change for both sexes, boys, in general, face a less complicated situation than girls. This parallels the greater complexity the girl experiences in early childhood when, unlike a boy, she has to switch her affection from her mother to her father. In general, early adolescence is not a particularly stressful time for boys but it can disorganise and distress a girl.

Chapter 3

Mid-and late adolescence

Mid-adolescence

Middle adolescence, or adolescence proper, starts at around the age of fourteen or fifteen in girls and fifteen or sixteen in most boys. By the end of early adolescence boys are still mainly homosexual in a social sense but an interest in girls has started to develop. Nevertheless the boy is still looking towards boys rather than girls for approval and friendship. Any social contacts with girls are usually undertaken along with other boys. Although for most girls the main friendship is with another girl, a girl's heterosexual drive and interests have been much greater than those of boys throughout early adolescence. A number are in heterosexual relationships, usually with older boys, and intercourse may have occurred. A girl with a boyfriend is likely to think of him as her best friend.

A recent survey of nearly 800 fifteen-year-olds revealed that girls, compared with boys, were more concerned about their personal safety, their 'looks', criticism from others, arguments with their parents, confusion about life, speaking-up in class, the health of their mothers, obtaining a job eventually and their ability to do it well. The concerns of girls are thus more mature and adult than those of boys at the same age. Worries about their mothers' health may reflect the reaction against that part of their unconscious mind which tends to hate their mother. It could also reflect the tendency of mothers generally to use emotional blackmail to control older girls by making remarks about the consequences of the girls' behaviour on their health. The phase of conflict between mother and daughter at this age can reach almost unbelievable levels of ferocity in some instances and contact with the family may even be severed by the girl running away. Alternatively a girl of this age may 'punish' her mother by becoming pregnant or in some other way.

As we pointed out above, girls have many concerns and, if they feel that they will only receive criticism instead of help and that their parents will make no attempt to see their point of view, a dramatic act or series of acts may be called for in order to establish their position. This happens in mid- or late adolescence. If a level of contact, no matter how tenuous, can be maintained between a mother and her daughter then everything usually works out well in the end, although it can take several years.

A lot of this kind of trouble could be avoided if parents

MID- AND LATE ADOLESCENCE

Who are the wallflowers here? In the late teens boys lag behind girls in their social development.

New attitudes and perceptions.

recognised that most girls are in a conflict over their desire to please their parents but also to grow up and fulfil their own needs. Adolescents, both boys and girls, criticise themselves enough and require little in the way of external help in the matter. Approval and success at home increase their self-confidence and protect them from excessive peer-group pressures and also from flagrant rebellion.

Survey evidence shows that the majority of mid-adolescents get on well with their parents and respect and admire them. A survey of 1000 teenage boys revealed that most felt understood by their parents, regarded their discipline as reasonable and were proud of them. Nevertheless, mid-adolescence is the time when the instinctual sex drive is finally withdrawn from the direction of the opposite-sex parent and is invested in the adolescent him- or herself. Masturbation rates tend to rise, as does a preoccupation with the self and the body. The capacity for abstract thinking which starts in early adolescence increases and results in mid-adolescence being a potentially creative period. Girls may begin to keep diaries recording their moods and activities. Emotional and romantic feelings can be inspired by things like literature and landscapes. Poetry writing may start. Although mid-adolescents can be savage, more in the way of mindless violence than for any purpose, the stage is usually one in which inner feelings of tenderness and beauty develop.

Sexual fantasies keep in step and although they may include unusual or even 'deviant' elements, active involvement with the opposite sex begins to emerge in fantasies. Although girls may have earlier explored their vaginas, and many may have used tampons, the vagina becomes more significantly incorporated into the body-image at this age. Earlier crude but situationally exciting fantasies of, for example, stripping, give way more to fantasies of 'making love'. Psychosexual history-taking from a spectrum of girls and women, not just those with sexual problems, shows that by the age of sixteen something like three-quarters of girls have included vaginal activity both in their fantasies and their masturbatory practices. The physically relatively insensitive vagina becomes psychologically sensitive. Thoughts of using her vagina to show her emotional feelings to a boy, and the pleasure his penis will obtain from it, become exciting.

Mid-adolescents may be involved in heterosexual relationships but intercourse is not at all common, especially for boys. It is more a time of sexual rehearsal in fantasy and self-generated romanticism which may be placed on a member of the opposite sex though almost always in a play-acting way. This is not to deny that, for example, a sixteen-year-old girl can love a boy, but it must be said that she can only love him to the extent to which a sixteen-year-old is capable. Although mid-adolescents may wax lyrical about their boyfriend or girlfriend, when seen a year or two later, they not infrequently have some difficulty in recalling their names. Early and pre-intercourse heterosexual experimentation may arise in this stage and fondling of the breasts and vulva may occur, but most girls are too shy and most boys too ignorant for this to progress to mutual masturbation. Most girls do not handle their boyfriend's penis during this stage. However, many mid-adolescent and some early-adolescent girls behave provocatively, not so much with the intention of having intercourse but more to reassure themselves that they can attract male attention. Such behaviour can be misunderstood by boys and men, and rape, or something close to it, may be the result. Probably the majority of such assaults are not reported to anyone at the time because the girls feel partially guilty or afraid.

Mid-adolescence is the true turning point from childhood to adulthood. As well as sexual, emotional, social and personality development taking place, career choices are usually being explored. It is a time of expansion, but the mid-adolescent still relies heavily on his or her parents. Moods can change rapidly from feelings of despair to exaltation and day-dreams are common. Everything and yet nothing seems possible.

Late adolescence

Late adolescence starts around the age of seventeen or eighteen in girls and about eighteen to twenty or later in boys. It is basically a time of changing relationships, even with the self. It represents the last days of childhood.

Independence from parents increases, although some late adolescents cling to their families and in some families the parents cling to the child. As at all stages boys are given more freedom than girls and usually still feel comfortable at home. Girls can be very conscious of their need to escape: into work away from home, into higher or further education and even into marriage. When they do escape they often pass through a phase in which they want to reduce contact with home to a minimum whilst maintaining a friendly relationship.

Parental criticism or disappointment still hurts the late adolescent but most consult their parents about important decisions and sooner or later do accept their advice. Some parents are excellent at giving approval and support to late adolescents without interfering but others try to exert total control. The latter court the risk of open or covert rebellion or, if the child submits, of changing his (more frequently than her) future growth. Open rebellion can take the form of delinquency or, in girls, unsuitable relationships, a premarital pregnancy and so on. Covert rebellion is sometimes expressed in failure of one form or another. Late adolescents are not fully realistic about their parents, but the old idolisation of the parents that was present in childhood is usually overthrown in mid-adolescence. The emotional feelings withdrawn from the parents (and especially the opposite-sex parent) into the self by mid-adolescence are available in late adolescence for investing in significant relationships outside the family.

From mid-adolescence the child increasingly creates his or her own social life independent of his parents, but in late adolescence the emphasis is on opposite-sex relationships. Progressively throughout adolescence the individual becomes increasingly cynical about friendships and by late adolescence, in contrast with early adolescence, feels that the chances of finding a new, good friend are increasingly remote. At this stage many girls say they dislike other girls but boys still mainly function in groups of one kind or another. Boys often see a girlfriend only as someone with whom they share sexual, but few other, intimacies.

Emotional development along adult lines proceeds rapidly but in girls, on average, it occurs two or more years earlier than in boys of the same age. Girls are more ready to commit themselves to a relationship, perhaps partly motivated by guilt over their sexual activities, and sometimes regard their boyfriend as being more committed to them than he really is. By the late teens some boys still look upon girls either as medals or as game to be tracked down. This is not so much the result of their insensitivity but rather reflects the more rapid progress of girls and poor sex education for boys. Misunderstandings are rife and more girls think of themselves as being engaged, to a greater or lesser degree, than do boys. Suicidal gestures can be the result of the rejection which ensues. Although adults can be very impatient with such gestures it is important to remember that the girl is really saying that if she cannot be loved she does not even want to live.

Girls, much sooner than boys, can become preoccupied with thoughts of loving and being loved, and they may cry themselves to sleep thinking about it. Late adolescence can be a harrowing time for a girl and bouts of depression are common. At this stage some girls become more or less passive, being chosen rather than choosing. Older and even married men can seem very attractive, not only because of their resources and experience but because ultimately the girl knows there is little hope of an enduring relationship, so ending the liaison distresses her less. Paradoxically, with older men she feels she is doing more of the choosing and is more in charge. As she becomes more self-confident her sights usually become set on men more of her own age.

Boys reach the same age of emotional development later (at around twenty-three to twenty-five), than girls, but because women tend to marry men a few years older than themselves, most men do not have to experience rejection distress. This is not to say that boys have less anxiety than girls; it simply takes a different form and is more concerned with approaching girls and, eventually, sexual-performance fears. Some late-adolescent boys conceal their anxiety behind aggressive behaviour towards girls.

The average girl today first has intercourse around her eighteenth birthday, and probably more than 95 per cent of girls first have intercourse between the ages of fifteen and twenty, whereas the range amongst boys is much wider. Male virgins of twenty-three to twenty-five are not uncommon. As a result, many young women today have had one or more fairly intense relationships before they finally marry. If this helps them to deal better with sex and any guilty feelings and so frees them to choose a partner based on personality factors rather than being swayed by an obsession with genitality, then this is beneficial.

Although most earlier sex education has been too little and too late, there is an intense practical interest amongst late-adolescent and young adults about the establishment and maintenance of relationships. Many really do want to know how to understand and please the opposite sex, and not just physically. They want to know if anything is wrong with them and if so how to correct it. Minor defects can be sources of agonising worry. In spite of being nearly adult they can easily be disorganised by anxiety and need parental support.

Various strands of their previous development now begin to be knitted together, for good or ill, but change, even dramatic change, is still possible. Although what happens in childhood has immense consequences, it is not necessarily permanent. New attitudes, perspectives and insights are possible and late adolescence is the last chance before the relatively fixed attitudes of adulthood overtake the individual. A lot of preventive work can be undertaken with late adolescents, but the majority have no readily available service to help them, unless they are in extreme distress. As a result, maladaptive attitudes towards the self and others are carried forward into adulthood where they ultimately cause trouble either for the individual or those around him or her.

Like most people, late adolescents need success but, because they are at the starting-line of adult life, their needs are particularly great. Although some may seem self-assured and even arrogant, typically under-confidence and self-doubt are never far away. They

(overleaf) *Young love*: She is obviously in love with him but is he sufficiently well developed emotionally to really love her?

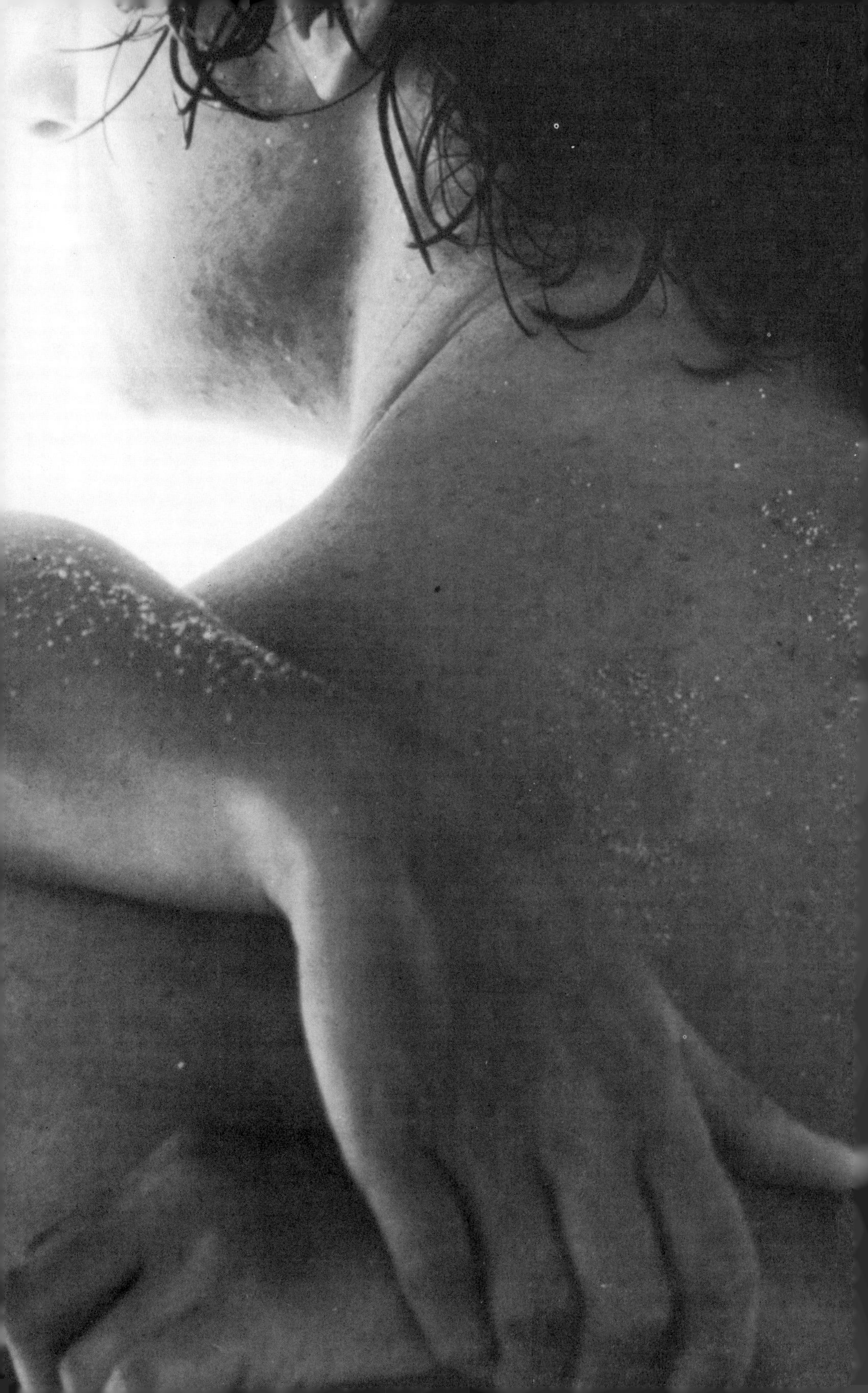

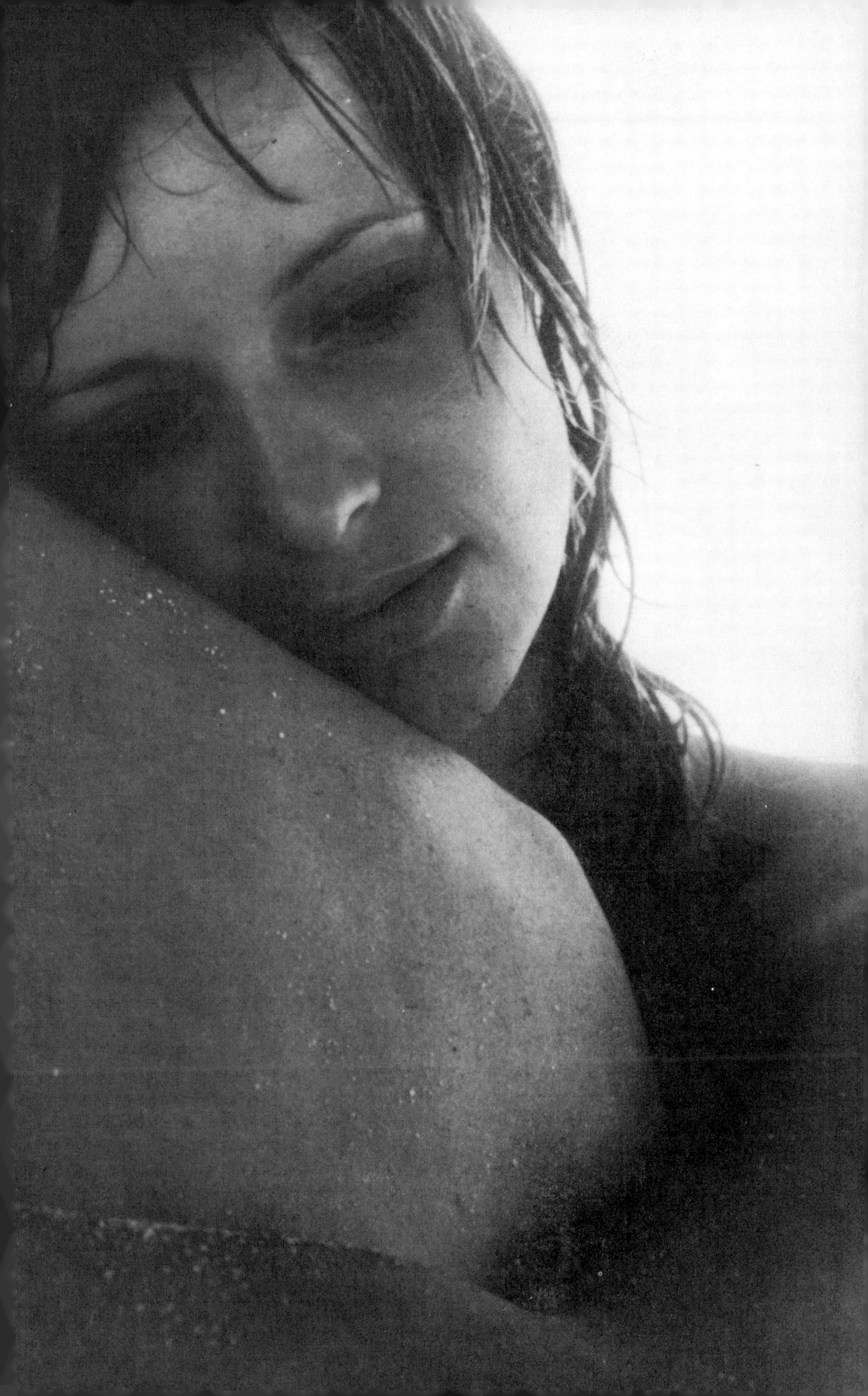

are in a difficult situation because they are becoming increasingly aware of their need for a relationship with a member of the opposite sex. This is more than a genital need, although men reach their lifetime peak of sex drive during this period. This is before many, or even most, of them have had intercourse. Contrary to survey evidence, girls probably reach their peak of masturbation rates earlier, perhaps in the late part of middle adolescence or early in late adolescence.

Young adulthood

Late adolescence ends around the age of twenty to twenty-one in girls but not until twenty-three to twenty-five in boys and for some well beyond that. It is succeeded by young adulthood. In this stage young women usually become less apprehensive about themselves, probably because of the confidence gained as a result of earlier successes (even if the relationship did not last) with men. They appear, in general, to be more philosophical and more capable of taking a long-term view of the future. In general, too, their relationship with their mother improves and most mothers appear willing to accept their daughter as an autonomous person.

Poor relationships between a father and his son can reach crisis proportions in late adolescence and early adulthood, as the son begins to feel more self-assured. Where it continues at a vicious level it is often found that Oedipal factors are still at work in the son and his relationships with women are often disturbed.

As a part of the late-adolescent process, the individual changes his or her relationship with society. Criticism and idealism may find expression in political or religious activity but also in good works towards others. The childhood tendency to divide the world into goodies and baddies still recurs and may cloud judgement, but it recedes throughout adolescence except in the politically disturbed faction of late adolescents and young adults. In the main there seems to be a working out—or not working out—of childhood grievances which are usually unconscious and elevated to some point of political principle which then has to be imposed on the whole community if possible.

Summary

Again, as in several other periods of psychosexual development, the girl has more complicated tasks to fulfil in late adolescence. In both sexes the stage is a heterosexual one although by far the most frequent form of sexual expression is masturbation. The sexualised love withdrawn from the opposite-sex parent is invested in the self and this makes late adolescence an important milestone in learning to love.

Late adolescence is also a time of great change, particularly in relationships, and young adulthood is the period of stabilisation which follows it. Romanticism is still rife in late adolescence but it is to be hoped that it is tempered a little by reason in early adulthood. Equally, it is to be hoped that it is never lost.

Chapter 4

Sexual attraction

Whilst it is obviously true that men and women are aroused by each other's bodies, arousal takes years of learning and there is a wide range of preferences for body and personality types. This is just as well given that 95 per cent of us eventually marry and preferably find a mate who is sexually attractive to us.

Choosing your type of partner

What happens normally is that boys and girls think about the things that interest or excite them while masturbating. The pleasant sensation of masturbation reinforces the enjoyment of the fantasised person, situation or object and the adolescent takes this image or fantasy 'on board' as part of the growing sexual personality. How and what the adolescent fantasises depends to some extent on his or her personality and several studies have been done in this area. In one, ninety-five men were shown silhouettes of female figures which had varied breast, buttock and leg sizes. The researchers found that different types of men emerged according to their preferences for the silhouettes. The 'breast men' tended to be *Playboy* readers, extrovert and masculine in their interests, and those who liked small-breasted women were inward-looking, submissive, drank little and held fundamental Christian beliefs. Men who liked large buttocks were also keen on neatness and order and those who liked small ones were work-centred and uninterested in sport. The most remarkable characteristic of those who preferred large legs was that they drank little and were shy in social situations. Men who preferred small legs drank very little but they smoked, and read sports magazines rather than *Playboy*. In general, a preference for large women was linked to ambition and a high consumption of alcohol whereas men who preferred smaller women were persevering and of a higher social class.

Similar studies of women looking at male outlines show that they prefer 'V's rather than 'pears' in male body shape. Women who liked large men were more likely to be interested in competitive sports. Smaller women preferred large men and so did those raised in fatherless homes.

There are definite class differences in likes and dislikes. In one study which involved psychiatrists, psychologists, porters, maintenance men and soldiers being shown fifty colour photographs of women, some women were found to have almost universal appeal regardless of the age, social class or marital status of the men. There were some interesting differences too. The porters and soldiers preferred the photos of naked, large-breasted women who were being sexy, and the psychiatrists preferred young, clothed girls who were 'unconventional' or 'provocative'. All the men tended to choose attractive and dressed women when asked to select a possible wife from the photos and they avoided those women shown in provocative or sexy poses. This and other work suggests that what a man finds attractive in a woman depends upon her age, social class, personality and to some extent on what he wants of her.

Research done with women looking at pictures of men shows that the professional and educated positively disliked the muscle-man type and preferred conventional, dressed men who were slim, dark and sensitive-looking. Men think that women like muscular, hairy-chested, broad-shouldered men with large penises, but studies have shown this not to be true. Women overall like men with small buttocks and a tall, slim physique and many in one survey said they were actually put off by the features men thought women liked.

Clothes

These set us apart from our immediate primate ancestors and most societies throughout the world cover up their genitals after puberty. Clothes do far more than keep us warm and cover our genitals. They can be used to change body shape and emphasise or exaggerate what Nature provided us with. Fashion is mostly about featuring favourably certain parts of the body or the proportions of the body, and both young and old use fashion to show off and improve their body appearance and attractiveness to the opposite sex. In one study, fifteen-and sixteen-year-olds were shown photos of very different female outfits and were asked what they thought about the person who would wear them. Not surprisingly they agreed on concepts of 'snobbishness', 'rebelliousness' and 'shyness' but they were also happy to make predictions about whether the person smoked, drank, had loose sexual morals or a lot of boyfriends.

Body odour

Our body's natural smells are an essential part of our attraction system, yet our culture has become obsessed with cleanliness and we seem to be intent on destroying or masking them. Certainly it makes sense and is pleasant to keep oneself clean but it is not necessary to overdo the deodorant or the perfume, because our own personal odours can have very powerful sexual properties.

As well as our obvious body odours there are other more subtle 'odours' called pheromones. These are chemicals produced by the body of an animal which have an effect on the behaviour of its fellows, as a form of communication. They are 'smells' which are not consciously recognised by the brain but nevertheless affect the behaviour of others. Pheromones have been widely described in various animal species and recent research has confirmed, not surprisingly, that humans have them too. A substance called andro-

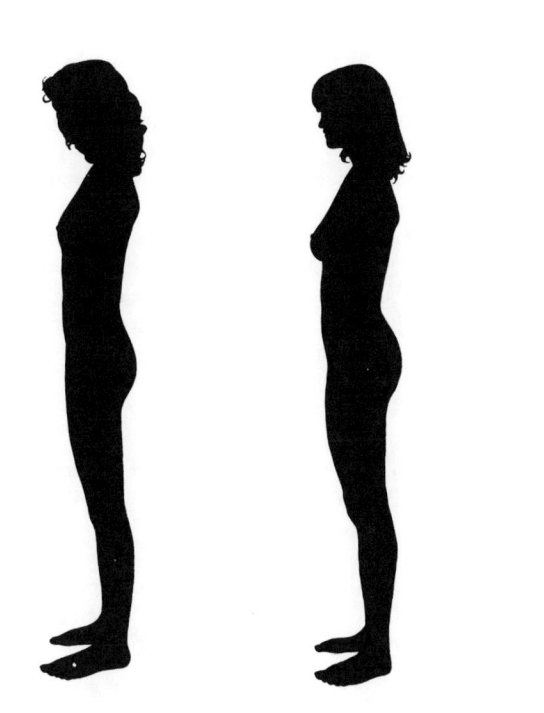

Different male preferences for the female body: Silhouettes used in one of the studies mentioned in the text to seek out male preferences for different female body shapes. Some of the findings were surprising

sterone occurs in male sweat and urine and has an attractant effect on women. Similar substances in women called copulins are vaginal pheromones which attract men. These are produced in increased amounts around the time of ovulation and arouse men most then. There are other fascinating pheromone phenomena. For example, women living together (in women's halls of residence, nurses' homes and convents, for example) tend to menstruate at the same time. Even though their menstrual cycles are quite different when they enter the community they tend to synchronise in time. One researcher spread male pheromones on the pillows of nuns' beds and found that those nuns' periods were disrupted from the 'norm' of the other nuns. This has now been called the 'strange male effect'. It has been found that telephones sprayed with male pheromones are used more by women than adjacent ones that are not sprayed; and that theatre seats sprayed with pheromones attract women. Even children can detect the sexual odour of adults and around the age of three sometimes have a distaste for the smell of the same-sex parent.

Faces

There is evidence to suggest that there is a widely held notion of the 'ideal' face. In one study people were shown photos of twelve young women between the ages of twenty and twenty-five and there was marked agreement as to which faces were the most attractive. The only people who disagreed to any extent were the over fifty-five-year-olds and some members of the unskilled occupations. As so many people agree about what is attractive they must clearly be making their judgement using certain shared standards. People shown photographs of physically attractive people readily assign them more socially desirable attributes than they do to photos of unattractive people. On balance, we also assume that attractive people will be more likely to hold top jobs, be better parents, be more happily married and have better lives generally. It also seems that we are more likely to trust physically attractive people on a first meeting than the physically unattractive. This confers a tremendous advantage on the physically attractive because by definition almost all contacts are one-offs and will never get any further if there is no immediate attraction. There is a greater chance that this immediate attraction will happen with attractive people.

Height

As a man's height increases so does our expectation of his socially desirable personal qualities. People tend to guess the height of authority figures and attractive people as taller than they actually are, and one researcher has noted that every American president elected since at least 1900 has been the taller of the two major candidates. Clearly, attractive people are viewed more favourably by society and not just by the opposite sex in the mating game.

Love at first sight

Many of us have been brought up to believe that the 'ideal' relationship starts with a glance across a crowded room. The eyes meet, it's love, and the couple live happily ever after. This can in fact occur, depending on how one defines 'love', because we can train ourselves to make up our minds about people on the slimmest of information. Almost all of us stereotype people and, using the flimsiest of information, make instant judgements about their personalities and characters. We meet many people in everyday life, and we cannot get to know them all in depth. We therefore have to use some kind of quick sorting method. Unfortunately, stereotypes can be harmful and can make us miss a good opportunity to get to know someone. This is especially true when it comes to occupations. Some men assume that women in certain occupations or jobs are promiscuous, so that the large numbers who are not either have to act up to their image or wait for a man who does not believe the stereotype and finds the woman attractive in herself. We have all heard that 'gentlemen prefer blondes' but in fact dark men seem to prefer brunettes and blond men's preferences are spread equally between blondes and brunettes. The majority of young women say they prefer dark men, with the exception of artificial blondes, who, according to one survey, do not care what colour hair a man has.

Once over our visual stereotypes we start judging people on their personalities. We tend to believe that people who get on well with others are intrinsically more attractive (or whatever we feel is important in life). In this way we link personal attributes to each other so as to build up a comfortable picture we think we can live with. So we arrive at suppositions such as 'a man who is this kind to children must also be . . .' Add to this a list of personal theories about people from past acquaintance (I once went out with a girl with long fingernails and she was awful, so this one with long fingernails probably will be too), and the field of choice one gives oneself soon begins to narrow. Some studies have shown that certain men assess women according to how similar or dissimilar they are to their own mothers.

Our reliance on judgements based on stereotypes can have unfortunate negative effects because we tend to behave in a way which fulfils our prophecies (and we all like that to happen). Studies have found, for example, that lovely clothes enhance a woman's social and sexual status. Even other women imagine well-dressed women to be more passionate, free, romantic, thrilling, approachable, adventurous, flirtatious and sexy than unfashionably dressed women. Media advertisements, showing women in glamorous settings with attractive men, confirm their view. One survey found that wearers of fashionable clothes were thought to have different dating patterns, sexual morals, and smoking and drinking patterns. But this can mean that unfashionable or unattractive women can find it very difficult to behave sexily, adventurously, romantically and so on simply because the rest of us do not see them in that sort of role. So the unattractive

Attraction? . . . Yes! But it could still be more physical and romantic than a true harmony of personalities.

and the unfashionably dressed are not encouraged to behave in these ways, and so they do not, which is then seen as proving that they are all the things they are generally held to be. This sort of self-fulfilling prophecy approach kills off perfectly possible partners at the starting post before we really know what they are like.

Getting to know your choice

Now let us assume that we are past the initial impression stage and things are beginning to progress. Based on first impressions a woman might think, 'He's a bit thick but I fancy him, so I'll pretend to be thick too so he won't be put off.' Armed with the 'knowledge' that Western men do not like their women to be brighter than they are themselves, she puts herself down and risks him being put off because she seems unintelligent. The man will unconsciously alter *his* behaviour to come into line with what he feels she expects and the charade gets off the ground.

Many men think that women most respect and enjoy the company of dominant men, and one survey found that girls certainly are attracted to competent men. But if men tried to overcome their incompetence by being dominant, the women found them more *un*attractive. The most appealing men were those who were competent and dominant. It does seem to be the case that men who have power and are good at what they do are very attractive to women.

So now our two individuals are talking and eyeing each other up. The main thing they are doing is making character and personality judgements, but they are also trying to find out if the other likes them. Smiles, nods, eye-to-eye contact and positive body language all help to build up a positive or negative picture. Some people are good at reading these tell-tales and build on them at once but others are very bad at it. If a girl finds a boy attractive there are common give-aways. She may, for example, tend to look into his eyes momentarily and then look away, or she may blush or she may giggle at the slightest joke or teasing.

The way we interpret these signs varies according to our mood from day to day. Studies have shown that aroused men (who had just read some sexy material) were more likely to see a girl as sexually attractive and receptive than were unaroused men. So we could meet someone on one day and be unaffected by them and then meet them again in a different and more receptive mood and really hit it off.

What you can tell by looking

In addition to possible physiological setbacks, which can include illness and family and money problems, there can be misunderstandings all through relationships but particularly at the beginning. Studies of what male college students wanted on a first date compared with what they thought the girls wanted show that they misunderstood each other right from the beginning. Whereas only half the men and women actually wanted or expected to kiss on this first occasion, three-quarters of them thought it was expected. Even

What do they really feel about each other? Everyone here is transmitting messages using body language.

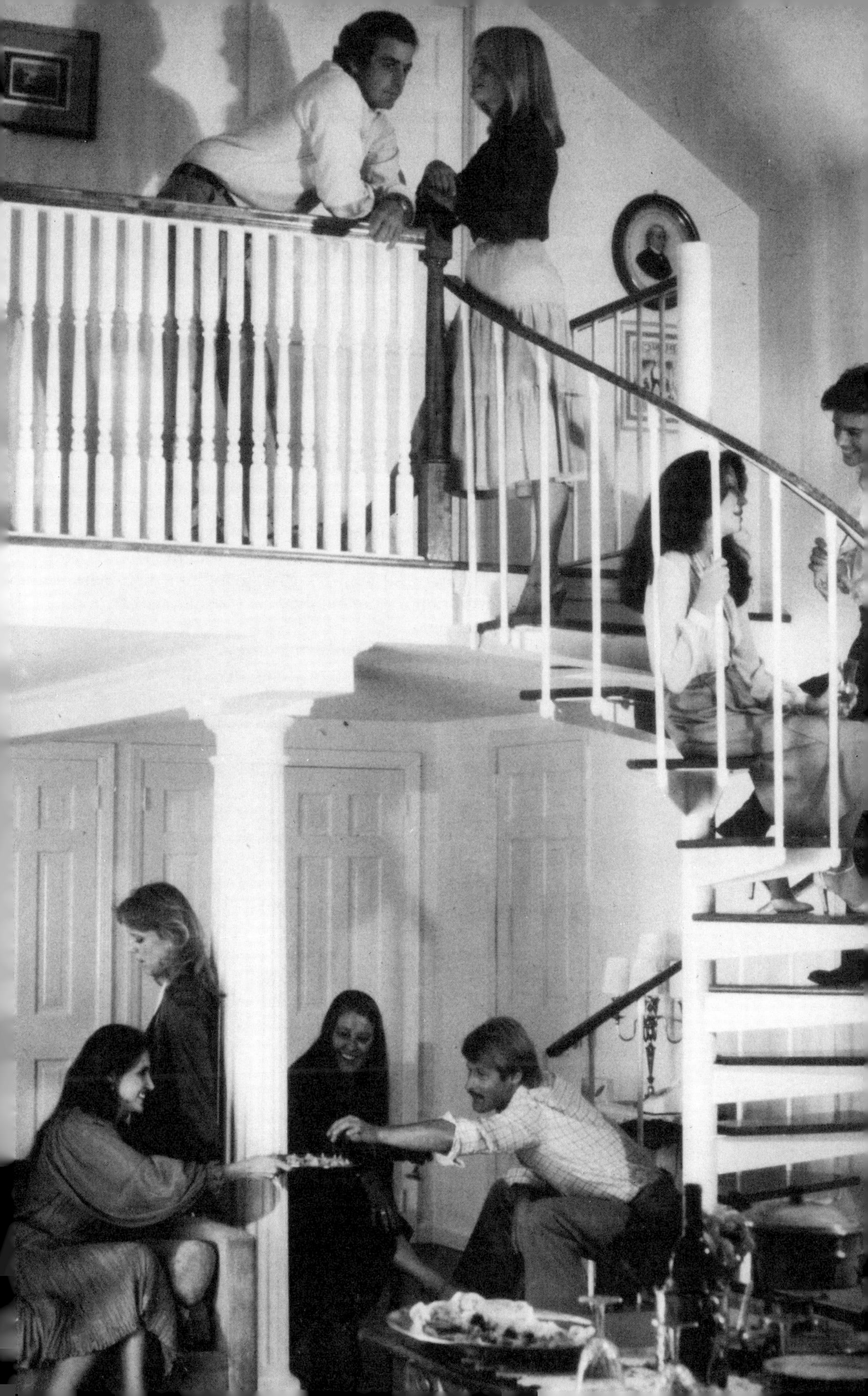

studies of engaged and married couples show tremendous areas of misunderstanding, so obviously there is room for a good deal more openness if relationships are to be successful and enjoyable.

Even if the level of communication between two individuals is not all that great there are certain things that one can learn from research and other people's experiences that help decide on a person's sexual availability.

Women of all ages are less permissive than men, but up to the age of twenty there is a slight rise reaching a peak then and declining thereafter, especially in those who have children. Women with girls in their late teens are least permissive of all, and are only exceeded by the deeply religiously committed.

The way people talk about sex can be revealing but it is a mistake to go entirely by what a person says on the subject. One study, for example, found that attractive girls were more likely to have premarital intercourse but that the attitudes to intercourse they expressed were no different from those expressed by unattractive girls. Similarly, studies of girls from religious families tend to show that they have intercourse younger than girls from non-believing homes yet their upbringing and outward signs would tend to point in the opposite direction.

Kinsey found that women living in urban areas were more sexually experienced. About 60 per cent of American men aged twenty to twenty-two admit to having had premarital intercourse (according to one survey), and the figure is about the same in Germany, Canada and Norway, rising to 75 per cent of English men. The English also lead this chart in 'one-night stands' especially among women, a third of whom claimed to have experienced one-night stands as opposed to fewer than 10 per cent in the other countries.

Once we get away from groups of people and consider individual *personalities*, things become more interesting. For example, studies have found that submissive girls are almost without exception virgins, whereas only about one third of dominant women are. Extroverts, hardly surprisingly, have intercourse much more often and do so at an earlier age, with more people and in a greater variety of positions. The differences are quite large. For example, 45 per cent of extrovert men in one study had had intercourse at the age of nineteen compared with only 15 per cent of the introvert men. The difference in women was even more startling—introvert women had intercourse three times a month whereas the extroverts experienced it on an average of seven and a half times a month.

Psychologically ill people tend to be promiscuous, have more premarital sex and have more 'hostility' and 'lack of satisfaction', according to one study. Very sensitive people tend to experience more impotence (men) or frigidity (women)—that is, failing to ejaculate and women failing to have orgasms. People with so-called 'hysterical' personalities were found in one study to be sexually very experienced but highly guilt-ridden.

Social give-aways that reveal sexual activity are fairly useful when assessing the field. For example, smoking and drinking are good clues to a teenager's sexual activity. Sexually inexperienced teenagers rarely got drunk and in one study sexually active teenagers smoked more than would be expected. Teenage girls who smoked more than twenty cigarettes a day were almost never virgins.

Girls who live away from home are more likely to be sexually experienced and girls living by themselves are least likely to be virgins. The lowest level of teenage sexual activity is found among girls living at home with both natural parents.

We have seen that attractive girls have more boyfriends but it does not stop there—they also have more intercourse. Attractive girls probably have a better sex life, twice as many male friends and have been in love more often. Attractive girls say that more of their friends have had intercourse but perhaps all their friends are attractive!

The subject of *virginity* comes high on the priority list of sexual attraction for many people and many men still want to marry a virgin. Very little is known about why boys remain virgins but some have religious scruples or other moral objections. It looks as though the vast majority simply have not had the opportunity.

Girls have been studied rather more, as one would expect. One study of adolescent girls suggested that there are three types of virgin—'inexperienced', 'adamant' and 'potential non-virgins'—and three types of non-virgins—'engaged', 'liberated' and 'confused'. The inexperienced virgin is the girl who simply has not had to make a choice because no relationship has ever got that far. The 'potential non-virgin' is much the same in that she has not met the right man in the right place at the right time; when she does she will probably have intercourse with him. The 'adamant' virgin believes in waiting until she is sure, for various reasons. Such girls were found to have a 'law-and-order' type of personality. The engaged 'non-virgin' is very common indeed. She will have intercourse only with her future husband, but the 'liberated' non-virgin enjoys sex for itself and does not insist on a meaningful relationship before she has intercourse. The 'confused' non-virgin does not know why she has sex but guesses that it will help her keep her boyfriend or get another.

In spite of all these apparently clear-cut categories it is probably true that, given that almost all women end up as non-virgins eventually, what the researcher is chronicling is the many stages of psychosexual development a girl goes through on her path to non-virginity.

In one survey of late-adolescent boys 58 per cent said they wanted to marry a virgin or, more exactly, to be the only sex partner the woman they marry has had.

Many girls (around two-thirds) who are not virgins on their wedding-day claim in surveys to have slept only with their husband-to-be but all such evidence must be taken with a large pinch of salt. Clinical experience suggests that this is much too low a figure and that many have had other sexual partners but dare not admit it—even to themselves on occasions.

What do you want in a relationship?

Even if on first meeting two people find they are attracted to each

Most people agree she was beautiful But what was she really like as a person?

other, it is essential before pursuing the relationship further that they sort out their ideas of what the purpose of the hoped-for relationship is. In other words, they should have realistic and mutually acceptable goals or they will end up wasting each other's time and even exploiting one another. Obviously, if either is thinking seriously of marriage as the end point, he or she will be looking for different things from someone who wants a short-term partner with whom to go to a social event or have sex.

Perhaps the greatest area of misunderstanding is over the subject of intercourse. Many girls will be displaying some of the pointers we have described in this chapter if they are potential sex partners. Some girls who are happy to get into quite serious petting would not consciously reveal a hidden wish to go further and others, in spite of their intention of being 'good', are frankly looking for their next sex partner—possibly one to marry.

So when a couple meet and start getting to know each other they have to make some rather quick and basic assessments of what each other's goals are. There are problems here because girls are occasionally misled by men—or even mislead themselves—into believing that the men want a long-term relationship and that they are in love when really all they want is sex (though not necessarily intercourse). A recent survey of what makes men and women unwilling to have intercourse at this stage of a relationship found that men said that fear of pregnancy and the inability to persuade the girl were top of their list, whereas women said that they did not have intercourse because they were not in love or because they would feel guilty afterwards, or because it was against their principles.

There is a lot of misunderstanding between the sexes. Men think women refuse to have sexual intercourse because of fear of pregnancy and for fear of losing their reputation rather than through shame or because they are not in love. The problem obviously lies in trying to assess such a delicate situation before embarking on the chase at all, and most of us try to do this along the lines described in this chapter.

Perhaps the last thing we should look at in the sexual attraction a girl has for a boy at this stage is the concept of love. Many youngsters, especially girls, find themselves 'in love' quite early in a new relationship. The most obvious thing about people who are in love is that they are blind to the faults of the loved-one even though these are pointed out by caring friends and relatives.

The infatuation stage of being in love is important in the context of sexual attraction because it can seriously impair one's ability to make reasoned decisions. There is no doubt in our minds, from clinical experience, that many girls of this age who feel sexually aroused by a man unconsciously generate feelings of love and protest them loudly so as to 'permit' themselves to go further sexually. After all, they have been brought up to believe that people only do 'that sort of thing' if they are in love, so they quite naturally assume they must be in love, because they are doing it. How much better it would be for many girls misled in this way if they could clearly see what they are doing and realise that they do not have to create a false emotion to excuse their natural biological drives. The sad thing is that such episodes debase the true concept of love between a man and a woman and make it even more difficult for people to recognise love when they see it in a potentially permanent relationship. On the other hand, if valuable lessons have been learned, all experience is useful.

Summary

Emotional and sexual attraction are complex issues of which we know only a few dimensions. Variations in taste between individuals ensure that almost any man or woman will be attractive to someone of the opposite sex. Hairy women, for example, often believe themselves to be unattractive but some men prefer them. Physical differences and even disabilities can be attractive to others. Physical attractiveness is the most important factor to young adolescents and to adults looking for brief affairs. Distinguishing emotional attraction from the physical is mainly an adult skill.

How attractive one feels depends enormously on how one feels generally. A recent good experience, such as a successful flirtation, can increase one's sense of attractiveness. For women particularly, how attractive they feel greatly influences how attractive they are. A good morale is vital to one's sense of attractiveness.

Chapter 5

Sexual encounters

So far we have taken our young man and woman up to the stage of finding each other attractive and wanting to take it further. What happens next and the speed at which the stages progress depend very much on the sexual experience of the two individuals and on their aims for the particular relationship. It would be wrong to suggest that all relationships at this stage have sexual implications; platonic (non-sexual) friendships are perfectly possible, as at any other age. Because of fears and anxieties many early relationships are platonic in the non-physical sense but the relationship is nevertheless based firmly on sexual motivation. In fact such platonic relationships in over-inhibited, over-anxious young people can be ways of escaping sexual activity. Many teenage relationships do end up with some form of sexual activity—even if it is only kissing—because the sex drives are high at this age and both sexes are out to learn as much as they can about each other in so far as their inhibitions and fears permit.

Late adolescents usually have a firm idea of their sexual identity and will be starting to fall in love, as well as having feelings for each other. Mid-adolescence is a time of self-centred sexual preoccupation but the late adolescent gets pleasure from shared sexual experience. His or her emotional feelings are more mature now, and tender affection, for most, goes hand-in-hand with an increasingly strong sex drive. This is the time when love can overwhelm a teenager. It sometimes consumes his or her life and is often quite opposite to what the rest of the world thinks—it is not simply a physical or carnal merry-go-round but can be a very beautiful experience.

There is little doubt that the majority of taboos about premarital sex originated for very good practical reasons, including fear of pregnancy (and the problem of illegitimate children), concern about VD, and the destructive influence of premarital sex on the family and other social values such as property rights and hereditary titles. There is no doubt that there was also a distinct feeling that the young ought to be 'kept down' and that making sexual intercourse the prerogative of adulthood was a very effective way of doing this.

As we saw in chapter 4, when we discussed virginity, a few young people today have good reasons for remaining virgins before marriage but such people are in a minority. Reliable figures are very hard to come by but one survey showed that 50 per cent of all seventeen- to nineteen-year-olds are not virgins, although this is an under-estimate.

So it is clear that whatever the so-called morals of the matter, the majority of young people are sexually experienced on their wedding-day. Before we look at the stages that lead up to intercourse, let us look at the arguments for and against premarital intercourse and try to draw some rational conclusions.

Premarital intercourse

The basic questions seem to be as follows. 1 Should adolescents at a reasonable stage of their maturity (say in the late teens) be allowed or even encouraged to have intercourse before marriage? 2 Does such experience make them 'better' adults and more meaningful marriage partners? 3 Does it help them make a better choice of eventual partner? If we believe that the answer to question 2 is 'yes' then surely we have a *duty* to encourage young people to have intercourse in a responsible way. But there are two opposing viewpoints that make answering these questions very difficult.

Some people claim that traditional moral rulings on the matter are seen by all but extremely religious Christians and Jews as being outdated. Unwanted pregnancies are now largely preventable and, the argument continues, there is a cure for most forms of VD. It is claimed that it is reasonable for teenagers who are biologically, psychologically and socially ready for intercourse to experience it in order to help complete their personal and sexual development. That we choose to marry rather late in relation to our biological and social maturity is, it is further claimed, unfortunate at best and damaging to young people's development at worst. Surely, it is argued, sex, which is a matter of such importance in marriage, needs to be experienced and practised, and perhaps being more experienced sexually one could make a more rational choice of partner. According to this view it is ridiculous and totally unreasonable to expect people to go into the most important relationship in their lives totally unprepared and inexperienced in one important area—rather like tying one arm of a boxer behind his back before a big fight. Those older teenagers who are in a stable relationship should be allowed, it is suggested, to enjoy this highly pleasurable experience, provided that it is done responsibly and in a way which encourages a growth of knowledge and understanding of the opposite sex.

The opposite view is partly based on traditional morals and on other, more modern, reasoning. Intercourse, it is argued, is not simply another pleasure but has serious implications for those who indulge in it. There should therefore be some culturally imposed restrictions that enable only people in mature, stable relationships to enjoy it. There is, such people argue, also a considerable danger that premarital intercourse will lead to a reduction in the quality of man–woman relationships because it will lead to a reduction of tenderness and affection and to more haphazard matings. Simply going all-out for pleasure is, it is argued, no guarantee of personal growth and to have a variety of premarital partners has been proved *not* to increase marital stability later. Such people accept that delaying first intercourse undoubtedly produces stress for the couple but they feel that such a

The public display of a private commitment (above).

The public display of a public commitment (right).

delay is necessary for social and psychological development to occur. Responsible sexual activity is an adult pursuit and indulging in it early will not bring maturity any sooner. Lastly, cultural pressures have been (and still are) so great against premarital intercourse that youngsters will inevitably feel guilty if they do go against such morals and this will be yet another negative factor in their growth and attainment of maturity.

The third major argument is centred around long-held beliefs or feelings (often based on religious taboos) that premarital sex, like murder, is simply 'wrong' and unacceptable on these grounds alone.

So what can we add to such a complex argument that could be at all helpful? There are several useful points that come out of many years' clinical experience.

First of all, anyone who has *strong* religious or moral qualms about premarital intercourse should stick to their views and remain celibate until marriage. Obviously the pressure comes when one of a couple has one view and the other the opposite. It is then up to them to sort out the question between them in a rational way. If the

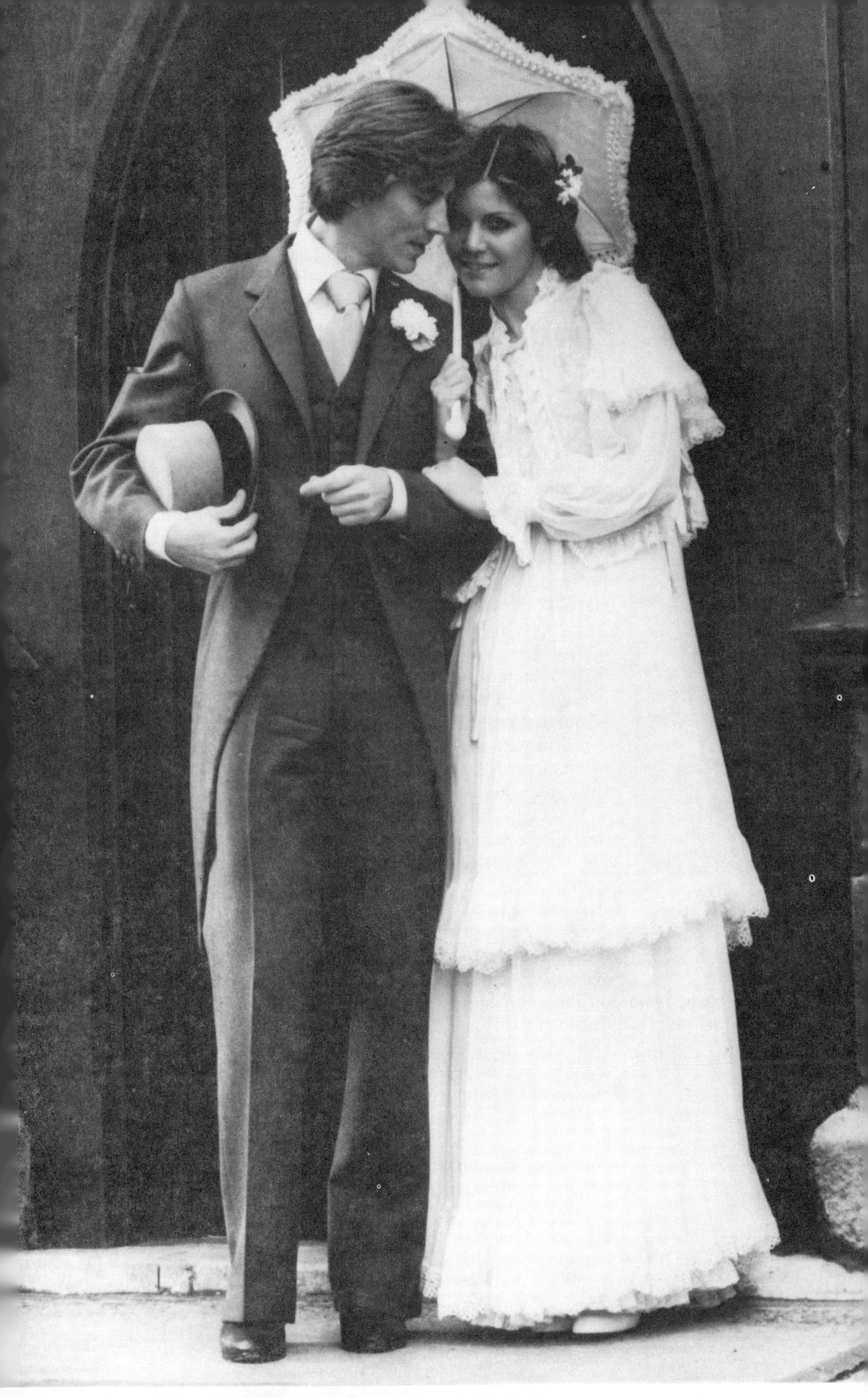

relationship fails as a result, so be it—it could have failed anyway at some later stage and most people who feel very strongly about moral questions end up feeling guilty or hating themselves for going against their better judgement. It is simply not worth doing this.

However, even this is not as simple as it appears. The young with psychosexual problems sometimes misuse religion as a refuge when their most sensible course would be to seek professional help. Apart from these youngsters there are those whose attitudes change enormously as they go through adolescence. Many girls, for example, assert during early and mid-adolescence that they will 'never do it' until they are married. By late adolescence they have almost all come to see sex as 'natural'—at least with someone they love.

The second point is that the average girl under the age of about sixteen to eighteen (and possibly even older for boys) simply is not mature enough to be able to cope with the depth of feelings involved in sexual intercourse and is better off without it. Intercourse too early (say under sixteen) is usually harmful, both at the time and later, and often brings more problems—emotional, physical and psychosexual—than pleasure. Intercourse should come as the natural end-point to an ordered and controlled psychosexual development which starts in the cradle. Jumping into bed in the early teens can hinder personality development and damage later capacities for heterosexual inter-personal relationships.

The third point is that adolescents all develop at different rates and many eighteen- or nineteen-year-olds (especially boys) are by no means ready for intercourse. Unfortunately, there is a tendency to conform with other adolescents and some may act precipitately as a result. Some teenagers overcome this by lying about their exploits and so protect their status within the group.

The fourth point to be made is that society has changed a great deal in the last generation or two and, whilst research shows that today's youngsters are in many respects very little different from their grandparents in their sexual activities, there is one big difference—they are more likely to go as far as intercourse. How each family comes to terms with these social changes in sexual fashions is up to them, taking into account their religious, cultural and moral views. We could not and would not want to impose some arbitrary standards on the many and varied readers of this book. Society is at present drifting further and further away from traditional moral codes in this area and little is happening radically to change the trend. No one would want to legislate further in this area, yet few families or teenagers are willing or able to discuss the matter openly or truthfully.

Drifting away from traditional morals.

It should also be realised that there is an enormous amount of hypocrisy on the part of parents who resent the opportunities of the young today compared with those of their own adolescence, and they frequently try (often unconsciously) to prevent their children enjoying the things they themselves enjoy as adults and as teenagers wished they could enjoy. If there was more honesty and discussion between teenagers and parents on this subject there would be a lot less rebellious premarital intercourse and a lot less emotional trauma for teenagers. Parents need to re-examine their views and be prepared to justify them to their teenage children if they are to have any hope of influencing their behaviour. It is hoped that this book will help promote discussion.

Finally, one sure thing is that if parents are overbearing and repressive about premarital intercourse, their teenagers are less likely to conform to parental requirements. On the contrary, evidence shows that they are *more* likely to rebel, so as to punish their parents, to express their individuality or simply to get their own way.

Sex has always been an 'adult' thing to do and late adolescents are keen to be seen as adults. So, they argue, sex is for them. If parents encourage their teenagers to see themselves as adults in other ways and give them responsibility in non-sexual areas then there is less likelihood that they will choose sex as their main way of demonstrating their 'maturity'.

Leading up to intercourse

Having grasped the nettle of premarital sex, let us now look at all the normal stages that lead up to intercourse, whether it occurs first in marriage or outside it.

No reasonable adult would expect their adolescent son or daughter to have no contact with the opposite sex—indeed it would produce a very unbalanced person if they were to. But between a boy and girl meeting and having intercourse there are many stages of sexual growth.

It is always difficult to know what is 'normal' in this area of human behaviour, so all one can do is to go by well-conducted research surveys and assume that they have not got things terribly wrong. Probably the best study of teenage sexuality was published in 1965 by Michael Schofield. Obviously things must have changed since then and without a doubt in the direction of slightly more sexual activity of all kinds, but probably not much more. This very substantial study, involving many experts and nearly 2000 single teenagers, is still a landmark in this field of research.

Let us look at the main findings and discuss their importance today.

Dating
Obviously dating is essential if one is to learn about the opposite sex and be able to choose a marriage partner. Girls started younger than boys, as would be expected, and over the age of seventeen the vast majority of teenagers, but by no means all, were dating.

Girls start dating younger.

Kissing
The first truly sexual experience most teenagers have is a kiss. In sexual terms Schofield and his team defined a kiss as one which carried at least a slight element of sexual arousal. Clearly a peck on the cheek at a party during a game does not count. The amount of kissing in both sexes matches very closely the amount of dating in both sexes and boys and girls usually experience their first serious kiss on their first date. Deep kissing (French kissing) is much more sexual and over

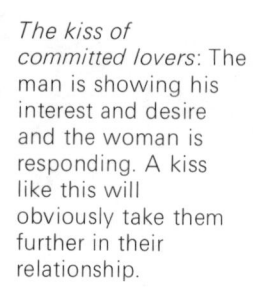

The kiss of committed lovers: The man is showing his interest and desire and the woman is responding. A kiss like this will obviously take them further in their relationship.

a third of the teenagers had never experienced it.

Kissing is a very interesting part of the sexual game, coming as it does first of all in the programme of social activity. Some people (teenagers and adults) do not like kissing at all, just as some do not smile much. Advertisers have so brainwashed us into believing that our mouths smell unpleasant that many people of all ages fear that they will be unacceptable to kiss. This is just one more way that advertisers can work on people's lack of confidence. Some people who have bad or crooked teeth do not like kissing, but a dentist can sort this problem out. Many a boy wants to kiss a girl but is afraid of rejection and fears that when he does she will find him not as good at it as she'd hoped.

When it comes to early kissing, here are a few tips:

1 Choose a moment when you are both relaxed and happy. Don't make a big production of it. Make it brief and sexless but on the lips.

2 If the girl (or boy) likes it, show your appreciation and do it again.

3 Don't do deep kisses at this stage.

4 Put an arm around each other and give a little squeeze or a cuddle.

A few boys describe how they become embarrassed if they have an erection when they kiss a girl and how they try to hide it. This is silly. A girl who likes you enough to want to be kissed will be flattered and delighted, even though at this early stage of the relationship she and you know you will not do anything about the erection. Girls are not sexless, but want to know they can turn men on. Don't worry unduly that the girl will think you're too fast—she may be pleased to discover the strength of her powers over you!

Kissing habits can be very annoying at any age so be careful how you kiss and try to modify what you do to try to please your partner. Slobbering noises and wet kisses are usually unacceptable and should be avoided. Having said this you cannot necessarily tell what sort of lover a person will be by the way he or she kisses. At this age he or she may simply be too inexperienced. Say what you enjoy and teach each other to do it. Also don't forget to kiss other parts of the body as the relationship matures.

As you start to kiss you will become pleasantly aroused and may confuse this with being in love. At this age (in your early teens probably) you will be sex-centred rather than love-centred and it helps to remember this, however cynical it sounds. Try not to say 'I love you' in the first flush of excitement. Love is much more than these sensations, however lovely they are, so don't debase it by saying something just for something to say.

Kissing is not an end-point but simply a stage on the way to a mature sexual relationship. Not every relationship is destined to have a future, so if you don't like things at this stage, for whatever reason, stop it and try again elsewhere or have a break from the opposite sex for a while.

In an established relationship, kissing is a means of communication and can take many forms according to one's health, emotions, feelings at the time, and what one is doing. Couples kiss differently when meeting in the street and when making love but it is always a way of transmitting information. Try kissing parts of the body that you know your lover is shy about. A scar, for example, once kissed is not thought so badly of by the owner. If you don't enjoy the way your partner kisses, gently and lovingly tell him or her so and practise until you both like it.

Petting

Kissing in our society is generally seen as acceptable even in public but anything more than this is deemed to be private. Any type of sexual contact short of intercourse is called petting.

Once a couple are kissing happily the man's hands tend to begin to wander and the girl tends to control how far he goes. When a girl is ready she will allow the boy to fondle her breasts outside her clothes, and this is very common. What girls like at this stage is gentle stroking and squeezing, with nothing at all rough. This is even more true when touching her breasts under her clothes. About half of all women do *not* find breast stimulation erotic and of those that do, many do not like what their men do. Except at the very last stages of sexual excitement before an orgasm (and this occurs very rarely in teenage sex play) most women want their breasts handled very gently and sensitively. We found in a survey of our own that most women like their breasts kissed (70 per cent) and sucked (68 per cent). Twice as many men squeezed their partner's breasts as wanted it done. All breast-play under clothes is best done with the girl's bra undone or it is uncomfortable.

Putting sex organs next to each other may be very pleasant but really has to be thought of as having all the dangers of intercourse. Don't forget that the first few drops of fluid that come from the penis before a man comes off (ejaculates) can contain sperms and the girl can possibly get pregnant. Also if one's partner has VD it can be caught like this (i.e. penetration is unnecessary).

Intercourse

The vast majority of teenagers do not have intercourse—they copulate. We shall see the difference between these two in chapters 15 and 17.

Schofield suggested that there are five main stages of sexual development in young people. By and large once a boy had gone through one stage he was unlikely to linger at that stage for long in that or in another relationship. With girls things are different. The fact that they are at one stage does not necessarily mean they can easily be persuaded to move to the next.

Schofield's five stages are as follows:

I   Little or no contact with the opposite sex; may have been out on a date but have never kissed.

II Limited sexual activities: kissing and over-clothes breast-play.

III More extensive experience: all activity short of intercourse.

IV Intercourse with one partner.

V   Intercourse with more than one partner.

A summary of some of Schofield's main findings.

1 Most teenagers had their first serious contact with the opposite sex between twelve and thirteen and fewer than three in 100 remembered being kissed before the age of twelve.

2 Breast-play was more likely to occur for the first time in a girl's home.

3 Very few girls had intercourse before the age of fourteen (one in 1000).

4 Girls who had intercourse before the age of seventeen almost always had an older partner.

5 Of those girls who had had intercourse, 82 per cent said they were going steady.

6 Most youngsters had intercourse in the girl's home or the boy's home and it most often took place in the house of the more experienced partner.

7 The first experience of intercourse for young teenagers was usually unplanned.

8 When asked why they had intercourse half the boys said they were carried away and half the girls said they were in love.

9 Fewer than half the boys and less than one third of the girls said they enjoyed their first sexual experience. In fact nearly two-thirds of the girls said they were disenchanted.

10 In spite of this, the majority of boys and girls were ready to try again and within one month 54 per cent of the boys and 61 per cent of the girls had had intercourse again.

11 Nearly half the girls had intercourse with their first partner on five occasions or more.

12 Boys who started going out with girls before fourteen were more likely to have premarital intercourse, as were girls who started under fourteen. Boys and girls who indulged in breast-play under sixteen were also more likely to have sex early.

13 Early sexual starters were more likely to come from less well-educated homes. Few early starters came from religious homes.

14 Girls sought a longer, possibly more mature relationship in their dating behaviour, while boys preferred to be more diverse and less committed.

15 Once girls had first had intercourse they had it more frequently than boys. Although girls took longer to commit themselves, once committed they were more sexually active.

16 The sexually experienced girl had an average of 2–3 partners in her teens and the experienced boy 6 partners.

17 There was no link between sexual experience and home background with the exception of social class among girls. Girls from higher up the social ladder were more sexually experienced.

18 There was a strong association between levels of sexual activity and the opportunity to entertain friends at home without parents there for both boys and girls.

19 There were almost no differences between the level of sexual activities in youngsters of the different religious denominations.

20 Over a quarter (29 per cent) of the boys and 50 per cent of the girls said they were in love at the time of their interviews.

21 Girls were much more likely to say they were engaged (16 per cent as compared to only 4 per cent of the boys). Obviously the girls had different perceptions of the nature of their relationships.

22 The most experienced girls had never had any advice about sex from their parents and such sex education as had been experienced by all the teenagers seemed to have had little or no effect on their behaviour.

23 The experienced, both boys and girls, seemed (from examination of their school records) to be more physically mature than the inexperienced.

24 Although far fewer girls than boys had been in trouble with the law, those who had been in court were more likely to be sexually experienced.

Girls want romance ... boys sex.

Of course the reader must remember that information about sexual behaviour obtained by surveys such as this, especially from young people, is very likely to be unreliable.

On balance girls think they are looking for a romantic relationship and boys for a physical one. Girls generally are hoping for their search to end in security, while boys are looking for adventure, but there are probably more girls around today in an adventurous frame of mind. Premarital intercourse is most likely when a boy makes professions of love and a girl believes that intercourse is a natural extension of her romantic feelings.

Summary

Sexual experience is gradually acquired in adolescents and very few social factors influence the situation. Society may find certain aspects of teenage sexual activity hard to accept, but it is a reality. Common sense suggests that it makes sense to accept the reality and to do our best to ensure that teenagers come to the least possible physical, emotional and spiritual harm. Total repression of emerging teenage sexuality is a forlorn hope and has negative side-effects both at the time and later.

A goodly proportion of teenage and late-adolescent boys who have had intercourse did not much enjoy the experience. Girls still exaggerate their romantic and loving feelings to justify their sexual adventures. Most boys and girls still have a lot of fears and guilt to overcome before they can enjoy sex and function properly.

The biology of growing up and the anxieties induced by our culture are in conflict and produce anxiety which in turn reduces sexual pleasure.

The adolescent has to pick his or her way through this sexual minefield and it is scarcely surprising that some are blown up. More rational attitudes could either increase or reduce teenage sexual activity but they would certainly inculcate a greater degree of responsibility into adolescents. Rebellious sexual activities would be greatly reduced; anxiety would be lessened, and youngsters would have a healthier and less confusing start to their adult lives.

Chapter 6

Who's best?

In short-lived premarital relationships when both of the people involved are learning about themselves and the opposite sex, all that matters is that they like each other, find each other sexually attractive and get along well when they are together. Such friendships rarely last long enough for the couple to make real discoveries about each other. Long-term relationships and marriage are based almost entirely on personality and it takes time to get to know what a person is really like. Most couples who end up marrying have been engaged or 'going steady' for at least a year. So with all the people we meet in our late teens and early twenties, we carry out a kind of repeated emotional and intellectual selection process to decide who seems worth taking from the short-term to the long-term stage.

To some people, even today, the concept of Mr (or Miss) Right is still very real and they have the notion that somewhere in the world is the perfect partner who will be exactly what they want. This is charmingly romantic but is not borne out by the facts. In fact one researcher in the field went so far as to say that about 75 per cent of all men and women in our culture are probably good all-purpose spouses and that with few exceptions any could marry any other and make it work.

The American sociologist Bossard found in 1932 that 17 per cent of 5000 Philadelphian couples had married people who lived within one city-block of where they lived and nearly a third married within four blocks. Only one fifth of the couples lived in different cities before marriage. More recent research has shown that while the distances have increased considerably since 1932 (because of better transport), we still tend to marry someone who lives within a very few miles of where we live. Other researchers have found that within a half-mile radius (and three out of every ten of Bossard's sample married someone that close) there were only five 'available' brides, so the man who marries the girl next door is very limited in his choice. The Bossard effect has also been noted in separate studies in London, Oxfordshire and Northumberland, and in France, Sweden, Finland, India and French West Africa as well. The effect is less now than it was, because people are more mobile, but it is still strong.

Why should we marry someone so close at hand when theoretically we could go to almost anywhere within our culture (not necessarily in our own country) and marry? The answer is complex and involves availability among other things. It is also intensely

Day dreams: Most people have some idea of what type of person they would like as an ideal partner and sometimes even fantasise the ideal type of relationship with them. One aspect of maturity is adapting to the realisation that there is no such thing as 'ideal' in this world.

practical. If one lives in London it makes sense to try to choose a mate from London rather than Toronto, or even Glasgow, even though there might well be many hundreds of suitable partners in either place. But one of the most interesting factors could be what sociologists call 'mere exposure'. If a man sees a girl regularly at work or at some recreational pastime he may not even talk to her over that time but his feelings about her are probably different after a year. Research has found that men feel more friendly towards the girl in such a situation; so simply seeing her a lot makes them more likely to find her approachable. Another study found that *other things being equal* a girl and a man who see each other every day for a year will come to like each other. Of course, this sort of exposure only makes the first approach more likely and does not guarantee anything after that. So apart from those who go to college or university, where the numbers of potential mates are very large, most people in fact end up choosing their mate from a very narrow circle indeed.

What influences choice?

A popular psychological theory for years was that men and women were looking for partners who would replace their opposite-sex parent—so a man would tend to marry someone like his mother and vice versa. Unfortunately, there is little evidence to support this long-held opinion and there is no evidence that people marry those who are like their sisters or brothers. Certainly people do not choose their spouses because of any physical resemblance to their parents. However, it has been found that men who had younger sisters and had married women with older brothers were happier than men with older sisters who had married women with younger brothers. In one study 600 college women were asked to describe and rate their ideal husband, their father, a male relative and their current male companion; none of the three people resembled their ideal mate closely but the current boyfriends just beat the fathers. Parents and the level of society in which one lives also determine the choice of partner. These constraints narrow the field considerably. Considerations such as age, class, religion, colour and social background all limit choice. Age is probably the biggest hurdle to jump because it is customary for men to marry women a little their junior and it is rare to find people marrying with ten-year age gaps. It is interesting that age differences do not seem to affect the success of marriages but it is not as surprising as one might at first imagine because marriages (between adults) are between personalities and these are largely independent of age. Nevertheless the happiest marriages have been found to be those between women whose husbands were four to ten years *younger* than they were. Several surveys have shown that people largely marry within their social class but that men tend to marry 'down' more often than women. All of these constraints seem to focus attention on the immediate geographical area and those available in a fairly restricted subsection of the community.

Not only do couples choose partners from those who are like them in the ways outlined above but they also choose those within this group who tend to agree on matters that are important to them. Several pieces of research have shown that people like and are attracted to others who are similar to them. Similarity of outlook and attitudes is more important but probably not very much so. What seems to count most is the subject's importance to the person involved and not its overall importance to others. So whilst a keen music-lover who was not very interested in current affairs would obviously agree that his interest is less important than say the nuclear-arms race, he would choose his friends or future partner from those who enjoyed music and would not care much about their views on nuclear weapons. It has been clearly shown that the more opinions are shared by a couple the more their attraction for one another grows. Having said this, there is a considerable tendency for couples to think they are more similar than they really are when predicting each other's attitudes and personality. If a couple are very similar they are said in psychological jargon to be homogamous.

But why should people choose those who are similar to themselves as partners—surely reason would suggest the opposite? Surely people with views that are not like yours would be more interesting and stimulating to be with, and you would learn such a lot. Although this might seem logical it does not work out this way at all. People tend to be attracted to groups of like-minded people of the same income, class, prejudices, race, religion and so on. It is common sense that if a couple spend a lot of their time disagreeing about things in life they will never have the time or emotional energy to devote to the things they agree on, and the relationship will suffer.

So homogamy makes good sense if only because like-minded people spend more time thinking and talking about things they have in common, which most of us find less threatening and more interesting. Apart from reducing conflict, homogamy makes mutual understanding and communication easier too. But it is not this simple. Most opinions about almost every subject are very difficult to prove and only have a value if another person believes in them. If I always disagree with what you say you will never be self-confident because your opinions will seem to have no value to me. So most people go for spouses and friends who will almost always reinforce their opinions and so build up their self-confidence. This gives them a sense of worth in their community. The reverse side of this coin is that most of us reject those whose opinions upset us and our social equilibrium. Because all our friends and our partner are roughly similar we can make assessments and judgements about them and their behaviour which would be impossible if there was little common ground between them. So by choosing people who are like us we reinforce our own ideas and 'prove' that what we are doing is right. This makes us feel good.

Unfortunately, what often happens is that a very dissimilar couple fall in love and one (usually the stronger personality) is determined to go ahead with the marriage on the assumption that he or she will be able to change the other. This change can happen but rarely does. Most people grow more like themselves as they get older. As long as the couple share sexual feelings for one another and there is some shared ground in other areas the relationship can survive for a while. Unfortunately many will end up fighting and subsequently get divorced. This is possibly only true for blatant mismatching though; most couples are not very similar and yet seem to cope well enough for most of the time.

For the purposes of our discussion so far, most men and women would agree about what they are looking for. But once we start looking more deeply there *are* differences in what the sexes are looking for. One survey found that American men wanted their future spouses to be affectionate, romantic, physically attractive and good home-makers, whereas the women wanted their future husbands to have conventional sex standards, good financial prospects, ambition and industry and to be considerate and sociable.

One British survey asked working-class people why they chose their spouse and got some amazingly 'trivial' replies. Many of those asked simply said it was because of his or her ways or because 'he wasn't like the others'. When they were specific they mentioned very minor details such as voice, manners or even resemblance to a film star.

Sexual behaviour is another area of behaviour which seems to influence partner choice. There are enormous differences in sex drive even in people of similar age and background. Some people are perfectly happy to have intercourse once a month whilst others want it several times a day. The classical story in this area tells of the sexual therapist who asked a couple (separately) about their sexual inter-

Choice: Obviously there is more to partner choice than the man's occupation—intelligence, appearance, personality, height, sexuality and availability are some of the other factors which will influence our choice. These in turn tend to influence the way we seek out our potential partners.

WHO'S BEST?

course rate. The woman said 'at least four or five times a month' with some pride while her husband's reply was 'only about four or five times a month, I'm afraid'. Perhaps couples select each other on their sex drive. Certainly studies have shown a high correlation in this area but there is more to sex than its frequency and better educated people everywhere seem to place a greater importance on variety than do their poorly educated brothers and sisters. Research has found that men think 'erotic ability' is very important in their fiancées and that their estimates of their own ability and that of their mates were closely related whereas girls' estimates of their own and their fiancés' ability were much lower.

More to sex than its frequency.

There have been some suggestions that people choose their spouses because of the same psychiatric symptoms and this has been borne out by several surveys which have found that husbands and wives do tend to share the same types of mental illnesses. No one knows whether this comes about because of 'like attracting like' or whether it is more a question of one 'drove the other mad'. However there is no conclusive evidence that people choose each other because of shared neuroses.

Intelligence does seem to be a potent factor in partner choice. Several studies have proven that people choose partners with a similar IQ. This argument is complex because social class and IQ are closely linked, and as most people marry within their social class it is probably inevitable that they will have roughly similar IQs. However, there is evidence to suggest that intelligence plays a more positive role in mate-choice. Interestingly, many highly intelligent women say that they want a man who is more intelligent than they are.

So far we have concentrated on similarity but everyone knows that opposites attract. We have already seen that if you are badly mismatched life can become unbearable, but many people with quite similar interests may have very different personalities. Indeed, some people go out of their way to find someone who will make up for their deficiencies, and women particularly can be attracted to a man who has a strength which she considers she lacks. Many such women say that children born of such a man would be better because these faults would be corrected. Such women often consciously choose an opposite and this can work very well. Unfortunately, it can become very complicated because a dominant wife may well want her husband under *her* thumb but may not enjoy having him under everyone else's too.

It is a pity that young people, when selecting a spouse, do not spend more time finding out in much more detail what makes their partner tick. There is no doubt that unsuccessful marriages are often based on quite crucial misunderstandings, some of which could have been sorted out before the couple got married. It is not very difficult to find' out what a person thinks about working wives, children, education, housework or other everyday subjects that people commonly disagree over, yet evidence shows that most couples do not discuss such things until courtship is well under way and the bond between the two is becoming rather too tight to break over a subject which seems at the time to be irrelevant to them. Unfortunately, five or ten years later when the sexual attraction has waned somewhat and the aggravation caused by the subject in dispute has magnified it can become a serious cause of rows and even marital failure.

A crucial part of deciding on a spouse is the 'getting-to-know-you' phase of courtship. During this time real problem-areas should be weeded out and the relationship ended or nurtured, according to the decisions that are made. But it is often not important matters that cause marital disharmony: many apparently minor areas need discussing early too. It is a pity that many men are so immature when they are about to get married that their fiancées cannot get them to discuss the realities of children and other matters which suggest domestic responsibility, for fear of driving them away completely. It is a terrible shame that the next time they find themselves in such a discussion it is often heated and causes a serious rift in the marriage. But interesting research has found that personality factors may not become important in their first year or two of a relationship when sexual attraction and romantic love carry the couple through. Indeed, researchers have found that certain women unconsciously delay the final stages of their personality development until they are in a permanently bonded relationship.

But 'beauty is in the eye of the beholder' and there are other compensatory factors that influence choice—factors which can

Come on, we're supposed to be there at 8.00': How do you rate their future together?

override the majority of those we have discussed. In some instances a partner who is completely opposite to the parents (for example someone of a different background, nationality or religion) appeals more strongly, perhaps as an expression of rebellion against parental rearing.

Certainly men are over-influenced by looks and sexual prowess in women and are prepared to write off other disadvantages if they think these obvious advantages compensate for them. Women, on the other hand are, after adolescence, more interested in the power they can sense in a man than in his looks. Under-confident women who fear that other women will easily take her man from her tend to choose timid men, assuming their shyness will ensure their faithfulness.

Summary

Although many people could establish a more-or-less workable marriage with a variety of members of the opposite sex, there are certain guidelines which are worth considering when choosing a marriage partner. Rushing into a relationship, an over-emphasis on romance, a restricted choice and sex probably all exert negative effects on making rational choices, and this is a pity because they can all be controlled. Boys with a poor self-esteem and girls who fear being left on the shelf are especially open to getting into unsuitable marriages.

Choosing a marriage partner should be a controlled, reasoned and carefully made decision. This chapter has outlined ways in which this can be achieved.

Chapter 7

Courtship

The concept of courtly love is a recent one, dating as it does from medieval times. Western women at this time were hardly respected at all, whereas Arab women were. Among Arabs there grew up the notion of an ennobling love that bore little relationship to their real personalities. From Arabia the idea evolved of love as something romantic—not a sordid sin but a divine mystery—and the lady who inspired it not a temptress but a goddess. This type of approach went down well with the ladies of French noblemen who saw the new concept of virtue as highly desirable. It is important to remember that until these times and indeed after, marriages were made for reasons that had little or nothing to do with what we would call love. Most often they were financial or inter-family arrangements that strengthened kinship. In fact in medieval times the concept of courtly love probably became so popular among women because it was thought that it was not an emotion they could have within marriage.

Today the concept of courting implies 'going steady' or, less commonly, one eager partner—usually the boy—trying to involve an apparently less willing girl. This latter situation is often known as wooing.

In many animal species a period of prolonged and more-or-less ritual courtship behaviour precedes the pair settling down to their reproductive life, and in many human couples it is really very little different. There are well-recognised phases they go through in the preliminary stages of a potentially serious relationship, and this process we call courting.

The way we are going to use the word in this chapter takes in all these meanings and implies that a certain amount of selection has already occurred between the partners. Courting starts beyond the stages of chatting-up, flirting, dating or going out together, at the point when there is a suggestion that there is potential for total commitment between the partners, usually to marriage but in cases where, for whatever reason, this is impossible, then to a deep and continuing love-affair and friendship. So courtship is not simply pre-copulatory and certainly is not a prelude to a one-night stand or to a brief fling. It is a natural follow-on from the subjects we have been discussing in the last few chapters.

Courtship is a time of exploration and adjustment. It is a time when the sexes can behave well and gracefully towards each other. Many a parent has been thrilled to see their oaf of a son or rebellious daughter become transformed almost overnight as he or she starts to court someone he or she is serious about. Not only do the young couple start to behave pleasantly and gracefully to one another but, ideally, they also start to share their secret and innermost feelings. This can be very difficult because most people's upbringing tends to make them secretive—partly because so many parents are negative in their upbringing methods and spend so much time telling their children off and putting them down. With this background it is understandable that many youngsters cannot readily trust someone to accept them as they are, warts and all. Trust, communication and understanding should all increase during a good courtship—indeed this is the main function of this stage of adolescent or young adult growth.

As these processes occur, vital questions need to be answered if the relationship looks like becoming permanent. Questions such as, 'Is it possible that I can feel the same about this person at 101 as I do now at twenty-one?' and 'Remembering that no one is going to be a perfect partner, are my capacities to adapt sufficient to accommodate to this person who is not quite my ideal?' Of course there are many other questions too, but the ones we have mentioned are cardinal to an on-going and loving relationship. In this respect the evidence suggests that females are more willing, or more able, to adapt than are males.

There is no doubt that the young, and the not so young, are best advised not to succumb instantly to their needs for sex and romance and thereby to short-circuit the courtship process. It is probably best to be a little sceptical and reluctant at first. The attitude should be, 'Go on, tempt me out of my freedom.'

Courtship, a vastly important stage.

Courtship is, as we define it, a vastly important stage where the partners test each other and themselves. This should be stressed in sex education and in the discussions parents have with their teenagers. Many bad marriages could be avoided if this were done. If the result of the testing, explorations and investigations is unsatisfactory to either party the relationship should be ended and not allowed to drag on. Even if the relationship ends at the courtship stage, the boy and girl should know more about themselves and the opposite sex, as well as having increased their skills of assessment and communication; they should also have a clearer idea of what type of person would be best for them. It is now time to try again with someone else and to be grateful that the wrong relationship ended when it did.

For these reasons we think courtship should be encouraged and the way to do this is to stress the pleasures it can bring. The cavalier poets were very keen to point out the pleasures of the chase and they were not wrong. Their nymphs and shepherds have now turned into the lyrics of pop songs.

While the amorous side of the relationship is progressing, other things are happening too. Almost anyone can be happy in bed with a new partner but it is much more important to discover whether it is possible to be equally happy when doing the widest possible range of other activities. Courtship is a time during which each partner should see if he or she can enthuse the other about things that interest them. If she goes with him to a rugby match, can he get her as excited about it as he is? And if she loves a particular type of music, can he share her enthusiasm honestly? It really pays to explore all the main areas of your life with your partner so that there will be no surprises later. This is one of the thrills of courtship—it extends one's horizons and opens new areas of experience.

On the sexual side what tends to happen when a couple meet, flirt successfully and then select the other as being 'special', is different for the sexes. Although boys usually make the sexual advances, as is culturally required of them, they often do not really want to succeed. They tend to 'idealise' the girl and their masturbation rate falls or even stops completely. Women, on the other hand, seem to envisage a total relationship from the start and their rate of sexual fantasy and masturbation usually rises. This is understandable, even in our culture, since from their youngest days girls, more than boys, seem to make more use of their bodies to express their feelings towards the things they like and love. The young man on the verge of courtship is probably reverting towards the time when he surrendered his childhood sexual interest in his mother at the beginning of latency (see chapter 1) and perceived her instead as being 'good'. It is therefore probably unwise for the young woman at this stage to be too open in discussing her interest in sex or her past conquests, because to many boys this can be unacceptably off-putting. The tendency for women to 'confess' at this stage, or perhaps at any other, can be unwise. Many do so because they feel they have sinned and want to clear the slate with their man. However, he wants her as she is now, whatever experience has made her the way she is, and it is this that he loves. Labouring an explanation or confession can actually do more harm than good.

When late-adolescent girls and women are asked how long they think they should go out with a man they like before intercourse occurs, the average answer is astonishingly short and is usually numbered in days. Promiscuous girls often entice men to have sex with them in an effort to divert attention from what they see as their other shortcomings, but studies of enduring, good relationships show that jumping into bed at the first opportunity is not the best way for most couples to behave.

Whilst we accept that there are numerous exceptions, by and large it is true to say that when successful relationships are investigated retrospectively it very commonly emerges that a gradual progress towards bed occurred rather than a headlong rush. This makes sense because it allows investigation of other aspects of the partner to proceed hand-in-hand with sexual progress. Unfortunately, our culture has for so long put restraints and restrictions on sex that this has created an artificial shortage of it. As a result, people are so preoccupied with the subject that it tends to get in the way of everything else. Thankfully, there are signs that the current generation of young people have the whole matter in better perspective than did their parents and grandparents.

Whilst accepting that some couples do not have intercourse during courtship (some do not even proceed beyond kissing), the

Stages of courtship

ACROSS A CROWDED ROOM.
*Attraction,
Approach,
Acceptance.*

Stages of courtship

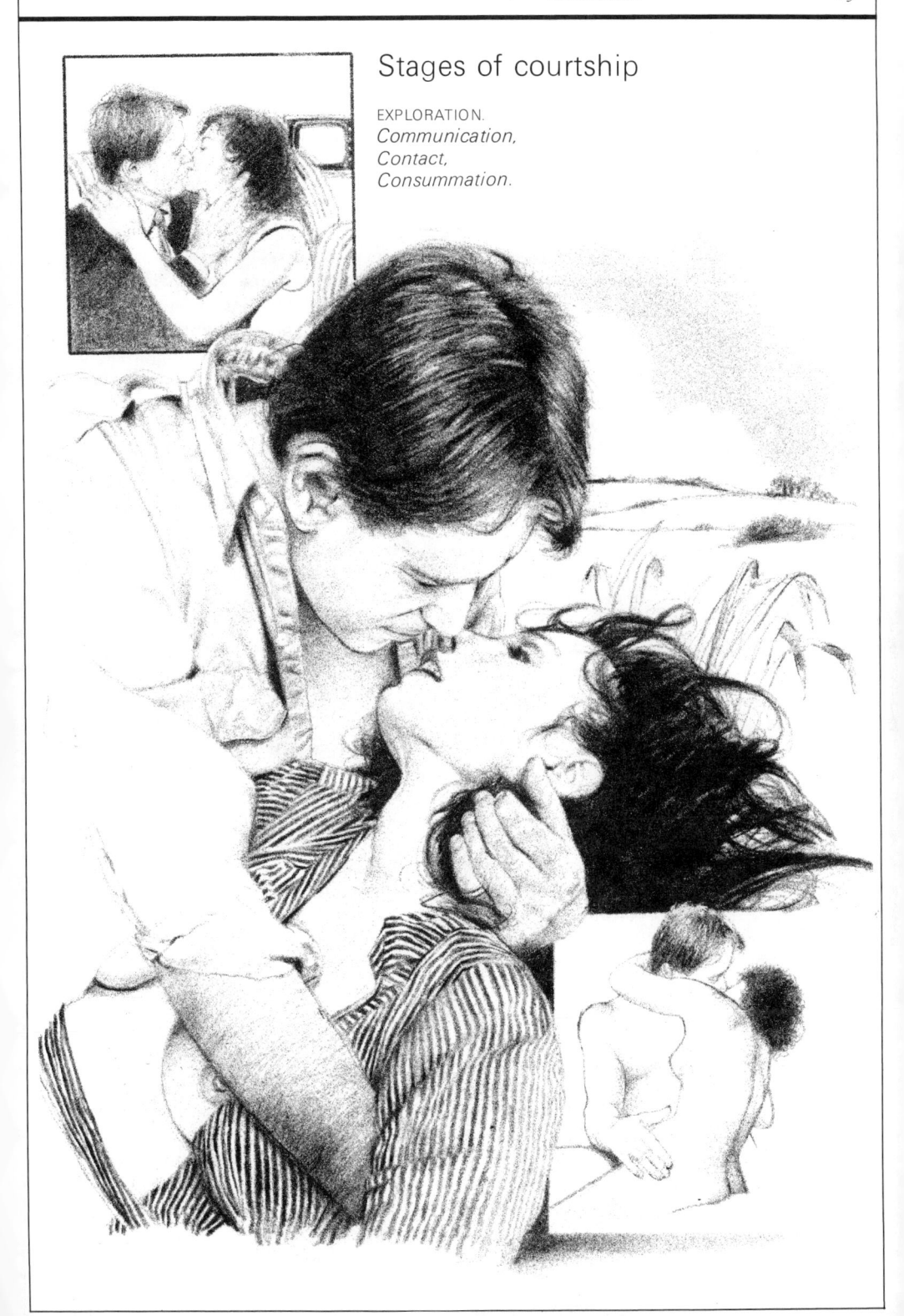

EXPLORATION.
*Communication,
Contact,
Consummation.*

majority do and this must now be accepted as the norm, whatever one's individual moral views on the subject. The majority of couples think that, if they are in love, intercourse is justified. Some men certainly exaggerate their loving statements so as to convince a girl that they are serious enough about her for her to agree to sex. Some such boys unconsciously regard women as being awesome and dangerous and therefore unconsciously try to disarm them by protestations of love.

Unfortunately, the man who professes no healthy sexual desires for his beloved and will not have intercourse with her 'because he respects her' is not always what he seems. Clinical experience shows that very often such males are unhappy about sex and their new brides frequently come for help some months later complaining that he still 'respects' her. This can easily occur because many girls are brought up to think that boys are only after one thing. Once she believes this, a boy who does not press her for sex can seem like a breath of fresh air. It may well be that he is, but beware, because he could also be very insecure about or afraid of sex and will not suddenly (or even ever) become the lover she wants. Very under-confident boys with a poor opinion of their masculinity will often marry early since, they feel, to 'own' a woman boosts their status. Such marriages usually end disastrously. The beauty of a properly conducted courtship for such a man is that he reduces his fears and anxieties about women and sex small step by small step. This is yet another reason for taking things slowly during courtship—after all we all have some fears and anxieties to overcome.

So clinical experience suggests that slow progress towards intercourse is advisable. The stages could each take weeks or even months but a steady impetus needs to be maintained so that adjustment can continue. The progress can, by mutual consent, be checked at any point (for example because of strongly held religious beliefs) but as long as the strong desire, although contained, is present it is not necessarily a sign of future troubles. Many couples with religious morals about premarital intercourse do just about everything else but stop short of intercourse, as did most couples in the days before contraception was easily available. There is no evidence that this is harmful to their future if they both agree that this is how they want to behave. It takes an almost superhuman feat of self-control to do this and some couples say later that it was not really worth the heartache it caused. These opinions are bound to vary greatly from individual to individual, even among those with strict religious views.

The stages of sexual advances may be: kissing, handling the breasts over clothes, handling the breasts under clothes, stripping to the waist, kissing the breasts, mutual genital handling, total nudity, mutual inspection and mutual masturbation—perhaps including oral sex. As well as revealing themselves physically the couple should also be revealing more of themselves psychologically, being open about approaches and stimulation they find arousing, saying how they like to be masturbated and sharing their fantasies.

Many benefits result from this slow progression: the acceptance and admiration of each other; the proof that they can excite each other; the confidence the man feels about his ability to satisfy the woman if he knows he can masturbate her; his becoming accustomed to erecting and ejaculating in front of her; and so on. Their sexualities are becoming fitted together so that when they do finally consummate the relationship, what they enjoy is intercourse and not copulation from the start. We shall see how different these are and why it matters in chapters 15 and 17. In this way patterns of arousal and satisfaction can be established. The couple learn to be mutually grateful and gratifying and so lay the foundation-stones for a successful marriage.

Many couples, unfortunately, only ever learn to copulate and their secret desires are never communicated. If courtship is properly carried out this problem never need arise. When the couple finally do have intercourse, whether before or after marriage, it stands the maximum chance of going well, which is good for them both. Shame, shyness and guilt will have been shed in the courtship stage and they should eventually be able to function without any restraint—physical or emotional.

When intercourse finally occurs it is not just the result of a desire for sex in its own right but sex *with the other person*. Ideally romantic behaviour should similarly increasingly be built into the relationship rather than, as usually happens, it being highly romantic for a short time at the beginning of the relationship only to die away as the years pass.

Pleasing sexual and romantic behaviour are good for full relationships, and progressively incorporating them into the court-ship stage should set the pattern for the future. To impose sex on someone at the outset of the relationship might work out but often it does not. Progressively incorporating sex and romance, based upon the exploration of and in communication with the partner, give them a foundation of reality rather than fantasy, and they are then better able to withstand the pressures of life over the years.

Another feature of courtship managed in this way is that in the sense that the relationship has not been ended by either or both parties it becomes a recommitment with every meeting. If communication is progressing satisfactorily the commitment is continuously strengthened. But snags can arise. Some, perhaps all, of us tend to display our good points and conceal our bad ones. A couple who really talk to each other during courtship eventually communicate everything, good and bad. In the end, if we love someone at all, we love the good and the bad. Real lovers often come to love the faults of the other as much, or even more, than their virtues. Many people feel that their partners did not truly reveal themselves in courtship but only after marriage. For many, too, romance ends on marriage or with the birth of the first baby and such reactions to these two events—each with its negative side as well as its positive side—are in part responsible for the very high divorce rates in the first five years of marriage.

Another way in which courtship can go astray is with the individual who is more concerned with the effect he or she is having on the other rather than vice versa. Women often seem to fall into this trap, believing that they can easily put right, through love and service after marriage, any imperfections in the man which they are ignoring at present. This is contrary to the spirit and function of courtship as we have outlined it. Courtship is not a prolonged con-trick with the couple acting out parts—or if it is the price will almost certainly be an unsuitable marriage.

Don't rely on change. Once people are adults they do not change dramatically, although personalities can of course be moulded and mellow with age, especially within a loving relationship. It is at this stage that one ought to look carefully at the other's parents and see what their relationships and personalities are like. Although it would be foolish to suggest that their personalities and behaviour are necessarily going to be reproduced in their child (the other partner) this is very often the case and it makes sense to be on the look-out for signs of things you could not live with. People do, after all, take after their parents and will certainly have been greatly influenced by them as they were brought up.

Summary

Courtship is, as we have described it, a phase of appraisal, approach and approval. It is, properly used, the transition stage between our promiscuous teenage desires and our hopes for a fulfilling one-to-one relationship. It is a process of exchange of one type of freedom for another and infinitely greater freedom—the freedom to be ourselves, to be understood, to love and to be loved, not in spite of ourselves but for ourselves. Couples who cut short or even forego courtship altogether miss out on this. Often they regret having done so for the rest of their lives.

Chapter 8

Engagement

Courtship is an intensely personal business but after a time, if the couple feel fairly sure that they are right for each other, they will want to start making long-term plans for being together. This will usually mean getting married. The bridge between courtship and marriage is engagement. Ideally this is a public declaration to the world that the two like each other greatly, are basically well adapted to one another, have done their 'homework' during courtship and are setting out to make a life together. Some people, especially in more formal times in the past, considered that engagement should occur before the intimacies of courtship, but this defeats a major purpose of courtship as we see it—the establishment of a degree of certainty about the relationship—and leads to unnecessary failed engagements and even to failed marriages. Once a couple have declared themselves publicly it is a lot more difficult (or even impossible) to go back and admit they were wrong.

It could be argued that our notion of courtship could open the doors for the promiscuous to exploit 'decent' members of the opposite sex but this is not possible if our advice about handling sexual matters is followed. Unsuitability would (or should) have been established well before the stage of intercourse is reached. If a man just wants a girl for sex (or vice versa) he is not going to be bothered with going through all our stages of gentle, controlled courtship and his real motives will all too soon become apparent. The girl who is being misled can then see this for what it is and is *less* likely to be taken in in this sort of courting—not more.

It is certainly wrong to hold an individual who wants to marry in a prolonged courtship situation without engagement, because if one partner has no intention of marriage but has not declared this he or she is exploiting the other and this is wrong. There are far too many men who keep a girl on the hook for years, only to go off and get engaged to someone else. This is horrible and uncaring behaviour. Less commonly it happens the other way around, but it is especially bad for women because they are in a more disadvantageous position as they get older because men choose younger rather than older women if they (the men) are still available later in life. This is why we said in the last chapter that courtship should always be on the move. If it is not, watch out, because you could be being taken for a ride.

Reasons for failure

Of course, not every courtship, nor even every engagement, ends in marriage and it is helpful to know what the commonest reasons for 'failure' are, so that a couple can see these worrying signs in their relationship and, it is to be hoped, avoid unnecessary problems. After all, all these early chapters are concerned not with getting people married to anyone approximately suitable at any price, but at finding as near an ideal mate as possible for a long and happy marriage. There are eight main problem areas seen in clinical practice.

1 One (or both) of the individuals is too immature in their personality development and simply is not ready to settle down. Such a person finds that he (or she) resents the thought of becoming linked to one person exclusively, talks a lot about the loss of freedom and wants to continue to play the field. Some people never get out of this phase and are never really happy in a one-to-one relationship at all. Perhaps they should not get married—they certainly cause a lot of marital havoc and form a substantial proportion of those with marital problems who seek help.

2 Often, a person will say, 'I love her (or him) a lot and we'd make a good couple, but do I really want to be married to him or her for years and so lose my freedom?' Such doubts are probably universal but fleeting. When they persist the couple are not keen *enough* on each other to want to make an exclusive commitment and should not get engaged.

3 Not uncommonly, because boys mature later and more slowly, the girl is ready, willing and able to go ahead with the serious commitment involved but the boy is not. This produces the situation in which the number of women who (when asked) say that they think they are engaged far outweighs the number of men who think the same. Clearly, women see the commitment as more serious and binding than do men—who, because of their immaturity and insecurity do not see the relationship as one of eternal commitment.

4 Unfortunately, some potentially very good relationships fail at this stage because they are unrealistically based from the start on romantic, instead of realistic, notions. As the whole thing becomes more public the over-romantic partner begins to see that it is a lot more serious and has much longer term implications than previously thought and cannot go on. This is the classic problem of being in love with love. A couple who discover their unreadiness at this stage are very lucky.

5 Some people are so indecisive that they simply cannot make important decisions of any kind and so back away from engagement.

6 Often one or other of the couple feels that the relationship is nearly right but is not quite good enough in some ways. This is a real dilemma because no one is perfect, and this goes for the person doing the agonising. There are two useful questions to ask yourself. The first is, 'Given that I'm not perfect, have my faults and am certainly not "ideal", have I the right to demand that someone else is all these things?' The second is, 'Given what I know of these faults and

shortcomings in the relationship, am I sufficiently flexible to be able to adjust?' In other words, 'Can I love him or her, warts and all?' Neither is easy to answer, unfortunately, but trying to answer them helps concentrate your thinking. Obviously the answer to the second question will depend on how great the differences are and how important the areas of disagreement are in your day-to-day life.

Many of us fear that if we give up a 'nearly right' relationship we will never get another that is better, but there is no evidence that this is so—at least not for the under-thirties who have a far wider choice of partners than they imagine.

7 Engyesis ('marriage sickness') is a medical term used to describe a cluster of symptoms (anxiety, depression and doubt) about one's partner which occur during courtship and engagement. When it was first described in 1888 it was thought that it was the sexual tensions of this group of people that caused these very real psychological problems. The main symptoms are inability to sleep, loss of appetite, weight loss, headaches, a feeling of tension and a lack of concentration. Almost all such people are insecure about their proposed marriage, and some have phobias, obsessions, feelings of unreality and even asthma. Some people become suddenly struck with one or more of these symptoms on making specific wedding arrangements—for example, booking the hall for the reception—or on finding an apartment to live in. The ill one then often says, 'You can see how ill I am, it wouldn't be fair to go on with the marriage,' to which the well partner says, 'I love you, I'll stand by you.' At this point the ill

Time for each other. During engagement it's important to make time for continued discovery and sharing in private amongst all the bustle of practical arrangements.

90　　　　　　　ENGAGEMENT

one becomes worse and goes to a doctor. The idea that sexual tensions are the cause of these problems is probably not true because in one survey at least half such couples were having intercourse. This same survey found that about half the patients had had a previous psychiatric ailment or illness for which they had sought medical advice.

The question is what to do in such cases. One survey found that the illness subsided more or less completely with the breaking of the engagement or on marriage, but that about a third continued to have symptoms after marriage. Medical opinion differs as to what should be done. Some doctors say that any relationship that produces illness must be basically unsound in some way and so should be abandoned and others that given that two-thirds seem to do well after marriage, perhaps it is simply a way of reacting to the common stresses of courtship and engagement, which go once the couple settle down together.

8 Parental opposition is, and always has been, a factor in the breaking off of courtship and engagements. Very often in our

Stages of Engagement

(opposite) The Early Stages.
A time for meeting each others' parents and friends and starting to become a part of each others' social lives. Most couples have a formal party or some kind of celebration to which the friends of both are invited. This is often the first time 'both sides of the family' get together formally.

(overleaf) The Later Stages.
This is a time for solving practical problems. Choosing a ring, a place to live and preparing for the marriage itself.

experience, parents do know best and usually have their child's future at the heart of their suggestions.

Many young people, unsure of themselves, cannot readily accept that their parents actually *might* know them better than they know themselves and so go ahead with an unsuitable relationship against lovingly given parental advice. Of course, by no means all such advice *is* lovingly given and some parents have all kinds of motives (which are too complex to go into here) for wanting to put their children off marrying *anyone*, let alone any one particular person. It really is up to the individual to decide.

If you have loving parents with whom you have a good, close relationship then it would be foolish to ignore their views. However, if in the past you have not been able to rely on them for help in any important area of life it would be foolish to expect meaningful help on such an important decision. Parents, it seems from research, approve of over 80 per cent of all engagements, so this is not a widespread problem. Also, it is important to bear in mind that parents have probably already exerted a very considerable degree of influence (far greater than either they or their child realises) well before this stage occurs. As a result most youngsters end up getting engaged to someone their parents basically approve of. The difference between these and arranged marriages are far fewer than one would at first imagine.

Preparation, planning and final commitment

In spite of all these possible set-backs engagement is still very much the norm though the form it takes can vary. Only about 4 per cent of those who marry have never been engaged at all but there are 'shades' of engagement between this and marriage. Engagements can be formal, with a notice in the newspapers, a party and substantial family involvement; or semi-formal with only close family being told; or informal, the couple arranging to marry but telling no one, or few people, about it.

In one survey, of those who were engaged, 8 per cent married within six months; 29 per cent married in six months to one year; and 28 per cent married within one to two years. Eighteen per cent of the men and 30 per cent of the women in this survey had seriously considered marrying someone else at some time.

Engagement then is a time of preparation and planning. It is a time for putting practical meat on to the bones (the plans and intentions) that developed during courtship. It is the couple working together in social ways, for example, planning housing, furnishing, wedding arrangements and so on. All these activities may reveal stresses, differences and difficulties not revealed or apparent in courtship. If such problems are great the relationship should end. After all, a perfect courtship is all very well but living together as a couple in society is a *social* business, not just a private one.

Because of this it follows that a successful engagement proves that the couple can work together in double harness and tests the

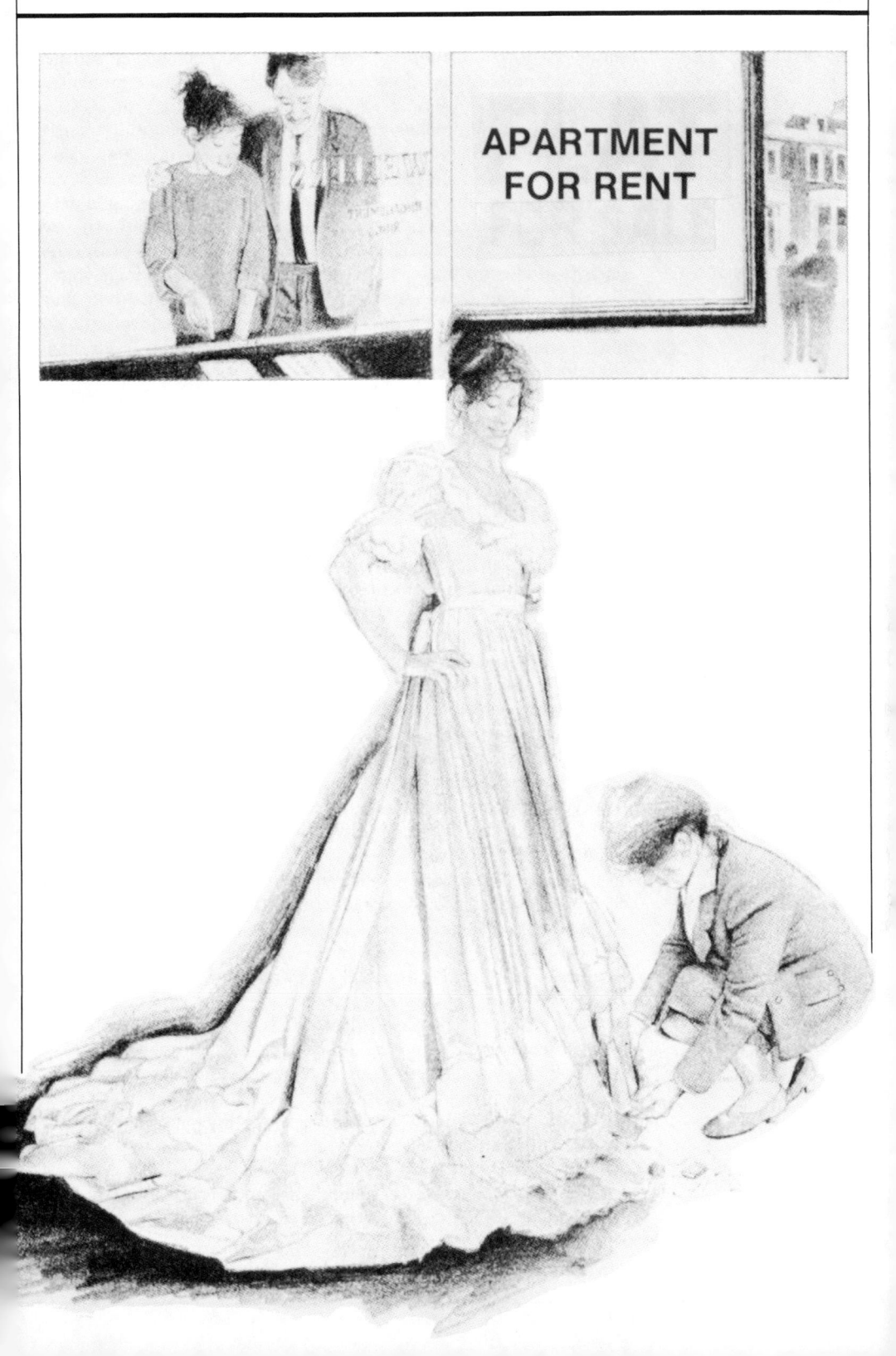

ENGAGEMENT

similarity of their attitudes towards the social management of their relationship. As a result, a successful engagement makes it more likely that the couple will have a happy marriage.

Engagement obviously tests another set of adaptive capacities in the individuals (the inter-personal and sexual ones probably having already been tested during courtship). It imposes stresses, and there are bound to be differences and difficulties, which the couple prove they can surmount. It is also a period of integration into the two families. With luck real friendships spring up with the prospective parents-in-law and the two families cooperate to help their young.

Engagement also tests the capacities of the parents to let go of their young. A mother who is emotionally over-dependent on a son may be unreasonably hostile to his fiancée and may even create situations in which her son is tested to see if his love for her is greater than that for his fiancée (or wife). If a problem like this becomes apparent the son will usually try to side-step the issue but it is a problem which is unlikely to go away. The capacity of the couple to recognise and cope with the problem in a way which does not involve making the mother unhappy is a test of their skill in managing relationships with others. The boy no longer feels bound to his mother but is more securely bonded to his fiancée and works with her to come to an amicable solution to the problem. This is a rehearsal for many similar situations that will certainly occur throughout their married life.

Similarly, a father may, out of unconscious jealousy, wonder what his precious daughter sees in her lout of a fiancé. This is usually less of a problem than that of the hostile mother but it is still a test of the social skills of the couple.

Many youngsters report that they can get on better with their parents-in-law (prospective or otherwise) than their own parents. This is probably helpful. By no means do all families side with their own child in difficulties which arise between engaged and married couples and such balances probably have a considerable stabilising effect on the relationship.

Many families grant much more freedom to engaged couples than was customary in the past and this now frequently extends to the couple living together and even sharing the same room in the parental households. The concept of trial marriage is hardly new and is usually harmless, but clinical experience shows that it should *follow* and not *replace* courtship and the engagement.

Some couples live together with no immediate intentions of engagement or marriage. It could be argued that all the purposes of courtship and engagement can be achieved within such a framework just as well as outside it. Unfortunately, this often turns out not to be true in practice and it can short-circuit the highly important phases of adjustment, communication and testing.

It is not uncommon, even in good, steady relationships or engagements, for one or even both partners, especially if they are young and inexperienced, to have doubts about the relationship. This sometimes occurs because they have very little against which to judge the value of their partner and the relationship. Temporary separations can help by reinforcing the relationship. We have looked at the main reasons for relationships failing at this stage and pointed out that this is no bad thing. Many experts working in this area think there should be many more abandoned engagements.

Sometimes engaged partners, both men and women, involve themselves in bursts of promiscuous behaviour. The unconscious or even conscious purpose may be to discover what sex with others is like before making a final commitment. Although this can eventually be seen simply as bad behaviour, and it may certainly suggest that the sexual aspects of the courtship have not been correctly managed, it is far better than sexual experimentation with others after marriage. Someone who has a continuing need for such promiscuous activity should be reassessed with the utmost scepticism by the other partner because, despite claims and promises to the contrary, this sort of behaviour will almost certainly continue after marriage.

How to cope with rejection

Where, during courtship or engagement, the relationship is seen to be wrong or unsuitable, it is best to end it in a straightforward way with a rational discussion of the reasons. However, having said this, not everyone is capable of dealing with rejection and tactics for ending the relationship may have to be modified. Threats and blackmail have to be resisted because an unsuitable relationship will only become more unsuitable as time goes by. Women especially may make suicidal gestures on such occasions and men may behave unsociably and even violently. In such cases they may need medical help or help from other caring organisations. If you are rejected, here are some helpful thoughts:

1 Considering how rotten a bad marriage can be, you have had a lucky escape.

2 You should be wiser and more clever in choosing your next partner and managing the relationship; after all if you have learned nothing of value to help you next time, you have only yourself to blame.

3 It is unrealistic, as often happens, to pick out one feature, physical or psychological, about yourself and blame it for your 'failure'—this almost never applies.

4 Even thinking about the situation in terms of 'failure' is wrong since relationships are about mutual compatibility and not about estimates of the eternal or absolute worth of the participants.

5 You are free for all the thrills and excitements of making another choice and testing it in courtship.

Having said all this, it has to be admitted that the abandonment that is involved, especially if the partner has left the relationship for someone else, and the sense of loss, exposes the individual to depression, mourning, self-criticism and a temporary loss of self-confidence and esteem. Women seem, on average, less able to cope with such set-backs than men and being rejected in this way *can* sometimes alter their self-esteem for life.

Immature marriages

Lastly, in our brief look at engagement, let us take a look at immature marriages because the seeds for these usually disastrous relationships are sown during the courtship and engagement phase of a couple's development.

By immature marriage we mean one entered into under the age of twenty. However, many much older people are so immature that they also have disastrous marriages for the reasons we outline here.

All the available statistics show that marriages entered into where the woman is twenty or under have very high failure rates indeed. Not only do at least one in three of these marriages fail but they still have an above-average failure rate as long as twenty to thirty years after the marriage. So why do youngsters do it?

Young marriages fare very badly.

One of the commonest reasons is that the immature man has a poor sense of his own masculinity and by marrying tries to prove something to himself and society. Girls tend to marry this young for many reasons including an over-romantic desire to 'be married'—one which is almost totally unfounded on reality; to escape from the sexual or other restrictions of their parents; to go along with their friends who have married young; because they desperately want a baby; because they desperately want sex and cannot have it outside marriage; because they are so immature that they cannot make a realistic choice between the options that are open to them in life and marriage seems a good way out of the dilemma; and because they can simply think of nothing they would rather do.

Because most young marriages are entered into for the wrong reasons and because the personalities of the couple are immature, they are almost doomed before they begin. Young couples think that difficulties and differences (often apparent, even to them) will be smoothed out as the years pass, but this rarely happens because all too often their personality developments do not bring them together but separate them further. Many such marriages end within five years and leave the couple free to try again, hopefully wiser and better equipped to do it better second time around. The tragedy is that many young couples in this group have a child as soon as they get married and a few are actually forced into marriage because the girl is pregnant. Marriages that are forced by pregnancy have terrible failure rates, the worst occurring if the girl waits until her baby is very nearly due before she marries. Young couples having children immediately may do so because in their immature way they see it as a way of proving to the world that they are really grown up. It is a sad fact that many of these couples are not at all adult and often have,to live with in-laws or parents because they are so poor. This is yet another nail in their marital coffin and things quickly go downhill. Young men in this situation are often very restrictive and jealous of their young brides and often become involved with other women. The marriage slowly, and—inevitably—painfully, drags to an end.

Any of us who are parents or have responsibility for the young will want to see such young marriages discouraged wherever possible. But handling the situation can be very difficult because parental friction is often at the heart of the problem anyway. If you as parents feel things are going this way for your under-twenty-year-old, it is best to get outside help unless you have such a good relationship that you can have a frank two-way discussion about the subject. The problems are ironically much more serious when immature thirty-year-olds want to marry because many of the problems rear their head yet no one but an expert in this field would see the reason why.

Immature marriage and all its dangers can be minimised by going through all the stages of courtship and engagement in the way we have suggested. The golden rule must be that if anything you have read in the last few chapters makes you unsure about your intended marriage—don't do it. Wait, think about it, discuss it with your parents, if you can, or with a friend or even a doctor or other professional who understands the problems.

Summary

Engagement is a social act which publicly states that a relationship is serious and that the couple intend to marry. It is a vital testing and learning phase but should be used as such and not viewed as a trial marriage. It extends and tests the abilities of the couple and their families to cooperate before the final act of marriage. In an ideal world, engagements would be broken far more frequently than they are. This, although painful, would ensure that more marriages remained intact. The further down the track one is, the harder it is to break off a serious relationship. So, if you are at all worried about your fiancé(e) and whether you could live together for a very long time, now, during your engagement, is the time to do something about it. Five or ten years from now with children, a home and many other complicating factors, things will be much more difficult and the toll on your life far greater.

Chapter 9

Romance

Although one would hardly think it possible in a society which seemingly puts such an emphasis on romance, most sex books do not even discuss it. Experience shows that romantic love is a vital part of most couples' lives and one on which they have very definite feelings.

It really is impossible to talk about love and sex without putting romance into perspective and that is what this chapter is all about. Although the message of today is 'play it cool' when it comes to displays of love and affection, a generation or two ago romance was a constant theme, especially in the cinema and fiction. To some extent this is still the case, especially in literature aimed at girls and women.

Romantic fiction, like pornography, has measurable effects on the sexual arousal system of women and men respectively. In fact, researchers have shown that in some ways romantic fiction is to women what pornography is to men. It is easier to fantasise with a romantic novel or to masturbate with a girlie magazine than it is to relate to real people and improve your skills with them. In an ideal world most people would not need either because they would be getting their satisfaction from their partners in a loving, mutually caring setting. This would mean that both sexes would have to care enough to want to please their partners in the ways they want to be pleased . . . and surely this is what should be at the heart of every man–woman relationship.

Curiously, asking women patients for details about their romantic fantasies produces more embarrassment than any question about their sexual fantasies. With men the situation is even worse because most of them are simply inarticulate on the subject. This is probably because as a culture we suppress men's tender emotions in boyhood and make such emotions out to be sloppy and unmasculine. The very strength of the feelings that are at the root of all this just proves how much romance affects us all.

A learning phase

Probably the need for romance and the search (or hope for) romantic love is best thought of as a stage in the development of the capacity to love in a mature, adult way. It emerges strongly in late adolescence as the love which used to be self-centred (in mid-adolescence) begins to be available for direction towards others. It would be extraordinary if people went from their self-loving, mid-adolescent phase straight to

Spontaneous displays of affection and romance can occur anywhere at any time in a loving and co-operating relationship.

an 'other-centred' type of love without some sort of intermediate, learning phase. Romantic love is this phase in adolescence. Romantic love is also a way in which we learn to bring together our sexual and loving feelings, for the first time 'aimed' at the same person.

This phase of romantic love, which many young people experience more in fantasy than in fact, and which others may never grow out of, is still very much concerned with the self—it is almost entirely a preoccupation with one's own feelings. This might seem strange at first sight because romantic love is, on the surface, very much concerned with the other person. Their virtues, real or imaginary, are extolled and their faults ignored. It is a feature of most of us that we tend to emphasise the positive points about people from the past during rows and deprecate those with whom we are having a relationship at the time. This facet of romantic love becomes important in those married couples (and especially women) who complain that there is no romance in their marriages, yet in previous relationships they had so much. Almost by definition the romantically loved person is seen in a shining and unique light as an ideal, and the protestations of the love felt emphasise its depth and durability: it will last forever. It will also overcome all obstacles. People in this phase of love write long letters and poetry describing their feelings towards the loved person.

In literature and in fact, this phase of romantic love can also be associated with bouts of anxiety and depression. The loving feelings may even be experienced as a form of agony and yearning. Romantic writers often talk of 'the agony of being in love' and in a sense suffering and tragedy are an integral part of romance. Some women

Is it total love or is it romance? The memory might live on, but will the relationship?

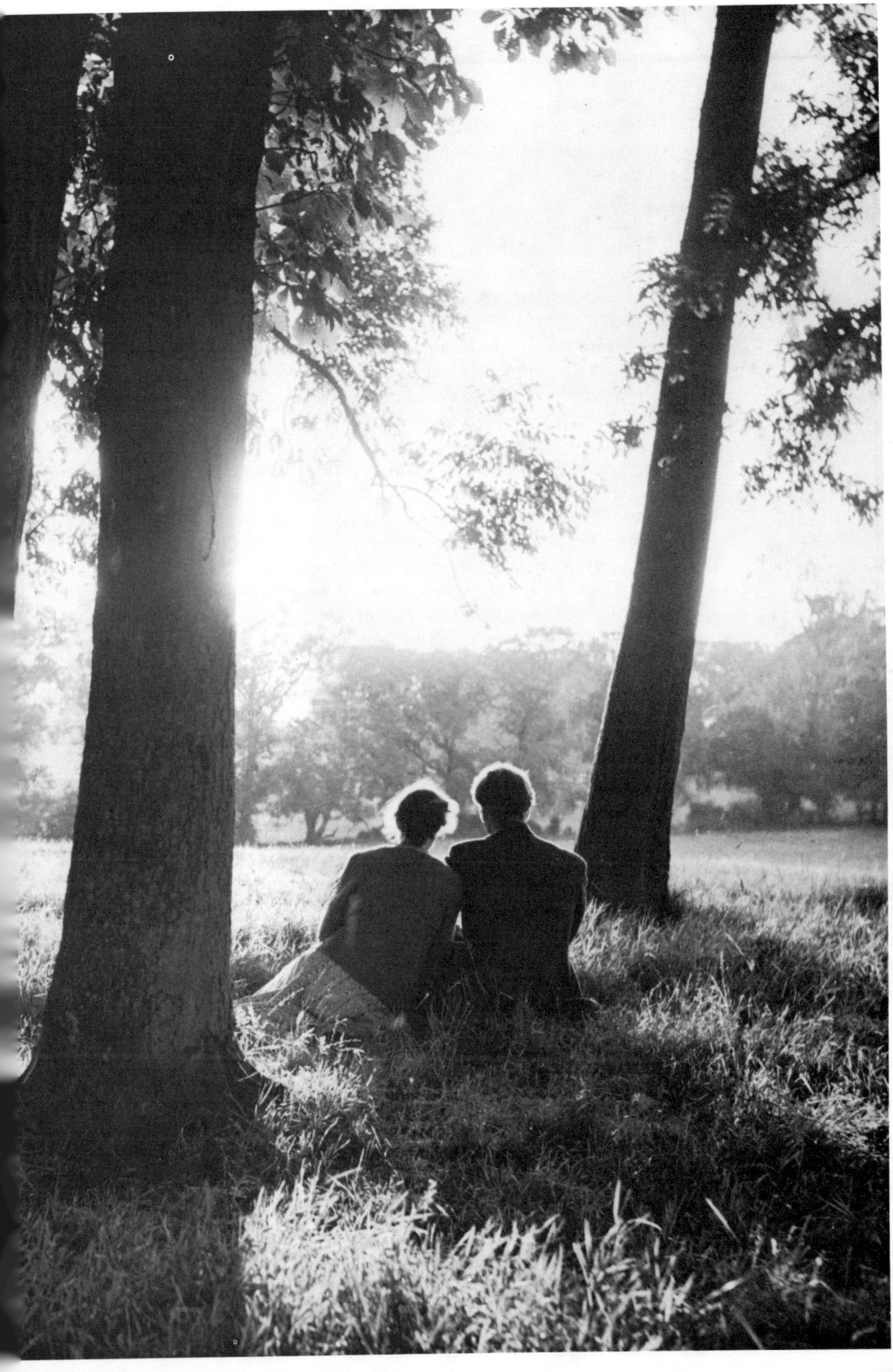

unfortunately never grow out of this phase and remain tragedy queens, as it were, all their lives. They have perfectly acceptable and enjoyable relationships yet spoil them by creating trauma and tragedies which they feel are necessary to their concept of romantic love.

Both the conviction that romantic love must ultimately be frustrated and the current trend for teenagers to be 'cool' are based on the fear of being rejected, which is common at this age. Obviously, the late adolescent experiencing this phase of romantic love is facing up to such fears, and learning to overcome them—and it is a valuable lesson to learn because by doing so he or she is also learning how to value, or over-value, a member of the opposite sex within a context which is not simply sexual. These teenagers are learning how to give up at least part of their own self-love and to invest it in another in the hope that it will be reciprocated.

So, it can be seen that the phase of romantic love is a learning one. Learning to love is much like learning any other skills: just as adolescents have to learn social skills, they have to learn the skill of love. Because it is immature love it is often described as 'calf-love' or 'puppy love' but this misses its importance. Unless one has come through this stage using it as a foundation, one cannot build the love structure an adult needs. Parents should never make fun of or put down their teenagers in this stage of puppy love—the teenager needs to go through it.

In some cases the individuals who happen to be involved in each other's romantic love phase may marry but this is not common. The couple are often simply in love with love and this is a very poor basis for marriage. It is interesting that fantasies (even if many are not conscious) about one's first experience of being in love may, in retrospect, be idealised more and more, and some individuals content themselves with these fantasies and take no further effective steps to establish new relationships—they are happy to live in the past.

Most people, however, progress to other relationships and, it is to be hoped, begin to get some idea as to what sort of partner would really suit them. The capacity to love develops more as discrimination increases and, with luck, a good and suitable relationship is eventually established.

Such a relationship once again releases romantic feelings, but now they are simply one component of the more complex emotional and sexual reactions of the chosen partner. Ideally the romantic portion of the relationship should be encouraged to emerge slowly so as to allow realistic assessments to be made. Romantic love then becomes increasingly added to the relationship rather than being its starting-point. In this way the objection that love is blind can be overcome. Unfortunately, many people get carried away with romantic love, which then clouds their abilities to make rational decisions about their partner even in the light of seemingly obvious evidence. If such a couple marry at this phase, once the romance has gone they have little left and wonder why the marriage has failed.

Romance in marriage

Usually, the romantic portion of love declines as a marriage continues. Some people (especially women) interpret this as meaning that love itself has gone from the relationship and this can start a search for a new lover or a divorce. In other cases the woman who feels this may meet the deficiency she is experiencing partly by addiction to media accounts of romance (in romantic novels, for example) and partly through her children in whom she invests over-

. . . on the other hand: A touch of romance as a part of total love helps a relationship to flourish and grow.

romantic feelings. Men often try to ignore their disappointment about the loss of romance and either become involved in affairs of the 'my-wife-doesn't-understand-me' type or take up compensatory pursuits such as absorbing hobbies and more work. Each partner may attempt to punish the other, using sex as the weapon, and the ultimate consequence can be that the real love in the relationship is in fact eroded, even though it was still there at the beginning of the problem. More couples should understand the link between romance and sex and how to put it in perspective so that its natural decline is not blamed unrealistically.

As we have said elsewhere, a well-developed man–woman relationship consists of several roles. One, and an important one, is the lover role. The romantic-love portion of their love for each other can easily be kept alive when they are functioning in the lover role. When a loving couple are making love they can recapture this late-adolescent phase of emotional development and again immerse themselves temporarily in the intense and passionate expressions of feelings of love, valuation of the other and commitment. We shall see in chapter 17 how important this is. After all, each time we make love we go back in time to our courtship days when romantic love played an important part in our lives. Regular top-ups of romance during love-making can be all that most couples need to keep romance alive in their lives.

Ideas of romance differ.

Many married women complain of the lack of 'warmth' in their relationship and many men wonder where the girl who loved them so intensely and of whom they have so many happy memories has gone. But when listening to the sexes talking about their notions of romance a difference seems to emerge. To men the word seems to imply a continuing, faithful, dedicated, trouble-free, sexually fulfilling and totally exclusive relationship. To the women the connotation seems to be more of occasion, of a particular set of events. So, for example, for a woman, it may be of a specific piece of music, a beautiful meal, the wine, the love-talk, the moon, the sea and the sand, perhaps culminating in sex on the beach.

Obviously, talking can resolve the problem but deeply romantic feelings cause embarrassment after adolescence and in any case if one partner has to tell the other what to do to show romantic love, they may feel that the very fact of having to tell shows that it was absent. 'Obviously he didn't care for me or he would have done (whatever) himself, without my having to tell him' is the sort of remark heard. But this is unfair because we are not telepathic and cannot hope to know by magic what our partners want. Loving discussion and the way the thing is done should easily overcome this problem.

Surprising though it may seem, *too much* romance can be a problem. The excessive expression of romantic loving feelings can mean that the individual is more in love with love (as are the characters in the late-adolescent phase of romantic love) than with the partner. As we have said earlier, some people never develop emotionally beyond this phase and this severely limits the love they can feel. It is a shame but a fact that these so-called romantics never really enjoy a natural, loving relationship and suffer accordingly.

So what are the answers? Perhaps the most important is for the partners to avoid assuming thoughtlessly that their notion of romantic love is identical with that of their mate. If each pays attention to what really gratifies the other in this area then they can build up an accurate impression of their individual needs. In this sense post-marital romantic love is not quite identical with the late-adolescent type, which is based purely on the notions of the individual. Post-maritally it needs to be adapted towards the needs of the partner.

Summary

Romance is, or should be, the mainspring of our emotional loves but not the whole of them. Romance is valuable and we should all try to sustain and nourish it if only because evidence suggests that it is very important to women. So men should not allow their romantic side to wither over the years and women should be more open in revealing their romantic needs. Only in this way can a couple keep the flame of romance burning over the years.

Chapter 10

Marriage as a relationship

It is probably true to say that with a few exceptions any marriage has the potential to be good. How marriage actually works out for any one couple is probably not so much governed by circumstances (which is what most couples believe) but by lessons learned in childhood and applied later. For example, a fear of the opposite sex, no matter how unconscious, can be learned early in life from indifferent or hostile parents or brothers and sisters of the opposite sex. Quite often a dominant, critical and punitive mother who wants (unconsciously) to take revenge on men generally for distress suffered in her own childhood brings up a son to be afraid of women. His male ego may be weak but he compensates by being bullying, dictatorial and inconsiderate to his wife. She may even have been attracted to him in the first place by his apparent 'masculinity', without realising that it was really a disguise for weakness. Unfortunately, by the time she finds out the truth the marriage is often on the rocks. Such a man dare not give in to a woman because in doing so he sees himself returning to his childhood and being submissive to his mother. Such men often batter their wives.

Wife battering

The universal feature of wife battering is that the husband thinks he is unable to control certain issues in the home without resorting to violence. Such a man is usually very inadequate, as we have seen, is a poor employee, earns little and supports the family very poorly. All of these are interlinked, of course, and an improvement in any one area makes battering less likely. Such couples have no talk 'safety valve'—they cannot discuss their problems. This often results in the wife nagging the husband until he gets so furious that he lashes out. Because communication is so poor within the marriage, and because such women often say nothing to outsiders, the problem easily escalates to violence with other members of the family. Unfortunately, being brought up in this kind of home virtually ensures that the children identify with the behaviour and that they are likely to copy it within their own marriages. The answer to wife battering is to get help straight away. Things rarely get better by themselves because the husband's personality is too deeply disturbed. There are refuges for battered wives all over the country now and local women's groups can help find one.

Not every inadequate man need end up battering his wife. Many do very well if their wives understand the situation. A helpful wife will boost her husband's confidence and build him up at every opportunity, so undoing the damage his mother did. The point we are making is that in a marriage the strong can afford to be gentle whilst the weak have to be vicious to achieve their goals or they end up effacing themselves completely. A couple who have such problems often find that their whole relationship is enriched if one can modify the other's personality in this way.

From this rather dramatic (but not uncommon) example we can draw a general principle which seems to hold good for marriage in general: that is that a couple should do everything they can to boost each other's ego (self-esteem) and never do anything that attacks the other's personality. Marriages are made between personalities and if they are attacked there may be nothing left. This works both ways, of course, with the wife constantly building up her husband and vice versa. It involves a gracious acceptance that one partner is better at some things and the other better at others. Each therefore feels strong and secure in certain areas of the marriage and can 'afford' to be weak in others.

Marriage and self-esteem.

How to cope with rows

Many a woman says that her husband will not row with her and that as a result she cannot clear the air on various subjects and her feelings become frustratingly bottled-up. This often happens because women tend to have superior verbal skills and, along with their female logic, defeat men, who then choose not to argue. There must have been a failure of communication somewhere along the line for things to have got this bad, and many a woman complains that her husband simply does not talk (or listen) to her enough. So great is her desire to clear things up (women have a tremendous need to keep the balance of emotions and feelings stable within the family) that she provokes arguments and becomes bossy. As a result she scares her husband off. Women are far better at assessing the real mood and the underlying feelings in a situation than are most men. Often a man does not see a problem as important and may not even see it *at all*. This does not mean that it does not exist. If one partner in a marriage has a problem they both have it.

Women also tend to perceive problems more than men, and they link them to the whole relationship. For example, a woman may say that if her husband loved her he would not do or say a certain thing. It may be a simple misunderstanding of the ways in which he believes he should demonstrate his love, and once again this is usually conditioned by what he learned in childhood. Such misunderstandings can lead to vicious rows and, if these areas are not disclosed and defused, can wreck a marriage. People cannot stand anything that seems to them to attack their love-bond; so it makes sense for couples to examine the real origins of their rows.

In such rows the woman, because she feels hurt or neglected, may, because of her greater verbal skills, say more wounding things than she really feels simply to provoke a serious response from her husband. Such over-dramatising of the argument would not be necessary if men were more sensitive to their wives' needs and feelings, and in a good marriage things should never get this far—but they often do.

Even if a man was not positively put down by his mother as a boy he may well still have problems in coping with his wife when she nags at him or provokes a row. Sometimes behaviour like this is produced by premenstrual tension or mental or physical illness. A sensible husband keeps a note in the family diary of his wife's premenstrual days and makes an extra special effort to be caring and supersensitive at this time. Premenstrual symptoms can now often be treated, so it is worth seeking medical help.

Whatever the trigger factor, many men actually revert to childhood when their wives become aggressive or seem to be provoking a row. They sulk, mooch around the house or go out to escape. This does nothing to help the situation because the woman still has not had her say and still feels scorned, overlooked, unloved, treated as worthless or whatever sparked off the row in the first place. She needs loving care and understanding but her husband, by behaving like a small boy, cannot hope to provide it. The underlying problem is thus not resolved and emotional tension results. The next time a problem area is aired the couple, already on a plateau of tension, spark each other off more readily and open hostility soon becomes the norm.

Often such hostility arises over what we call 'no-go' areas within the marriage. Subjects as diverse as children's schooling, the woman's weight, his drinking friends, religion, oral sex and so on are out of bounds, skirted round and never actually discussed. One partner (or both) harbours strongly held views, yet cannot get the other to discuss them or come to an agreement at all. Slowly these 'no-go' areas within the marriage grow in size and number until the couple are only relating in the most superficial way, skimming over the surface of life. As soon as any discussion gets valuable it hits a 'no-go' area and hostility or silence breaks out. Eventually such a couple end up saying little to each other and rowing when they do speak. The cure for this state of affairs is to have a minimum of 'no-go' areas in the first place.

Clearly no two people will agree on everything, but a loving, caring friendship can withstand a fair amount of disagreement. There are usually no absolute answers to the problems being discussed and one person's views are worth about as much as another's. Many 'no-go' areas are not really serious anyway: they are simply the pretext of the current battle. The war is already raging deep down in the couple's lives. End the war and the mini-battles cease. It is not a bad idea to discuss 'no-go' areas with a third person with both parties present. A marital therapist is obviously ideal but they are few and far between. A caring doctor can be good; a marriage guidance counsellor or even a good friend can help. A third person's views can often soften the arguments, and he or she can get reluctant spouses to open up and really say what is bothering them.

MARRIAGE AS A RELATIONSHIP

|——— WRONG ———|——— RIGHT ———|

A small change in attitude and behaviour can make a world of difference.

Once 'no-go' areas begin to intrude on a couple's life, sex is the first thing to suffer. Professionals working with marital problems never accept sexual problems at face value because they are so rarely the cause of marital disharmony. Sex, as we have said, is usually the injured bystander as the marriage crashes on the rocks, but in a society so over-concerned with sex it is understandable that people who go for professional help often complain of a sexual problem first.

Rows and an extension of 'no-go' areas within the marriage reduce the tenderness each feels for the other, and usually the woman is the first to go off sex. Men see this as a sort of punishment and indeed some women do use sex to punish their husbands. A woman who argues with him and has rows is one thing but one who is reluctant or refuses to have sex as well is the last straw. The husband sees himself as no longer loved because in our society men are trained to think that a woman shows her love by her willingness to have sex with him. He progressively withdraws from the relationship, 'de-loves' his wife and escapes into gardening, 'the boys', a time-consuming hobby away from home, or a considerable increase in work. The woman's fears that she is no longer loved, appreciated and wanted are confirmed for her too and the marriage spirals downwards.

So far the reader could be forgiven for thinking that we have painted a very negative picture of marriage as a relationship, but we have done so quite deliberately. By understanding how things can go wrong one can more easily find answers to prevent and cure the problems. At the first sign of emotional dis-ease within a marriage we would like to see the 'unaffected' partner say, 'Let's sit down and you tell me about it. You're obviously upset, I'll try to help.' The listener

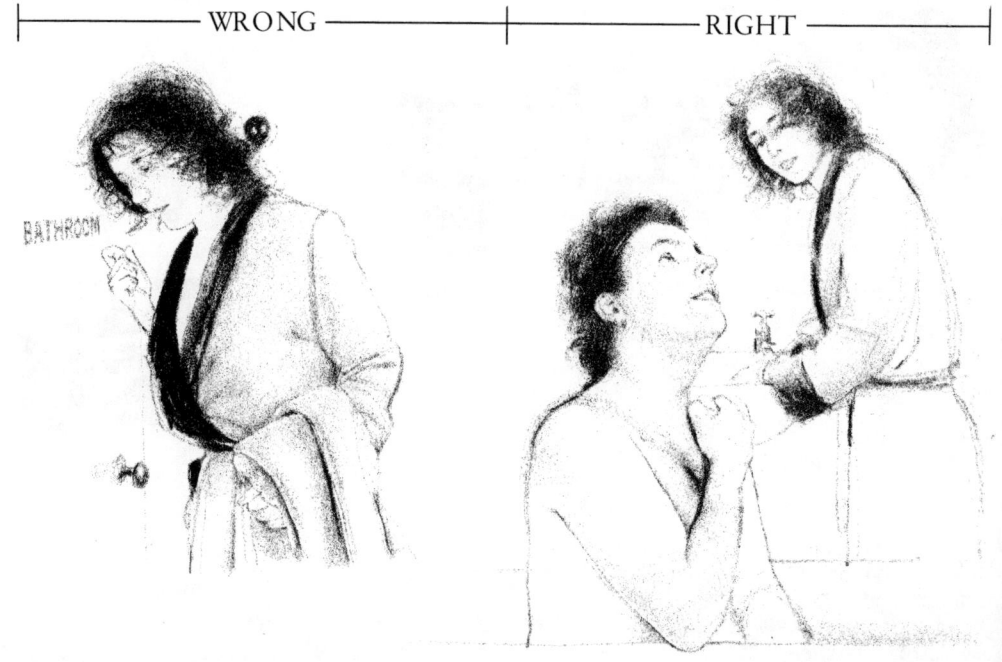

|—————— WRONG ——————|—————— RIGHT ——————|

then allows the 'complainer' to get the problem off his or her chest without interruption and then negotiations start with real care and warmth. Such behaviour defines troublesome situations early and major 'no-go' areas never get a chance to take root. Each person sees the other behaving in a way that is compatible with the way they think someone who 'really loves them ought to behave, and such tolerance breeds tolerance in return. In this way fights and rows, being unnecessary, become rare, and the couple can devote their energies and emotional strengths to positive outputs which will benefit themselves as individuals, their family and society. A couple who are always quarreling simply drain themselves dry and everybody suffers. Their quality of life becomes unbearably poor. There must be a way out of this and we have suggested one that works.

Quite quickly in a marriage run along the lines we have just described a fund of goodwill builds up and the couple can make concessions to each other on certain matters (that could easily have become 'no-go' areas), can overlook peccadilloes and can even delight in each other's shortcomings. In general, women are better able (or are more prepared) to adapt to men in this way than vice versa but obviously there are exceptions.

Most problems in marital relationships probably come about as a result of the negative emotional attitudes we have described, or as a result of variations on the same theme. However, a marriage full of bad emotional tensions can give one or both of the partners the opportunity to latch long-held grievances on to the current trend of unhappiness and non-communication. So, for example, a man or woman who has been refused intercourse may, if he or she feels hurt by it, the next day or even later try to hurt his or her partner by raising a subject he knows to be painful.

Another category of rows may then emerge which is not primarily brought about by the apparent cause, which in turn becomes concealed and unresolved. It is at this stage that many couples seek professional help or see a solicitor about divorce. It takes a really skilled professional to find where the problems lie in such cases and all too often couples have the wrong (more superficial) problem treated only to return home to continue their unhappy lives. Often such professionals attach blame to the partners involved, but this can be very unfair because the answers are rarely clear-cut and the obvious 'offender' in the marriage is often the weaker and needs help more than (even implicit) condemnation.

Men and women have very different ideas as to which faults are killers of marriages. One survey found that women thought that selfishness and inconsiderate behaviour were the most important faults in their husbands and that men rated nagging and moaning top of the list. The old fears of sexual incompatibility, too many or no children, drunkenness and lack of trust, so commonly found to be problems in past surveys, have now virtually disappeared in favour of selfishness, money problems, conflicting personalities and jealousy among wives of husbands paying attention to things other than them.

But rather than simply rowing about these areas we suggest couples use the technique known as 'shaping-up'. The idea behind

No-go Areas

The Growth of 'no-go' areas within a marriage can ruin even the best relationship.

this concept is that rather than falling out over minor areas of disagreement one makes a conscious effort deliberately to ignore them or to treat them neutrally. When the 'offending' partner behaves in a way which the other wants to encourage he or she is rewarded by signs of pleasure, affection, flattering comments and even sexual favours. This technique can also be used to modify sexual behaviour which a partner does not like.

A good way of training this shaping-up ability is to learn sensual massage. This is a very pleasurable pursuit that greatly increases a couple's powers of communication. Once they are talking to each other again on mutually rewarding subjects they find it easier to discuss more difficult subjects. Also, if one is having a wonderful time physically with someone it is much harder to row or even to ignore each other.

Sensual massage

This is basically a type of massage performed first by one partner on the other and then the other way round. There is only one rule—the partner who is being massaged has to tell the other exactly what feels nice and what does not. The only goal is for the massager totally to devote him- or herself to pleasing the other, whatever it is that he or she asks for. Sensual massage is not genital. In fact we suggest that nipples, breasts and genitals are avoided. It also is not a prelude to intercourse, although sometimes intercourse will follow naturally. The very fact that the couple end up pleasing each other, yet do not *have* to go on to intercourse can be a wonderful relief for both and it often defuses the sexual situation greatly.

The massaging is done in a warm room with both partners completely naked and baby oil or special, warmed massage oil can be used. Take the phone off the hook, put on some music you both enjoy, and put a sheet on the floor or massage each other on the bed. The key to really good sensual massage is that there must be constant feedback—at least for the first few times, until each knows exactly how to please the other. In a couple who massage each other several times a week, the need or desires of one partner may change, and, again, the change should be picked up and acted upon by the one who is massaging. Be careful that you do not fall into the trap of one partner always being the 'giver' and the other the 'receiver'. The one who finds it more difficult to 'receive' often needs help and loving care more than the other partner.

Sensual massage is not something that one partner does *to* the other—it is a two-way team effort. It is very pleasant just to cuddle up together afterwards and go to sleep, although sometimes the massage ends up with intercourse.

A couple doing this several times a week are making time for each other, caring about each other's responses, talking to each other more and, as a result, finding it harder to be angry, especially over little things. Their quality of life is improved greatly as a result.

MARRIAGE AS A RELATIONSHIP

Before starting sensual massage it is pleasant to relax a little, perhaps with a drink, while your massage oil is warming.

You can start wherever you like and every couple has its own routine. Firm grasping of the neck and shoulder muscles is often exquisitely pleasurable but, as always, be guided by what your partner wants.

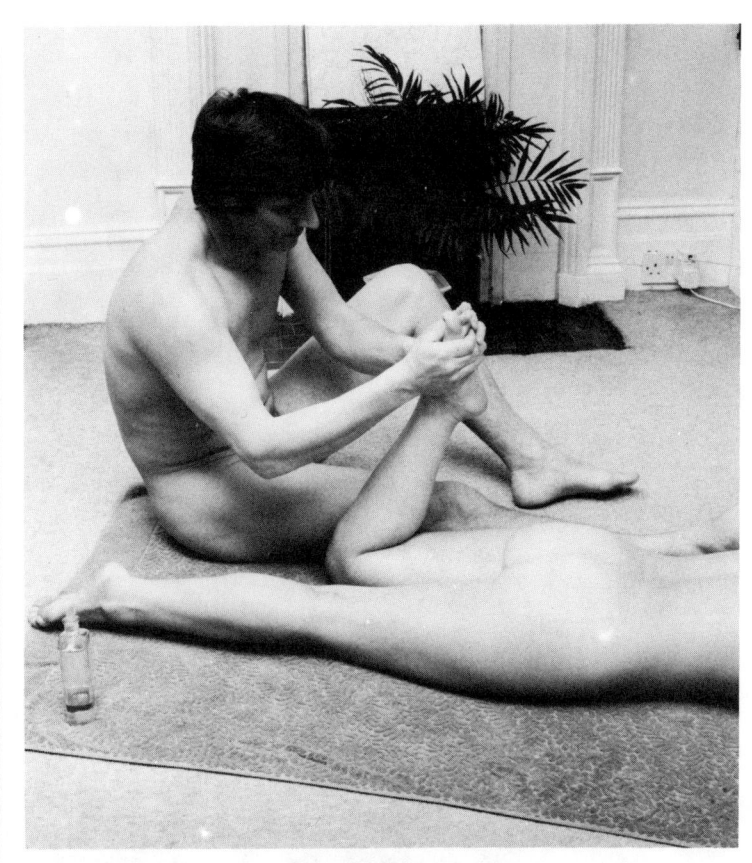

Many people find having their feet massaged a very sensual experience. Work firmly with the balls of your thumbs under the arch of the foot. Run your fingers in between your partner's toes and gently pull them. Experiment to find out what your partner enjoys best.

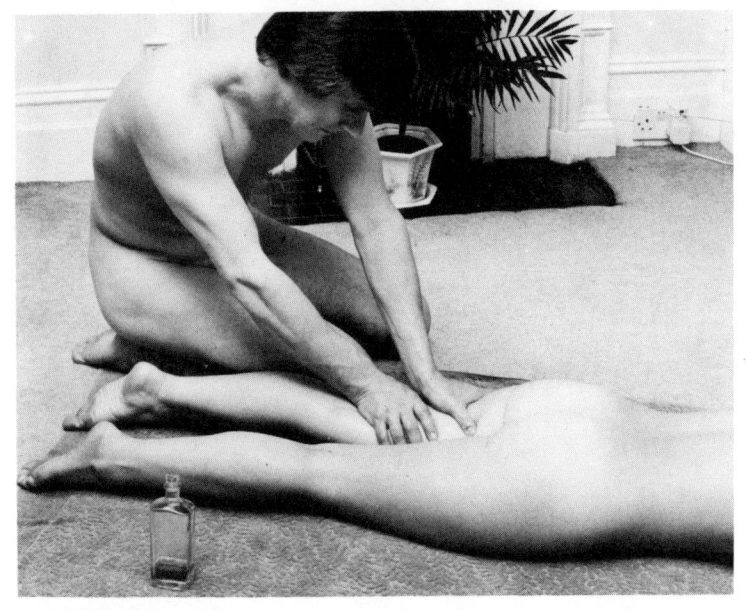

When massaging the legs apply firm pressure from below upwards and gentle pressure when your hands are travelling in the opposite direction. Firm repeated upwards motions along the calf muscles are often very pleasant and many women enjoy the tops of their thighs being massaged.

116   MARRIAGE AS A RELATIONSHIP

This is a particularly enjoyable manoeuvre but takes some practice. With your hands well oiled ensure that there is always one hand on your partner's body so that each takes over from the other in a continuous motion of skin contact. Each hand starts near the towel and pulls firmly but gently upwards as you work down your partner's side from chest to thigh.

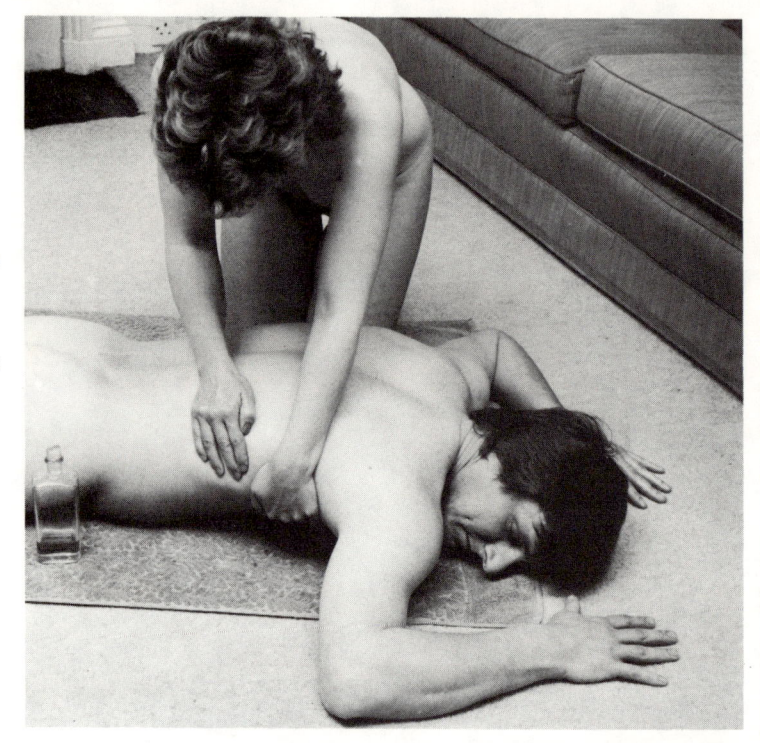

Massaging the buttocks is a manoeuvre some people enjoy. Use the tips of three fingers firmly over the hip joint. A variation of this involves using the same fingers and plenty of oil a few inches above this area to each side of the base of the spine. Many people have 'knots' in their muscles here.

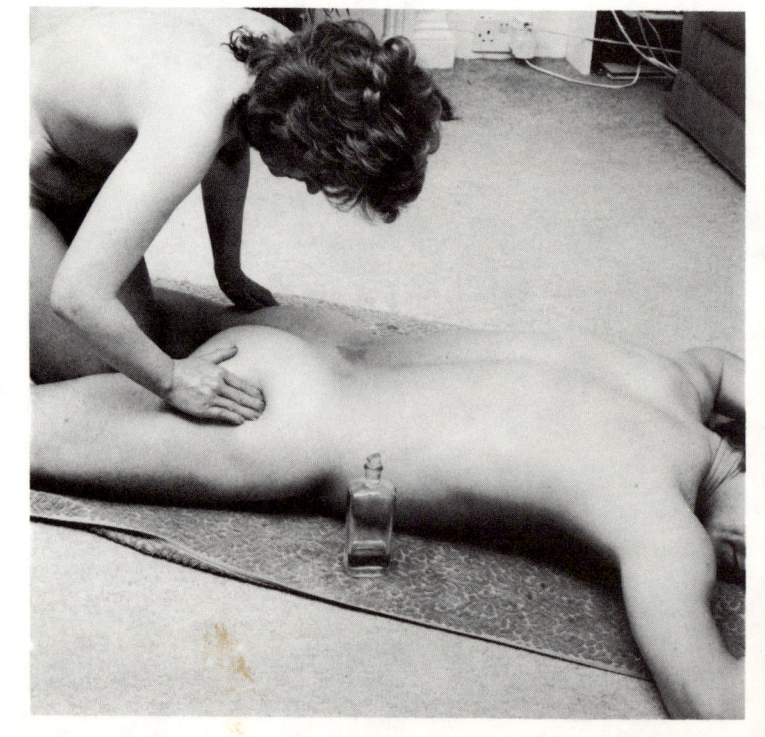

MARRIAGE AS A RELATIONSHIP

Sit astride your partner's thighs using both hands flat on the abdomen and massage in a clockwise direction.

Hand massage can be very relaxing if sensitively done. Massage the palms, run your fingers through those of your partner, firmly gripping the fingers with yours as you do so and gently pull each finger in turn. Some people, especially women, find foot and hand massage almost orgasmic.

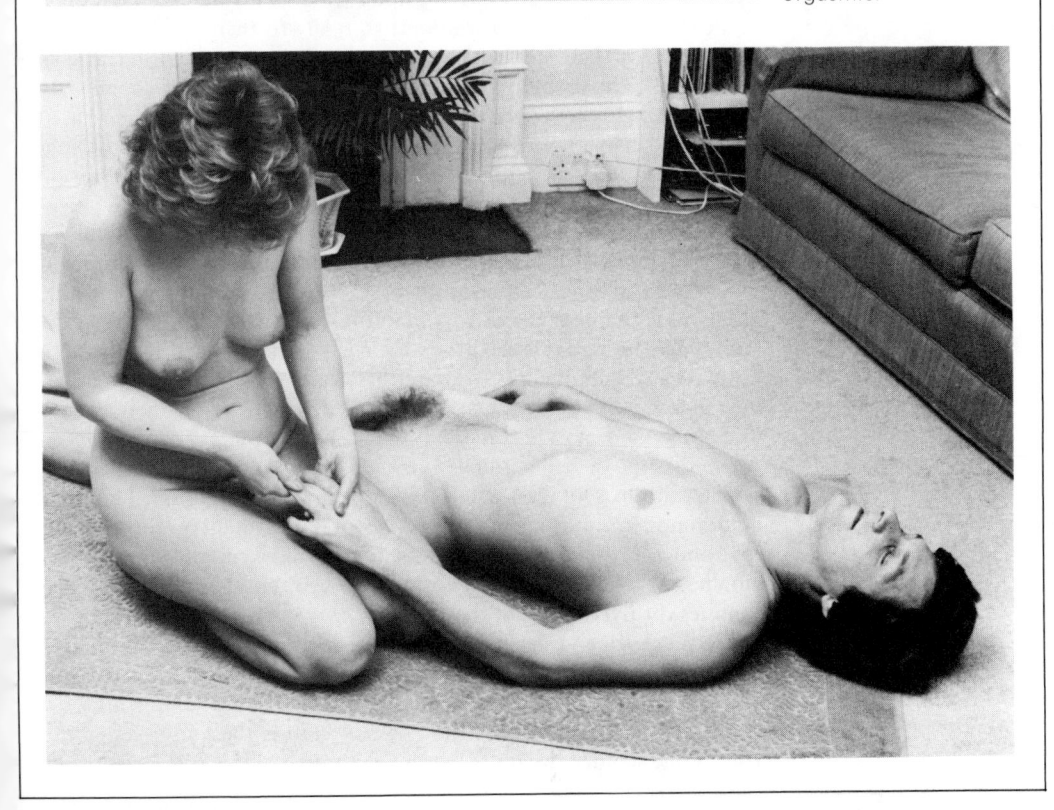

Shifting roles

Marriage is more difficult to manage well than other situations in life because there are many roles involved in any one marriage and because the nature of the relationship keeps changing. Unlike many other social situations where roles are clearly defined, within marriage the roles are often shifting and confused. Which role is played at any one time depends both on deep internal needs and desires and on the circumstances operating in the marriage at the time.

Four basic roles are seen in most marriages. The first is the *mother–son role*. It seems to be a feature of female behaviour from childhood onwards for a woman to want to care for the things she loves. She expresses her love in very practical, often domestic, ways and wants to be loved in return for her efforts. If her caring and loving activities are ignored or rebuffed then she fears she is being taken for granted and bad emotional tensions build up. She interprets her husband's lack of appreciation as a lack of love for her. This caring she needs so badly to express is a form of mothering. Some men, as we have seen, cannot allow themselves to be dependent and to accept this mothering for what it is, and they thereby deprive their partner of a major source of satisfaction. A woman thus deprived will be unfulfilled unless her life is filled with children or others whom she can mother. In reality all men need *some* mothering from their wives, but if this behaviour oversteps the mark and becomes bossy and overbearing as opposed to loving and caring, many men cannot cope, and they rebel. Some men respond so badly to their wife's needs to mother them that this becomes a real source of contention in the marriage. Unfortunately, it is one which goes largely unrecognised. Such marriages often take on a new lease of life if the man is ill or has a coronary, for example. Now his wife is really needed in her mothering role. She comes into her own and her husband loves her for it. Even when her husband is dead and her children gone, many such women channel this mothering role into caring for others or for animals.

The arrival of children disturbs the mother–son role in many marriages and this is why so many problems arise around the time of a first baby. A woman who is very maternal (and many are) will be quite happy mothering her husband in the early years of marriage. Once a baby comes along he has to share this mothering with someone else and many men cannot cope. They feel displaced from their wives' affections, and may become depressed, have an affair or indulge in other disruptive behaviour—much of which is in a vain effort to register the 'loss' of their wife's total affection and attention. This is so commonplace as to be considered normal. Fortunately, the cake of love and affection does not necessarily have to be cut into smaller and smaller pieces as children are added to the family, because in many families the overall size of the cake enlarges and as a result everybody gets a piece which is as good or even better. A man who goes off in a huff and thereby makes it impossible for his wife to act in a motherly way towards him is digging his own grave within the marriage.

The other side of the mother–son coin is the *father–daughter role*. Some women do not believe in the worth of this role—asserting that it simply amounts to men being dominant and patronising. This view unfortunately deprives their men of a vital function they feel the need to fill in relation to their wife, that of caring for her as if she were a child, protecting and cherishing her. Many marriages work for a good deal of the time in this role without friction, and the father–daughter role-play is implicit rather than obvious. This works well because the man is not endlessly dominant and the woman endlessly submissive—there is a shifting dominance within the overall roles. Some women, once they have children, start to call their husband 'Daddy' along with the children. Such women have reverted to the blissful stage of their own lives when they were happy to be loved unconditionally by their father, whose rules and regulations they accepted, but within the confines of which they knew they could get their own way most of the time. They flirt with their husbands more or less continuously, whilst at the same time regarding them as someone whom they can trust always to love them and who will be kind to them.

Some women find such a picture quite disgusting but most of those who adopt this role do so knowingly and find that it suits them best. In this role they boost their husband's self-confidence, and he in turn behaves better to them and to their children.

The third, and probably most basic, role is the *friendship role*. We have discussed this in detail on page 121.

The fourth role is the *lover role*. The emotional aspects of loving are discussed in the chapter on Romance (page 98) and the physical aspects are dealt with in chapters 16–18 but here we ought to look at the damage that is done even before the couple meet and marry. We saw in chapter 1 how Western child-rearing tends to make sex out to be nasty or even dirty, and then we wonder why it is that teenagers start on their careers as lovers with negative ideas. Unfortunately, one cannot just shrug one's shoulders and say 'So what?' because the way we behave in the lover role greatly influences the way we behave as parents, and the vast majority of married couples have children.

A lot of research has proved beyond doubt that a woman's sexuality is inextricably tied up with her mothering abilities and vice versa. A woman who is at ease with her body, who is orgasmic, and enjoys intercourse and her relationship with her husband, also finds childbirth, breastfeeding and the rearing of babies easier and more enjoyable. This all has deep implications for the way she thinks of and cares for her babies. A woman who is a good lover is almost always a good mother, so it makes great sense for couples to work together to ensure that the woman enjoys all aspects of her sexuality so that her confidence and enjoyment of them are boosted. We have had extensive experience with young babies, mother–baby interrelationships and breastfeeding counselling over several years and are no longer reluctant to make very early predictions about such women. The sexually 'together' woman is by and large the one who enjoys her pregnancy, birth and breastfeeding experiences. She sees them as extensions of her sexuality—which they are. Researchers have shown that some women experience clitoral enlargement during birth and some women consciously experience giving birth and breastfeeding as sexually arousing. The sexually inhibited woman could also experience such pleasant feelings but she cannot cope with them, feels guilty for having them and so unconsciously suppresses them. This is a shame (especially as it leads many women to get less out of birth and breastfeeding than they could) but is typical of what our Western culture has done to women's sexuality. After all, a woman's sexuality is not simply manifested by her intercourse performance; it is a continuous facet of her personality, expressed by her clothes, the way she walks and sits, her hairstyle, the way she cares for and feeds her babies and what she does in bed with her husband. To confine the concept of a woman's sexuality to her performance in bed is to misunderstand the whole subject and to underestimate women as highly sexual creatures in everyday life. Most men are guilty on this count, at least to some extent.

So, being good lovers and encouraging each other in the lover role is very important, not only for immediate pleasure but also as a rehearsal for and reinforcement of the parenting role. A woman who is a good lover often behaves in a loving, motherly way towards her husband before and especially after intercourse, and a man who is a good lover practises his powers of tenderness and affection, which can then be shared with his children.

Summary

Marriage is the framework within which most of us express our sexuality for much of our lives and, as we have seen, it is a relationship basically between personalities rather than genitals. Our sex organs were designed to work without constant attention and fussing. They are simply used to express our personalities in a genital way. We express our personalities in other sexual ways all the time.

There are no magic rules for a successful marriage except that ideally the couple's personalities should be in tune with each other for as much of the time as possible. Only by entering the marriage scene well prepared as personalities can we hope to make a real success of it. Change is possible in marriage but it occurs slowly if it occurs at all, and unless both partners are patient and prepared to work at it the pressures in society are so strong that the chances are that it will end before it has been given a serious chance.

We like to see marriage as a way of life that offers the best possible relationship a man and a woman can enjoy and the ideal background for the rearing of children.

Chapter 11

Marriage as a way of life

Marriage, or the close man–woman relationship that exists whether or not it has been dignified by the marriage ceremony, can be an enormously strong bond. It can withstand long-term illness, mental and physical disabilities, sexual deprivation, addiction to alcohol in one partner, unemployment in the breadwinner and so on. All of this suggests that a good marriage is much more than simply a long-term commitment to sexual exclusivity. We see marriage much more as an enduring friendship—an alliance between a man and a woman who work together as friends—in a completely self-contained team of two.

Unfortunately, the concept of a husband and wife being each other's closest friends seems rather odd to many, so it is hardly surprising that once the romantic feelings of the first year have died away, some couples complain that they have little left. There is evidence that where a woman sees her husband as her best friend, she feels understood and says that things get better year by year. She finds she can tell him anything, even things she cannot relate to her closest woman friend. No direct similar evidence exists in respect of men but what men are known to think of a good relationship leads us to assume that they see things in much the same way as women.

As in any close alliance there are bound to be 'frictions of association'—troubles caused by being together for much of the time, but in a good marriage these are kept to a minimum by a sensible division of labour between the sexes which is roughly the same in all cultures. Although many of us curse the lot of our own sex from time to time, wishing we were the opposite sex, in a good marriage the tasks that have to be done are divided up according to who does them best and the marriage not only survives but thrives.

Once we start to think of the man–woman relationship as a kind of super-friendship it begins to alter the whole subject of sex. It is possible to have sex with anyone but there are very few people who could be life-long friends.

Once a friendship is formed it is in the interests of the couple to please each other and to respect the interests and feelings of the other. So, for example, the husband of a woman who does not like fellatio (oral sex with a man's penis) respects this restriction and does not use it to 'prove' that she does not love him. If, then, one day she decides to try it with him, yet cannot go through with it, the 'loving friend' type of husband is not angry but would see her effort as endearing and, for her, a sign of love and effort.

Affairs

Affairs are said to be increasingly common, though all the statistics about their prevalence are misleading because affairs tend to be under-reported in surveys. The impression of clinicians working in this field, however, is that women are as likely, or nearly as likely, as men to be, or to have been, in such relationships, and that possibly by the age of, say, fifty-five around three-quarters of married individuals will have been involved in one or more affairs although they may not have gone as far as intercourse. In fantasy, if not in fact, virtually everyone will have had several.

A few people find a kind of sexual refuge in marriage and have little practical sexual interest in other members of the opposite sex, but for most marriage does not reduce the attraction of others. The attraction may be expressed only in fantasy, friendship or mild flirtation with limited sexual aims, but it is still there. A few immature people are incapable of making serious attempts at sexual commitment in *any* relationship, and so affairs continue regardless of marriage. Some people, by divorce and remarriage, perhaps several times, 'legalise' their affairs in a way that would not really have been possible in the past, except for rather special cases such as Henry VIII.

A few couples who feel they cannot tolerate the sexual restrictions of marriage reach an agreement or 'contract' which specifies that extra-marital relationships are acceptable within certain constraints and rules. Sometimes a condition of such an agreement is that the partner be informed, although many people are inclined towards the opposite in that they do not mind their partner having such a relationship provided they do not know of it. Either way, it is, perhaps, a better alternative to repeated divorce, especially if the individuals believe that their relationship is worth preserving. In several Western cultures in recent times it has been considered to be socially acceptable for a man to have a mistress and for his wife to accept it as a fact of life. Today, the true mistress is a rare creature but men (and increasingly women) who find one sex partner for life insufficient look outside marriage for this variety. It is scarcely surprising that affairs are as common as they are today—in the absence of any culturally acceptable way of coping with a need for sexual adventure and variety over a married lifetime, many people are likely to seek alternatives. Unfortunately there is only one current alternative, the 'hole-in-the-corner' affair, and this is intrinsically dishonest and unattractive to many because of the deception it involves. Such deception, especially if maintained over a long period, must destroy something in the marriage which a more open 'mistress and lover' system would not. Both sexes would probably tolerate a culturally sanctioned mistress/lover system of extra-marital affairs with far less danger of divorce than the current secretive and dishonest arrangement. After all, whatever some people may think, most individuals find it impossible to sustain a solely one-to-one relationship for the whole of their (increasingly long) married lives, and there may be a better way of coping with this reality than the rather shabby system that our culture reluctantly accepts today.

Affairs are a threat to marriage.

For most people an affair is simply an adventure and is never meant to replace their marital relationship—in fact, most individuals involved in an affair, when asked, say that they want *both* the new partner *and* their spouse. Of course a few of those having affairs are either consciously or unconsciously on the look-out for a new partner because of underlying dissatisfaction with their marriage.

This puts the finger on the real difficulty. In our culture marriage carries the implication, and even the promise, that the relationship will be sexually exclusive. In an age of efficient contraception old objections about reproduction (and inheritance) confusion which could result from extra-marital sex have lost some of their validity. They have not lost all of it, as is shown by the fact that a substantial proportion of married women seeking an abortion do so because they are pregnant by someone other than their husband. Increasingly, however, marriage is being seen as a relationship which does not necessarily confer exclusive ownership rights on the partners.

A related aspect is the view that if a man marries a woman she has the right to be maintained by him for the rest of her life, regardless of separation or divorce. Views on this are also slowly changing. Although many people will find these changes unacceptable for themselves, and will try to run their marriage on traditional lines, which is fine if they have a like-minded partner, the changes in attitude which are now occurring could actually strengthen marriage as an institution because extra-marital sex would not be seen as a mortal blow to the relationship. Almost by definition in the past such an event meant the marriage had ended. Greater toleration may be good for marriage overall but obviously individuals must still be able to feel secure in spite of their partner's—or even their own—adventures. Human nature being what it is, this does not seem very likely.

Conventional attitudes are perhaps harmful in another way to some good marriages. Many people (especially women) are brought up with the belief that it is wrong to have sex with more than one member of the opposite sex. This leads to what is termed serial monogamy; that is, over a period of time a woman will have intercourse with several partners, abandoning one before starting with the next. Combined with the belief that you can only have intercourse with someone you love this paves the way for unnecessary divorce.

The motives lying behind affairs are many. They include: the search for ideal love, sex or romance; curiosity, especially in those who had little or no experience before marriage; confirmation of attractiveness in women or masculinity in men; poor sexual self-esteem for whatever cause; sexual boredom; experimentation; revenge on the partner (even if the affair is not made known to him or her); the sudden opportunity to fulfil a fantasy; and testing to see if a sexual problem in the marital relationship is due to the partner or oneself. Promiscuity as such is not a frequent cause although an unfilled sexual need is commonplace. Travel, holidays, being away from home ground, alcohol and parties all have potential for leading to affairs, but these are often brief. With increasing numbers of women working there are more opportunities for men and women to spend long periods working together. This increases the opportunity for intimacy to occur and would seem to make affairs more likely. An affair, after all, requires both time and opportunity if it is to develop.

More permanent affairs are a greater threat to marriage because of the possibility that the relationship could become more than sexual and might turn into a full-blown love-affair. Here, a woman, probably in an unconscious move to reduce her guilt about her sexual activities, often emphasises the love aspect of the relationship and, if she believes (as is common) that it is only possible to love one person, then divorce may be the end result. In such cases the original relationship (or relationships if both are married) may be destroyed, only to be replaced by one which is not much better and may even be worse. If both parties were to make their intentions clear to each other at the start of the affair such situations could often be avoided. In these circumstances men may mislead women by initially displaying more emotion than they really feel so as to get them to agree to sex, and women may mislead men by behaving more sexually than they really feel so as to establish an emotional relationship. As in most facets of man–woman relationships, greater honesty between the sexes could avoid unhappy outcomes.

Most affairs are probably kept secret, unless they are discovered, and the realisation that the marital partner may be involved in an affair can lead to destructive suspiciousness even in a good relationship. In some instances, however, one partner may egg the other on into an affair. Sometimes, a partner who cannot have intercourse for one reason or another may, out of consideration, urge the other to have an extra-marital relationship. In other instances the reason is sexual weariness with one partner on the part of the other; an attempt to reduce guilt about having had an affair; the desire on the part of one partner thus to obtain justification for an affair they intend; or, occasionally, to have the partner reveal in minute detail what happened as a form of vicarious sexual pleasure.

More uncommonly, one partner wants to be present and participate as an additional stimulation. This leads to troilism in which an additional man or woman may be added to the couple's sexual relationship. A man, for example, may be aroused by watching his wife undertake lesbian acts with another woman, and may then want to have intercourse with both. However, sometimes it is the wife who enjoys watching her husband have sex with another woman or vice versa. This type of arrangement may only be fleeting but in a few marriages it is a more or less permanent feature. Such marriages are rarely happy deep down in spite of outward and often vociferous claims to the contrary.

An extension of this is into wife-swapping on a casual or permanent basis. This could be called a joint affair if it is permanent, since the husband and wife are both involved. Oddly, such openness can lead to jealousy; for example, the husband may become jealous because he believes, or even sees, that his wife is more sexually aroused by the other man. It is not therefore surprising that 'swinging', as it is called, is in decline and is destructive to relationships.

For some people the very secrecy of an affair is part of its attraction—they say they find 'naughty' sex more satisfying than 'legal' sex. This is understandable because 'naughty' and 'sex' are notions which are commonly combined during childhood. It is also understandable in those who have been brought up with the belief that they will not be loved if they behave sexually. So they subsequently behave (with the person they love) in an inhibited way because of the fear that they will no longer be loved if they reveal their real sexual needs. For some people sex with a stranger is infinitely more gratifying, since they are more uninhibited.

Perhaps the biggest single dilemma facing the person who is having an affair is whether or not to tell. There are no easy answers to this but it is probably wise to err on the side of *not* telling. 'Coming clean' may make you feel good (or even self-righteous), but it can have a devastating effect on your partner who, especially if it comes as a surprise, may react more dramatically than you imagine. Some people tell in order to take revenge on their spouse, but this sort of relationship is doomed by this stage anyway. There is little doubt that keeping the whole thing to yourself is best of all, but this can put incredible stress on the marital situation because you will be living on a tightrope which makes 'telling' seem attractive. As we have said, in practice it is rarely the best course. Few people really want their spouse, once told, to accept the situation with equanimity—simply because this would show that he or she does not care about the relationship. A massive over-reaction with talk of divorce or even suicide is not uncommon and can permanently damage the relationship. Discretion, secrecy, lying and subterfuge then are the prices one has to pay to keep an affair from one's spouse, and for many these outweigh the advantages of the affair itself.

The discovery that one's partner is, or has been, involved in an affair is usually a shattering blow—sometimes more to one's self-esteem than anything else. However, calm discussion should reveal whether it resulted from a real dissatisfaction within the marriage or was simply an adventure. If it is the former, it may be an opportunity to sort the marriage out, perhaps with professional help; if it is the latter, there would seem to be little point in any extreme reaction.

Apart from the suspiciousness, jealousy, distrust, anger, divorce and unwanted pregnancy which may result from an affair, the most solid objection is probably that of venereal disease. If everyone followed the traditional pattern of no sex before marriage and no sex with anyone else afterwards, then VD would die out. The fact that it has not, either in the past or now, shows that many people find it difficult or impossible to keep to the straight and narrow path.

For all the hurt and harm they can cause affairs continue now as in the past. Changing attitudes towards marriage and affairs, no matter how unwelcome and unacceptable to some, are, at least, one answer, even if not the complete one, to the problem of divorce. That the acceptance of affairs could reduce divorce is a total reversal of the traditional view of marriage but for some it works.

Sexual difficulties

A woman who has no orgasms is often seen to be 'unloving' by her husband just as she can be critical of his sexual capabilities. Unfortunately, such couples rarely discuss their problems and because of a shortage of trained professional help often find it difficult to sort them out. It is easy for a couple to get out of tune sexually, often because of erroneous notions and expectations. The frustrations that ensue can lead to a search outside the partnership for what seems to be lacking within it as we have just seen.

Clinical experience shows that sexual problems are not usually the bogey-men they are made out to be. Most couples complaining of sexual problems have other underlying problems that are far more important. Most often the sexual problem is a symptom of their inability to communicate their sexual (and other) needs. A woman's prevailing attitude to sex may prevent her from asking her husband to indulge in some activity which she would love to try but cannot bear to ask for in case he thinks she is perverted.

Prostitutes are known to provide men with sexual favours their wives and girlfriends will not provide—a sad reflection on the lack of communication and caring over sexual and other matters in many marriages. Often a woman is interested in a varied and exciting sex life, yet her husband complains that she is 'uninterested' in sex. Clearly they have never sat down and talked it over.

Sometimes, the reason for this is that they love an image of the other rather than the reality of the individual. For example, a man may unconsciously attribute to the wife he loves the same characteristics of prudery that he thought his mother possessed. In consequence he thinks his wife would repel sex-talk as 'dirty' and so never broaches the subject.

Marriage in name only

Some marriages, of course, endure for the sake of the children, for financial reasons or because of strongly held religious views. The couple have to all intents and purposes secretly divorced or agreed to get a divorce at a later date. Such a couple usually maintain a façade of friendliness but satisfy their needs for love, companionship and even sex elsewhere. This sort of marriage is remarkably common. After all, about one in three marriages end in divorce in the Western world today and many more continue in the way just described. Such figures and clinical experience suggest that only about a third or a quarter of marriages are what most would call successful. Some research indicates that the proportion of totally satisfactory marriages may be as low as a tenth.

A large number of unsatisfactory marriages continue for very obscure reasons. The partners remain involved with each other but bitterly, and almost all areas of conflict remain unresolved for years. Possibly these are good marriages that have simply moved in the wrong direction as we described in the previous chapter. People involved in these marriages have a most unsatisfactory way of life and often have physical or psychosomatic illnesses as a result. Many are on drugs that alter the mind and many are frankly depressed. Psychosexual and marital counselling can help a lot of these couples, but the going is tough because they may have been living in this unsatisfactory way for years and their desire to improve things may be long dead. Having said this though, there is no doubt that a few couples actually seem to thrive on friction as a way of life.

This brings us to the subject of the 'good' and the 'poor' marriage. A marriage is good if the couple think it is, even if it seems poor by comparison with others. A good example is the marriage between two sexually inhibited people. Such people please each other yet may never have discussed their attitudes towards sex. Before marriage they do little (if anything) sexually and afterwards intercourse may well be infrequent and of poor quality. In some cases these couples hardly ever have intercourse at all, yet are quite happy. This way of life suits them and that is all that matters.

'Good' and 'poor' marriages.

Some good marriages run along very odd lines compared with many people's notions. They work because they answer one (or both) party's psychosexual needs, albeit in a rather unusual way. For example, a woman whose sexuality is such that she can only express herself through mothering may have lots of children and even mother her husband too.

The reverse of this model can occur if a girl marries a 'daddy' figure and this too can bring similar joys and problems, with such marriages being more often successful than not.

The phases of marriage

Marriage, like all human endeavours, never stands still: it evolves with time.

Phase one
This first phase lasts until the couple start a family. Changing homes, friends and life-styles to accommodate the marriage can be difficult. However, for many, the first few years spent together—with the wife working and no children—providing themselves with a home and preparing for a family, can seem, in retrospect, to have been the best years of their marriage. Sex is usually frequent and experimentation commonplace, but sexual difficulties arising from sexual inexperience and the lack of a will to learn are widespread. Many young women complain that their husbands do not do what they like most, that they are too rough and that they are selfish. In spite of all this most young couples at this stage say that sexually they are happy and they look forward to their problems disappearing as they mature and get used to each other. The fact that the divorce rate is highest in this phase of marriage would appear to contradict what we have just said but, as we shall see, this is not as surprising as it at first seems.

Ideally, during this phase of married life the couple are learning to resolve conflict and should be getting used to communicating with each other before children come along. Children make conversation more difficult and increase problems. If the couple cannot sort out the problems of living together, tensions arise and anger, resentment, and misunderstandings are common.

During this stage some young people become ill physically or mentally, and depression is not at all uncommon. Once things begin to go bad, sex, rather than being the cause of the trouble as many couples think, becomes the victim. Provided the basic relationship is good, nearly all these early problems can be resolved by the couple themselves or with professional help.

All these adjustments take a long time and it is essential to allow plenty of time between getting married and having a first baby. Far too many couples have a baby so soon after marriage that they have hardly had time to get used to each other as partners, let alone as parents. In most couples it is the woman who starts putting on the pressure for a baby, and often the man, not nearly as sure of himself in the relationship, simply cannot cope with the thought, let alone the reality.

Whether this pressure comes about because of the intrinsic biological yearnings of women or whether it is the result of our apparently baby-centred culture is hard to say but the result is the same. The couple, who hardly know each other, have to take another human being into account and have to adapt to quite different roles too soon. Many couples deeply resent this later in life—when they are free of their child-rearing responsibilities in middle life they are bitter that they now no longer feel the same about each other and yearn for their early child-free days when they were both young. At this stage, if not before, one or other takes off for a romantic affair outside the marriage and the result can be disaster for the family.

Some young couples imagine, quite wrongly, that once the wife becomes pregnant all sex should cease. This is bad enough in a long-established relationship but in the first few years of marriage it can lead to trouble. After the birth, the sleepless nights and new-baby routines stress even the mature married couple but they particularly take their toll on the recently married. The new mother needs plenty of help but the young husband, still seeing himself as a grown-up boy with a permanent live-in girlfriend, often is not ready or able to cope with new burdens. He has hardly had any time to be at the centre of his wife's world when he is displaced in favour of a baby that needs a lot of attention. The woman, fearing that the baby will change her body for the worse (the vagina, stomach and breasts are now irrevocably altered in many women's view), fears that after only a few years of marriage her husband will go off and find another woman whose body is still in good shape.

The rejection women fear.

Is it surprising with all this going on that couples in their first seven years of marriage are so prone to divorce?

Phase two
This lasts about twenty years, covering the period during which the children grow up and leave home. In general, dissatisfaction with marriage increases during this period and most couples tend to draw apart. Earlier problems that were not resolved are aggravated, intercourse rates frequently fall and experimentation declines. Ironi-

cally, sex now rears its head in a rather unexpected way. The man, who in the first years of marriage felt he was getting less sex than he thought he needed (because his wife was inexperienced or reluctant), is now amazed to discover that she wants more than he can supply at a time when he is under increasing pressure at work and at home. Many women really come into their own sexually in their late thirties and their forties and begin to worry about the onset of the menopause and what it will do to their attractiveness. Some women have a mad fling at this stage for fear that it will be their last chance before their charms fade away for ever! Often such women simply want to take advantage of what they see as remaining of their active sex life and do so with their husbands, but others look elsewhere. Of course, there is no evidence that women are less sexy or less interested in sex after the menopause—on the contrary, many are so relieved at the fear of pregnancy being lifted from them that they blossom as never before. Two useful signs that a woman of this age is looking outside her marriage for sex are the onset of effective dieting after many years of unsuccessful efforts and suddenly finding endless fault with their husbands. The latter is a commonly used way of 'de-loving' her husband, because in our culture, if she still loved him, she would not be 'free' to fall in love elsewhere.

Women in their 30s and 40s.

A common factor that links the first two phases of marriage is that the two partners may not see themselves as equal in attractiveness and value. More attractive spouses can come to see themselves as under-benefiting from the relationship and less attractive ones as over-benefiting. Either way, couples often start to count the cost and this is a bad sign. The relationship no longer seems to be a good bargain, benefiting each equally. The under-benefited one becomes less willing to please and eventually starts having affairs, scarcely caring about the effect on the other partner. The over-benefited partner is less likely to object for fear of losing the (too good) spouse and is unlikely to have an affair to retaliate for fear of being totally abandoned by the erring spouse. This is another reason why couples should be as nearly equal as possible in the attractiveness league.

Phase three
This lasts from about the age of fifty until the death of one of the partners. It is usually a phase of togetherness and increasing satisfaction. The couple have no fear of pregnancy and their sex lives often improve. Unfortunately, some older couples still feel that sex is for the young and so do not enjoy sex nearly as much or as often as they could. Thankfully things are changing in the right direction as far as this is concerned. It is worth taking care not to lose the habit of intercourse if one partner has to go into hospital or is ill for a long period. We will look at this more in chapter 33. It is also interesting to see that evidence suggests that an active sex life is linked to a long life. People of this age often have grandchildren who bring pleasure with few responsibilities (a rare combination in life), and no longer have to worry about being competitive at work. The man will have got as far as he is going to and is either settled in his career or is either running up to or already in retirement.

Throughout all these three stages of marriage there is a biological need for attachment. In the good man–woman relationship this attachment grows, particularly at times of stress when the couple think about each other, want to be with each other, communicate distress to each other and are comforted by one another. Separation from someone to whom one is attached in this way causes anxiety, protest and even physical illness. The bond that forms between long-married couples can be formidable. They tend to think along the same lines; can know what each other is thinking or is about to say; suffer with each other mentally and even physically; and seem to be 'one body' as described in the Bible.

Anything that persistently disrupts attachment can damage a marriage. Men who work away from home have a lot of problems—problems which have little or nothing to do with their seeking sex outside marriage. An individual who as a child experienced threats of or the actual divorce or separation of his parents (especially being separated from his mother in the early years) reacts, when his attachment in marriage is threatened, by going in one of two opposite ways. In the first the individual craves attachment but can only function by caring for others, whether they want it or not. (Some people go into nursing and the other caring professions because of this deeply felt need.) Conversely, the individual may be unhappy about the threatened loss but, fearing abandonment, is jealous, possessive and controlling. Is it surprising then that children with attachment problems in early life continue to have problems within marriage? Unfortunately, the children of divorced parents are likely to repeat the cycle for these and other reasons and themselves produce children who are more likely to divorce. We ignore this basic biological attachment need at our peril and this is one of the many reasons why we believe that couples should stay married and patch things up rather than get divorced at the drop of a hat.

Types of marriage life-style

When two people live together for a long period, married or not and even if they are of the same sex, they need to work out some kind of structure which will enable them to function as a unit. Many marriage 'experts' have classified such relationships within marriage in great detail but because of shortage of space we will look here only at the four commonest types.

The patriarchal marriage

This is the most common marriage structure today, even with the tremendous growth of women's power and influence. In this the woman looks to the man to be the stronger (physically and mentally), the breadwinner, the leader (most of the time), the more intelligent, the decision-maker and so on. The husband in a marriage like this perceives his wife as a little girl—though not overtly so most of the time. This need not be nearly as awful as it sounds because the man's ego is boosted so much that he rises to the occasion and carries the marriage along very much on his own shoulders. Also, many men feel

Marriage Styles

Although the marriages shown here and on the next two pages look very different the couples may (or may not) be equally happy and fulfilled.

PATRIARCHAL MARRIAGE.

threatened by signs of what they take to be female oppression of them—decision-making and so on—and react by coping badly as husbands. This is clearly to the detriment of the family but is not necessarily the wife's fault. It usually comes about because of the man's immature personality. A lot of this immaturity is hidden under the mask of the patriarch and this can be no bad thing in many marriages. In order to be gentle you have to feel strong and this may be a hidden advantage of the patriarchal system.

Surveys show that most women want (or have been conditioned into wanting) this type of marriage. The intelligent, independent woman can have the best of both worlds by going about her life very much as it suits her for most of the time whilst avoiding direct challenges to her husband so that he feels patriarchal enough of the time to keep him happy. Undoubtedly many marriages thrive on this form of tact in the woman.

The board-of-directors marriage
This type is increasingly common and is seen to some extent in all marriages. In such a marriage there is a sensible division of labour (often in fact dictated by convention) and by and large decisions are made jointly after discussion. The person best at a particular task does it. There are certain areas of married life which men seem to tackle better than women and vice versa. This, of course, does not mean that women cannot mend cars or that men cannot make dresses but, on balance, given the way we are made and brought up, certain jobs remain culturally attached to each sex.

The marriage of equals
In this the woman and the man are completely interchangeable in daily-living terms. Biological sex differences (except, of course, for reproductive functioning) are ignored. Couples who adopt this form of marriage seem to have more problems than others, but, with careful arrangements for outside child care to enable the woman to work as an equal to her husband, a good working arrangement can be achieved. Such a marriage can work well for child-free couples or the childless.

The role-reversal marriage
With the increase in unemployment and the high earning potential of some women, it is occasionally economically necessary or sensible for the man to be the person who looks after the children and the home. There is an obvious social strain in this arrangement, but it can be made to work.

The mother/father relationship
We have discussed this already earlier in the chapter. In this type of marriage the person unconsciously marries his dominant parent and can only happily function in this context. This means at its most simple that a man who had a very dominant mother might well choose a similar 'motherly' type to marry. We have seen how troublesome this type of marriage can be because few people want the parental role to be absolute (or even present) in *every* dimension of their lives.

MARRIAGE AS A WAY OF LIFE

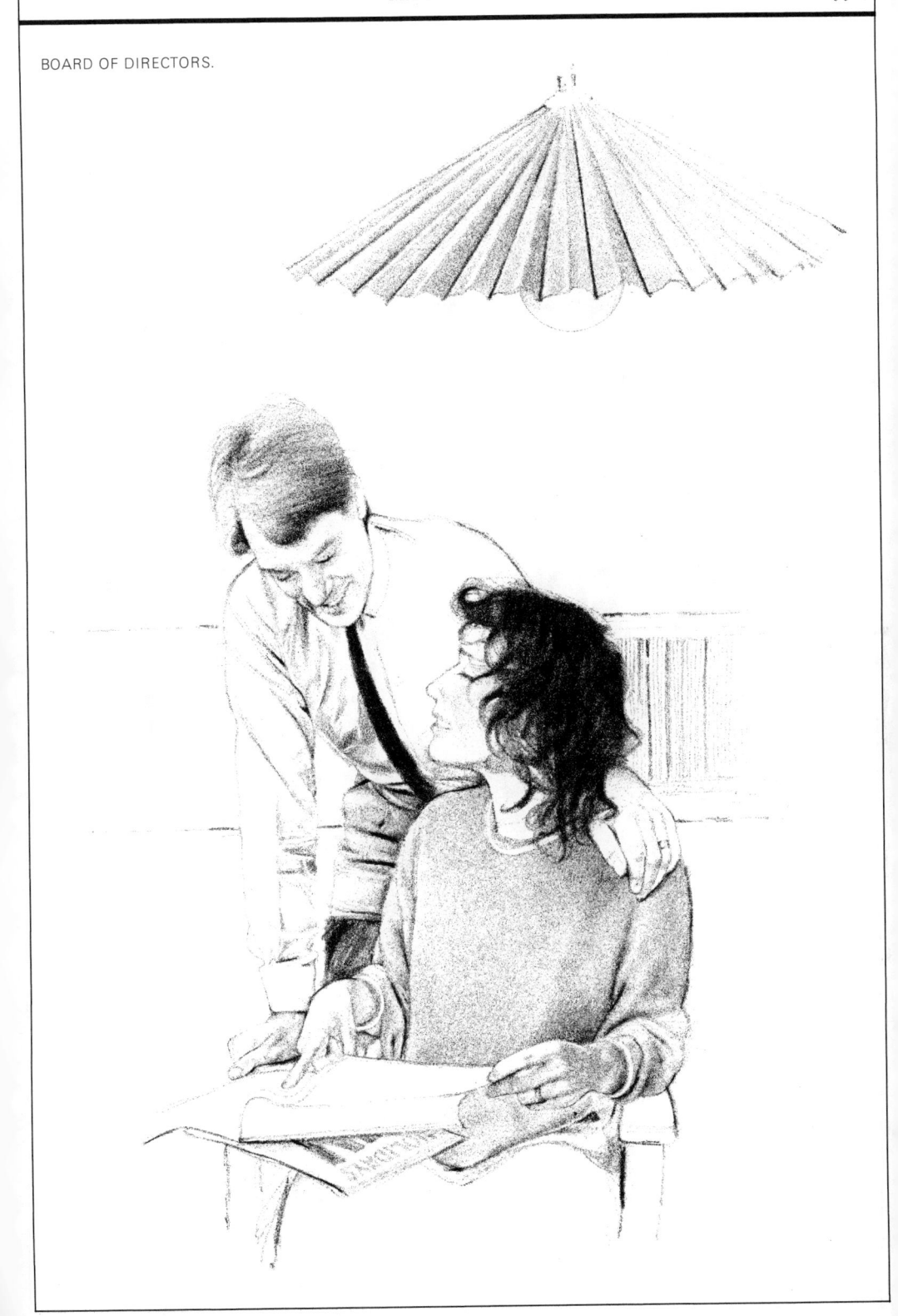

BOARD OF DIRECTORS.

MARRIAGE AS A WAY OF LIFE

ROLE REVERSAL.

Alternating dominance

A good marriage is one in which the partners switch roles a lot. In some situations male-type skills are needed and without further consideration the man begins to take control. In other situations the woman, again without thinking, takes the lead. No conflict arises in such situations because the couple are switching roles in a reflex manner. In other, less clear, situations, both might attempt to be dominant or both might respond submissively, in which case conflict or indecision results. Once attention is focussed on this feature of the male/female relationship it is easy to see it at work in a good relationship.

None of this means that either party is intrinsically inferior or superior—when one partner is away or ill the family continues to run smoothly because the remaining spouse can usually fulfil the role of the absent one with ease. Sometimes a man will want to 'mother' his children and on occasions a woman will have to be the strong one, perhaps even the breadwinner.

In a well-balanced marriage no one keeps a score but the partners work together in tandem, building up each other's self-confidence and sharing the benefits equally. Such a couple's marriage, based as it is on mutual respect and friendship, improves as the years go by and sex takes its place among the many other activities which express their love and friendship. In whatever way society changes, it is extremely unlikely that marriage will go away. We sincerely hope it does not because experience suggests that it is the only hope for a sane future in our culture. The natural unit of humankind is a woman and a man complementing each other's skills, talents and resources.

Summary

Marriage, or any other close man–woman relationship, offers a whole range of wonderful options as a way of life. Provided expectations are not set too high and the couple keep their feet firmly on the ground, marriage can be a friendship; a source of attachment; an alliance against a hostile world; a source of companionship; a mutual admiration society; a therapy group of two; a work group with each member specialising in jobs they do best; a source of tender, loving care; a means of keeping adolescent romance alive; a secret society with its own language and history; a child-rearing group; and a means by which we can increase the love we feel for ourselves indirectly by putting someone else first in life.

Chapter 12
Marriage, divorce and society

Although marriage is a personal contract between two people it is also a social act because it is the way in which we choose to organise men and women in family units to bring up children. Around the world different cultures have very different ways of organising family life and child care but in the West we have arrived at the nuclear family, in which, typically, two adults live alone with their children. The heart of this type of family structure is the parents, not only because they are the starting-point but also because they are the only consistent source of adult company for the children. The vast majority of people, even if they do not believe in marriage in other ways, still think that children should ideally be raised within the context of marriage. Many young couples throughout the Western world live together, but once they decide to have children they usually get married. This is changing slowly as society's ideas change. After all, it was not long ago that people got married in order to copulate. The trends are not likely to parallel the premarital sex question though, because child care needs a long-term commitment of the adults to each other and their children, whereas copulation does not.

There is no need to 'sell' marriage. It is as popular as ever even at a time when its failures are so apparent and seemingly inevitable. The vast majority of people want to be married or, one could argue, have been conditioned to want it. Marriage is, unfortunately, still portrayed as some kind of fairy-tale ideal rather than the reality of two people living together and sharing their lives for a long time. The thing is that today, with age expectancy rising all the time, a couple married in their twenties can expect to be together for forty to fifty years or longer, which is more than twice as long as they would have only a few hundred years ago—simply because one or other of the couple would have died.

Statisticians and analysts looking at the mid-life peak in divorces (second only to the first-five-year peak) suggest that it could be a sort of natural break point for many people. After all, they argue, had they lived a few centuries ago they would have been 'divorced' by death.

However marriage is 'sold' or 'over-sold' culturally, most of us end up thinking of it as a passport to eternal bliss in the physical, social and psychological sense. As a result many, if not most people, (and especially girls) go into marriage with expectations that are far too high and as a result all too often come down to earth with a bump. This really should not happen in the eighties but it still does. What most people do not realise is that by idealising marriage as an institution they trivialise the man-woman relationship. This comes about because it is intrinsic in our culture to regard marriage as the *ideal* manifestation of the man-woman relationship. Until recently it was the only social structure within which men and women could enjoy each other's company *and* have intercourse. Reliable contraception and the women's movement have changed all that, probably for ever, and now most people do not get married *solely* to have intercourse or to have a close, meaningful relationship with someone of the opposite sex. Even so, most people still see marriage as their preferred life-style, even if children are not involved.

Why marriages go wrong

Marriage has many enemies today. The politicians and legislators formalise it and constrain it; taxation makes it financially beneficial not to marry; the churches impose rules to try to regulate it yet few adherents to their faiths live by them; and so on. The greatest of all enemies of marriage is society itself. In a world in which we change our cars every couple of years and move home every seven, is it surprising that we have come to look at life through 'disposable' spectacles? People are more mobile now, they change jobs frequently, move from their communities and have less sense of belonging; so is it surprising that the pressures to stay with one's partner are not as great as they were? Of course there were bad marriages in the past but most stayed together for religious, moral, financial or practical reasons, sometimes in a state of armed neutrality but often simply because they realised that the grass would not necessarily be greener on the other side of the hill. Easier divorce has undoubtedly ended a lot of very unpleasant marriages, but it has also given a couple with too high an expectation of marriage as an institution and of each other as individuals, a way out which is sometimes too easy.

Research shows that most people are no happier once they are divorced than they were within an unsuitable marriage, and the best thing to do is almost certainly to patch up existing marriages whenever possible. After all, presumably the couple must have had a certain amount going for them at some stage or they would not have got married at all. Having changed or having fallen out of love with marriage are not necessarily good reasons for divorcing. Professional help to keep them together (especially when children are involved) is the best prescription in our view but, of course, better education for marriage is the best preventive.

If there are no children, the couple are freer to split up but even so there are very real pains caused by the loss of someone one has been loving and living with. Divorce may be *technically* easier today, but in human terms is every bit as hard and probably worse, especially for women. A century ago, one third of women of marriageable age were not married and had no opportunity to be. Today, over 90 per cent of women are married (or have been), so the unmarried state is no longer an acceptable one. Life is far from a bed of roses for the unmarried older woman—at the very least there are considerable social and personal disadvantages.

When one considers the tremendous amount of goodwill, excitement, and appreciation of the opposite sex there is in the teens, it seems incredible that things should go so disastrously wrong for so many marriages. The truth is that the trouble starts much earlier than this. All through childhood we are rather poor as a society at helping the sexes enjoy and understand each other.

Things can go disastrously wrong.

Wherever the blame lies we need to change things for our children and their children. We need to reappraise for ourselves the long-held views of the man-woman relationship and question them logically. If the long-held beliefs and prejudices do not stand up they should be rejected, just as one rejects other illogical facets of life. We cannot fight Nature, which intended that men and women should get on well together and form bonds to give children a stable and loving environment in which to grow up.

When looking at marriage as a social institution we have, unfortunately, no way of defining 'good' marriages. Divorce is a measure of dead and terminally ill marriages, but in between the extremes of these and the good marriages are countless millions of very poor or ailing marriages. It has been estimated that for every divorce (about one in three or four marriages) there is a similar number of poor marriages which are sick but not terminally ill. Even though the divorce rate is so high, there is evidence that many so-called 'good' (i.e. not divorced) marriages are less than ideal. This is in itself a cause for real concern.

People's attitudes vary according to when you talk to them. Many people are desperately unhappy with their marriage one month or year and content the next. One survey found that over 80 per cent of women said that given their time again they *would* marry the same man. In another survey 75 per cent of married people said they had seriously thought about divorce at some time. These two supposedly contradictory findings are, in fact, not incompatible. Contact with young couples suggests that the numbers of good marriages among the young are rising, so perhaps the divorce rate will fall soon.

Certainly in today's society as a whole, youngsters are less willing to buy a pig in a poke and get married as inexperienced (not just sexually) virgins. However, there is no evidence that being sexually experienced in one's adolescence makes for a better marriage. Nevertheless, totally inexperienced couples who cannot relate well to the opposite sex do have more problems. This has probably always been the case but in the past such couples worked harder at making things work or stuck it out.

What to do when marriage goes wrong

Probably about two out of three marriages have serious problems at some time although, as we have seen, only half of these will end in divorce. So what can someone who is worried about his or her marriage do?

Talk it over between yourselves
If you have bought this book and read this far you will already have learned enough to have answered some of your main problems (we hope), and throughout the rest of the book you will find answers to many others, which you will be able to discuss with your partner. Ignorance of the facts is only one area of trouble, albeit an important one. Feelings are the biggest problem when things go wrong and often one cannot share one's feelings about someone else with them. At this point a third party becomes almost essential.

Talk to a close, loving friend
Don't go around sharing your marital and relationship problems with just anybody or you will receive so much conflicting and unprofessional advice that you will be even more confused. Also, it will be humiliating for you and your partner when things improve, if your friends and acquaintances know all your business. Seek out a trustworthy friend and talk things over rationally and confidentially. Bear in mind that by definition a friend will tend to take your side because he or she likes you and will not want to offend you. A true friend will tell you the bad news along with the good, but such discussion can put intolerable stress on the friendship and can even kill it completely. Because there are so many problems with all this, lots of people do not confide their marital problems to friends or family but go straight to professionals.

Not just anybody.

Talk to a professional

Your general practitioner
He or she will probably have no specialist training in this field but should be quite helpful as a result of dealing with similar problems time and time again. A general practitioner can rarely spare much time but can sometimes refer you to other people who are more expert and have more time. A marriage that has been going wrong for years

before help is sought (which is usually the case) cannot be sorted out in a few minutes but often needs hours spread over several months. People cannot change their ideas and feelings quickly, and glib answers, however well meaning, are useless and often fuel the fire rather than quench it.

Marriage counsellors

These counsellors offer a realistic service to the married, the single, the divorced and separated, homosexuals, and anyone who needs personal counselling. These counsellors are all trained but are not specialists in the medical sense of the word. Their training is by definition fairly restricted, and they are taught not to tell patients what to do. They work in forty-to-fifty minute time slots, which many people find too short to be really useful. However, many of the commoner and uncomplicated marital and sexual problems can be dealt with by these counsellors, and these counsellors usually charge modest fees.

Psychosexually trained doctors and psychiatrists

Psychosexual medicine is a new branch of the medical profession in the UK and at the moment has attracted very few practitioners full time. The majority of 'experts' working in this field are consultant psychiatrists who, because of their understanding of psychological and emotional problems, tend to deal with sexual and relationship problems too. Many do not particularly want to deal with sexual problems and their patients share their reluctance. Few people with sexual or marital problems *are* mentally ill, and psychiatrists are by definition doctors who deal with mental illness. Going to a psychiatrist still has something of a stigma attached to it and there is always the suggestion (not from the doctor, of course) that one might actually have something 'wrong' with one's personality. The burden of sexual and marital problems is so enormous that the number of psychiatrists who deal with this area is small in comparison and help be difficult to find. A few psychiatrists offer psychoanalysis for such problems but only a tiny fraction of 1 per cent of all marital problems need or receive true psychoanalysis.

Psychoanalysis is not the answer.

Psychologists can actually be more helpful than doctors in many cases because more often than not individuals with sexual or relationship problems are not *ill* and do not need a medical mind to sort them out. The strength of the nonmedical specialist is that the patient does not go along thinking that there is a magic operation or bottle of pills to answer his problems.

Psychologists also have a different point of view from that held by most doctors in that they do not see themselves as authority figures who have to tell patients what to do. Most doctors find it very difficult, because of their training, not to tell people how to behave—after all they do this all day and every day in other areas and it is what is expected of them. However, in this area, the effective therapist has to be a superb listener and interpreter, not an authoritative, standing-in-judgement figure. Most psychologists are better trained not to take this approach than most doctors, though of course there are exceptions.

Psychiatrists who specialise in these types of problem can be reached through your general practitioner, through a marriage guidance counsellor, through self-help groups and through personal contacts. Talking to someone about such sensitive and difficult areas of your life is painful, and doing so to someone who comes highly recommended is a helpful start. How much they charge and how they work varies enormously and some run group sessions which can be very helpful.

Sex therapists

The vast majority of the 'treatment' of marital and sexual problems is done by talking and listening and by the partners discussing things they have learned when they go home. We find that the majority of the real work a couple does happens in between consultations. All professionals can hope to do is to dispel some ignorance, get the couple talking again, help give them insight into their problems, show that they are not alone with their problem (millions of others have been down the same path before) and that they, the professionals, care enough to listen and really to try to help. Once they have recognised at least some of these things most couples are ready to work hard between consultations to build their marriages up again.

A small percentage of couples (or individuals) need more specific physical help with sexual problems. A woman who has never had an orgasm, for example, can, by having the blocking anxieties instilled in childhood removed, have her inherent capacity to do so restored to her; an impotent man or one with premature ejaculation can be helped; and couples with similar problems can be shown how to overcome them. Sex therapy is often highly effective and results can be obtained remarkably quickly for most problems. Some sex therapists use surrogate partners to teach inexperienced and fearful patients how to behave with the opposite sex. We do not favour this method because very often the real underlying problem is not a sexual one (their genitals are working well enough), but a personality one. Such individuals have a much greater need of treatment to improve self-confidence and social skills rather than their sexual ones. It is not uncommon for them to 'fall in love' with the surrogate who has been provided for them, and their condition then can be even worse than at the start of therapy. We consider that many sex therapists pay insufficient attention to the background of an apparent sex problem—but simply prescribe sexual exercises for all and sundry regardless. To be fair, though, this can frequently be successful for a variety of reasons.

None of these helpers can work miracles for a marriage. The couple has to want the treatment or counselling to work and they have to be prepared to put a lot of themselves into it. Results can be quick but rarely are—it usually takes several sessions to make any impact on a problem and progress is then dependent upon the ability of the parties to change and adapt to the suggestions made by the counsellor. The best time to catch any marital or sex problem is early, preferably in the twenties or thirties when the couple are still emotionally and intellectually flexible enough to be able to change their behaviour and their ideas.

Given that the vast majority of young couples are sexually active (though not necessarily having intercourse) before they marry we would like to see more care being given to good foundation-stones being laid at this stage. Many a couple can see later in their marriage that it was during their engagement and in the early married years that their troubles started—in fact a lot of those we see say that they knew from very early on that they had made a mistake. It is then, in the early years, that unrealistic expectations build up and the marriage begins to falter. With a little help at this stage it need not do so.

Social skills may be at fault.
Lastly, none of this section should make the reader think that marriages stand or fall because of sexual problems. They don't. Marriages are between personalities—not genitals. The sexual relationship is the innocent bystander that is demolished as the marriage gradually runs out of control. On the very few occasions when a pure sexual problem *is* the cause of the trouble it is usually fairly easy to sort out.

The truth about divorce

Most young couples getting married have few conscious thoughts about divorce but the facts are that about a third will end up seeking one. Divorce rates have been increasing since the end of World War II—as divorce laws have eased. The rate increased by three times in Britain between 1965 and 1975 and by two and a half times in the US over the same period. The troubles that wreck marriages, it has been found, usually start early. One study found that the problems became apparent in the first year in well over a third of marriages even though the couples struggled to save the marriage, and divorce is seen equally across all the socio-economic classes.

In the US in 1970 the average length of marriage at divorce was six and a half years, but in Britain the average time has remained stable since 1965 at about thirteen years. The countries with the highest divorce rates are the USSR (where an enormous number of marriages end in the first year), the US, Hungary, Egypt and Denmark. England now leads Europe in the divorce league tables.

As we have said, we are not in favour of couples divorcing 'at the drop of a hat' because it is likely that they will suffer greatly (even if there are no children involved, there is pain and a sense of failure) and that they will often find themselves less well-off in every way than they were before. Far too many couples see divorce as an easy way out of their less than perfect marriage. In the main, nothing could be further from the truth.

Those who divorce very early and very young (because they have made a 'mistake' or fallen for someone else) usually fare well, and by their later twenties cannot remember much about their previous partner. These really cannot be called marriages in the true sense of the word. Strange as it may seem, marriages that have gone on for forty or fifty years can also be painlessly dissolved because the couple have spent such a long time drawing apart and 'de-loving' each other.

Between these two extremes lie the vast majority of divorces— those between people who have lived and loved for some years and have children—usually still at home. It is impossible accurately to assess the harm done to the millions of children around the Western world affected by divorce but several surveys show that it is often very severe, as we shall see.

A few people experience an enduring feeling of elation at being rid of their troublesome and unsatisfactory relationship, but these are rare. For the vast majority, divorce is extremely painful.

Many studies have shown that people do not realise how awful divorce really is. Perhaps the most universally experienced feeling is one of overwhelming *loneliness.*

Long marriages are usually the most painful to break and many such couples feel exactly the same as if they had been bereaved. *Suicide* and suicide attempts are not at all uncommon. One US study found that suicide rates among divorced people were three times higher in women and four times higher in men than in their married opposite numbers. If the separated are added to the divorced, as they should be, at certain times the suicide rate for the divorced can be ten times those of the marrieds. Married men usually have the lowest rate of suicide in society and divorced men have the highest.

The divorced and separated are also a very illness-prone group. Of course there are the psychological and emotional problems, including a sense of rejection, despair, loneliness, feelings of failure, protest, anger, guilt, anxiety and depression, and all of these can be bad enough to need treatment. One study found that marital problems were the factor most commonly associated with psychiatric illness and that women were more often affected than men. Many wives seek help for such problems within their marriage because they want professional reassurance that their husbands' claims that they are 'going mad' are wrong. All kinds of physical symptoms, including headaches, abdominal pains, painful periods, bouts of diarrhoea, palpitation and very many others, can also be seen in those who are in the early phases of divorcing or separating.

One of the earliest casualties of all this disruption is sex. The pain of divorce extinguishes or impairs the sex drive, often for months.

Some individuals seem to give up interest in the opposite sex, perhaps thinking 'once bitten—twice shy'. Others live in passive hope that a new and perfect partner will come along, but some become frantically involved in the search for a partner. Rebound relationships may be formed which are worse than the original marriage. Perhaps all divorcing individuals should be offered counselling to help them avoid repeating earlier mistakes or committing new ones.

On a day-to-day basis things are not easy. Separated or divorced men are supposed by their married friends to be having masses of sex and their female counterparts to 'be crying out for it'. Many divorced

All too often the 'deserted' partner fantasises about the idyllic life the other must be leading. Realities are often harshly different.

lessening social stigma attached to divorce, but, whatever society thinks, it will never be possible to extinguish all the sense of failure and shame. Unfortunately, society adds to this shame quite unnecessarily, which does not help the recently divorced couple. Much of the social stigma comes from the long-held view that divorce lets women down and somehow threatens marriage as an institution. To some extent these are valid points but they have been over-stressed and in today's world are no longer nearly as true as they were. The Church of England has the option to refuse, and the Roman Catholic Church refuses to remarry divorcees in church—and this too further condemns and shames those involved. Clinical experience suggests that of the 50 per cent of marriages that are solemnised outside a church, many would like to have had a religious ceremony but could not because of the Church's ruling. There are signs that this ruling will change soon but, as things stand, the recently divorced feel they have 'sinned' rather than made a mistake and society believes to some extent that they should suffer for their sin.

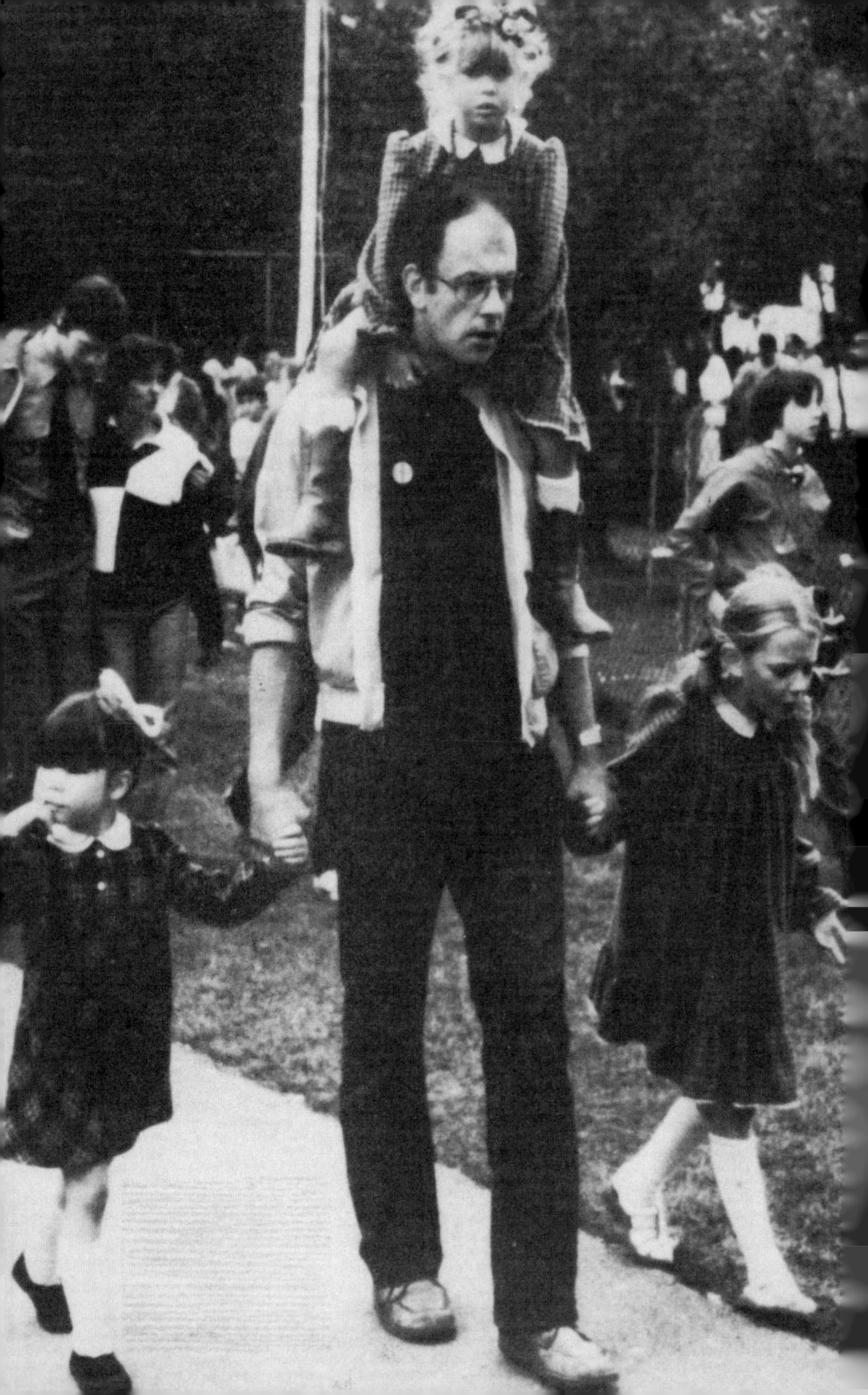

withdrawn. Of those who go through with it one in ten would remarry their ex-spouse and one in fifteen in fact do so, having been apart for an average of three years. Fewer than half of such remarriages are happy, according to one survey.

As well as all the hate, anger and other feelings, there are the many practical problems of housing, moving and child care. Divorce affects the pocket just as much as the heart and everyone involved is financially worse off. The basic problem is clear. Two households have to live on the money that previously supported one and almost all divorced couples experience an immediate fall in their standard of living.

In our apparently child-centred society, many people worry about the effects of divorce on the children involved. In the USA, researchers feel that the poverty caused by divorce is as much to blame for the delinquency rates as the divorce itself. What seems to be more important for the delinquency figures is the after-care by parents. One study found that delinquency rates were related to a lack of visiting by the father and showed the importance of good relationships with the stepfather.

The conclusions of all the research are not clear-cut. Is an unhappy home with fighting parents worse for children than one in which the parents get divorced? A 'bad' after-divorce is most upsetting; a 'good' after-divorce perhaps has no serious long-term effects; and the effects of a conflict-filled home are no doubt worse than a good divorce. Unfortunately, it is very difficult to organise a good divorce, even with the best will in the world.

Delinquency is only one extreme end of the spectrum, of course, and varying degrees of disturbance are almost universal in the children of the divorced. Things are very difficult for mothers who run a family single-handed and one study found that in one third of such families total chaos was the norm. Children of the recently divorced tend to have more tantrums and school problems, cry a lot, wet their beds, go back to early childhood behaviour, run away and so on. Children hate divorce and most say that their homes were happy before the divorce. They yearn for the departed parent and probably never get over the loss. Children of divorced parents are far more likely to get divorced themselves than are other children.

Second time around

Once all the natural grief and suffering are over (and this can take a couple of years or more), society begins to put pressure on the divorced to remarry. Most people would rather function as part of a couple and the natural instinct for most is to try to make something work again.

Because there are now so many people around in the remarriage

Dad's doing his best: An outing with the divorced father. Is anyone really enjoying this part-time fathering?

market a whole new industry has arisen to cope with them. Marriage bureaus are, of course, not new but they are increasing in numbers and some deal with specialised groups of the population. Computer-dating is popular and singles clubs and those for the divorced and separated are commonplace. The middle-aged single again have particular problems because, although the media often portrays them as having all the advantages of being single, the reality is very different. Confidence may have been lost and, as they are older, adjustment to a new potential partner is harder. Divorced women are often seen as a threat by married women and so may have difficulty in meeting suitable men.

However, it appears that about half of divorced people find their second partner through informal sources (friends and relatives) and half through formal ones. As we have already seen, the divorced tend to fall away from the friends and acquaintances they had during their marriage and enter the divorced-and-separated sub-culture. This is probably just as well because married people are usually hopeless at producing new partners for their divorced friends. The sex lives of the divorced vary greatly—some abstaining because they feel so wretched about it all (though their feelings change over the months and the normal sex drive returns in most people) and others for religious and moral reasons. Those who can only have sex in the context of romantic love often remarry very quickly to legitimise their need for sex.

The speed at which people get back to dealing (sexually or otherwise) with the opposite sex depends greatly on their sex drive, their personality, how much they were hurt by the divorce and on many other factors. Divorced people on the look-out often spend a lot of time sleeping around in an effort to experience some love without having to recommit themselves. This is probably essential because one thing a divorce certainly does is to knock one's self-esteem as a man or a woman. In a sense one has to relearn the old lessons of adolescence but against a background of a one-to-one relationship that was, for a time at least, acceptable or even wonderful.

About 60 per cent of remarriages are to other divorcées. This is probably no bad thing since they recognise the problems and pitfalls and can understand each other's situations better. They reassure each other that they are not unique in their problems, or unstable, and a bond is more likely to form as a result. Unfortunately, most people are unaware of the real reasons for their marriage failure and so make exactly the same mistakes again. Nearly half of all remarriages fail, mainly because people choose those who are similar to their first spouse (although this may not necessarily be obvious to those involved). Those who have been married twice have a divorce rate fives times the norm.

Summary

Divorce is bad news and little or nothing is being done to prevent it. Easier divorce legislation increases divorce but it also opens the possibility of men and women behaving better towards each other and making some effort to please each other, for fear of divorce. However, only the legislation is easy—everything else about divorce is almost inevitably bad. More realism about the sexuality of men and women, and their needs, might result in less divorce, as might the education of the sexes about each other.

Chapter 13

Some sexual anatomy

Although many sex books seem to put too great an emphasis on the basic plumbing of sex, it helps to understand at least a little of the basic anatomy (structure) and physiology (working) of the sex organs, if only because so many men, women and adolescents worry so much about things that really need cause them no concern at all. So let us look at the sex organs of men and women, bearing in mind people's commonly held fears and misconceptions.

The male sex organs

A man's sex organs seem at first sight to be rather simple, lying as they do mostly outside the body where they can be seen and handled. This is a tremendous advantage to boys who can easily see how they are made and do not have any concern about what is inside them in the way women do.

Basically a man's sex organs consist of his penis and his scrotum, which is a bag hanging from below the penis and containing the testes that produce sperms and male hormones. There are 'hidden' parts of his sexual anatomy—the prostate gland, for instance, which lies deep in the pelvis—but most men are not even aware that they have such a gland unless it begins to give trouble in old age.

The penis is a man's most obvious and talked-about sex organ. Most men at some time or another have worried about the size of their penis, just as women concern themselves with their breast size. Surveys of women who have had many sex partners show that a man's penis size really does not matter when it comes to sexual satisfaction, but even though most men know this, about a third still wonder whether things wouldn't be just that little bit better if they had a longer or thicker penis. The size of the un-erect penis does not seem to matter very much because, apart from very small and very large ones (which are somewhat uncommon), the majority of penises erect to about the same length and circumference. Just as we cannot possibly say how often a couple 'should' have intercourse, we cannot say how long a penis 'should' be. Men's erect penises in fact vary in dimension less than other parts of their bodies.

There are all kinds of myths connecting penis size with the size of a man's body, his race, his amount of sexual activity and so on but careful research has shown that all such old wives' (or husbands') tales are based on hearsay. There is no definite correlation between

SOME SEXUAL ANATOMY

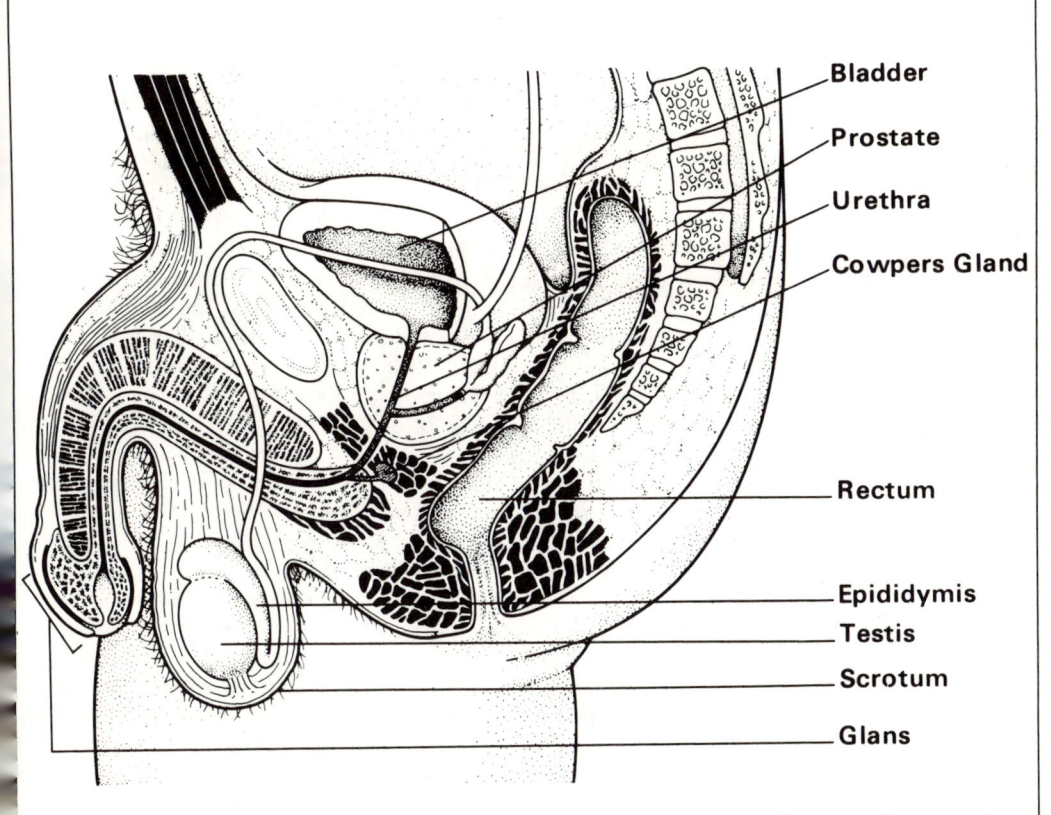

- Bladder
- Prostate
- Urethra
- Cowpers Gland
- Rectum
- Epididymis
- Testis
- Scrotum
- Glans

Cross-section of male pelvis to show both internal and external sex organs.

penis size and body size, and black men do not have longer penises than white men. One of the many clever things about the vagina is that it can adapt to a penis of any size and can do so painlessly and pleasurably. So the same woman can get exactly the same level of vaginal pleasure from a five-inch and a seven-inch penis.

The penis is a tube-like structure, but although it looks like one tube, it is in fact three. As you look down on the penis from the top there are two tubular masses of tissue under the skin called the *corpora cavernosa*. They are called *cavernosa* because they are cavernous in structure and can swell to accommodate large volumes of blood. The third cylindrical structure in the penis lies on the under surface and is called the *corpus spongiosum*. It ends in a bulbous swelling (the glans) which is the sensitive tip of the penis.

The corpora cavernosa swell when a man becomes sexually aroused and an erection occurs because more blood flows into the penis than is allowed to flow out. The penis has to swell and become rigid to fulfil its sexual function—that of placing semen high up in a woman's vagina near the cervix.

The *urethra* is the tube that carries urine from the bladder to the outside. It terminates at the tip of the penis in a thin, slit-like opening. Semen comes out of this same opening, so the urethra has a dual urinary and sexual function in men (though it does not in women). During ejaculation the muscle at the base of the bladder, which is normally contracted except during urination, compels the semen to travel down the penis instead of entering the bladder. Certain medical disorders and some drugs can so alter this muscular mechanism that the man ejaculates semen into his bladder instead of down his urethra.

The shaft of the penis is covered with dark, loose skin which looks rather delicate and thin, and this skin continues below over the scrotum as a more wrinkled, thicker and hairier covering. The skin protrudes over the tip of the penis as a loose fold called the foreskin.

The *scrotum* is a bag of skin inside which are the sperm-producing organs, the testes. The skin of the scrotum is composed of several layers, the most important of which is muscular. The position of the testes in the scrotum is controlled by the cremasteric muscles which contract, pulling the testes up towards the body when cold and lowering the testes into the scrotum when hot. By adjusting the height of the testes their temperature is kept slightly lower than that of the rest of the body. This is important because normal sperm development can only occur if the testes are maintained at a temperature of about 2–3° lower than that of the core of the body. Both fear and cold cause the cremasteric muscles to contract and so draw the testes nearer to the body. A mass of veins surround the artery that supplies the testis on each side, producing a heat-loss system which also helps to reduce the temperature of the testes. In this way the testes receive blood at a lower temperature than that supplied to the rest of the body.

Each testis is composed of several hundred little lobes, each of which contains a number of highly convoluted seminiferous tubules. These eventually straighten out and converge to form the five or seven ducts that open into the epididymis. The testis produces not only sperms but also male hormones, the latter in special cells called Leydig cells. Testosterone is responsible for a man's secondary sexual characteristics (his muscular body, beard growth, distribution of body hair, deep voice and aggression), affects his metabolism and his psychological behaviour and also stimulates the formation of various chemicals in his reproductive tract, that ensure the production of sperms.

The formation of sperms takes about two weeks. When they are first produced, they are not motile (do not move). After passing through the tubules that form the testis, the sperms are collected in the epididymis where they are stored. While they are here they mature further and become motile. From the epididymis the sperms enter the vas deferens, a fine, muscular tube, and travel along this up out of the scrotum and into the abdominal cavity. It is the vas deferens each side that is tied off in a man undergoing vasectomy. The vasa deferentia gently milk the sperms along by muscular action to their upper ends where they widen to form the ampullae. Most sperms are stored in the epididymis, as we have seen, but the ampullae act as secondary storage sites. Beyond the ampullae are two blind bags off the vasa deferentia called the seminal vesicles. They are important because they produce a fluid containing a sugar called fructose which is the fuel sperms need to enable them to live on on their journey to fertilise an egg.

The prostate gland, which makes about 10 per cent of the seminal fluid (semen—the ejaculated fluid that contains the sperms), lies at the base of the bladder and surrounds the first part of the urethra. The prostate produces substances which act as a vehicle for the sperms, supply them with nutrients and buffer them against attack from the acid vaginal secretions. It is because it needs to counteract acid vaginal secretions that semen is so alkaline.

Beyond the prostate is a pair of small glands called Cowper's glands. These produce a small amount of lubricant which is added to the seminal fluid before ejaculation takes place. Rather less than 10 per cent of the volume of any ejaculate is composed of fluid from the testes and epididymides; about 80 per cent comes from the seminal vesicles; and the remaining 10 per cent from the prostrate.

The whole process of maturation of a sperm from the day that it starts in the testis to the day it is ejaculated takes about three months, most of which is spent in the epididymis. Once a man becomes sexually excited, his penis enlarges and the vasa deferentia increase their muscular milking action and send more sperms into the ampullae. A combination of muscular contractions of the pelvic structures produces an ejaculation of the semen and when this happens the seminal vesicles and the prostate add their secretions to the sperms which are discharged as semen via the penis. Sperms form only 5 per cent of the volume of semen and a normal man ejaculates between two and five millilitres (or even more) of semen after a day or two of abstinence. Men who have large volumes of semen are not necessarily more fertile than those who do not, but volumes of less than 1 ml are sometimes associated with infertility because there is not enough fluid to maintain contact with the cervix.

Controversy rages on the subject of circumcision and its effects on a man's sex life, so it is worth a mention here. Circumcision is an operation carried out to remove the foreskin and so leave the penis head uncovered all the time. Circumcision is now a rare operation and is usually only carried out for medical or religious reasons. Routine circumcision is a thing of the past. There is absolutely no problem in having a foreskin left intact when it comes to sexual functioning provided that the man keeps the head of the penis underneath the foreskin clean. This is not only more pleasant for the woman who may want to kiss or suck the penis, but is also thought to be safer because it has been found that the wives of uncircumcised men are more likely to get cancer of the cervix than those who are married to circumcised men.

When it comes to sex and circumcision, men vary greatly in their views on the subject. Some uncircumcised men claim that because the head of the penis is covered all the time it is more sensitive and so gives them more pleasure, and some circumcised men claim that because their penis head is rubbing against things (underpants usually) all the time it becomes de-sensitised and so allows them to enjoy longer vaginal stimulation before they come off. Clinical experience shows that whether or not a man has a foreskin seems to make very little, if any, difference to his enjoyment of sex. Obviously if the foreskin is so tight that it cannot be pulled back and it hurts him, it would make sense to discuss it with a doctor but this is not common. So, in summary, the evidence seems to show that boys do not need to be circumcised, and that if their foreskin can easily be pulled back at five years old (do not fiddle with it before) and they are taught to pull it back to wash underneath, this is all that is needed for health and sexual pleasure.

Sex play and a man's sex organs

A loving couple who really care for each other and who have intercourse rather than copulate are likely to get to know each other's sex organs intimately and will learn exactly what each likes most. When it comes to handling a man's sex organs there are a few hints that might help lovers. First, a man's penis can be very small at times, especially if he is cold or anxious or not feeling at all sexy. There is no need for concern because the penis will come back to its normal size as soon as it is stimulated. Similarly, a man's scrotal contents appear to vary greatly in size and still be perfectly healthy and normal. If one side swells up or is tender, even on gentle handling, get medical advice (see also page 401).

Once a man is aroused sexually, his genitals can stand a lot of quite hard and vigorous handling, but be guided by him as to what he likes. Many men complain that their women are too gentle and do not, for example, rub hard enough when masturbating them. A woman is unlikely to do any harm unless she does something very rough.

Although a man's penis is the most obvious part of his sexual anatomy he will enjoy being stimulated along the whole length of his sexual tract too. Many men enjoy the root of the penis (between the penis base and the anus) being rubbed and massaged as there is a large amount of erectile tissue there. Some men like their prostate massaged by the woman inserting her finger into the anus (beware of long fingernails and be sure to lubricate the anus well first or it will be uncomfortable). This can be especially pleasant when a man is being masturbated. The prostate is easily felt as a small, hard, rounded object at the base of the penis inside the man's rectum.

Apart from putting things inside the urinary passage and squeezing the testicles too hard, there is really no harm that can be done during love-play or intercourse and, if a man keeps his sex organs scrupulously clean, his partner will enjoy stimulating him in a wide variety of ways, learning from experience which he enjoys most. All men are fairly similar in the way they prefer to be stimulated but individual variations do occur.

The female sex organs

A woman's sex organs are rather more of a mystery than a man's because many of the important parts lie inside the body and so cannot be seen, and even those that are outside are not easy to look at. As a result some women have some very strange notions about their sex organs. In addition to these problems a woman's vagina lies only a matter of centimetres away from her anus (back passage) and so may become mixed up in her mind with dirt and stools. A man's sex organs are well away from his anus and so do not produce quite the same hang-ups. Also, of course, girls in our society are brought up to be more concerned about and ashamed of their genitals and this is another reason why many claim never to have looked at their vulvas even though they very much wanted to. But even though many of a woman's sex organs are hidden, it is essential that a loving couple get to know all they can about them because only then can they really enjoy sex to the full. A woman who has irrational fears and suspicions about how she is made will not function well sexually and her partner will not be allowed or encouraged to enjoy her body as he should.

Breasts

In other societies other parts of the body are considered to be a greater 'turn-on' but the breasts have eclipsed almost all of these in the West, and a woman's most easily observed signs of sexual arousal take place in her breasts.

Whilst about one third of men have some kind of hang-up about their penis size, about three-quarters of all women are dissatisfied with their breasts. This has come about partly because of men being misled by pictures of women in girlie magazines and because of the advertising world's emphasis on large, provocative breasts. Whilst it is probably true that men tend to prefer (and probably have been conditioned to prefer) large-breasted women, the variety of taste is wide and, anyway, no thinking man judges a woman solely by her breast size. There is no evidence that big-breasted women enjoy sex or breast-play any more than do their smaller-breasted sisters.

Interestingly enough, it seems that society's ideal breast image is slowly changing anyway. The ideal woman as currently portrayed by the media is neither very slim nor very curvy. Her breasts are neither particularly big nor particularly small. This perhaps reflects the enormous variety of fashion, hairstyles and make-up available today, most of which are incompatible with the concept of a stereotyped woman.

Breasts and sex

Unfortunately, society has become so hung up on intercourse as the only form of sexual expression that many people ignore or deny the

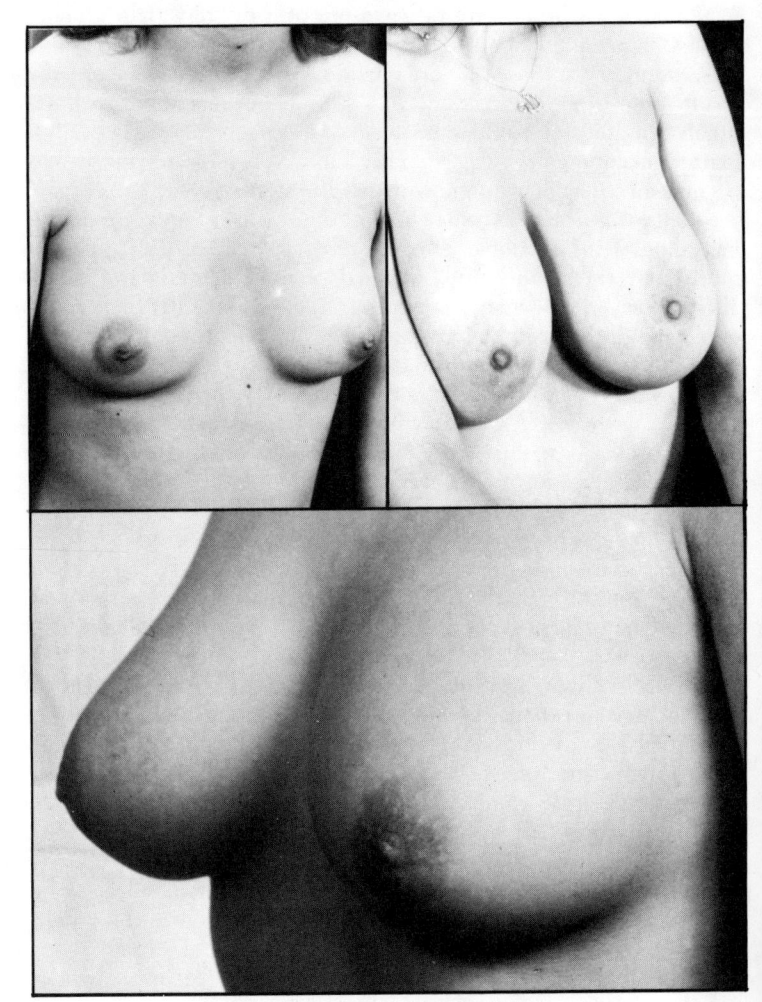

There is a lot of variation between the shape and size of women's breasts and this is one reason why woman-watching is a subject of fascination to both sexes.

richness and variety of sexual feelings that are available. Women especially are plentifully endowed with several different ways of obtaining sexual pleasure, all of which are inextricably interlinked. Men by comparison have a very poor repertoire, concentrating as they do on their penis as their main source of sexual enjoyment.

During the earliest phase of sexual arousal the first visible sign that anything is happening is that the nipples become erect. This comes about as the tiny smooth muscles in them contract. One nipple often erects before the other and erection can occur without physical stimulation. Stimulation either by the woman herself or by her partner usually hastens erection but is not essential. The nipples increase in length and diameter as the woman becomes more excited and blood collects in and around them. This mechanism is rather like that which causes the penis to become erect.

Women are exceptionally sensitive about the appearance of their breasts in a sexual setting. Women with small or markedly asymmetrical breasts feel they will be at a disadvantage, as do women with inverted nipples. Those with large, pendulous breasts fear they will put men off and those with scars after surgery are even more upset. A woman who has had her breast removed by mastectomy has special, and understandable, problems.

There is no evidence at all that any form of sexual activity (including practices in which the breasts come into contact with the penis or semen) causes cancer or any other disease. A woman who is destined to get some kind of breast condition will get it anyway, whatever her sexual practices. In fact there is some evidence that intercourse without the use of barrier methods (that is methods that allow semen to bathe the woman's cervix and vagina) might even have a protective function against breast cancer. Similarly, there is no evidence that powder, perfume or anything else used on the breasts does them any harm. Perfume should be kept off the nipples because it is not pleasant for the man to taste but that is the only reason. Nipple stimulation may become unpleasant because of tenderness around the time of ovulation, a period or the menopause but a loving couple will find ways of overcoming this problem. Anyway, nipple- and breast-play have no effect on the progress of the menopause and can, of course, be continued after it.

A woman's genitals

Breasts are, of course, easy to look at but when it comes to a woman's genitals she needs a mirror to see what's what. If you want to understand and make the best of your sexual anatomy, make some time for yourself, remove all your clothes from the waist down, lie down somewhere comfortable (half-sitting up is best) and look at your genitals with a hand mirror.

First, with your legs together look at the pubic hair. This covers all the *vulva* (the outer parts of the sex organs) and forms a fairly neat triangle with its base just near the pubic bone. The extent of the spread of the hair is very variable and some women's hair grows on to the tops of their legs and even up the abdominal wall a little. Both are perfectly normal. Some women like to keep their pubic hair trimmed but there is no necessity for this. Some shave their pubic hair completely, or just around the vaginal area so that with her legs together there is still a triangle of hair but none around the actual vaginal opening. If a couple enjoy oral sex the woman's pubic hair will have to be kept fairly short or it will get in the way of oral stimulation of her clitoris. If you feel under the pubic hair you can feel the pubic bone.

Now open your legs. There are two fairly thick, fleshy lips, the *labia majora*, which are covered with hair. If you pull these apart you will see two inner lips inside. Sometimes one lip is longer than the other and the inner ones sometimes hang down more than the outer ones. The inner lips are much thinner than the outer ones and come together around the clitoris. At the bottom the lips separate to go around the vagina. As you part the inner lips you will see three things from front to back. First the *clitoris*, a little knob-like structure covered with a hood of tissue; second, the urinary opening (very small and closed off except when passing urine) which lies in the front wall of the vagina; and third, the opening of the vagina itself, an opening that will admit a finger tip even in a virgin. If you are a virgin you will probably see that there is a veil of thin skin almost closing off the vaginal opening. This is called the hymen and can come in lots of different shapes. Many girls today use tampons and some put things inside their vaginas when they masturbate so, even if they have not had intercourse, they may not have much in the way of a hymen left. Usually, in such girls and in all women who have had intercourse, all that remains are a few tags of pinkish skin around the vaginal opening. We look more at first experiences of intercourse in chapter 17. Almost all hymens break (or the hole stretches) with heavy petting or on first intercourse, but if there is any difficulty consult your doctor.

Even further behind the vagina is the anus or opening to the rectum but this is not a part of the sex organs although it may be of erotic value. After looking, get ready to feel inside.

The *vagina*, contrary to many people's belief, is not a rigid tube inside a woman's body but is a flattened cylinder whose walls touch each other all the time unless something is inside. The vagina is about three to four inches long but during sexual arousal it lengthens and widens at the top. To all intents and purposes no woman's vagina is too small to accept a penis. If a penis cannot go in, either the woman has a tight hymen that has not been broken; has a condition that causes pain on attempted intercourse; or is suffering from a condition called vaginismus.

Now put your middle and/or index finger inside your vagina and feel the walls (damp and moist) and the direction in which your vagina goes (upwards and backwards). Also find your G-spot (see page 191 for details). When you have a finger inside contract the vaginal wall muscles around your finger. At first you will not be able to do this well, so it will need some practice. Start by sitting on the lavatory and pass a little urine. Then in mid-stream stop the flow—

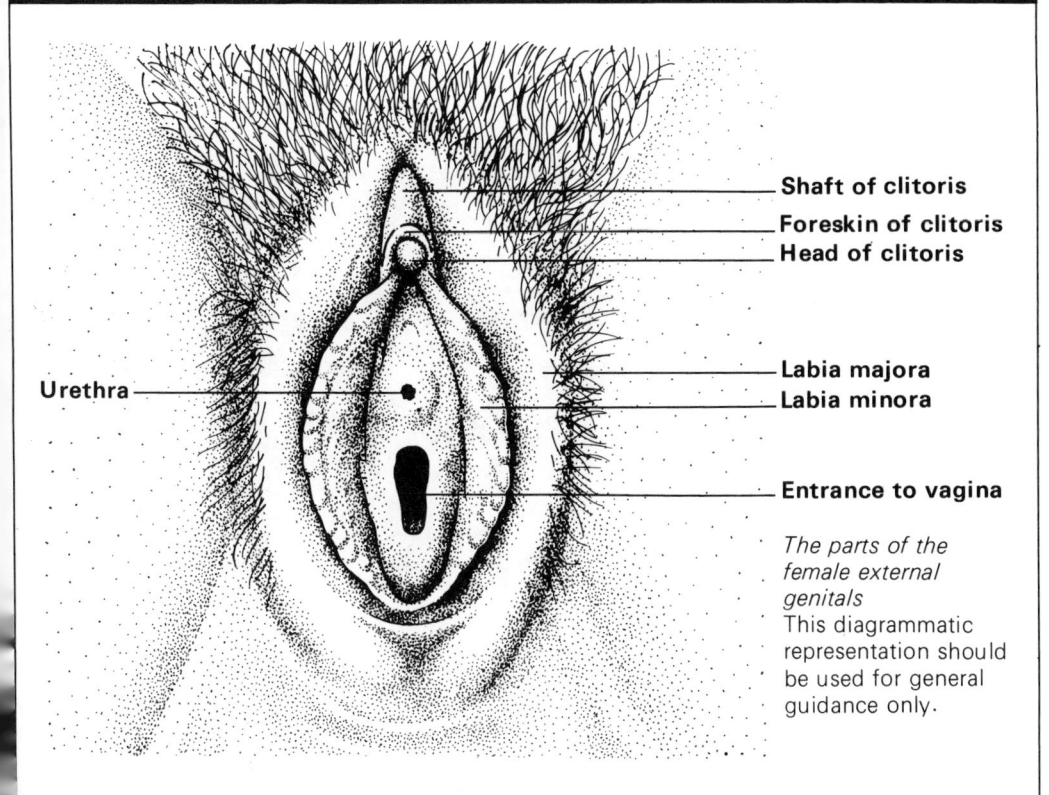

Shaft of clitoris
Foreskin of clitoris
Head of clitoris

Urethra

Labia majora
Labia minora

Entrance to vagina

The parts of the female external genitals
This diagrammatic representation should be used for general guidance only.

and practise this until you can do it at will easily. Now with two fingers inside the vagina contract these same muscles around your fingers. If you have had a baby there are good reasons to learn to do this because it will help strengthen the pelvic floor muscles and it will make intercourse more pleasurable for your partner. Some women routinely use these muscles during foreplay and intercourse to increase their partner's pleasure. There is no acceptable evidence that a woman can clamp down with these muscles on a man's penis and so keep him inside her!

Next put your finger deeper inside till you can feel the *cervix*—the part of the womb that lies in the top of the vagina. This feels a bit like the tip of your nose and is rather firm with a dimple in the middle. From a sexual point of view the uterus does not do much (except that it contracts during an orgasm), but any considerate and caring lover will get to know what his partner enjoys and will experiment with stimulating her cervix or womb with his fingers by stroking it, grasping it between two finger tips or moving it. You will only get to know what is pleasurable by experimenting.

At the top of the vagina at the side lie the ovaries, but it takes an experienced gynaecologist to be able to feel these, so do not worry about feeling them. Some women enjoy having their ovaries stimulated but not many men can do it and it is probably not worth expending effort on them.

This is all that you can actually feel but inside there are other parts of the reproductive system. The uterus is a pear-shaped,

SOME SEXUAL ANATOMY

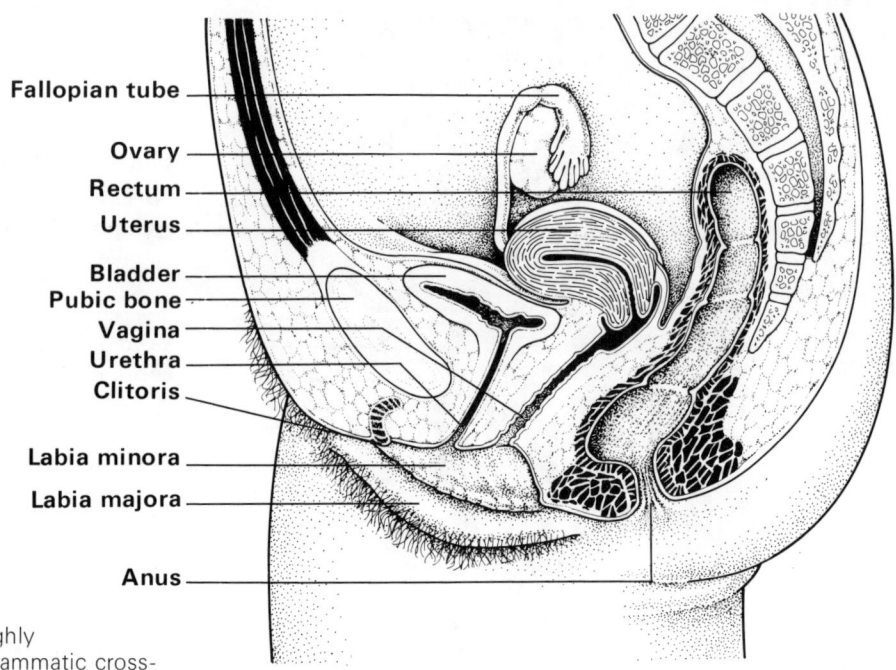

Fallopian tube
Ovary
Rectum
Uterus
Bladder
Pubic bone
Vagina
Urethra
Clitoris
Labia minora
Labia majora
Anus

A highly diagrammatic cross-section through a female pelvis. The pads of fat and tissue between the pubic bone and urethra, urethra and vagina, and vagina and rectum have all been deliberately exaggerated so that all these organs can be more clearly seen. In many women the vagina is not a straight tube as shown here but curves backwards in an S-bend.

muscular organ about three inches long and two inches across at its widest part (the fundus). The pointed part of the pear shape points down into the top of the vagina and the body of the 'pear' lies above the vagina in the pelvis. The neck or cervix of the womb (the narrowest part) lies within the vagina and it is this that can be felt with your fingers. In most women the uterus is angled slightly forwards but in about 20 per cent it is tipped backwards (retroverted). It used to be thought that women with retroverted uteri were more likely to be infertile but this is now known not to be so. Occasionally a woman with a retroverted uterus may have another reason for her infertility that is also causing her uterus to tip backwards. Endometriosis or adhesions secondary to pelvic infection can cause this but it is not the backward tilt of the uterus that causes the infertility.

The *uterus* has a cavity which is triangular and flat, the point of which ends in a narrow canal inside the cervix. It is lined with a special type of cellular tissue called endometrium and the cervix is normally plugged up with mucus. Suffice it to say on this subject that when a woman is most likely to conceive (around the time of ovulation) her cervical mucus is most encouraging to sperms and that when this mechanism fails in some way, her partner's sperms, however plentiful, may not get past the cervical mucus barrier.

At the sides of the top of the wide end of the uterus two tubes enter. These are the fallopian tubes that run from the ovaries to the uterus. Each fallopian tube is about four inches long and is thinner in diameter than the lead in a pencil. The tubes have very muscular walls lined with hair-like projections. Both walls and projections move in such a way as to waft ova (eggs) progressively along from the ovaries to the uterus. Cells lining the tubes produce substances that alter sperms so that they can fertilise an egg—indeed, fertilisation of an egg by a sperm occurs in one of the fallopian tubes. The open ends of the tubes are called fimbriated ends and are a sophisticated collection apparatus which ensures that eggs are caught and channelled down into the fallopian tubes. There are numerous nervous, hormonal and chemical mechanisms at work in normal fallopian-tube functioning and we still know very little about exactly what goes on. But just as the structure and physiology of the fallopian tubes is vital to the downward passage of an egg, it is also important for the upward progress of the sperms. Subtle chemical changes take place in sperms as they travel along the tubes to meet the egg, changes which are essential if the sperm is to be in a condition to fertilise the egg it meets. This process of sperm maturation is called capacitation.

The ovaries lie below the fimbriated ends. They are paired organs about the size of walnuts lying one each side of the pelvis. They have two functions. First, they release a ripened egg each month and, second, they produce progesterone and oestrogen—two important female hormones. The ovaries are remarkable organs—when a baby girl is born she already has all her eggs (30,000–40,000) in her ovaries. After puberty the eggs begin to ripen or mature under the influence of complicated hormonal changes that occur cyclically. This happens every month (unless the woman is pregnant or on the pill; nor does it happen for some of the time she is breastfeeding) until the end of her reproductive life, the menopause, intervenes. In practice, several eggs begin to mature each month but for some unknown reason only one actually ripens. The average woman has 400–450 cycles in a lifetime. The ripening and release of an egg each month is called ovulation.

A woman's body functions in a cyclical way, each cycle lasting about a month. It is important to remember that this is only an average and that there can be large variations in cycle length that are still quite normal. In a classical 'text-book' cycle the events run as follows. The first day of the cycle is taken as the first day of menstruation. This is the day when the lining of the womb, now that it is not going to be needed for pregnancy, starts to be shed in the form of clots, cells and blood. The brain (particularly the hypothalamus) influences a tiny gland that lies near it (the pituitary gland) to produce a hormone called follicle-stimulating hormone (FSH) which stimulates the ovary to ripen an egg that month. Another hormone, luteinizing hormone (LH), is produced by the pituitary during the whole cycle. A surge of LH is produced around the middle of the cycle (day 14) which helps release the ripened egg. This release of the egg is called ovulation and it is at this stage that a woman is most likely to conceive. Some women experience abdominal discomfort at this time (*mittelschmerz*—a German word for middle-of-the-cycle pain).

Each month, then, an egg is released from one of the ovaries and is 'collected' by the fimbriated ends of the tube. It takes at least three days for an egg to pass along the tube. While this is going on, the ruptured egg sac on the ovary turns into a functioning gland called the

Schematic representation of various events during a woman's menstrual cycle.

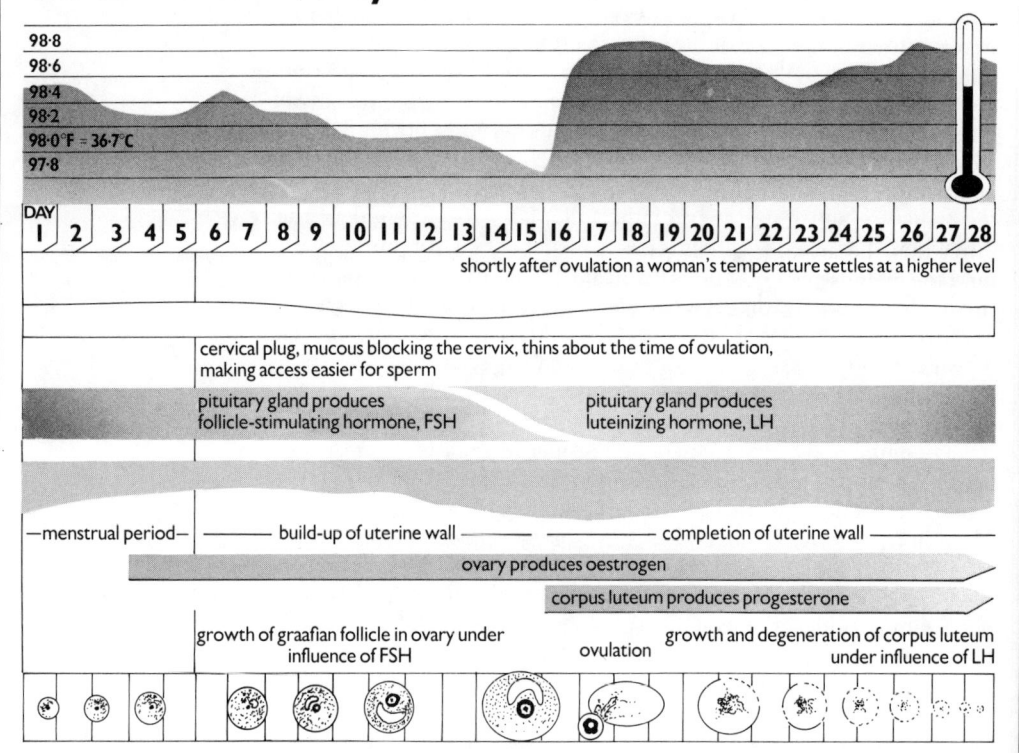

Temperature	
98·8	
98·6	
98·4	
98·2	
98·0°F = 36·7°C	
97·8	

DAY 1 2 3 4 5 6 7 8 9 10 11 12 13 14 15 16 17 18 19 20 21 22 23 24 25 26 27 28

shortly after ovulation a woman's temperature settles at a higher level

cervical plug, mucous blocking the cervix, thins about the time of ovulation, making access easier for sperm

pituitary gland produces follicle-stimulating hormone, FSH

pituitary gland produces luteinizing hormone, LH

—menstrual period— ——— build-up of uterine wall ——— ——— completion of uterine wall ———

ovary produces oestrogen

corpus luteum produces progesterone

growth of graafian follicle in ovary under influence of FSH

ovulation

growth and degeneration of corpus luteum under influence of LH

corpus luteum which produces another hormone called progesterone. Progesterone, together with oestrogen, acts on the lining of the uterus in such a way as to build it up, ready to receive a fertilised egg. Oestrogen produced in the first half of the cycle primes the endometrium and encourages growth. Without it, progesterone produced in the second half of the cycle could not act properly to ripen the endometrium ready to receive the fertilised egg. If the egg is not fertilised, the corpus luteum, which has an independent lifespan of only about fourteen days, begins to cease functioning. Progesterone and oestrogen levels fall, causing the lining of the womb to slough, thereby starting a menstrual period.

Periods (menstruation)

From puberty until the menopause women have a period each month as the lining of the uterus (womb) is shed if an embryo has not implanted. There are many reasons for periods not appearing in normal women, the commonest of which by far is pregnancy, but others include an emotional shock, physical or mental ill-health, a change of time zones, a woman's fear that she might be pregnant and all kinds of stress.

Women's periods can vary greatly in their duration and in the heaviness of the blood loss. Normal periods can last for anything from two to eight days and the amount of blood loss is usually between five and six tablespoons. It seems a lot more because blood spreads over surfaces easily. If you ever have bleeding between your periods, see your doctor.

The beginning of a girl's first period is a momentous day in her life because it marks her entry into womanhood and tells her that she could soon be fertile and so able to have a baby. The sensible mother starts talking to her daughter well in advance of her first period and probably before the age of ten, as many girls start menstruating soon after this. To an unprepared girl her first period can be frightening and the memory can stay with her for life. There are many old wives' tales about menstruation which should be dispelled to avoid the danger that the girl will hear them at school and worry quite unnecessarily. In this connection it should be emphasised that the blood lost is not 'bad' blood—it is good blood which is simply used to wash away the lining of the womb.

One of the earliest practical considerations is sanitary protection. Sanitary napkins or tampons have to be used to absorb the menstrual blood. Sanitary napkins are pads of highly absorbent material—often paper. Today's slimmer pads are unobtrusive even under tight clothes and many come with a waterproof backing film to prevent leaking.

Tampons are more convenient and comfortable for many girls. These are small plugs of absorbent material about the size of a finger that are inserted into the vagina where they expand and absorb the menstrual flow. If the girl is a virgin she may find it difficult to push the tampon into her vagina at first but most hymens already have a large enough hole to make it fairly easy. On first inserting a tampon the girl may actually break or stretch the hymen and this can cause some soreness for a day or two. It may be helpful to get a mirror and put your first tampon in whilst looking at what you are doing. For the first few times a tampon is used it can help to smear its tip with KY jelly or something similar. Follow the instructions on the packet as these vary according to the type of tampons you are using. The most helpful thing of all when putting a tampon in the first few times is to relax. It cannot get lost inside you. It is relatively easy though to forget that it is there, especially when the period ends and there is no leakage.

What goes in must come out but sometimes it is a problem to pull a tampon out. All tampons have a string attached to their base which when pulled brings them out of the vagina. Squat, or stand with one leg raised, and pull gently on the string. Tampons very rarely get stuck but if they do don't worry. Just ask your mother to help you or go to your doctor.

Whether you use a tampon or a sanitary napkin it should be changed several times a day and more often if the flow is heavy. Lots of girls and women put a stick-on 'pant liner' inside their pants to mop up the inevitable occasional leak. It is a good idea to have a wash or a bath each day of your period to keep fresh.

Many girls and women wonder about sex and their periods, but even though many cultures have a taboo on sex with menstruating women there is no reason to avoid intercourse during your periods. Of course some women use their periods to avoid having sex for a quarter or more of the month. An orgasm can help to reduce some of the symptoms of premenstrual tension and the cramping pains some women have in the first couple of days of their periods. Research has proved that many women are most interested in sex around the time of a period and actually during it, and again at around ovulation (in the middle of the month); so clearly there is no reason to believe that nature meant sex to be a no-go area because of a period. This is just as well because women can spend one quarter of their reproductive lives menstruating. Many women report how much they like to be made love to during a period. They also mention that a man really has to love them to want to put up with any messiness involved.

Although there is an ancient Jewish notion that menstruating women are unclean, no medical evidence has ever been found to support this, though some doctors persist in talking about menstrual 'toxins', the existence of which has never been proved. In spite of the advertising world's suggestions, and many women's suspicions, that menstruating women smell and that men are likely to find the woman unattractive, this is not true if reasonable rules of hygiene are observed.

Having periods affects women in many different ways. Some are completely unchanged physically or mentally and others are tired, grumpy, irritable, have a lot of lower abdominal pain and back pain, and feel bloated. Considerable research shows that women are more likely to be ill, to be admitted to hospital, to have acute medical and psychiatric illnesses, to crash the car, to hit their children, to be off work, and a host of other things, around the onset of their period. Men (including male doctors) for years thought that these problems were in the mind but research has now proved that the signs and symptoms are indeed very real. From a family point of view it makes sense to mark the family's calendar with the mother's period times (and a few days before) if she has mood changes or feels off-colour, so that the whole family can take these into account and make allowances. Explaining all these premenstrual troubles to children can be a problem and should be done in a way that does not make them think of menstruation as an illness. Girls raised to think in this way often end up with intolerable premenstrual symptoms themselves because they expect to be *ill* when they have a period.

Obviously having periods can be messy and some women consider them a misery and indeed call periods 'the curse'. However, this certainly is not true for most. In some classes in the West and in many cultures around the world the onset of menstruation is welcomed. Periods are simply a part of every woman's life in her fertile years. However, if she is pregnant or breastfeeding on an unrestricted basis she will not have periods at all for some time and possibly for several years on end if she has several children. Today's Western woman will have 400–450 periods in a lifetime, but her ancient ancestors would only have had about thirty cycles, partly because of a later onset of periods and an earlier menopause and partly because all the others would have been suppressed by having many pregnancies and breastfeeding on a prolonged basis.

Sex play and a woman's sex organs

Apart from putting his penis inside his partner's vagina, which if done gradually in an aroused woman produces no problems at all, the next most important thing a man should do to ensure his partner's pleasure is to stimulate her clitoris. There is only one rule about this and this is to build up the kind of relationship with your partner which makes her feel free to communicate her wishes to you. A woman's pleasure from her clitoris will be highly personal as will the way she obtains it. This will be based on her masturbation practices, and she will want her lover to go along with these well-tried techniques as much as possible. We discuss all this more in the chapter on foreplay (page 186).

Some women experiment with putting things inside their urinary passage but this is very dangerous and we suggest that you do not do it.

As with a man's sex organs, all that is required for the normal healthy working of a woman's external sex organs is to keep them regularly washed. A woman need never do anything to clean inside her vagina; it is self-cleaning. Simply clean the vulval area when you bath or shower. Don't use vaginal deodorants or perfumes on the delicate inner lips of the vagina itself, as they will sting badly. We discuss basic genital hygiene on page 367.

Summary

Genitals tend to have a bad reputation in our culture and frequently their existence is completely ignored or denied in child rearing. They are often called 'private parts', but as human beings come in one of only two genital forms this description seems a little misplaced. Our mouths ensure our personal survival and our genitals the survival of the species. Genitals also help to improve the relationship between the sexes. Whilst we believe that preoccupation with genitals and genital functioning is a form of inhibition (because it takes the mind off the central matter of intercourse) a reasonable and unobsessed knowledge of and acquaintance with sexual anatomy and physiology is both healthy and helpful.

Chapter 14

Sex differences

That man and woman are anatomically different is obvious and we have looked at the differences in chapter 13. The question we are looking at in this section is, 'Are they different in other ways?' Let's see if there is in fact any evidence to suggest that women are essentially different creatures from men.

'Measurable' differences between men and women

When one starts looking at men and women and comparing them, the first thing that becomes apparent is that man is a more vulnerable creature.

At every age from conception onwards more males die than females and to compensate for this more males are conceived (the ratio is 130:100). Male babies are more likely to be miscarried, to be stillborn, to have birth injuries and to have congenital disorders. Even so, about 105 boys are born to every 100 girls.

Throughout life about 4 per cent more males die at any given age than females, and whilst our life expectancy has been rising the most striking advantages have been to women, who are living longer than men (currently, on average, seventy-five years to men's sixty-seven). Men are more likely to die younger because they have more illnesses, more diseases and more accidents than women. Men are more prone to ulcers, heart attacks, virus infections, cerebral palsy, bronchitis, sex-linked diseases (such as haemophilia) various infectious diseases, lung cancer, successful suicide, mental retardation, autism, speech defects, visual and hearing defects, truancy, delinquency, alcoholism, anti-social behaviour and many other conditions. Ironically, although men spend less time in the home they have more domestic accidents!

From birth, and even before, boys and girls are constitutionally different. Male foetuses grow faster than female ones and at birth boys are on average longer and heavier than girls. Boys grow faster up to the age of about seven months after which girls grow faster to the age of four years.

Boys eat more food than girls and at all ages females have a greater proportion of fat to muscle than males. Males have a higher blood pressure, perhaps linked to their greater physical strength and capabilities. But although boys start off larger at birth, girls are always more mature up to and past adolescence. Girls' bones and teeth mature earlier and they experience puberty earlier.

As well as these developmental differences there are sensory ones that are well proven. Girls are more sensitive to touch and pain stimulation (right from birth). They can also hear and smell better. Boys tend to do better at visual 'tasks'.

Of course there is considerable overlap of all of these characteristics between males and females, but on balance the differences are measurable and meaningful.

Most people are happy enough to accept that such physical differences exist, and it is when it comes to less tangible things such as psychological differences that the controversy really begins.

Basically the controversy revolves around the question as to whether women are inferior intellectually to men. One cannot go far in this discussion without grasping the nettle of intelligence. Men have, on average, measurably larger brains than women and this fact has led researchers over the years to the assumption that this automatically makes men more intelligent. In the middle of the last century, anthropometry (measuring things about humans) was all the rage and a lot of it was aimed at proving that women were inferior. This kind of thinking was understandable at a time when mankind was using his new-found ability to quantify everything and was really only an extension of ancient beliefs which had never died. After all, in the Dark Ages there were serious academic debates among churchmen as to whether women were even really *human*—debates that went on for decades formally and for hundreds of years informally.

So, against this background, what do we find today? Unfortunately the concept of intelligence is a complex one and ways of measuring it almost unbelievably poor. As a result we arrive at the seemingly Alice in Wonderland, but widely accepted, statement that 'intelligence is what we can measure with intelligence tests'. These tests measure abilities such as breadth of vocabulary, general knowledge, comprehension, concept-formation, memory and abstract reasoning. These items have a strong verbal component. Of course we all have non-verbal abilities as well, and these too can be tested.

Although most males and females score roughly the same at the same age and with the same education, the pattern of scores is different. Girls on average score higher than boys on tests which measure verbal fluency, short-term memory, speed and deftness, and boys tend to score higher on arithmetic, block design, maze tests and assembling objects. This can all be seen by perceptive parents who notice that their daughters speak earlier than their sons, and use longer sentences and speak more fluently from an early age. In addition, girls are on average better at grammar, spelling and fluency throughout their school life. On balance more males than females lie at the extremes of intelligence (that is, having very high or low scores) and females tend to group nearer the average of the total population.

Personality is another area to look at when comparing men and women. There are undoubted differences between boys and girls even very early on. Boys are more active (could this be because mothers are more active with them?) and more liable to explore in play, and girls are less active and sit still for longer. Boys run, jump, push, pull and are rougher, whilst girls tend to choose cutting-out, modelling, drawing and other sedentary pursuits. A mass of personality-difference studies come basically to the same conclusions. Women tend to be 'inward looking', more concerned with people and relationships, more sympathetic, more tearful, more easily disgusted, weaker, more helpless, more emotional, more passive, moodier, more suspicious and more susceptible to social pressure than men. Men, on the other hand, tend to be more aggressive, more adventurous, more assertive, more exhibitionist and boastful, more rebellious and revengeful and more tough-minded.

Men and women *are* measurably different, but that does not make either sex better or worse. In certain circumstances a woman's intrinsic personality traits are particularly valuable and in others a man's are needed. In raising a family both are *essential* because it has been proved time and again that balanced children need an adult of each sex to bring them up as they will have to live in a world populated by males and females and the characteristics of the sexes are unlikely to change dramatically one way or the other inside a few generations.

The biological approach

If inadequate studies such as intelligence and personality tests cannot convince us about the differences between men and women, perhaps the truly scientific world has the answers.

Biologists differentiate between males and females in seven main ways: 1 the chromosomes; 2 the sex organs; 3 the sex hormones; 4 the internal reproductive organs; 5 the secondary sex characteristics; 6 the gender role; and 7 sexual identification. The sex organs and secondary sexual characteristics are discussed in detail in chapter 13, so let us look at the rest here.

Chromosomes

All living organisms are made up of cells, each of which has a nucleus which contains chromosomes. These complex protein structures carry the genes which contain the blueprint which defines every detail of each organism's structure and function. These genes are inherited, thus explaining how it is that physical and psychological characteristics can be passed from generation to generation. Genes control the myriad complex enzyme systems in the body, some of which are responsible for brain and hormone metabolism—both of which probably affect behaviour to some extent. So via our genes we inherit our physical, and some psychological, characteristics from our forebears. Every cell in the human body contains twenty-three pairs of chromosomes, each of which in turn carries thousands of genes. The exception to this rule are the sex cells (sperms and eggs) each of which contains twenty-three *single* chromosomes. When an egg is fertilised by a sperm the two sets of twenty-three link to form a complete double

The chromosome pattern of a man: There are 22 pairs of 'body' chromosomes and one pair of 'sex' chromosomes. Of the latter the presence of the large X and the smaller Y shows that the owner is male. A woman's body cells have two large Xs and no Y.

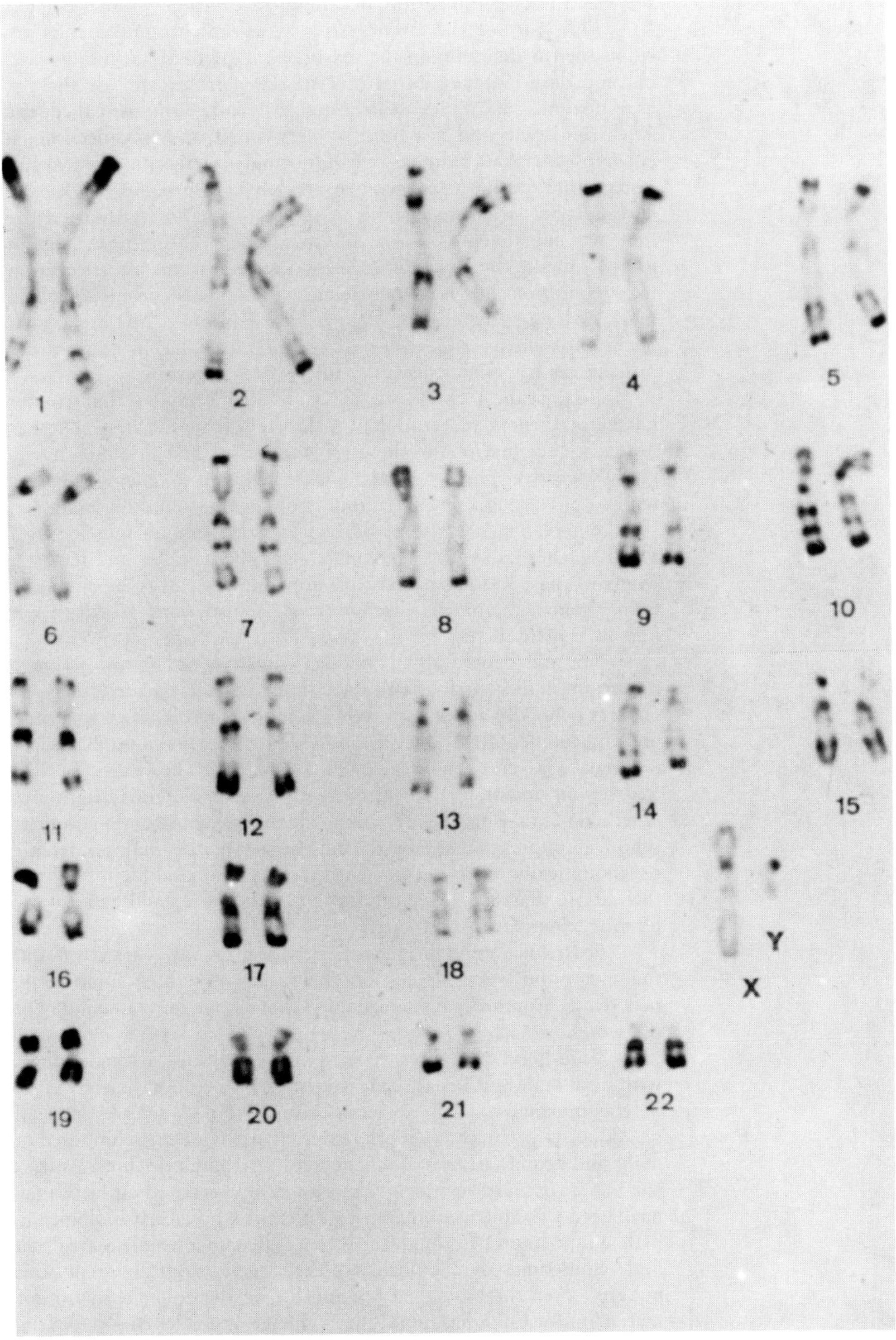

1
2
3
4
5
6
7
8
9
10
11
12
13
14
15
16
17
18
Y
X
19
20
21
22

set which is essential for the development of a new human being.

One pair of the twenty-three pairs of chromosomes is responsible for determining the sex of the individual. Generally each chromosome matches its partner in the pair, except for the sex chromosomes in males which are different. One is called the X chromosome and the other is very small and is called the Y chromosome. A woman has two X (normal-sized chromosomes) and a man an X and a Y. So women are XX and men are XY in sex-chromosome structure. From the very moment of fertilisation the male and female embryos are different. The Y chromosome's main job is to make the developing embryo male and this occurs even in freak conditions in which there is more than one X chromosome in a male. As long as there is one Y the baby will be male. An absence of a Y chromosome produces a female even if one of the chromosomes is missing (as sometimes occurs) with an XO pattern.

Because the Y chromosome is so small it is obvious that females have more genetic material than males right from the start. There is now evidence that one of these Xs is repressed and that only one is really operative. This would make sense in that both sexes would thus tend to have roughly equal amounts of chromosomal material.

But Nature plays some odd tricks from time to time and as a result teaches us some interesting things about males and females. Many of these lessons go to prove how difficult it is to be dogmatic even about something as seemingly straightforward as whether a person is male or female.

The old debate about whether 'nurture' or 'nature' is more important in its contribution to sex difference is less heated today, as experts generally agree that highly complex factors, both inherited and environmental, produce the individual's final make-up. But when it comes to psychosexual identity, the debate is as fierce as ever. The 'old school' maintains that at birth the genetic material determines whether a child is male or female while the 'psychosexual neutrality' school maintains that at birth the individual is neither male nor female psychologically but is neutral with respect to sexual identity. They then argue that sexual identity is acquired by the child as a totally learned experience.

Be this as it may, the debate will rage for many years yet. But in the meantime some babies are being born with spontaneously occurring chromosomal abnormalities that help our understanding of the whole subject.

True hermaphrodites (a very rare condition) are individuals with both male and female characteristics. Sometimes they have two X chromosomes (as in a female) and normal female internal reproductive organs but with the external genitals being composed of male and female organs. Such people can thus have both ovaries and testes. Because such babies cannot easily be 'sexed' at birth they have been valuable in studying sex difference, because a biologically male infant could be brought up as a female and a female reared as a male. Sometimes the illogicality of the rearing is not apparent until puberty when the biological sex and the gender role clearly do not match up. Research has found that a change of gender role before the age of two and a half years is easily tolerated by the child and no harm is done. After that age there are increasing emotional and psychological disturbances which can last into adult life. So this type of evidence suggests that sexual identity is firmly established in the first three years of life. First signs begin to appear as early as one year old.

In hermaphrodites there seems to be a considerable preference for the gender role that they have been given at birth and by which they have been brought up—even when this goes against the obvious physical sexual identity.

Turner's syndrome is a condition that arises when the fertilising sperm has no Y chromosome. The child is therefore chromosomally XO (instead of XY or XX). Such children are female but fail to develop or to mature sexually and may be mentally retarded. One study of thirteen such girls showed that although they had no functioning sex tissue and no sex hormones they all had 'typically feminine' day-dreams, fantasies of marriage, romance and heterosexual eroticism. So in spite of having only one X chromosome they behaved in certain ways like females with two. This, of course, plays right into the hands of those of the psychosexual neutrality school who say that these girls simply identify sexually as a result of their rearing in spite of their genetic make-up.

However, this may not be enough to clinch the argument where sexual abnormalities do not exist. Where a child is for some reason brought up contrary to his or her biological sex (a boy brought up as a girl for example) he or she does in fact want to change to come into line with their biological sex. A fascinating study of certain Dominican families throws some interesting light on this. The families had a rare enzyme defect which meant that at birth the boys were thought to be girls. They were raised as girls until puberty at which time they grew a normal penis. Despite their rearing as girls they all went on to function normally as men. This and other work seems to suggest that biological sex is much more important than gender-allocated sex.

Transsexualism occurs when a person feels that he or she belongs to the opposite sex in spite of perfectly normal physical evidence to the contrary. No one has any certain idea why this occurs and it is nothing to do with transvestism (dressing up in clothes of the opposite sex) or homosexuality.

Sex hormones

From the sixteenth day after the fertilisation of an egg a female embryo is detectably female as determined by the presence of Barr bodies (the repressed X chromosomes mentioned earlier). By the seventh week ovaries or testes are beginning to develop, and in the male testosterone, the main male hormone, is produced.

Hormones are complex chemical messengers produced by one part of the body to be active somewhere else. The release of such chemicals is under the control of an area of the brain called the hypothalamus. Girls who have feared that they might be pregnant will tell how psychological events can switch off their hormones—

periods may fail to happen in such circumstances. An embryo has to have male hormones (mainly testosterone) to become a male and animal work has shown that if you transplant a testis from a male to a female rabbit at birth the female will behave as a male. On the other hand, removal of the female's ovaries at birth does not interfere with the femaleness of the animal. So for a foetus to develop into a female neither female hormones nor ovaries are required, but male hormones are essential for the development of males.

In the foetus the hypothalamus is cycled. That is, its activity switches on and off spontaneously for some as yet unknown reason. In females this cycling continues and controls many body functions, including ovulation and the menstrual periods during their fertile life. The male hypothalamus becomes uncycled at some stage, probably under the influence of testosterone. In practice the story is probably a lot more complicated, and it appears (from animal work) that some homosexuals still have cycled hypothalamic activity like that of women (see page 360).

So it is the absence of testosterone that makes a foetus female. In a condition known as *testicular feminisation* the genital tracts and external genitals are female and breasts appear at puberty. The person is genetically a male, with XY chromosms, but looks like a female. The same thing can occur in reverse with 'women' who look like men.

All of this begins to raise some very fascinating questions. If, as we have seen, the brains of male and female foetuses are behaving differently (one cycled, and the other not) might there not also be other differences in brain function? It is already known that certain brain centres are influenced by sex hormones as well as influencing them and micro-anatomical research has shown that some areas of the hypothalamus are larger in women than in men, and that the connections between the cells of this area of the brain and the brain itself are different in the sexes. Just before puberty both sexes produce some male hormones but girls produce more *female* hormones than do boys and so develop as characteristic females. Sex hormone output is, contrary to popular belief, a very unreliable way of judging sexual identity at the best of times.

It is interesting, before leaving the subject of hormones, to look at a rare condition called the adrenogenital syndrome. Girls with this condition are exposed to abnormally high levels of male hormones right from foetal life, because their adrenal glands over-produce these particular hormones secondary to an inborn error of metabolism. These girls have an enlarged (penis-like) clitorisad, compared with their sisters, spend more time in rough-and-tumble play, are athletically orientated and less interested in playing with dolls. In other words, they are tomboyish in every respect. This (and parallel animal work) seems to prove that levels of male hormones from birth affect the developing brain in a way that changes a child's behaviour.

Sexual identity and gender role

Sexual identity is the way in which a person sees him or herself as male or female, and gender role is the way society sees him or her in the cultural setting (as masculine or feminine). Gender role is stated at

(opposite) *Are we born with our sex roles or do we learn them?* Two boys 'playing' with a doll—but what are they really doing to her?

(overleaf) *Boys and girls 'cooking' together*: Will this blurring of roles help to make a Brave New World as some people claim; will the boys be less manly in the future or will it make no difference? Or will the boys become great chefs!

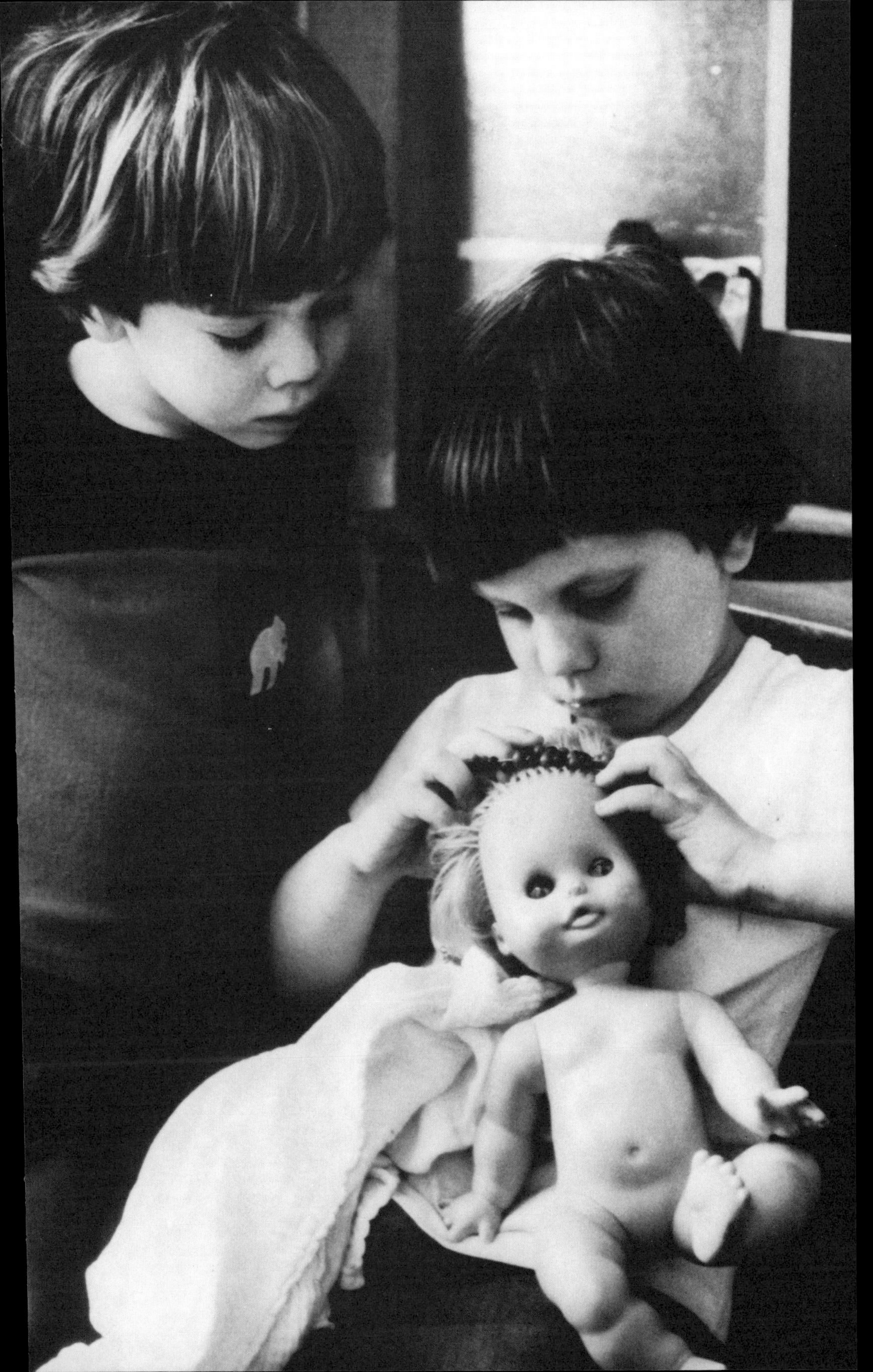

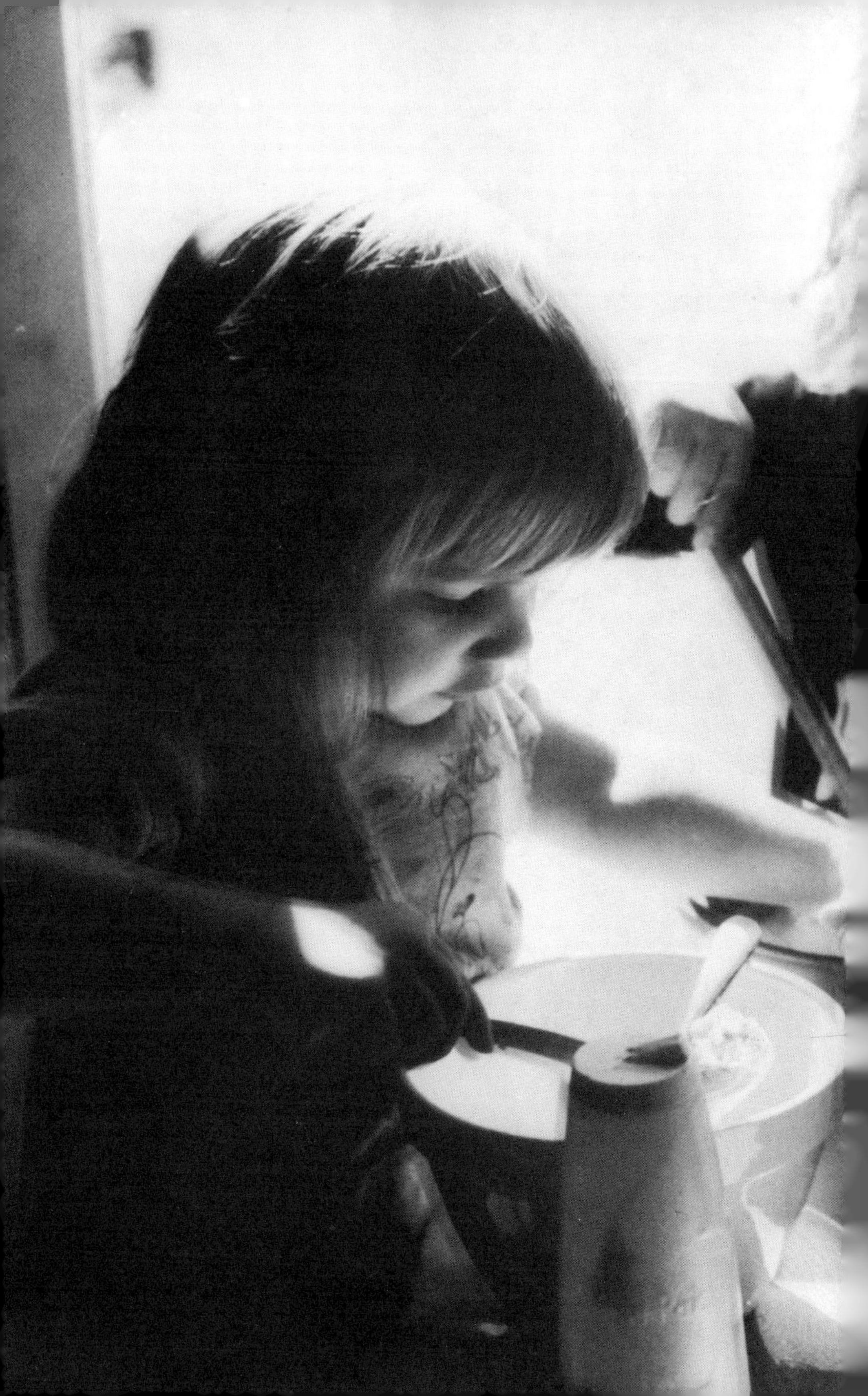

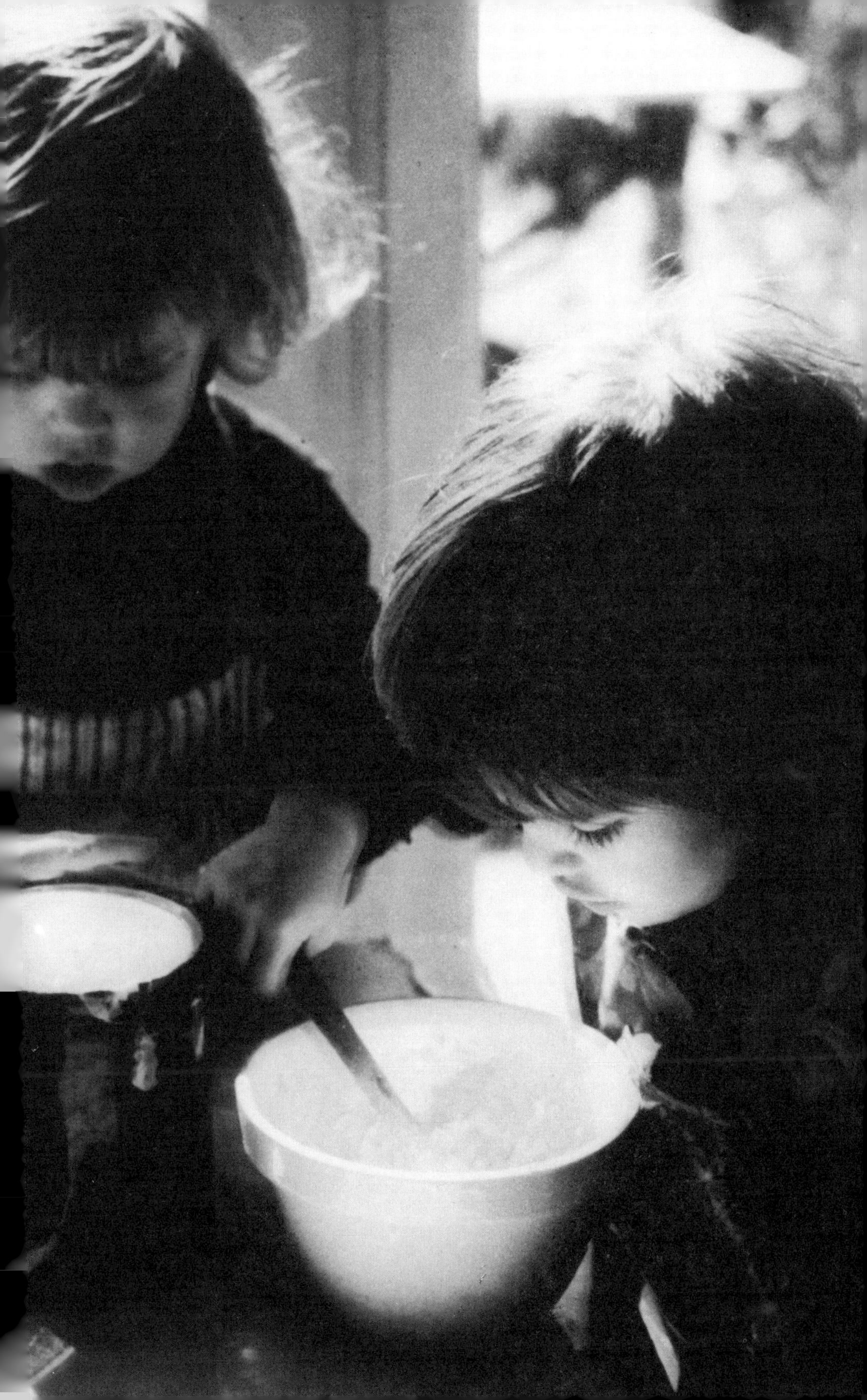

birth; sexual identity takes several years to develop, as we have seen.

Obviously the two are closely linked because the way society labels you has a considerable effect on what you feel about yourself. Many of these areas become shrouded in greyness when one comes across people who are ascribed a gender role but are confused about whether they feel masculine or feminine. Any parent of several children will be amazed at the tremendous variations there are between the behaviour patterns of children brought up in the same home by the same parents. We all, quite unconsciously most of the time, encourage certain types of behaviour and discourage others.

Babies and young children learn their gender role and sexual identification by several methods including trial and error, direct parental teaching and imitation. By judging their parents' reactions they learn by trial and error what seems to be 'approved' and what does not. By a system of rewards and punishments (many of them unconscious in the parents' minds) the child learns to differentiate between what is acceptable behaviour for his or her gender and what is not. A major variant of imitation is role-playing in which a child acts out the role society expects of him. Common roles are doctors and nurses, mommies and daddies, and teachers and pupils, and children swap around their roles with brothers and sisters or friends. Although the roles come and go most children intuitively play most of the time true to their gender role. Few boys pretend to be mothers (although they sometimes do and this is perfectly healthy as a stage of development); most will be fathers or other 'authority' figures such as a doctor. This is almost inevitable because it is based on what they see in the world around them.

Quite quickly society stamps the gender role firmly on a child and girls begin to be labelled 'tomboyish' and boys 'sissy' if they show signs of imitating the opposite sex. A girl imitating male behaviour (being a tomboy) is much more acceptable to society than a boy being a sissy, though undoubtedly lots of little boys feel more feminine in many ways than many little girls. This does not mean that they are in any way 'female'. Most people when questioned would still choose to have a boy child first, and those who have a boy first have a longer gap between him and the next child than those who have a girl first. These ideas are changing slowly though, and a recent survey found that only one in five women would rather be men than women.

Hard and fast distinctions between boys and girls of all ages are changing, albeit fairly slowly, with the result that today's young people are perhaps less sex-stereotyped than their parents and much less so than their grandparents.

Summary

As we have seen then, there are more differences between the sexes than the obvious genital ones, and although some of these may be passed on from one generation to the next in early training there is no doubt that many are inborn. Some of the same differences can be observed in animals and are probably best regarded as 'design-features' of the sexes.

/ Chapter 15

Copulation

In the next four chapters we are going to look at what most people call 'making love'. Experience shows that the majority of couples are not making love most of the time they are having intercourse—they are just copulating. The reader may at first think that we are splitting hairs and simply defining the words differently from their common usage, but we hope that by the end of chapter 18 you will see why we have approached the subject in this way. Most 'sex' books spend a great deal of space (usually most of it) discussing the 'plumbing' of copulation, as if a knowledge of 150 different positions in which to have sex would answer every problem for the readers. We have made the point repeatedly that it is rare for sex technique to be a serious problem in a partnership—personality problems are infinitely more common. Although many couples complain (or one partner does) that their sex life is poor, dull, boring or non-existent, the answers are rarely to be found in the marriage manuals that mostly simply suggest different ways of making the plumbing work.

So what is copulation? The word is the scientific term used to describe the act of putting the penis in the vagina. As any penis will go into any vagina there is nothing very special about being able to copulate. Any man who can have an erection and any woman who can open her legs can copulate. Most people learn to copulate in their teens or early twenties and then progress to intercourse and making love, as we shall see. Unfortunately, many couples stop at the copulation stage, where they remain for the whole of their married life.

Since Nature gave us penises and vaginas and a sex drive to want to use them, we must assume that to copulate is normal and a part of Nature's plan. How and with whom we copulate is quite another matter and is discussed elsewhere throughout the book. Most copulation and intercourse takes place within marriage, so understandably this is where the pains (and the pleasures) are usually to be found.

Given that we all have an interest in and a potential for sexual activity at almost any time, the reasons that we all have such different appetites for sexual expression in the form of copulation and intercourse are many. The most important brakes on our sexual expression and appetites are those imposed in childhood. Most children are brought up to think of sex as dirty, and that 'nice' girls do not do it. Much of this negative influence towards sex is unconscious

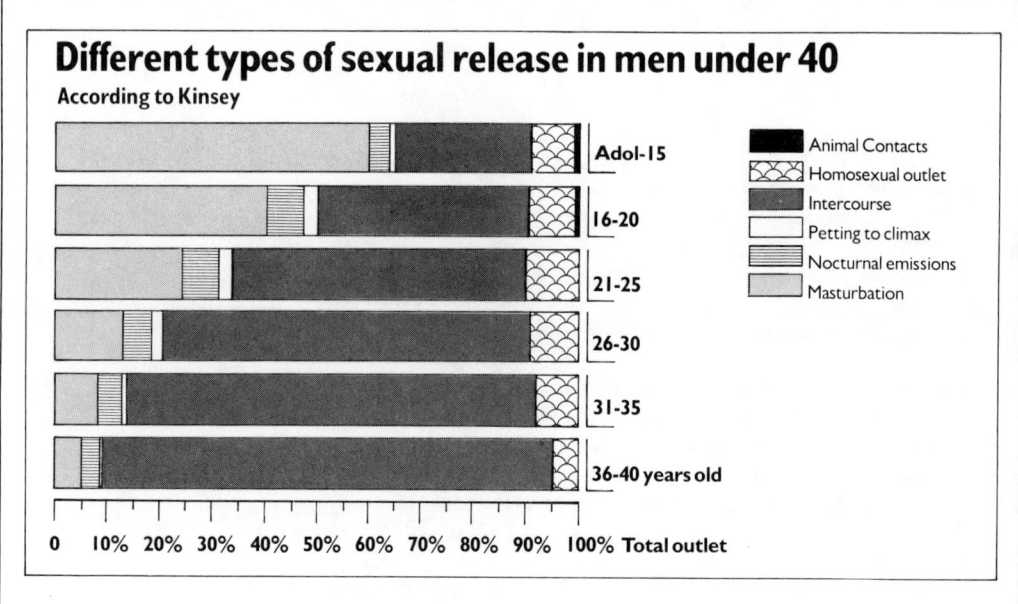

Different types of sexual release in men under 40
According to Kinsey

Legend
Animal Contacts
Homosexual outlet
Intercourse
Petting to climax
Nocturnal emissions
Masturbation

Bars: Adol-15, 16-20, 21-25, 26-30, 31-35, 36-40 years old

Scale: 0 – 100% Total outlet

on the part of the parents and, on questioning, even the most liberated and 'with it' of young people (let alone older ones) tell of the negative effects their upbringing had on their sexuality. The parents of such people often think they were open, honest and frank about the subject. All parents repress their children's sexuality to some extent, even though they do not consciously realise it most of the time, and the way in which they react with each other as parents (whether they are cold and uncaring, or loving and physical, in front of their children) also has an important effect on the children's subsequent attitudes. One way in which parents unconsciously repress their children's views on sex is simply by *not* talking about it. Children sense that something strange or wrong must be involved when their parents say nothing. As a result of this cultural attitude most people (and girls especially) grow up to enjoy and indulge in sex less than they otherwise would.

So the amount of sex anyone has depends on the balance struck at any one time between the anti-sex attitudes of society and their upbringing, on the one hand, and the pro-sex drives of Nature on the other. Take the brakes off the anti-sex mechanism (by falling in love, getting drunk, going on holiday or whatever) and the real sex-interested self emerges to enjoy itself as it could have all along. So cultural conditioning in a sex-negative culture such as ours is a starting-point in determining how often people have sex.

Although cultural conditioning is by far the most important factor and is obviously infinitely variable between people and even within any one person from time to time, there are many other factors that control the frequency of sex. Availability of someone to have sex with is an obvious factor. Many—those in prison and some single, divorced, separated and widowed people (not to mention priests, nuns and monks who choose celibacy)—simply do not have a sex partner and may seek sexual release through masturbation. Tiredness is a common cause of—or excuse for—a poor sex drive. This comes about most commonly because of the pressures of work and those of caring for young children. Babies often keep couples awake at night and a tired couple may not feel like sex. Illness (physical and mental), a fear of rejection, a poor view of oneself (because of being fat, for example), living with in-laws and scores of other reasons can all determine the amount of sex any one couple has.

Some couples are perfectly happy having intercourse once a month or less and others need to do so several times a day. Both frequencies are normal for them and, provided they are both happy, who is anyone to say they should not be? Within the lives of any one couple the picture can change dramatically over time anyway. A young couple, just married, may well have intercourse every day, or even several times a day. They then have a baby and may have intercourse a few times a month or less during the early years. In middle age their intercourse rates will possibly rise again as the woman becomes keener, and in old age they may have far more sex than they did as youngsters in their twenties and thirties.

The concepts of 'highly sexed' and 'undersexed' are harmful and silly. There is an infinite variation in people's drives for intercourse and these change. A man's 'needs' for sex seem to be linked only to one measurable thing in his past: his masturbation rate during adolescence. Similarly the terms 'frigid' or 'nymphomaniac' are redundant. These are words used by men to describe women who have a lesser or greater sex drive than they (the men) think they should. A 'frigid' woman in the arms of one man can become a 'sex maniac' with another. Having said this it can be very frustrating and can create serious physical and emotional tensions in an individual or a couple who are used to a certain frequency of sex if for some external reason their intercourse rate falls, especially suddenly. Often it is the imbalance between the drives and needs of one partner and those of his or her spouse that causes problems, but even when this appears to be a real problem the underlying trouble usually lies elsewhere. Most loving, friendly couples, even if they have very different needs for intercourse, cope perfectly well and develop a pattern of mutual masturbation or find other methods of sexual release that are satisfying to them both. Even in less 'ideal' marriages women may agree to sex more often than they say they would ideally like, to please their husbands. While the 'not tonight, I've got a headache' story certainly occurs, clinical experience suggests that it is not very common and that most women are more accommodating than they are given credit for.

Which partner controls the intercourse rate within any one couple is difficult to prove. Women are classically thought to do so because they can say 'no' at any time and men are popularly supposed to be forever keen to get at their wives. Clinical experience shows that this is far too simple and rarely true. Many women never refuse their husbands sex and research has shown that many wives are unhappy because their husbands do not want to have sex nearly often enough.

It has long been suggested that intercourse is 'good' for you. This is a debatable topic. Let us make it plain that intercourse can enhance the sense of well-being of most people but that some seem perfectly all right without it. Some tentative medical evidence is beginning to accumulate that suggests that people with a good sex life tend to live longer. Also, there is strong evidence that women who have a satisfactory sex life are less prone to heart attacks.

Certainly sex makes most people feel 'good' as opposed to 'bad' but even this (because of long-held cultural views that intercourse and masturbation weaken a man) raises problems. Of course, certain types of intercourse (such as extra-marital sex) can make people feel unhappy and guilty. Many men quite consciously, if unwillingly, abstain from intercourse before important business meetings or sporting events (to name but two such activities) as a result of these inbuilt fears. Some men, fearing that sex will weaken them so much that they will be unable to function in the world, abstain from intercourse or masturbation often so as to have 'enough energy' to put into their careers and other important activities. There is no evidence that sex in itself is weakening or damaging (though guilt after masturbation can make men feel off-colour, and obviously VD and unwanted pregnancies can be negative side-effects of intercourse), but there is little evidence, either, that it affects physical health positively even though a person's emotional and psychological life may well be improved.

Couples copulate for many different reasons. Sometimes it is purely to release sexual tensions; on other occasions to show their love and affection; on others deliberately to try to conceive; on others to punish the partner in some way; and on others to reward. Sex can even be used as a weapon in bad marriages.

Copulation is a complex business.

In summary, copulation is a highly complex business. The act itself is simple—nearly anyone can do it—but the reasons people do it and the implications for the couple are not so simple. Whether, when, how and why a couple copulate depends on their upbringing, their needs, their drives, their partner's needs and drives, external factors, the behaviour of their friends and acquaintances and many other things. Why then do sex manuals make the whole thing seem so mechanical and matter-of-fact? In truth few things we do in life are less matter-of-fact.

Understanding the mechanics

Any reader who has come this far will know that our approach to love and sex is not purely mechanistic. We do not believe that just because a couple are copulating successfully they will necessarily be happy—nor do we believe that the reverse is true. This having been said, it makes sense to know a little about what happens in the body during sexual arousal so that a couple can better understand themselves and their bodies. Ignorance is nothing to be proud of—but knowledge of the plumbing does not guarantee sexual enjoyment either.

Our knowledge of the details of what really happens during sexual arousal was, until about twenty years ago, very patchy indeed. The pioneering work of Dr William Masters and Dr Virginia Johnson changed all that and now many other researchers have

Male responses during sexual arousal

ejaculation
heavy breathing

glans penis
and testes swell

penis relaxes

'sex flush' appears

loss of erection

testes rise

scrotum thickens

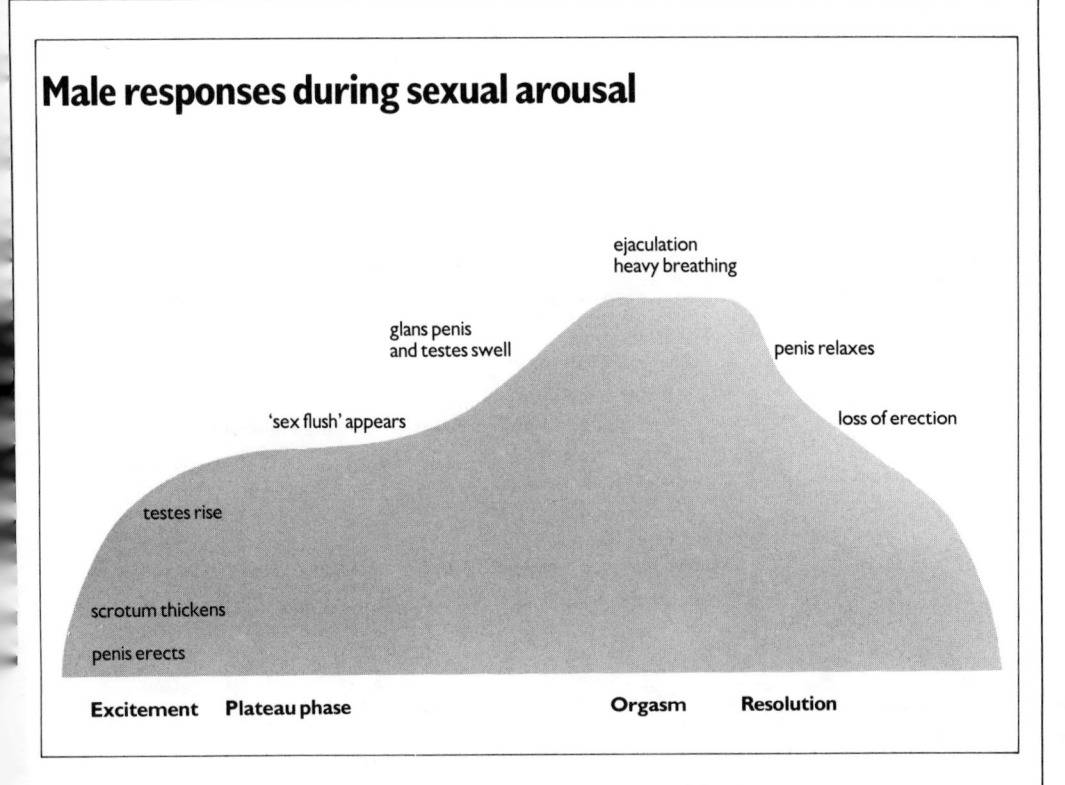

penis erects

Excitement **Plateau phase** **Orgasm** **Resolution**

repeated and extended their work. Up until the 1960s medical books and many marriage manuals were full of enormous errors of fact and the public clung to some even stranger ideas. Let us look at men and women in turn.

In a man

A man usually starts to become sexually aroused in his head. He is 'turned on' by something erotic (either in reality or fantasy) and this mental change sends nervous impulses down his spinal cord to his genitals. In response the spongy tissue of his penis becomes filled with blood, causing the organ to stiffen and change from the limp, downward-hanging organ it usually is to a protruding rod-like one. This is called an erection. During these changes the man's heartbeat quickens, his pupils enlarge, his blood pressure rises, his breathing quickens, his nostrils flare, his muscles tense, he sweats a little and he feels sexually excited. This is called the excitement phase of his sexual response. His scrotum (the pouch containing his testes) becomes tenser and thicker and the testes themselves are drawn up tightly against the body.

It is possible for all these changes to occur and the man then to go back to his normal pre-excitement phase. Apart perhaps from feeling somewhat let-down, he will return to normal within minutes. Most often though, having got this far, he will go further either by masturbating or by copulating.

The penis now swells even more and its tip (the glans) becomes

Female responses during sexual arousal

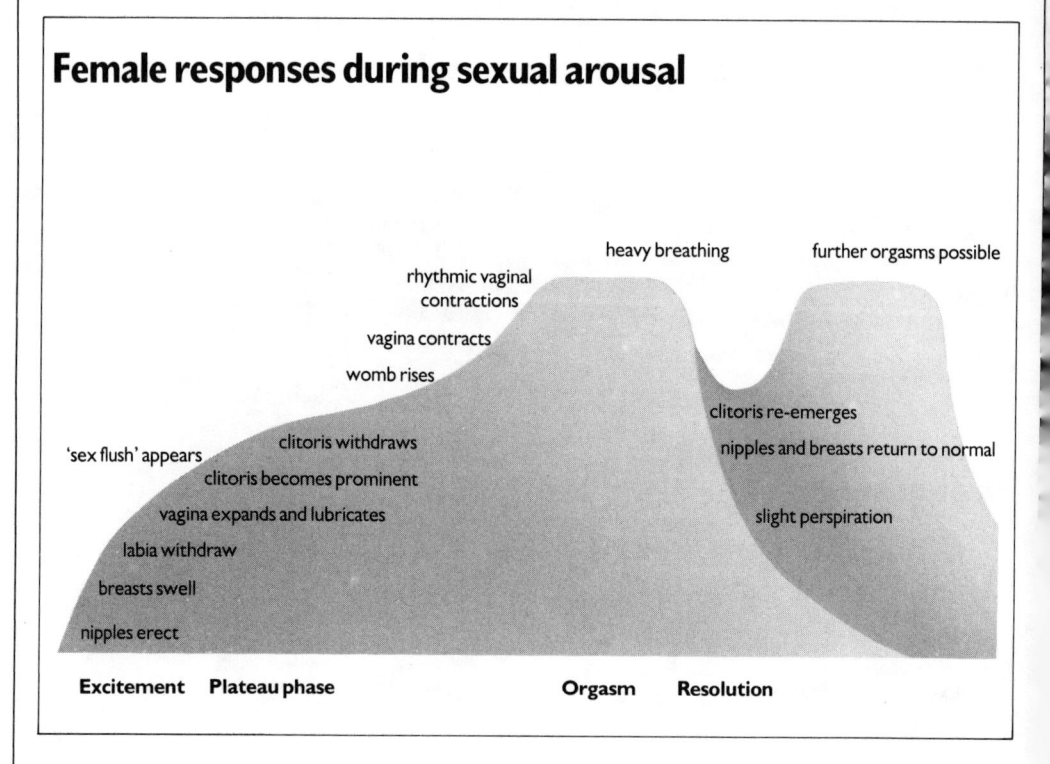

- heavy breathing
- further orgasms possible
- rhythmic vaginal contractions
- vagina contracts
- womb rises
- clitoris re-emerges
- 'sex flush' appears
- clitoris withdraws
- nipples and breasts return to normal
- clitoris becomes prominent
- vagina expands and lubricates
- slight perspiration
- labia withdraw
- breasts swell
- nipples erect

Excitement **Plateau phase** **Orgasm** **Resolution**

purplish blue and the contents of the scrotum increase in size. This is the plateau phase and it is more difficult to return to normal from this than from the earlier excitement phase.

The next stage is the orgasm itself. The intensity of sexual arousal is now so high that the man *has* to come off (ejaculate). Surges of nervous impulses now run back and forth from his nervous system to his genitals and the passages that run from the testicles to the penis contract (along with local muscles) to squirt semen out of the end of his penis. Once an orgasm is near there is nothing a man can do to stop it—it takes him over. At ejaculation a small quantity of semen shoots out of the penis often for some distance and is associated with a wonderful sensation deep in the pelvis as the prostate gland (previously swollen with fluid) discharges its contents. A series of four or five contractions follows at a rate of about one every 0.8 of a second, each producing a smaller volume of semen than before until the tubes carrying the semen are empty. Eventually the contractions cease and the man relaxes. His erect penis returns to its normal size and he feels relaxed and even sleepy. The amount of semen a man ejaculates depends mainly on how recently he last came off and says nothing about his 'virility'. Similarly, the colour and consistency varies a lot with how long he has been continent. There is no way of judging the quality of semen by its appearance or its volume. Each ejaculation (about a teaspoonful) contains millions of sperms, any one of which could make a woman pregnant.

Once the man has ejaculated, he may take several hours to

become arousable again. Younger men have a shorter refractory period and are arousable again sooner than older men. Some boys can have repeated orgasms just like most women. There is absolutely no harm or danger in ejaculating several times a day but it can be tiring. There is no truth at all in the notion that men only have a certain fixed amount of semen which can be ejaculated—every healthy man can ejaculate semen many times a day for the whole of his life and still suffer no adverse side-effects.

The whole male cycle can be achieved very quickly, especially in teenagers and young men who become aroused and ejaculate in a few minutes. Things are rather different in women.

In a woman

In many ways the body-changes that occur in a woman are very similar to those in a man but the whole cycle usually takes longer to get going, lasts longer and is capable of near-instant repetition—which a man's is not. Some women say that under certain circumstances they become aroused and have an orgasm very quickly indeed.

During the excitement phase in a woman her nipples erect, her breasts swell and the veins in her breast skin become more readily visible. The skin of the whole body becomes slightly dusky because of an increased blood flow and there may be a sex flush—a faint measles-like rash over her stomach, chest and neck. This rash disappears at orgasm.

During the excitement phase the woman's genitals become engorged with blood. The inner lips of her vulva (labia minora) and clitoris swell and become darker in colour. As the clitoris is stimulated it becomes erect (like a miniature penis) but usually does so very slowly compared with a penis. Some women's clitorises swell to over twice the size of the resting state but others even when fully aroused are much the same size as before stimulation began. If stimulation is continued a 'plateau' phase is reached in which the shaft and the tip of the clitoris go back under the protective foreskin. This makes it appear that the clitoris has disappeared. The tip and the shaft reappear if stimulation stops and the process is repeated if stimulation stops and starts. After orgasm only about ten to fifteen seconds are required for the clitoris to return to its normal, resting position and size.

The outer lips (labia majora) swell and pull back so as to open up the vulva a little. The vaginal walls start to 'sweat' and the fluid lubricates them and appears at the vaginal opening in some women. At this stage the woman feels moist inside as her sexual tension grows. The vagina now relaxes and becomes 'tented' at its top end. The womb (uterus) is pulled upwards and makes the vaginal cavity larger. Further breast-swelling occurs, the areolae round the nipples swell so much that sometimes the nipples seem to disappear and the woman may begin to twitch all over her body. Sometimes this twitching starts in a toe or a leg, or her stomach muscles may give fluttering twitches. Her pulse rate, breathing, pupil size and so on all change and she is ready for an orgasm. As she has one, her body arches, her muscles tense, her face may draw into a grimace and her vagina and uterus

contract rhythmically along with some of her pelvic muscles. Her body may be thrown into spasms of violent contractions or she may sense very little. Some women scream, cry out or bite their lips as they come off—the response depends almost entirely on the personality and experience of the woman, her early masturbation practices and the circumstances in which she finds herself during that particular orgasm. Once the intense contractions of the vagina and uterus are over, the woman quietens down to her plateau phase and is usually able to have another orgasm very soon.

Most women are capable of having several orgasms one after the other but many say that one is quite enough and that they feel perfectly satisfied and have no need for more. Some women can have twenty or more orgasms one after the other but between one and three is the most common number. How many a woman has depends on her masturbation practices in her teenage years, her in-built sexual inhibitions, her partner's ability and willingness to continue stimulating her and, of course, her own desire to have more.

This then describes the basic mechanics and we shall see in chapters 19 and 32 what can go wrong. Overall, it is probably fair to say that in our teens we experience intense, quick-onset orgasms and that as we mature arousal takes longer, lasts longer and produces better quality orgasms. This is certainly true up to old age for most of us and continues well into old age for many. Young boys and even some girls tend to be trigger-happy and to come off quickly. This is fine during early masturbation practice but is not so welcome when one has a partner to consider. A loving couple will know how to arouse each other and will take great pleasure in doing so, so that their orgasms are the best they can possibly be. Orgasms vary in intensity and quality from person to person and even within any one person. If a woman has a series of orgasms, any one of them can be the best. As in any other sphere of life, practice makes perfect. Only by sharing with each other what they like best can a couple hope to enjoy high-quality orgasms most of the time. But this takes us out of copulation into intercourse.

By our definition copulation may not involve the full spectrum of female arousal—though some women have orgasms when copulating. A man, on the other hand, has to be fully aroused in order to penetrate a woman.

One of the bridges that convert pure copulation (which one can have with anyone) into intercourse (which is a loving, caring and sharing of one's sexual personality) is foreplay.

Summary

A knowledge of the sexual-arousal mechanisms can be helpful to enable both partners to know that each is properly aroused and excited by what they are doing during foreplay and intercourse. For example, a man skilled in his partner's sexual response can tell by feeling her nipples or clitoris exactly where she is in the cycle and so knows how best to caress her or whether to go on to intercourse. Obviously a preoccupation with bodily changes at such a time is unhealthy and unloving but a little knowledge, practically applied, can improve the quality of one's foreplay and intercourse enormously.

The missionary position: This position for copulation or intercourse is often frowned upon in sex books but nevertheless remains the favourite of the majority of women.

Chapter 16

Foreplay (love-play)

This is the highly personalised and enjoyable behaviour that takes place between a man and a woman before penetration occurs. It is an extension of the love-making that ideally goes on throughout their everyday lives and we will talk more about this in chapter 18.

A lot of nonsense has been written about foreplay. The received wisdom perpetuated from sex manual to sex manual is that the secret of good sex is preparation. Unless, it is claimed, you spend hours preparing a woman's genitals (and the rest of her) she will have no orgasm, poor orgasms, or will not even want sex at all.

Many women sometimes like to enjoy extended love-play before having intercourse and at other times enjoy a 'quickie' in which the man simply thrusts his penis into her straight away. These women tell how they like sex in this way even before they have started to become aroused and lubricated. This sort of 'kitchen-table' unpremeditated sex can be thoroughly enjoyable for both partners, yet it involves little or no foreplay.

Most couples though do not practise this kind of 'quickie' sex every time and usually enjoy some form of foreplay before they have sex.

Foreplay has many functions. It makes the couple relax; it gives them an opportunity to talk 'sweet nothings' to each other; it makes them aroused; it prolongs the pleasure of intercourse (which would otherwise be over quickly); and it makes the pleasure of intercourse more intense. It is a time when a couple can lose themselves totally in each other, forgetting the rest of the world entirely. Foreplay also postpones the onset of intercourse, which is a good idea on the basis that something lovely is always better if you have waited for it.

Some useful hints

A couple who make love to each other all day, every day, as we describe in chapter 18 will be almost always ready to have intercourse. But even they will enjoy some special foreplay before intercourse. A couple who live their lives on different planes, see little of each other, or do not get on especially well, need to spend more time in foreplay to bring the whole relationship to a more loving level before they can enjoy intercourse at its best. Many women complain that their husbands spend too little time in love-play and many men complain that they simply want to get down to business, and not bother too

FOREPLAY (LOVE-PLAY)

much with the preliminaries. Only a frank and loving discussion can sort these things out within any relationship and each couple has to find its own best way of coping. There are, needless to say, no absolute rules, but the following hints might be helpful, at least on some occasions.

1 Most foreplay begins with kissing and cuddling and progresses to petting and it can be very arousing to undress each other slowly or to strip in front of each other. Some couples like to prepare for foreplay on their own, each bathing or washing and then presenting themselves 'ready for action', while others enjoy the preparatory stages as part of the love-play itself.

2 Have a bath or shower together (or separately). You may choose to use perfume as a sexual turn-on but it is not necessary to use anything at all. This frees your body's natural scents for turning each other on. Don't be obsessional about washing your sex organs but make sure they are clean and fresh. Their natural odour is designed to excite the opposite sex, so don't destroy it.

3 Make the surroundings as relaxing and arousing as possible. If you like music, put on some that you enjoy; dim the lights (love-play in the total dark reduces the enjoyment because you cannot see your partner's pleasure). Spend time massaging each other and simply lie down together, naked or lightly clothed, and talk or drink a little alcohol. Take the phone off the hook and lock the door if the children are likely to come in and disturb you.

4 Tell each other what you feel—praise little things about one another and kiss, especially parts of the body you know your partner is embarrassed about (a scar, a fat stomach or whatever). Be gentle, tender and affectionate and share each other lovingly. Don't rush; give yourselves time and don't touch each other's sex organs until you are both ready.

5 Be unashamedly romantic—go back to your courting days and relive the romantic love you felt for each other. Tell each other that you love each other (if it is true). Being told you are loved is a great sexual turn-on. If you enjoy using swear words, and some couples do, go ahead. Anything you want to do that you both enjoy is all right. It is at this stage that many couples talk to each other in their private language and praise each other's bodies in endearing terms. 'You've got the most lovely thighs' and similar loving remarks are always welcome.

This first stage of love-play should not be genitally centred; it should have no goals other than sharing each other's company and luxuriating in the closeness of each other.

Things that women like

Obviously women's likes and dislikes are very personal and individual when it comes to love-play and the loving man finds out what pleases

188 FOREPLAY (LOVE-PLAY)

Male and Female Erogenous Zones

Note how much more of a woman's body is erotically sensitive than that of a man's.

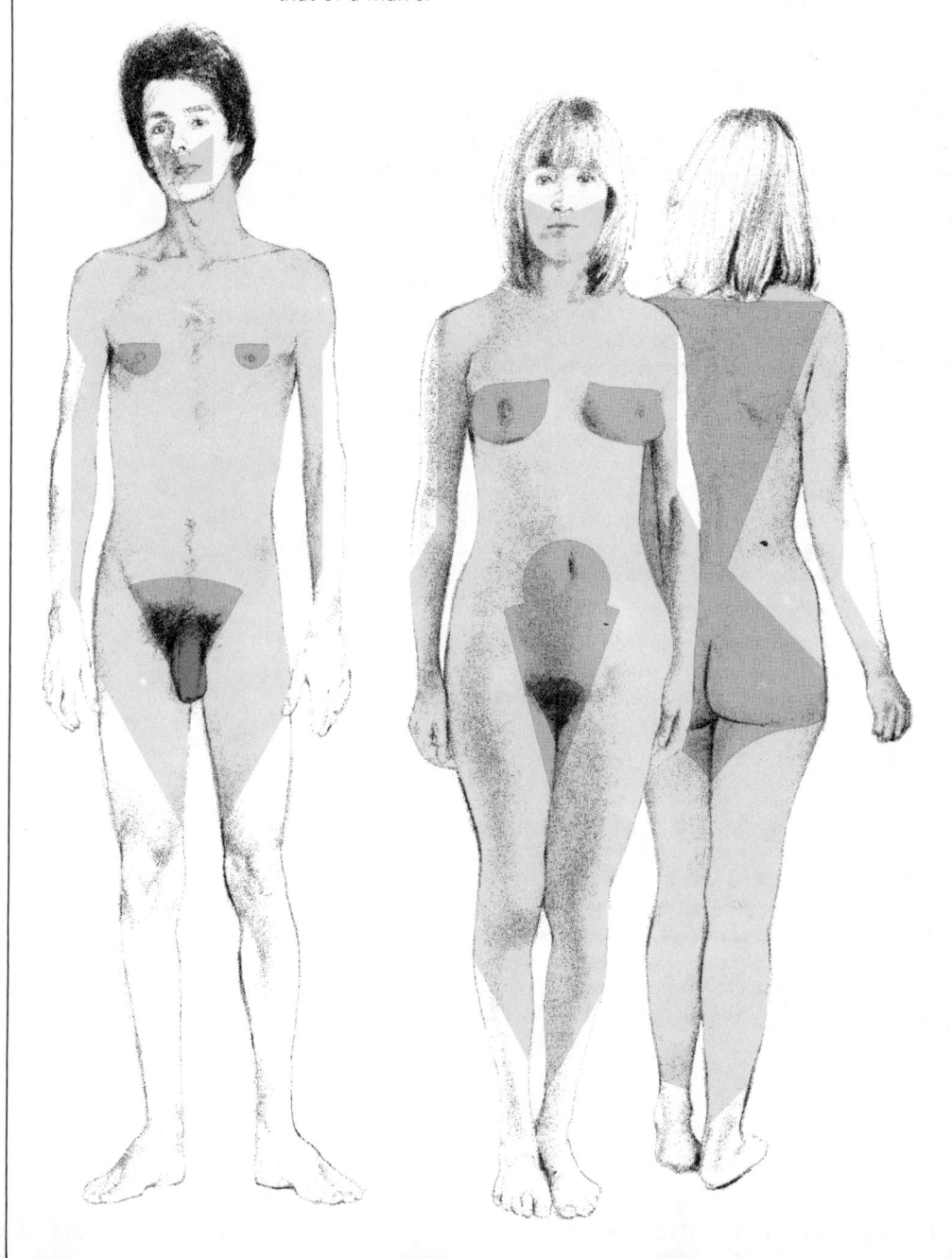

Moderately erogenous zones **Erogenous zones** **Highly erogenous zones**

his partner most by asking her to tell him and by experimentation. We cannot stress enough how different women are one from another in what they like, so don't go by your previous experience of women and simply repeat your foreplay 'patter'. Your partner may not like it. If she does not, don't be offended or think she is 'frigid' but ask her what she does like and then do it.

Kissing and caressing

Almost all women like being stroked and caressed and kissed all over their body. Usually it is best to start furthest away from her sex organs and work towards them slowly. Find areas of the body which she especially likes being stroked and concentrate on these. The feet, behind the knees, the insides of her thighs, the shoulders and the ear lobes are areas where many women like to be stroked and kissed yet they are often ignored by men. The nearest you should get to genital stimulation at this stage is to run your fingers over and through her pubic hair.

Women like being caressed and kissed.

Next, go on to caress other more specifically erotic areas such as her breasts, mouth and bottom. When kissing these, or indeed any areas, be careful not to tickle your partner because this can break the relaxing spell. The mouth is highly erotic for most women. Kiss, of course, but also see if she likes deep kissing (many women do not), running your tongues over each other's, and running your tongue around her lips gently—the possibilities are many. Breasts need to be approached gently at first. Many women complain that men are too rough with their breasts before they are aroused. Kissing and sucking is what most women like best and stroking is pleasant too. Never bite the nipples (especially when a woman is highly aroused) because you could easily hurt or damage them. As you caress and kiss the woman's breasts, her nipples will stand out and become hard and her breasts will swell slightly. About half of all women say that they enjoy their breasts as erotic centres during love-making. Of the remainder, some are excited more by their partner's obvious enjoyment of them than they are by the direct stimulation he gives them. Many women's breast sensitivity changes in the course of their menstrual cycle and what can be very arousing at one time of the month can be annoying or even painful at others. It is therefore very important that men learn about their partner's breasts and vary their love-making techniques to take these changes into account.

A woman's buttocks are also very sensitive and arousing for her during foreplay. Most women like their buttocks caressed and squeezed. This also gives the man an opportunity to get very near her vaginal area with the woman face down and this can be very arousing because of the promise it brings.

When caressing your partner you may find you get carried away and that you bite or suck her so hard that she is marked. Be sensitive about this. First, never bite too hard but keep it playful and, second, don't bite her where it will be seen by others, which will embarrass her. Some women enjoy gentle smacking on their bottom. This is in no sense related to the sado-masochistic pursuits we will consider later.

Caressing the clitoris.

By now your partner should be very relaxed and pleasantly aroused and her excitement phase will be well under way. The time all this takes varies enormously from couple to couple and even within any one couple, depending on the circumstances. When you both feel ready, let your hand go down to her vaginal area and start to caress her clitoris. This is the little knob that lies near the top of her vulva way above the actual vaginal opening. If you have been caressing each other, by this stage she will be ready for your attention to her clitoris and will slightly open her legs to make it easy for you to find it. Some women are so aroused by what has already happened that they will guide your hand to their pubic area. The whole area should be fairly moist from the woman's vaginal fluids which are produced as she becomes aroused, but KY jelly can be useful if the woman lubricates slowly. If she is still dry, use some saliva so that as you caress her clitoris your finger does not feel rough but slides more easily. What you should do to your partner's clitoris depends entirely on what she likes and you should ask her, but most women like the pressure to be gentle and the movements slow at first, building up to harder and more vigorous movements as they near orgasm. What a woman likes is based on her unique masturbation method. This is why we encourage couples to watch each other masturbate, so that each partner learns what pleases the other most.

Now as the clitoris enlarges and becomes excited, 'dip' your fingers into her vagina to keep the vulva moist with vaginal fluid. You really should not need any lubricant other than saliva or the woman's natural fluids. Once she is very excited don't delay but bring her to a climax and be sensitive to her needs for this. Many women want their partner to put his penis into their vagina while continuing to caress their clitoris, others need manually produced orgasms before the man enters, and others like to have one orgasm without the penis inside and then to have others with it inside with either the man or the woman herself caressing her clitoris.

Stimulating the vagina.

Either before caressing the clitoris or even after an orgasm (depending on what your partner likes or asks for) you can use your fingers to stimulate her vagina. Always make sure that your nails are well cut and that you have not got any obvious infections on your fingers before doing any of this. Many men assume that because they enjoy their sex organs being stimulated by hand that women will too. This is by no means true and many women dislike fingers inside them. If your partner *does* like to be stimulated in this way, and most do, don't thrust several fingers in at once or do it when she is dry. This is a recipe for disaster and can be very painful. Get her well lubricated as we have described above, then lick your middle finger and gently insert it with your palm upwards. You may be able to feel the neck of the womb (cervix) as a hard knob with a dimple in the middle. Some women very much like their cervix stimulated when they are very aroused or like the finger to sweep around inside the vagina. Some like their ovaries stimulated (at the sides of the top of the vagina). Some women like their partner to use his fingers in a sort of thrusting (penis-like) movement and others like the fingers simply inserted and kept nearly still. Many women use two fingers inside their vaginas when

———————— G-spot

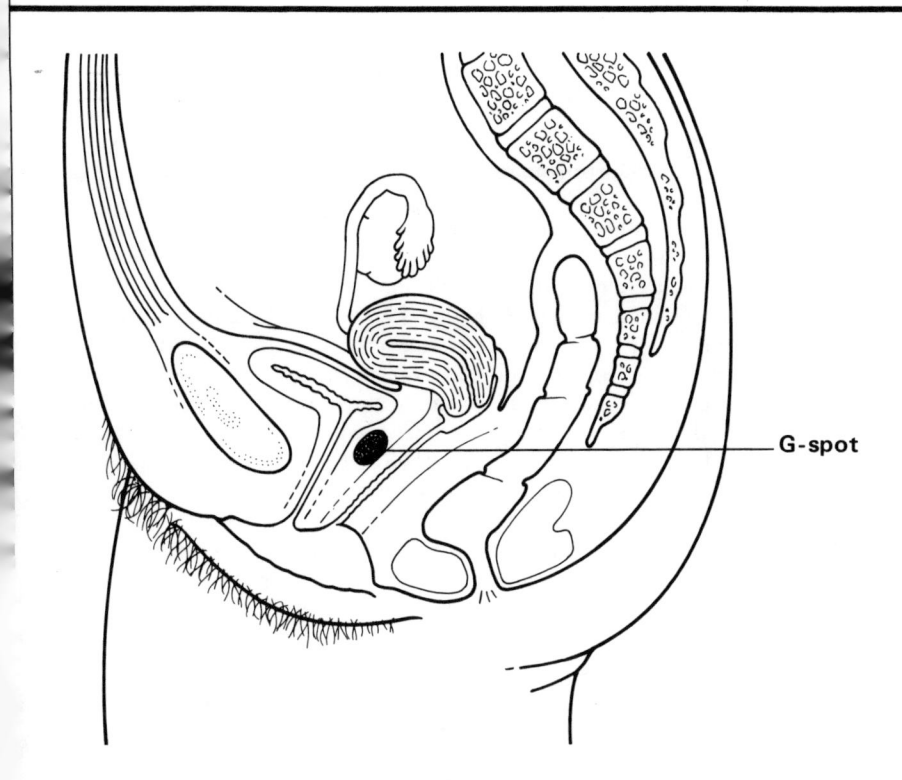

Highly diagrammatic representation of the female pelvis to show the approximate location of the G-spot.

they masturbate and so may well want more stimulation than one finger can give, especially if they have had a baby. Find out how many fingers your partner most enjoys: though it may be different from one time to the next. A few women like their vaginal opening stretched with several fingers, especially just as they come off. Many women can take three or four fingers as they climax, especially if they have had a baby. Some women, once sufficiently aroused, can have very enjoyable orgasms from being stimulated using the fingers alone but many enjoy the combination of fingers inside and other things such as cunnilingus (oral stimulation of the vulval area).

The G-spot

Recent research has confirmed what many women have known all their lives, that the front wall of the vagina can be very sexually sensitive and can even produce orgasms when stimulated in the absence of clitoral stimulation. This area of the vaginal wall has been called the G-spot after the German obstetrician and gynaecologist Ernst Gräfenberg. It was he who suggested that there might be other orgasmic centres other than the clitoris and many women know he was right—in fact some women can only have pleasurable intercourse in positions in which the penis stimulates the front wall of the vagina vigorously.

The G-spot is probably composed of a complex network of blood vessels, nerve endings and the tissue surrounding the bladder neck. When a woman is unaroused it can hardly be felt but once aroused it can be felt as a hard area with defined edges. If the woman is very aroused this transformation takes place very rapidly. Although not all women have a G-spot, it appears, the majority do, but because it is a structure that is only usually apparent during sexual excitation it is hardly surprising that obstetricians and gynaecologists have not described it.

Finding your G-spot.
A woman can find her own G-spot, though, and so can her lover. When a woman lies on her back this is almost impossible because gravity tends to pull the internal organs down and away from the vaginal entrance, so she would need very long fingers and a short vagina. The best position is sitting or squatting. Insert one or two fingers into your vagina and experiment with stimulating the front wall. The first sensation is usually one of wanting to urinate and it is sensible to try your first experiments with the G-spot whilst sitting on the lavatory. If you pass water before trying to find your G-spot you will not worry that the sensations mean you have a full bladder. Explore the upper part of your vaginal wall, perhaps even applying some pressure with your other hand on the lowest part of your stomach just above the pubic bone. As the G-spot begins to swell you will feel it as a small lump between the two sets of fingers.

To the finger the G-spot feels like a small bean, but when swollen it can be an inch across. The size of the spot varies from woman to woman, as one would expect, and women vary in their enjoyment of their G-spot just as some like their nipples played with and others do not.

As you continue stroking the area you will probably notice some pleasurable contractions in your uterus. Experiment with this area, just as you did with your clitoris in the past, until you learn what is best. You will probably need greater finger pressure on your G-spot than on your clitoris to produce the same pleasant sensations and the sensations will be felt deeper inside you than when you masturbate clitorally.

As you get beyond the sensation of wanting to urinate you can move to a bed or somewhere more comfortable. Continue stimulating the spot while kneeling or sitting on your feet with your knees apart. Some women ejaculate a clear fluid from their urethra (urinary passage) as they have an orgasm from stimulating their G-spot.

Of course you can share the discovery of your G-spot with your partner. The best position for doing this is with you lying face down, legs apart and your hips up on a pillow. Ask your partner to insert two fingers (palm down) and explore the front wall of your vagina with a firm touch. You can move your pelvis to enable his fingers to get the best possible contact with your G-spot. He can later insert his penis and stimulate the spot this way too. Another good position for finding the spot is to lie on your back and then have your partner insert two fingers palm up. He will feel the spot about half-way between the back of the pubic bone and the end of the vagina where the cervix is. Putting his other hand above your pubic bone at the very bottom of your abdomen and pressing firmly can also help him find and stimulate the spot more easily.

Unfortunately, because many women, especially in the early

days of discovering the G-spot, have a sense of wanting to urinate (which they will not do if their bladder is empty) they block the pleasant feelings and so prevent themselves from having an orgasm. A loving partner can help a woman overcome these problems by also caressing her in the other ways that she enjoys, perhaps by orally stimulating her clitoris and vulval area before and during stimulation of her G-spot. Incidentally, it is probably worth remembering that many women who use a diaphragm as a means of contraception lose sensitivity in their G-spot as a result, because it cannot be adequately stimulated through the rubber dome. If you want your partner to stimulate your G-spot, wait until the last moment until inserting your diaphragm—just before he puts his penis into you. For the woman who greatly enjoys stimulation of her G-spot during intercourse another method of contraception will be more suitable.

While we are on the subject of something that the medical profession has been ignorant of yet many women know only too well exists, let us say a few words about female ejaculation—a more controversial topic than the existence of the G-spot.

Aristotle and Galen both described female ejaculation, yet most doctors today would claim that it is a fantasy. Thousands of women know they are wrong. One pair of researchers, when trying to find out several years ago how many women ejaculated, found that only about 10 per cent admitted to doing so. More recently this figure has risen to 40 per cent. Clearly this cannot be a change in female physiological functioning; women are simply more willing to admit to what they think may be a rather oddball experience. Certainly the majority of women in our culture do *not* ejaculate, but for those that do the passing of a small quantity of clear, odourless fluid from their urinary passage during orgasm can be baffling, worrying or even alarming, especially if their doctor does not believe that women can ejaculate. Research has found that the fluid is definitely not urine but that it is more like the secretion from the prostate of a man. This is fascinating because it is now thought by some researchers that the G-spot is a sort of prostatic structure in women—so perhaps it is its stimulation that makes some women ejaculate. Some women, like men, report having wet dreams—they wake up in a puddle of fluid which does not smell or stain like urine. A few remember an erotic dream but others have no recollection of any kind.

Female ejaculation—fact or fiction?

Obviously, female ejaculation is normal and perfectly healthy and need cause no concern. The only possible 'problem' it could be confused with is stress-incontinence, in which urine is lost in small amounts when the woman coughs, sneezes, laughs or strains. It is usually very obvious to a woman who is ejaculating during an orgasm that she is not 'leaking' urine, once she knows about female ejaculation. Unfortunately, most doctors, knowing nothing of female ejaculation, send their female patients who experience this natural phenomenon to surgeons who operate on them for stress urinary incontinence which they do not have.

So if when you are stimulating your partner she produces a spurt of fluid at orgasm, she is ejaculating. The fluid is odourless and not unpleasant to taste if you are caressing her orally.

Cunnilingus: Not all men enjoy doing this to a woman and not all women enjoy having it done, yet it is an increasingly popular type of foreplay. Some women can only have an orgasm with a man in this way.

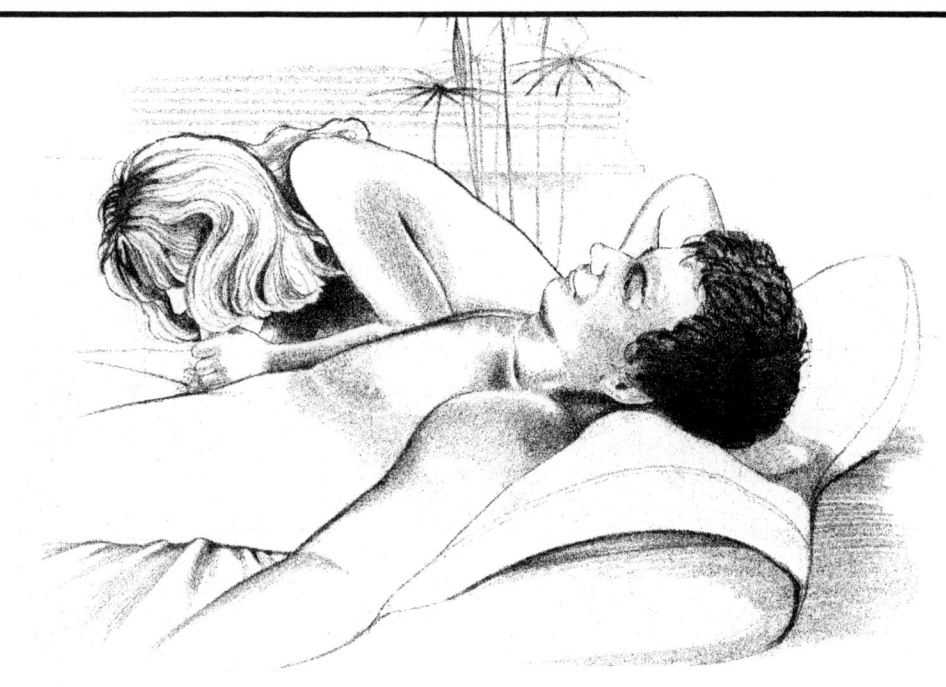

Oral stimulation

This is extremely pleasant for both partners and many women who cannot have an orgasm in any other way often do so with their partner caressing their clitoris with his tongue. There is absolutely nothing revolting or dirty about kissing a woman's genitals. After all you would kiss her everywhere else and this is simply an exquisitely loving continuation of that. Either lie between her open legs with your head coming from below or crouch over her with your penis on her upper chest or face and kiss her vulva like this. It helps to have a pillow under her bottom to raise the whole area slightly and to prevent you from breaking your neck! Lick the whole of her vulval area with your lips and tongue and dip your tongue into the vagina and stroke it upwards towards her clitoris. Caress the clitoris with your tongue as if you were using a finger and keep doing what she likes until she comes off. Most women who have orgasms in other ways, and many who otherwise would not have one, have extremely good orgasms from such oral caresses. There are lots of other positions (such as sitting on a chair and kneeling on all fours) in which you can kiss your partner's vulva, so experiment and find what you both most enjoy.

This sort of foreplay will almost always arouse a woman, and will show her that you love her and care for her enough to take time over her. She will respond by loving you in return.

Anal stimulation

Many women enjoy having their anus stimulated, especially as they near orgasm. How you do this will be dictated by what your partner wants, but a finger (or tongue) encircling the anus can be very stimulating. Some women like to have a finger tip inserted into the anus itself and others like a lot of anal sensation with several well-

Fellatio: As with cunnilingus, not all women are keen to do it (especially to ejaculation) and not all men are keen to have it done to them. Fellatio is, however, increasingly fashionable.

lubricated fingers. Whatever you do, be sure not to put the same fingers into the vagina after having been in the anus, as this can cause an unpleasant infection.

Vibrators

Something else enjoyed by some women is to have a vibrator or dildo used on their vulval area generally or inside their vagina as part of foreplay. Most women, once proficient' at having self-induced clitoral orgasms, are not very keen on the orgasms produced by a vibrator but there are exceptions to every rule and some enjoy their partners using a vibrator on them whereas they would not particularly like to do so themselves. Once a woman is very aroused she may like a vibrator or dildo inside her vagina to add to the quality of her orgasm, and some women are so vaginally orientated that they can only really enjoy a clitoral orgasm if their vagina is actually being stimulated by fingers or a penis substitute of some kind.

Be guided by what your partner wants but do bear in mind that her experiences of vibrators and dildoes will be in a different (masturbation) context, and she may need to experiment with these things in a different way if they are used during foreplay. For example a woman who never puts her vibrator inside her vagina when masturbating may have extremely powerful orgasms if her partner is caressing her clitoris with his fingers while giving her vaginal sensations with a vibrator or dildo.

Things that men like

Women are luckier than men in that the whole of their bodies are highly erotic, especially as they get aroused. A man's erotic areas are fewer in number and his most erotic zones by far are his genitals. Many women can and do have orgasms by having their feet, ear lobes, ankles, anus and many other areas kissed or stimulated, but a man will usually only get aroused and ejaculate if his genitals are stimulated. This is not to say that men do not also enjoy having their bodies caressed and kissed—they do. Some men, for example, enjoy having their nipples kissed.

Over the years many sex manuals and doctors have given the impression that sex would be wonderful for any couple if all *men* knew how to please their women. This is now seen to be much too narrow a view. Women need to know just as much about how to please their partners, partly because it turns their men on, which is nice for them, but also because doing arousing things to their partner is highly arousing for the woman herself. A woman who lies back and lets it all happen in loveplay is missing half the fun! Men today expect women to play at least some part in love-play and the commonest complaint about wives in this context is that they are too passive. There is no reason for this to continue. Sex is not something a man does *to* a woman; it is something they enjoy *with* each other, trying to make it pleasurable for each other every time. This by definition becomes teamwork, not a solo performance.

We think that every woman should learn to excite and arouse

her partner just as he should learn to please her. This is especially true as the man gets older when he will need increasing amounts of stimulation to become aroused but his erection will last longer and be more satisfying for the woman. By and large, though, a man is more quickly and easily aroused than a woman and the problem, if there is one, is to prevent him from coming off too quickly, before you are ready. Once a man has an erection he is raring to go, so your activities should not be aimed at arousing him physically by bringing him to ejaculation too easily or you will be disappointed. Of course sometimes you will want him to come quickly and so will not hold back his progress. What will turn him on most is seeing that you love him and want to caress his body. Kiss him just as he does you.

In the early days of your sexual relationship, until you have got the measure of each other's arousal responses, you may find that your partner comes off or wants to put his penis in you sooner than you would like. Either allow this and then come back later when he is less 'trigger-happy' and make love in a more controlled way, or stop the action on him completely while his erection subsides a little. A good trick that works well is to take the glans (head) of his penis and squeeze it with your thumb over the ridge (frenum) and with two fingers on the opposite side of the penis. This slows his progress to orgasm for a few minutes while you get further excited and are ready to take his penis, have an orgasm or both.

Caressing

Don't forget to tell your man that you love him, compliment him on his body and tell him what a lovely penis he has. Cuddle and caress him in ways you both enjoy or even play games based on shared fantasies.

As we said at the start of this section, although a woman can be turned on by almost anything if she is in the mood, a man is mainly turned on by having his genitals stimulated. This means that he will want his partner to get to his penis as soon as possible. Don't be hurried but tantalise him and make him wait. He will caress you longer and better if he is aroused and wanting to come off.

How to handle a penis

It takes just as much time for a woman to learn this as it does for a man to learn how to handle a woman's clitoris. Many women think they can do anything to their partner's penis and he will ejaculate. They are right to some extent because most men do come off easily. What we are saying, though, is that men do not just want to ejaculate at random—they want to look forward to it, be teased a little and have good-quality orgasms. The quality of orgasms varies enormously in both men and women at different times and loving partners should aim to give each other the *best* orgasm, not just any orgasm, when they make love. Here then are a few tips about caressing a man's penis.

First of all, talk about it. Ask him what he most likes. Get him to masturbate in front of you and then learn from him how to do it. After all, he is the expert on his penis, just as you are on your clitoris. There are no absolute rules about penis stimulation but many women are too gentle, do not rub fast enough, or use an unnatural grip. All of

Foreplay: A position in which a man can comfortably pleasure a woman. This is a particularly good position for helping her to experience orgasms from the stimulation of her clitoris yet leaves her feeling unthreatened.

these can be got around, especially if you kneel between his legs. There is little point in giving any specific instructions here because any loving couple will soon work things out for themselves. Just try things out if you are in doubt and see what the effects are. Of course once you become experienced with each other you will know exactly what to do.

Men very much like their penis stroked and caressed by their partner's breasts and many men greatly enjoy having their balls (testes) squeezed too. The undersurface of the man's penis, right down to between his balls and into the area between the balls and his anus, is also very pleasant when stimulated and many men like their anus stimulated. We talk about anal stimulation on pages 195 and 387.

Just as women can be driven wild by oral caresses of their vulvas, so men love to have their penis kissed and gently sucked. 'Oral sex' has become enormously commonplace in the last twenty years but is not, of course, new. Unfortunately, a lot of women are unhappy about performing oral sex (fellatio) on their partner because they fear he will ejaculate in their mouths. Some women enjoy this oral intercourse, but most find they choke if the penis goes to the back of their throat, or they do not like the taste of the semen. Some women are perfectly happy if their partner ejaculates into their mouths as they kiss his penis but do not like swallowing the semen. They keep a tissue handy or go to the bathroom to spit it out and rinse their mouths. You cannot get pregnant from swallowing semen; it is non-fattening and there is no proven health hazard, unless the man has a venereal disease which can be transmitted to your throat.

Most women who enjoy kissing and caressing their man's penis with their mouths use such play as part of foreplay and not as a type of intercourse. A very substantial proportion of men going to prostitutes ask them to kiss and suck their penises, clearly having an unfulfilled need that any woman can cater for with her partner.

Start off by simply kissing his penis lightly and gently, and then slowly take the head of the penis into your mouth. Keep your mouth wide open, keep your teeth out of the way and then start to run your tongue around the rim of his penis and all over the tip. Push it into the opening a little and do whatever the man enjoys. Push your head up and down so that the penis goes in and out of your mouth, first deeply and then more shallowly. Use your tongue to stimulate the little ridge on the underside of the tip of the penis—most men find this very exciting. Although many women think they should be sucking their men's penis when doing this, it is not necessary or even desirable though a gentle suction can be pleasant. Never, ever blow down the penis.

Kiss the penis lightly and gently.

If you sense that your partner's breathing is getting heavy and you feel that he is about to ejaculate, take his penis out of your mouth and caress him to orgasm (particularly with your breasts) or slip his penis into your vagina. Most men get an enormously powerful erection when stimulated in this way, and a man who has problems with getting an erection may very well not be able to get one at all without oral stimulation. Older men respond very well to oral stimulation.

Unusual love games and foreplay

Let us make no bones about it: Nature meant a man and a woman to have intercourse with a penis going into the vagina. Unfortunately, because of their rearing, some people find that they cannot get sufficiently aroused to have intercourse unless they do things beforehand which many people would consider 'odd' or 'kinky'. These include sado-masochistic practices (hurting and being hurt); dressing up, for example, in leather, sexy outfits or furs; and having to have intercourse in strange locations. Many couples flirt with things like this on the odd occasion but they never become compulsive or an essential part of their love-making. This is covered in much more detail in chapter 32.

Foreplay, by definition, leads to intercourse and is not an end in itself. Unfortunately, some people get hung up on the sorts of practices mentioned above and substitute unusual foreplay for sex. Sex becomes totally out of balance—the pleasure now comes mostly from the furs, the dress, the place, or whatever and not from the person. Such people do not enjoy the pleasures of intercourse for its own sake and can also experience two other problems. First, they seriously reduce the numbers of partners they can hope to find because there are very few who enjoy wearing leather or making love in the bedding department of a store, for example; and, second, such

Foreplay leads to intercourse.

practices can actually be dangerous if they get out of control. Many of the people who need such turn-ons during their foreplay are very inhibited. They are not sex maniacs, as people generally think, but they get more pleasure from their particular turn-on than from intercourse. We would like to see a new generation of adults who never need such stimuli—not for any moral reasons but simply in human terms because it is so restricting and can be harmful.

Summary

Whatever method of foreplay one uses and however loving it is, it is a prelude to intercourse and not a substitute for it. Some couples (especially modern men who have been terrified by the women's press into trying too hard to please their women) get so involved with the technique of foreplay that they stop enjoying sex as a result. People who learn enormously elaborate foreplay may seem to be very at ease sexually but often they are not—in fact they are often inhibited people who cannot let themselves go and enjoy sex. They are permanent spectators at their own copulation. Many men cannot actually enjoy having their penis in a woman's vagina because their upbringing has made them so guilty. These men compensate by being foreplay *experts* but rarely enjoy actual intercourse or even the foreplay itself.

The most important thing about foreplay is that it should show real love and affection for the partner and enhance the quality of orgasm at the end.

Lastly, it is important not to judge people by appearances and practices when it comes to foreplay. Some of the sexiest women who have powerful orgasms do not want to give or receive much foreplay and the apparently sex-mad person who will 'do anything' is often not what he or she seems. Many's the patient who has said, 'But I'm the most uninhibited person I know—I'll do this, that and the other and even so I don't get an orgasm (or have very poor or inefficient ones).' Anybody can *do* anything. Being uninhibited deep down so that you can *enjoy* it is quite another thing.

Chapter 17

Intercourse

What intercourse is all about

Anyone can copulate with a willing member of the opposite sex, as we saw in chapter 15, but the act is not necessarily based upon an intimate knowledge of the sexuality of the partner and, although it can be exciting and gratifying, in reality it amounts to no more than masturbation using the genitals of the opposite sex. Unfortunately, a lot of couples, married or not, spend much of their sexual lives copulating with one another and not having intercourse, let alone making love. This can come about because of shyness, inhibition, lack of courage, knowledge or imagination, a lack of sexual attraction, or simply because one or both partners have little love to express.

For most couples, however, the desire to please and to give pleasure, along with the desire to experiment, leads to the elaboration of simple copulation into intercourse. This elaboration expresses the needs and the sexual personalities (sexualities), of that particular couple. As they develop and grow together as a couple they develop a pattern of sexual behaviour which is unique to them. Copulation at its most basic is almost entirely a physical experience but intercourse is much more. It involves the personalities and intimate needs and desires of the people involved.

Any couple who understand each other and can communicate anything to each other, in words or other ways, can have satisfactory intercourse provided they are sexually turned on by each other and have sufficient concern and interest to do so. On the other hand, some couples who enjoy excellent intercourse claim to like rather than love each other. Love is certainly not a prerequisite for enjoyable and fulfilling intercourse—but it helps. Some people even find it difficult to express themselves sexually with someone they love. This is one of the many ironies of sexual dysfunction.

As we have already seen, foreplay is the arousing activity in which most, but not all, of us like to indulge before we actually go on to have intercourse. Just as intercourse could be described as personalised copulation, so foreplay can be seen as personalised, pre-intercourse behaviour which is adjusted to the preference and mood of the partners. On balance, women want more foreplay than men are prepared to give and this can be a real problem in many relationships. Men who are afraid they may lose their erection prior to penetration usually try to keep foreplay as brief as possible, as do those who fear they may ejaculate prematurely. Both these groups of men find the additional stimulation of foreplay unwelcome or simply too much to bear. Women who think, however unconsciously, that touching is 'dirty' also try to keep the preliminaries short so as to get on with the 'permissible' act itself.

Some women are so excited by the thought of intercourse that they have an orgasm at or soon after penetration. Many men have the same experience but if they can develop an attitude of mind which thinks of penetration, at least initially, as being a continuation of their foreplay techniques, they find they can make intercourse last as long as they or their partner wishes. It is possible to do this by accepting the pleasurable sensations in the penis and, instead of trying to suppress awareness of them by thinking of something non-sexual, trying to focus attention on the partner and her responses. When they finally decide to 'let go', perhaps on some mutually agreed signal from the woman such as, for example, her stroking him in some particular way, they can unleash their sexual desires and start to move in a way which produces maximum penile pleasure. At this stage the man often becomes relatively unconscious of the woman's reactions because his own pleasure is so intense. On the other hand his mounting passion, tension and vigour may be more than sufficient for his partner to obtain an (or another) orgasm. Trying to obtain a simultaneous orgasm by any other means can all too easily reduce what should be a spontaneous pleasure to a series of predetermined goals which have to be worked hard for. Most people find this takes the fun out of sex, even if on occasions it results in them coming off together.

From the point at which he 'lets go', the man is no longer concerned with how long he lasts, and the time it takes him to have an orgasm is likely to be somewhere between a half to three minutes. The average man on the majority of occasions ejaculates within two minutes or less, unless he learns to control the situation. Exceptions are those men mentioned in chapter 19 who suffer from a form of impotence known as retarded ejaculation. Any man can teach himself to establish ejaculatory control and there are several well-tried techniques available. These include the determination of a frequency of ejaculation reasonable for the individual man (if he goes too many days between orgasms he will be too 'trigger-happy'); the rehearsal in fantasy of the technique we have just described when he masturbates; and the practice of semi-masturbation in which he rubs his erect penis with accompanying fantasies but does not allow himself to reach orgasm (see page 237). By doing these things the average man can easily get used to maintaining an erection for long periods without ejaculating and can then ejaculate at will. Most experts would agree that being able to do this is valuable because most, if not all, women enjoy some prolongation of the act and many complain that their men come off too quickly. Premature ejaculation as such is a somewhat different problem and is discussed in chapter 19.

Women too can train themselves through masturbation to develop attitudes and practices of value in intercourse. For many women their desire for intercourse rises with the amount they masturbate. Through masturbation and fantasy any woman can develop her potential for excitement during intercourse, and most can reduce the time it takes to have an orgasm by practising these fantasies when they masturbate. As far as we know, those women who have a capacity for multiple orgasms establish it first by masturbating. The ability to masturbate well is basic to intercourse, just as learning to talk is the basis of the ability to converse. In a way successful and enjoyable intercourse could be described as two masturbators comparing notes about practices and fantasies and then making it perfect for each other. In fact, unless you know exactly what your partner likes when masturbating the chances are you will not get the best out of intercourse.

But this view of intercourse reveals a common difficulty. For reasons discussed elsewhere in the book, some men find that they perpetually prefer to adopt a passive role in intercourse. This may be one reason why prostitution is popular—the man can pay a woman to do things *to him*. In some cases all that can be done to help such couples is to suggest that they each take it in turns to be active and passive. Most men have occasional masturbation fantasies of the woman taking charge and most women have occasional fantasies of being in charge. So most couples are likely to enjoy occasional role reversal in intercourse and this of course doubles their repertoire. Some women, on the other hand, have a need to be totally passive, since to behave in any other way would raise their sense of guilt to a point where they can no longer enjoy themselves. Such women can often be unsatisfactory partners, especially for the older man who needs prolonged stimulation from the woman if he is to function well.

A very common attitude is that sex is something that men do *to* women. This arises from the age-old Western notion that 'nice' women are basically sexless. The total sexual dependence that this ultimately implies can make it difficult for her to have an orgasm with a penis in her vagina. A very common inhibition tucked away in the depths of many a man's mind is that his woman *really is* sexless and only has sex to please him—provided she is pleased with him. Many women speak about their sexual needs in a way which is sanctioned by cultural conventions, and this reinforces the man's beliefs. Unfortunately, inhibitions such as these often prevent copulation from developing into intercourse. It is vital to understand that sexual inhibitions do not necessarily adversely affect sexual desire or the frequency of intercourse but they *can* adversely affect performance in the man and sexual pleasure in the woman.

'Nice' women are sexless.

To some degree we are all reared with inhibitions about intercourse. One effect this has is to raise anxiety, which in turn tends to make men ejaculate earlier than would otherwise be the case and to delay orgasm in women. Good masturbation can help to master and dispel these inhibitions but both sexes also need their partner's help to abolish them. So, a woman who understands her sexuality and the needs of her body should educate her partner, and her partner, by encouraging her to develop her capabilities, can liberate her from her inner inhibitions. After all, between the two of them there should be complete openness and a willingness to do what the other wants.

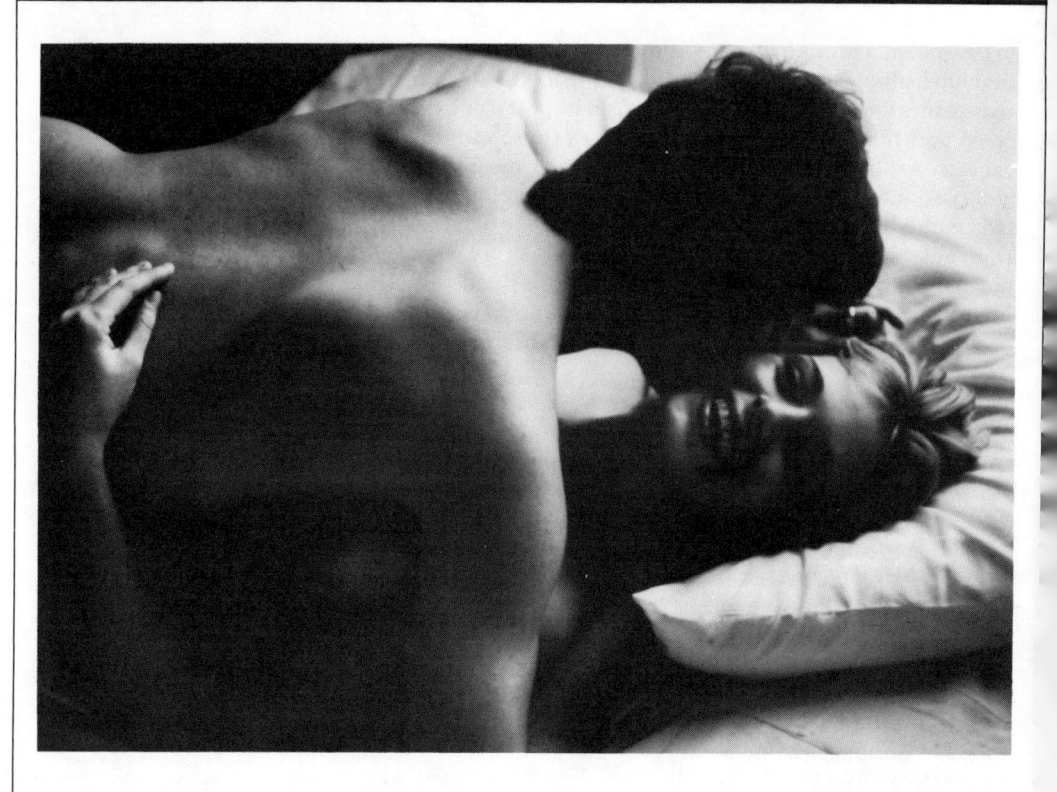

Communication and intimacy: Although what this couple is doing may appear to be fairly ordinary, in fact they are arousing and exciting each other in ways based on their unique knowledge of each other.

The trouble with inhibitions is that they tend to increase one's awareness and vigilance. The individual, so to speak, 'watches' him- or herself for any infringement of the unconscious 'rules', and this is exactly the opposite of what is needed for good intercourse. What we need to do is to cut off our earlier taught restraints so that we can totally lose conscious control of what we are doing during intercourse. In this sense, good intercourse is a kind of regression to babyhood and this may be the reason why some couples indulge in baby-like talk and noises when making love. After a certain point in the proceedings rational talk reimposes awareness of the real world and undermines the other-worldliness so vital for good intercourse. Some people, especially women who fear total sexual abandonment, continue to talk, as a defence against this loss of control. The same end can be achieved if a woman self-consciously concentrates on having an orgasm instead of relaxing and letting it happen. An inhibited man too may over-concentrate on the state of his penis or his partner's physiological responses, or the mechanics of intercourse. Although he achieves his unconscious inhibiting aim of pleasure reduction by doing these things, the consequence is likely to be poor performance and early ejaculation with a poor-quality orgasm.

So much for the background factors so vital to success in enjoyable and fulfilling intercourse. Realising they exist, recognising them and dealing with them can help a man and woman help each other. *The overwhelming principle, contrary to what most sex books would have you believe, is that attitudes are more important than techniques*. The most powerful sex organ of the body is the brain. Too many 'experts' have put far too much emphasis on genital technique and positions during intercourse. The vast majority of couples with good, enjoyable and lasting sexual relationships do not spend their lives changing techniques but eventually learn to make love in a very few tried and tested ways that they find mutually enjoyable and satisfying.

Having said this, it is helpful to be aware of some of the many ways in which it is possible to have intercourse, because most couples want to experiment from time to time and need to be aware of the alternatives there are at special times of life, for example, during pregnancy.

What about positions?

There is nothing magical about the choice of position for intercourse. There is no virtue whatsoever in experimenting for the sake of it if you are both happy with the way things are. The problems arise when one partner is happy with the status quo and the other wants more variety. There is only one way out of this dilemma and that is to talk it over and to come to an understanding about the reluctance of the wary partner. It may be that his or her reluctance is based on a deep-seated fear or a sense of shame, either of which may have arisen as a result of influences from childhood onwards, but often it can simply be laziness or the lack of a real desire to be a complete sex partner in that particular relationship.

Any position in which the penis and vagina can be brought into approximate alignment can be used. Rather than catalogue all the possible positions it is probably more useful to consider the various central factors involved. These can be summarised as the alignment of the penis; its penetration; body contact; the movement of the penis in the vagina; and special methods of stimulation.

Obviously the easiest way to put the penis into the vagina is straight in, so that the length of the penis goes in parallel with the woman's vaginal walls. This will mean the couple getting into various positions which become obvious when you try them out. In some positions the penis does not go straight up the length of the vagina but goes in at an angle. Inserting the penis at an angle to the line of the vagina is usually uncomfortable, but some women enjoy it because of the greater distension it produces of the vaginal opening or even because of the slight pain. It is important to bear in mind that the only part of a woman's vagina that is at all sensitive is its opening and a little way inside—the depths of the vagina are virtually unable to sense anything, apart from movement. Deep inside, the vagina is probably even less sensitive than the skin of the shaft of the penis. It is because of this that the size of a penis does not matter to a woman. Forward angulation so that the tip of the penis presses hard on the front wall of the vagina produces sensations in the urethra (urinary passage) which can lead to orgasm in some women. This comes about because it stimulates their G-spot which can bring them to orgasm without any clitoral stimulation at all. In many others it is unpleasant

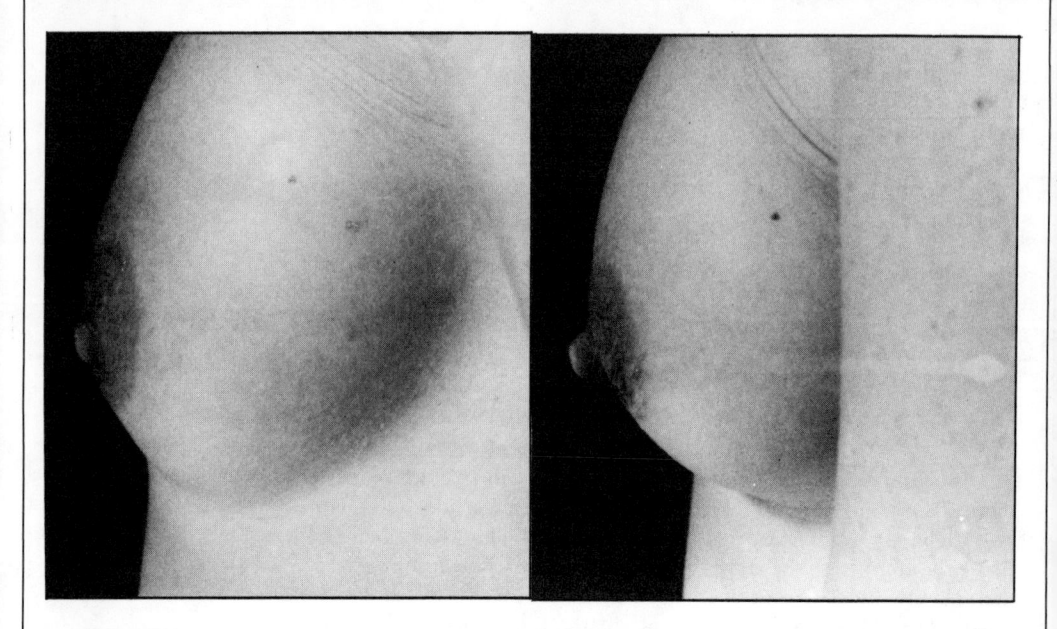

The breast of a non-sexually-excited woman (left).

The breast when the same woman is becoming sexually excited. The nipple is erect. Later the breast will swell, making it appear that the nipple has lost some of its erection. Immediately after orgasm the swelling disappears so making it seem that the nipple has become erect again. Once all sexual excitement is over, the breast returns to the resting stage (left)

because it makes them want to pass water. Backward angulation so that the rear wall of the vagina is jabbed by the penis can be uncomfortable or even painful if the woman is constipated, but such a position brings the base of the penis into closer proximity to the clitoris and so is more likely to stimulate it. When the man is in a position in which he controls the angle of his penis, such as when he is on top of the woman, he is unlikely to make much use of it but when the woman is on top she can stimulate the front wall of the vagina by leaning backwards, or the clitoris by leaning forwards.

Most, if not all, men like deep penetration, especially as they come off. If a woman is nervous of deep penetration the couple can use a position in which she controls it. Man-below, woman-on-top positions are good for this. If her partner is on top, a woman can also control penetration at any time, by closing her thighs. Because of the tenting effect which occurs at the inner end of the vagina during peak excitement, the tip of the penis probably receives less stimulation in deepish penetration, provided the to-and-fro motions are not too great. This can help men with ejaculatory control problems.

The deepest penetration is possible in positions in which the woman's thighs are bent towards her body. Positions such as those with the woman on her back with her knees on her breasts, or on all fours (particularly if her forehead is on the bed) allow the penis to be deeply inserted into the vagina. The more her thighs are in line with her body and the more they are closed, the less the penetration. Men who masturbate by clasping their penis between their thighs (see chapter 26) usually have difficulty in getting sufficient stimulation from the vagina to reach orgasm. They, and men who tend to lose their erection after penetration, can be helped by having the woman beneath them with her legs out straight. After the penis has been inserted, she then closes her legs and the man places his thighs outside

Intercourse positions

	Man's position	Woman's position	Woman's legs	Vaginal entry from	Advantages disadvantages recommended for
	Standing	standing	apart	front	A/C/F/G/J/L/N
	Standing	legs wrapped around his waist	widely apart	front	B/F/J/P/R/d
	Standing	standing, leaning forward	slightly apart	behind	B/E/G/J/N/S/T/a
	Standing	facing away on all fours on bed	widely apart	behind	B/E/G/J/L/N/P/S/a
	Standing	on all fours with straight legs, hands flat on floor	widely apart	behind	B/P/S/a
	Standing	lying on back on table	widely apart	front	B/C/D/E/F/G/H/N
	Sitting on chair	sitting on penis facing him	widely apart	front	A/B/F/G/J/P/b/c

INTERCOURSE

	Man's position	Woman's position	Woman's legs	Vaginal entry from	Advantages disadvantages recommended for
	Sitting on chair	sitting on penis back to him	apart or together	behind	A/B/E/G/J/L/M/N/b
	Sitting on chair	sitting across his lap with one leg over chair arm	apart	front	C/E/F/G/J/L/M/R/b/d
	Sitting in narrow armchair	sitting facing man	widely apart, knees resting on arms of chair or on seat	front	B/F/G/J/N/ a/c
	On back, legs straight and together	Kneeling over penis facing his feet	widely apart, knees or feet on bed	behind	A/C/D/J/M/P/d
	On back, knees bent or straight	squatting over penis facing him	widely apart, feet on bed	front	A/B/E/F/G/H/J/M/N/R/c
	Kneeling, leaning back on hands for support	she sits on his penis facing him	apart, astride his closed legs	front	A/B/F/H/J/M/N/R/c
	Kneeling, facing woman	flat on back on edge of bed or low table or sitting in a chair	apart, feet flat on floor	front	B/D/F/G/H/K/M/N/O/a

INTERCOURSE

	Man's position	Woman's position	Woman's legs	Vaginal entry from	Advantages disadvantages recommended for
	Kneeling, facing woman	sitting in a chair or on edge of bed	pulled up to chest, heels on man's buttocks	front	B/D/G/H/K/M/N/O/a
	Kneeling, facing woman	lying flat on back on edge of bed or low table	apart, ankles locked behind his back or neck	front	B/G/H/K/M/N/O/b
	Kneeling, behind woman	kneeling, facing away from man, trunk supported, on bed or table or simply on all fours	together or apart	behind	B/N/G/J/P/ a
	Face down, body weight mainly supported on knees and elbows	flat on her back	apart, flat on bed	front	B/F/K/N/O/Q/b
	Face down, body weight mainly supported on knees and elbows	flat on her back	together	front	F/K/N/O/Q/ b
	Face down, body weight mainly supported on knees and elbows	flat on her back	widely apart, feet flat on bed, bent thighs	front	B/F/K/N/O/ a

INTERCOURSE

	Man's position	Woman's position	Woman's legs	Vaginal entry from	Advantages disadvantages recommended for
	Face down, body weight mainly supported on knees and elbows	flat on her back	knees on breasts, ankles over his shoulders	front	B/K/N/S/a
	Face down lying on top of woman, supporting weight on elbow	face down	wide apart	behind	C/S/T/a
	On side	on side, 'moulding' into his body contours, facing away from him	together, parallel	behind	B/D/E/G/N/ b
	On side	facing away from him, bending top leg and resting foot flat on man or bed	apart, with top leg raised	behind	B/D/E/G/L/ M/N/O/T/b
	On side, thighs bent upwards	on side facing him, legs apart, man lying between them	apart	front	F/M/N/P
	On side at right angles to woman's body	on back, legs drawn up, feet flat on bed or held up by woman grasping behind knees	apart	behind	B/D/E/G/J/ K/L/N/O/Q/T/ d

Key to symbols used in intercourse position chart

A Woman can move
B Allows deep penetration
C Shallow penetration only
D Good during pregnancy
E Allows access to clitoris
F Couple can kiss
G Man can caress partner's breasts
H Man can see vulval area
J Needs little undressing
K Good for conception
L Woman can reach scrotum
M Stimulates G-spot
N One partner can stimulate body of other
O Good for learning sex with a new partner
P Anus accessible in woman
Q Anus accessible in man
R Tiring
S Stimulates back wall of vagina
T Good for female orgasms in some inexperienced women

Movement
a Allows full stroke movement
b Full penetration with slight movement – also allows control of speed to orgasm
c Woman can move – can greatly assist women with orgasm problems during intercourse
d Neither can move much – woman stimulates man using pelvic muscles
e Both can move well

---

hers. Another variation on this suits those men who say they need general muscle tension if they are to obtain a good orgasm. Rear entry with both partners standing but the woman bending forwards is an example of how this can be done, especially if he has to stand on tiptoe to bring the penis level with the vagina, perhaps because she is wearing high-heeled shoes.

For those who get a lot of pleasure from cuddling and close physical contact, the man-on-top and the 'spoons' positions are best. Rear entry, woman-on-top, and the left-lateral positions involve less body contact, as does that with the woman sitting with her legs apart and the man kneeling between them. The chart on pages 207–210 outlines the commonest intercourse positions and their advantages and disadvantages.

Movement

A common notion in Victorian times was that *'ladies* do not move'. This may well be true but only *women* can have intercourse. However, a man with difficulties in controlling the time of ejaculation can find that passionate movements by his woman destroy his control. On the other hand an older man or a man with a tendency to slow ejaculation or a loss of erection may benefit from his partner's movements. A woman can move most freely in positions in which her body is free. These include positions such as the rear-entry, woman-on-top and left-lateral. Women like to move in all kinds of ways during intercourse and movements include thrusting and rotating the pelvis so that the penis is swept around the interior of the vagina. The best way to imagine this is to think of the base of a felt-tip pen inserted into the vagina. The woman then draws circles with the tip. A woman can also contract the muscles around her vaginal opening. If this is done as the penis moves inwards and if they are released as it moves outwards, it greatly enhances the sensation for both partners.

A little practice during masturbation or during intercourse pays real dividends. A variation of this is for the penis to remain motionless in the vagina and for the woman, by repeatedly contracting and relaxing her pelvic muscles, to bring her partner, and herself, to orgasm.

In positions in which the man mainly controls the movement he usually wants to move at a speed which corresponds to the one he uses when masturbating. Some like short, rapid movements and others slow, long ones. Women have their preferences too and a loving couple will tell each other what they want. Quick, teasing movements at the vaginal opening without full penetration and even total withdrawal from the vagina, for example, can at the early stages of intercourse bring some women to orgasm.

Adding to the excitement

Special methods of stimulation can add pleasure to either or both partners, but some people worry about them in the belief that they are perverted or somehow 'wrong'. It is commonly accepted that no sexual activity is wrong between a loving couple in private if it harms neither of them and they both willingly agree to it. A woman wearing special clothes can greatly please some men. Hearing their partner use words such as 'fuck', 'cunt' or 'spunk' during intercourse can bring some people to near-instant orgasm. Neither of these need influence the position a couple chooses but other wishes such as the woman's desire to have her breasts held can do so. This can be achieved in the 'spoons', woman-on-top and rear-entry positions. Some men like their scrotum held or their testes (balls) squeezed and this is easy in the rear-entry, the left-lateral and man-on-top positions. Since the vast majority of women do not have an orgasm with penile thrusting in the vagina alone, they will need their clitoris stimulated if they are to have an orgasm at all. This is easily achieved in the left-lateral position and to a lesser extent in the rear-entry and woman-on-top ones. The best thing is to experiment and find a position you both like.

Seeing is an important source of sexual stimulation to some people and not being seen to others. Women especially may not want to be watched and this can easily be achieved by turning off the light or using positions in which her face is turned away, such as the rear-entry, 'spoons' and woman-on-top positions, where she faces the man's feet. The left-lateral and woman-on-top positions allow the man to watch his partner and this can powerfully affect some men. Watching their partner's movements and facial contortions at orgasm is intensely exciting for some women and a man who particularly likes to see his partner's bottom or to watch his penis moving in and out of her vagina will find rear entry particularly exciting. A couple who like to watch can use mirrors.

Although each couple should find for themselves the positions that give them most pleasure, certain deserve a few special comments. The missionary or man-on-top position is often condemned as unimaginative yet well over half of all women say it is their favourite. If the man takes some of his weight on his elbows and knees so as to form a bridge over her, she is not crushed too much. She can reach her clitoris and the man has a fine degree of control over the alignment, movement and penetration of his penis. Whilst still taking his weight on his arms he can place one behind her upper back in order to bring her (and especially her breasts) towards him, and with the other under her bottom he can control her movement and even stimulate her anus if she likes that. Kissing and biting her ears and neck, which some women find very stimulating, is possible and this position is probably best for those who like intercourse to be romantic. Women whose inhibitions prevent them from being too active or who enjoy feeling helpless particularly enjoy this position, but it is also suitable for those women who like to move—this is possible if the man bridges over her.

The 'spoons' position, in which the woman lies curled up on her side and the man lies behind her and curled around her, is a rear-entry position and therefore allows the man to stimulate her breasts and clitoris. In the 'reverse spoons' the woman faces the man on her side and the man, also on his side, lies between her legs, one of which is under his waist and the other over it. Some women have a marked preference for this position, perhaps because they masturbate on the side. If the woman sits with her legs apart on the edge of a chair and the man kneels between them this is really a 'reverse spoons' position but with the couple vertical rather than on their side.

The left-lateral position is used by right-handed men and the right-lateral by left-handed ones. It is an excellent position for the early days of intercourse and for getting a woman used to having an orgasm during intercourse. It is easiest to understand by imagining the man sitting on a chair with his penis erect and his thighs together. The woman sits at right angles to him on his lap so that his penis enters her vagina. She faces to his right and her legs are widely separated. If it is now imagined that the couple fall through a right angle to his left so that the woman is on her back and he curled round her right side and lying on his left side. Her clitoris is nicely exposed and he can easily stimulate her with his right hand. She is free to move and can control their joint movements by holding his scrotum and testes in her left hand. He can kiss her right breast and fondle her left one and also assess her stage in the sexual-response cycle from the changes in her nipples and breast.

Rear entry, with the woman bending forwards or on all fours or draped over some suitable object, allows very deep penetration and a lot of exquisite genital sensations for both sexes. It was especially condemned by the medieval Church for this reason, because it was considered a sin to enjoy sex too much. Many women regard it as dog-like and so unconsciously discourage it—often by unconsciously contracting their vaginal muscles, thus causing pain.

Woman-on-top positions are often preferred by passive men, by women who like to control penetration, alignment and movement and perhaps by women who still have unconscious childhood fantasies about having a secret penis. A woman's thrusting may activate the pleasure of her fantasy. Many women who can only get

A variation for intercourse: Experimentation can greatly add to excitement and pleasure during intercourse.

orgasms during intercourse in this position are often curiously inhibited and even tense in other positions. As a variation the man can hold the woman by her buttocks and then move himself.

Something that works well for the woman who wants to obtain an orgasm actually during intercourse but has difficulty doing so is for the man to get her to masturbate herself in her usual position and then to adjust his own position as best he can so as to put his penis into her. Studies of the fantasies of many women show that they want their men to take charge and even to order them about sexually. This is usually a way of overcoming their guilt feelings. By being 'ordered' to do something she would otherwise not do she feels freed from the responsibility of her action. If such a woman wants to have an orgasm during intercourse it is probably wise for the man always to suggest that she stimulates her clitoris (when he is not doing it for her), whatever position is used, because cultural inhibitions make it essential for her to have a lot of stimulation if she is to overcome the barriers to orgasm during intercourse.

After intercourse many women like to masturbate—not because they are dissatisfied but because the orgasm feels different and completes the session for them. Because so many women are shy or because they think their men will be cross or offended, some go to the bathroom to masturbate or even wait until he is asleep. It makes sense then for such women to masturbate after he has come off while he helps her by fondling and kissing her. Few men are selfless enough to do this but it is well worth the effort, in the interests of the loving relationship.

Not all intercourse has to be genital to genital. It can be mouth to genital, hand to genital or genital to anus. (Anal sex is discussed in more detail on page 387.) Most couples use these methods as foreplay techniques but they can be used right up to orgasm as well. A woman who has difficulty in having orgasms by any means other than masturbation probably has the best chance when the man stimulates her clitoris and vagina with his lips and tongue (cunnilingus). Similarly, a man who has trouble with obtaining or maintaining an erection can be greatly helped by his partner kissing and caressing his penis in her mouth (fellatio).

Not all genital to genital.

Location can affect the pleasure of intercourse. 'Naughty' sex pleases certain women, most of whom occasionally fantasise about intercourse out of doors or in situations in which they might be discovered. Hotels and holidays promote intercourse for the same reason and because the lovers are relaxed. Intercourse whilst travelling on ships and trains can also be especially nice. Intercourse when the couple are close to others (such as under a blanket on a crowded beach) is a real turn-on to some but may verge on exhibitionism. Although people enjoying such situations may appear at first sight to be 'oversexed' they are, in fact, often highly inhibited. They do what they do because they need extra stimuli to get aroused.

Many people have a marked preference for intercourse at a certain time of day. Usually, they are also most likely to masturbate then. A couple may be out of phase on this, however, and compromises will be necessary if they are to have a successful sex life.

Some couples have intercourse on a pre-planned basis (for example every Friday night), but most simply go by their instincts and feelings at the time. There is nothing wrong with premeditated intercourse—looking forward to anything is always half the pleasure—but if intercourse becomes so stereotyped that it is forbidden (or even if it is only unlikely) at other times, this is probably harmful to a couple's sex life. If pre-planning is tantalising, spontaneous 'quickie' intercourse is delicious. There really should be no rules—if a couple feels like having intercourse, whether the woman is pregnant, breastfeeding, having a period, ill or whatever, they should do it if it is acceptable and pleasing to them both. Most couples have intercourse on their bed but, as we have seen, this is by no means essential. Varying the place can be far more stimulating and fulfilling than varying the position for the sake of it. If you always wait until the circumstances are 'just right' for intercourse (people's definitions of this, of course, vary considerably) you could be waiting a long time and your sex life may suffer, especially if you have young children, are ill or have social or work circumstances that make it difficult to have intercourse as often as you would like.

Shared fantasies

Fantasies aren't all suppressed desires.

Perhaps one of the greatest misconceptions about fantasies is that they are all suppressed wishes or desires. Many people have fantasies that they enjoy at the personal level (either during masturbation or intercourse), yet they have no intention of acting them out, nor do they even have a need to do so. Many couples are confused on the subject—if they have an honest and close relationship they often feel, 'Since this is how I really am, I'd feel better if you knew.' This attitude is, alas, self-centred rather than partner-centred and may well (like 'coming clean' over an affair) clear *your* conscience but do untold harm to your partner. Sharing fantasies is therefore not always a positive business.

The problem is how to decide which fantasies to share and which to keep to yourself. This is never easy and involves a deep knowledge and understanding of your partner. Our advice would be to tread carefully, always erring on the cautious side. If you declare your fantasy it puts a tremendous pressure on your partner to accept it, because what you are really saying is, 'This is the way I am, and you have to accept it all and not get angry or stop loving me.' A current myth is that lovers should have no secrets from one another, but we would seriously question the wisdom of this in *real* relationships (as opposed to story-book ones). Often the knowledge that one's partner really wants something one can't or won't supply can niggle away in the back of one's mind and work adversely in the relationship. A man might say, 'If you really loved me you'd do such and such,' but women see things differently. To a woman the idea that her love should be judged by her willingness to dress up as a schoolgirl to have intercourse, for example, is outrageous. In fact many women see their man's fantasies, if acted out, as threatening their love bond and thus to be discouraged. Few women want to hear about their man's fantasies for the girl next door because it arouses fears that fact and fiction might just become the same, given half a chance.

The secret of sharing fantasies is to be sure that you both really want to indulge—coercion plays no part in this game. Take it gently and raise the subject indirectly at first. If your partner can cope with this without getting edgy, then start off by discussing one of the fantasies that involves him or her. If this goes down well you could cautiously proceed to declaring other areas. A good way of letting your fantasies be known is to encourage your partner to read a book or see a film centred around your fantasy and watch his or her response to it. If the film or book causes anxiety or anger you are best advised to keep your fantasies to yourself.

Sharing must involve caring.

In clinical practice it is usually found that individuals in a good, satisfying relationship very commonly use fantasies involving members of the opposite sex other than their partner. These may be well-known figures such as film stars, friends, acquaintances or even strangers encountered in everyday life. Of course men and women also commonly have fantasies involving faceless, non-specific members of the opposite sex. This, along with occasional flirting, can be protective to the marital relationship because it is less threatening than actually having intercourse with others. Although many couples do discuss their fantasies concerning other members of the opposite sex, not everyone is sufficiently secure to be able to stand it; so in some relationships it may be wiser not to mention them.

Other difficulties can arise from sharing fantasies. Some individuals, both men and women, have been brought up to be so inhibited about sex that they consciously restrict their fantasies or even abolish them from their consciousness altogether. In this way a woman may feel that prostitution, for example, is so revolting that even if a prostitution-type fantasy came into her mind she would banish it at once.

Some men's fantasies are perpetually passive—the woman always takes charge of them. This is a form of masochism, not necessarily because they want to be sexually hurt but because they need to surrender the initiative. Women often fantasise that they are in a passive role because they have been brought up to believe that sex is something men do *to* them. Obviously, if both partners fantasise passively they cannot really satisfy each other. The best solution in this situation is for them to agree to take it in turns to have their fantasy indulged.

A similar type of difficulty can arise when one partner, usually the man, always has fantasies of activities that do not culminate in intercourse. Some individuals are inhibited about intercourse and so encourage activities close to it, such as oral sex, which avoid the act of intercourse itself. Sometimes, although intercourse is what they would like, their most arousing fantasies are about, for example, dressing in women's clothing, or the woman being tied up and/or beaten. Such fantasies may be repugnant to a man's partner but can be modified with professional help.

With these difficulties in mind, the sharing of fantasies allows the circumstances and types of intercourse to be so adjusted as to give maximal pleasure to both partners. It means that intercourse becomes unique to that couple and adds to their sense of private adventure. It also, perhaps, makes it less likely that either partner will seek adventure elsewhere, because they are both totally pleased and catered for within their sharing relationship. Nevertheless, a surprising number of couples, even young ones, do not share their fantasies to any significant extent and their experience of intercourse is consequently impoverished. When couples who are in an otherwise good communicating relationship do begin to share their fantasies they frequently discover that they are remarkably well-matched.

Adding to your stock of fantasies.
The sharing of fantasies not only provides information about the most desirable way of conducting intercourse with respect to such things as position, movement, simultaneous stimulation and, perhaps, the use of obscene language, but also includes things such as dress, location, approach and foreplay. Explaining and working out the fantasies together, perhaps with some modifications, can provide, in all their permutations and combinations, a considerable array of sexual games and behaviour. This stock can be added to as new fantasies occur to the individual partners. One value of masturbation after a sexual relationship has been established is possibly that such new fantasies can be incorporated into their sex life (via the masturbation fantasy), perhaps in response to erotic material one person comes across or even in response to his or her partner's fantasies. Sexual boredom can be relieved in this way, especially if the partner's fantasies, or some of them, are stored away for future use when the circumstances seem suitable. Women frequently say that if they have to tell their man what to do it reduces their pleasure. This problem is solved if the man reserves some of her fantasies for occasional and unexpected use, especially if he adds a few variations of his own.

Good sex is neither exclusively of the mind nor of the body—it is a blend of both. As a result intercourse proceeds at least as much at the psychological level as at the physical level. The sharing of fantasies teaches partners about each other and this can be very important for men, who are frequently brought up to believe, usually unnecessarily, that women are really sexless and only have intercourse to please a man or because they love him.

How often?

Numerous surveys have been done on this subject and they all tend to show certain things. First, people have intercourse at very different frequencies, from once a month to several times a day. Second, younger men want intercourse more often than they have it (they want sex twice as often as they get it, according to one recent US survey). Third, men underestimate how often they have had sex and women overestimate. Few couples agree on how often they have intercourse.

Clearly there are no rules or regulations at all on the question of frequency, and even within any one relationship intercourse frequency will depend upon how the two people feel about each other at the time, how tired they are, whether they are physically ill or worried about something, their domestic circumstances, their worries about contraception, the time of the month (for a woman), their age and a host of other individual factors too numerous to mention. Having intercourse, unlike copulation, involves so many emotional, psychological and physical factors that an imbalance of any of them can disrupt the best-laid plans or spontaneous desires. In an ideal world most couples would probably have intercourse much more frequently than they do but the world is far from ideal and this is reflected in our sex lives more than in most other pursuits.

Given that men generally (especially when young) want more sex than their partners do, it may fall to the woman to go along with these wishes when she would perhaps ideally not want to. This is perfectly acceptable in a loving relationship. Sometimes one will feel more like intercourse than the other and both should be prepared to accommodate the other's desires within reason. This means that many intercourse experiences will be less than perfect but this is a hard fact of life. Anyone who goes into a permanent sexual relationship thinking that each time they have intercourse it will be an earth-shattering experience is either going to end up having sex very rarely or will be married to a very unusual spouse. One of the greatest problems in modern marriage is that the sex books have so conditioned people to believe that everyone else is having a stunning sex life that the average couple having intercourse moderately satisfactorily a couple of times a week feel that they must be abnormally under-sexed or even no good at all. This leads to a general aura of dissatisfaction and perhaps even to a quest for 'better' things outside the relationship. By the time the 'honeymoon period' with the new lover is over and a different sort of ordinariness has set in, the individual has lost his or her original partner and often a family.

Sex for most people is unambitious and routine for most of the time, and the constant quest for what *could* be can be harmful and wasteful of human emotions.

The first time

Although many people talk about the first time a girl has intercourse in hushed tones as though it were something to be feared, most modern girls do not find it a problem at all. A few experience some pain as the man's penis stretches and breaks the hymen (if it is still present, see page 158) and some of these are put off sex for a long time, but most find that any discomfort there may be quickly disappears and that by the third or fourth time they have no unpleasant sensations at all. Clearly if you are scared or worried about sex, perhaps because you are not sure about contraception, you will be tense, and this can make intercourse painful or difficult. Persevering in spite of the pain is not sensible. Try to relax more and spend more time on foreplay. If sex hurts after the first few times it probably makes sense to see a doctor, unless you notice that it is at the same time of the month each time, in which case a change of position may prevent the penis from hitting the slightly tender womb.

There is no way anyone can tell that a girl has had intercourse for the first time just by looking at her. She may have some temporary soreness in her vagina but no one else will be able to tell this.

Today's young woman does not necessarily have any discomfort when having intercourse for the first time. As we saw in chapter 13 girls are born with a tight membrane of skin (the hymen) that partially covers their vaginal opening. A girl who is a virgin may well have a broken hymen even though she has not had intercourse. In the past a girl had to produce proof of her virginity on her wedding night, but today this is not required in our culture and anyway would be impossible to prove. Many hymens get stretched and broken by the use of tampons at period times; and other girls will have broken their hymen by putting one or more fingers inside their vagina when they masturbate (or their boyfriends will have broken it when petting).

A girl can find out if she still has an intact hymen by pushing her finger into her vagina gently. If it will only go in a little way or not at all, her hymen is intact. She can leave it as it is, to be broken by the first intercourse; can break it, or stretch the hole herself by gently pushing a finger deeply into her vagina; or she can encourage her lover to stretch her as part of their petting prior to intercourse. Although many girls dread the pain and bleeding there is usually very little of either and only very rarely is there enough blood to call for the use of a sanitary towel or tampon.

First-time anxiety.

If your vagina is dry the first time you try having intercourse use a lubricating jelly such as KY jelly or some saliva—if you are apprehensive you will be relatively unrelaxed and may not have produced much vaginal secretion. Most people are anxious the first time and many girls do not like intercourse much the first time—it has often been built up in their minds into something unrealistically special, and when the bells do not ring and they feel a bit sore, they wonder what on earth people have made all the fuss about. Certainly do not try anything 'clever' the first time around. Have intercourse in a simple position (the missionary position is good at first), spend a lot of time kissing and cuddling and go gently. It is relatively easy for the girl because she can just lie there, but the man has to get and maintain an erection and some find this difficult the first time around. Alternatively the man comes off so quickly that it is all over in a flash and the girl hardly knows what has happened.

Intercourse, like everything else in life, improves with experience and practice—nobody expects to become a champion in his first race and sex is much the same. Your love, care for and enjoyment of your partner will mean that intercourse will become increasingly enjoyable. As you relax, are secure with your contraception and experiment with what you most enjoy you will get more and more out of it. Being brought up in the way we are, it takes about five years for the average couple to become really competent at intercourse with each other. Copulation, on the other hand, is easily learned.

Always remember that in a good relationship intercourse is just a part of making love—and by no means the only important part.

Chapter 18

Loving behaviour

With all the emphasis on genitality in modern life many couples lose sight of the possibilities there are for loving behaviour on a day-to-day basis. Many people start off their married lives being very loving and close and romance abounds. As the years trickle by and children put stresses and strains on the marriage, loving behaviour is often the first thing to suffer. This is a terrible shame because unless one feels loved and loving the physical side of sex means little and often slowly fades.

Loving behaviour involves both feeling lovable and feeling loving and both are equally important to a good loving relationship. The phrase 'making love' is a particularly useful one but has now become synonymous with having intercourse, which is a pity because couples can make love all day but having intercourse is a rather specific and small part of the business of making love.

Making love the way we define it has to do with a couple's whole life together, physical and emotional. Couples who make love according to our definition do not copulate—they always have intercourse. So what do we mean by making love?

First, it is a continuous, on-going process that is ideally an important part of every couple's life. Obviously none of us can spend all day having intercourse, nor would we want to, even if we were physically capable of it, but we can spend all our time together making love in the widest sense of the word. Everything a couple does together should show their love for each other—affection should not be something we switch on when we want sex. A couple who live like this might not have intercourse very frequently but they are constantly tuned in to each other's physical and emotional wavelength and intuitively know when they want sex and when they don't. Such a couple have a mutual language, share their thoughts easily, and sometimes know what the other is thinking. As a result, they are so much at ease that they can communicate about anything without fear of rejection.

When two people get married they are two individuals. Slowly, the marriage takes on a personality of its own. It is the loss of this extra dimension that helps make divorce so painful. Losing a person is difficult enough (as anyone will know who has been bereaved) but the loss is sometimes worse with a failed marriage. This is why it has been called a kind of 'living death'.

But how can one go about creating a marriage in which lovemaking goes on all the time? First, let us say straight away that there are many ways, and a loving couple will arrive at their own ways. However, clinical experience shows us that many cannot do so alone, so here are a few practical guidelines.

There are two especially important aspects of the subject. First, you have to be able to love yourself and your body and, second, you have to know how to make love to your partner.

Getting yourself fit to love

Many people we see have very poor opinions of themselves and their bodies. Is it surprising then that when we get down to tough talking about their marriage problems, they complain that deep down they consider themselves unlovable and unattractive? How can they possibly hope to be able to make love all the time as we are suggesting?

There are lots of practical things one can do to improve one's own self-image. Ask yourself the following questions. Have you let yourself go looks-wise? If so, rethink your clothes and appearance, with good advice if necessary. Have you put on too much weight so that your clothes look small on you? If so, go to a health club, see your doctor or buy a good book and get those pounds off. Is your job dull? If so, consider whether a change is possible. The number of people who have told us how their unsatisfactory jobs make them feel worthless is enormous. Once you get out of a rut you begin to have more self-esteem and this improves your love-making. Are your children or family getting you down? If so, see your doctor or another professional adviser and get things sorted out. And so on. Go through your life, talk it over with your partner, item by item, and see how you can improve your self-image.

One of the killers of self-image for many people today is that many of us are so busy, especially if we have families. Being too busy can leave one feeling like a drudge, and can kill self-confidence and many of life's pleasures. Decide between the two of you how you are going to organise things practically so that you can take up an interest or hobby. Go to an evening class, start up a home business, do anything which *you* enjoy. Do something that your partner has no specialised knowledge of and give yourself the confidence of doing something alone and independently. You will find that this will provide a new interest for you and will give you new things to share with your partner. Of course, none of this means you should start spending so much time apart from each other that the relationship suffers, but you don't have to—an evening or two a week will do.

Once you have started to sort out your life and your physical appearance you will feel so much better that you may well feel more loving and lovable and, incidentally, you will probably find that sex is better too. But this is not enough. In parallel with these changes start a programme of improving your physical lovability. You can do this on your own at first. If you are already a very loving, physical person, skip over the next part and go on to the next stage.

Put aside an hour or so for yourself when you know you will not be disturbed. Take the phone off the hook and make sure the bedroom and bathroom are warm. Draw the curtains and run a hot bath. Stand completely naked in front of a full-length mirror and get to know your body. Imagine that it is the first time you have seen yourself naked and look at yourself as you never have before. Don't gloss over the things you don't like about your body. Try to see the good points too and remember that you are you and no one else. Be honest about anything you could improve (a flabby tummy or fat thighs for example) and decide to do something positive about it. If you don't like what you see in the mirror, no matter how much your partner loves you, you will continue to be disappointed until you come to terms with it or change it. You don't have to have a 'perfect' body to be highly attractive. You don't have to apologise for being you, but if you are unhappy with the way you look, do something about it. Concentrate on your good points though and put your bad ones (especially if they cannot be altered) into perspective.

Look at your body and when you have explored every inch, get into the bath, soap yourself all over and start exploring your body physically. Go through the motions slowly and systematically, letting your hands run all over you, using your fingers to go into all the hollows, folds and creases of your body. Close your eyes if you want and luxuriate in it. See how different the skin feels in different parts of your body and see what you most like done to each area to produce the most pleasant sensations. Keep the water hot and keep on exploring until you are relaxed.

Get out of the bath and dry yourself gently, then lie on your bed and try to think about your feelings about what you have just done. Did it make you feel good, bad, guilty, silly? If so, why? And how do these feelings relate to the way you feel when you are with your partner? Did you think it a waste of time? If so, why? Don't you see yourself as important enough to spend time on, or would you rather be watching TV? Think about the fact that many of us have become so unused to giving ourselves pleasure that we are almost incapable of really pleasing someone else or receiving pleasure from others. Compare how the feelings you have just had are compared with other loving, sexual sensations you have had with people in the past. How do your current feelings match up?

All of this should make you begin to question how you feel when you are with your partner in bed. Have things become slipshod, hasty and makeshift? If so, how about changing things now—today—so that your physical love-making does not slip away from you further.

Now that you are beautifully relaxed you can repeat the whole bath routine but with body lotion. At the end, if you feel like it, masturbate and luxuriate in the wonderful feelings.

Once you have done this a few times and your partner is equally practised, the time will have come to start doing exactly the same things together. We described sensual massage on page 113 and you can now have a go at that. Get your partner to do to you what you find is sensual and exciting and do it for long periods of time, talking and sharing your thoughts and feelings as you do so. Guide each other as to exactly what is *best*, not just pleasant, and learn over several

Getting to know each other.

sessions exactly how best to please each other. *Don't have intercourse for the first few sessions* and keep away from breasts and genitals. Keep the relationship on a loving, caring, affectionate plane. If you get really aroused, masturbate each other if you have to, but better still get used to pleasing each other physically without *having* to have sex. When and only when you can both give each other beautiful sensations that are an end in themselves, start having intercourse at the end if you want to. Many couples don't want to—they simply enjoy the stroking, cuddling and massaging as an end in itself. There is no goal to aim for in this sort of love-making and it can be as relaxing as intercourse and just as pleasurable.

LOVING BEHAVIOUR 225

Love and desire: Even if this affectionate and erotic sequence does not end in intercourse it will cause a degree of sexual arousal...

226   LOVING BEHAVIOUR

Now that you are well on the way to being what you want, get started on your communication with your partner. Sensual massage is a very real and valuable form of communication. In the early days at least you will be talking a lot, telling each other exactly what you like and don't like. When you feel more at ease with yourself you will find it easier to communicate on other things too.

Go to bed, cuddle and perhaps massage each other and, when you are relaxed, get a piece of paper each and write the following words down the left-hand side. Copulation, intercourse, masturbation, oral sex, orgasm, genitals, penis, vagina, clitoris, anus, testicles, breasts, nipples, menstruation, semen. Now both of you, each on your own, write against each of these what your shared private words are for every one of these sexual terms. Before you start, decide on a prize for whoever gets the most in the column. Once you have finished, swap your pieces of paper and take it in turns to read out what the other has written. This is a good way of breaking down the unspoken barriers that have arisen during your relationship and can spark off all kinds of discussions from which you can both learn. We all have our private language as loving couples, and also have unspoken ways of communicating loving intentions. But in many couples one or other has forgotten the language and cannot communicate. When a husband says, for example, 'I'd love an early night tonight,' he almost certainly does not mean that he is going to bed at 9.30 to sleep. He really means, 'I'd like to make love to you tonight.' The couple probably used to understand this language but have now got to the stage where they take the words literally and cannot actually bring themselves to say what they really want.

An extension of this word game can be played using other words (not necessarily of a sexual nature) about other important areas of life. Give yourselves prizes for getting right your partner's views on, say, private education, capital punishment, Mr Jones' new car, simultaneous orgasms, or whatever you think matters to your spouse. Once again this is simply a device to get talking and to show each other just how you really do think about things that matter.

Making love all day

A couple who have been through all this preparation and learning may start to feel like romantic teenagers about each other again, yet they are mature, capable adults and active members of society. During their day-to-day lives they lose no opportunity to kiss each other (at any excuse); they touch a lot physically; they tell each other sweet nothings every so often; they tend to compliment rather than put down each other; they never forget anniversaries and birthdays because they really matter to them; they never attack each other's personalities; and they almost never fight. Quite incidentally they have intercourse much more than most couples and enjoy their orgasms much more. If one partner does not want sex the other does something else to relieve him or her, and there are no ill feelings because they are making love all the time—intercourse becomes the icing on the cake, not the cake itself. Such a couple never force each other to do sexual things that one does not enjoy because the love and friendship between them makes refusal not only possible but acceptable. There is no question in such a marriage of the man thinking that a woman who refuses to have oral sex with her husband does not *love* him—he *knows* she loves him because she shows it in a million other ways. She simply does not like oral sex—just as he does not like roast duck. Of course, if there are many sexual 'no-go' areas, there may well be trouble afoot and professional help may be needed. This is unusual in this type of love-making relationship.

Simultaneous orgasms. We would like to say just a few words here about what to many people is seen as the pinnacle of love-making—the simultaneous orgasm. A loving, caring couple who have orgasms in sex (before, during, after—or all three) will usually be totally satisfied. In the past some 'sexperts' and many others in the medical profession have put about the story that the ultimate goal, which demonstrates that a couple are really tuned into each other, is simultaneous orgasm. We know from experience that this is fallacious, and even makes people feel failures when they are not. The intense psychological, physical and emotional effort needed to have simultaneous orgasms (both coming off at the same time during intercourse) is so great for most couples that it actually detracts from their enjoyment of intercourse. If it can happen spontaneously and readily it is certainly very pleasant but it is not worth striving for it as an end-point—though couples often pretend to each other that it was worthwhile.

Any two people living together will have problems because of the hundreds of sources of friction in any one day. Making love all the time reduces the friction, defuses situations before they flare, provides a self-rewarding system for our secret society of two lovers and, incidentally, makes them better parents because they have a stable, loving bond between them. Loving couples miss love-making much more than they miss intercourse when they are apart. After all, you can copulate with anyone of the opposite sex and have intercourse with quite a few, but there are very few people in one's life with whom one could make love every day, for years on end.

Summary

Most people marry full of good intentions but these can soon slip so that after a year or two either or both partners feel they have a marriage in name only. By following the tips in this chapter such a deterioration can be avoided or an impoverished relationship revived.

The actual ways in which this is achieved are not important—we have simply outlined some techniques that have been proved to work for many couples. The main thing is to get your self-love right first so that you can extend it to your partner.

Few couples find that behaving in this kind of loving way is easy to keep up, given the hurly-burly of everyday life and the pressures of family life in particular. However, it is well worth the effort and the time and effort you put in is rewarded many times over.

Chapter 19

Sexual difficulties

It has become fashionable in recent years to talk about people's sexual problems as if we were being afflicted by a new epidemic. To some extent we may today be in the throes of a period of more prevalent sexual dysfunctioning, but on the other hand, because of the publicity sexual problems now receive, people who in the past would have kept quiet about them now feel willing to discuss them or seek help. Also, the apparent increase in sexual problems may to some extent be the result of an increased level of expectation, brought about by the increased discussion of sex. However, sexual problems are not new: they have always been around.

Today, many young and middle-aged couples strive after improved sexual pleasure and many worry that they are inadequate. In the not-too-distant past people just got on with it and assumed that they were much like everybody else. Today, though, with much greater openness on the subject, many people are no longer prepared to settle for what they see as second best.

Public awareness and the pressure of the women's movement over the last twenty years has definitely and provably increased men's anxieties about sexual performance, and many are now so concerned about their ability to give their partners an orgasm that they have impaired their ability to enjoy their own sex lives. The assertiveness of women outside the bedroom has also adversely affected many men and this is reflected in their reduced practical interest in sex. Modern middle-class men are under tremendous pressure to perform in and out of bed, at work, in the home, socially and at play, to such an extent that sex is pushed to the end of their list of priorities. There is evidence to suggest that intercourse rates are falling and some researchers now believe that the male population is in sexual retreat.

There are many causes, both psychological and physical, for sexual problems and more are recognised each year. In a book such as this we can only give the briefest outline of the main problem areas.

Underlying causes

Although some sexual difficulties are the result of physical illness, the majority are of psychological origin. It is always possible that discoveries such as the fact that high prolactin or oestrogen production in some men can produce impotence will explain some sexual difficulties which would previously have been thought to be of psychological origin, but such discoveries are unlikely to be the answer to many couples' sex problems.

It is not only an absence of hard biological evidence that leads us to say that most sex problems originate in the mind; there are two other reasons too. First, when investigated, most people's sex problems show sufficient evidence of a psychosexual origin to make it worth considering this as a serious possibility. Second, psychotherapeutic techniques (talk therapy), perhaps combined with other non-drug or surgery techniques, often relieve the problem. Clearly most sexual problems have little or nothing to do with the body's basic plumbing. This is not to pretend for a moment, however, that all problems are 'in the mind' (imagined) or unimportant. They certainly are important and can ruin a person's life and a couple's relationship. Unfortunately, some people see sexual problems as unmentionable, or possibly even imagined, and so they put up with them for months or years longer than they would put up with a problem affecting any other system of the body. Many people with problems are reluctant to consult a doctor, sometimes because they feel that he or she will think badly of them or has not the time to treat them, while others put off seeking help because they do not believe help is available or effective. Unnecessary shame is often a deterrent too. Many sexual problems can be adequately treated but, because they are usually deep-seated, time-consuming therapy is usually needed.

At the heart of the psychological factors that prevent sexual success and produce sexual casualties is the anti-sexual nature of our culture, which demands that female sexuality especially be restricted and suppressed from an early age. As we have mentioned elsewhere, conservatism on the subject of sex in child rearing leads to the unconscious transmission of sexual suppression from one generation to the next and sex education, at least as it is practised at present, does little to redress the balance. Normal religious beliefs affect the situation very little except that children brought up in religiously extreme homes have more than their fair share of sexual problems as adults. A girl or, less commonly, a boy who is exposed to oppressive sexual behaviour as a child may later experience sexual problems. Seduction whilst he or she is still immature can also produce problems later, as can shaming or direct punishment for childhood sexual behaviour. In fact so many obstacles stand in the way of full and normal psychosexual development that the wonder is not that so many people have sexual problems but rather that so many turn out to be normal!

Increasingly today drugs, pharmaceutical preparations and chemicals also interfere with sexual performance (see page 403). More subtly, unconsciously perceived chemical messengers called pheromones may also be involved. For more about these see page 000. Psychological 'messages' can also be transmitted by one partner and picked up unconsciously and yet still influence sexual behaviour. Body language is one example. It is quite possible that such psychological and pheromonal messages, if negative and transmitted over a long period of time, might adversely affect the sexual capacity of one's partner.

Another example of how one partner can influence the other is sexual apathy, which starts, for example, in a man whose wife, because of her upbringing, has to express opposition to or unwillingness over intercourse she really wants because her conscience would object if she enthusiastically accepted his advances. Some women who from their responses obviously do enjoy intercourse may nevertheless, in obedience to unconscious anti-instinctual forces implanted during rearing, offer no stimulation or cooperation to their partner—some even enquire whether he will be finished soon! The effect on the man, especially as he gets older, may make it seem that he is uninterested or even has an impotence problem, but in reality it is the wife who has the difficulty in many such couples.

The emotional relationship between a couple can express itself as a sexual problem—indeed most so-called sexual problems are probably the result of emotional and interrelationship problems. A failure to erect or lubricate, premature ejaculation, or failure to have an orgasm can be expressions of resentment, as can the rejection of advances.

The root of most sexual problems.

A false perception of the sexuality of the partner, as in the case of, for example, a man who unconsciously identifies his partner too much with his mother, and a failure to communicate may result in rare or unenjoyable intercourse, leading eventually to a lack of interest or frank sexual problems. Along the same lines, a woman having a baby can change in her husband's eyes from a lover to a mother and he may well then see her as relatively (or totally) undesirable. He may even become impotent if they do try to have intercourse. A loss of sex drive, or even completely going off sex, after the birth of a baby is common in women too, for reasons which include pain from an episiotomy, a birth injury, hormonal disturbances, post-natal depression, fear of a further pregnancy, tiredness, over-occupation with the new baby, or an unconscious identification with the woman's own mother, now that she has become a mother. Many, if not most, women perceive mothers in general as sexless.

Misperceptions and false perceptions, no matter how unconscious, affect sexual performance in other ways. Some women see sex as something some *to* them by a man, and while they never refuse to have intercourse they may never be capable of anything better than basic physical cooperation, and so they become sexually boring. Some men unconsciously see intercourse as something women endure solely to please them, and may be nervous in their approach and premature in reaching orgasm so as to impose minimal demands upon them. Other men who unconsciously see intercourse as an assault on women, perhaps as a result of witnessing parental intercourse even before their conscious memory began to work, are afraid of retaliation from women and so need the most direct forms of encouragement from them if they are to erect.

There are men and women who see themselves as sexual enthusiasts but who, when the subject is examined more deeply in therapy, are found to be continuously putting sex last on their list of priorities in life. It is not, they say, that they don't *want* to have intercourse but there is 'just no time for it' and in any case they are 'always too tired'. Also, they often add, 'sex isn't everything'. Where both of the partners want to avoid sex such a situation is satisfactory. It is not at all uncommon for the inhibited to choose other inhibited people as partners, but if this is not the case sexual problems can result. For example, many a man takes the view, again mainly unconsciously, that if a woman really loves him she will nearly always want to have intercourse with him and will always have at least one orgasm. If she places a low priority on sex, or at least continuously finds other things she would rather do, he sees this as rejection, loses interest or performs badly when she does agree. Many women too measure their attractiveness, and therefore their value, by the ardour shown by their partner. If he puts everything else first (late night movies on television seem to be a common culprit here) she may respond by getting angry, becoming sexually uninterested or performing badly. Believing herself to be unwanted she may even fall out of love with him. A sign that this is occurring is a sudden loss of her ability to have orgasms.

Measuring attractiveness by his ardour.

Stereotyped, habit-ridden copulation and insensitivity to the needs of the other partner both sow the seeds of sexual difficulties, as do relatively minor problems such as bad breath and, for many women, the man being unshaven. Sometimes even just loving the partner can produce problems. As we have mentioned already, some men perceive the woman they love as sexless and put her on a pedestal in their minds, so that they are impotent with her but not with others. Some women are inhibited and sexually shy with the man they love, having been reared in childhood to believe that sexual activity leads to a loss of love, but can perform with efficiency and abandon with a stranger. Other women overcome this by fantasising about other men when having intercourse with their partner. In any case, for reasons which are largely unknown, everyone finds certain members of the opposite sex infinitely more desirable, arousing and exciting than others. Some men and women can perform perfectly well with some members of the opposite sex but not with others.

Many people who talk continually about how much they want intercourse are unconsciously trying to avoid it. Such people may fix on a physical event such as having a baby, a sterilisation operation or the onset of some disability as an excuse to avoid intercourse, sometimes permanently. For women who see sex as being mainly for reproduction, sterilisation can disturb them anyway. Disturbances of body-image also affect sexual performance. Women who have not accepted their vagina as part of their body (usually as a result of sexual suppression, fear of pregnancy, or fear of the penis, induced in childhood) psychologically do not have a vagina. Attempts at intercourse are experienced as being like a knife being pushed through an intact body surface, and they suffer from a condition known as vaginismus. A man who has incorrect or fear-inspiring images of the female body can, unconsciously, think of the vagina as a whirlpool or a mouth with biting teeth. Placing his penis inside it is like putting his head in a lion's mouth, so it is avoided by failing to erect or by ejaculating before entry or soon afterwards.

Avoidance of intercourse.

So the background to sexual problems is very varied and is often very time-consuming to sort out, if only because basic causes are often overlaid with conscious excuses and explanations that first have to be stripped away. Some problems are the direct result of the rearing and training of the individual: the potential problem existed long before that person met his or her partner. It was lying dormant but ready to bloom. In some cases an apparently normal sex life may be sustained for months or even years before a 'sexual breakdown' occurs. This happens because for a time the person's sexual desires exceed his underlying fears and guilts and he can function perfectly well. Once desire wanes even a little all the inhibitory forces take over and the person develops a frank sexual problem. An unhappy example is seen in those women who have been brought up to the 'sex is naughty' view of sexuality. They function well before marriage and enjoy sex but lose orgasmic capacity and interest in sex afterwards, when it is legitimate. In other cases the problem reflects a difficulty within the relationship. Sex itself may be the primary cause of the problem or it may, so to speak, simply be knocked down as a bystander.

Psychological illness, personality factors and problems with religious beliefs may or may not contribute to sexual problems. For example, a person who is prone to excessive anxiety about life generally may or may not be anxious about intercourse: sex can provide a refuge for such people. Conversely, someone who displays low levels of anxiety in the rest of his life can show signs of alarm, muscle tension and sweating as sexual contact becomes imminent. Men and women with personality disorders run the risk of retaliation through a sex problem in the partner. For example, a critical, domineering or excessively maternal woman may come to be seen by her partner as an unpleasant mother figure. In these cases where the 'sex-is-sin' view has been heavily instilled in childhood problems commonly result.

What can be done?

Obviously, from what we have already said, some sexual problems need expert handling just like any other medical or emotional problem. Self-help is the obvious and most common place to start. Discussing the subject can help if the couple are not so far down the tracks that talking is impossible or fruitless, and a good book can give one or both of the partners insight into their problem and can help show them that others have been down the same path and come out on top. At this stage the couple can often get real benefits from returning to courtship, taking the pressure off sexual performance, favouring the non-physical side of their relationship and reading and discussing what they have learned.

If help is needed there are three main sources. Relatively untrained and well-meaning counsellors, professional or not, can help with superficial sexual problems and indeed many people find a satisfactory result in the hands of such counsellors. However, the majority of sexual problems only receive superficial first-aid when treated like this, and such 'cures' may last only for a short time. The two provably useful approaches to sexual problems that now have a track-record worthy of the name are psychosexual therapy and sex therapy. Both need to be practised by the fully trained professionals if they are to be effective, mainly because untrained people dabbling in these areas of people's lives can do damage—often without realising it. Those who think the answers to all sex problems are easy and quick to solve simply do not understand the problems.

Some changes are not easy. Both forms of therapy involve the person making changes to the way he or she behaves or thinks and this is never easy, even for a motivated and intelligent person, partly because of the complexity of the problem and because the partner is necessarily involved. This does not mean that the partner necessarily has to be involved in the actual treatment, but his or her reaction to the problem will undoubtedly affect the situation and the results of the therapy. A doctor can treat one's gall-stones perfectly adequately without ever seeing one's partner. This is just not so with many sex problems, which by definition involve two people.

Psychosexual therapy

This is all about searching for the contributory causes of the problem and then treating it in as precise a way as possible. Such therapy is, of course, highly personal and unique to the individual or couple being treated. Nearly always the unravelling of the problem involves uncovering layer after layer of complexity and is something like solving a detective mystery. As in the practice of medicine generally, making an accurate diagnosis is the key to success, but one difficulty is to assess the importance of the mass of symptoms and material which is produced. Almost anything *could* have contributed to the current sexual problem and, often quite unconsciously, many patients, whilst wanting to be helped, put all kinds of difficulties in the way of establishing the truth. The examples of the underlying causes of sexual problems we have outlined in this chapter are very elementary. They do nothing to show how complex the origin of all sexual problems really is. Frequently there are several contributory causes and these are further affected by interactions with the partner. The sexual problem is often the final symptom produced by a host of varied underlying problems, many of them nothing at all directly to do with sex.

Sex therapy

This is much less concerned with the cause or causes but more with the actual problem itself and what can be done to overcome it. To a psychosexual therapist a sexual problem is simply a symptom of some other underlying difficulty or problem, whilst to the sex therapist it is the main focus of attention. But, although the sex therapist may think that the treatment techniques he or she uses are simply concerned with the problem, they may be successful because they unwittingly and incidentally relieve the underlying problem. So, for example, being instructed by the therapist to masturbate or mutually masturbate can undo old harm by removing guilt and anxiety from the act and thereby making it pleasurable. For this reason some psychosexual therapists 'borrow' the techniques of the sex therapist and incorporate them into their overall treatment plan. Some degree of education, or rather re-education, the relief of anxiety, encouragement and mutual trust are common to both therapies. Both have their successes and failures.

Because sexual and psychosexual problems are often so closely bound up with the person's personality, there are no potions, magic pills or speedy therapies. Almost all sex problems need time, care, trust and confidence between patient and therapist if they are to be at all successfully treated. It is scarcely surprising that Masters and Johnson are as successful as they are—they have patients in their clinic for days and even weeks, which is hardly surprising when one remembers that the original problem probably took years or even decades to germinate.

No potions or magic pills.

How common are sexual problems?

Very little information is available on how commonly sexual problems and difficulties occur, and there is no way of getting accurate figures on the subject. In the USA it is estimated that sexual problems affect half of all marriages at some time or another and one survey in Britain found that 57 per cent of twenty-five-year-olds had some sort of sexual difficulty—yet only 2 per cent had consulted a doctor. Sex problems are far commoner than measles and produce much more heartache, yet they do not get the prominence they deserve in medical training and the provision of services.

In an attempt to find out how common sexual problems were in the USA, 100 volunteer 'normal', happily married, middle-class couples were recently investigated in considerable depth using a questionnaire which was completed separately by the partners. One finding was that 10 per cent of those questioned thought that their marriages were satisfactory, without realising that their partner did not agree. Twelve per cent of the couples had received some kind of marital or sexual counselling during the marriage, but no couples who were currently being treated were included. Over 80 per cent regarded their marriages as being happy or very happy, and nearly 90 per cent said they would marry the same person again. As has been found in a number of other surveys, 10 per cent of the women but only 5 per cent of the men said they would marry someone else if they had their time again.

'Sexual problems' in this survey were defined as being disorders of erection or of ejaculation in men and disorders of arousal or of orgasm in women. 'Sexual difficulties' included such things as: an inability to relax; the partner choosing the wrong time; lack of interest; not enough foreplay; a distaste for sex; different sexual habits and practices; and so on. Each person reported not only their own problems and difficulties but also those they thought were present in their partner. Women, it turned out, know of the existence of problems and difficulties in their men but the men seriously underestimated them in their wives. Of the men, 60 per cent said they had no problems and 50 per cent no difficulties. In contrast, only 37 per cent of the women reported themselves free of problems and only 23 per cent said they had no difficulties. As a result of the greater sexual suppression of girls and women it comes as no surprise that women have more problems than do men, but it is also possible that men are more reluctant to mention or even recognise theirs since their manliness is at stake.

As to the actual problems themselves, the most common by far in men (36 per cent) was ejaculating too quickly. Much less common were problems in maintaining an erection (9 per cent); in getting an erection (7 per cent); and in being unable to ejaculate (4 per cent). Eight per cent of men had more than one problem whereas 63 per cent of the women had more than one. These latter were problems in getting excited (48 per cent); in reaching orgasm (46 per cent); in maintaining excitement (33 per cent); and in being unable to have an orgasm (15 per cent). However, 11 per cent of women complained of reaching orgasm too quickly.

So if all these sexual 'problems' were present in allegedly happily married couples, just think how many problems there must be around.

What can the average couple hope to achieve themselves if they have a sexual problem? The next section of the chapter looks at the main sexual problems with a special emphasis on self-help. Obviously this review is brief but it is a first step, before you take your problem to a professional.

Helping yourself overcome your sex problem

Sex problems in men

Premature ejaculation Sex therapists argue about the definition of premature ejaculation. Some say it is present if a man comes to orgasm in less than thirty seconds and others if orgasm is reached less than two minutes after penetration. Others say five minutes and yet others assert that the problem is present if the man cannot contain himself sufficiently to enable his partner to have an orgasm on at least half of all occasions. Another definition says that it is present if orgasm occurs with ten or fewer thrusts of the penis. Most psychosexual therapists see all this as rather pointless and instead look for psychosexual evidence of a need or wish to avoid intercourse, or intercourse with one particular partner. They also take account of the woman's orgasmic capacity before arriving at the conclusion that the man is a premature ejaculator.

As for causes, sex therapists regard hasty, early acts of intercourse—such as, for example, might occur with prostitutes or when it is feared that parents will return home—as being important, whereas psychosexual therapists concentrate more, for example, on even earlier rushing into masturbation as a result of a desire to get the guilty act over. They would then search for the original, pre-masturbatory causes of such guilt and try to defuse them. A man who ejaculates before he wants to has 'trained' himself to accept orgasm at the earliest possible moment and has no control. Men who feared their first experience of intercourse and rush to orgasm in the same way later may not display the same characteristic in masturbation—they are not guilty about sex generally, just fearful of intercourse. Similarly, marital difficulties may lie behind the problem, especially if it is intermittent. Such differences are important to the psychosexual therapist because, he argues, they need different treatments.

A premature ejaculation is less enjoyable an experience for the man than a 'normal' one. This is probably the result of the underlying anxiety and is why so many inexperienced men suffer from it. As confidence is gained it is usually overcome, especially if the woman is reassuring. A critical woman, however, can easily convert premature ejaculation into impotence simply by helping to build up a type of secondary anxiety in the man. He becomes more anxious and so performs less and less well in an ever descending spiral.

A range of treatments alone or in combination can be used for men with premature ejaculation. Men whose problem stems from the unconscious notion that intercourse is an imposition on a woman (and many women for their own unconscious reasons tend to encourage this view) can be cured simply by listening to their wives giving their psychosexual histories and talking about their masturbation and fantasies. The next step is to apply this information to the run-up to intercourse and foreplay so that the woman is near orgasm before they start having intercourse. This increases the chance (especially if stimulation of her clitoris continues during intercourse) that she will have an orgasm, which in turn increases his confidence.

Fantasies about successful intercourse when the man masturbates help, as does starting to masturbate but stopping when near to orgasm, then starting again, and repeating this cycle so that he becomes able to remain sub-orgasmic for increasing periods of time. Eventually, after several weeks of practice, he will be able to control his rate of coming to orgasm during masturbation and will be able to come off at will once he is sufficiently aroused. The next stage is for his partner to do the same to him, but he has to say when she is to stop for a while. When the couple have worked together for perfect ejaculatory control, the woman can cover the man's penis with body oil, KY jelly or talcum powder and help him get control with the enhanced slippery feelings these substances produce. A further refinement is for her to place her thumb on his frenum (the little vertical ridge on the underside of the tip of the penis), with her index finger on the rim of the opposite side of the penis and her middle finger just below it, and then to squeeze the penis just before orgasm is reached. This reduces the man's erection. After a while stimulation of the penis is started again and the procedure repeated until the man can 'last' for as long as they both want. This training can be successful after just a few sessions in couples in whom the underlying causes of the problem have been detected and explained.

The Squeeze Technique: This specialised form of masturbation carried out by a man's partner is useful in helping the man with premature ejaculation.

Masturbating your partner: Getting your partner's genitals close to yours in this way lets you see what's happening and makes it easy and relaxing to stimulate them.

Other techniques which some men find useful are: avoiding excessive stimulation before penetration; using a sheath; thinking about some non-sexual subject; covering the penis with a mildly anaesthetic ointment or spray; tightening the anus by squeezing the internal muscles; and pushing the penis very deeply into the vagina so that the tip lies in the expanded upper portion, and then making only small movements. Other recommendations are to keep fairly high orgasm rates and to have an orgasm by masturbation before having intercourse.

However, the easiest way of all involves simply a change in attitude. This change is not usually difficult for premature ejaculators to make because it often fits in with the underlying cause of their problem. The man must think of putting his penis in the vagina as being an extension of foreplay. In this way he uses his penis instead of his hands or mouth to stimulate the woman. This gives him the impression of being in emotional and psychological control and he now finds that he can last for as long as he wants or even not ejaculate at all on a particular occasion. If he does want to have an orgasm he can still enjoy intercourse if he has developed the right attitude. By using one or more of the many techniques suggested here, many premature ejaculators can be performing to their perfect satisfaction (and that of their partner) within weeks.

Problems with erection An erection in the presence of a woman is a biological compliment to her but both men who want to have intercourse and those who unconsciously want to avoid it can have problems. Sometimes no erection is possible or it may be insufficiently strong to be of any use for penetration. Some men find their penis becomes very hard during foreplay and then they lose their erection before intercourse starts or soon after insertion. In some cases the man ejaculates whilst his penis is less than fully erect and, because of the poor orgasm resulting, may scarcely know he has done so.

The word impotence is often applied to these problems but this is only partially correct as the term also covers and includes problems with ejaculation too. Probably the word is best dropped from use and, like the female equivalent—'frigid'—should never be bandied around loosely nor used to attack a partner.

Erection problems can have physical causes. More than twenty types of drug, especially antihypertensives, tranquillisers and antidepressants, can cause impotence, as can alcohol and perhaps even excessive cigarette smoking. Diabetes eventually produces impotence in a third or so of affected men, probably by damaging the nerves. Diseases and injuries of the nervous system and diseases of the arteries supplying the pelvic region are also causes of impotence. Disorders of the hypothalamus and the pituitary gland, under-functioning testes and an over-functioning thyroid gland can result in impotence, as can surgery carried out on the bowel or the prostate. However, the fact that any of these conditions is present in an impotent man does not necessarily mean that his impotence is solely, or even mainly, attributable to that cause. Psychosexual or sexual therapy can improve the performance of at least some of these men with this problem.

Erection problems which are only present intermittently, or in which a full, hard erection occurs at some stage in the proceedings, can be, but rarely are, of physical origin (unless they are attributable to intermittent medication with the offending drug). Men who can masturbate satisfactorily and who wake with a hard erection or have one during the night are also unlikely to be impotent as a result of a physical cause. However, the fact that a man has erection problems in both masturbation and intercourse does not prove that the cause is physical; in fact it is commonly a result of depression, sexual despair or high levels of anxiety from previous failures in intercourse which have spilled over into masturbation as well. Such men are usually said to have psychological causes for their impotence, although in older ones the problem may partly be a natural part of ageing.

Inexperienced men.   Erection problems are common in inexperienced men and simply reflect their anxiety about the situation. The problems become more serious when the man reacts badly to the problem, feels his masculinity is being questioned, or develops secondary anxiety and then tries to avoid the 'test' of intercourse. The best thing, of course, is to prevent the problem arising in the first place, by making slow progress towards first intercourse, step by step, so keeping anxiety within controllable limits. This can be seen as a type of courtship behaviour, an important stage of which is mutual masturbation. This accustoms the man to erecting and ejaculating in front of his partner and, provided he learns to masturbate her appropriately, it gives him confidence that he can make her orgasmic before they even attempt intercourse.

At the end of this learning process, which may take weeks, most of the anxiety will have disappeared and the desire for intercourse, other things being equal, is considerable. The problem is that in such cases the woman usually wants to get to the stage of intercourse before the man is really ready. Better sex education for girls could relieve most young men of this problem.

In couples in whom the problem has persisted or for whom it suddenly starts after a period of adequate functioning, the psychosexual and emotional state of both partners needs to be assessed, as do their personalities and the relationship. In some cases the briefest assessment reveals the nature of the problem, which is usually something along the lines given earlier, and leads to a prompt cure. In others it can be much more difficult.

In general, the couple are best advised to avoid intercourse and return to courtship. Where the basic relationship is sound, most couples take to this happily and usually with much more enthusiasm than in their original courtship. A holiday often helps. Encouraging total communication and then giving each other physical pleasure, perhaps using sensual massage, all helps. The man learns, often for the first time, of his partner's real eroticism. Learning how to read her signs of sexual arousal (see page 183) comes as a revelation to many such men. It is also a good idea to introduce more eroticism into your life generally, perhaps including books and films. If a woman is underconfident or prudish about her body, as some are, her partner will have to persuade her to see it from his point of view. In this way he can make her more confident and increase their eroticism. Most men are aroused by watching their partner masturbate and this can be incorporated into foreplay. Very often a couple need to be persuaded to set aside time to tease, undress, explore and investigate each other. Once they have got used to doing it they never look back.

Many man with erection problems fear having an erection because they think that this will lead to their partner expecting, attempting or even demanding intercourse. Once intercourse has been 'prohibited' by a therapist he is free to erect and does so readily. Confidence in his ability to erect can be increased by the woman repeatedly rubbing his penis, stopping, letting the erection subside and then restoring it. The man's attention can be increasingly distracted from the performance of his penis by encouraging him simultaneously to concentrate on giving pleasure to his wife. A penis which is fearfully watched by its owner never erects, just as a watched pot never boils!

When his secondary anxiety and fears have gone and he is more confident about his penis, the man usually (provided any underlying problem has been treated) begins to suggest intercourse or has a try at it. In collusion with the therapist the partner may have been instructed to avoid it. Eventually the man reaches a point where his desires so exceed his fears that he can tolerate his frustration no longer and he 'forces' the woman to have intercourse. At this point the confidence of both partners greatly increases, the man's for obvious reasons and the woman's because she sees herself as desirable and desired. Most partners of men with erection problems consider, at some point, either that their loss of attractiveness is to blame or that the man has another woman. Usually neither is the case.

An understanding on the part of both partners of the nature of the balance between the unconscious forces which promote and oppose sexual functioning is often extraordinarily helpful to those who can grasp its significance and elaborate upon it. In essence treatment consists of increasing the man's instinctual forces and diminishing the strength of the anti-instinctual (culturally imposed) ones.

In some cases a variety of pills and potions will help if the patient thinks they can but none can 'make' him have intercourse. Using Anglo-Saxon words for the couple's sex organs and sexual functioning has an aphrodisiac effect on some men (and women). Sex aids can help (see page 386), as can the woman playing with the scrotum and compressing the base of the penis during intercourse.

Retarded orgasm and an inability to ejaculate Some men suffer from a delay in reaching orgasm and cannot ejaculate with their penis in a vagina. Some can be masturbated or fellated to orgasm by the woman if they withdraw, whereas others cannot be brought to orgasm by a woman at all, by any means, and may not be able to ejaculate if a woman is even in the same room. Some men who are successfully treated for premature ejaculation then suffer from retarded orgasm and vice versa. The majority of the partners of such men are distressed by it. Some women conclude that they have over-stretched their vagina during masturbation or childbirth and this is the explanation.

However, the problem sometimes presents itself indirectly in the form of complaints that the vagina is too large and unstimulating or that the penis, or some portion of it, has lost its sensation. Some men in this group are discovered to compress their penis tightly during masturbation. They have simply mis-trained themselves and now cannot respond without tight penile pressure. Others complain of intense penile pain, which they naturally want to avoid, at orgasm.

Diabetes and various drugs can be the cause in men who complain of a lack of sensation, but more often their ultimate unconscious need is to deny that they are having intercourse. It is only by doing this that they can function at all. Some very religiously inclined men, especially if they are unmarried, suffer in this way. Some, who unconsciously equate genital fluids with excretion, want to avoid soiling the woman and others unconsciously equate the woman with their mother. Their response is not to stop sex with her but not to ejaculate inside her. Others who, it is easily imagined, were rebuked and punished by women—sometimes even older sisters—for genital activity in childhood, are simply afraid to lose control and reach orgasm in the presence of a woman.

Relatively inexperienced men who have this problem say that at some point during intercourse the whole business loses its excitement and that distracting thoughts enter their minds. The explanation is that as their level of pleasure and therefore, to them, sinfulness, rises, so does their anxiety, so reducing the pleasure. Some maintain their erection but have difficulty in having an orgasm, if they have one at all, and others simply lose their erection entirely. This situation is exactly the same as occurs for some women during intercourse—excitement is lost as a result of anxiety. Although most, but not all, men enjoy intercourse more if the woman also moves her pelvis, this activity or what she says can be the distraction which intrudes into the man's mind. It increases his self-awareness and thereby his anxiety about what he is doing by bringing him back to earth, perhaps by interrupting a fantasy or other erotic activity that was increasing his level of excitement.

Fears of VD and pregnancy.
Various fears can cause the same problem, although they may only be vehicles for yet deeper fears. These include a fear of making the woman pregnant, a fear of VD and fears about other men with whom the woman has had intercourse. Thinking about other men may make him jealous or make him worry that her previous lovers were better endowed sexually than he or better lovers.

Treating the underlying cause, together with re-education, a decrease in anxiety, a reduced emphasis on orgasm, and an increase in penile pleasures and eroticism, all with the involvement of the woman, with the aim of increasing the efficiency with which the man responds to her manual or oral stimulation, forms the first stage of treatment. Once the woman can reliably bring the man to orgasm she, without saying anything, can on occasions, when he is near orgasm, quickly get on top of him and thrust rapidly so as to make him ejaculate in her vagina.

Sexual problems in women
The enormous numbers of sexual problems in women as revealed by

the survey we quoted earlier in the chapter suggest that all the clinics and therapists dealing with them are doing no more than scratching at the surface. When one bears in mind that women, in the absence of a deficiency or disease, are biologically endowed with an enormously greater sexual capacity than are men, the enormity of the present situation is impressive and a cause for concern. There are many ways of tackling the problem. The best course, in our view, is prevention, by bringing up children differently. Better sex education for girls from the cradle onwards is becoming an urgent necessity in an age when men are becoming increasingly desperate to perform to their partner's satisfaction and when women have increasing sexual expectations. The discrepancy between what women are capable of and what they can achieve may in itself account for the marked difference between the sexes in the prevalence of emotional illness.

Women would probably perform better if they were able to communicate more to their partners and if men were educated to understand them better.

To say that men suppress women is provably wrong. Their mothers probably suppressed them far more as girls—and much more than they did their brothers. Men often complain that their women undervalue themselves and so underachieve—they tend to see more potential in their women than the women do themselves.

These influences and many others, exert negative influences on female sexuality generally. It could be that human females are designed to be sexually dissatisfied, at least to some degree, so that they have an incentive to have further sexual activity. Human females are, in effect, permanently 'on heat' or in season because humans are capable of rearing their young in any season of the year in which they are born.

Most women seem to be in touch with a deep inner sexuality which they fear because of the consequences which could result if they were really to let go. In fact many sex problems in women are the result of what is called 'reaction-formation' against their own sexuality. They have learned that it is bad to be sexual and then have realised how sexual they are. Thereafter their interests, attitudes, behaviour and pleasures all have to be presented, even to themselves, as the opposite of what they really are.

Re-education can rapidly and dramatically alter this situation, especially if the woman's partner is encouraging. Many women are afraid to be themselves for fear of earning condemnation and this is one reason why bold, self-confident and sexually dominant men, who expect a woman to be very sexual, appeal to so many women. Under-confident, shy and embarrassed partners simply make most, but not all, women feel inhibited as well.

If men were educated to know about and accept female sexuality there would be fewer sex problems in women and any man who does not take the trouble to learn about the sexuality of his partner cannot be said to love her in a meaningful way.

Orgasm problems Any woman who cannot masturbate freely and enjoyably proves that, for one reason or another, she is unable fully to accept her genitals, her sexuality and her right to have pleasure. Sex for her is something a man does *to* her. Some such women claim that they have never ever been at all sexual. They deny ever having experienced sexual arousal, sex dreams or desires. While some say they have always been like this, others trace it back to some event such as the loss of a particular partner, a rape, having a baby and so on. Their genitals are perceived as being totally unpleasurable. Depending on her personality a variety of strategies such as explanation, education, careful history-taking, clinical examination and so on, can be used by a therapist to demonstrate the fallacy of her belief. Starting from her positive thoughts about what might turn her on, however meagre these may be, the therapist then expands her sexual consciousness gradually until she blossoms in a way she never dreamed of. A depressed, drab, under-confident and sexless woman can rapidly become a new person, as suppression, shame, guilt, self-detestation and reaction-formation are lifted. Such a change is often not as welcome to her partner because he may have chosen her *because* she was so inhibited, and her new self puts him in a dilemma. At this point psychosexual therapy may be necessary for them both.

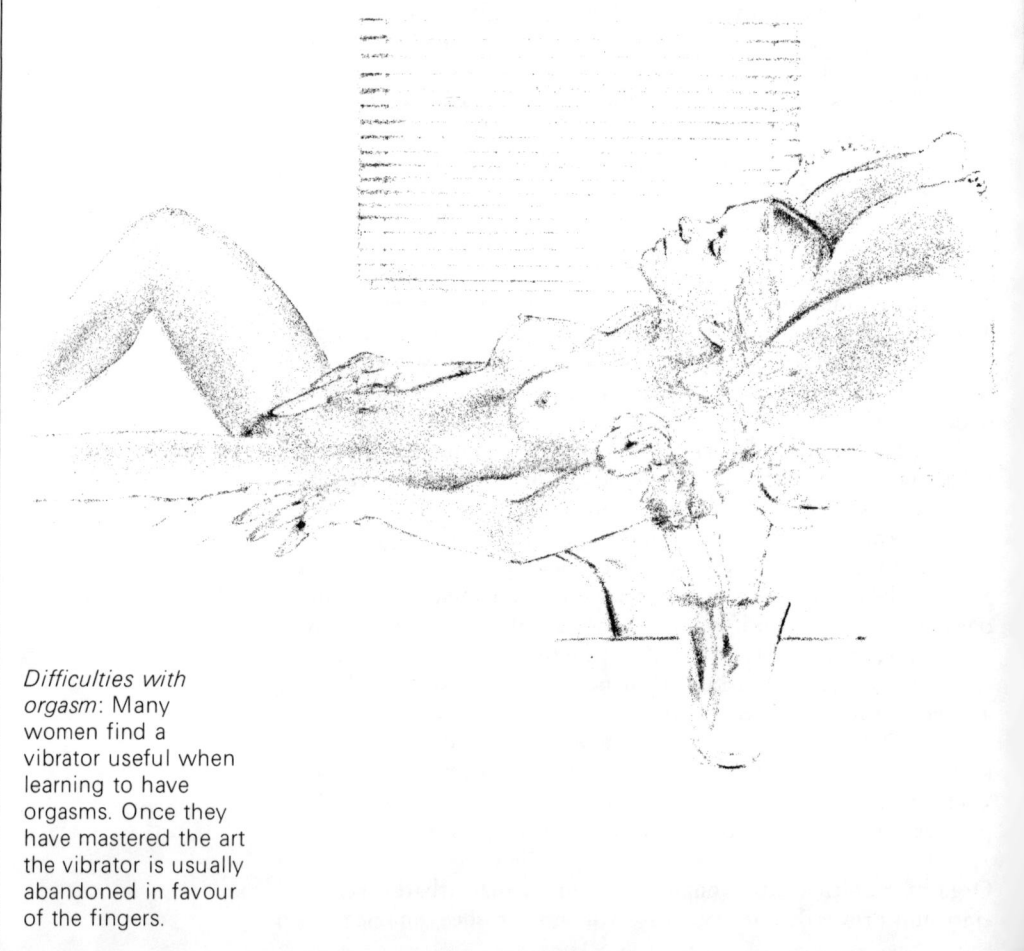

Difficulties with orgasm: Many women find a vibrator useful when learning to have orgasms. Once they have mastered the art the vibrator is usually abandoned in favour of the fingers.

The next step in helping such a woman to masturbate is to establish masturbation using any device, circumstances, fantasy, erotica or movements which appeal to her. When she has achieved masturbation on her own and is confident, she can then demonstrate her ability to her partner who should encourage and help her, perhaps sharing some of his fantasies with her. Gradually he takes over and learns to masturbate her as well as, if not better than, she can herself. He encourages her to masturbate regularly and shows his pleasure at her success. Intercourse, which has usually been quite deliberately stopped during treatment, is resumed with either partner continuing the masturbation of her until she learns to have an orgasm with the penis inside her vagina. The left-lateral position is ideal for this (see page 213).

After this the couple can find the particular positions for intercourse which suit them best whilst being encouraged by their therapist to expand their erotic lives, to experiment, to use whatever sex aids appeal to them and to devise sex games if they want.

In all this it is important for the man to discover or work out as much as he can about the woman's real sexual inclinations and wishes whilst unobtrusively monitoring her sexual responses to a variety of situations. Obviously the above outline is very basic and personal elaborations are endless, but if things go well the man becomes an expert on foreplay *for his partner*, rather than following advice in books, which may work well for other women but not necessarily for her. Since a woman will do almost anything for the man she loves and enjoys earning approval by giving him pleasure, the scene is set for a deeply satisfying sex life for them both.

These techniques are applicable to all the sex problems listed by women in the survey we mentioned earlier. Occasionally, physical illness such as diabetes or any condition which reduces the woman's levels of testosterone can account for some problems and these will need appropriate medical treatment.

Pain on intercourse In the majority of cases the cause of the pain is physical. A woman may have pain or discomfort if she has a vaginal discharge (see page 368); immediately after having a baby; for weeks or months after an episiotomy; for some weeks after a vaginal operation; as a result of internal disorders of her reproductive organs; if intercourse is attempted too quickly, before she is lubricating; after the menopause; and for a host of other reasons. Any persistent pain for which there is no obvious cause should be reported to a doctor. If when intercourse is attempted the muscles surrounding the vaginal entrance go into an involuntary spasm, this is called vaginismus. Some women also suffer from vaginismus because, for example, they do not 'accept' their vagina, or fear the penis or getting pregnant. Latent or actual lesbians may suffer from the same problem when heterosexual intercourse is attempted. Other women experience vaginismus for some time after being raped or after similarly unpleasant sexual experiences.

Treatment, which can be very difficult, consists of persuading the woman to accept vaginal penetration by, for example, fingers (first a doctor's and then her own) at first and then, perhaps, objects of increasing size or a vibrator, ideally helped by her husband. When eventually penile penetration is attempted some women fare best if they control it by being on top of the man whereas others function best underneath or on all fours. If the vagina is well lubricated and the penis inserted slowly and gently, pausing for a moment if any painful spasm results, full penetration can usually be achieved. One technique which sometimes works well when all else fails is to instruct the woman in the voluntary control of her vaginal muscles (we have described this in detail on page 158). When penetration is attempted she contracts them as firmly as she can momentarily, whilst her man pauses. As she relaxes the man pushes his penis in a little further and so on.

Summary

Sexual problems vary from a total lack of interest in sex to its inefficient or unenjoyable expression. In general men express their sexual inefficiency as performance problems and women as sensation problems. The inefficiency may only amount to a slight brake on pleasure but in the end the person's interest usually remains fixed on intercourse. Sex is more in the mind than in their genitals but the central problem is one of sexual inefficiency. Some can overcome their problem and function well if certain conditions, or partners, are available.

For some unfortunate people, the desires never exceed the fears and they never function well, or even at all, with another human being, either heterosexually or homosexually. Sometimes the cause is no more than a belief, in a shy and inhibited person, that there is something unacceptably wrong with their body, such as a small penis or different-sized breasts. In some, the feared defect is not even really there, or it is trivial and is simply being used as an excuse to mask a deeper fear.

Fortunately, more help is available today than ever before and a person with a sex problem can usually find some answers, if not necessarily a complete cure, at a special centre.

Chapter 20
Contraception and planning a family

Contraception literally means 'against conception' and any practice, device or substance which prevents conception is said to be contraceptive. So, clearly, abstaining from intercourse is a means of contraception, as is oral intercourse, anal intercourse, mutual masturbation and, for that matter, homosexuality or any sexual activity that does not involve intercourse between a fertile man and a fertile woman. The practice of sterilisation, in which the tubes delivering the eggs or sperms are interrupted, can be used to make either sex permanently infertile. Avoiding intercourse at and around ovulation, or the man withdrawing his penis from the vagina before he ejaculates, are both contraceptive practices. The use of devices which allow him to ejaculate in the vagina but which prevent the sperms reaching the cervix are also contraceptive. Although abortion is sometimes spoken of as being a form of contraception, it clearly is not and, since it often allows conception to occur, the IUD is probably not really a method of contraception in the strict sense but is included here nevertheless. No one really knows how the IUD forces the lining of the uterus to eject the fertilised egg—it should be considered as a kind of extremely early method of abortion rather than a type of contraception.

We have called this chapter contraception *and* planning a family because the two are rather different. Contraception is by definition simply a way of preventing the conception of a baby, but family planning may well involve the planned spacing of children. Many women attending so-called 'family planning' clinics are not planning a family at all—they are looking for a 100 per cent successful way of not getting pregnant, often for the many fertile years after they've finished having their children.

If words mean anything, and contraception means 'against conception', then any method with a significant rate of failure is clearly not truly contraceptive. We feel this point is worth making because the topic is often discussed as if there were a wide choice of safe (i.e. efficient) methods. This simply is not so.

At this point it is worth mentioning that contraception can be viewed in two main ways. First are the population-control methods, such as prolonged breastfeeding (still the most widely used contraceptive method in the world), the rhythm method and the mucus method. These are fine when used by a section of the population of, say, Third World countries when the aim is a reasonable fall in the birth rate which is what such countries need and want. However, they are not really suitable for an individual woman who wants to be *sure* she does not conceive. The second group of methods are the 'personal' contraceptive methods. These are the well-known ones that are commonly used by women in the West who want to be sure that they will not get pregnant unless they specifically choose to.

If a couple want to avoid conception but also want to have intercourse freely, the method they use should ideally be 100 per cent effective. To some extent the method they choose will depend on the woman's age since most women are increasingly less fertile after thirty or so.

Maximum fertility in Western women is between twenty and twenty-four. For the first year or two after a girl starts having periods she is relatively infertile because most of her cycles do not result in an egg being produced, but it is not advisable to rely on this 'juvenile sterility'. Only the most effective contraceptive methods should be used if a girl of this age is having intercourse. For the older woman a less efficient method can be used yet still be highly effective because her fertility is less high.

As well as being efficient, the 'ideal' contraceptive method needs to be acceptable and simple. A 100 per cent efficient method which is so complex that only 10 per cent of the population are intelligent enough to use it properly is only 10 per cent effective. Similarly, a 100 per cent efficient method which is unacceptable to 90 per cent of the population because of, for example, religious reasons, medical fears, messiness, or interference with sexual pleasure, is again only 10 per cent effective.

So obviously the effectiveness of any particular method is influenced by many things apart from its actual efficiency as a method. For this reason effectiveness is measured as the number of pregnancies arising in a population of 100 women using any particular method for a year. So, if five pregnancies occur amongst 1000 women who use a particular method for two years, its effectiveness is 0.25 pregnancies per 100 woman-years. Put another way, it means that an average woman could expect one pregnancy every four centuries if she used the method. Sometimes, especially in trials of the pill, the number of twenty-eight-day cycles is counted instead.

However effective any given contraceptive method is in theory, it is only as reliable as the person using it. A major and powerful influence affecting personal efficiency in the practice of contraception is motivation. The essential point to grasp here is that unconscious factors can so easily alter a person's conscious intentions. Many so-called 'method failures' in which the individual woman claims to have used the method conscientiously but nevertheless has become pregnant, are probably caused by unconscious deliberate intent. The topic is a large but often ignored one and it is only possible to give a few examples here.

The young are particularly likely to be victims because, although they may consciously believe that they are free from guilt about intercourse, unconsciously they are still strongly influenced by the moral teaching of our culture instilled into them in their childhood. A sexually inexperienced girl may say to herself, out of guilt, after each time she has intercourse, that she is not going to do it again until she is married, so there is no need to go to a doctor or a clinic to get a safe method of contraception. Indeed, to take such a step, she may well think, will only encourage her to 'sin' again. This accounts for the apparent paradox of the young girl who will not use contraception until she is 'going steady'. The point is that she has been taught that sex is only justified if you love a man. So before that blessed state arrives she is constantly trying—and failing—to avoid sex by avoiding contraception. It is because of this that many girls reared with excessive and unreasonable moral restraints are among those most likely to have unwanted pregnancies. Such girls often deny to themselves, as much as to others, that they have sexual desires, and so they, unlike girls who can accept their sexuality, never prepare for sex. The all too obvious point that only those who thoroughly accept their sexuality have any hope of controlling it is largely overlooked, both in child rearing and sex education, especially as far as girls are concerned.

Contraception and 'going steady'.

Along the same lines, a boy who, for example, doubts his fertility, perhaps because of earlier mumps orchitis (inflammation of the testes) or because he fears his penis is too small, may consciously intend to use the withdrawal method but, because of his unconscious desire to prove himself, is slow in doing so in the unconscious hope that the girl will become pregnant.

One of the first things that girls are told about their sexuality in our culture is that they will grow up and one day have babies like mommy. The strong unconscious notion is thus implanted—and later greatly reinforced—that sex is for babies. From this it is a short step to believing that sex other than for babies is sin and pregnancy is the punishment. This view lurks behind much anti-abortion propaganda.

The consequences of all this for contraception and family planning are enormous. Some women cannot enjoy sex unless there is a chance of pregnancy. This leads to contraceptive fecklessness such as stopping the pill on the most trivial of excuses. Often actions like this are rationalised on the grounds of medical fears, or the fears of fatness, for example, but the real underlying fear is that of sin; the woman has not fully accepted her right to sexual pleasure although at a conscious level she may regard herself as completely uninhibited. Eventually her fear of pregnancy will drive her back to the pill, but she will be vaguely unhappy and may even say her sex drive or her ability to achieve orgasm has gone. In this way she writes off the only 100 per cent effective method and her unconscious desires will have been fulfilled. Other consequences are that such a woman will unconsciously see a pregnancy as punishment, and accept it, even though it does not fit into her plan for her family; for the same unconscious reasons (i.e. needing a possibility of pregnancy) a woman may lose all pleasure in sex after she has been sterilised or reaches the menopause.

Other unconscious motives for frustrating contraception whilst consciously trying to 'contracept' are: to escape from a work situation; to punish parents; to provide a dependent baby who will *really* love her (she thinks that no one has *ever* really loved her); to give her partner something to worry about; to compete with a sister or a friend or colleague; to prove her fertility (many women fear that small breasts, scanty periods, a previous abortion or using the pill have impaired it); and so on. When having intercourse with a man they particularly admire some women are contraceptively slack because they feel it will not matter if they became pregnant because any baby by him would be likely to possess the admired features which she lacks.

Contraception and childhood ideas.

All this leads us to the conclusion that effective contraception starts with sensible child rearing in respect of sex. Beyond that, and provided that the underlying attitudes are satisfactory, then it is true to say that the only true contraceptive we possess at the moment is the pill (oral contraception). It is the only method which approaches total efficiency. Unfortunately, recent evidence has found that there are real, if small, health hazards in women over thirty-five who use the pill and are fat, have high blood pressure or smoke, so this makes it only suitable up until this age. After thirty-five it is probably best for women to use a progestogen-only pill (the so-called 'mini' pill; it is the oestrogens in the pill that are mainly suspected of causing the problems in older women) or another method. Let us now look at the main types of contraceptive.

The pill

In its commonest and most effective form the pill contains the synthetically produced female hormones, oestrogen and progesterone. Because these two are combined in the one pill it is called the 'combined pill'. The hormones these pills contain are very similar to the natural ones produced by a woman's body but are different enough to allow absorption from the stomach and intestines. Natural hormones would not be absorbed if taken by mouth. The pill's constituents are, after absorption, so similar to the natural hormones that they influence chemo-receptors (specialised monitors of blood hormone levels) at the base of the brain in the same way as natural hormones. If they were not identical or nearly so they would not work because chemo-receptors are so specific. Because of this it is not quite right to think of them as totally alien chemicals, which is how they are sometimes represented. The reason the pill works so well is that it copies Nature. Its effect is to convince the pituitary gland that a pregnancy has already occurred and in this state the pituitary suppresses the release of the hormones which normally make the ovaries release an egg each month. It is a form of false pregnancy.

It sometimes happens that whilst a woman is on the pill an egg *is* produced, but conception still does not occur because one effect of the progesterone in the pill is to make the mucus in the passage through the cervix so thick that no sperms can penetrate it. A further effect of the combined pill is to prevent the development of the lining of the uterus, the endometrium, so that even if conception were to occur the embryo could not implant and grow there. Although there have been tremendous advances in oral contraception some improvement is still possible. Pill manufacturers are always trying to improve the

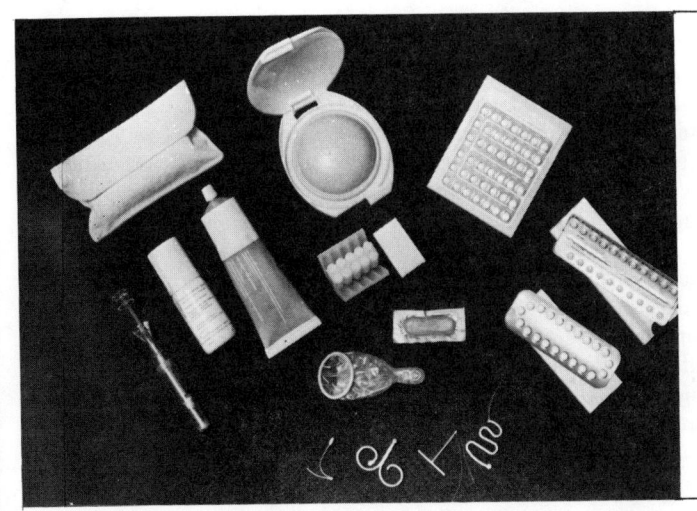

CONTRACEPTION AND PLANNING A FAMILY

Reliability of various contraceptive methods

Combined pill . . . 100%
Mini pill . . . 98%
IUD . . . 96–98%
Diaphragm plus spermicide . . . 97%
Condom (sheath) plus spermicide . . . 97%
Safe period (using temperature and cervical mucus combined) . . . 85%–93%
Sterilisation . . . 100%

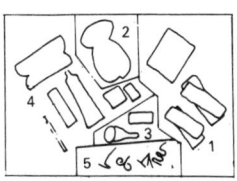

Some of the more popularly used contraceptives: 1 pills, 2 diaphragm, 3 sheath, 4 pessaries, foams and gels, 5 IUDs.

specificity of the pill so that it acts where it is most needed in the hormonal cycle.

Several varieties of the combined pill are available and those women who are not quite in hormonal balance can benefit by having one particular formulation as against others. For the majority, though, a pill containing around thirty millionths of a gram of oestrogen and around 150 millionths of a gram of progesterone is suitable and highly effective, and produces very few side-effects.

One pill a day is usually taken for twenty-one days and then there is a seven-day break to allow 'withdrawal bleeding' to occur. This happens two to four days after the pill is stopped. Withdrawal bleeding proves to the woman that she is not pregnant and mimics a normal period, but it is not in fact a true period and a few women choose to go for several months on the pill continuously, only rarely having a withdrawal bleed. If you decide to do this it is probably safest to allow a withdrawal bleed to occur about every three or four months.

Withdrawal bleeding has advantages over a normal period in that it is predictable, is less in quantity (and so does not make the woman anaemic) and is usually painless. Premenstrual tension rarely occurs.

The pill's constituents are broken down by the body over twenty-four to thirty-six hours and are excreted via the urine and stools. Some women metabolise the pill more rapidly and so need higher doses. Others who are on certain drugs such as anti-tubercular, anti-epileptic or anti-fungal drugs and antibiotics also metabolise the pill more rapidly. This could mean that they need a higher-dose pill to be safe. If these women are on a normal-dose pill, it, so to speak, 'runs out' before the next one is due. Women who, perhaps for the psychological reasons mentioned earlier, 'forget' the pill or who are very late taking it are also exposed to the pill running out. In all of these cases the sign to go by is the spotting of blood or even a full withdrawal bleed. If a pill has only been taken, say, six hours late, spotting is not inevitable, but if it does occur it happens two or three days later. In other words it is a 'mini' withdrawal bleed. The reason why a full bleed does not occur as a rule is that the woman continues to take the pill. The correct reaction to repeated spotting or withdrawal bleeding at unexpected times, provided it is not caused by interference from other drugs, is *not* to change the pill you are on, as many doctors and clinics suggest, but rather to be scrupulous in taking it within, say, an hour of when it is due.

The pill is a very safe and efficient contraceptive but problems can and do sometimes occur. Problems mostly arise in those who are found on psychosexual investigation to have unconscious difficulties about accepting their sexuality, as we mentioned earlier. These should be cleared up before a change in method is seriously considered, simply because all other methods are less efficient. Depression, irritability and bad dreams can be due to unconscious self-detestation for pill-taking and depression often results in a loss of sex drive, a failure to have orgasms, and over-eating, leading to the marked weight gain sometimes reported on the pill. This is not to say that *all* pill symptoms are emotional or psychological but many are and can be prevented or cured by psychosexual counselling alone. It is interesting that studies in which women who have been given a placebo yet were told it was the pill had pill-like symptoms which went on until they stopped taking the tablets! Although it is disputed, some evidence suggests that the pill is actually medically beneficial, for example, in reducing the occurrence of lumps in the breasts and in reducing the risk of cancer of the ovary and the lining of the womb (endometrium). There is no indisputable evidence that the pill permanently impairs fertility or damages future babies.

Obviously careful medical supervision is advisable because this ensures correct usage, is reassuring for the woman, provides an opportunity to disentangle psychosexual factors which may greatly benefit the patient and her partner in other ways, and provides a basis for regular health checks. Most of the things which are wrong when doctors carry out routine pill checks are nothing to do with the oral contraceptive.

Unless there is some medical reason to the contrary, such as recent jaundice or a history of thrombosis (blood clots), the pill is undoubtedly the best contraceptive for women in the highly fertile years of their lives.

For years there has been talk of a male pill but there are considerable technical problems and even more psychological ones because it is still a fact that most men are keener to see their partners take the responsibility for contraception than they are to do so themselves. Technically, too, the male pill presents more problems, because a man produces millions of sperm per ejaculate as against a woman's single egg per month.

Sterilisation

Next to the pill in efficiency is sterilisation. One could be forgiven for thinking that sterilisation should be 100 per cent effective since it involves an operation. However this is not so because there is a measurable failure rate for the operation for both men and women. This is caused by poor operative technique and not because the method itself is at fault. Overall, sterilisations fail in less than 1 per cent of cases but, of course, one partner being sterile does not prevent the unsterilised one from being involved in a pregnancy with a third person.

Male sterilisation can be achieved by removing the man's testes or by damaging them with large doses of oestrogen or X-rays. None of these is a common procedure. The method used in common practice is to sever the vasa deferentia (the two tubes which deliver sperms from the testes to the prostate). The operation is known as a vasectomy.

Female sterilisation

Almost all sterilisation procedures in women involve doing something to the fallopian tubes down which eggs travel from the ovaries to the uterus. These fine tubular structures, one in each side of the pelvis, are so delicate that their cavities are no wider than a bristle from a brush. The traditional sterilisation operation involves cutting these tubes. Through a small abdominal incision made under an anaesthetic, the surgeon takes each fallopian tube, ties it in two places and cuts out a section about two to three centimetres long between the two ties. The skin incision is closed as usual and the patient is discharged home in two or three days.

A second type of sterilisation procedure involves the use of a laparoscope. This is an instrument that is inserted through a one-centimetre-long incision in the abdominal wall just below the navel. The instrument has a telescope and light which enables the surgeon to look directly into the abdominal cavity and also has a tubular cavity down which fine instruments can be threaded so that operations can be performed inside the abdomen without opening it up. Laparoscopic sterilisation is simple, safe and quick but is highly skilful and needs an experienced operator if it is to be done well. It rarely involves more than one night in hospital, if that. The technique is performed as follows.

The laparoscope is inserted, together with a fine instrument to enable the surgeon to grip the fallopian tube. An electric current then fuses the tissues into a solid mass, so closing off the tube completely. The procedure is then repeated on the other side. It is quick and almost totally safe. The only problems are that women who have had bowel operations before may not be suitable (because old scar tissue makes the procedure technically difficult to perform) and that fat women may also be difficult to laparoscope.

About one third of women report that they are unaware that anything has been done; about a third have period-type pains but can carry on as normal; and the remaining third take a couple of days off to recover.

Other common sterilisation procedures carried out under laparoscopic control involve the placing of tiny elastic bands or plastic clips on the fallopian tubes. This is quick and simple and means only one night in hospital.

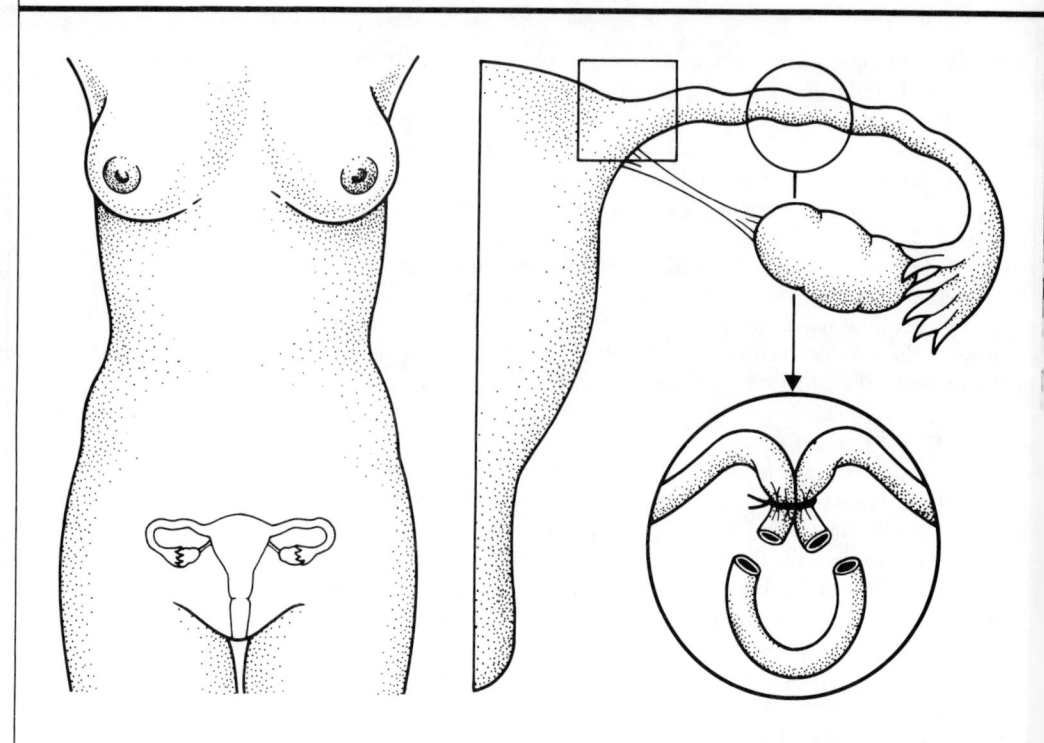

Diagrammatic representation of one form of female sterilisation: In the diagram on the right the fallopian tube on one side has been severed and tied.

Some women consider the desirability of sterilisation and give permission well in advance of the birth of their baby so that if a Caesarean section becomes necessary, they can be sterilised at the same time. This should not, however, be a last-minute decision taken by a couple when they hear a Caesarean section might be necessary. Research shows that women who undergo sterilisation immediately after the birth of a baby or after an abortion are more likely to regret it later than those who have made a more considered decision.

Once a woman has been sterilised (other than by laparoscopy) she will be home again within two to three days and there are no changes in her menstrual cycle or her sexual functioning except, of course, that she cannot conceive. The egg she produces each month is reabsorbed by the body just as a man's body reabsorbs his sperms after a vasectomy. Some women are very upset at the thought that they can no longer conceive but most are happier than before because they no longer need bother with contraception. Because of this, some couples' sex lives are greatly improved as a result of sterilisation.

At present, sterilisation is best thought of as being virtually irreversible. Many researchers are working on reversal and reversible procedures but the task is technically very difficult because the fallopian tubes are so tiny and the operation to sew up the ends involves operating under microscopes and using stitches little thicker than a human hair.

The placing of clips or elastic bands on the fallopian tubes damages a much smaller length of tube and so may improve the chances of reversal if the woman decides she wants more children. Younger women seem to regret having been sterilised, a fact which is causing concern among gynaecologists because the age at which women are being sterilised (currently thirty-two to thirty-six) is falling.

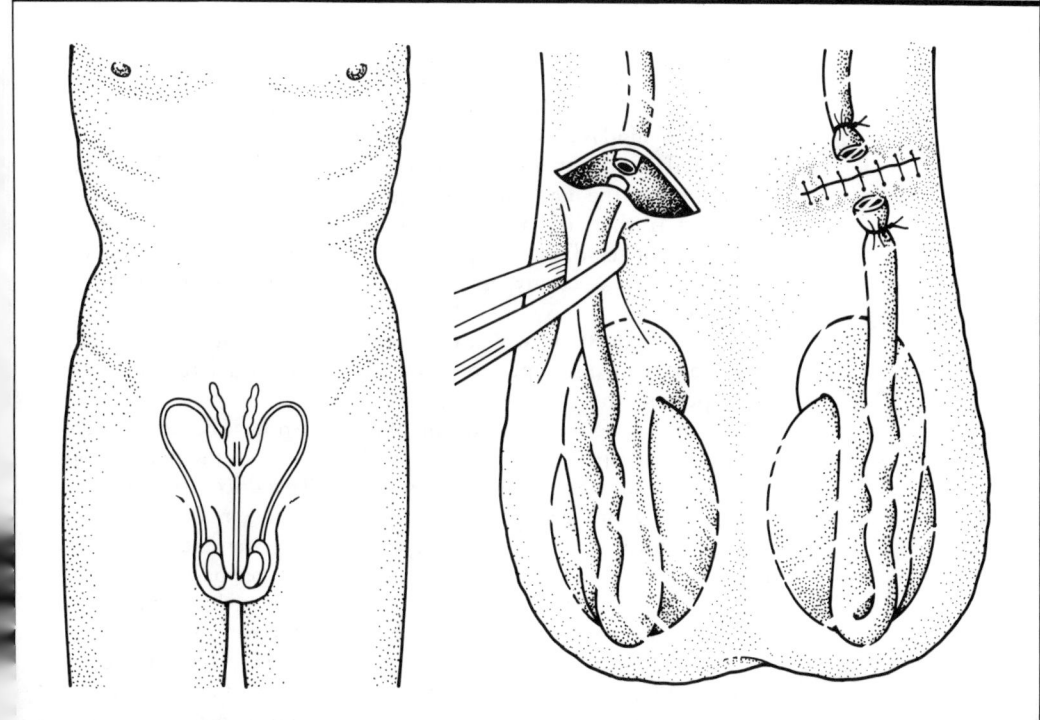

A poor marriage is a bad reason for seeking sterilisation, especially now that divorce is so common. As many as one in seven women bitterly regret having been sterilised.

Male sterilisation

As we have already seen, the vast majority of men who choose to be sterilised have a vasectomy. A vasectomy is an operation in which the sperm-carrying duct (vas deferens) is cut and tied off on each side as a means of permanent sterilisation.

Increasing numbers of men are concerned that their wives should not have to bear the burden of long-term contraception and find the sheath cumbersome or unsatisfactory in other ways. For such men a vasectomy is a very good operation. Like the female forms of sterilisation, though, it must be thought of as irreversible and so deserves very careful consideration by both partners before action is taken.

A vasectomy is a simple and quick operation, usually performed as an out-patient. There is no special preparation necessary but a little shaving either side of the top of the scrotum is often suggested.

After thoroughly cleaning and disinfecting the area around the scrotum, the surgeon injects a small amount of local anaesthetic into the areas where he will make his incisions. These incisions are small (about one centimetre long) and are made about five centimetres above the testes, where the root of the scrotum joins the lower

Diagrammatic representation of vasectomy: The diagram on the left shows the spermatic pathways in a man and on the right the point at which the vas deferens is severed and tied.

abdomen. The vas is very superficial and easily found. It looks like a thick piece of yellowish string. The surgeon ties the vas in two places and cuts out a piece about a centimetre long. Any bleeding is stopped and the wound is closed with two small stitches. The procedure is then repeated for the other vas. Both sides together only take about twenty minutes and the man can go straight home but has to wear a scrotal support (rather like a jock strap) and avoid lifting and strenuous exercise for ten days. It is probably sensible to have a day off work following a vasectomy but after this everything should be back to normal.

To understand why a vasectomy works we need to look at the male anatomy (see page 150). Obviously if the vasa deferentia are tied off sperms cannot get to the penis.

In a vasectomy, the cutting of the transport tubes from testes to penis means sperms are trapped in the testes and the man becomes sterile. A man who has had a vasectomy still produces sperms as usual but they cannot get out—they dissolve and are reabsorbed by the body. However, unlike women, who become sterile as soon as the fallopian tubes are cut (because no eggs can get past the block), a vasectomised man can be fertile for weeks or months simply because he has some sperms 'in store' in his reproductive tract.

Complications after the operation are very few indeed. Any pain can be controlled with simple painkillers and any bruising will soon disappear. Very rarely a large bruise can form in the scrotum and some men complain of pain at the vasectomy site.

As with any kind of sterilisation procedure, the most crucial question is—does it prevent pregnancies? As we have seen, the answer is not as simple as in the case of women. Because a man can remain fertile for so long after the operation, two or more sperm counts are carried out between eight and sixteen weeks afterwards. The man supplies a specimen of semen which is examined microscopically for sperm activity. During this four-month period, the man (or his partner) has to use an alternative method of contraception. Once the hospital has given the go-ahead, these other methods can be abandoned and the man can be sure that he is not fertile.

Conception can still occur.

Most men are concerned about their sexual potency and those who undergo vasectomy are no exception! One of the commonest questions men ask is, 'Will it affect my sex life?' Unfortunately the answer is not simple. Many surveys have been done on the subject and they seem to show basically the same thing—that men whose sex lives were satisfactory before the operation rarely have problems but those who had difficulties before may have problems after. There is nothing physically damaging to a man's sex organs about a vasectomy: a simple tube that carries sperms is cut and none of the erection-producing mechanisms are touched. So if a man becomes impotent after a vasectomy it must be for psychological reasons and not physical ones.

When it comes to reversal, things are not so good, although in the best centres success rates of 50 per cent are claimed. Numerous studies have been and are being done to try to devise a truly reversible vasectomy. Some researchers have even worked on a small, magnetically operated tap that the man could switch 'on' and 'off' by placing a magnet over the tiny equipment in his vas deferens. Sewing the small-bore vas tubes back together again is very difficult technically and anyway a proportion of men whose 'plumbing' is put back to normal again still do not produce fertile sperms. It is thought that this is because they have produced antibodies to their own sperms.

A vasectomy is a very safe and effective sterilisation procedure, but should only be carried out in men with normal sexual histories and currently satisfactory sex lives, and must be considered to be permanent.

Much less research has been carried out on sterilisation than on the pill, mainly because there are no pharmaceutical companies backing sterilisation as a method of contraception. However, several studies are under way in which men who have had a vasectomy are being followed up to see whether any rare or long-term effects occur.

IUD (intra-uterine device; coil; loop)

Although it has its fans the IUD is less satisfactory than the pill, especially in young women who have not yet had a baby. The method probably works by dislodging any embryo which arrives in the uterus. Because of this it is really a type of early abortion—not a method of preventing conception.

The insertion of an intra-uterine contraceptive device (coil, loop, IUD) is, in good hands, a simple and usually trouble-free procedure. There is no space in a book such as this to go into the advantages of the coil as a means of contraception; suffice it to say that for many women it is an ideal alternative to the pill. It is especially suitable for women who have had families and do not want any more children.

There are basically two types of coil—the first generation of simple, inert, plastic devices and the second generation of devices that are either coated in copper (the copper-7 for example) or impregnated with hormones. The insertion method is much the same no matter which device is used.

An intra-uterine contraceptive device should only ever be inserted by a trained person because putting something into the uterus is a skilled, though simple, operation. An experienced operator will also know how to get the woman to relax, which is very important if the procedure is to be successful. The woman is placed on a couch with her legs up in stirrups, or lying on her side, and the vagina is swabbed with a mild antiseptic. The doctor does a vaginal examination to ascertain that everything is normal, and inserts a speculum so that he or she can see the cervix (the opening to the uterus). He or she then inserts an introducer, from which the IUD will pass into the uterus. This introducer is very narrow and does not stretch the cervix nearly as much as does a D and C, for example. Most women do not need any local anaesthetic around the cervix, but if the procedure does cause pain it can perfectly well be given.

Once the introducer is in position the plunger on the end is pushed. This discharges the coil from the end of the introducer into the cavity. The natural elasticity of the IUD springs it open and keeps it in the uterus. The introducer is withdrawn gently and the string or the protruding 'tail' of the device cut to the right length. There has to be a tail or string protruding from the cervix into the vagina to allow the device to be removed easily. The introducer and the speculum are removed from the vagina and the procedure is over.

Bleeding, mainly in the form of heavy or prolonged periods, is the main after-effect of the coil. Sometimes bleeding even occurs between periods. Nearly one in ten of all coil users have to have it removed in the first year for this reason alone. Prolonged bleeding can be caused by too big a device or by the right device slipping out of position. Unfortunately, some women have to have several devices fitted before, by trial and error, they find one that suits them.

Bleeding and the coil. Recent research has shown that the copper-containing devices cause less bleeding than the larger devices. If bleeding persists and the woman is very keen to carry on with an IUD, drugs can be taken to stop the flow. This, however, negates one of the main reasons for having a coil—*not* going on long-term medication. The newer hormone-impregnated IUDs do not seem to produce as much bleeding, but here again the body is absorbing small doses of hormones over a long time and some women do not like the thought of this.

The coil is especially suitable for women whose cervix has been enlarged by giving birth, but today there are coils that can be inserted through the relatively tighter cervix of women who have had no children. Pain may be a greater feature among these women and they may indeed expel the device altogether. If this happens, it is probably better to use another method of contraception until after the first baby. Most women feel some period-type pains after the insertion of an IUD but this is usually easily cured with simple painkillers.

The most unwanted side-effect of all is, of course, another pregnancy—so how does the coil perform? The Lippes loop (one of the simple plastic types) has a pregnancy rate of two or three pregnancies per 100 woman-years and the copper-7 a rate of 0.7–2.2 per 100 woman-years but these may be underestimates if expulsion rates are included. As a figure of 2.4 per 100 woman-years can be obtained with a condom and spermicide (properly used) one could be forgiven for thinking that the coil has nothing to be said for it, but this is not so. IUDs have the advantage that once they are satisfactorily in position they can be forgotten (which cannot be said for condoms and spermicides). Having said this, though, any woman using an IUD must realise that it is possible to get pregnant with it in place or because it has accidentally been expelled unknown to her. Some women use spermicides as well, as a safety measure, and it is always a good idea to feel inside the vagina every month after your period to check that the tail or string of the device is still there.

IUDs are still in their relatively early days, so the long-term effects of irritation of the lining of the uterus for several years are still unknown. Studies looking for increased cancer rates have as yet proved negative. When a pregnancy occurs with an IUD in place there is a greatly increased chance of spontaneous miscarriage, though it is possible to remove or retain the device without damaging the foetus. With more and more chemical-impregnated devices coming on to the market it makes sense to ask how these might affect the foetus, but at the moment no evidence points to abnormal babies being born to coil-users.

There are a few serious complications that can occur with the coil. First, because of poor insertion techniques the device may inadvertently be pushed right through the uterine wall and into the abdominal cavity. This is obviously undesirable and the device has to be removed in an open abdominal operation or using laparoscopy. Second, in the presence of an IUD, a pregnancy may occur in the fallopian tubes that lead from the ovaries to the uterus. If you ever suspect that you are pregnant with an IUD see your doctor *at once*. Lastly, infection can occur in the uterus or fallopian tubes in a coil-wearer. This is somewhat uncommon but if you have a history of pelvic infection you should tell your doctor—he or she will not then put a coil in in the first place. IUDs themselves probably do not produce infection but they may activate old infections. Either way sterility can be the result.

Chemical and barrier methods

Various substances kill sperms and, if put into the vagina before intercourse, reduce the chances of conception. Vaginal foams and pessaries are probably the most effective but any of the chemical methods can cause irritation. A possible advantage of these methods is that as well as killing sperms they may kill gonococci—the germs that cause gonorrhoea. A possible disadvantage is that there is some evidence that the chances of foetal deformity, if a pregnancy should occur, are increased.

The effectiveness of such chemical methods is increased by using them along with a barrier method, such as a condom (sheath, rubber, protective) or a cervical cap (diaphragm), all of which are intended to prevent the sperms reaching the cervix.

The correct-sized cap has to be selected and instructions for its use given by a clinic or general practitioner. Although inserting it takes a little getting used to, once the woman has the knack it can be in place in half a minute. Its efficiency, used along with a spermicide, can be as good as two to three pregnancies per 100 woman-years, but in practice its effectiveness is often a good deal less. Some couples find a diaphragm robs intercourse of its spontaneity but many, especially those who are having intercourse fairly infrequently, or are on the downhill slope of their fertility, find it ideal because it is safe, easy to use and has none of the male loss-of-sensation problems associated with using a sheath. Loss of spontaneity can easily be overcome simply by putting it in place every night as a part of the bedtime ritual. It is important not to forget that it is there and leave it in for days or an unpleasant-smelling infection can occur. Research is being under-

CONTRACEPTION AND PLANNING A FAMILY

The use of a sheath: Used carefully, a sheath can be a very safe method of contraception.
1) Squeeze air out of teat and apply sheath to penis after placing a few drops of spermicide inside.
2) Unroll the sheath along the length of the penis (3) using other hand to ease it back towards the head of the penis.
4) When the sheath is on completely it should be totally unrolled and the packing rings should still be visible.
5) Withdraw shortly after orgasm keeping a finger or two on the base of the sheath as you withdraw.

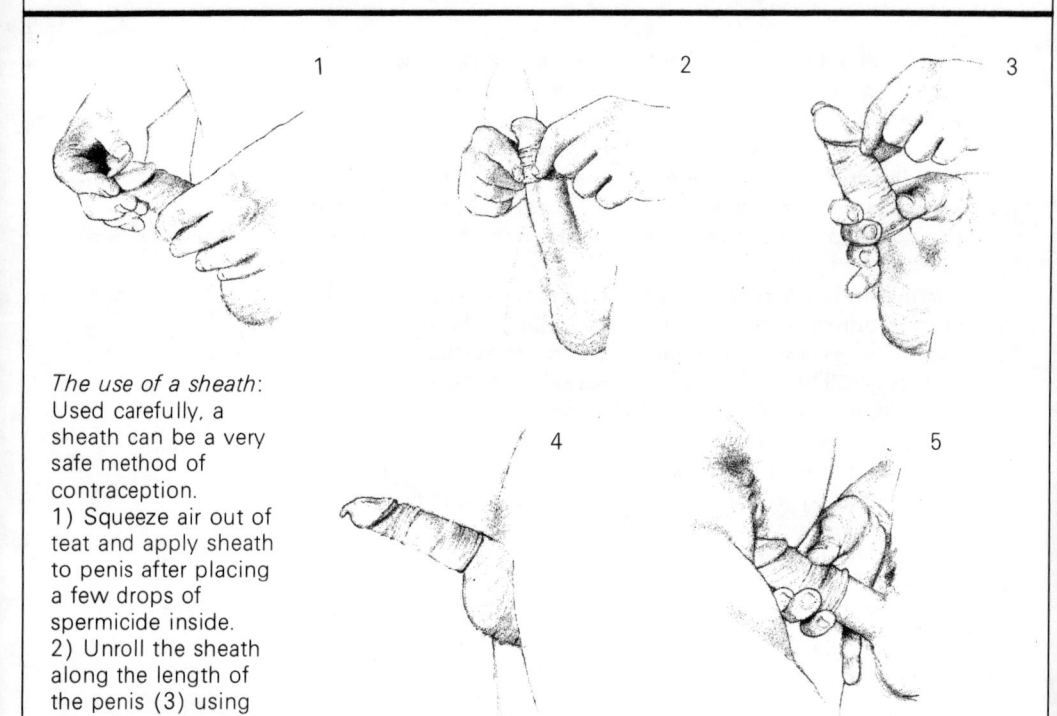

taken to try to improve the method but it is unlikely ever to rival the pill for efficiency.

The sheath can also be very efficient, especially if a teat model is used and a little spermicide placed inside. In practice its effectiveness is considerably reduced because so many people put it on wrongly (see above for the correct way). Quite a lot of men also fail to withdraw shortly after ejaculation, and as their penis shrinks the sheath comes off and semen leaks out. Its great merit is that it very considerably reduces the spread of VD, especially if it is worn for the whole sexual encounter. This makes it the ideal contraceptive for use in casual sex situations regardless of whether another contraceptive is also being used. Many women dislike condoms because they say their use is 'unloving' but some who have a fear of semen can enjoy intercourse more if one is used. Men often complain of a lack of sensitivity when using condoms, but for some this can be an advantage—the speed at which they get to ejaculation is lessened, allowing a better performance.

Provided it is used sensibly and conscientiously the condom is probably the best alternative to oral contraception, especially for the young. If a woman puts it on her partner, this in itself can become part of foreplay.

Natural methods

By 'natural' we mean the absence of pills, potions and devices, and several methods are available. They are all best regarded as inefficient for the woman who is determined not to get pregnant, but they are useful for population control or for the couple who is not too worried about having another baby. A simple method is for the *man not to ejaculate*. Provided the woman knows this is his intention she can still enjoy intercourse and have an orgasm. The method suits many older men who enjoy vaginal stimulation of the penis but do not necessarily want to ejaculate on every occasion they are aroused. Once the man has made up his mind to use this method it is easy to master if he is determined. It can allow intercourse to continue for as long as the woman wants and it makes it possible for the man to have intercourse more often. On occasions when he does want to ejaculate, of course, contraception must be used if his partner is still fertile.

Having said all this it must be remembered that there are sperms present in the pre-ejaculatory fluid (the few drops of liquid that emerge from the tip of the penis before a man comes off) and that this might, rarely, get a woman pregnant. Because of this, this method is fraught with danger for a fertile couple.

Withdrawal

This is a simple method but it can be frustrated by either partner. The man withdraws his penis during the interval between his orgasm setting in and ejaculation starting. Since his instinct at this time is to thrust his penis deep into the vagina he may fail to withdraw in time. As the first few spurts of semen contain most of the sperms this is potentially dangerous. Some women so much hate the thought of withdrawal that they try to prevent it in the heat of the moment. Again, this is a very unsafe method and can be emotionally unpleasant for the couple.

The rhythm method

This essentially consists of trying to predict when ovulation occurs from a study of the woman's menstrual cycle. To do this properly she has to have an accurate record of her periods over the preceding year. Only then can she see a reliable time pattern. Going by what has happened over a few months is simply not accurate enough. The first day of the cycle is taken as being the day menstruation starts and the last day is the day menstruation next commences. The life of the egg is thought to be one to two days (although it may be as short as twelve hours) and that of the sperms in the tubes two to three days. Adding a day either side for safety means that intercourse has to be avoided for seven days around ovulation. This means that you cannot have intercourse between the eighteenth and eleventh days before your next period starts. To allow for variations in cycle length, the first unsafe day is calculated by deducting eighteen from the number of days in the shortest cycle in the last twelve months. The last unsafe day is found by deducting eleven from the number of days in the longest cycle. After every cycle the numbers should be worked out again so as to cover the last twelve cycles. This is important because very few women are regular as clockwork and many things, such as stress and illness, can alter cycle length. If you work on the assumption that your cycle is twenty-eight days long all the time you will definitely expose yourself to getting pregnant.

The temperature method

In this the body temperature is taken daily, first thing before getting up, by inserting a thermometer into the mouth, rectum or vagina. The result is plotted on a chart. The temperature recorded like this is seen to rise over the two or three days after ovulation to a plateau about 0.4C above the temperature recorded in the early days of the cycle. After the temperature has been at this plateau level for three days intercourse can be resumed. If intercourse is avoided for four days (the longest reasonable life of a sperm in the female reproductive tract) before the predicted date of ovulation (as calculated from several months' charting of your temperature) and resumed at this later point in the cycle the method can be reasonably effective.

The mucus method

As menstruation stops the vagina is usually 'dry' for some days. This is followed by a phase in which the vaginal mucus is found to be thick, whitish or yellowish, opaque and sticky. As this starts you have to stop having intercourse. Around the time of ovulation the mucus becomes clear, slippery and watery. It is now like the white of a raw egg. In the next stage the mucus changes and becomes tacky and opaque and the feeling of vaginal wetness diminishes. The last day of the clear, watery, slippery mucus is peak mucus day and intercourse is not allowed until four days after that day. In practice this turns out not to be a safe guide, so the method should be combined with the temperature method and intercourse resumed when three consecutive daily temperatures have been above the level of those on the previous six days. These methods produce an unplanned pregnancy rate of twenty to twenty-five per 100 woman-years.

Post-coital contraception (the 'morning after' pill; inserting an IUD)

If there is a chance that fertilisation may have occurred as a result of sexual activity at around the time of ovulation, as a result, for example, of a burst sheath, synthetic hormones can be taken within seventy-two hours, (preferably within forty-eight hours). Alternatively an IUD can be fitted. Four out of five women choose the hormonal method. Inserted at this time the IUD has a very low failure rate. If at all possible young women who have not had a baby and victims of rape should not have an IUD inserted in this way.

Planning a family

Having a baby is nothing like buying a TV set or a car and a couple's urge to produce a baby should ideally be controlled until the man and woman know they are secure together; that they can cope with the bad times as well as the good; that they want a baby for the baby's sake only and not to please themselves, to keep up with the Jones's, improve their own self-esteem and so on; and until they can provide for it without undue sacrifice on their part.

Having a child and producing another human being who may well live for eighty or more years is becoming an increasingly awesome undertaking. Most couples are having fewer babies and having them later. This is surely responsible. An increasing proportion of couples (up to 10 per cent) are choosing to have no children at all for various reasons.

The ideal way to space a family is not known. Nature's way, which depends on long-term, unrestricted breastfeeding, ensures that babies are born at intervals of about two and a half to three years but this is not suitable for most Western parents because the mother cannot usually breastfeed in this way and anyway does not want a baby every three years throughout her reproductive life.

If children are born too closely together the mother may be over-taxed, but longer intervals can increase rivalry between the children. Spreading them out with very long intervals means the family is committed to child rearing for years on end, but this suits some women who are at their best when caring for babies. Longer intervals also reduce the severity of the economic effects of having children on the family. Small families tend to be more favourable to intellectual development of the children than large ones.

Every baby a wanted baby: The world would be a happier place if every woman and her family could hardly wait for the new arrival.

Making a contraceptive plan.

Whatever plan is adopted it has to be related to contraception. Ideally, a highly effective contraceptive such as the pill should be started before the couple first have intercourse. The woman should continue taking the pill until about six months before the couple want to conceive their first baby. At this time the pill should be stopped and a condom or other barrier method used to allow time for the pill's effects on the body to wear off. After about three months the couple can start having unprotected intercourse, but it is important to remember that many couples do not conceive at once, whether or not the woman has been on the pill. A woman having intercourse on an unrestricted basis and not protected by any contraceptive takes an average of 5.3 months to conceive. Twenty-five per cent of couples will have conceived in the first month, 63 per cent by the end of six months, 75 per cent by the end of nine months and 80 per cent by the end of one year. A further 10 per cent will have conceived by eighteen months.

If a couple decide to have a second child but timing is not too important then relatively ineffective methods such as vaginal foams, a cervical cap or one of the natural methods could be used. If no further children are wanted at all, the pill should be used again until the woman is about thirty-five years old. Alternatively, one of the partners could be sterilised. After the age of thirty-five less reliable methods can be used, such as the progesterone-only (mini) pill. This has to be taken *every* day continuously whether the woman is menstruating or not. It does not contain oestrogen and is thought to be less likely than the combined pill to cause thrombosis and similar troubles. It is taken daily and bleeding tends to be irregular but its reduced efficiency compared with the combined pill is offset by the woman's declining fertility at this age. An alternative is the IUD. Pelvic inflammatory disease is a less likely complication at this age, and once her children have been born it is of little or no consequence at this stage of her reproductive career, if the IUD impairs a woman's fertility.

Contraception needs to be continued until about a year after the periods end at the menopause, but as fertility is falling rapidly by this age in most women less efficient methods can be used.

Summary

It is probably true to say that anyone who is fertile, or likely to be fertile, and who has intercourse without using efficient contraception, unless they want a baby is, in today's overcrowded world, behaving irresponsibly. We owe it to future generations not to produce so many children that there are not sufficient resources for them.

Education about contraception involves far more than the dissemination of facts about various methods. It starts in infancy by avoiding instilling notions that sex is mainly about having babies. This approach is no longer necessary or pertinent to our culture today. Historically it had a place, of course, but today sex can be entirely divorced from child production and should be seen as such from a very early age.

Chapter 21

Conception and infertility

Conception

In practice the words conception and fertilisation are used interchangeably. On certain occasions the terms are taken to mean just the fertilisation of the ovum (egg) but on others they include all the events leading up to the embedding of the fertilised egg in the wall of the uterus. It might be less confusing if the word conception were reserved for the process in which the egg settles in the lining of the womb (implantation), and the word fertilisation simply for the joining of the egg and sperm.

For conception to occur a sperm must reach an egg and join with it. Usually only one egg is released during each menstrual cycle and roughly speaking each ovary takes it in turn to produce one. The release of an egg at the middle of a woman's menstrual cycle may be accompanied by cramp-like abdominal pains, usually felt on the same side as the ovary producing the egg. This is called mittelschmerz pain and is experienced by half of all women at some time. Women do not release an egg when they have an orgasm but there is no doubt that emotional and psychological factors can influence ovulation profoundly. Many women who are not ovulating when they go to an infertility clinic start to do so and conceive after their first visit. About 40 per cent of all infertile women conceive in this way, before any real investigations or treatment have been completed. Another interesting phenomenon is known as psychic ovulation. It has been noticed for decades that the wives of men returning from war (or other long periods away from home) are more likely to conceive at once than would be expected on a calculation of the number who would normally have been at or near ovulation at the time. It seems that the highly charged emotional state of these women and their husbands' eagerness to have intercourse with them have an effect in bringing on ovulation prematurely. This can be explained by the fact that the brain centres for emotion lie very close to the pituitary gland that controls the body's hormones.

As the time of ovulation approaches, the fimbria (finger-like projections at the end of the fallopian tubes) 'sweep' the ovary so as to locate the Graffian follicle where the egg lies. If the fimbria cannot do this because, for example, scar tissue from a previous operation is immobilising them, the woman could be infertile. When ovulation occurs the egg is more or less swept from the ovary along the tube by

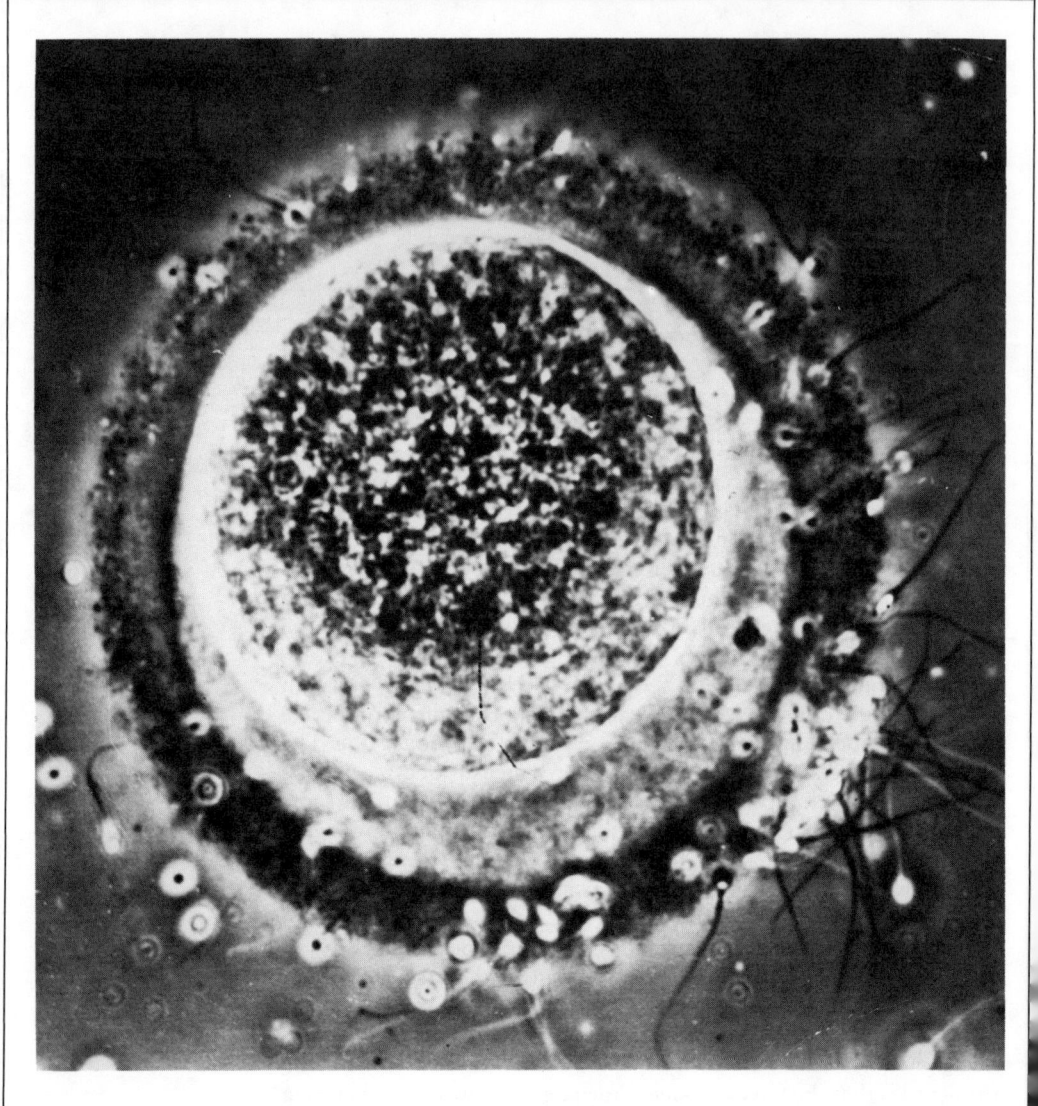

The moment of fertilisation: The sperms arrive at the egg but out of the millions in the race only one will win. If the winner is an X-carrying sperm the result will be a girl, or a boy if it should be a Y. Note the size of the egg compared with the sperm.

the action of small hair-like structures, called cilia, which waft it in the direction of the uterus. The egg lives, it is thought, for only twelve to twenty-four hours, so fertilisation has to occur fairly rapidly whilst it is still towards the outer end of the fallopian tube.

Sperms have a hazardous journey to reach the egg. When a woman is lying flat on her back the semen released by her partner at ejaculation collects in a pool in the top end of her vagina. Unless the uterus is abnormally positioned (which can be a cause of infertility), the cervix is immersed in this pool. The acidity of vaginal fluids is not favourable to isolated sperms and, if they were to remain there, most would be killed within two hours. However, certain components of semen produced by most men reduce vaginal acidity to counteract this killing-off effect. Good sexual arousal of a woman, with plenty of lubrication, also helps by diluting the acidity.

Some sperms tend to find their way into the cervical passage within two or three minutes. In women who have not had a baby the passage stays open for half an hour or so after an orgasm and this may help sperms to enter. If a woman does not have an orgasm the lower portion of her vagina remains congested and may act as a sort of plug, reducing the leakage of semen to the cervical passage. If she does, the spasmodic contractions of her uterus during orgasm create a negative pressure inside it, thereby sucking up semen from the pool. This is interesting because some women say that even if they have an orgasm during intercourse they sometimes like to masturbate afterwards. It is possible that this orgasm after intercourse may help women experiencing difficulties conceiving.

Around ovulation time the mucus in the cervix is copious, slippery and alkaline, and is favourable to the passage of sperms upwards into the uterus. At other times of the month it is gelatinous and tends to trap them. Nevertheless, even around ovulation the cervical canal still acts as a filter, killing off poor-quality and abnormal sperms. As soon as sperms have been ejaculated they acquire the power to swim but they do not yet have the ability to fertilise an egg. This they start to obtain as they pass through the cervix. If they are injected straight into the uterus they may not be capable of fertilising an egg.

Sperms can also be killed around this time by the action of antibodies. Some women are allergic to their partner's sperms and so cannot get pregnant by him. Usually sperms do not cause much in the way of antibody formation in women but the gradual accumulation of antibodies on repeated exposure to sperm could be part of the explanation for the decline in fertility of women with age. Some women produce antibodies in sufficient quantities to immobilise sperm in the cervix and make them clump together by their heads. Such women may be infertile or sub-fertile. Men too can form antibodies against their own sperm (sperm cells are genetically different from the rest of the body's cells and this is what usually triggers off antibody formation in the body), which causes sperms to clump together by their tails. Depending upon their antibody level, such men may have difficulty in fathering a child. Such antibodies are common after a vasectomy (see page 255).

What happens in the cervical canal is therefore crucial to fertility and can be investigated, if necessary, by removing some of the mucus after intercourse undertaken in the middle of the cycle and inspecting it under a microscope. Finding sperms moving in the mucus shows that Intercourse has in fact occurred, that antibodies are absent and that the man produces sperms of sufficient quality to penetrate the mucus. This is called a post-coital test and is done in certain cases of infertility.

Any man who is unable to produce sperms or to produce them in sufficient numbers and quality, or any man who can make them but cannot deliver them to the vagina, will be infertile or will have difficulty in producing a child. Over 80 per cent of couples who try to have a baby conceive within two years; 10 per cent take longer; and around 10 per cent are infertile if no treatment is given. In this last 10

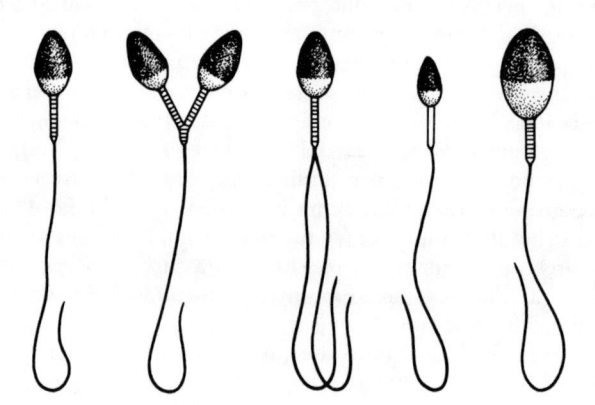

Some abnormal sperm forms which can result in difficulties in conceiving.

per cent male factors are predominantly to blame in just under half; female factors in the same proportion; and in the remaining 20 per cent there are problems in both partners or no cause is ever found.

At one time great attention was paid to the sperm counts of infertile men. A count of less than 60 million sperms per millilitre of semen was thought to make conception unlikely, but it is now known that men with less than 10 million per millilitre can succeed. It is now considered that a count of 20 million, with over half of the sperms showing movement an hour after the semen was collected, and a semen volume of 1.5 millilitres, is sufficient for fertility. One problem with all such tests is that the man has to produce semen by masturbation, usually at the hospital, and this may well inhibit normal ejaculation and so reduce his count. Men with absent, immature or otherwise defective testes are infertile and men who have an obstruction of the vas deferens (after a vasectomy or due to scarring as a result of a previous infection of the tube, such as may occur in gonorrhoea, for example), will not be able to transport the sperms they do make to the penis and are also infertile. They are, of course, able to ejaculate normally and the semen appears normal.

To function correctly the testes have to be at a temperature of $29.35°C \pm 0.18°C$. This is lower than body temperature, so the muscles that control testicular distance from the body relax when it is warm so as to increase the distance and so cool the testes. The reverse happens in cold weather. Although it does not matter much with normal men, an infertile man should avoid wearing Y-front pants because they keep the testes close to the body and warmer than they should be for the ideal conditions for sperm production. Such men are often advised to pull their testes down and to hold them under the cold tap or sit in a cold bath twice a day.

Men with a varicose vein adjacent to a testis, called a varicocoele, also have testes that are too warm and may need an operation to tie off the varicose vein if infertility is a problem. The results are excellent, with half of such men fathering a child within a year of the operation. This is the easiest and most treatable form of male infertility.

Sperm production is under the control of the same pituitary hormones that control the menstrual cycle in women, the only difference being that sperms are produced more or less continuously.

Exposure to certain hormones, drugs, pesticides and industrial chemicals can reduce the sperm count and cigarette smoking can increase the number of abnormal sperms. Pregnancies caused by men with a high incidence of abnormal sperms in their semen have a higher chance of miscarriage, stillbirth and handicaps in the child. Although the cervix should filter out such abnormal sperms, a few can evidently get through and fertilise an egg.

If a man can produce excellent-quality sperms in abundance but is impotent (cannot obtain or sustain an erection), he is, in effect, infertile. Similarly, if he cannot ejaculate when his penis is in the vagina he is, strictly speaking, infertile. Some men with serious damage to the spinal cord after a car accident, for example, cannot get an erection or ejaculate, and a similar condition exists in others who suffer from illnesses affecting the autonomic nerves in the pelvis. The most common of these is longstanding diabetes. The passage of controlled electric currents via the rectum can produce an ejaculation in such a man, often without an erection. The semen obtained in this way is usually of poor quality but it can be used to inseminate his partner artificially and so enable apparently hopelessly infertile men to father a child.

Collecting the husband's sperms for use in inseminating his wife is a useful technique in cases where the man cannot deliver them to the cervix. This can be done with impotence, vaginismus in the woman, hypospadias (a congenital deformity of the penis in which the opening is underneath and not at the tip) and in cases where the sperm count is low. A technique that has been found to be very successful is to collect only the first portion of the man's ejaculate, produced by masturbation, and to use it to inseminate the woman. The first spurt or two of semen contains the most sperms and produces much higher pregnancy rates than whole ejaculate collections. If this sperm-rich portion of the semen is collected from several ejaculations and is used at the time of ovulation, the woman's chances of getting pregnant are greatly increased. The semen can be introduced into the woman by placing it inside a cap which is then fitted to her cervix or it can be injected into the lower part of her cervical canal. This is called AIH (Artifical Insemination by the Husband). If the man cannot produce any sperms, semen from a suitable donor can be used instead. This is called AID (Artificial Insemination by a Donor).

Once through the cervix, the sperms tend to make the two-inch journey through the uterus fairly quickly, perhaps helped by uterine contractions, hormones and sexual arousal in the woman. Entry into the fallopian tubes is thought to be another point at which any defective sperms which have survived their passage through the cervix may be destroyed, probably by white blood cells. Once in the tubes, capacitation (the capacity of a sperm to fertilise an egg) is complete and the sperms make their way along the tubes against the beat of the hair-like cilia which line it and which are wafting the egg down towards the uterus. Sperms can live in the cervix and the tubes for a considerable time and research suggests that the cervix may even act as a sort of sperm reservoir. However, they probably do not maintain their capacity for fertilisation for longer than two to three days. Out of the millions ejaculated into the vagina probably only a hundred or two finally reach the vicinity of the egg and only one enters the egg itself. This first sperm to reach the egg produces a rapid change in it which prevents a second sperm from entering. So out of all the millions of sperms there is only one winner (unless, of course, more than one egg is fertilised to produce non-identical twins or triplets etc). This joining of the sperm and the egg is called fertilisation and it occurs, as we have seen, in a fallopian tube.

At conception, the genetic material in the egg and sperm fuse and a new human being starts to grow from a single cell. Since sperms and eggs each contain only half the necessary number of chromosomes for a human being, the fusion of the two restores the number. The sex of the individual is also decided at this instant and depends upon whether the successful sperm was the carrier of an X (female) or a Y (male) sex chromosome.

Changes after fertilisation.
The fertilised egg now starts to divide and this is the beginning of the process that turns a single egg into a complex human being. Sometimes the two halves, after the first division, each develop into a baby. In this case the twins are of the same sex and are identical. Why this occurs is unknown but there must be a genetic basis because it runs in families and some men produce twins from different women. If two eggs have been released, an event which increases in frequency with the advancing age of the mother, and both are fertilised, then non-identical twins are produced.

The first cell division occurs within twenty-four hours and thereafter the fertilised egg divides about once every twenty-two hours. As this process goes on the embryo is wafted along the fallopian tube by muscular contractions of the tube and by the movements of the cilia. Secretions produced by the tube probably nourish the embryo on its journey to the uterus, which takes a week or so. On arrival it implants itself in the lining of the uterus (the endometrium), which has been primed for its reception by hormones. If conception has occurred, the corpus luteum—the area in the ovary where the egg comes from—continues to provide hormones to maintain the growing embryo in the first few weeks.

Problems in a woman can prevent or disrupt conception. In a fifth of infertile couples the fault is found to lie with ovulation. Just as the testes can be absent or defective in a man, the functioning of ovaries can be faulty. Even if the ovaries are intact ovulation may still not occur because of disorders of the pituitary gland which lead to disturbances in the release of gonodotrophic hormones. Many of these disorders are emotional or psychological in origin; those that are not can often be helped by modern drugs that stimulate the ovary or produce eggs.

In another fifth of infertile couples the problem lies not with the ovaries but with the tubes. Usually these are blocked by scarring from earlier infection (often gonorrhoea) or surgery. Tests can be carried out to see if the tubes are open, but even if they are, and if tests show that the woman ovulates, this does not necessarily prove that she is fertile. Unlike for a man, in whom it can easily be demonstrated that he can produce a good-quality ejaculate, the only ultimate proof of a woman's fertility is pregnancy itself.

If the tubes are blocked, surgery—and particularly microsurgery—can help to overcome the problem by various methods. Test-tube babies are increasingly a way out of the problem for these women. If only the techniques were less costly, less cumbersome and more reliable (only about one in fifteen women using this method produces a full-term baby), it could easily become a widespread method of overcoming this very common cause of infertility. In the test-tube method an egg is obtained from the affected woman's ovary using a laparoscope. The egg is then mixed with sperms outside the body in a test tube. The developing embryo is implanted back into the uterus through the cervix when it has divided into about sixteen cells (which is about the stage of development the normal embryo is at when it reaches the uterus). There is little doubt that, as technology develops, increasing numbers of women will be able to benefit from this medical advance.

The worst outlook for infertile couples is when there are faults on both sides. Nevertheless, even in these couples pregnancies have occurred in many cases where the medical situation originally looked bleak.

Faults on both sides.

In the vast majority of healthy couples conception occurs within a few months and there is no problem. However, for increasing numbers infertility is a very real problem. Infertility is defined as the inability to achieve a pregnancy after a year of unprotected, unlimited intercourse or the inability to carry a pregnancy to birth. It is not uncommon and is becoming more common. About six in 100 young women are infertile but this figure rises in the older age groups, as a result of many factors, so that in all about one in seven of the whole adult population of childbearing age is infertile. Add to this the numbers of couples who have had one child but cannot have another (secondary infertility) and the number of people involved runs into millions.

Infertility is becoming more common for several reasons. First many couples are choosing to remain child-free until their late twenties or early thirties and by this age a woman's fertility is on the downhill slope. Maximum fertility in the West is in the early twenties and after that fertility rates decline. One survey found that three-quarters of mothers having their first baby when they were thirty or more had been having unprotected intercourse for more than two years before they conceived. Second, VD is on the increase and gonorrhoea undoubtedly causes many women's fallopian tubes to block. The sad thing is that many women do not know they have the disease and so can be infertile without knowing it when they get married. Third, prolonged use of the pill delays the return of periods in 2 per cent of women. As there are about three million women on the pill in the UK this adds up to a lot of individuals who cannot conceive exactly when they want to. The IUD is popular as a form of contraception, and it has been shown to delay conception for a short while after its removal, and in some cases it blocks the tubes by causing an infection and the blockage results in infertility. Fourth, exposure to drugs, environmental pollutants and food additives is also rising and any or all of these may play a role in infertility. Experts estimate that all these factors will push the proportion of infertile couples up to one in five by the end of the century.

If you are having trouble in conceiving there are several things worth trying before going to your doctor.

Helping yourself

Masters and Johnson found that simple advice on and attention to technique, such as in the list below, provided the answer for one in eight of their so-called 'infertile' patients.

Sex technique To have the best chance of getting a woman pregnant a man's penis must penetrate her vagina deeply and he must ejaculate while it is there. Oral sex or intercourse with any other part of the body will not result in a pregnancy.

Timing For most sexually active couples it does not much matter how often they have intercourse, because if they do so often enough then by chance alone they will soon hit the time around ovulation and the woman will conceive. However, if a man is a shift worker or works away from home a lot, if either partner is ill, or if for any other reason they do not have intercourse often, their chances of the woman getting pregnant are greatly reduced. The best time to have intercourse in order to stand the best chance of pregnancy is around ovulation (day fifteen of the woman's cycle if it is usually 28 days long). Ovulation usually occurs 14 days before she is next due to have her period no matter how long her cycles are.

Frequency As we have seen in chapter 17, there is no 'normal' number of times a week to have intercourse. However, if you are having intercourse very infrequently you stack the odds up against yourselves very heavily when it comes to conceiving a baby. Many of the couples attending infertility clinics are having intercourse once a month or less. Given that the couple having intercourse about two or three times a week will take 5.3 months to conceive, on average, once a month is not giving yourselves a fair chance. For many couples low intercourse rates are what they want and trying to increase the frequency can produce all kinds of problems in the marriage. Such couples may benefit from professional help. Some couples worry about saving up sperms to produce a better quality ejaculate and so increase their chance of conceiving. There is some truth in this because sperm counts are reduced in a man who ejaculates every day, but there is no point in 'saving up' for more than two days.

Sex positions If you are fertile it does not matter in what position you have intercourse, but if you are sub-fertile it can make all the difference as to whether or not you will conceive. The first thing to try is to put a pillow under the woman's hips so that the pool of semen ejaculated into the top of her vagina does not run straight back out again. The woman lies down after intercourse for half an hour and should not get up to pass water or to wash. Ideally, she should go to sleep in this position, but this may be inconvenient.

For a woman whose uterus is retroverted (tipped backwards), raising the hips takes her cervix out of the pool of semen in her vagina and so makes a pregnancy less likely. These women are more likely to conceive if they use an 'all-fours' position for intercourse. The woman kneels on the bed with her elbows and forearms on the bed. This allows exceptionally deep penetration of the penis and bathes the cervix in semen.

Generally speaking, if you are having difficulty in conceiving you should use the positions that give the deepest possible penetration and you should see your doctor if deep penetration is painful.

Orgasm is not necessary in order to conceive but it may help in two ways. First, during an orgasm the uterus definitely sucks up any sperms bathing the cervix and, second, a woman who is orgasmic is more likely to enjoy sex and so will have intercourse more often, which will increase her chances of conceiving.

Not damaging sperms Never douche or wash the vagina immediately after intercourse, and never use creams, petroleum jelly or other lubricating fluids during intercourse because they all damage sperms to some extent. If you need lubrication, use saliva. Prolonged foreplay is a good idea because this increases the production of a woman's natural lubricating fluids.

Causes of infertility

Female Conditions	Cause	Treatment
Ovulation problems	Usually unknown	80% of women ovulate with the drug clomiphene.
	'Normal'—most women don't ovulate every month.	None
	Poor quality egg as woman ages.	None
	After coming off the Pill	Time usually cures
	Hormonal dysfunction	Sort out causes
	Certain tranquilisers	Stop drug
	Psychological stress or shock.	Periods return spontaneously but clomiphene can be used.

Female Conditions	Cause	Treatment
Fallopian tube	Blockage secondary to VD. As a long term result of the coil (IUD). After an abortion Any pelvic inflammatory disease causing blockage of tube (appendicitis, for example). Deliberate damage to sterilise a woman.	Use surgical techniques to unblock fallopian tubes; replace them with a transplant or remove pelvic adhesions where present.
Endometriosis	Unknown	Pregnancy The Pill for 1 year continuously Male hormones (Danazol) Surgery
Infections of the genital and urinary systems	Gonorrhoea causing blocked tubes.	Treat gonorrhoea but surgery usually necessary too.
	T-mycoplasma	Tetracycline
	Thrush/trichomonas	Treat vaginal infections
	Urinary infections	Treat infections with drugs
Cervical factors	Cervical infection	Drugs and/or local minor surgical treatment.
	Narrowing of the cervical opening.	Dilate it under anaesthetic (D & C); if unsuitable can have AIH.
	Thick cervical mucus	Oestrogen therapy
	Hostile cervical mucus	Use condom for 1 year to allow antibodies to sperm to disappear or use drugs that suppress the body's immune mechanisms.
Abnormalities of the uterus	Inborn abnormalities	May be none
	Fibroids	Surgical removal
Polycystic ovaries	Unknown	Clomiphene, gonadotrophic hormones or surgery.
Turner's syndrome	Congenital	None
X-rays	Usually women working with x-rays.	Remove source of problem

Female Conditions	Cause	Treatment
Menstrual back-flow	Unknown	Surgery to pull up tubes
General diseases	TB Diabetes Any severe illness Severe malnutrition Severe depression Anorexia nervosa Gross obesity	Usually only temporary cessation of ovulation.
Vitamin B12 deficiency	Unknown	Give vitamin B12
Stress	Many	Cure cause or use tranquilisers if necessary.

Male Conditions	Cause	Treatment
Varicocele	Varicose vein around testis.	Surgery, results excellent
Testicular failure	Mumps	None—few men permanently infertile as a result.
	Klinefelter's syndrome	None
	Accidental knock or trauma during surgery.	Sperm count returns to normal with time.
	Twisting of testis	If caught early, sperm count not permanently harmed.
'Glandular'	Usually unknown Thyroid gland underactive.	Treat if possible
Obstruction of vas deferens	Vasectomy	Can be reversed in about 50% of men.
	TB or gonorrhoea	Relieve blockage of vas deferens by surgery.
Poor semen volume	Unknown	Use small volume for AIH
Ejaculation problems	Sperms go into bladder not down penis.	Retrieve urine and separate out sperms which are then used for AIH.
	Premature ejaculation	Man comes off too soon and sperms never get into vagina. Sex therapy useful.

Male Conditions	Cause	Treatment
Undescended testis	Developmental	Surgery or drugs in little boys but no treatment satisfactory in men.
Sperms agglutinate (clump together)	Immune disorder	Wash sperms in laboratory and use for AIH.
Necrospermia (man produces dead sperms)	Unknown	None
Genito-urinary infections	TB, Gonorrhoea, Colon bacteria	Treat infection
Zinc deficiency	Many. Usually poor dietary intake.	Give zinc tablets
Drug allergies	Sensitive to drug	Stop drug
Ageing	Normal	None
Stress	Many	Remove cause
Severe malnutrition	Usually enforced	Give nourishing food
Heat	Tight underpants, frequent hot baths/showers.	Wear boxer shorts, bathe scrotum twice daily in cool water.
Drugs	Many drugs dangerous to sperm production—ask doctor.	Stop taking offending drug

Joint Male/Female Conditions	Cause	Treatment
Sex at wrong time of month	Ovulation around day 15—must have intercourse around then.	Have intercourse every other day from day 11 to day 18 of cycle.
Sex too infrequent	Many	Have intercourse more frequently, especially around middle of cycle.
Poor positions	Woman gets up after intercourse and 'loses' all semen.	Woman stays lying down for $\frac{1}{2}$ hour after intercourse with hips on pillow.
	Uterus tilted backwards.	Intercourse in rear entry positions.

Joint Male/Female Conditions	Cause	Treatment
Lubricant jellies washing/douching etc.	Obvious	Stop all these practices—they can kill sperms.
Sexual performance problems	Many—see doctor or marital therapist.	Treat individual sex problem.

If after trying all these simple measures for six months you still cannot conceive it is worth talking to your doctor about it, especially if you are much over thirty. With medical help six out of ten infertile couples end up with a baby and things are improving all the time, so it is well worth going for help and not putting it off too long.

Infertility and its impact on couples

Infertility is seen by most affected couples as a major life crisis which is hardly surprising in a culture that is so baby-centred and with a history in which barren women were treated as outcasts. Fertility is a deep-seated concern for most of us—even the 10 per cent of couples who choose to remain child-free mostly say they would like to think they *could* have children if they wanted. To be unable to conceive puts an enormous burden on the couple and changes their relationship in many ways. But no one can live in a state of crisis for ever and the way each couple reacts depends on their psychological make-up, the type of marriage they have, their personalities, their family support, their previous ideas about family life, and so on. In response to infertility couples go in one of several ways. They may come through with a stronger bond between them; they may find the whole thing too much and break up over it (though this is rare); or one or other may become permanently affected by the problem in a way which endangers their inter-personal relationship, though not enough to break it up.

The personal and emotional problems of infertility emerge slowly, thankfully, and this gives the couple time to come to terms with their state. When a couple cannot immediately have a baby they assume that there is some temporary hold-up and that eventually all will be well. As the months go by the subject becomes more sensitive and the woman begins to dread her next period because it seems to prove her worst fear—that she cannot become pregnant. Soon the couple start wondering about the old wives' tales they have heard and are plagued by well-meaning advice from parents and friends.

The next step is to take the problem out of their hands and give it to a professional. This compounds their emotional problems because the previously normal couple now become 'patients' and are treated accordingly. People repeatedly say how inadequate they feel at this stage—especially a young, healthy couple who have probably hardly seen a doctor for anything in their adult lives. Many fear that people's reactions will be that they 'aren't doing it properly', that they are sexual cripples, and this can be very hurtful. The merry-go-round of infertility tests brings its own emotional traumas with raised hopes dashed time and again as tests fail to find answers. 'I only hope he's normal,' is a common remark women make as their husbands undergo tests. Deep down many fear they have chosen a 'dud' and would almost rather that the trouble was with them.

When the diagnosis is finally proved and the couple is told that they are likely to be infertile, denial is often the first emotion. 'It can't be true', 'They must have mixed up the tests,' and so on, are common reactions. Very soon this denial gives way to anger, frustration and desperation. 'Why us?' is the commonest question couples ask; and 'What have we done to deserve it?' Religious women, especially, often recriminate themselves for previous sexual misdemeanours and ask God if this is some kind of punishment. Both men and women who have had extra-marital affairs question whether these could have had any effect on the situation and if so, how. This is a time when the couple need love, comfort and support, to help them through their pain.

Women start to avoid children.

At this stage women especially start to isolate themselves from children and situations in which they might meet children. Anger sets in at the doctors who are 'useless'; at the health services which are a 'dead loss'; at parents who are 'horrible' in putting pressures on them to have children; at friends who tell them to 'pull themselves together and learn to live with it'; at neighbours' and friends' children who are even more unbearable than usual; at their spouse's habits and idiosyncracies; and so on. Many a 'guilty' party (the one who is 'at fault' in the infertility problem) feels angry with him- or herself and this is not helped by the other partner being loving and understanding. On the contrary, this often makes things worse. Grief sets in but unlike losing a child in a car accident there is no tangible loss. This unfocussed grief is especially difficult to deal with because so few people really understand what the couple is going through. Such grief is perfectly normal and has to be worked through just as after a bereavement—and in a sense that is exactly what it is.

Eventually, over the months and years, the conflicts resolve but not without taking a terrible toll in the bedroom.

Although some couples claim that their infertility brought them closer together, this is not the normal story. Most infertile couples have sex problems which first emerge as the tests and treatments are being carried out. This is hardly surprising because infertility is a body blow to anyone's sexuality. One of the most powerful concepts we carry from childhood into adult life is that we will marry and have children, and most people do just this. Not to be able to do so is a major set-back. It is quite usual at this stage for even a healthy, well-balanced couple to go through a stage when they lose all confidence in their looks, sexual attraction and their ability to do anything right. Trying to have intercourse 'to order' at certain times of the month, ejaculating into bottles in hospital clinics, having tubes and instruments pushed into one's sex organs and generally concentrating too much on sex takes the pleasure and spontaneity out of it for the vast majority, and eventually sex becomes a chore to be endured. The man feels like a robot, only to be encouraged at the most fertile time of the month and the woman becomes obsessed with temperature charts and the onset of her period each month.

The best thing to do is to follow your normal sex urges and make love whenever you feel like it. Don't lose sight of your original aim of sex—pleasure—just because you are trying to get pregnant. Get away together on a holiday to break the downhill emotional spiral and have the odd drink before intercourse to reduce your inhibitions. Devices like this can help bring back the sparkle to your sex life.

Once the diagnosis has finally been confirmed, most couples go off sex completely for weeks or even months. They are angry at all those years of wasted contraceptive effort and reflect on what a mockery it all was. The fertile partner often offers sex as a softener to the infertile partner but the recipient cannot cope with this gesture until some long time has elapsed and he or she has worked through the grief.

It sometimes helps *not* to have intercourse in bed if this reminds you of sex for babies. Oral sex and mutual masturbation are a good way of getting started again, are not linked to 'baby-making' and encourage sex for its own sake. Once you can come to terms with sex for its own sake, you are well on the way back to a normal sex life and you will be better able to cope with your long-term infertility problem. Infertility is a crisis but it is not a terminal illness. Most couples come out of the problem to lead vigorous, healthy and optimistic lives if they work hard to rebuild their lives.

Summary

Although conception is a complex business it is all too easy for most couples to conceive. However, when conception does not happen easily it can cause real distress. Fortunately, research is improving the situation all the time and female infertility especially is more treatable than ever and male infertility better understood. There are several exciting developments in the pipeline for the infertile today, with test-tube babies becoming more widely available for women with blocked fallopian tubes.

But having said all this, about four out of ten infertile couples end up with no baby from any source at all (including adoption and fostering), so there is still a large area for concern. Such couples are increasingly being helped by society's more accepting attitudes to the child-free (those who choose to have no children). Acceptance of them is rubbing off on the child-less (who would like children but cannot have them).

Chapter 22

Abortion

Abortion is an emotive and therefore a controversial subject. By removing the embryo (which is the name given to the fertilised egg in the first eight weeks of the baby's life) or the foetus (which is what it is called thereafter), a potential life is lost.

However, Nature also makes use of abortion. In some unknown way, a pregnant woman's body 'inspects' the embryo and if it is defective it is likely to be rejected without the woman even necessarily knowing she has conceived. It is thought that a half to three-quarters of all fertilised eggs are lost like this. Later, when the pregnancy is recognisable and established, a further 10 to 15 per cent of pregnancies fail, mostly between the second and third months. Many such foetuses are found to be visibly defective. Sometimes, the woman herself, rather than the foetus, is the cause of the abortion in that she may be hormonally deficient or may have fibroids, for example. All such naturally occurring abortions are labelled 'spontaneous' and the public calls them miscarriages. The spontaneous abortion rate is slightly lower in that around 2 per cent of babies are born with congenital defects but most of these are slight. Nature may be a little more 'strict' in her scrutiny of female embryos, in that they are probably rejected earlier than male ones. This may account for the preponderance of male births of around 104 male to 100 female.

Abortions which are caused by human intervention are called induced abortions. In an ideal world no woman would become pregnant unless she wanted a baby for its own sake and was able to provide an emotional and physical environment in which it could prosper. But there is evidence that up to a quarter or so of all babies born are not wanted in this positive way although, one should add, they may not be completely *un*wanted.

Women who have abortions are sometimes represented as being unnatural or frivolous, but there is another way of looking at the subject. The age group which has most abortions is the late-adolescent and young adult one. There is no evidence to suggest that these women are trying to avoid pregnancy *altogether*, only *this* pregnancy. Presumably, a strong motive for seeking an abortion is that they cannot provide properly for a child at the particular time and so want to defer pregnancy until they can. From this point of view having an abortion is a responsible act.

The younger generation, contrary to appearances perhaps, is the one which encounters the most problems arising from psychosexual conflicts and confusions. They are not alone, of course, and many long-married women with families also have abortions because they cannot face another baby for a whole range of reasons. Whether or not such women should be 'allowed' to use abortion as a form of birth control is a debatable subject, which we do not want to go into here, but some women only come to the decision after much heart-searching and agonising. Almost all women are disturbed by the event.

If an abortion is the decision, then good counselling can reduce anxiety, guilt, misapprehension and the possibility of depression later. An experienced counsellor may also be able to detect unconscious motivations, a knowledge of which may prevent the woman starting another unwanted pregnancy.

Over the years the techniques used to carry out abortions have become more refined and safer. In ordinary, uncomplicated, early cases, an abortion is safer than having a baby, even though having a baby is itself now a very safe process.

Methods

Usually a general anaesthetic is given but local anaesthesia is sometimes used. In most cases the vacuum aspiration method is used, by which the embryo is sucked out. The canal through the cervix does not have to be stretched very much during this technique, unlike older methods in which the canal was opened wider so as to introduce instruments. Overstretching the cervix can result in it becoming loose, which increases the chances of a spontaneous abortion in any subsequent pregnancy.

If the pregnancy is further advanced the prostaglandin method is the one usually used. The prostaglandins, which are introduced into the uterus, encourage it to go into labour prematurely. The contractions slowly enlarge the passage through the cervix, in the same way as in labour, and the foetus is eventually passed. This slow enlargement of the passage does little or no subsequent harm to the cervix.

Various abortion techniques have been used around the time a woman's period is due and before it is possible to know whether she is pregnant or not, just in case she might be pregnant. This is known as menstrual regulation and both a vacuum method and a method which involves placing prostaglandins in the vagina have been tried. Although they have their strong advocates these methods are still controversial.

Another technique is to insert an intra-uterine contraceptive device in the hope that it will dislodge any embryo which might be present.

Apart from making the cervix incompetent the other physical complications of abortion are infection and/or haemorrhage. The first can lead to infertility but both are relatively rare when the operator is skilful and experienced. Similarly, the uterus may be perforated by the instruments used, the operation may fail and there are risks, however small, from an anaesthetic. These are infrequent occurrences in skilled hands, but they do occur occasionally. Failure to remove the embryo is understandable when one bears in mind how small it actually is in early pregnancy. Also, the operation is not done under direct vision but by touch. Some women have a double uterus or twins and these again can occasionally mislead the operator into thinking the operation has been successfully carried out when in fact a foetus remains.

Late abortions carry more risks, and unfortunately are common among the young who often 'deny' they are pregnant and not uncommonly even deny having had intercourse. It is only when the woman faces reality that an abortion is sought. Another situation which leads a woman to go for an abortion very late applies to older women. Since the chances of mongolism and other genetic defects rise with maternal age, some obstetricians use the technique of amniocentesis to obtain cells for culture to discover whether the foetus is abnormal and then offer the woman an abortion if something is wrong. Since culturing the cells and then studying the chromosomes takes a long time such women tend to come for an abortion late. The ideal time is thought to be about eight to ten, or even up to twelve weeks. At this early stage the operation can be undertaken on an out-patient basis if certain conditions are fulfilled. The prostaglandin method is used after about the fourteenth week in a woman who has not had a baby but later in one who has.

Summary

No woman has an abortion for pleasure and nearly all feel anxious and guilty. If a woman really wants her baby but has an abortion because of her circumstances or ill health she often gets depressed afterwards. However, the majority feel that an enormous weight has been lifted off their minds and some even feel a little guilty about their lack of distress. Her relationship with her partner not infrequently improves because it is an adversity shared and surmounted. Contrary to what is often said, the partner also feels guilty about the situation in which the woman has been placed and by enduring it she earns a new respect from him. Sometimes the relationship collapses. This is especially likely when either partner made the pregnancy 'happen' in an attempt to secure the relationship.

Chapter 23

Pregnancy and childbirth

After her own birth having a baby is the most important milestone in the life of most women and even though today about 5 to 10 per cent of the married population opt to have no children at all, the remainder do so. There are numerous books about pregnancy and childbirth which cover the day-to-day events in detail, and we cannot hope to include this sort of information in a book like this. What we will look at in this chapter is the couple as a sexual unit. Let us start by looking at why women have babies, because understanding the real motives for having a baby helps one understand the feelings, emotions and problems that can arise.

Reasons for having a baby

The first reason to consider is the cultural pressure to do so. The majority of people do get married and a large proportion of them have one baby or two. Our culture is still 'pro-natalist'—that is it reveres babies and makes them seem desirable objects. This is, of course, healthy and normal because the human race has to continue and even if we in the West stopped having babies the world's population would still continue to rise alarmingly. Most people feel that it is reasonable to have up to two babies to 'replace themselves' but in worldwide population terms this is no longer necessary or desirable. An average of one more baby (to make three people per family) represents a 50 per cent growth in population within a generation, and this, if repeated worldwide, would be disastrous.

Most couples are brainwashed by our culture into believing that having babies is what happens to people when they get married. This certainly used to be the case and clearly still is to some extent because the average couple still has children, though a quarter to a half of all pregnancies are unwanted or unplanned. Increasing numbers of couples are choosing not to have children but they are still in a tiny minority, as we have seen.

Within the cultural norm of having babies, couples have babies for all kinds of different reasons, many of them quite unconscious. Some have them to prove to themselves and the world (although they do this unconsciously, of course) that they are grown-up and adult people. A person doing this usually has a poor view of him- or herself sexually or as a personality, and wants to do something the world cannot ignore. This motivation is fairly common in teenage preg-

The magnificence of the pregnant woman: Many women do not much like their bodies when they are pregnant but the large quantities of circulating oestrogen accentuate their femaleness and many men are greatly turned on by this.

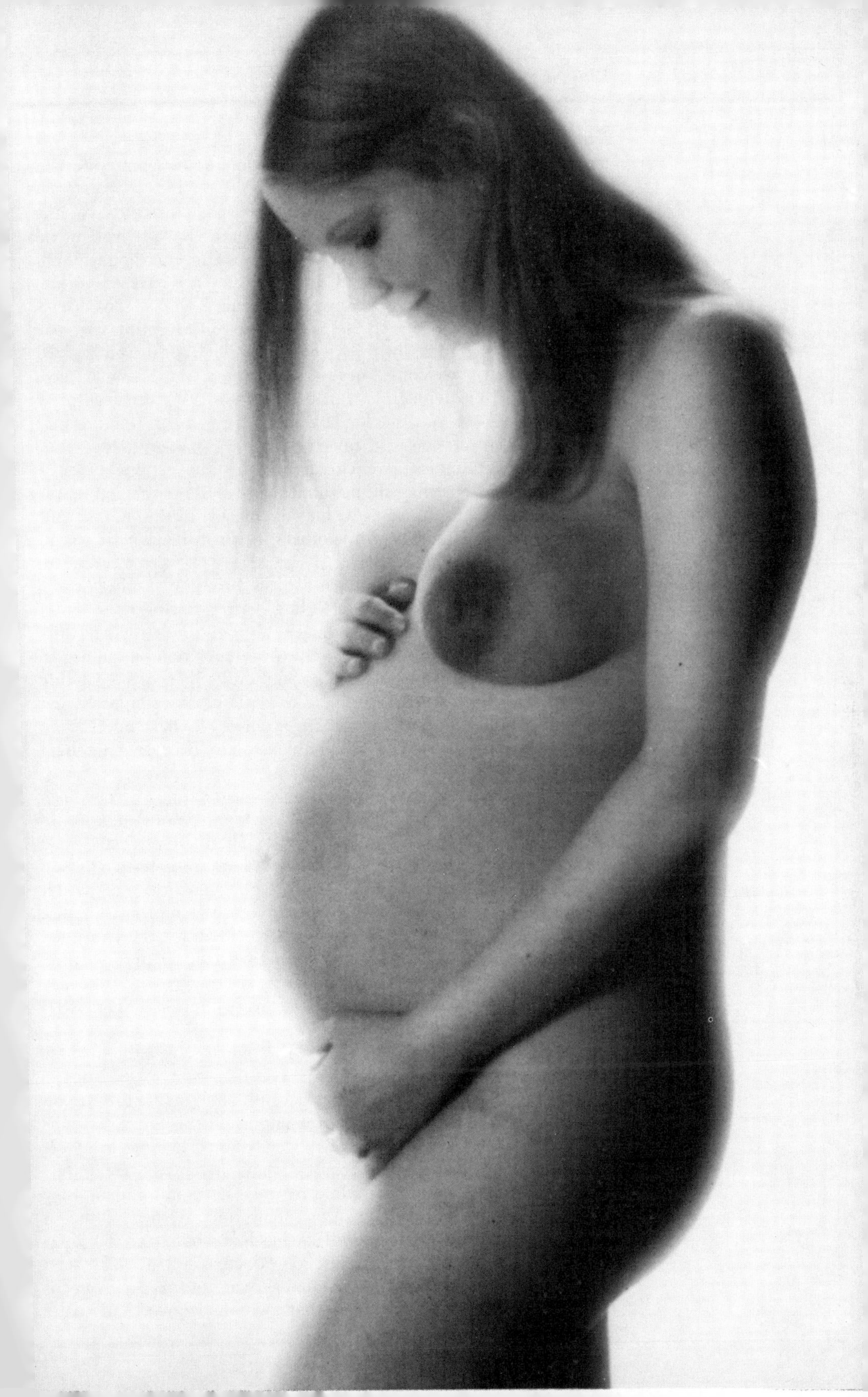

nancies. Some couples have babies to secure a relationship. Before marriage a girl sometimes gets pregnant to make a man marry her but this is increasingly uncommon.

Within marriage some people have a baby to 'save' the relationship, thinking—usually wrongly—that a baby will mend their problems and bring them closer together. Once the 'honeymoon' period is over after the birth of the baby they are back to normal again. Many women have a baby inadvertently—it does not matter too much if they have one so they do not use contraception seriously and as a result get pregnant. Such a baby may not be positively wanted or planned but is welcomed nevertheless. Some young women have babies to keep up with friends or others at work. More accurately perhaps, their friends having babies makes them think about motherhood in relation to themselves.

An unfortunate motive, closely linked to the last one, is that a baby is sometimes seen as the next milestone in life—often under the influence of parents. For some women having a baby is a sign that she really loves her partner, and for others it proves her female status. Whilst it can be true that a baby is a sign of love between a couple, to use a pregnancy alone to do this is foolish. Bringing another person into the world to 'prove' such a feeling is irresponsible.

Another group of women simply want to prove their fertility and having a baby does this in a way with which no one can argue. Today, with increasing propaganda about the dangers of VD making young girls infertile and the pill and the IUD having similar effects, increasing numbers of girls and young women who have never had a baby begin to wonder if they will be able to do so. Becoming pregnant settles the question.

Hard though it may be to believe, some doctors advise women to have babies for a variety of reasons from painful periods to 'nervous' disorders. This is unacceptable. There are perfectly good medical ways of treating such conditions and bringing another person into the world should not be seen as a type of medical therapy. Of course a few women do produce psychological symptoms because they are yearning for a baby—perhaps for them a baby is a good 'medical treatment'. Certain ethnic groups are required to prove their ability to have children before they marry on the grounds that they would be a bad marriage prospect if they were infertile, so here is yet another motive for having a baby.

There are many other reasons why couples have babies. There are, for example, genuine failures of contraception. Also, some— perhaps most—women have babies because of an innate drive to do so. It is almost impossible to say how important this latter reason is because the cultural pressures are so enormous. Instinct arguably plays a relatively small part today. If having babies were purely instinctual many women would probably have more than they already do. Many people, including some doctors, believe that a woman is not a 'real' woman until she has had a baby and that deep down all women really want babies. Some doctors even go so far as to claim that women *ought* to have babies. We cannot agree with any of these sentiments. There is no doubt that a woman who has had a baby is *different* in many ways from how she was before but to say that a baby is essential to make her whole in some way is to pervert the evidence. If our culture stopped claiming that babies were the magic answer to so many ills, then many women who really should not be having children—or so many children—would not have them and the world would be a happier place—for them and their children.

Ideally every baby should be a positively wanted baby and it is the duty of every engaged couple to discuss carefully and lovingly their views on the subject. There is little point in getting married to someone crazy about babies if you cannot stand them or only want one or two. Every couple should carefully evaluate their motives for having a baby and unless they both agree on them they should not have one. A baby is not a thing; it is a person who is going to live for scores of years and starting that process off is an awesome responsibility—not a decision to be taken lightly.

Preparing for pregnancy

Most of us go into parenthood pitifully unprepared. Culturally we are led to think that it is a blissful state in which we will have endless joys, with a text-book baby that sleeps and eats regularly and smiles and gurgles the rest of the time. Preparation for parenthood should start *before* a woman gets pregnant. We have heard some parents say that if they had known what babies were like they would have opted for none at all. Sex educators and parents should tell young people about to embark on parenthood what it is really like. Most parents minimise the hardships of child rearing (such as interrupted nights) when talking to the young about babies, possibly so as not to discourage them. Then when a young girl has her baby she is perhaps fearful, disappointed, amazed, anxious, depressed, lonely and a host of other things because she imagines she must be at fault, since everyone else seems to be coping so well, and that she is a failure.

Parents minimise the negatives.

So during preparation for pregnancy young parents-to-be should be told that babies have unwelcome aspects some of the time. They are tyrannical; do not care for your feelings; tire you out; leave you with little or no time to think, let alone do anything else; wake you at night; get ill; seem ungrateful; act irrationally; and can be generally fairly annoying. Working from this basis, whan a baby *is* pleasant it comes as a bonus. Unfortunately, most young couples probably would not listen to such talk because they would feel things will be different for them for a whole list of reasons. When they have a baby that behaves normally (in the very ways we have just listed) they are very upset, and their sex lives and even the marriage itself can begin to falter. A first baby can put tremendous strains on even a good marriage, but a shaky marriage can crumble completely. This is the reason why we say, from bitter clinical experience, that it is best to leave having a first baby until the relationship is really sound and has proved its strength and capacity to cope with the bad times as well as the good.

We would like to see every couple attending a pre-conception clinic, where they would not only be given all kinds of medical advice but would also have an hour or two with insight-trained counsellors who would look at their personalities and psychosexual development, to help them to decide whether they were really ready for children. Of course no counsellor can be 'sure' all the time, but he or she could advise the really unsuitable couple against having children at that time and guide them along paths that would help their personality growth towards successful parenthood.

Some regret having children. Some people tell us that they wish they had never had children and knew all along, deep down, that they did not want them, but felt they ought to have them. Unfortunately having children is not like having the 'flu—you cannot have 'a touch of it'. Of course being pregnant and having babies can be a wonderful, fulfilling and enjoyable experience, but we have not played on this aspect because there are plenty of books and magazines that stress these aspects of pregnancy and childbirth. From our experience there seem to be certain characteristics that help a woman become a mother more easily.

First, because motherhood is an extension of her sexuality, she should be at ease with herself as a sexual being. Many troubles occur in pregnancy, during childbirth and after because women go into the baby business still unsure of themselves and their bodies. This puts them at a disadvantage and leads to unnecessary pregnancy and labour symptoms, poor birth experiences, failed breastfeeding and eventually poor baby care.

The 'ideal' mother is at ease with her body, has a strong view of her body image and is not 'uptight' about her figure. She has an active, happy sex life, enjoys orgasms and enjoys her breasts being played with by her husband. She has intercourse rather than copulates, is at ease with her genitals and lets her husband see them and play with them. (A woman who has never had a man's fingers inside her vagina during love-play will be in for a very rude shock when it is done in semi-public with her legs up in the air and with half the world walking through the labour ward!)

Women and their own mothers. Psychologically the woman who is ready for motherhood needs to have a good relationship with *her* mother. Many women have some negative thoughts about their mothers, even though these feelings are held in their unconscious for much of the time. It is an interesting fact that many women tell their own mothers last of everybody that they are pregnant. This dates back to the childhood repression of their sexuality when they were told off for touching themselves and showing an interest in boys. Such a woman joyfully tells everyone else that she is pregnant but her mother she informs with some guilt because it so obviously confirms that she is sexually active. Almost all girls and young women believe that their mothers are asexual or do not masturbate or think that, if they do so, it must be very rarely. So it is hardly surprising that they do not think that their mothers could understand or cope with their sexuality.

Lots of women, as pregnancy advances, begin to fear that the baby will be abnormal, that it will be born dead, or that they will die while giving birth. Others worry about the pain of birth—to quote just one source, the Bible says that women shall bring forth the next generation 'in pain'. Very articulate women sometimes say that they feel they die a little each time they have a baby because they are now the older generation and a new generation has taken over. All of these conflicting emotions add to the real physical burdens and joys of pregnancy and make it a complex time.

Pregnancy is a worrying time for lots of women who have, or imagine they have, family diseases or traits. The time to get these worries sorted out is before getting pregnant. If, for example, there is spina bifida in your family, get your doctor to send you to a genetic counselling service to have the subject discussed, if it concerns you. There is no point in worrying throughout pregnancy as many women do about something you could have had explained easily. The vast majority of non-physical family traits are environmentally caused, so if, for example, your mother is very nervy and your father irascible, don't worry that your children will necessarily be the same—they probably won't be unless you are too.

All of these fears are perfectly normal and need discussing, yet according to one survey of women who had various anxieties during pregnancy, fewer than half ever discussed them with anyone, even their husbands, probably for fear of appearing silly or unmaternal. Only later, once they were confident enough of themselves as mothers, could they bring themselves to admit that they had the fears. This is a shame. Surely it is the duty of all health professionals to seek out such fears and to help women come to terms with them. Why should as many as six out of ten pregnant women suffer in this way just because they cannot bring themselves to tell anyone?

All of these fears are normal.

A less common but not totally dispelled fear is that of producing a baby of the 'wrong' sex. Although most women say that the first time round they do not much mind whether they have a boy or a girl as long as it is normal, the picture changes for later children, when parents have stronger opinions as to the sex they would like. Surveys have found that the average woman wants two children, 1.3 of whom should be boys! Although social pressures are changing, the picture tends to suggest an in-built desire to have a boy first, and a girl second. The historical, family and cultural reasons for having boys are now all but gone (families no longer need many hands to work in the family business, to farm, to produce food or to fight), yet there is still a slight preference for boys in Western society. Possibly, with the coming of vaginal jellies that will enable a couple to determine the sex of a baby, they might be able to choose with some certainty what sex they will have. This will be especially helpful for the couple who have already had two or three children of the same sex and who now go on having more children, hoping for one of the opposite sex. Many such couples would probably only have two children, if they were able to choose the sex of each. In some parts of the USA, amniocentesis is being used to discover the sex of the foetus, with abortion if it is the 'wrong' one, but we sincerely hope this practice will not catch on in Britain. Some parents 'choose' the sex they want their child to be on the basis of their love of themselves or based on their fantasies of life as it 'should' be. In the former, a man who loves himself may feel (unconsciously) that he will love a boy better than a girl because a boy is more like him. Other fathers (and mothers) fantasise that they will do all kinds of male (or female) things with a same-sex child and that this will make up for things they themselves never did as children.

Unwanted pregnancies

The majority of babies are born to married couples yet between a quarter and a half are not wanted or are unplanned. In addition to these unwanted babies within marriage a sizeable minority are born outside marriage. Given that half of all women admit to an extra-marital affair (and many have several), and that over 90 per cent of people are sexually active before marriage, there is a very considerable chance of extra-marital pregnancies occurring. Most babies born to a married woman are assumed to be hers and her husband's but the unmarried girl has very different problems.

'Bad luck' Some research shows that women having abortions are psychologically just like other women but have simply taken more risks or have used inefficient contraceptive methods. Other research suggests that this is too simple a view and that most of the women got pregnant to prove their love for their man, to add satisfaction to a relationship, or to secure a failing one. Some women were found to have got pregnant to punish themselves for sexual misdemeanours or for a previous abortion. Sometimes it is to replace a dead child or a lost boyfriend. On investigation most of the 'bad luck' category can be re-allocated to other causes.

Depression leads to carelessness over contraception and a hope that a baby will improve things.

Uncertainty over sexual identity A few women have to prove that they are really female by having a baby.

To punish their parents A teenage girl often wants to punish her repressive parents, especially if they have implied that she is promiscuous when she isn't. Some of these girls also see having a baby as a way of getting away from home.

Trying to trap an unwilling or hostile partner This is much less common than it was.

Wanting some fun and freedom before 'settling down to middle age' is not an uncommon story in older women who have an extra-marital pregnancy.

Deliberate non-contraception is remarkably common. Many women either don't like the method of contraception they are using, or really want to get pregnant, however unsuitably, or follow a moral or religious code that bans contraception.

Personality problems Women who seek abortions are found to have different views on sex compared with those who go through with their pregnancies. Abortion seekers often don't see themselves as instrumental in their unplanned pregnancy.

Changes in circumstances after conception—for example the collapse of a relationship.

Partner factors are not all that common but must be thought of. Some men deliberately get their partner pregnant to test their own fertility; to try to secure the relationship; to give themselves added personal status; to give the woman something to worry about; because of an inability to keep away from intercourse during unsafe periods; because of a weak personality development; or because of a refusal to let the woman use oral contraception (a virtually 100 per cent safe method), supposedly on religious or medical grounds but really because they fear her fidelity or the demands for sex she might make on them, and so on.

Psychosexual problems As we have said on many occasions, sexuality is simply one aspect of a person's personality and women who get pregnant when they know they shouldn't often have some kind of psychosexual problem of which they may be unaware. The types of psychosexual disorder involved are numerous but a few of the commoner ones are: a woman who believes that reproduction is the only justification for sexual pleasure. Such women may have had several babies yet deny that they are interested in sex. A second category includes those women who unconsciously believe that sex is sinful and that pregnancy is a punishment for their sin. This means that there must be a risk of pregnancy if they are to enjoy sex. Other women believe that sex is something done to them by a man and is therefore something for which they have no responsibility, so they don't bother with contraception because to do so would be a contradiction. Many young women who believe that love is the only justification for sex refuse contraception until they are sure of the man and then get pregnant in the intervening time. Some women who don't accept their sexual drives deny them consciously yet unconsciously try to indulge them (by getting drunk, losing control and then getting pregnant, for example). A small proportion of women can't tolerate any sort of contraception because they feel guilty enjoying any form of sexual pleasure. Some women are so filled with shame about their sexual drives that they don't seek contraceptive advice.

Another common fear is that to accept effective contraception is to open the floodgates to promiscuity. Such women (especially when they are unmarried) refuse all contraception and then get pregnant. Some women are unconsciously incited to pregnancy by their mother (who wants a baby for herself) but then regret the conception when it has occurred. And lastly there is the teenage girl who has just started having intercourse. Such adolescent girls frequently refuse to accept that their status has changed and even though they are *not* virgins can't bring themselves to accept the fact and continue to live with the fictitious belief that they *are* virgins. Many such girls say that they are better able to keep up the lie to their parents and themselves that they are virgins if they don't use any contraception. Such a girl believes she is still a virgin (albeit a part-time one) and for this reason doesn't really need contraception. Such a delusion in a part-time virgin unfortunately leads, all too often, to unwanted pregnancies.

Many of these reasons for being unwantedly pregnant can be prevented with professional help and better sex education but parents certainly ought to be aware of them if they are to help their daughters both before and after marriage.

Accidental pregnancy is rare.

The truly accidental pregnancy is probably rare among the married and uncommon even in teenagers. As parents we owe it to our children to bring them up in a way which makes it unlikely that they will have unwanted children, if only because they are a burden within any relationship and to society and could well end up making the couple regretful at the very least and desperately unhappy at worst.

Pregnancy

For most women who want to be pregnant and who have no particular fears or anxieties, pregnancy is an enjoyable time. The first three months produce most of the classic pregnancy symptoms, but during the middle three months most women find themselves well and content. Increasing research has shown how important the psyche is in pregnancy and there is little doubt that many pregnancy symptoms are produced or made worse by a woman's psychological state. Psychoanalysis of women with strange cravings (for eating coal, soap and so on), for example, or excessive vomiting, shows that these women often have deep psychological problems, which are at the heart of their troubles.

One of the most interesting psychological phenomena of pregnancy is the 'phantom pregnancy' (pseudo-cyesis). This is the condition in which a woman believes she is pregnant, and even has pregnancy symptoms, when she is definitely *not* pregnant. She may have a swollen stomach and can even produce milk, but there is no medical confirmation of the pregnancy and she never produces a baby. This phenomenon is also seen in animals. In women it is found both among those who desperately want or do not want a baby, and some such women insist on having an abortion, so convinced are they that they are pregnant. A few of these women, under treatment, say how they believe that sex is sinful and that they must be punished for it. Pregnancy is this punishment, so they must be pregnant.

At the other end of the scale are the many psychological and emotional causes for miscarriage. But this raises the question about how a woman knows she is pregnant—many women think they are pregnant and are having a miscarriage when in fact they are just having a heavy period. As so many women worry repeatedly about whether or not they are pregnant we will discuss the subject in some detail here.

Every day of the year millions of women in the Western world worry about whether or not they are pregnant. There is one easy and cheap way to find out—unless you are prepared to wait and see—and that is to have a pregnancy test. A doctor cannot tell with certainty whether you are pregnant or not until ten to twelve weeks after the first day of your last missed period, but many women know within days or at the latest in a couple of weeks, especially if they have been pregnant before.

Most women, though, will need a chemical pregnancy test. This can be done by a general practitioner, a hospital pathology laboratory, with a do-it-yourself kit from a pharmacist or—most reliably—by a pregnancy consultation or advisory centre or service. (All major cities have at least one. They go under various names—look them up under Pregnancy Test Services in the Yellow Pages.) The best of all these is the last because it is only here that full-time skilled staff spend all day doing the tests. As a result their accuracy rates are extremely high (over 90 per cent). The thing about being pregnant, or thinking you might be, is not to sit around worrying but to have a test done. The sooner you know, the happier you will be. If you want to have the baby then you will be pleased to know and can book into a hospital, and if you do not want it, you can have an abortion all the sooner.

Today's tests are generally positive at forty-two days after the first day of your last period, and the newest tests are positive even before this. The secret of getting good results is the careful collection of the specimen of urine. Be guided by the following rules:

1 Don't drink any fluid after 6pm the night before the test. Not drinking produces a very concentrated urine next morning which makes the test more accurate.

2 Collect the specimen properly. Sit at the back of the lavatory seat with your legs one on either side. Use clean tissues soaked only in water and wash your vulva from front to back once only with each clean piece of tissue. Separate your inner lips with the fingers of one hand and then start to urinate. Once you have a good stream don't stop but collect a small bottleful of urine as you continue to urinate. When the bottle is full take it out of the stream and continue to urinate as usual. Cap the bottle, write your name on it, the date of your last period and any drugs you are on. If you have been on the pill in the last three months the test will be difficult to interpret and other drugs could interfere with the pregnancy test too.

3 Send or take the urine sample to the testing place. Many of the best centres have postal testing services.

Sex during pregnancy

Pregnancy can be a wonderful time for a couple sexually, especially if the baby is wanted. In the first three months many women have unpleasant pregnancy symptoms, but after this things greatly improve and many women are happy and enjoy sex a lot. Some women enjoy sex more when they are pregnant than at any other time, possibly because there is no need for contraception and because deep down she knows that sex can now be for pleasure only. In general a woman's sexual interest falls as pregnancy progresses.

Most men enjoy their wives being pregnant—many of the body changes (rounded figure, larger breasts, fuller face, shiny hair, better skin condition, no periods and so on) make a woman more physically attractive. Some men with a poor opinion of their masculinity now really come into their own because they have achieved a tangible landmark as a man that no one can argue with. This makes them more at ease and less anxious about their sexuality and can have a pleasant effect on their wives. Many women say that from the twelfth week or so onwards they feel more cuddly and physical than usual (though not necessarily wanting more intercourse) and many women want more breast and clitoral play than intercourse, perhaps because they fear that intercourse will harm the baby. There is no truth behind this fear unless the pregnancy is unstable for some reason already.

Intercourse during pregnancy does no harm either to mother or baby (except possibly very late on, as we shall see) and we think it actually does the couple good for a number of reasons. First, a couple who is enjoying a lively sex life will be preparing themselves as a partnership to be good parents. Remember that a substantial proportion of all men who ever have an affair do so when their wives are pregnant or soon after. This suggests that such couples are not being as attentive to one another as they might be. During pregnancy, as at all times, married couples should release each other's sexual tensions. So a couple enjoying the woman's pregnancy will quite understandably want to show their love for each other *more* and not less often and will do this in many ways, one of which is having intercourse more often. All of this makes it more likely they will enjoy the birth of the new baby.

The second reason why sex is good during pregnancy is that an orgasm is actually a mini-labour, so frequent orgasms may help to increase uterine efficiency and blood flow to the area. It has been suggested that such an increased blood flow might help the development of the baby's brain, but this is speculative at the moment. Certainly many women enjoy orgasms greatly during pregnancy even if they have never previously done so. There is no evidence that this does harm and orgasms *may* actually be advantageous to mother and baby.

Up until the last few weeks have intercourse in any position you feel comfortable with—you will find the spoons position (see page 213), the various rear-entry positions and the woman-on-top positions most easy to get into and most comfortable when the woman's stomach is big. The penis cannot do the baby any harm as it hits the

Sex in pregnancy: In this restful position the woman can be massaged and masturbated even very late into pregnancy.

PREGNANCY AND CHILDBIRTH

Sex in pregnancy: In this position, provided deep penetration is avoided, both partners can enjoy a lot of pleasure with no risk of harm to the baby.

uterus, but it makes sense to avoid any positions that cause the woman pain or discomfort.

When it comes to the last six to eight weeks, it is probably best to go a little more gently because research has shown that intercourse may possibly cause the baby distress, though this does not cause any real medical problems as far as is known. During this time it may be found preferable for the couple to masturbate each other. Oral sex and swallowing semen late on in pregnancy and especially very near term (delivery) can possibly start off labour because of the uterus-contracting substances in semen called prostaglandins. If your general practitioner or pre-natal clinic doctor tells you to avoid sex for a particular medical reason, then of course it makes sense to follow his advice. Also, be sure not to have intercourse if you have vaginal bleeding during pregnancy. See your doctor at once if you ever bleed during pregnancy.

Enjoy other types of love-making.

If you have had a previous miscarriage it is probably best to keep off intercourse for the first twelve weeks and especially around the time when your period would have been due, but you could discuss this with your obstetrician.

Though most couples enjoy love-making during pregnancy, a few find that things go wrong. Some women become unresponsive and uncomfortable when they know they are pregnant. Such women need professional help. Also a man may have potency problems once his wife has conceived. Sometimes there are fears relating to hurting the baby in the womb but often the causes are much more complex and need sorting out by a psychosexual expert. Such women (or men) often feel that sex is OK when it is for a bit of harmless fun but once they get on with the serious business of children they should (they believe, unconsciously) behave differently.

The birth

Birth, like the love-making that started it all off, is primarily a sexual event. Unfortunately, with pre-natal care which treats women like objects on a conveyor belt and with delivery rooms like operating theatres, much of modern obstetrics has lost sight of this fact. The fact that so many women have such unhappy memories of their childbirth experiences says little for our Western obstetric system, but things will undoubtedly change as public pressure increases.

From an emotional point of view there is little doubt that it is most pleasant to have a baby at home, but hospital is safer in some cases for both mother and baby. The difficulty in choosing whether to have a baby at home or in hospital lies in the fact that apart from the group of predictable high-risk births, it is impossible to know whether any one labour is going to need urgent medical attention or not. Some mothers are happy to take any slight risk there may turn out to be in having a baby at home and believe that for them this is the best place. A book like this is no place to go into all the detailed arguments for and against home and hospital deliveries, but wherever the birth takes place the couple should be allowed to be together if they want to all through the labour, the entire birth and afterwards.

(overleaf) The interested father-to-be: By taking an interest in her body changes a man can help his woman to adapt psychologically to the physical changes taking place in her body.

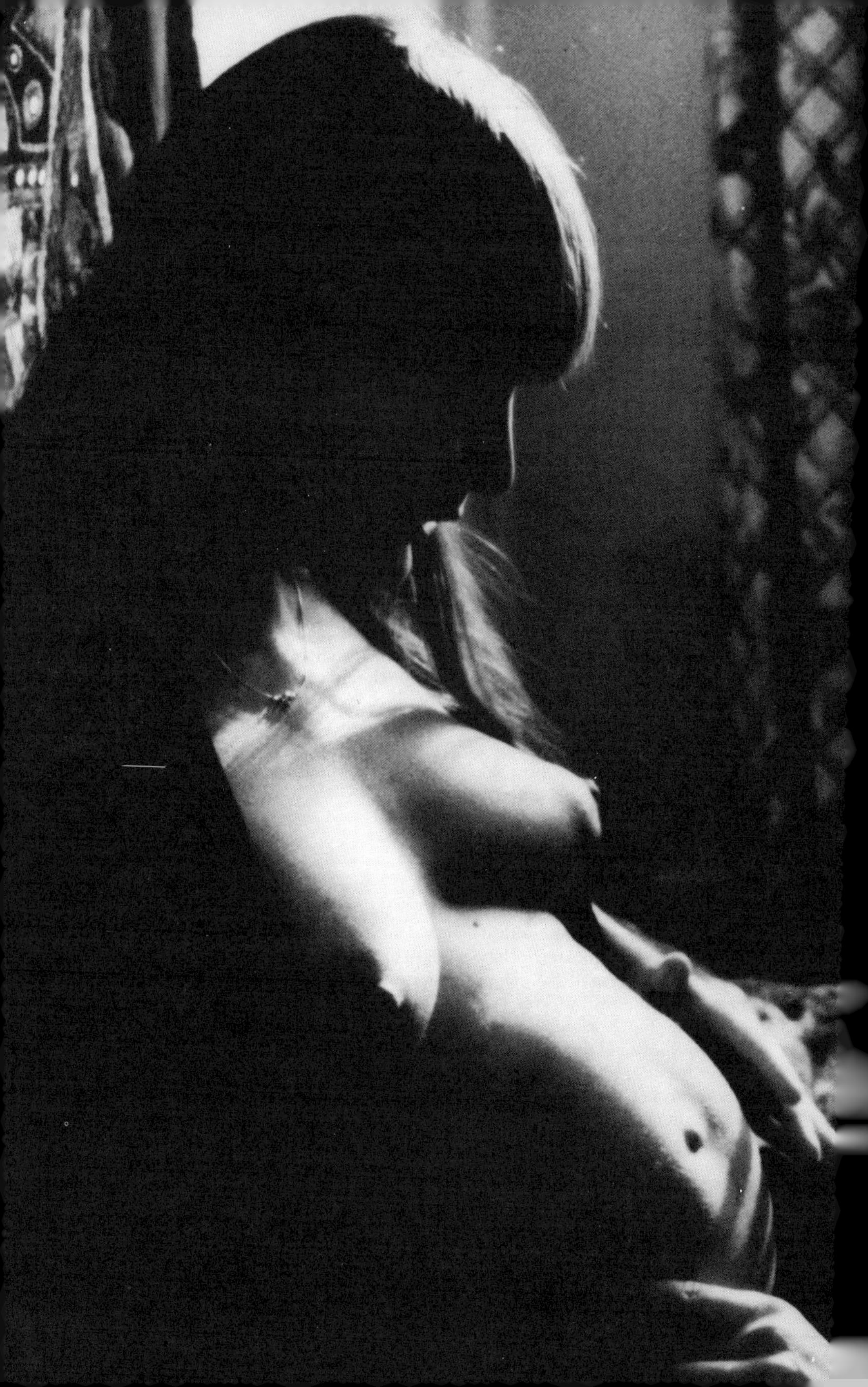

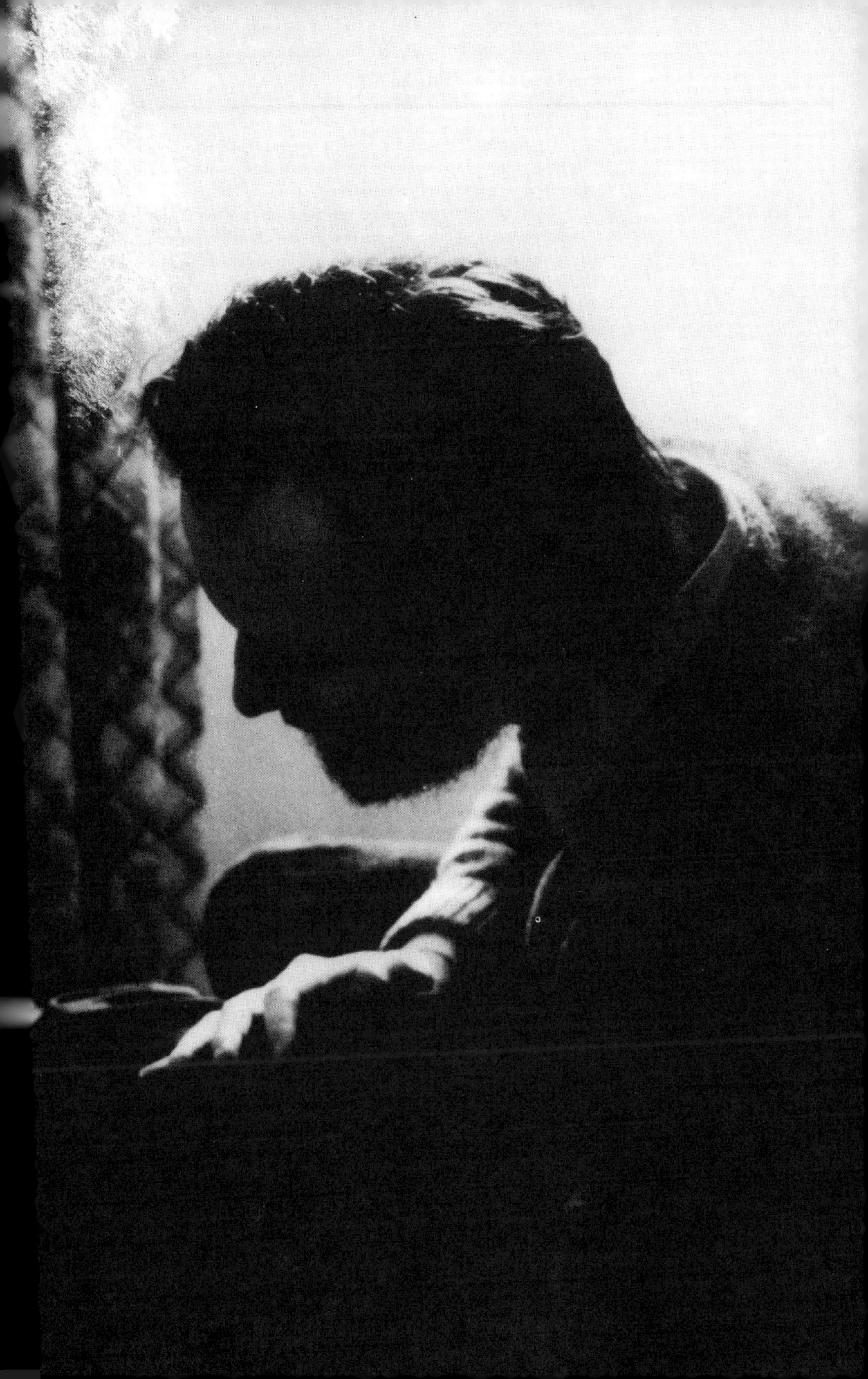

Assuming a woman has a normal birth, there are some guidelines that can make the whole thing more enjoyable and memorable—for the right reasons!

When the woman gets to term and assuming you have not been told of any medical complications, go about intercourse gently, and if there is any pain or discomfort try another position or stop altogether. If the woman enjoys oral sex but has been avoiding swallowing semen, she can start again now. As mentioned on page 297, semen has been used for thousands of years by people all over the world as a way of starting off babies when the woman is ready to give birth. Semen by mouth and in the vagina helps, and orgasms will also almost certainly help start off labour if the cervix is 'ripe'.

We favour natural birth situations that involve the minimum of intervention unless medically necessary (when all available help should be at hand) but such methods are, unfortunately, not widely available yet. Ideally the woman should be able to walk around for as long as she wants to and should adopt the positions that are most comfortable for her during each stage of the birth. The majority of women around the world, given a choice, do *not* choose to lie down. Giving birth flat on your back in the 'stranded beetle' position is a modern Western notion that most women accept because it is what they have been conditioned into believing is right. Most women, given the choice, crouch or kneel down and let gravity help the baby come out more easily. Using such methods research has found that less pain relief (if any) is required; that Caesarean sections are rare; that episiotomies are hardly ever needed; that the babies are better oxygenated (have a better blood supply); that labours are shorter; and that the mothers enjoy the birth more. During the whole of the birth the husband should be able to be present but if the 'business end' upsets him he can stay up the head end and talk to, cuddle and massage his wife.

Once the baby is born, rather than a midwife giving the mother an injection of a drug to make the uterus contract to expel the placenta, the husband can enhance normal physiological uterine contraction after birth by playing with his wife's nipples. You will both need to be fairly uninhibited to do this but it usually works well. You will want to cuddle each other after the birth, and look at and stroke the baby (still attached to the cord). Once the cord has stopped pulsating or once the baby is breathing well it can be cut. To do so before robs the baby of valuable oxygen-carrying blood.

Immediately after the birth a couple should ideally be together all the time with their baby, simply relaxing and enjoying each other's company and getting to know the baby. Assuming that mother and baby are both well there is no reason why they should not leave the hospital within twenty-four hours or even less, if the woman wants to—then the couple will be at home again with their baby in their own nest. This is important for the success of breastfeeding and enables the husband to be with his wife and the baby. Many couples may not be able to arrange this but it is becoming increasingly possible and is even encouraged in more enlightened centres.

Having a baby is not an illness—it is a normal physiological event. What is needed is more home-like privacy within hospitals, where expert staff and equipment should be available if needed. Unfortunately, medical and nursing staff have been trained into thinking they are essential even for the average, normal labour and birth and so find it almost impossible not to intervene with one 'essential' procedure or another. All of these disrupt the couple's inter-personal relationship, infantilise the woman at a time when she, obviously, feels vulnerable and even possibly harm the mother or the baby. Babies usually deliver themselves and simply need supervision in case of trouble but sometimes a professional will be necessary to help with problems. Women allowed to give birth in the way we have described have fewer problems and so need less help.

At first a lot of women find the whole idea of birth being a lovely, sensual and even sexual experience rather strange or even impossible to believe, but there is plenty of evidence that it can be. A few women describe labour as the most exhilarating orgasm they have ever had! Some women have clitoral enlargement during childbirth, some feel pleasantly sexually aroused when breastfeeding and some even have orgasms. None of this should come as any surprise to a reader who has come this far in the book because pregnancy and childbirth are simply another manifestation of a woman's sexuality, like her clothes, her walk, the way she makes love and the way she cares for her children. All of this sexual behaviour is modified (if not actually caused) by oxytocin—the 'love hormone'. When a woman has an orgasm, is breastfeeding, is in labour, or gives birth, her blood oxytocin level is raised. This makes her feel loving, motherly and caring. Even before the levels of this hormone were measurable in the blood, people had noticed that women felt similar in these situations involving their sexual physiology, so it is hardly surprising that labour and birth are so sexual an experience for some women. It is not being sentimental to say that birth under the right conditions *can* be a beautiful, memorable and uplifting experience for both parents.

Sex and breastfeeding

There is now no doubt in the minds of the medical profession (and most women agree) that breastfeeding is best for a baby, yet few babies are still being totally breastfed at one month. It is true that about 70 per cent of mothers breastfeed their babies in hospitals in most of the Western world today, but as soon as they get home 'problems' intervene and the babies are soon on the bottle. Husbands are well known to influence their wives' choice of baby feeding method and successful breastfeeding is really only likely if a woman's husband is supportive. Years of breastfeeding counselling experience indicate that breastfeeding is not so much a matter of nutrition as of sex.

There can be few people who would disagree that a woman's breasts are probably her most obvious sexual signal, and certainly they are used more in advertisements to entice than any other part of her body. So it is hardly surprising that most women think of their breasts as having a sexual function first and a nutritional one second.

The other function of the breast: Many men find the changes in lactating breasts enhance their attractiveness—contrary to what women think. Sometimes, however, a father is reluctant to share 'his' breasts with his baby.

And of course they are right because for the majority of their lives this is true. However, because of the sexual nature of breasts in our society, many men and slightly fewer women feel that their breasts (and therefore their sexual attractiveness) may be permanently affected for the worse if they breastfeed. Research shows that this is not so. It is pregnancy with its breast enlargement that causes sagging, if it occurs at all, and not breastfeeding. Letting the breasts become over-full (engorged) can probably make them more saggy too.

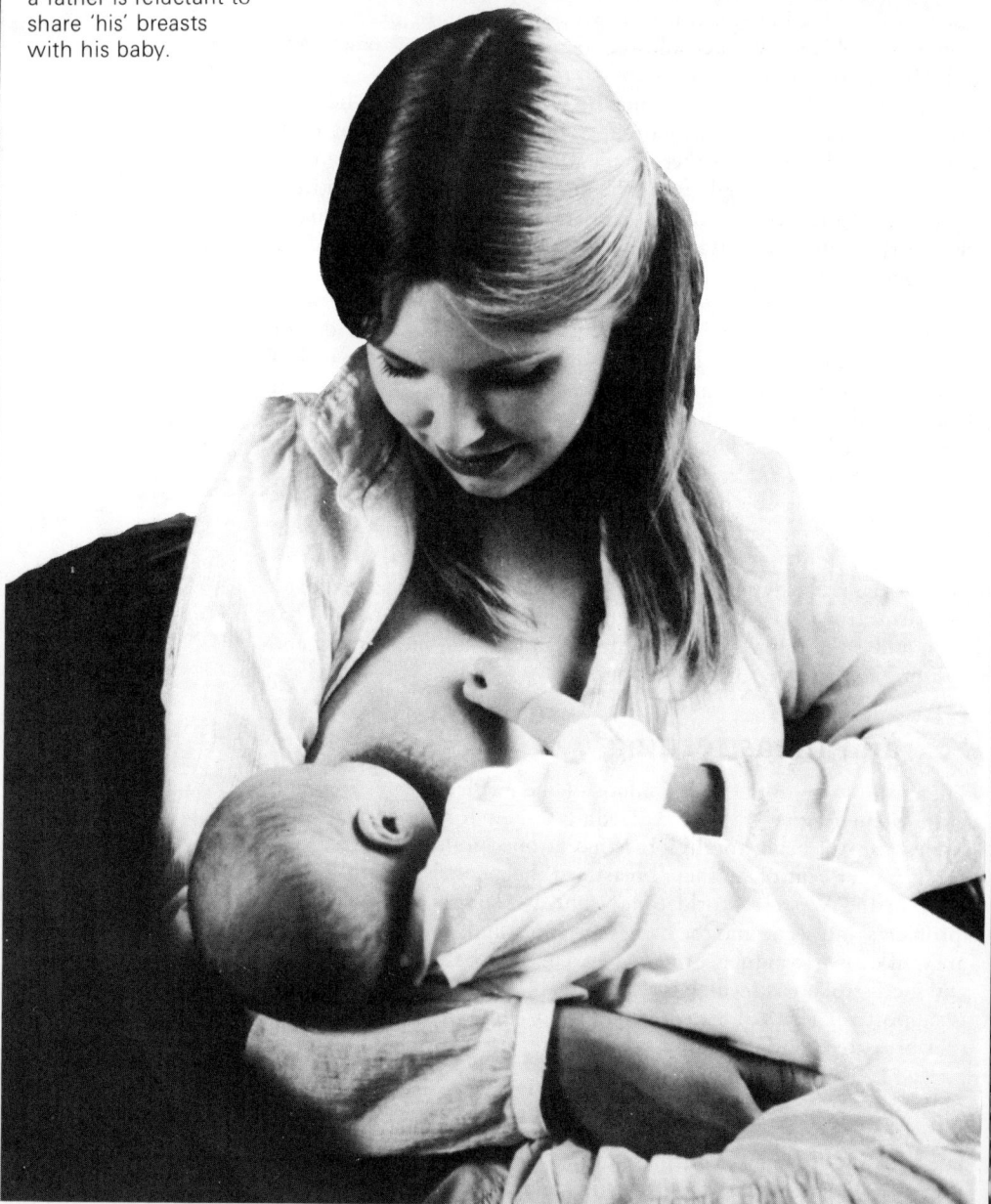

Certainly it makes sense to wear a well-fitting bra in the last few months of pregnancy, even at night, so that the breasts' natural supportive tissues are given some help, and of course a sensible woman wears a bra all the time she is nursing for the same reason. Apart from this though, there is no reason to suppose that breastfeeding needs any special breast preparation or that it does the breasts any permanent harm. On the contrary, most small-breasted women say that they prefer their breasts when they are bigger during pregnancy and lactation and so do their husbands. Some women have permanently larger breasts after stopping breastfeeding.

Many men are unsure about breastfeeding because they are jealous of the baby being at their partner's breasts so much. Some create a great fuss and issue an 'it's him or me' ultimatum. This is a pity because a happy, loving couple can share the woman's breasts in three ways. The woman herself, her husband and their baby can all enjoy them. There is no reason why a man should not continue to kiss and caress his wife's breasts when she is breastfeeding; in fact a lot of women feel more sexy and breast-centred when they are breastfeeding than they ever usually would and this can be to the husband's advantage. If you have a baby in bed with you, your husband can even suck your milk from one breast while the baby sucks the other!

Making love while lactating needs a few words. Many women's breasts, especially if they are full a long time after a feed, become tense and uncomfortable, especially if squeezed or played with sexually. The answer is to express some milk or feed the baby before making love so as to reduce the tension. This also makes milk leakage less likely if the woman has an orgasm. Often at orgasm she will leak or even spurt milk as the sexual arousal hormones surge around her body. One answer is to encourage her husband to suck her nipples while making love. There will be plenty of milk left for the baby. Intercourse positions will have to be chosen so as not to squash the woman's full breasts but this is usually no problem for most couples.

The main thing about breastfeeding from a sexual point of view is for the woman to encourage her husband to fondle her breasts, even if he is reticent or shy. Don't let him feel completely left out.

After the birth

If you go home early as we have suggested, you will be back in your own bed and able to cuddle each other and be especially loving towards the baby. Breastfeeding will proceed easily with the baby in bed and you will have fewer broken nights than you would getting up to get bottles ready. Many women who feed their babies in bed hardly wake up at all—they usually turn on to one side and the baby feeds on and off all night in the early weeks. This is also pleasant for the husband who does not lose his wife to another room for half the night and can cuddle his baby too. You should not take a little baby into bed with you like this, though, if you are very obese, or if you are drunk or on sleeping pills. In any of these circumstances you could suffocate the baby. The vast majority of people around the world have their babies in bed with them and no doubt always have done.

If you are in hospital, be sure to see plenty of your husband and cuddle up to each other and to the baby as much and as often as you can. Look after your baby all the time and keep him with you twenty-four hours of the day, in your bed if you are allowed to.

The return to sex after birth is very much a personal matter. Some women who have had no stitches (an episiotomy can leave a woman sore for many months—one reason why we are against routine episiotomies) can be back to sex in two weeks, but most do not feel like intercourse this early. Breastfeeding makes a woman's sexual organs return to normal more quickly than would be the case had she started to bottle-feed, and totally breastfeeding women return to intercourse earlier. By about six weeks the majority of women feel ready for intercourse again but if there is any pain you should talk to your doctor or obstetrician at the post-natal check-up. While waiting for intercourse to be comfortable again you can enjoy other types of love-making. Many women want to return to having orgasms a few days after birth and there is no harm at all in this. In fact it is probably positively helpful because it seems to help the uterus to return more quickly to its normal state. But whenever you return to sex be sure to be well protected with contraceptives. Whilst you would be extremely unlucky to conceive in the first month or two after birth it can and does happen. Women who breastfeed exclusively and on demand, whenever the baby or they want, on average do not ovulate for about fourteen months after the birth, but the bottle-feeding mother and the woman who breastfeeds on a restricted basis can do so within a few weeks. Talk to your doctor at the post-natal check-up about which form of contraception would be best.

Parental reactions to pregnancy and childbirth

Having a baby puts a new mother and her relationship with her husband to the test. It tests her maturity; the strength of her identity as a woman; her ability to be both dependent and independent; her capacity to cope with anxiety; and her relationship with her own body. Quite understandably, many women find all this too much and do not enjoy their first baby as much as they could.

Even a woman who really wants a baby may become anxious and depressed early in pregnancy. The food hates and cravings which occur in some pregnant women are usually quite normal but they may express an unconscious need for the woman to baby herself; she may be eating in this way to offset her depression; or the symptoms may have a sexual significance. The often secret and much rarer eating of peculiar substances, such as coal and soap, may express unconscious desires to humiliate or punish herself. Much of this is very complicated psychologically and most doctors have neither the training nor the time and inclination to sort out such problems.

Most husbands today are willing to understand and help their wives during pregnancy but the majority do not do as well as they could because they are not sufficiently well informed about the real fears and anxieties of pregnant women. Virtually all husbands regard the pregnancy as very much their concern and nearly all want to learn how to help. Unfortunately, they are often excluded by health professionals and have only fairly recently been admitted to the labour ward, for example.

About one in ten expectant fathers produce symptoms during pregnancy for which no physical explanation is found. These include abdominal pain, nausea and vomiting, toothache and so on. This condition is psychosomatic and is known as couvade. The symptoms occur most in the early months but recur at the end of pregnancy and end with delivery.

As the birth approaches most women seem to regress psychologically to a child-like state of dependence. Whether this is natural or is the result of the way the culture and health professionals treat them is hard to say. If she is adequately prepared psychologically her understandable anxieties will be under control by now, which will help to reduce any pain or distress during labour. Obviously, expectations are important and here again both the culture to which she has been exposed since childhood and the professionals around her have an effect.

Baby-blues

Three or four days after delivery more than 80 per cent of women develop the 'baby-blues', with weeping, anxiety, confusion and fears of incompetence. This temporary state of post-natal depression is probably more common in women in hospital than in those at home and is thought to be less common among mothers who breastfeed on an unrestricted basis from birth. Usually it is short-lived and could be partly due to the dramatic hormonal changes following delivery.

Although some mothers seem to fall in love with their baby at first sight, others question their feelings, waiting for the overpowering love our culture has taught them is felt by all 'normal' women. Women who have had a baby of the 'wrong' sex may take time to adjust and those whose children have any blemish, no matter how slight, may also have difficulty at this stage. These doubts may contribute to a feeling of depression. All this is hardly surprising when one remembers that the average woman is emotionally vulnerable immediately after the birth and that for as long as she stays in hospital she is not the baby's responsible mother—the midwives are. Once home she is in charge and handles and cuddles her baby more. This is undoubtedly one reason why depression is less common after a home birth.

Baby battering

If the pressures on the woman from the baby, from herself and from those around her are considered and if we bear in mind that her relationship with her baby is a straightforward inter-personal one rather than an overwhelming instinctive form of mother-love, then baby battering becomes easily understandable. Increasing research is now suggesting that the way a baby behaves influences its mother's reactions and not just the other way round, which was the way most experts considered the situation until recently. The way a baby responds to what its mother does greatly influences the way she in turn behaves. So, as in any inter-personal relationship, both parties are responsible for the actions and reactions of the other. In contrast to the typical picture of an indifferent, neglectful mother, the battering mother is often one who *does* care. She desperately wants the baby to love her but it may seem to her not to do so. It cries inconveniently or incessantly after she has done her very best for it and this she sees as rejection and criticism. Babies are designed to cry instinctively to ensure their survival, and though experienced mothers are very sensitive to these calls the inexperienced mother can have real problems recognising them or knowing what to do.

Hostility versus cooperation. The baby itself will eventually gain some control and will learn, when it is older, that screaming the place down when it wants something may well lead to hostility rather than cooperation from its parents. This learning is likely to be the result of a certain amount of parental irritation, and so the dividing line between the normal parent and the battering parent can be a fine one.

As far as prevention is concerned it is known that anything which fosters the inter-personal relationship is protective for the baby. Keeping the baby with its mother all the time right from birth is important in this context, as is encouraging her to experience maximum physical pleasure from it. Both of these things help the bonding process between them. Because of our cultural attitudes battering parents are far more likely to be punished than helped, especially if they are men. Often the circumstantial odds are so stacked against them that at the particular moment when they resort to battering, they seem to have no other option. Parents Anonymous is a self-help organisation run by parents who have been in this position, for others who fear they might batter or who actually have battered their babies.

Although mothers are usually more tense with first than with later babies, subsequent babies tend to over-tax them more, so children of any birth order can be battered. Whether or not physical battering occurs, thousands of children each year suffer damage to their personality as a result of serious emotional abuse.

Men's role

The arrival of the first child signals a tremendous change from the man's one-to-one relationship with his wife and is the start of increasing detachment from her unless they both work hard at keeping emotionally close. Alternatively, the man may compete with the baby or may try to form an exclusive relationship with it so as to have it for himself.

One of the most common problems seen by marriage guidance counsellors is the young couple who have just had their first baby. The woman is baffled, tired, anxious, possibly depressed and is trying desperately hard to be a good mother as she has been brought up to think she should be. Her husband often feels impotent (and not necessarily just sexually); cannot think what he could do to make the unique and exclusive relationship between mother and baby work better than it is doing; and often feels shut out if his wife is coping perfectly well without him.

Obviously a woman who makes her husband feel unwanted or pushed out by the baby is foolish, not only because he will feel bad but because she is at a time when she needs a friend and someone who cares for and loves her. Having a baby is a joint affair—it is not something a woman does on her own.

First-time parents-to-be have fantasies, fears and concepts of 'ideal' parenthood which influence their attitudes towards their new baby and all that surrounds it. These areas are rarely investigated or even acknowledged by those caring for the pregnant woman but they need to be discussed fully by the couple and problem areas taken further with a professional where necessary. When this advice is followed the couple can anticipate problem areas and can do something about them, so enhancing their enjoyment both of the events and of each other. We live in a strange world—women receive more counselling for abortion than they do for childbirth!

Summary

Pregnancy, childbirth and motherhood all suffer from culturally inspired fears, myths and expectations. Good sexual attitudes and satisfactory sexual practices are the background, preparation and key to happy pregnancy, childbirth and especially to good mothering. Women not only have a spiritual bond with their babies—they also have a powerful biological one. The damage we do to girls by ignoring the physical and biological side of mothering is enormous and leads many of them to get less out of pregnancy, birth and motherhood than they could. This is not simply of academic interest, though, because it deeply influences how they behave to both their husband and their baby and the way they view themselves.

Chapter 24

Other people's children

Adoption

In its widest sense adoption is not an uncommon practice world-wide; many children are mainly reared by grandparents and other relatives, though this is now uncommon in the West. A form of adoption has been practised by some of the wealthy for centuries in that their children have been handed over to the care of wet-nurses, nannies, governesses and other parent substitutes. The child of a working mother today spends the major part of its waking day in the care of others and so may be influenced by them more than by its parents.

More formally and legally, adoption means that a child is handed over by its biological parent or parents to adoptive parents, and that thereafter he or she is legally the latters' child and their responsibility just as if he or she were one of their own. Because of previous abuses (some children have simply been sold in the past), the law controls the situation and adoptions are now legal only through recognised adoption agencies. Private adoptions between individuals are illegal.

Because of the advent of abortion, more effective contraception, the greater social acceptability of the unmarried mother and the willingness of the welfare state to support her if necessary, fewer babies are now available for adoption. About 60 per cent of all adoptions, however, are now 'in-family' adoptions in which one or other parent is the child's natural parent.

Obviously we cannot go into the mechanics of adoption in a book of this scope but some of the problems associated with adoption are of more general interest because of the light they throw on normal development and attitudes.

The shame of having a baby illegitimately can continue for years and the rights recently given to adoptees over the age of eighteen to have access to their original birth records, through which they can often trace at least their mother, have inspired terror in some such mothers who have established a new life in the meantime and have kept the adoption secret.

The courts, various religious organisations and the local authorities are all involved in adoption but this does not necessarily make the task of matching children to families any easier. From time to time courts have been reported as being rather offensive in the comments they pass in adoption cases, and local authorities are not

One father . . . two mothers? The older children are by the father's first wife. His new younger wife is the mother of the small child. Unless this is carefully handled the situation can become explosive.

organised in a way which makes for consistency in the care they provide for the children in their charge whilst awaiting adoption. For example, children in residential nurseries have, on average, been handled by at least fifty different people for a week or longer by the age of four and a half years.

Religious bodies involved in adoption often insist that the child be brought up in their faith and the mothers who give up the babies to them expect their wishes to be honoured on this matter. It is only rarely that such societies accept adoptive parents of other religions. Moral and religious attitudes probably tend to influence decisions as to which couples are chosen and which are rejected when applying for a child even where a religiously based adoption society is not involved. Children are much better off being adopted than remaining in the care of a local authority, regardless of their age at the time of adoption. As a rule, also, children who are adopted rather than being restored to their natural parents are usually better off. Adoption is an extremely difficult area to work in. There are simply too many people choosing too few babies and unpalatable decisions have to be made. The problem is that the adoption society's first duty is to the child and they owe it to that child to find a family that will suit him or her. This is never easy and, given the shortage of babies, is bound to produce heartaches.

Another practice that is worrying in some instances is for the organisation responsible for the adoption to insist that the biological mother has contact with her baby after the birth. They argue that the woman's decision is not realistic unless she has had contact with the baby. Women given time to make up their minds once the baby is actually there are sometimes tempted to change their minds and keep the baby. This is probably no bad thing because quite often the woman does not know if giving up the baby for adoption is the best thing and needs more time to decide. However this practice can be criticised as cruel if the child becomes attached to the mother and the mother bonded to the child before the decision to give him up is made. This could then be harmful to them both.

Another subject of possible concern is the current advice to adoptive parents to inform their child at the earliest possible time that it has been adopted. Pre-school children often are not psychologically equipped to cope with the knowledge, and the trauma of it may run through their lives from then on, often leading to damage to their self-esteem and to a general sense of worthlessness. The evidence suggests that children should not be told until they have the verbal skills to communicate any distress they may feel. The adoption agencies claim that children informed early, simply accept it and regard it as being of no consequence but the medical evidence is against this view. Perhaps all that young adopted children need to know, like all others, is that they belong to their family, that they are valuable and valued, and that they are loved. Of course a child who is adopted when not a baby (and these are greatly in the majority) may remember his other family so the argument is then academic.

Fostering

Adoption is, of course, only one way in which children other than one's own come to live under one's own roof as part of the family; fostering, a system in which one or more children come to live in a household for a very variable length of time, is even more commonplace than adoption. Foster parents do not usually have quite the same problems as do adoptive parents because fostering is not a lifetime's legal commitment and foster children usually have more contact with their natural parents. This puts the foster parents in a difficult 'piggy-in-the-middle' situation, though, because they have to take not only the child and his parents into account but also the welfare agencies involved.

Step-families

Although children living in step-families are still, of course, a minority, they are a growing minority and one that causes more than its share of heartache. In the past most step-children resulted from remarriages caused by death but now divorce has overtaken these figures.

People who go into a second marriage with high hopes are often horrified to find that the situation is difficult and often actually hostile and that their children actively threaten the new union. Quite a few marriages break up for this very reason, yet few people want to talk about it. As well over half of all divorces involve children and most divorcees remarry, there are large numbers of step-children in the community at any one time (about 20-30 million in the US in the seventies).

To see why step-parenting is so difficult, let us compare it with adoption. The parents of adopted children are seen as having equal status by a child but clearly a step-child will feel very differently towards his or her 'new' parent compared with the biological parent. Some adoptions are of babies or very young children but step-children can come on to the scene at all ages—often quite old—and after having had good relationships with the parent who is lost. Also, adoptive parents get plenty of professional help and support, but the step-parent does not.

The sad thing about much step-parenting is that both parties (children and adults) are usually so hurt from their family break-up that they are all crying out for love and affection. Often all are trying desperately hard to be lovable yet they find that they cannot receive or give love. Research has found that most remarrying couples desperately want their new partner to love their children, and loving her children has become an integral part of wooing the divorced or widowed woman. Many people remarry to make up for the loss of a father or mother in the family even if they do not consciously admit it. This creates all kinds of problems about how to refer to the children. 'My children', 'our children' and 'the children' are all used, but 'my children' often takes a long time to come for the step-parent.

One practical step that is often helpful is for a new couple to have another child. This cements the union in the eyes of the couple, the world and the existing children, who seem to like it because a half-brother or sister links them. This seems to be particularly important if the new mother has not had any children before.

Slowly as the months and years pass it is possible, and even common, to build up a real feeling of love for one's step-children even if at first it seems rather unlikely. In fact many people enjoy a different, more relaxed and more adult loving relationship with their step-children than they do with their own. Perhaps the fears of loss of love are not present in the same way, allowing the step-parent to be more open and so freer to love.

Summary

Adoption should ideally offer a symmetrical solution to the twin problems of the child who is not wanted and cannot be cared for and the couple who want a child to add to their existing family or because they cannot have their own. Although most adoptions are relatively trouble-free adoption procedures still cause some concern.

Having a child or children who are not one's own flesh and blood in the family is always bound to present problems—especially when parents are involved. As millions of children are involved throughout the Western world, these are problems we all have to be aware of.

Chapter 25
Teaching children about sex

Sex education

Unlike animals and some human communities, we in the West do not allow children to learn about sex from direct observation and subsequent experimentation. Whatever the merits of this course of action, it can expose our children to misunderstandings, misleading fantasies, misinformation and a general state of ignorance and confusion. It also raises questions about the age at which children should be taught, what they should be taught, by whom and how, and what rights, if any, parents should have in deciding these issues. Some people believe that the child or adolescent should not be taught anything at all but that they should be left to find out for themselves—after marriage, of course. Their underlying fear is that if children are taught anything before marriage they will go straight off and do it. Others, more realistically, believe that it is impossible to keep knowledge about sex secret from the unmarried and that the best course is to try to inculcate a sense of responsibility, along with accurate information and a knowledge of contraception, before it is too late. Reason is on their side because ignorance is more likely to lead to sexual irresponsibility or incompetence than to provide a firm basis for prevention.

The term 'sex education' is a woolly one. In this chapter we are dealing with formalised sex education in the teacher–pupil sense—although the teacher may of course be a parent. The vast majority of 'education' about sexual matters occurs informally in the very earliest years of life—in fact sex education starts in the cradle.

That harm can come from sex education is indisputable. Individual children can be greatly disturbed by it but this is not usually the case. Such vulnerability may spring from problems unique to a particular child and may be associated with his or her rearing, but sex education may not be the best way of helping the child at a particular time. In any case, education about sex, like education on other topics, can be done well or badly, and sensitively or insensitively. It may not be done at all—this happens especially for boys. This is illogical because when it comes to sexual behaviour the human male depends more than the female on learning. Sex education is more common for girls and its covert aim is usually to deter them from sexual activity. In some schools sex education is so vague that the child does not realise it has been given.

Our only hope for a better future in sex, as in everything else, is

Sex education in the home: Although she does not realise it this mother will communicate more sex education messages to her children unconsciously than she ever will on an occasion like this.

through education in its various forms. It falls to all of us to ensure that accurate knowledge and sensible attitudes are taught to the young.

However, the situation is not as simple as this. Even before a child starts school his or her psychosexual development is well advanced. The child will have seen how his or her parents show affection (or do not) and he or she will have been rebuked or restrained over sexual matters many times. Attitudes about sex, which will affect sexual behaviour later, have already been instilled into the unconscious mind, largely from the unconscious minds of the child's parents.

There is considerable discussion among sex-educators as to the best age to start formal sex education. Various ages are suggested. A favourite choice is some time in the junior-school years when the child is in the stage of latency and therefore unlikely to become obsessed with the topic. However, such discussions overlook the fact that the foundations for sexual attitudes in subsequent life were laid years earlier. The parents, wittingly or unwittingly, have already established the basis of a moral code in the child. The fact that this is frequently unsound in that it adds negative emotions to sex is discussed in chapter 1. A sound programme of sex education might try to establish more rational attitudes, but the difficulty or impossibility of achieving this in formal teaching situations will be understood by everyone who realises that it is the unconscious which largely governs sex rather than superficial 'intellectual' attitudes. Only psychotherapy can effect such a change and this clearly is not practical for millions of children.

Sex education in school: Schofield (see page 65) found that this can be so oblique that the child does not realise that he or she is having sex education.

However, this raises two points. First, any realistic sex-education programme should be based on the establishment of insight. To explain to the young what has basically happened to them during their psychosexual development and what will happen in future is to provide them with a powerful means of self-control. If they can also be given insight into the opposite sex they will be better placed when it comes to partner selection and entering into marriage.

The second point is that formal sex education should not be thought of in the context of school alone. Most mothers want to do their very best for their babies and guidance on sex education as a part of pre-natal classes would be less controversial than sex education in schools and would be aimed at the one segment of the community who really are in a position to influence the next generation. Moreover, even at a factual level mothers themselves often benefit from such education. Surveys of the knowledge of simple anatomical facts in this group have revealed appalling ignorance. A recent survey of 127 working girls aged sixteen to twenty-one showed only minimal knowledge about contraception and over two-thirds had run the risk of pregnancy. Obviously the sex education they had received was ineffective, insufficient, or both, and required supplementation.

This, however, points to a further difficulty in sex education. Those girls may have been given adequate contraceptive information but may have chosen (unconsciously) not to incorporate it into their body of knowledge. This ineffectiveness arises from the fact that, because of attitudes instilled during rearing, some children do not want to know about some aspects of sexuality and even when told in a

Sex education for girls: Girls are much more likely to be given sex education than boys—a lot of it aimed at attempting to control their sexuality. Instruction such as this could well convey little or no information about the wonder of sex.

clear and pleasant way repress what they have been told. Studies have found that many children shown sex-education films in the morning cannot say what they were about later the same day. Clearly their unconscious minds have suppressed the information.

Another problem with sex education is that a child's perception of the individual who is putting across sexual information affects his or her readiness to accept it. A teacher who is open and friendly is likely to be more effective than one who is moralistic and religious.

Perhaps the best solution would be to train specialist teachers who would move from school to school to give lessons in the presence of the usual class teacher who would then be involved in the subsequent discussion. Perhaps 'sex-education classes' could be established independently of the formal education system. Probably many parents, and teachers, would welcome such a development.

A great proportion of sex-education material, even for adults, let alone for the young, treats the recipients as if they were fools. The consequence of treating people like fools is that they are likely to behave foolishly. On these grounds alone sex education should be fully factual and should use photographs or films whenever possible. Such material can easily be labelled obscene but with care suitable illustrations can be found. Obviously it should not be horrific. Some films of childbirth, for example, are fully realistic but manage to be more reassuring than frightening. Others put some girls off childbearing for life and frequently make both girls and boys faint. Some teaching materials about VD are so horrific that the children are frightened off the opposite sex. This is totally inexcusable. Surely the idea of sex education in the widest sense must be to encourage the sexes to think well of each other and to enjoy each other. Shock-horror propaganda will never do this.

The knowledge given should match the stage of development of the child to whom it is addressed and should aim to deal with the myths and false fantasies that arise in that particular stage of development. For example, pre-pubertal children, especially girls, are interested in relationships and mating. A simple but complete overview of sex and the man–woman relationship should be given in these years, and sex should be set in a biological perspective. Early-adolescent children need to understand the changes in their own bodies and in those of the opposite sex. These should be illustrated with photographs. The guilt which arises at this age about masturbation needs to be recognised and ideally eliminated, but masturbation also needs to be placed in perspective. The romanticism of mid-adolescence can be expanded so as to place sex in relation to emotion but should be combined with warnings about the dangers of using loving feelings to justify sex. Contraceptive information is likely to be well received at this age (although the age at which some girls now become pregnant raises the possibility that it should be taught earlier), but it should be clearly stated that intercourse at this age can harm subsequent personality development.

The young will listen to good, sensible-sounding advice but frequently reject moral prohibitions and judgements. Encouraging the young to take responsibility for their own sexual behaviour tends to instil a sense of caution and removes rebellious motives from sex.

Late adolescents, most of whom have left school before reaching this stage, require, above all, practical advice on how to seek, establish and maintain relationships which are suitable for them. Fuller details of sexual communication and techniques are best left to this stage, although an outline idea of intercourse as an act should first be mentioned in early adolescence. This is essential to combat the many harmful and misleading myths and sexual jokes that abound amongst early adolescents. Although the topic of venereal disease should have been discussed earlier, but without being used as a deterrent, it is in late adolescence that the young person really needs to know how to suspect the presence of VD both in himself or herself and in a potential partner.

Summary

Although many may object, the aim of a sound sex-education system should be to help the young eventually establish a good, full, heterosexual life. The erotic nature of the subject has to be faced rather than side-stepped, and in any case a part of sex education is concerned with the erotic potential of the recipients. Sound sex education would also stress the range and diversity of human experience whilst avoiding too much attention to statistics about what is average. Everyone is as unique in his or her sexuality as in their personality.

Questions children and parents ask about sex

Once children get to school they discuss sex just as they would anything else but as they are in their latency stage it does not have anything other than academic interest to them. Both during this and the later phases leading up to puberty we feel that a child's parents are the best people to give information because they know the child and what he can cope with day by day and year by year. Parents also have the advantage over formal systems in that they can take opportunities as they arise and use them to talk about sex in an informal, unplanned way. Satisfying a child's curiosity should ideally be done in a spontaneous way and the old notion of saying nothing until you sit your child down to talk about 'the birds and the bees' is not only unfashionable but far less pleasant for both child and parent.

There is so much in daily life that raises questions about sex that can be dealt with in a low-key, matter-of-fact way that the average child can end up very well sex-educated without even realising it. TV, shopping, people a child meets and his or her mother's experiences with carrying, bearing and rearing a baby can all lead to questions which are best answered simply at the time.

Some general guidelines about answering children's questions about sex

Don't say too little. This is a common mistake. The child then becomes even more confused but will probably never be able to verbalise his confusion, especially if you have been dismissive or made it all sound so simple that he or she feels they *should* have understood what you were talking about. On the other hand:

Don't take the opportunity to deliver a lecture on the subject. Most children are simply looking for a straightforward, uncomplicated answer to what seems to them to be a very simple question. By going on at too much length you will confuse them, especially young ones. Gauge your replies according to what you know the child can cope with intelligently and emotionally.

Try very hard not to colour every answer with your personal views and hang-ups. We all have some negative or downbeat views about sexual subjects and it takes a real effort to try to counteract them for the sake of our children.

Ask the child a question in return and use the answer to teach on. When a child asks where babies come from you could, for example, ask, 'Where do you think they come from?' The child might say, 'from the tummy button' and you can use this to teach the true facts and to dispel false beliefs and notions, so killing two birds with one stone.

Always answer sex questions at the time and so so spontaneously. Never put off the answer or the child will imagine there is something strange going on and that you cannot answer straight away.

Bear in mind that a sex question from a young child simply does not have the same overtones and connotations it would have coming from an adult. If an adult were to ask you, 'What's a homosexual?' your answer would be very different from the one you would give to a six year old, yet the question is exactly the same.

If you don't know—say so. This raises the general question of honesty. We feel parents should never lie to their children about sexual matters. Children look to us as sources of trustworthy information on most things in life and we owe it to them not to lie or mislead them with half-truths.

Questions children ask . . . and some suggested answers

Where do babies come from:
They grow in mommy's tummy after daddy puts a seed in there.

Where does daddy get the seeds from?
They grow inside his body in the things that hang down behind his penis.

How do they get into mommy's tummy?
Daddy and mommy cuddle up together and he puts his penis into her vagina and the seeds come out inside her.

Can I watch you do it?
Well we'd rather you didn't because we like to be alone when we're doing it—it's nicer for us to be undisturbed.

How does the baby come out?
Mommy's tummy pushes it out down the same way that daddy's seed went in—down the vagina.

Why haven't I got a penis?
Because you're a girl and girls have a vagina instead. There has to be a place for the daddy's penis to go to get the seeds inside the mommy. If they both had penises there'd be nowhere to put the seeds and she couldn't get a baby.

Does it hurt having a baby?
Yes it does for some women, but some have no pain at all and if the pain is too bad then doctors can help.

How does a baby breathe inside you?
It doesn't breathe because there's no air inside mommy's tummy. It gets all its food and things to grow down a cord that joins it to mommy inside.

What's a tummy button for?
When a baby is inside a mommy it's joined to her so that it can live. When it's born it comes out with this tube still attached to its tummy. The tube is cut near the baby's tummy but this doesn't hurt. After a few weeks the tube drops off the baby and leaves a mark called the navel, tummy button or umbilicus.

If a baby dies inside the mommy does she die too?
No, the mommy will be all right and can try to have another baby later on.

Do you let daddy put seeds into you only when you want a baby?
No. It's so nice when he puts seeds in me that we often do it even if we don't want a baby.

Why don't you get a baby every time then?
Because a lot of the time a mommy's body can't make babies and sometimes we use special things to stop the seeds making babies. They're called contraceptives. If we had a baby every time we made love we'd end up with so many children we wouldn't be able to look after you all properly.

Why do you call it 'make love' when you do the seeds?
Because when we cuddle up together we feel very loving towards each other. Putting seeds inside mommy makes us both feel lovely. That's why we do it even though we don't want to make a baby.

When will I be able to make love?
One day when you're older and you meet a man/woman you love who loves you too.

Do you have to be married to have a baby?
No you don't but if the mommy is all alone she might have difficulty getting enough money to look after herself and the baby. It's really best if there's a mommy and a daddy because then they can look after each other and the baby.

Why do you have to go to hospital to have a baby—I thought only people who were ill went to hospital?
Yes, it's usually ill people who go to hospital but when a baby comes out of a mommy's tummy it's best to have a doctor or nurse there just in case anything goes wrong with the baby or the mommy. Most mommies have their babies in hospital though some choose to stay at home. Anyway mommy will come out of hospital ever so quickly.

Why does the baby's head look so funny?
Because it was a bit squashed as it came out of mommy's tummy. It'll look perfectly normal in a few days.

Why does the baby have a bracelet on?
So that every one knows who it belongs to. The nurse puts the bracelet on very soon after the baby is born. It doesn't have the bracelet on when it's inside mommy's tummy.

What's an incubator?
A special little house over a cot for a baby who is ill and can't live very well without doctors and nurses helping him. Most babies who have to go in incubators are perfectly well afterwards.

Why don't men have babies?
Because you have to have a thing inside you called a uterus which is where the baby grows. You also have to have a vagina so that the baby can come out. Men don't have these things. They have a penis so that they can put seeds into mommy's tummy to start the baby. Daddies start babies off and mommies have them. Then they both look after the baby together.

Why do some babies drink from a bottle?
Because their mommies have chosen not to breastfeed them. They give them cows' milk instead in a bottle.

Is it nice breastfeeding a baby?
Yes, very nice. You can cuddle the baby a lot and the milk mommies make in their breasts is the best food for a baby. Milk in a bottle comes from cows and is very different from mommies' milk. After all it was made by a mommy cow to feed her babies and our babies aren't at all like baby cows are they?

Why can't daddy breastfeed, he's got nipples?
Because you need breasts to feed a baby and not just nipples. It's the breasts that make the milk for the baby.

When a daddy puts his penis inside a mommy does he do a wee inside her?
No he puts seeds inside her.

Does it hurt when a daddy does that to a mommy?
No—in fact they both like it a lot.

Where do you and daddy do it?
Usually in bed because it's warm and cuddly there but we could do it anywhere when we're on our own and quiet.

Mrs Jones has got three babies, does that mean that she has only done it three times?
No, she's probably done it lots of times but it doesn't make a baby every time. (Explain more as above).

How old will I be before I can have a baby of my own?
Well you could have a baby when you are a teenager but it's best to wait until you are married so that the baby has a mommy and a daddy to love it and look after it. After all, you like having a mommy and a daddy don't you?

Can I have a baby with daddy (mommy)?
No, mommies and daddies have babies together but brothers and sisters and parents and their children mustn't have babies together because the babies might not be normal. Mommy and daddy love you but they love each other in a slightly different way. Anyway, its best to have a baby with someone you're married to and you can't marry your mommy (daddy) or brother (sister).

What does having a period mean?
Every month mommy makes an egg in her tummy and if it doesn't meet a seed from daddy it doesn't make a baby. Then her tummy leaks blood for a few days to make it ready for another egg. The bit of blood she loses is called her period.

When will I have a period?
When you're about twelve or so and your body starts getting ready to make eggs.

Where does the blood that she leaks go?
Mommy has to wear a pad of cotton inside her panties or something inside her vagina to soak up the blood. She throws away the things that are wet with the blood. Her body makes more blood, so the bleeding doesn't matter.

Do boys have periods?
No they don't because they don't make an egg each month like a woman. They make seeds (called sperms) all the time and never bleed.

Why do I sometimes have stuff leaking on to my pyjamas at night?
Because you're leaking semen in your sleep. It's produced now that your body is getting ready to be a man. Some people talk about 'wet dreams' because they probably happen while you're dreaming. It's nothing to worry about and happens to most boys of your age.

Why does my penis look different from other boys'?
Because you haven't been (have been) circumcised. Some boys have had the skin on the tip of their penis removed. Some do it because their parents' religion says so and others do it because their father was done. Doctors don't think it's necessary to have it done if the skin is loose enough to be pulled back by the age of five.

Questions parents ask

Should we let the children see anything of our sexual relationship or should we hide the fact that we are sexual from them?
It is really entirely up to you to do what seems natural. There is no point going out of your way to show off your sexuality to your children but it is certainly helpful and valuable for them to see you kiss, cuddle and be intimate with one another. This is how they will learn to be loving one day themselves. Some parents are so hung-up about their own sexuality that they never show any affection to each other in front of the children. This is a shame as parents are the models for their children's future. However, how far you go must be a matter of personal choice. On balance genital activity of any kind is probably not sensible in front of children, especially when they are in the Oedipal phase.

If you feel you want to have intercourse while the children are around simply say, 'Mommy and Daddy want to have a rest,' or 'We're going to have a cuddle,' or something similar. Bring up your children to respect your needs to have a 'cuddle' when you both want to. Most parents of young children are exhausted by nightfall and often end up not having intercourse at all if they do not take their chances during the day.

How about making love with a baby in the bed?
There is no problem at all with this provided that your bed is big enough or that you can put the baby on the floor on a pillow or comforter if he or she is sleeping. Up to about a year there is probably no danger of your baby seeing you have intercourse but it is impossible to prove this one way or the other.

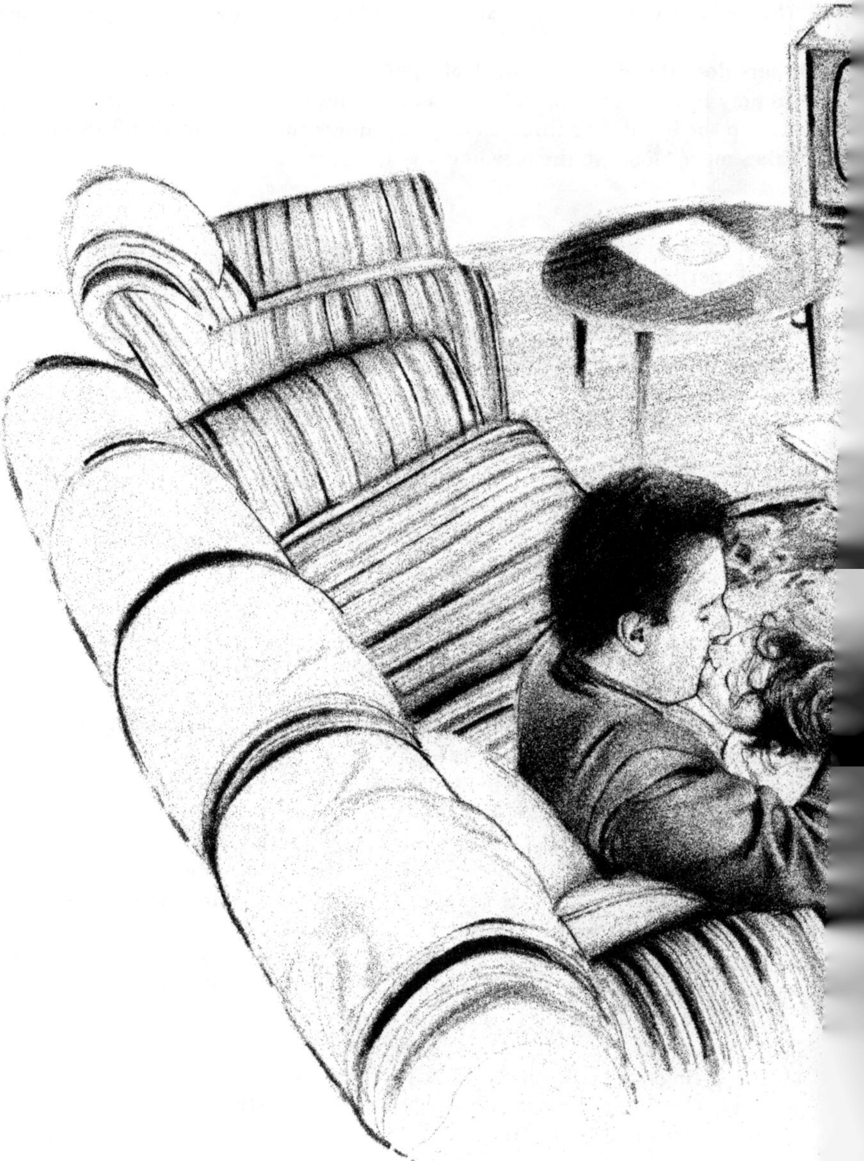

TEACHING CHILDREN ABOUT SEX   323

Sex education: Children learn about sex education in many more ways than most parents realise. With parents like this children will grow up to be physically affectionate.

Many couples find that if they have intercourse with a baby under a year or so old close by he or she becomes excited or restless and may even wake as his mother has an orgasm. This can even happen if the baby is in another room.

What about locked doors to our bedroom?
It is probably reasonable to have a bolt or a lock on the door because children are thoughtless and forgetful and may barge in when you don't want them to. Having told the children that you are going to have a cuddle, enforce your own privacy—you deserve it and should not feel bad about excluding the children, provided they are old enough to be left safely and are happy playing.

What should we do if the children burst in when we're making love?
This depends on the age of the child. Babies and toddlers cannot be expected to look after themselves safely so you cannot make love when they are awake anyway. Pre-school children may have to have some attention paid to them before you ask them to go and play while you cuddle, but older children can be handled more firmly but kindly. Very young children can mistake a man on top of a woman as an act of brutality, especially if she is noisy when having orgasms. Older children who know that you are having sex can be quietly and firmly asked to go because you are making love.

Most parents are embarrassed, shocked or angry but this is not the child's fault. If you are likely to react in this way lock the door beforehand so that you don't take your feelings out on the child. Explain as soon as you can afterwards why you were cross and don't make him or her feel bad about it.

Does it matter if the children hear us making love?
No, not really, but if they are very young or might think the mother who is noisy on orgasm is being hurt, then it is best to have sex when they are asleep or out of earshot.

Is it true that some people use their children as an excuse not to have sex?
Yes, it is and this is especially true of women. Ideally a woman should discuss with her husband why she does not want sex or get help from a professional. Keeping quiet and making the children an excuse is damaging to the relationship and makes the man resentful about the children.

Does our sexual relationship have to suffer because of the children?
No, but it may change. Many couples change their ideas of their sexuality (for better or worse) after having children. The average couple with young children are very tired (especially the mother) and this colours their appetite for and enjoyment of sex. Many young men at this stage of their careers are very busy and have little time to devote to their wives and this too alters their personal relationships. Anyway as the years pass things change between you, and sex changes with time. Even without children sexual relationships between a couple can change over the years. Certainly it is more difficult to be spontaneous with children around, and you cannot pet as openly as you could before. There is little doubt that children around cause inhibitions, but there are ways around this for the couple who want to make their sex lives work.

Why should I tell my children anything about sex at all?
Because if they do not hear from you in a loving, caring, balanced way they will hear from someone else in a much less attractive and informative setting. Parents greatly underestimate the misconceptions children have about sex and leaving the subject untalked about actually does more harm than good. Research has shown that a part of the

body that does not have a label (the sex organs, for example) are thought by the child not to exist. Just think how extraordinary it would be if a child grew up having no word for his feet. The sex differences between men and women (and boys and girls) are so compelling that children have an insatiable desire to learn about them and all that results from them. Many of the subjects in the sex area are baffling and amazing to adults— imagine how much more so they must be to children, with their natural curiosity and delight in the unknown, who are as yet untainted (we hope) by the negative attitudes our culture has towards all things sexual.

What age should we start sex education?
Sex education begins at birth. From the cradle until mature adulthood children need information, a source of dependable reference when told nonsense that frightens or alarms them and a haven of love on which they can rely no matter what. In addition to all this they need to see a close, loving relationship at work in their parents' lives because the parents are their models for the future.

What if they don't ask questions?
If the child is young leave the subject alone rather than force discussion on matters that he or she couldn't care less about. In time most children want to know and they will ask you or someone else. Unfortunately, so much of our sex-negative thinking comes across unconsciously to our children, just from the way we react or behave, that they feel sex is a 'no-go area' and so do not feel like asking questions. A child's questions may have been discouraged by a parent or even another adult, or he or she may have been fobbed off in the past and now does not know how to ask about something that obviously upsets his or her parents too.

A lot of parents find that bringing up the subject under some other pretext works well but if you do this, don't make the mistake of taking any spark of interest the child shows as an indication that he wants a full-blown medical prize-winning lecture on the subject. Some children are naturally more shy than others and others are less inquisitive about everything; others think they know it all anyway (even a seven year old may say that the subject is boring and that he knows all about it). The main thing is to encourage and reward curiosity.

Why can't I just leave it all to the school or someone else?
You can if you want to and many parents do. But if you do, don't then get upset if what they tell your child is not what you would have said. If you have specific ideas about any area of sexual knowledge you should ensure that your children understand your position, even if one day they choose to reject it. Young people will eventually make up their own minds about sexuality just as they do about everything else, but if you want to influence them because you care for and love them it is silly to leave the imparting of sex information to others—they simply will not understand, love or care for your child in the way you do.

Of course there is no reason why the two options should be mutually exclusive. Start off by answering all your children's questions when they are young and then help them to understand what they hear at school and discuss it with them if they want to do so.

Are pets any help?
Yes. By having pets and watching them mate and have their young, children of all ages can learn a great deal about sex in a gentle, natural way. Of course, watching rabbits teaches nothing about human inter-relationships but it helps get the plumbing sorted out in their minds and this in itself is a help. Research shows that country children are much

more at ease with physical sexuality, and that this is probably because their experience of animal sex has made them see the whole thing as natural and normal, which it is.

How useful are books for children?
That depends on the book and the child. Some children are happier to learn from books than from adults, so for them a good book can be just the job. However, you cannot ask a book a question, so the flow of information is very much one-way. There are lots of good books around for children of all ages, but be sure to read any book first so that you know what your children are learning. If there are things you do not like about the sex-education books they use at school, take up the subject with the head teacher. There are books available for parents to read with their children and this can be a very good way of handling the subject.

How do we handle the dirty jokes from school?
When children are about six or seven they start to giggle at 'dirty' words like 'underwear', 'penis' or 'naked'. Early dirty stories do not necessarily have a sexual component but the child gets a great kick out of telling them. The next stage is to find excretion and sexual functioning hilariously funny. There are now some sexual overtones. Swear words become incorporated in the stories and even the un-funniest of stories causes the child to fall about with laughter. It is interesting how little dirty jokes have changed over the years. Today's nine year old laughs at exactly the same things as his grandparents did and for the same reasons. Dirty jokes are an early sign of the child's growing independence and preparation for the adult world. Sometimes the jokes are defiant and rebellious but most often they are geared to shock the 'stuffy' adults around him. Often they laugh because everyone else is laughing (it is simply a social pursuit) even though they may not really understand the joke. All of this is a part of growing social confidence and enjoyment and acceptance of becoming part of a peer group.

With all this in mind it is possible to stay calm and to put dirty jokes into perspective. By all means enjoy a joke with your young children, if only to show them that you know what they are on about and that you are not dead from the waist down—as they often think. Dirty jokes, if they are not actually harmful or worrying your child, are simply a passing phase and will do no harm.

Supposing our child finds one of our girlie magazines?
Assuming that the magazine is not frankly pornographic (these should be kept locked away so that the children cannot get them) there is no point making a fuss.

Parents may worry when they find nude magazines hidden in teenagers' rooms and are terrified that this might be the signs of early depravity, or the prelude to a teenage pregnancy. Usually, they have no need to worry because a child's idea of what is in a girlie magazine and a parent's are very different. The child thinks of the girl with no clothes on as being naughty and exciting because in our culture nakedness is so uncommon. In other cultures children would learn about the bodies of the opposite sex from real life and no one would worry. But in our culture children and young adolescents often have to resort to magazines, newspapers and so on to get an image of nakedness (or femaleness) against which to judge their own body image. Young children (under the age of ten) often will not even see such pictures as "dirty," but older ones, especially boys, will be frankly turned on by them. Most children of all ages are fascinated out of sheer curiosity and soon become bored. Older boys in their early teens use them to assist in masturbation fantasies.

This does not mean that you should go out and buy such magazines to educate your children, but if you would normally buy them for yourselves (as millions of couples do) you should be prepared to discuss them with your children in a calm way. You can always tell your children that such magazines stress the physical attributes of the person and say little or nothing about feelings and emotions. If, on the other hand, you become anxious and secretive about such magazines, your child will be more anxious, will wonder what you have got to hide and will get them one way or another. After all, they are widely available. Try instead to be easy-going and to take it in your stride—the child will soon get bored with them.

Should I allow children to play doctors and nurses?
Young children are learning all the time and are naturally curious. They particularly like the differences between male and female bodies, and children from four to eight like to explore everything. Part of this involves exploring their own and other children's bodies. Unfortunately most parents are so anxious about children showing each other their genitals that they do not cope very well and so pass on negative attitudes to their children. Almost all children undress in front of the opposite sex and play 'doctors and nurses', 'mothers and fathers' or something similar, and no harm comes of it. They are all ways in which little children try to mimic the sex roles of adults, if only for a few minutes. They also enjoy the exciting feelings it produces.

What *is* harmful is the guilt the child feels if his parents are cross or make him feel wicked. Lots of children, realising that it is not what their parents want them to do, try to get caught so that they *have* to stop what they are doing. This sense of wanting to be caught because of the "indecency" of it all is made far worse by heavy-handed telling off.

Some control may be helpful in some circumstances because some young children get excited and alarmed by the feelings of excitement (even though it is not usually genital excitement) that such play can sometimes arouse and they need to know that their parents can cope with the situation and control it. These are big feelings for young children and they need help in handling them. Often a child will be far more guilty-looking and embarrassed than the true nature of the sex games warranted.

A very few children's sex games are a sign of a disturbed child, but such games are usually imposed on other children rather than enjoyed mutually, and the other children tell their parents. Such disturbed children need professional help, as do children for whom sex games have gone wrong and caused distress. Apart from keeping an eye open for any negative effects sex games may be having, also make sure that the children are not doing anything dangerous to one another. A young child who has had its temperature taken rectally may, for example, introduce other children to things being pushed up their bottoms and this should be discouraged because of the possibility of physical damage.

Sex games among young children are simply a prelude to other much more sexually explicit discovering 'games' they will be playing ten years later, so it is just as well to come to terms with your curious, enquiring child because this is the first step on a long ladder and if you worry and fuss at every rung you will both end up anxious and neurotic over sex.

What are the commonest misconceptions children have about sex?
Children (like adults) have all kinds of strange ideas about sex, mainly because they feel it is a 'no-go area', about which they cannot ask, or that if they do they will not get an honest answer.

Here are some of the most common misconceptions, so that you can work them out before them come up. (They are arranged approximately in order of the child's age).

A woman gets pregnant by swallowing the man's seed.
Babies come out of eggs like chickens.

You can buy a baby at a shop.
Babies come out with urine from a woman's body.
Babies are born from a woman's anus (back passage).
Babies come out of the navel.
Even if a man and woman only kiss they will have a baby.
Every time a man and a woman have sex they have a baby.
Girls used to have a penis but it was cut off for some reason.
Men have nipples so they must be able to breastfeed.
All fat women are pregnant.
Only women who are married can have a baby.
Only women who love their partner can have a baby.
The only time a man and a woman have sex is when they want a baby.
Masturbation will make you homosexual.
Masturbation will give you spots.
Girls can keep your penis in their vagina and even cut it off in there.
Girls who have just started having periods cannot have babies.
The only time a woman can have a baby is when she is menstruating.
A girl cannot get pregnant unless she has an orgasm.
You can only get VD from toilet seats.
French kissing can get you pregnant.
Orgasms can make you pregnant.
Being in love means you ought to have sex with someone.
Sex is the best way of proving you are in love.
A boy who gets you pregnant will marry you.
Parents cannot possibly begin to understand what you are going through because they are too old-fashioned.
No mothers masturbate and they are too old for sex.

Summary

Sex education should prepare the young for the conflicting and difficult emotions they are about to experience (or actually are experiencing) and should help them cope with them. Adolescence is a difficult enough time for parents and children alike and to add to their troubles by ignoring the real problems and simply teaching the bald facts is to do them less than justice.

An ideal sex-education programme would undo previous harm, correct tendencies towards perversions and detect children who need more personal education and care or perhaps even therapy. Through insight it would simultaneously maximise both the child's potential and control—these, surely, are sound educational aims whatever subject is being taught.

Chapter 26

Masturbation

Masturbation is an inexhaustible subject of increasing public interest. The reason for this is that it is, in one form or another, universal, but because of centuries of religious opposition it came to be regarded as sinful, shameful, harmful and secret. The removal of the veil of secrecy has led to the altogether healthy increase in interest.

It is widely agreed that almost all men masturbate, but statistics gained from surveys purport to show that masturbation is less common in women. This is because female masturbation is very difficult to define. It is an infinitely more variable sensation than in men and all that can be said with reasonable confidence is that it consists of some recurrent psychological and/or physical activity, undertaken consciously or unconsciously, resulting in signs of sexual arousal (signs which in themselves might not be recognised by the woman) and perhaps resulting in an identifiable orgasm. This highlights another area of difficulty. Male sexual arousal is easy to recognise but female arousal is not obvious except on close inspection. This is probably why boys are said to masturbate more than girls in childhood.

The next problem when considering the subject is to account for the diversity of female masturbation and its relative inefficiency in some women. The answers can be found by considering three related phenomena. The first is the greater parental suppression of genital activity in girls than boys. Parents of both sexes are more tolerant of genital handling in boys than in girls, although the more educated a mother is the more likely she is to accept sexual expression in her daughter. Because they are more affection-dependent, girls may also be more willing to try to conform. They may, as a result, find ways of masturbating that do not lead to easy detection. Instead of lying on their backs, opening their legs and touching their vulvas, many routinely adopt other postures such as lying face down, lying on their side, sitting or even standing. Muscular contraction or rubbing the vulva against an object (including the heel) may be substituted for direct touch methods. If genital stimulation is not abandoned altogether, as it is in some girls, it can occur through clothing, or a whole variety of objects may be used as a substitute for the girl's hand. Alternatively masturbation may become attached to 'legitimate' pursuits such as washing the vulva or even urination. Although many women claim to be able to masturbate by more than one method, women who carry into adulthood, as most seem to, any of the less

Proportions of Masturbation by age

Single Men Average Figure/week	% of total outlet	Age groups	Married Men Average Figure/week	% of total outlet
1.86	60.22	Adol.–15	....	....
1.23	38.5	16–20	0.14	2.95
0.86	29.52	21–25	0.17	4.4
0.75	26.94	26–30	0.16	4.57
0.59	24.94	31–35	0.11	3.79
0.58	29.09	36–40	0.07	2.95
....	....	41–45	0.05	2.43
....	....	46–50	0.05	2.53
....	....	51–55	0.03	2.13
....	....	56–60	....	....

obvious methods mentioned above can find themselves unable to reach orgasm except in that position or by that method. As a result their husbands and even the women themselves claim they never masturbate.

The second explanation of the diversity of female masturbation lies in the fact that the female body can respond sexually to stimulation in almost any anatomical area. This also happens in pre-adolescent boys. This is also of more value in sexual relationships with others and some women can have an orgasm from the stimulation of areas of the body well away from the vulva, including their breasts. Muscular movements such as rotating the pelvis, rhythmically contracting the vaginal muscles or making thrusting movements with the pelvis can bring on an orgasm in some women. Being rocked about on buses, bicycles, motorcycles and trains, for example, can lead to orgasms in others. Even movement of the vulva against underclothing is reported as being arousing to the point of orgasm by some women.

The third reason is that female orgasms are very variable in intensity. One factor here is the number of throbbing muscular contractions which occur during an orgasm. If there are only a few of these contractions it is experienced as only a mild sensation, and if the woman has been taught that sexual pleasure is naughty or sinful, the anxiety associated with the act may stop the contractions entirely. Something similar can happen in anxious men. Similar muscular contractions to those which women enjoy at orgasm eject semen in men, and under some circumstances ejaculation can be reduced to a few little dribbles. Since most definitions of masturbation refer to orgasm as the end-point, a woman who when masturbating can only achieve a minor sensation may think of herself as not masturbating at all. The point here is that the anxiety earlier instilled into her gives her an unconscious incentive to play down her responses so as to avoid too much guilt. Similarly, the women mentioned earlier who use somewhat obscure masturbation methods are using less than the best method (direct stimulation of the genitals) to get an orgasm, and as a result are inefficient. Unfortunately, for these women, direct methods would arouse anxiety to a point where it would be impossible to have an orgasm at all.

Men, of course, or some of them, have the same difficulties. Men who have been strictly reared with regard to masturbation (parents sometimes even make them promise never to do it) masturbate the way many other men do yet can block off the consciousness of orgasm and although they ejaculate they still claim not to masturbate. Although older men often rub their erect penis with no intention of reaching orgasm (which according to most definitions would not amount to masturbation, though it clearly is), some guilty young men do so too and later have a nocturnal emission (wet dream). These men also deny that they masturbate.

Guilty women will, in a similar way, confine their masturbation to the twilight state between sleeping and waking (or vice versa) and so deny masturbation on the grounds that it does not occur when they are fully conscious. Some women who deny masturbation do so on the basis that they do not fantasise while doing it. However, they often have a rich fantasy life which simply does not coincide with when they stimulate the vulva.

A substantial minority of women claim never to have masturbated, as do a tiny percentage of men. When the factors we have outlined are taken into account, however, it can be seen that the denial does not necessarily amount to a deliberate lie. In our clinical experience, at least, and regarding those people in whom it is important that the subject of masturbation be clarified, it is true to say that virtually everyone masturbates in some way or another.

The less direct the method used, the more the individual shows that a difficulty exists about sexual expression. It could be argued that

A pleasant way for a woman to fondle a man: With both man and woman comfortable this can be pleasant and stimulating for them both. It is relaxing for the woman as her hands are in a restful position that she would use to masturbate herself.

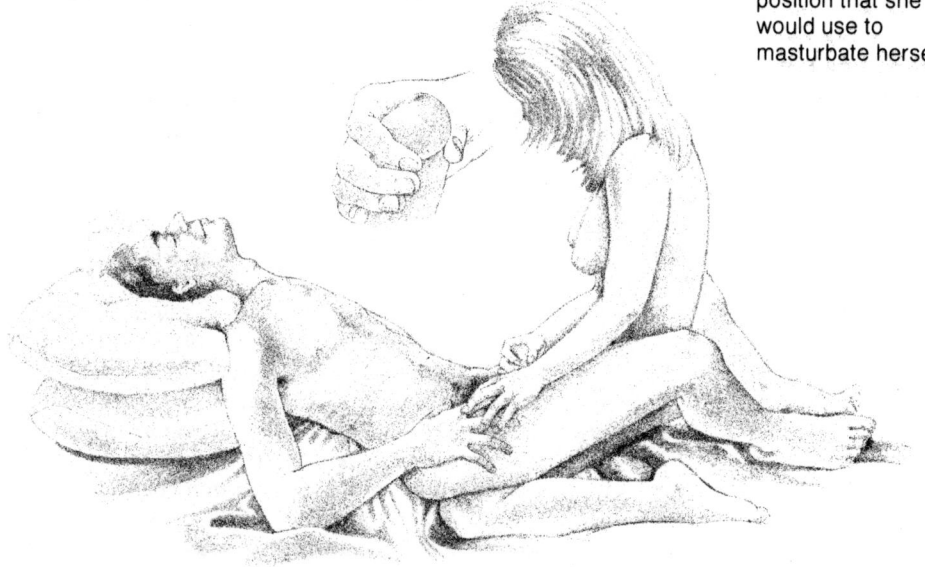

the less direct methods have been learned by chance and have then become fixed in preference to more usual methods. Such an argument does not fit in with clinical experience which shows that unusual masturbation methods are almost always associated with a difficulty. This is serious because learning to masturbate bears the same relation to intercourse as does learning to speak to conversation.

As well as being a form of sexual training, masturbation, or rather its associated fantasies, helps to bring images of the bodies of the opposite sex and of intercourse with them to mind, especially in the young. This is a learning process and is a kind of sexual rehearsal for the adolescent. Some males of all ages, but especially younger ones, rely on girlie magazines to get clear images for their fantasies, and this must be better than reliance on fantasies which could well otherwise be warped or perverted. Learning to masturbate is simply a part of what a growing man has to learn. Girls and women may also be aroused by girlie magazines because they identify with the girls in the pictures but more commonly they find titillating stories more of a turn-on. This may reflect the concern that is instilled into girls about their behaviour with men—tales of seduction excite them more.

Amongst adults today, married men are often found to be more reluctant to talk about their masturbation than are their wives. Less well educated men are particularly likely to regard it as an abnormal and childish habit. However, it has a real place in married life because it allows differing sex drives to be accommodated without looking inside the partnership. This may be the reason why, on average, surveys report that women masturbate more frequently than men. Also, a man can either have intercourse or masturbate, but not both in a short space of time, unlike a woman, so there is less of a restriction on female masturbation. In fact, women are perhaps, other things being equal, more likely to want intercourse after masturbation because sex is in their minds. This is useful clinically in women who have lost their sex drive. Encouraging them to masturbate can rejuvenate their sex lives. Clinical experience with large numbers of couples who are happily married and enjoy sex with each other shows that on average the wives masturbate about as often as they have intercourse, whereas only every fourth orgasm in the husband is produced by self-masturbation. One value of masturbation in marriage may be that material from the accompanying fantasy may then be available for incorporation into marital sex. Even the fantasy itself may be used during intercourse because many women and particularly older men need to use fantasy to sustain their arousal and have an orgasm. Some people with deviant sexual needs can function satisfactorily in intercourse only by using an appropriate fantasy. Masturbation, fantasy and, perhaps, a little flirting may also be a defence against extra-marital sexual intercourse. If partners take steps to learn about each other's masturbation fantasies they have the key to their sexualities and can often thereby harmonise intercourse.

Women say they masturbate to relieve emotional tensions, and some boys and men use masturbation to blot out anxieties in the same way that alcoholics and drug-takers do. This is really a misuse of masturbation. Other men find masturbation more gratifying than intercourse itself—this is a sign of the presence of an inhibiting anxiety. Women, especially young ones, tend to get more satisfaction from masturbation than they do from from intercourse and frequently display greater physiological body changes during orgasms induced by masturbation. This may come about because of residual inhibitions about intercourse; a lack of skill in her partner; her perception of her partner; or because she can stimulate herself in her favourite way during masturbation whilst fantasising a scene that arouses her. This does not necessarily mean that such women prefer masturbation to intercourse—they like both.

Some men, on the other hand, routinely masturbate and never attempt to have intercourse with a woman. They are frightened of intercourse, women, or both, and are passive. Their hope, and usually their fantasy, is of a woman carrying them off and raping them one day. Some, however, are socially skilled with women, attractive and effective in all other areas of their lives. The reason for their behaviour is simply their excessive fear of intercourse.

How men masturbate

The most usual method of male masturbation, at least from adolescence, is to stimulate the rim of the head of the penis by encircling it with the index finger and thumb and then moving the hand in an up-and-down pumping type of action. The remaining fingers tend to encircle the shaft lightly, although some men squeeze it tightly. Some use the other hand to play with their scrotum or, less commonly, their anus. Many stop occasionally during the act and others stop for a while before orgasm and then restart, so as to prolong the pleasure. Variants of this behaviour consist of lying face down and then using the flat of the hand to press the penis on to the mattress whilst making copulatory movements. Objects such as a pillow folded over or even aids from sex shops may be used to form an artificial vagina. Some men masturbate sitting down, pushing their penis down between their thighs, crossing them and then stimulating the penis by moving the thighs and trunk towards and then away from each other. Unusual methods such as this seem frequently to be associated with difficulties in intercourse and undue guilt about sex.

More worrying signs of trouble are where the adolescent boy (or the man) dresses in female clothes to masturbate or reduces his level of consciousness by over-breathing, taking alcohol, glue-sniffing, using drugs or by other means. Individuals of both sexes who are guilty about masturbation or intercourse sometimes express their guilt by having bouts of sexual activity interspaced with longish periods of abstinence. Another sign of difficulty in either sex can be elaborate rituals, sometimes based on washing, after masturbating.

How women masturbate

Unusual practices, although less bizarre, are more widespread amongst girls and women, as we pointed out earlier. The most basic pattern though is to lie in the normal female intercourse position and stimulate the vulva directly with the hand. The variations thereafter are immense. For example, the whole vulva may be massaged or one specific area of the side of the shaft of the clitoris lightly stroked. The edges of the inner lips may be specifically rubbed or they may be trapped between the fingers. A vertical or circular motion may be used. Some women press so hard that their knuckles turn white and this may be because their clitoris has fewer nerves than average. On reaching the plateau stage of sexual response many women change their type of stimulation. As orgasm approaches the area stimulated may be well away from the clitoris. Intermittent stopping is characteristic, although guilty women may race to have an orgasm as quickly as possible to get it out of the way. Intermittently, one, but more commonly two, fingers may be inserted into the vagina and rotated rather than moved in and out. Since only the entrance of the vagina is very sensitive the purposes are to delay progress to orgasm, simply for the pleasure of it, and, frequently, to act out a fantasy of penetration. Objects may be used to stimulate the vulva and are sometimes inserted into the vagina. The commonest object used like this today is probably the battery-driven vibrator, but in the past a huge variety of objects has been used if articles which have had to be medically removed from women's vaginas are anything to go by.

Women are more reluctant to admit that they do anything to their vaginas when masturbating than they are to massaging and caressing the vulva. Some women use only the vagina when masturbating. It is in masturbation rather than in intercourse that women demonstrate their greater sexual capacities than men—although of course they may not fully use them. Women have been known to obtain fifty and (many) more orgasms in a single session. Such sessions are sometimes repeated frequently, especially if a vibrator is used. Clinically such women are no more likely to be 'neurotic' or 'obsessional' than other women (as has been suggested by 'experts' over the years), nor are they more likely to show overgrowth of the inner lips or clitoris than are other women (as some women fear). Such an over-growth, which many women attribute to masturbation, is probably part of the normal anatomical variation between individuals. During early adolescence the labia may be more vulnerable to such enlargement.

In later life many women who have nothing physically wrong with their uterus or their hormones, but who nevertheless menstruate so heavily and so frequently that they are likely to end up having a hysterectomy, are, on psychosexual investigation, found to be poor and inadequate at having orgasms when masturbating and during intercourse. They often express strong opposition to masturbation. Psychosexual therapy designed to reverse the opposition to indulgence in sexual pleasure can sometimes bring the situation under control without a hysterectomy being needed. The underlying cause of the bleeding is possibly the continuous congestion of blood rarely relieved by orgasm.

Fantasies

Masturbation is a psychosexual act which incorporates both fantasy

Male sexual fantasies: In general men seem to be less ingenious than women in their sexual fantasies and seem, oddly, to stop short of intercourse.

Female sexual fantasies: These are many and varied but many women inhibit them because of their feelings of guilt and shame.

and physical stimulation. Some men and women claim never to fantasise during masturbation. As a rule they seem to fare as well as anyone else both in masturbation and intercourse, so the deficiency is apparently not usually serious. Presumably their fantasy is unacceptable to their conscious mind and so is repressed into the unconscious. The dissociation of the act and the thought is presumably the result of guilt, and sometimes the point of the repression appears to be to avoid a particular situation or homosexual or incestuous thoughts. Fantasies are, of course, a rich source of information about the sexuality of an individual and can be of tremendous importance in the treatment of sexual problems.

Allowing for the shame people feel about discussing fantasies they regard as unusual, the range of sexual fantasy is enormous. The same fantasy theme may be used for a period of time but usually varied slightly. Reliving previous sexual experiences, possibly in an elaborated form, is a common source of fantasy material. Most fantasies can be grouped into people fantasies and practice fantasies. In the first, the fantasy is of sex with someone the person knows or members of the opposite sex in photographs or stories. In the practice type of fantasy the person concentrates on the sexual activity rather than on any particular partner.

In men with sexual problems the fantasy often ends in foreplay activities and no penetration is involved. Often the fantasy is of being fellated. In people fantasies, men who are scared of women often use either schoolgirls or much older women. This is commonplace in adolescent boys who want intercourse but are still at the stage where their fears are greater than their desires. Passive men who have not fully resolved their early attraction to their mothers often have fantasies of being in the total control of the woman. Deviations and perversions reveal themselves in fantasy. Sometimes they only reveal their presence in a sudden change in fantasy as orgasm approaches. Some individuals, more often men than women, see someone else instead of themselves performing sexually in their fantasies. This usually points to excessive anxiety about intercourse, which may be the basis of voyeurism.

To generalise from large numbers of individuals it seems that women fantasise more extensively but less deviantly than do men. In spite of the oft-made claim that women's sexuality can only be expressed in the context of a loving relationship, this certainly does not seem to be the case, to judge from their fantasies. Adult women usually start the fantasy with themselves naked in the presence of the man without 'explaining' how it came about. Adolescent and pre-adolescent girls may find fantasies of being naked exciting and often use stripper fantasies. In their fantasies women often portray themselves as being overwhelmed. This is evidence of their residual guilt about sex and reduces objections from their consciences. In this way fantasies of being forced to have sex; the use of restraint; of being had by many men; and of being a slave-girl commonly arise. As well as these fantasies many, if not most, women also have fantasies about one or more men they actually know.

Summary

It is difficult to escape the conclusion that if masturbation, in the full psychosexual sense, proceeded with less difficulty in adolescence, then intercourse would be improved to the benefit of the man–woman relationship. Opposition to masturbation may have made sense to some people in the past as a control against sexual expression becoming rampant, but there is no justification for repressing it today. In fact the reverse is the case; those individuals who are most accepting of their sexuality in all its forms are the ones who are most responsible about its expression.

Chapter 27

Sexual morals

The historical background

It is characteristic of human beings to have beliefs about how they and others around them should behave. This leads to concepts of what is right and what is wrong; what is good and what is bad and the way we 'ought' to behave in general. One workable definition of a nation or a culture is 'a group of people who share the same moral codes'. Morals are simply codes of behaviour that a given nation or sub-group within a nation agrees are acceptable. Such codes differ greatly around the world today and have probably been even more different over the centuries. Morality does not only cover matters to do with sex, of course. People make moral judgements about the upbringing of children, the conduct of business affairs, matters of government, and gambling and financial matters, among other things. Often the morals in such circumstances can be agreed upon fairly readily and adhered to or not according to the individual. When it comes to sexual morality the story is rather different because our sex lives put such urgent pressures on us that exceptional codes of behaviour are called for if we are to run a tolerably pleasant community.

Early men and women probably thought little about the morality of sex. It was as 'natural' for human females (like other animals) to be pregnant or breastfeeding for much of their short lives as it was for a man to have intercourse with a female simply for the physical pleasure of it. According to the available records sex and morality came together much later in civilisation. Such considerations began to arise once men realised that they were responsible for making women pregnant (evidently a fairly recent discovery in the history of mankind)—only then did they have any concept of fatherhood and of 'their' female being special. Until this time a woman had intercourse with men in their group, became pregnant and mothered the resulting child, with—it is thought—no concept of it 'belonging' to anyone, except her.

Primitive man took great strides as soon as he caught on to the concept of 'his' child and from here on women became men's chattels, along with other possessions. Slowly, as societies developed from small family groupings, men began to limit sexual activities that seemed disadvantageous to their particular society. Quite naturally many such 'rules' centred around the importance of the tribe's survival at a time when fierce battles for territory and resources were common and when disease and infant mortality took a terrible toll.

Over thousands of years people have considered various sexual practices 'immoral' but it was not until the coming of Christianity that *all* such practices were forbidden. Throughout history, societies have usually condemned adultery; have sometimes condemned homosexuality and abortion; and have never condemned masturbation. At a stroke the Christian Church declared all these pursuits to be immoral and, what is more, sinful. Not only did they, it was agreed, have adverse effects on society but they also offended God and cut the offender off from his maker until he repented. In the first few centuries after the death of Jesus, early Christian thinkers virtually outlawed any form of sex other than that within marriage for the procreation of children. Some of the greatest Christian proponents of these ideas could hardly bear to accept that men and women had to have intercourse to keep the race going, so fervently anti-sex were they. Most of these moral rulings had little or nothing at all to do with the teachings of Jesus, but were an embellishment of basic Judaeo-Christian thinking by over-enthusiastic authorities such as St Jerome, St Augustine and, to a lesser extent, St Paul. Jesus, perhaps surprisingly, said very little about sex (though he specifically condemned adultery and divorce) and was loving and forgiving to those that broke the moral codes of the day. The Church over the years since his death has reinterpreted much of what He said, often to suit its own ends. This has resulted in the Church having basically negative and prohibitive views on sex and sexuality, though views vary considerably from sect to sect within the Christian Church world-wide. Even among members of one Christian faith (for example Catholics) there is considerable breadth of interpretation among both clergy and laity.

This has led to a situation in which Western cultures usually discuss morality solely in relation to sex. A woman can be a wonderful mother, never steal, cheat or lie and be a good housekeeper, but if she is unfaithful to her husband, then she is immoral. On the other hand as long as she is faithful to her husband, she can be a slut, a spendthrift, a poor mother and never out of the courts, yet she will not be labelled 'immoral'. This state of affairs has come about because of the exceptionally harsh views of sex held by early Christian thinkers, as we have seen, which have distorted the original Jewish and Christian codes of behaviour on which Western society was based.

The original Hebrew (then Christian and eventually Marxist) moral rules were aimed at providing four main things. First, in a hostile world they were aimed at maintaining and increasing the numbers of the nation. From this real need arose rules that forbade any form of sex that did not result in children (such as homosexuality, masturbation and, of course, contraception). By going against these rules the person not only did himself 'harm' but also damaged the group or the race.

The second aim of traditional sexual morality was to strengthen the family unit because the family was the main structural unit of society. Marriage developed as a way of giving the children resulting from sexual intercourse a secure base from which to grow up, and this

The Church, sex and sin.

tended to have a stabilising influence on society generally. At this time, most women died in their thirties or forties, not long after their procreative function had ended (the menopause was earlier in pre-Christian times). This meant that women saw their sexual role as inextricably linked with childbearing from when they were sexually mature until they died. This led to the view that all forms of sex that did nothing to promote family and marriage were 'wrong'. Sex outside marriage was therefore 'wrong', as were all types of sex (such as homosexuality) that took men away from their main duty in life—that of supporting women within a family.

The third area of traditional morality is not so practically or socially based but involves the philosophical concept of asceticism. The argument runs as follows: given that sex is so pleasant, is it not 'better' in moral terms to prove to yourself that you can do without it and that it does not rule you? The acceptance of this principle led quite understandably to the state of affairs we have already discussed in which sex was ideally to be avoided at all costs. The early Christians were particularly influenced by this line of thought because they had seen the sexual excesses of the Roman empire which, they argued, had led to its downfall. After such a libertarian system people all over Europe were ready for something more sober. As a result Judaeo-Christian asceticism over sex came at the right time and the seeds fell on fertile ground. People had seen the terrible problems of libertarianism and did not want to pay the price themselves. The emerging Christian Church, like any other clever political institution, saw the advantages of taking this line, latched on to it and promoted it.

The concept of asceticism.

The fourth aspect of Christian sexual morality has occurred more recently in Christian and Marxist writings. It is suggested that too great an emphasis on sex is bad in a purely practical way because it takes people's eyes off the production of material things for the community (in the Marxist version) or God (in the religious version). So either way sex 'gets in the way' of the real business of living and is therefore to be avoided.

For hundreds of years these attitudes were so ingrained in society that they became accepted as essential for all human beings—a view which is patently nonsense. Other societies all over the world have developed very different sets of morals, all of which are perfectly acceptable to them, yet many of their 'norms' are quite unacceptable to societies based on Judaeo-Christian principles. Clearly, then, morality in sexual matters in any one society is not necessarily based on concepts of absolute 'rights' or 'wrongs'. Sexual morality, like all morality, is based on practical considerations, the origins of which are often forgotten as the centuries pass. New codes of behaviour are constantly emerging and in a highly complex society such as ours in the West today there are many sub-groups whose concepts of sexual morality are developing at a different rate from those of others.

What then is happening today in the Western world? Quite simply, although we live in a notionally Christian society, few people adhere to Christian principles to any degree and as a result a secular collection of 'morals' has developed by common consent. This in itself would be fine but unfortunately things are not as clear-cut as one might think because, although most people do not follow Christian precepts, they have an uncomfortable feeling, deep down, that they should do so, because our culture is still inextricably tied up with Judaeo-Christian concepts of sexual morality irrespective of our individual religious affiliations. The problems arise when new or different concepts of morality, no longer based on the traditional ones, start to conflict with what we have been brought up to believe are unshakeable truths. If for all of your life you have been brought up to think of masturbation as immoral or sinful (for the historical reasons we have outlined), it is not going to be easy to unlearn this programming and suddenly to accept it as OK.

We live in a changing world in which many of these traditional morals are being questioned. This does not mean that the new morals are necessarily right, or that we are necessarily any happier because of this questioning, but it is undoubtedly happening and is producing all kinds of problems. The old objectives of traditional morality seem quite irrelevant to many today, when population growth is, if anything, anti-social; when marriage is a frequently short-lived undertaking with a decreasing success rate; and when asceticism is a very unfashionable concept. Today's moral principles seem to be based more on the increasing of pleasure for the majority and, perhaps even more important, on the *right* of each individual to express him- or herself in the best way he or she can. Because sex is an important form of self-expression it has become a very important part of this way of thinking.

Babies not an inevitable outcome.

These ideas have taken root and grown all the more quickly because we live in a world in which we no longer need so many children and in which we have effective contraception and abortion. These changes have freed us to have intercourse without worrying about what was, until very recently in human evolutionary terms, the inevitable outcome—children. Now that babies are no longer the inevitable outcome of intercourse, sex has taken on a new function which traditional moralists did not have to face. Add to this the fact that in today's society women (perhaps with the help of the state) can support themselves, and it becomes relatively unimportant for them to marry men in order to be supported. This has led to concepts of more temporary support and even to a reversal of the roles with some women supporting their partners.

Only a tiny minority even of so-called 'religious' people today adhere strictly to traditional Judaeo-Christian morality in all its details, and the law of the land certainly no longer upholds such morals as being essential for the maintenance of the fabric of society. Adultery, homosexuality and prostitution, for example, are not *illegal*, even in so-called Christian countries. What we see is a situation in which even religious people (a small minority of the whole population) adhere only to those parts of traditional morality that they choose. Clearly the average man and woman in the street are running their lives according to a set of moral codes that they have to some extent defined for themselves individually. Morality thus has become 'privatised' to a great extent. But even such a private system of morals is passed from generation to generation, so let us see how this happens. As we live in a basically Judaeo-Christian society, let us start by looking at the Christian moral code.

The Christian code

The Bible is a large and complex book, compiled from many different sources originating long ago. It is therefore subject to dispute about the exact meanings of many of the words originally used. It is possible, by out-of-context quotation and by misquotation, to support almost any point of view. Biblical 'authority' has been used by some Christians to create a system of sexual tyranny, complete with punishments both in this world and the next. In history this has inspired great fear amongst largely illiterate populations who could not read the Bible for themselves. Even today some self-appointed Christian moralists try to find ways of bringing individuals they see as sexual transgressors before the courts in the hope that the law can be used to punish them. More importantly they seek, by making an example of such people, to deter others. They are really moral bullies who are motivated by the belief that they are undertaking God's work.

It is little wonder that the negative attitudes and moral self-righteousness lying behind such behaviour eventually appeared repellent to many. Some of the attitudes were so unrealistic and so extreme that they led to an equally extreme response on the opposite side. The extreme moralist and the extreme anti-moralist are but two sides of the same bad penny. The truth lies elsewhere.

Individuals who find both sides equally unattractive and who have returned to the Bible itself to see what it actually says claim that on balance it is not against sex. Jesus himself, unlike all subsequent moralists, seems to have been little concerned with sex. His forgiveness of the prostitute (Mary Magdalen) after she washed His feet with her tears conveys a message which has not yet been accepted, after nearly 2000 years. His statement to the mob howling for the blood of the woman taken in adultery, 'Let he among you who is free of guilt throw the first stone,' is an utterance of the utmost humanity and, considering that the mob was endeavouring to trap him, bravery. His moral courage stood against the viciousness and hypocrisy underlying the morality of the crowd and he thereby saved the woman. Although the context was adultery, the principle behind his statement is capable of endless application in most moral issues today.

In the book of Genesis the Bible says, 'The man and the woman were both naked, but they were not embarrassed.' No Victorian prudery here! The Songs of Songs in the Old Testament contains some of the most beautiful and erotic love poetry ever written. Throughout the Bible there are positive comments about sex and in St Paul's writings in particular there is a good deal of helpful advice. Paul sees marital love as an art which can be taught (just as many marital therapists do today). He suggests that both partners should behave in such a way as to create a relationship of openness, sharing and caring, in which each is seen as part of the other. Paul recommends regular sex and also tells husbands to be as concerned about their wives' sexual enjoyment as the wives are about that of their husbands. The Bible mentions the fun of sex and stresses that marriage is first and foremost for companionship and only secondarily for procreation. Nowhere does it forbid *any* form of sexual behaviour between a man and a woman who are married to each other, although over the centuries the Church has sought to regulate even sex between husband and wife.

Premarital sex and the Bible.

However, whilst all this reveals an acceptance of a happy sex life within *marriage* it relates only to marriage and nothing else, either premaritally or extramaritally. If one interprets the word fornication as meaning any sex outside marriage, then one has to agree that premarital sex is wrong according to the Bible, which continually warns against fornication. The condemnation of sex outside marriage by the early Church was eventually overtaken by the notion that all, or at least most, sex was sinful unless it was intended solely for procreation within marriage.

Imagine what would have happened if the extremists in the early Church had not been so influential and a different path had been pursued. If, instead of the populace being treated like children to be terrified into obedience, sex had been regarded as something infinitely precious to be constantly enjoyed, and if masturbation had not been condemned, then today a situation could have existed in which individuals, and especially the young, might have listened and acted upon advice as to how to maximise sexual pleasure. At this point we would argue that the tenor of this whole book and 'traditional' Christian advice can be reconciled into a pattern of behaviour which might well suit many individuals.

If positive attitudes were instilled into the unconscious minds of children instead of negative ones, then most of them would enjoy the capacity for full sexual expression on achieving maturity, (see chapter 28). Adolescents might then accept masturbation as training for intercourse instead of resorting to intercourse out of guilt arising from masturbation, before their personalities are fully mature. Youngsters brought up in such a way would stand a better chance of reaching true maturity and would thereby be more capable of supporting a mature relationship.

Emphasis on the point that intercourse is an inter-personal, and not solely an inter-genital, activity would tend to reduce the Church-inspired preoccupations with genitality and direct attention towards a more 'Christian' concern with relationships. Advice to avoid full intercourse until marriage and then to confine it to marriage, which is, in essence, the Christian code, could then be put forward in its own right, not solely as a moral issue, but as an important option for everyone. It is interesting that the sexual freedom accepted by many in the West today does not seem to have led to any *more* happiness or personal fulfilment; in fact the opposite could be said to be the case.

This is not to say that a return to a repressive sexual code would be a good thing, but just that there is a middle path which may be inherently better for us. There is a considerable reawakening of Christianity throughout the world at the moment, especially in the

USA, and this, together with the spread of troublesome and even incurable forms of venereal disease, is leading increasing numbers of people to question the wisdom of the sexual freedoms advocated in the sixties and seventies. There could well be a beneficial effect on the sum total of human happiness if the basic concepts of Christian love were applied widely to inter-personal and sexual relationships. Several impressive advantages could result. First, much sexual dissatisfaction could be avoided because the couple would never look outside their marriage for sex; second, the man or woman's sexual confidence would be increased because he or she would know that he or she was not being compared (perhaps adversely) to another lover; and third, such a couple would eventually develop a style of intercourse between themselves which was totally 'uncontaminated' by sexual contact with others. These are weighty considerations which, if adopted, could, at least for some couples, increase their chances of happiness or, more to the point, reduce their chances of unhappiness. To a sensible person all of this is at least worthy of consideration.

How children learn about morals and how we can help them

Philosophers will argue for ever about the existence of inborn morality and a book such as this is no place to take sides. It could well be that children inherit certain concepts of right and wrong, but there is little doubt that they learn such things in the early years of life—usually at home. Experiments have been done in which children of very different societies were posed moral dilemmas and their responses analysed. It seems that, irrespective of culture, children seem to go through three quite distinct stages as they learn to become moral beings.

In the first stage, the emphasis is centred on the child him- or herself. Good and bad, right and wrong, are labels fixed to actions because of the effects they have on the child him- or herself. At this level it is simply a matter of, 'If you are nice to me, I'll be nice to you.'

At the second level, right and wrong are determined according to the rules the child sees to be beyond him or her. Quite regardless of the consequence to him- or herself, what mom thinks or what the school or the law says, certain things seem to be right or wrong.

Finally, the child reaches a level of independence in which he or she questions the validity of the rules and values. Now he or she judges right and wrong independently. Hand in hand with all this go his parents' reactions (and those of other authority figures in society) to 'moral' questions. The child sees what produces approval or punishment and quickly learns what to do to make life pleasant for him- or herself and others. He or she also, by the same argument, learns what makes others unhappy, and this too is an important part of moral training.

In order to develop in this way and to be able to learn what morals mean in the real world, children have to be able to play roles within the safe context of the family and school so that they can test out the rules for themselves. But as with learning anything a child can only go from step to step on a ladder—he cannot take leaps that are beyond his ability to understand and cope with. So what we have to do as parents is to pose questions which our children can understand, yet which will bring them up against moral questions to which we can help them find answers. Only by being taken a step at a time like this can children ever hope to learn to make rational moral judgements. And judgements they will certainly need to make, because traditional concepts of sexual morality will be seen to be largely redundant by many of them, and they will need to think things through for themselves from rational basic principles.

Judgements have to be made.

The fundamental rule of moral training then must be that it is rational. Children do not know how to cope with irrational parental behaviour in any field, and in an area such as this it is especially confusing for them. Unfortunately, a lot of moral training is not done at the conscious level—all those who are parents know how easy it is to influence our children with a look or the way we instinctively behave or react to certain situations. Our own moral programming is so deeply ingrained in our personalities that it is only with the greatest difficulty that we can stand back from it and give our children an unbiased and rational start in life.

Unfortunately, the outcome of our, often unconscious, 'moral training' is to produce a child who believes that he or she is bad because he or she goes against our codes. A child is not bad or evil because he or she masturbates, for example, even if masturbation is thought to be unacceptable. The practice might be considered to be evil, but not the child. Alas, millions of children, girls especially, are brought up to think that they are bad because of their awakening sexual feelings and behaviour. This is hardly surprising in the light of the historical trends we have outlined, in which all forms of non-procreative sex were thought morally wrong, but it does untold harm to the child, who associates sex with naughtiness at best or evil at worst, often for life.

Children are made to feel dirty.

How in the 1980s can we possibly justify or even live with a situation in which our children are made to feel dirty or guilty about their sexuality? Is sex really dirty? Can a young child discovering his or her sexuality be said to be evil? Surely not any more, but owning up to this means that parents have to make enormous strides in their honesty. No longer can we live under the 'because I say so' umbrella; we owe it to our children to be honest and rational in the way that we treat their sexual questions just as we are in other spheres of life. Time and again we see perfectly normal, intelligent, well-meaning parents, who are normally straight and honest with their children, go completely to pieces on sexual matters. Surely this vicious circle has to be broken, and this is the generation to do it.

None of this means that we have to throw up our hands and tell our children that anything goes when it comes to sex, but it does mean an honest questioning of what we *really believe* and what we would stand by if it came to the crunch. The facts of life are that a child's sexuality grows gradually over the years and is enormously affected by the way his or her parents behave and think. At a time of sexual change in society, we must fit our children for that change and help mould their moral sense so that they are able to cope with it. If we do not they will simply grow up ill equipped to deal with the world as they see it, and we will have failed in one major duty of parenthood. *Raising our children to be able to live in the world as we would like it to be is a disservice, because long after we are dead and buried they will be struggling to cope with their inadequate training.*

So what then is the overall principle that we should aim for in moral training? Surely, if it is one thing, it must be that we do not do anything that harms other people. Very few, if any, moral rules stand alone as absolute truths, most were, or are, about the consequences of behaviour.

Even the traditional laws as set out in the Ten Commandments, viewed by many as absolute truths, are clearly not so. There are times when many a traditional moralist would consider it morally right to kill (during war), to steal, or to lie (to save someone's feelings) and once one starts to examine such laws clearly, whilst admitting that they form an excellent basis on which to run a society, even so-called believers find them unworkable or inappropriate some of the time, and the vast majority of people are not believers anyway.

As society becomes more secular, which it has been doing for centuries, the more its social and moral life becomes determined by what is acceptable to all, no matter what their religious beliefs. This has led to the current situation in which morals have largely become separated from religion, which in turn has become a largely private affair, as we have seen. Modern society tolerates widely varying religious beliefs but understandably draws the line at their influencing society as a whole. Surely a sign of a balanced modern society is that it can tolerate and contain such variations yet still function as a workable whole. None of us wants society to rule out *our* particular religious or moral beliefs, yet we are often all too ready to behave in exactly this way towards our neighbours.

By the same token we have a moral responsibility not to harm our children by what we do to them, however well intentioned. As a society we should be mature enough to devise a system of morality backed by law (because people seem to need laws to help them curb their sexual behaviour in a social setting) that puts sex into its place as a natural, ordinary part of everyone's life from the cradle to the grave.

None of this means that 'permissiveness' should become the norm. On the contrary, thinking through what we teach our children and young people in a logical way that takes account of the facts as we know them, encourages them in turn to be more questioning and critical.

It soon becomes apparent that a lot of so-called sexual 'morality' questions cease to be questions of morality in the widely accepted sense. They become questions of human behaviour in the current situation. Many a modern moral decision based on rational reasoning will of course overlap with biblical codes simply because human beings do not change, and their problems remain much the same over the centuries. It will always be morally wrong to kill, to lie, to cheat and so on because it is impossible to run a society as complex

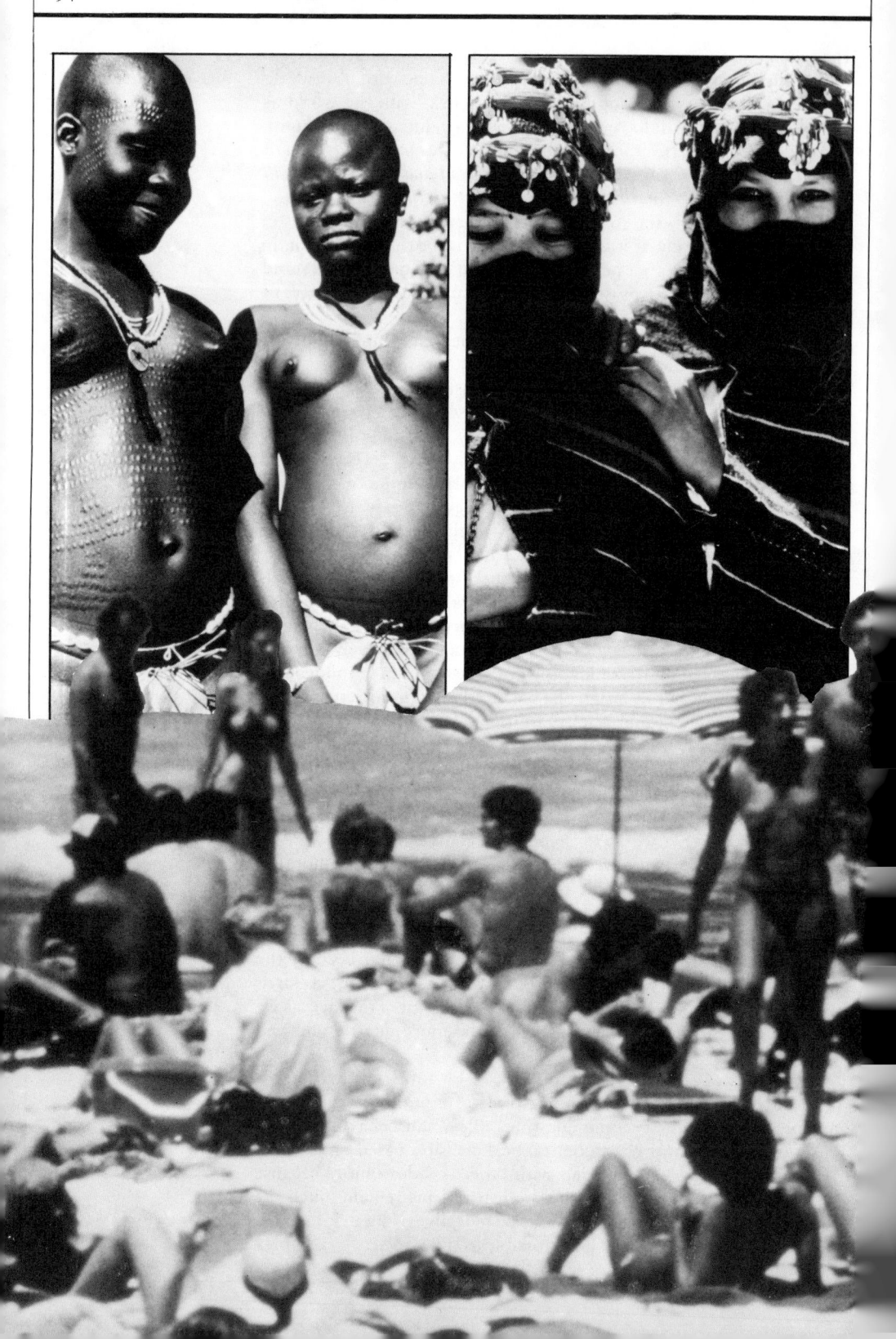

SEXUAL MORALS

SEXUAL MORALS 349

Different cultures—different centuries—different ways: 100 years or 100 miles can make all the difference to what is considered moral or immoral.

as ours if people behave like this on any scale. When it comes to sexual morals, though, the rules of the game have changed so much that we owe it to ourselves and our children to be sure of what we are perpetuating into the next generation.

A book such as this cannot and should not lay down what parents should tell their children about sexual morals. What it can do is to outline the facts as they are currently understood, so that those of us who have responsibility for the moral training of the young can do our jobs from a well-informed base.

Some parents are too bigoted.

Some parents will be so bigoted that they will continue to perpetuate old myths and moral teachings simply because they cannot or will not accept the truth as it is currently understood. Such people will not be influenced by anyone—they 'know' that certain things are 'wrong' (such as oral sex, homosexuality, masturbation or whatever) and no rational explanation will influence their thinking. This is a cruel shame because *their* programming as children is going to be passed on to their own children who are brainwashed into all kinds of irrational beliefs, many of which will stay with them for life and reduce the quality of their lives and that of their future spouses.

Today's thinking, caring parent must surely accept sex as a natural, normal part of a child or young person's life and act accordingly.

Summary

The most convincing argument in favour of the conventional moral code is that of 'ancient wisdom'. The idea here is that, for reasons which may now be lost to us, our forebears, over thousands of years, discovered the best ways of regulating society and constructed these discoveries as moral codes. If this is so, we break or alter them at our peril.

By extension, the rule-makers or moralists, then claim that God will favour those individuals or societies which keep to the rules and perhaps destroy the rest. At this point it becomes impossible to subject the rules to rational scrutiny and assess their worth.

Parents, of course, are gods to a small child and whatever rules they choose are instilled into the child's mind whilst he or she is incapable of critically questioning them or even of consciously remembering that they are being inserted.

Obviously, it is better to educate the young not to make the mistakes of their forebears, but once the rules have passed beyond rational thinking it becomes impossible to know whether they are doing more harm than good.

Probably the best course is not to regard moral codes as being absolute but rather to subject them to recurrent scrutiny in the light of the changes which occur all the time in the community. If they have lost their point they should be overruled.

Chapter 28

Maturity

All parents bringing up their children want to see them grow up to become well-balanced, mature adults, and much of what parents do for and with their children has this end in view. They are children for so short a time and it is the duty of parents to prepare them adequately for the future. But 'maturity' can be difficult to define.

When it comes to concepts of physical maturity definitions are relatively easy. A person can be said to be physically mature when he can reproduce himself or when bone growth has stopped. These two ages do not coincide in man, so even physical maturity is not a simple concept.

But if physical maturity is difficult to pin-point, emotional and psychological maturity is nearly impossible to define. All of us eventually mature physically but many people never fully mature emotionally and psychologically—they remain as children in certain respects all their lives and often this is to their disadvantage. It is even more difficult to define psychosexual maturity, but it is worth trying to lay down some guidelines for emotional and psychosexual maturity even though some people would contest certain of them in detail.

Two interlinked themes are involved in the concept of emotional maturity. One relates to the development of the individual as such and the other is concerned with the way he or she relates to others. So clearly, any definition or concept of maturity has implications both for the individual and for society at large. On the whole it is a grossly neglected topic, and at present appears to concern mainly those involved in relieving psychosexual and marital difficulties. This is a pity because immature behaviour in its many forms affects us all.

Central to the personal aspect of maturity is the comparison between a child and an adult. A small child is totally dependent on its parents, particularly its mother: it takes rather than gives; consumes rather than produces (except for noise and body-waste); is unreasonable and unreasoning, being governed solely by instincts; is intolerant of discomfort and frustration; is egocentric (being concerned only with its own feelings and having no concern for the welfare of those around it); and is prone to outbursts of rage and anxiety. Yet within the child lie blueprints for physical and psychological development, and under the influences of these blueprints a child gradually progresses from childhood to adulthood.

From the biological point of view the function of an adult is to reproduce and rear children. Obviously, a child cannot fulfil these tasks. The process by which he or she becomes fitted to do so is what we call maturation. The maturing child eventually turns into an adult but, in order to fill the adult reproductive role successfully, he or she must have certain attributes.

So far, most readers will agree with what has been said, but when it comes to the details of the attributes required we get into trouble and often prefix them with the word 'ideally'. This implies, and it is true, that few individuals, if any, are fully mature and that the 'ideal' parent does not exist any more than does the 'ideal' child. However, if systems of rearing in which children are communally cared for are discounted, it is widely agreed that children are best produced and reared by a mature man and a mature woman who love each other and have a sense of commitment to each other and to their child. For such a state of affairs to come about, the two individuals obviously have to have the necessary confidence and social skills to attract a mate in the first place; sufficient inter-personal skills to keep him or her; a sufficient degree of emotional development to love and be loved; and sufficient sexual skills to have intercourse. In order to continue the relationship in a reasonably happy and efficient way they, as a rule, need to be able to give and receive support and love and they need to be reasonably independent, so as not to overburden each other or anyone else, and yet be capable of asking for help when they are confronted with situations which are beyond their capabilities. They are helped in their relationship if they can evolve a style of sexual behaviour which allows free expression and mutual satisfaction. If the couple are to avoid unnecessary conflict they should be capable of consideration and communication and should be in fundamental agreement regarding their joint aims in life.

As far as their child is concerned, they need to be able to provide for it, protect it, accept its independence and not to have unrealistic expectations of it. They should be sufficiently close to each other not to want to make a special love-object of the child or to use it as a weapon against each other, nor to take out on the child the anger they may occasionally feel towards each other. Each must accept that they have responsibility for it, and that in this respect, over the years, the father's role is no less important than the mother's. They should be sufficiently secure to allow the child to be, within reason, itself and not to try to turn it into some form of apostle for, or replica of, themselves.

Our children are a part of us genetically, but they are totally unique and will be around long after we, the parents, have gone. A mature couple do not 'own' their child. They are simply custodians for about a quarter of that person's life. That this happens to be the most important quarter of most people's lives has great significance for the future of the child. The opposite-sex parent must not try to seek revenge on the opposite sex generally through the child and should not try to resolve his or her problems with the opposite sex through the child. In this way problems are perpetuated from one generation to the next.

The child's interests, which are not necessarily synonymous with the child itself, usually need to be placed first and foremost, especially when he or she is very young and, above all, the child needs to be loved not because it is good and pleases its parents, but because of itself.

All this demands emotional maturity in the parents. Unfortunately many cannot come anywhere near to fulfilling this very reasonable list, mainly because of inadequacies in their own rearing.

Much more is needed for successful human reproduction than just genital contact, and if adults retain too many of the characteristics of childhood themselves adequate child rearing is impossible.

However, another set of factors influences progress towards maturity. A child is exposed to his or her family and to the experiences of life. Such exposure affects personality, psychosexual, emotional and other development. The topic is vast but a few examples might help by way of illustration.

Being born largely unwanted and subsequently being less than adequately loved exposes a child to feelings of inadequacy and uselessness which undermine all other development, even physical. Children who are severely neglected emotionally, or are unloved, do not grow physically the way they should, boys being worse affected, at least physically, than girls. The situation is complicated because the child may not obviously lack for anything: in fact it may be spoiled by the parents out of guilt. As adults such people may be less than mature because they demand rather than give love or compassion. Frequently they become 'neurotic' about love, perpetually demanding proof of it, and watching the partner for any sign of what they regard as evidence of not being loved. Most commonly they are depressive, self-critical and generally unable to love themselves adequately. They may be suicidal or promiscuous. Where a mother is generally unmaternal, it is thought that schizophrenia may result in the child, as may alcoholism. A boy reared in this setting, for example, may subsequently fear all women or hate them overtly or covertly, and children of either sex may later display 'mother-hunger' or 'father-hunger' in which they seem to try to revert to childhood to be loved by a woman or a man as a parent. All shades of such effects can occur and in some instances the child's perceptions of reality are governed by rivalry with brothers and sisters more than by any defect in its mother or father. On the other hand, over-close, over-demanding, over-indulgent, seductive, remote or rejecting parents of either sex can distort the psychological development of a child of the opposite sex.

The effects of emotional neglect.

As a rider to all of this, common sense and the opinion of many psychiatrists and psychologists indicates that emotional problems and neglect started in early childhood can be effectively plastered over by subsequent good treatment and/or by the capacity of the individual to bounce back. This latter varies enormously of course. Whilst people may cope very well much of the time, in times of stress their negative rearing comes to the fore as the 'plastering' cracks.

Parents who refuse to allow their child to grow up, and treat him or her perpetually as if he or she were younger than its years, who oppose independence and, in an effort to meet their own needs, encourage the child to cling to them, run the risk of producing an immature adult who will always want to be dependent on his or her spouse or anyone else (perhaps including those from the social services or psychiatrists). Such individuals regress to childhood as soon as they encounter any difficulty in life.

The 'rules' of behaviour are taught to a child in many different and frequently unobvious ways, including by identification with its parents, experience of life, formal and informal education, exhortation, rewards, punishment and so on, but the majority originate in the unconscious mind of the child's parents and go directly into his or her own unconscious. (There is a rather nice definition of a university lecture that illustrates this process well. A lecture, it is said, goes straight from the notes of the lecturer to the note book of the student without passing through the minds of either!) Much behaviour and many attitudes are taught in exactly the same way within families.

In a household in which rules are few and lax, children remain impulsive and self-indulgent, and in one in which they are over-harsh, they become inhibited and anxious. Where the rules are inconsistent the children become indecisive and confused. Attitudes are conveyed in a similar way. Thus a child may, for example, be taught to fear failure, ill health or a lack of money more than anything else. Alternatively, he or she may be trained to have excessive fears about the opinions, real or assumed, of others, or may develop an undue fear of or contempt for authority. In a similar way a child may learn that sex is excessively private, dirty or sinful, and so on. If children develop serious inhibitions about sexual matters they may later lack sufficient drive to overcome their fears, which will impair their social and emotional as well as sexual development.

A child's capacity to experience anxiety, which has a natural survival value for the human species, is probably over-utilised by most parents in child rearing. It is very easy to do this, especially if the parents were reared this way themselves, but it is a real disadvantage to the child, who will grow up to become anxious about almost everything. Instead of inducing anxiety, try to give positive reasons why your child should or should not do things. If you are always threatening ill effects as the result of various activities it will be hardly surprising if the child actually believes that most behaviour produces a negative outcome and then grows up to fear or be anxious about most things.

In the same way parents can teach their children to be hostile to others, but even more commonly they fail to deal adequately with the hostility that arises in their children towards their brothers and sisters and even towards themselves. Behind this is probably the failure to deal with fear, especially the fear of the loss of love. Many parents are so love-dependent that they are not able to discipline their children adequately because they fear that they, the children, will stop loving them. On the other side of the coin, many parents threaten to stop loving their child if he or she does things they do not approve of. This is especially harmful behaviour. Whatever the child does, especially a young one, he or she needs to know that he or she is loved, and to threaten to withdraw that love—or to do things which make the child feel it has been withdrawn—is a form of psychological torture which is harmful if frequently repeated. If you get to the state in which the only way you can control your children is to threaten to stop loving them, get professional help. You may not mean much of what you say, especially in a fit of temper, but the child will remember it all too vividly—even if only in the unconscious mind—particularly if you tend to say it often. The chronic hostility that this can produce can lead to excessive and uncontrolled aggressiveness, rage, unfairness and cruelty. The hostility may then become generalised and so have to be directed against others in the same category as the original object of the hostility. In this way all women, men or authority figures, for example, become hated figures, and this gets carried through into adult life.

These and similar concepts obviously have implications for society and inter-personal relationships within it. A lack of maturity damages the individual, the institution of marriage, parenting and society in general. Emotional immaturity is often the root cause of criminality, social inadequacy, disruptive politics and extreme religious fervour. At the same time we have to admit that emotional immaturity can sometimes be a spur to achievement which is creative rather than destructive.

In one sense we never grow up—we simply become more elaborate. The child is as present in every adult as it was in childhood. A truly mature individual is still in contact with the child within him- or herself and can allow it out to play occasionally without becoming childish. Retaining the child-like capacity to experience total pleasure, to give total love, to be free of all criticism of someone who is loved, to be full of curiosity and excitement and to retain a sense of wonder are all, paradoxically, elements of maturity. Presumably, too, progress towards maturity involves the shedding of the unpleasant results for the personality of the bad aspects of one's rearing.

Apart from hatred and envy, already mentioned, and an undue fear of condemnation by others or God for natural behaviour which is harmless to others, senseless shame, especially about sex, and inappropriate guilt, need to be controlled. The tendencies to tell lies to avoid trouble, to denigrate others out of fear or jealousy, to be spiteful over minor wrongs, to be unduly suspicious over the motives of others and to need to obtain love and approval from all, thereby leading to insincerity, should ideally be eliminated. A capacity not only to accept failure without disintegration or discouragement but also to learn lessons from it and to be stronger needs to be developed especially in a culture such as ours in which the middle classes at least give children the impression that what they achieve is the true measure of their worth.

Most importantly of all from the point of view of maturity, in our culture there is a need to control unreasonable, unnecessary and excessive anxiety. Anxiety is a natural and protective emotion which should mobilise the individual's resources to deal with real or realistically possible threats to his comfort or security. Its perpetual misuse leads to inefficiency, inappropriate action or inaction, the reduction of happiness and, eventually, to psychosomatic illness, which can cripple the person just as surely as any other illness.

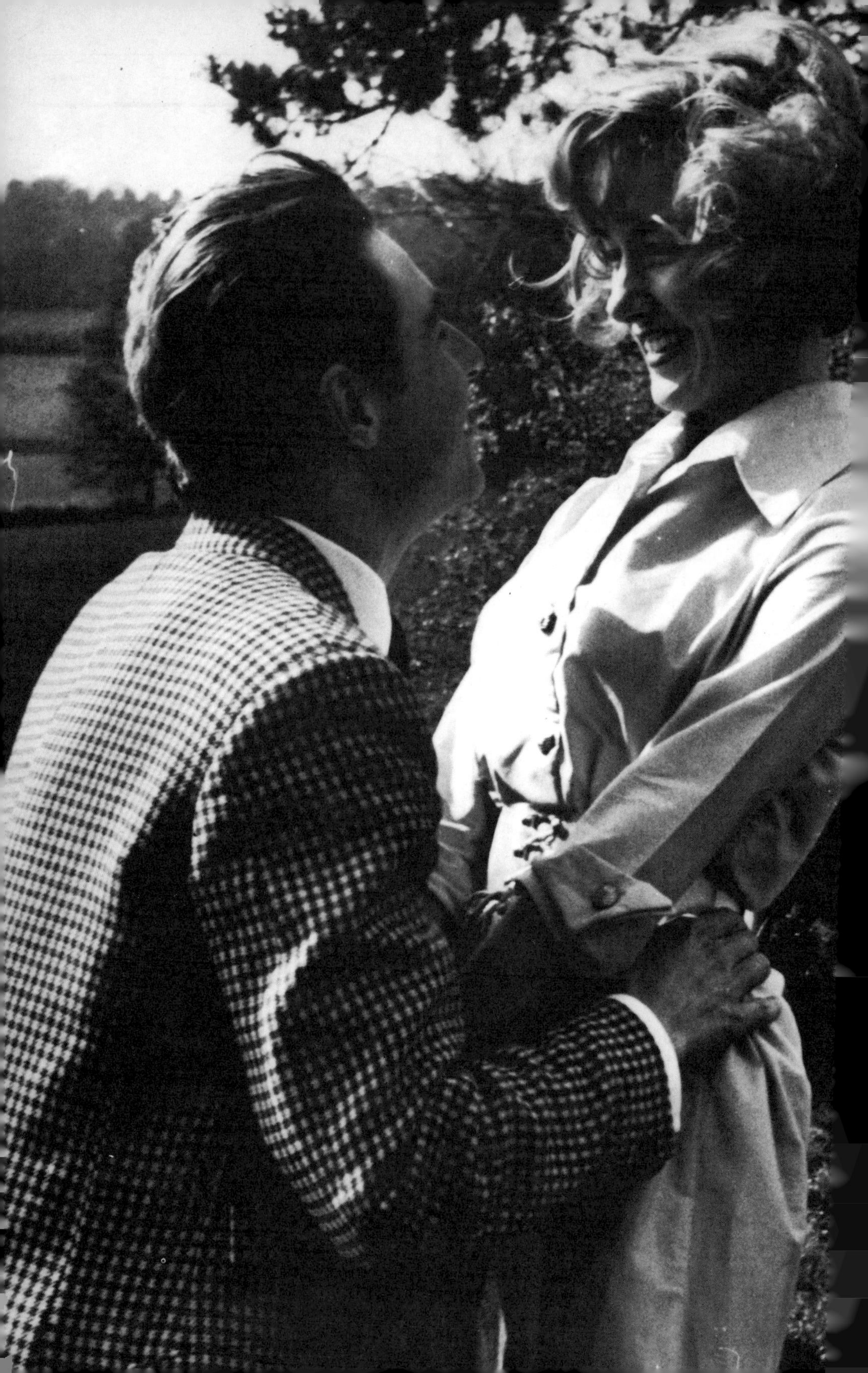

Characteristics of a mature person

Bringing the strands together then, the characteristics of a mature person could probably be said to be that he or she:

Is reasonably independent but not excessively so.

Is capable of giving as well as receiving—emotionally as well as in other ways.

Is free of undue aggression and competitiveness and is able to put such feelings to constructive use.

Is productive as a member of society.

Is cooperative.

Is mainly realistic and is not too much governed by self-deception, fantasies and unrealistic perceptions.

Is largely free of childhood feelings of inadequacy, self-centredness and inferiority.

Is capable of controlling impulses and of converting the energy they contain to more socially acceptable ends when necessary.

Can tolerate frustration for a reasonable period of time, or even for ever, by coping with it in another form.

Is flexible and adaptable, not responding neurotically to changes in circumstances.

Is, eventually, fairly well aware of his or her true capabilities and faults, neither unduly exaggerating nor minimising them.

Is capable of dealing with individuals as individuals and not as if they belonged to stereotyped categories of individual.

Mature lovers: Mature people who love each other in some way love everyone. Such lovers are the very foundation of society.

Maturity in women

In discussions about maturity in women two special problems are often raised. In the first it is sometimes claimed that if a woman can not obtain orgasms from her vagina she is immature. However, so many obstacles are placed in the way of the sexual development of girls that whereas they can, as adults, function genitally and copulate, their capacity to acknowledge and experience sexual pleasure is often grossly impaired. The inhibition is not on doing (they can 'do' anything)—but on pleasure (they get far less pleasure than they could). The problem for many women is not whether they are mature and can experience orgasm from vaginal, as opposed to clitoral, stimulation, but whether they can experience an orgasm at all.

The other topic affecting women and maturity is the view that until a woman has had a baby she cannot be regarded as mature—in other words she has not proved her capacity to fulfil her reproductive role. Apart from the fact that an addiction to babies can in itself be a sign of excessive guilt about sexual activity, it is obvious from earlier parts of this chapter that the argument could equally well apply to both sexes. Maturity, however, should not be regarded at the level of the individual as revolving around whether they have reproduced or not but their fitness to do so should they decide to.

Summary

Because of the variations between people, and their experiences of life, maturity is hard to define. Its main, and necessary, characteristics can be outlined, but even these do not have to be on display all the time. Paradoxically, the retention of an ability to return to one's childhood is a sign of maturity in itself and is probably basic to good, unselfconscious intercourse. Thus, 'mature' is not synonymous with 'adult' in the psychological sense.

Unfortunately, the topic receives little attention, to the detriment of good education, and the term 'immature' is brandished about as one of abuse. However, many of the individuals who want to alter the world want to do so out of immature impulses. They need the world to fit them and their childhood problem but, of course, they dignify their cause by enlisting their religious, political, social or moral theses. This probably explains why political movements and so on can harbour so much hatred, sometimes of a murderous variety, against 'enemies'. Immaturity is the root cause of most problems in the world at large and explains why no one is left in peace for long.

Chapter 29

Homosexuality

What is homosexuality?

The word 'homosexual' has nothing to do with the Latin word *homo* (man) but comes from the combination of the Greek word *homo* (same) and the Latin-based word 'sex'. So it means sexual activity between people of the same sex. This can take many forms, just as sexual activity between people of the opposite sex does.

Current research suggests that there are about 2 million homosexual men and women in the UK today.

Why is homosexuality such an emotive subject?

In the Western world homosexuality is generally thought of as unacceptable, even if it is reluctantly tolerated in some countries. A few countries have legitimised the act between consenting adults in private but it is still a long way from being sanctioned as socially acceptable behaviour.

Why should homosexuality raise so many hackles and create such strong feelings? There are probably three main reasons. First, it tends to reduce the increase in population because men who are exclusively having intercourse with one another are not fathering children. Second, it undermines the position of women and the institution of marriage because men are getting sexual gratification outside marriage. The third reason is that it is thought to be 'unnatural' and disgusting.

There are two basic types of homosexual behaviour. One is that indulged in by most boys and some girls in their development as described in chapter 2. The other is that found in adults who have elected to run their lives in a way which means they are sexually active with one of their own sex. Some of this latter group are bisexual (they have sexual intercourse with both sexes). For many girls of about eight to eleven and boys of about thirteen to sixteen, homosexual encounters, usually with children of their own age, are a normal part of growing up. Ninety-six per cent of boys and girls come out of this phase to become substantially heterosexual adults.

Why are some people homosexual?

The short answer is that no one knows. As we have seen the vast majority of boys go through a developmental stage around puberty during which some degree of homosexual behaviour is normal, and many experts believe that most adult homosexuals have remained frozen at this stage of their development.

Recent evidence has found that a specialist area of the brain (the hypothalamus) that controls all the hormones of the body is 'cycled' in its activity in all young foetuses. In male foetuses it normally becomes uncycled but in some male homosexuals it may remain cycled. Perhaps this points to something happening early in pregnancy that prevents the developing male foetus from becoming a typical male.

Some young people and, indeed, adults of any age, have problems with narcissism—that is, they are only attracted to someone

HOMOSEXUALITY

like themselves. They are consequently predisposed to choose a sex partner from their own sex.

Many people deprived of sex with the opposite sex for long enough (for example in prison) will turn to some kind of homosexual activity, even if it stops short of intercourse. Some women turn to homosexuality after bad experiences with men and many more at least consider doing so. These homosexuals often return to heterosexual life once the balance of their lives returns to normal again.

Sometimes homosexuality arises in a man because he is so tense with women that he cannot relax and so never has satisfactory sexual relationships with them. Such men turn to other men and find that

Those who love their own sex: Although the heterosexual may never fully understand the homosexual, the mark of a civilised society is to be tolerant of the ways of others. (Wide World Photo)

they have better quality, more enjoyable orgasms with them. The 'cure' here must surely be to ensure that boys are not brought up to fear women, as too many have been. Thankfully this is less true today than it was in the past. A similar situation also lies behind some lesbianism—some women can relax more with another woman, and so come off more easily.

Lastly, experimentation in sexual matters has become a feature of the current scene and experimenting with homosexuality is sometimes simply a part of this. Some youths, frightened of getting girls pregnant or simply wanting to sample both sides of the fence before deciding, try a homosexual relationship. Unfortunately, there are real dangers in this because, at this young age, a boy can become locked into the homosexual sub-culture all too easily and so does not get a chance to develop his heterosexuality. An extension of this type of homosexuality is that in which a rebellious teenager uses homosexuality to punish his or her parents and rebel against society.

If all of these 'causes' seem to point to a clear, black and white picture of homosexuality, this would be wrong. Certainly, about one in twenty-five adult men choose to be exclusively homosexual, but there are many others who have fleeting homosexual experiences. People have different levels of responsiveness to people of the same sex. Among those who declare themselves to be homosexual there is more evidence of heterosexual behaviour among the women than among the men, but further analysis shows that the heterosexual activity provides little satisfaction and sexual release and is taking place for the sake of appearances.

Broadly speaking, homosexuality can be latent (beneath the surface) or openly expressed. Many people are latently homosexual and with very little provocation demonstrate their homosexual side on occasions. (Incidentally, the fact that many people, men and women, find anal stimulation erotic does not make them homosexual.) Overt or expressed homosexuality is less common and is unfortunately plagued with unhelpful stereotypes in many people's minds.

What do homosexuals do?

Male homosexuals most often use one or more of the following sexual techniques when making love: reaching orgasm by rubbing their bodies against each other; masturbating a partner; being masturbated by a partner; sucking the other's penis (fellatio) or having their own sucked; and performing or receiving anal intercourse. According to one study almost all homosexuals indulge in at least five of these practices in any one year and about a quarter will have done them all.

Women homosexuals' practices are mainly: reaching orgasm through body rubbing; masturbating their partner; being masturbated; performing cunnilingus (licking the clitoris of the partner), and receiving cunnilingus. Most female homosexuals experience masturbation (both doing it to their partners and having it done to themselves) more commonly than other physical practices. The thing they like best (according to the above survey) is cunnilingus.

Problems of homosexuals

Homosexuals have problems just as heterosexuals do but they have additional troubles because of society's attitudes to them. Although most male homosexuals report that they are in good health and happy overall, they are also more likely to be lonely, depressed and tense than heterosexual men. They tend to worry more and to feel persecuted. On the other hand they tend to be more exuberant than heterosexual men. Homosexuals are more likely to consider or attempt suicide (though this may have nothing intrinsically to do with their homosexuality—it may be related more to the sub-culture they find themselves in or the social and other pressures on them because they are gay). Homosexual females were also found to be slightly less happy than their heterosexual counterparts and to have had more contact with professional counsellors. Close-coupled lesbians, however, were found in one survey to be less lonely and happier than heterosexual women.

The problems start for teenagers when they declare to their parents that they think they are homosexual. Most parents are upset and understandably find it difficult to know what to say other than to be negative. The best way to handle this problem is for parents and child to discuss it fully and then to get professional help if there is still concern. The best place to start off is probably with the family doctor or marriage guidance counsellor locally. Either of these will hopefully provide a relatively unbiased approach to the subject. By going straight to the many homosexual organisations a young person runs the risk of being welcomed with open arms and their homosexuality confirmed and celebrated. We feel this is bad for the young person, who might well just be going through a temporary phase in his or her development because it might preclude or hinder heterosexual development in the future. Only if it seems clear that the young person seems convinced of and is happy with his sexual orientation does it make sense to contact a homosexual group so that he or she can start off his or her sexual life prepared for the problems and able to meet like-minded people. Until homosexuality becomes totally acceptable (which is still a long way off), this sort of situation will always be a terrible dilemma for the average parent.

Is my child going to be a homosexual?

As was pointed out earlier, it is perfectly normal for young people to go through a homosexual phase during their sexual development. This should not be seen as the prelude to a lifetime's homosexuality (which it very rarely is) but as a safe way of discovering about one's own sex.

The stages differ in boys and girls, so let us look at them both briefly. Girls go through this stage in their pre-pubertal phase (eight to eleven) and boys in their post-pubertal stage (thirteen to sixteen). Girls will play dressing-up games, which include undressing and perhaps smacking each other's bottoms; kissing 'like a boy'; putting a finger in a friend's vagina; or playing with each other's breasts.

The homosexual and lesbian pair: Some people can only find fulfilment of their loving and/or sexual needs with a member of their own sex.

Rarely, though, do girls teach others to masturbate. Boys talk a lot about sex, have competitions as to who can ejaculate first, have mutual masturbation sessions, compare penis sizes, count hairs and so on. Boys of this age usually do all these things with boys of their own age and as long as this happens all will be well. When older boys or men are involved there are legal and personal problems and such contacts should be vigorously discouraged.

Many girls at this stage, and later, have a crush on older girls or school teachers. Such homosexual crushes are rarely overtly sexual in content (except perhaps in the girls' fantasies). They usually fulfil an unconscious need the girl has to identify with a woman she sees as likeable or successful in a quite non-sexual way.

All of this means that it would be harmful and pointless to punish a child found enjoying homosexual experiments within these

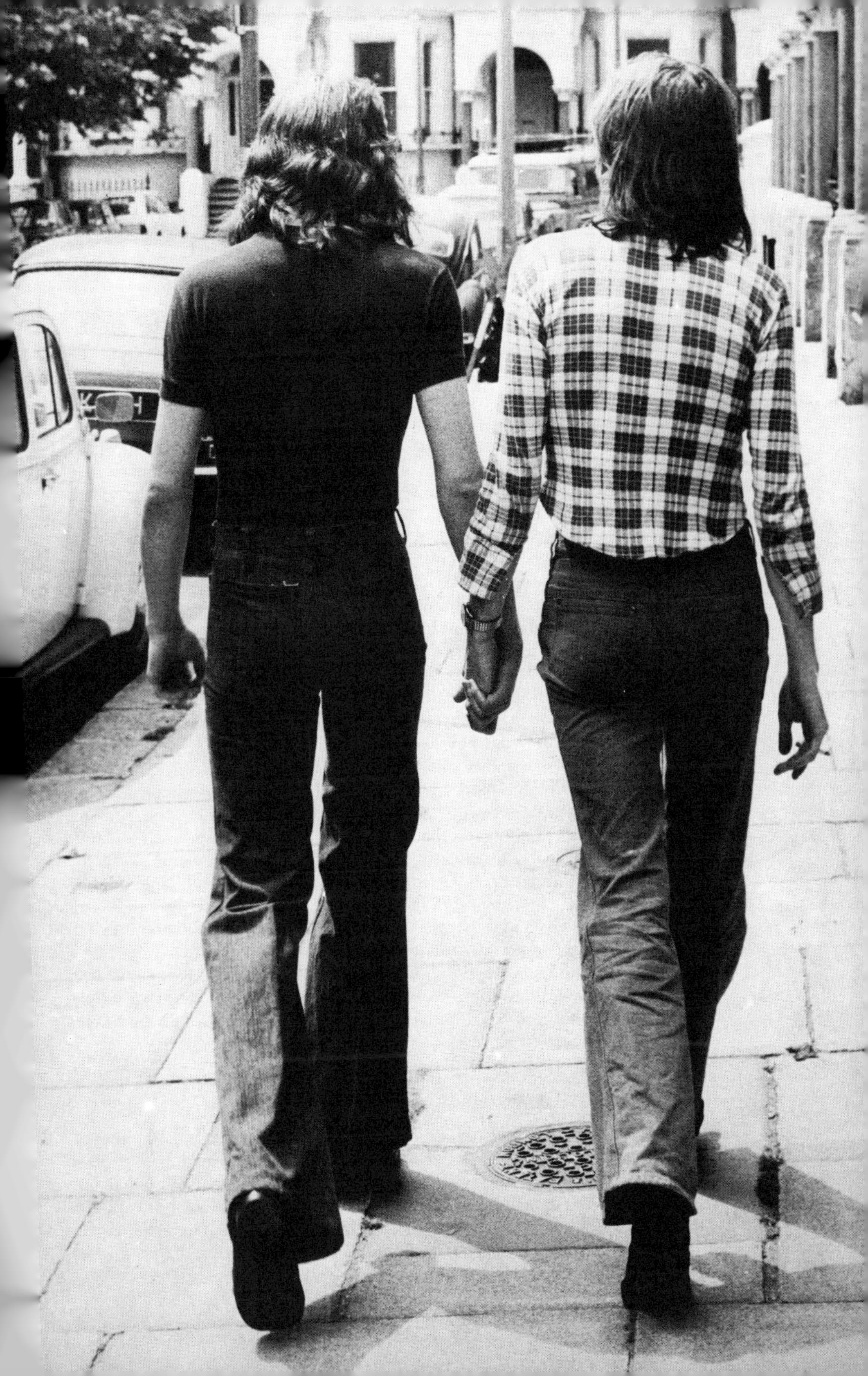

age bounds. Two girls aged sixteen found mutually masturbating, for example, *should* be a cause for concern, though, because unless it is a one-off game it could well mean that one or both will have problems in relating to men.

What to do if you think you are a homosexual

Obviously if you have chosen to follow a homosexual life-style as a mature adult, it is your choice and you should be allowed to live with it. The problems arise for those (men and women) who find themselves turning towards same-sex partners without being happy about it. This can happen for many reasons, as we have seen. A woman whose husband is away a lot or is in prison may turn to another woman; men thrown together without women indulge in more sexual activity with each other than they would otherwise ever contemplate; the happily married person suddenly finds him- or herself attracted to someone of the same sex and so on.

Very few spouses can cope with the thought of their partner being or becoming homosexual, so the best place to start is probably your general practitioner or local marriage guidance counsellor. You do not have to be married to go to the latter. Some basic help from such people will often put your mind at rest, but if you need more detailed or specialist help you can contact a specialist psychosexual therapist either through the marriage guidance organisations or through a referral from your physician.

There are thousands of men living secretly with their homosexuality within marriages and the going can be very tough without outside help. Once you have had some professional help you (or your therapist) may suggest that you discuss it with your spouse. How this is done will vary greatly from couple to couple. Some perfectly happily married couples continue to run a normal and happy family life with one of them conducting a secret homosexual love-affair, but they are few and the stresses usually tell in time. The odd homosexual encounter (especially for women) may well not threaten a marriage but anything more serious will need professional help. Remember too that many male homosexuals have or have had VD, and that if you have a homosexual affair you run a considerable risk of giving VD to your wife.

Summary

A homosexual orientation can probably result from a large number of factors. It is said to be rare in communities which—unlike our own—do not make an endless song and dance about heterosexual behaviour. In any reasonable society an individual's sexual orientation would be his or her own concern. Today, the majority of the population probably accept homosexuality, believing that it is up to the individual to make his or her own choice.

Chapter 30

Sex-related diseases

Our sex organs, just like any others, need basic care and attention if they are to remain healthy. The majority of men and women who have one sex partner never have any trouble with their sex organs—at least not from infection. Sometimes a woman (and her partner) can get monilia (thrush) without having caught them from someone sexually (by having sex), and a woman can have a vaginal discharge for all kinds of reasons, as we shall see, but in general venereal infections come from someone outside the one-to-one relationship.

Look after yourself

Apart from using a sheath, you cannot do much to prevent yourself from getting VD if you have sex with someone who is infected. There are a few basic hygiene rules which are worth following to reduce your own risk of infection. Following them also means that you will notice any trouble as soon as it occurs.

1 Keep healthy and fit. Anyone who is run down or seriously ill is more vulnerable to any infection. Stress too seems to predispose to infections.

2 Always report any discharge, inflammation (painful redness), pain (especially on passing water), or bleeding from the sex organs to your doctor at once or go to a special clinic at your local hospital.

3 Wash your genitals and around the anus every day. Keep a sterile wash cloth for this. Boil it regularly and don't share it with your partner. If you use a shower or a bidet you will not need a cloth for this purpose.

4 If you are a woman, always wipe yourself from front to back after opening your bowels and use each piece of paper once only or you could transfer bacteria from around the anus to the vulva.

5 Wear clean pants every day.

6 Men who have not been circumcised should pull back the skin every day and wash the penis tip well. There is some evidence that poor hygiene can cause cancer of the womb (cervix) in a man's sex partner.

By doing these simple things you will keep clean and fresh and will notice any abnormalities *at once*.

Let us now look at the sexually transmitted diseases in turn. But before doing so let us consider vaginal discharges because they can cause such confusion and worry.

Vaginal discharge

The normal, healthy vagina produces a whitish secretion with a characteristic odour. The amount of this fluid produced varies considerably from day to day and with the stage of the menstrual cycle. This discharge is different from the lubrication which occurs during sexual arousal, when all healthy women produce clear fluid. Normal vaginal secretions have a very characteristic smell which turns many men on sexually. Unfortunately, the advertising industry has done its best to portray the vagina as needing frequent cleaning, and many women believe they should wash out their vagina with a douche or a bidet or mask their natural odour with deodorants. None of these is necessary. Simply wash the outside regularly and leave the inside to take care of itself. If you think you have too much of the normal secretions, or if the secretion smells unpleasant or makes you itch, see a doctor. Also get help if (especially around and after the menopause) you have too little natural wetness.

Two common diseases produce a vaginal discharge. One is thrush (moniliasis or candidiasis) and the other trichomoniasis.

Thrush

This is a fungus which infects humans. A woman can get it in her vagina where it causes intense itching, soreness and a thick, curdy, white discharge. A doctor can confirm the diagnosis by taking a swab and examining it under a microscope. In men, thrush may produce no symptoms or there may be slight soreness or redness of the penis.

Thrush is often but by no means always caught venereally (from other people's sex organs). Quite a lot of people carry thrush fungus in their bowels and elsewhere but have no symptoms. Women who are pregnant or on antibiotics, or who are diabetic, are especially prone to it. If you have thrush time and again it is wise to have your urine checked for sugar just in case you have become a diabetic.

Treatment is fairly simple. A drug called nystatin cures almost every case if taken exactly as directed. Some doctors give tablets by mouth to clear the bowel of the fungus too, but most simply prescribe pessaries (vaginal tablets) which have to be inserted every day and night, for two weeks. You may need to wear a stick-on pantie liner while this treatment is going on. Nystatin cream or ointment applied to the vulva is soothing and should be used on the man's penis as well whether or not he has symptoms. Other preparations are also available and some act faster than nystatin—talk to your doctor.

If you have thrush, even if it is being treated, don't have sex for at least ten days from the start of the treatment. This is no great hardship because most women are so uncomfortable with thrush that they are not inconvenienced by this restriction on their sexual activities.

If you get thrush, don't assume that your partner has been

unfaithful—you have probably caught it from yourself, from your own bowel infection, as we have explained.

Trichomoniasis
This is the second most common cause of an abnormal vaginal discharge. Again it is an infection that is carried without symptoms by many people (one survey suggested that 23 per cent of women carry it), so do not jump to conclusions about venereal spread. In women the infection causes a painful and irritating discharge of a yellowish-green bubbly fluid. It is sometimes offensive to smell. The vulva is usually bright red from being inflamed and intercourse is unpleasant because of the pain. The diagnosis is made by a doctor who takes a swab.

In men the infection can produce a slight irritation in the urinary passage (urethra), but usually the partner of an infected woman carries the bug without knowing it. This means that a woman with trichomoniasis must ensure that her partner is treated if she does not want him to reinfect her.

Treatment is simple and effective. Both parties are given a course of a drug called metronidazole (Flagyl) as tablets to be taken three times a day for a couple of weeks. Flagyl can cause sickness and headaches, especially if combined with alcohol. The couple should avoid sex until the treatment is over. Other newer drugs which are effective more quickly are now available. Flagyl is also used to treat *Gardenerella* infections in which the resultant discharge often has a fishy odour.

Foreign body in the vagina
This is the third commonest cause of an abnormal vaginal discharge. Usually it is a forgotten tampon. Other things put into the vagina can also be forgotten and cause a discharge. Such discharges are usually yellow and smelly and need to be sorted out by a doctor if you cannot easily get the foreign body out yourself.

Disorders of the cervix
These are a fairly common cause of vaginal discharge and there are many of them. The fluid tends to be brown or blood-stained, and slimy. Any such discharge *must* be seen by a doctor at once. Many a simple condition can be diagnosed and dealt with by out-patient treatment.

Gonorrhoea
This is the second most common of the 'real' venereal diseases. It is frequently called the 'clap' and its incidence has risen alarmingly throughout the world. World-wide it is the second most common infectious illness after measles, and in countries such as the UK it is now even more common than measles. Even with efficient tracing of the contacts of those with the condition and with effective treatment this infection is still very common.

Gonorrhoea is caused by a germ called a gonococcus which is

mainly transmitted by sexual intercourse. It is possible to catch the disease via infected towels and other household items, and this is the way babies and young children sometimes catch it. The bacteria grow in and on the sexual organs but they can also grow in the throat (after oral sex) and rectum (after anal sex). Homosexual men are very likely to get gonorrhoea. If you have sex with someone who has the disease you stand a 70 per cent chance of getting it, but the risk is greatly reduced if the man wears a sheath. If a man urinates *immediately* after intercourse with an infected woman he stands a fair chance of escaping infection.

The symptoms differ considerably in the two sexes. In men they are usually fairly obvious. A few days after intercourse with an affected woman the man has a severe burning pain when passing urine and then develops a yellow discharge of pus from the penis. These symptoms must be taken seriously, so go to your doctor or local VD clinic at the hospital at once. Early treatment will not only cure the disease and stop it spreading to anyone else but will also prevent long-term complications of the disease, such as eye trouble, arthritis, painful swelling of the testicles, or a narrowing of the urethra (urinary passage).

Unfortunately, as many as half of women with the disease have no symptoms and as a result may infect others unknowingly. This is why gonorrhoea is such a widespread disease and is so difficult to eradicate. Others get the same sorts of symptoms as men but the gonococcus also affects their fallopian tubes and ovaries. These can also become inflamed and produce lower abdominal pain, fever, menstrual irregularities and a vaginal discharge. Later still the fallopian tubes may become blocked off and the woman is then infertile.

Treatment is relatively simple and effective and if started early prevents the long-term effects we have outlined. It is really best to go to a VD clinic or to your doctor if you have any suspicion that you have this disease or if you have had intercourse with someone you suspect could have had it. Simply ring your local hospital and ask for the 'Special Clinic'. Such clinics maintain absolute secrecy and discretion, and your partner or parents (if you are a teenager) will never be contacted without your permission. There is no need to give a false name as many young people do. If you have any symptoms that could be gonorrhoea, for goodness sake don't have sex of any kind until you have been checked over by a doctor. Almost every infection caught early can be cured.

The cure for gonorrhoea involves having a course of antibiotics. Although it is true that certain strains of gonorrhoea are difficult to treat, the vast majority can be effectively treated. You will have to go back for tests to check that the infection is in fact cured. Don't have sex of any kind until you are given the 'all-clear'.

Syphilis

This used to be an extremely common disease until the coming of penicillin in the 1940s, but is happily less common today. In the past, when treatment was poor, the long-term effects (both physical and mental) were atrocious. Today such effects are extremely rare.

About a month after having sex with an infected person (often a homosexual man) the contact gets a chancre (pronounced *shanker*) at the site of the infection. This can be on the penis, vagina, nipple, finger tip or lip. Before it ulcerates it is a hard, painless sore the size of a fingernail. A woman may not know that she has it because it could be deep inside her vagina. The sore goes away after a few weeks. This stage is called primary syphilis.

The second stage starts with a copper-coloured skin rash produced as the germs spread throughout the body in the bloodstream. There is also a fever, sore throat, swollen glands and a loss of hair. These symptoms go away too.

The third stage is a hidden one that can last for years. There are no symptoms but the germs are working their way into almost every organ of the body.

The fourth stage of syphilis which affects about a third of all cases is the one described in historical records with such horror. This stage damages the nervous system, along with most of the other organs of the body, and the person can be paralysed, go blind, go mad and eventually die.

A woman who is pregnant and has syphilis can pass the disease on to her baby who will be born dead or diseased. This disease can be detected easily by taking a swab from the sore and blood tests can help too. Treatment with antibiotics is effective, especially in the early stages. Any long-term changes that have occurred in various organs cannot, of course, be reversed.

NSU (non-specific urethritis)

This is now the commonest of all venereal diseases and can be very difficult to treat. It is mainly a disease of men (women can certainly carry it but often do not show any symptoms). There is considerable medical debate as to what organism causes NSU but whatever it is it can be very difficult to find.

NSU develops seven to ten days after having sex with an affected person and the symptoms are similar to those of gonorrhoea. The discharge may be white, yellow, green, grey, or streaked with blood and must be reported to your doctor. The first sign may be pain on passing water.

The VD clinic will do tests to rule out other types of VD and you will be given a long course of antibiotic tablets. Repeated courses may be necessary as the disease can take months to clear. This makes it very wearing to suffer from as repeated visits to the clinic are essential.

Genital herpes

Until recently the existence of this condition was hardly known to the public but the disease has now reached epidemic proportions in the USA and is fast on the increase in the UK. It is caused by a virus (the cold-sore virus) which produces painful, burning, fluid-filled genital blisters. There may also be burning pain on passing urine and painful lumps in the groin. The sores can become infected. About 30 per cent of sufferers have other symptoms such as tingling pains down the legs, back pain, a fever and swollen lymph nodes (glands). The blisters may recur several times a year and some people have as many as twelve bouts a year with stress and menstruation seeming to act as triggers.

There are more than seventy similar viruses known to man, the most common being the chicken-pox virus and the viruses causing shingles and infectious mononucleosis (glandular fever). Genital herpes is caused by the herpes simplex virus which is closely related to the virus that causes cold sores. Of babies infected during birth (as they come down their mother's infected vagina), about half die or are severely retarded—so it is a serious disease for them. In women, recurrent attacks are thought to increase the risk of cervical cancer five- to eight-fold and sufferers are advised to have a smear done every six months.

Probably the most unpleasant thing about the disease is the terrible psychological and emotional effects it can have. These have been aggravated by exaggerated propaganda about the disease. However, the thought of having to declare that one has an untreatable venereal disease before having intercourse with someone is a tremendous strain and carries an enormous responsibility. In the US so great is the problem that special self-help herpes groups have been formed. A new drug (Acyclovir) is available to help cure the disease but it is only really effective intravenously and at the moment this means a short stay in hospital while the drug is given. Various other treatments including diets, locally applied yoghurt, whisky and ether have been tried but have proved ineffective.

Pubic lice (crabs or nits)

These parasites live in pubic hair and suck human blood to live on. Their eggs are called nits and look like small white blobs attached to the pubic hairs. Infestation makes the pubic area itch like fury. You cannot wash out the eggs: you need a chemical which can be bought without a prescription from any chemist. Chemical preparations are also available from your doctor or VD clinic. They kill off the tiny crab-like insects and the nits, and cure the condition. The infestation is caught by being in contact with someone who has the condition or from close contact with infected bedding, clothing, towels, or even a lavatory seat.

Unfortunately it can take some time to kill every last nit, so while this is happening wash all your clothes, underwear, towels, sheets and so on and don't have sex until you are completely in the clear. Be sure to see that all your close physical and sexual contacts are treated.

Scabies (the itch)

This is a similar infestation but usually causes itching, often in the webs of the fingers, around the waist, on the wrists and under the armpits. Tell your doctor or special clinic—treatment is simple and effective.

Hepatitis B

A virus disease which it is strongly suggested can be transmitted via saliva, semen, menstrual blood and other body fluids. To this extent it can probably be transmitted sexually. Homosexuals are more likely to be affected than heterosexuals and the disease is important because it can cause chronic damage to the liver. Having said this, the majority of infections are symptomless and self-limiting. Unlike with other types of venereal disease there is no way of detecting carriers of the disease nor is there any way one could suspect a potential partner of having it.

AIDS (Auto-immune deficiency syndrome)

This is being increasingly diagnosed, especially in promiscuous homosexual men. In this condition, the exact cause of which is still in dispute, the antibody defences of the body are impaired, so reducing resistance to infection and even cancerous changes.

Summary

Venereal diseases are increasingly common but the commonest condition associated with venereal disease in any Western community is VD anxiety or phobia. Although it is obviously common sense to check up at a special clinic if you have the slightest suspicion that you have been in contact with an infected person, many of those who go to VD clinics are simply worrying unnecessarily.

If everyone simply had intercourse with the individual to whom they were married then VD would probably die out. However, a large number of people have intercourse with more than one person and many people have sex with many partners.

In the last analysis all that is special about venereal diseases is the way they are spread. There are lots of factors involved in the increased spread of VD and the so-called copulation-explosion brought about by the pill may not be the main cause. The control of VD has always been seen as a job for the moralists. They have had little or no success. We would rather see it as a job for sex educators and those who can actually cure the diseases.

Chapter 31

Prostitution

It might at first sight seem that prostitution is a rather strange topic for a family book of love and sex, but we have good reasons for including it, beginning with the fact that the majority of men who go to prostitutes are, or have been, family men.

Prostitution is an important part of our story because it sheds light on a very difficult subject that is capable of ruining relationships and breaking up marriages and families—men's *real* sexual needs and desires—and the fact that they are so often unfulfilled within their marriage.

Whether we like it or not we all have slightly differing sexual needs and requirements. For those who are happily settled in a caring and truly loving relationship all these needs are met within the relationship. However, for many people—men especially—these needs are not met in this way and they choose to seek out someone who will indulge them with them. Sometimes this is done in an extra-marital affair, of course, but millions of men around the world choose not to go down this path and instead pay a professional woman who sells sex for a living. This has very obvious advantages and no emotional overtones or complications.

Of course, in an ideal world there would be no need for prostitution because every man would have a loving partner who would do exactly as he wished and would therefore answer all his needs, preferably in a loving and caring setting. That this is not the case is very sad and reflects two things. The first is that many men simply imagine that their wives would not want to do certain things, even though in fact the wives would but get no chance to say so. The second is that many women, reared as they are in our culture, *are not* willing to answer certain sexual needs and desires in their partners. As long as both of these conditions apply there will always be a need for prostitutes.

What is a prostitute?

A prostitute is a person, male or female, who, in part or in whole, makes a livelihood by gratifying the sexual desires of other individuals, either male or female, within transient relationships, in return for remuneration. Although male prostitutes and even brothels exist to satisfy women, and although homosexual and lesbian prostitutes are available to members of their own sex, by far the most common form of prostitution is that in which a man pays a woman. This has been used to 'prove' that men have greater and less discriminating needs for sex than women. On the other hand it can be explained with equal ease and conviction as a consequence of the behaviour of any society in which the sexuality of the sexes is differentially suppressed. Since most cultures, and especially ours in the West, suppress women more, man-pays-woman is bound to be the commonest form of prostitution. If a woman in a culture like ours wants casual sexual satisfaction and is not too inhibited about seeking it, she can easily get it without having to pay for it. If all the conditions were reversed, including the economic ones, then perhaps woman-pays-man prostitution would flourish. Prostitution takes the form it does in our culture because of the economic and sexual suppression of women, and the very existence of any form of prostitution is probably the product of sexual suppression in general.

Most prostitutes do the job to make money—and it can be very lucrative. More basic reasons for going into the profession include a lack of training for anything else, boredom, loneliness, being drawn into it by friends, and sexual gratification (this latter is usually, but not always, strenuously denied by the prostitute).

Almost all studies of prostitutes take their word for it when they say they hate men and cannot bear sex with their client, and only a few individual psychoanalysts have taken the trouble to go deeply into the unconscious realities behind such statements. When this is done the results are quite surprising. A woman prostitute may be punishing her mother or taking revenge on her father who she felt could not possibly love her. Some may not have resolved the problems associated with releasing the childhood bonds they had with their father, and for them taking money from men is a symbolic, child-like way of taking love.

Some prostitutes think they can meet 'better' men than would otherwise be possible and some hope for a marriage to a rich and powerful client. Others who feel, or used to feel, unattractive as women can get repeated boosts to their morale which seem to them to prove they are desirable. A number of prostitutes who work heterosexually (with men clients) are lesbian and yet others may be latently lesbian and use heterosexual prostitution to ward off the tendency. Women prostitutes who cater for both sexes are becoming increasingly common.

Male homosexual prostitutes, who are usually young, are said to pay more attention to the physical appearance of would-be clients than do their female counterparts. Like the latter they usually deny any desire for sexual pleasure themselves and they also often deny that they are actually homosexual. Nevertheless, they erect and ejaculate with male clients and, it is said, usually pursue a homosexual life-style when they have to give up prostitution. Although some dress and behave effeminately, most try to emphasise their masculinity.

Since at least some prostitutes are unconsciously motivated to take up the job because of childhood problems such as a poor relationship with their mothers, unresolved problems over their relationship with their fathers, excessive guilt about early sexuality leading to extreme masochism and so on, they often have impaired

The oldest profession: In spite of opposition, prostitution still continues to flourish nearly everywhere in the world.

psychosexual development. If this is so, as well as having an understandable willingness to satisfy most clients' demands, if only to ensure their return (because most prostitutes like a regular clientele), such prostitutes probably have a greater capacity to undertake and even enjoy a diversity of sexual behaviour than does the average woman. This is fortunate because many prostitutes say that the majority of their clients want something in addition to, or even in place of, normal intercourse. A prostitute may have to dress up in special clothes, provide special facilities, possess special equipment, utter special words, undertake special acts, and be prepared to bring her client to orgasm by a whole variety of means. Of these, oral sex, carried out by and to her, is increasingly popular. The customer might simply want to look at her (she need not necessarily be naked) whilst he masturbates himself (sometimes he will not even want to do that) or he may want to watch her undertake lesbian acts with a colleague. He may want to bath or massage her, beat or masturbate her, urinate or ejaculate on her. More commonly he wants her to carry out these acts on him. Some men ask prostitutes to have anal intercourse with them using a dildo or a vibrator. Yet others may only want, they claim, to reform or rescue her, whilst others again just brutalise her out of a hidden religious motivation or in symbolic revenge against all women. As a result of these many, often strange, requests, the average prostitute has to be able to look after herself and to remain in control of the situation. This she can do very well because as a matter of professional pride she only occasionally gets 'carried away' by what is going on and she knows exactly where to draw the line. Even so, prostitutes are open to danger from their more weird clients and this is a danger of which they are only too well aware.

Fantasies of being a prostitute are commonplace amongst women and adolescent girls. Sometimes they are pushed back into the unconscious because, in our culture, whilst women are allowed to do almost anything to attract sexual attention to themselves, actually to solicit sex earns condemnation. Our society has a multiplicity of names with which to reproach sexually forward women, and deter others, such as whore, tart, harlot, slut, and hooker, to name but a few of the 200 or so.

Probably the safest conclusion about prostitutes is that they are much like other women and it is only circumstance, past and present, which pushes them over the boundary beyond which they stifle moral scruples and actively seek sex for pay. The reason why so many strenuously deny that they get enjoyment from sex with clients is that the denial reduces their guilt and moral objections to their own actions to a level at which they can live with themselves. However, prostitutes are a valuable source of information about the sexual preferences and practices of the male population and their activities may represent the true, if only occasional, needs of men, unmet at home because of the unwillingness—real or imagined—of their wives. Often it is not really the case that women do not want to meet their partners' special needs, and several surveys have shown that women would like their men to be more adventurous. In the marital bedroom a wise wife could do far worse than regard herself as a prostitute specialising in one customer!

Some prostitutes specialise in particular areas of sexual behaviour, common examples being humiliation, bondage and flagellation, all of which are much more widespread than is generally believed. A variant of this is the 'mistress' type of prostitute who has an on-going relationship with her submissive clientele which may even be carried out through the post. Others specialise in using pornography to arouse and excite the man. More specialist set-ups also exist such as saunas and massage parlours where the clients are eventually masturbated, the euphemism for which is 'hand-relief'. In others the clients are in separate rooms and look at naked women through a window. Other prostitutes may be specialised in the way they get their clients. Call-girls and women who work through an escort agency are two common examples.

The clients of prostitutes are said to come from all walks of life but increasingly come from the older segment of the community, because free sex, it is said, is more easily available to the young today than in the past. Older men, especially if they are concerned with their respectability, are often unwilling to make advances to women of their acquaintance and may be happier to patronise prostitutes. Older husbands are more likely to be sexually bored with their partner than are younger men and are often less willing to run the risks of emotional entanglement with a non-prostitute. Men with more 'deviant' needs, with physical handicaps, or with a penis they regard as unusually small, may all be more attracted to prostitutes rather than face rejection, or exposure, by a non-prostitute. If you are paying the woman (they argue) she cannot refuse you. This is not in fact true and prostitutes will refuse clients with whom they do not feel safe or who do not fulfil other criteria.

Because prostitutes are available in all age groups and in all variations of body-form and colour, the patron of prostitutes can choose what he wants, as opposed to picking from what happens to be available in the non-prostitute population he meets. Some men who have been reared to believe that sex is unacceptably sinful can only get normal sexual pleasure when with a prostitute and some men who are emotionally immature may prefer prostitutes to other women.

Whereas it could be argued that other trades and professions are subject to regulation and restriction and therefore so should prostitution be, the law and its current implementation are designed to make it difficult or near impossible for the prostitute to function at all, and there are some who would like to see even more control.

Legal control. Obviously the underlying ultimate aim of all this regulation is to eliminate prostitution. Eliminating prostitution has been tried throughout history but has never really worked and is certainly not working today. On the contrary, while controls are as tight as ever on full-time professional prostitutes the part-time 'amateur' flourishes as never before and is uncontrollable because she works in private homes. The reasons put forward to justify the expenditure of resources on the harassment of prostitutes include complaints from the neighbours, the necessity for the law to be upheld, and the view that prostitution goes hand-in-hand with organised crime and the drug world. This seems to be yet another example of the confusion which excessive moralising brings about—it reverses cause and effect. In practice, the law appears to be tough on prostitutes and often deprives them of basic rights and fair treatment. It can be this type of attitude that pushes prostitutes towards crime and criminals. In the end, the vast majority of activities involving prostitutes end up with consenting adults having sex in private, harming no one (at least not directly), and it is hard to see the justification for increased state interference.

Perhaps it should be said here, if only for the sake of completeness, that increasing numbers of perfectly 'ordinary' women all over the world are turning to part-time prostitution to make money in a quick and easy way that is often approved of or even encouraged by their husbands. These semi-professionals form a small but growing proportion of all prostitutes and are part of a trend that would have been unthinkable even twenty or thirty years ago.

No longer therefore should prostitutes necessarily be seen as different from other women—women with the same psychosexual make-up and background as others who think they would never contemplate prostitution are increasingly turning to multiple partners as a source of income. The growth of contact magazines has made this practice easier to carry out even though such magazines are supposed not to carry adverts from prostitutes. Quite a lot of women have multiple sex partners in 'commercial' settings, but as they do not charge their partners, they cannot really be said to be prostitutes. Many of these do, however, make their living out of the 'sexploitation' business and sleep around with whoever needs to be influenced, in order to get on in their career or job. Thus, some models, actresses, dancers and even secretaries could, in the widest sense of the word, be said to be prostituting themselves, by using sexual favours (often short of actual intercourse) to obtain what they want from the men who have the power to give it. The fact that no money actually changes hands is somewhat academic—services such as jobs, promotion, accommodation and meals out come into the deal.

In a society such as ours, in which sex is widely available and women are prepared to use their sexual favours to get what they want in life, the line between the actual 'prostitute' and the girl who is out to get the best for herself in life is somewhat hazy. The major difference is that a prostitute makes her living mainly by giving sex in return for money and thus has relatively little choice over her clients, and the 'good-time' girl makes her living mainly from a 'legitimate' job and can usually exert some sort of choice as to who she has sex with.

Summary

Prostitution is probably as old as the human race and will always be necessary as long as men have sexual needs that are not otherwise met. Prostitution is almost entirely a private business indulged in by two consenting people. This makes it difficult to see why it arouses such hostility, except on the religious or moral grounds that sex between two people who are not married is in itself unacceptable.

Surely it would be wiser to leave prostitutes and their clients alone and to try to find out why men need to use them at all. If such research could throw light on men's unmet needs and future generations of couples could be helped to be self-sufficient sexually, prostitutes would diminish to a number which would cater almost exclusively for single men.

Chapter 32

Am I odd?
A brief look at some more unusual aspects of sex

Unbelievable though it might seem to many people, there are individuals, lots of them, who believe that any form of sexual expression other than putting the penis into the vagina, and even doing that with foreplay involving the genitals, is a perversion. For some women, to enjoy sex simply for the pleasure it gives them is near perverse and religious authorities over the centuries have claimed that any woman who enjoys sex is as good as a prostitute and is therefore deviant. Even today some religions assert that sex for pleasure is wrong and that it should still be carried out with reproduction as its main aim.

Such notions still underlie our cultural heritage, no matter how unconscious we are of them, and it is easy to see how people can be ashamed of, for instance, an interest in erotic material or masturbation, let alone anything else, as a result of these underlying notions. Unconsciously, many people, including those who think of themselves as sexually liberated, believe that any indulgence in sexual pleasure is likely to bring punishment from God, perhaps in the form of mental illness—which is greatly feared, especially by some women—or disease. Our laws and customs also reflect the view that sex is sinful and harmful.

Our sexualities work against this suppression imposed in childhood and adulthood. But the desires and instincts that are blocked may have to find an outlet in some closely related form and this, by definition, is a deviation. However, our sexualities are as various as our personalities, so some people all of the time and all of us some of the time are going to be attracted to activities, either as a prelude to intercourse or as a substitute for it, which do not conform to the basic cultural norms of copulation. Because there is often so much shame attached to the desire it may not be admitted to the individual's partner or, if it ever is acted upon, it may be regarded as very secret and shameful. Some partners cannot cope with the request for what to them is very odd behaviour and sometimes use a deviation like this as a reason for divorce.

Because the whole subject is so shrouded in secrecy (the only people who ever hear about such things in detail are sexual and marital therapists) the public's knowledge of what 'normal' people do or would like to do sexually is poor, and it is easy to denounce the sexual behaviour of others as abnormal, deviant or perverse. Such condemnation used to be very prevalent, but many activities that used to be thought of as unusual or perverted are now known to be widespread and well within the range of acceptable and 'normal' behaviour. Oral sex (fellatio and cunnilingus) is an example.

Many people never feel like kissing or orally caressing their partner's genitals and the idea does not excite them. Some, both men and women, see their genitals and their fluids as dirty and untouchable and so would not kiss or suck their partner's sex organs or allow them to be caressed in this way, although they may fantasise about oral sex. Some women who would really like to have oral sex performed on them are deterred by the thought of the smell of their vulva and think men will be put off, whilst other women who, perhaps because of being reared with excessive guilt about it, have difficulty in obtaining real pleasure from intercourse, can have an orgasm quickly and easily with oral sex.

Today the topic of oral sex has been so widely discussed that it has become a positive fashion. Most couples use it simply as a sexual

A touch of sado-masochism: Many couples increase their pleasure by playing games of this type during foreplay.

enhancer before actual intercourse, but still a great proportion of all male orgasms are induced by fellatio ('sucking off', 'a blow job', 'giving head') than was ever the case in the past. By definition this is a deviation from normal intercourse. So long as it remains a form of foreplay to arouse or an occasional change from vaginal intercourse it is probably perfectly normal but a person who can only have orgasms as a result of oral sex needs professional help to sort out his or her hang-ups about intercourse.

It is probably also the case that many more female orgasms are being induced by cunnilingus than was ever the case in the past. The main explanation, other than the fact that inhibited women can often succeed in having an orgasm only with oral sex, may be that the male population collectively is losing its self-confidence with regard to penile performance and is increasingly depending on the more reliable tongue, which does not lose its erection or come too quickly. In the end, though, we are mammals and mammals suckle their young. So our first physical pleasure in life is oral and this involves sucking another person. It would be surprising if orality were not important in our sexuality—it certainly is in some other mammals. Its practice in the past has been denounced as a perversion simply because it seemed to lead to 'pleasure sex' rather than furthering copulation as a reproductive duty. As the present over-reaction towards oral sex subsides we will undoubtedly reach a point of reasonable balance on the subject and people who feel they want to kiss and orally caress each other genitally will do so and not worry about it.

What we have said about oral sex can be used as a model to discuss almost any sexual activity other than basic and unadorned copulation. Nearly all the activities involved can be used as a part of foreplay (as a sexual enhancer), as an occasional alternative to penis-in-vagina sex, or in a more or less perpetual substitution for it. In foreplay we tend to re-enact not only our psychosexual development but also the stages which most young people go through between first sexually kissing a member of the opposite sex and having intercourse. So foreplay usually contains elements of pre-genital behaviour (oral, anal and phallic) and to this extent could be (wrongly) regarded as perverse. Good foreplay also contains an element of courtship too. Everyone, or nearly everyone, unless they repress them into the unconscious, has sexual fantasies which they, or others, would think of as perverse. Foreplay can be the way in which couples, especially younger ones, both express and contain their perverse thoughts and fantasies. This explains why young couples tend to experiment more sexually and this is good because they should in this way slowly evolve a pattern of sexual behaviour which suits them both. In general, a sensible rule is that anything which helps one's partner to greater arousal and better quality orgasms and satisfaction is not only permissible but welcome. So voyeuristic, exhibitionist, oral, and even minor sadistic and masochistic acts as well as bondage could well be involved.

What is perversion?

Although it is difficult to define, we think that the word perversion should only be used, if at all, where heterosexual intercourse is consistently bypassed in favour of other sexual activities. Perversions can, rarely, be the result of a personality disorder, mental illness or disease of the brain but apart from these causes, perversions are in theory caused by one of two things. First, the person's psychosexual development may have gone ahead more or less normally but, because of previous experience or suppressive rearing with regard to intercourse, intercourse causes too much anxiety for it to be really pleasurable. This can result in sexual dysfunction of various kinds or a tendency to go off at a tangent from intercourse into activities which approach it, purely for pleasure. In this way, a man may be willing to have intercourse but in fact enjoy orgasms more when mutual masturbation or oral sex is involved. Many cases of non-consummation of marriage fall into this category. 'Deviation' seems an appropriate word because the aim is right yet it slightly misses its target.

The other basic causes of deviations are distortions in psychosexual development (see chapter 1 for more details). In these types of perversion the person grows up fixed at a certain stage of childhood sexual development or returns to it because progress to a later stage involves too much fear, guilt, anxiety or pain. After a difficult time with a member of the opposite sex an individual may return to an earlier stage. Usually, he or she recovers rapidly but the examples show how we can move up and down the ladder of psychosexual development. When psychosexual development goes awry like this the individual is a good distance away from heterosexual intercourse and the term perversion is probably more appropriate. We think that it is important to point out that the word applies to a perversion of *development* rather than the actual practice involved. Certainly the person him- or herself cannot be condemned—on the contrary, they should be pitied because of what their past has done to them. The term 'deviant' and 'pervert' are hurled about quite unnecessarily and can cause real harm to the individual involved.

Apart from the most commonplace of perversions there are several real disadvantages to being locked into non-intercourse sex as your main or only means of sexual release. First, many of the opposite sex will find you strange or unacceptable; second, you will have difficulty finding suitable sex partners; and last, you could get drawn into all kinds of sub-cultures in society, many members of which are unusual or unacceptable in other ways. Many 'normal' couples see those with deviant or perverse sexual appetites as being more 'turned on' or highly sexed but often the opposite is the case. Such people do not get their best pleasure from straightforward intercourse and need other things to function well sexually. This is a drawback socially and personally and not an advantage to be admired.

Deviations and perversions are usually thought of as being the almost exclusive preserve of men but the causes from which they spring apply to both sexes and, in our culture, even more to women.

Women may, because of their nature, be less prone to respond to the damage inflicted on them during rearing by becoming deviant. They simply become less sexually efficient. Alternatively, they may be more ashamed of the need and so repress it more, or they may be better able than men to meet the need in fantasy during intercourse and masturbation. Men anyway tend to be the 'operators' in sexual activities and so are more likely to go out and make their fantasies come to life, whereas women (mainly because of their conditioning) will keep them as fantasies. As women become increasingly liberated this picture could change. Men also have more to learn about sex than women and as a result are more vulnerable to mislearning.

One theory of perversions in men attributes it to repeated masturbation while fantasising perversely during adolescence; the resulting orgasm acts as a reward and reinforces the tendency to enjoy the thought of the perversion. Because perverse fantasies are common in adolescence but perversions in adults are comparatively rare the theory is unlikely to hold true for the majority, but it can be applied in reverse when treating deviants. In this technique, which is applied to both men and women, the patient is advised to masturbate frequently to their usual perverse fantasy but to change it at the last moment before orgasm to a fantasy of normal intercourse. By association with orgasm the heterosexual fantasy increases in strength and erotic power. Gradually it is extended backwards in masturbation so that, eventually, the whole of the associated fantasy is of intercourse and the interest in the perverse activity fades out.

The characteristics of a full-blown perversion are its compulsiveness and its fixity. The person *has* to do it and cannot easily stop doing it. He cannot overcome it by reason, fear, shame, threat of punishment or even by exposure. Lesser degrees, which can be described as borderline cases of perversion, exist, particularly in women. Women in this category can and do function 'normally' but they do not enjoy it much. For them really to enjoy sex their perversion has to be incorporated into their sex lives. The distinction between such women and the 'normal' person who occasionally enjoys 'perverted' activities as an alternative to intercourse is a fine one but they can be distinguished on the basis of the compulsiveness and fixity of the true perversion. Let us now look at some of the commoner practices.

Sado-masochism

In sado-masochism there is an erotic association between pain and sex. The sadist inflicts pain and perhaps humiliation and restraint on the partner and the masochist pleasurably endures it. The accepted generalisation is that men are sadistic and women masochistic. Whilst it is undoubtedly true that many women enjoy having intercourse in a brisk, no-nonsense way which brooks no objection, and some claim to like rough treatment, which may include having their bottoms smacked, there are probably reasons involved other than masochism. The main one is guilt reduction. A woman who has been brought up to think of sex as dirty and sinful, yet really enjoys it, gets most pleasure when she is 'forced' to have sex because it takes her actions out of her own hands and this excuses her otherwise inexcusable (to her) behaviour. Many women find it flattering and exciting to have their desirability confirmed by being wanted urgently and passionately, especially if they have been married a long time and think their husbands may be going off them. Many women say that sexual situations are the only ones in which they enjoy being subordinated entirely to a man's will. Most hope that their partners will do something new to them, and many say that it is best if it just happens to them, without their being notified in advance. This state of affairs arises more because of passivity than masochism, and it could also be a consequence of the way our culture shames women, which results in their being inhibited in expressing their more unusual needs. If a woman is taken and told what to do she does not have to feel ashamed or guilty, because she is not the one who initiated it. As a result, in many couples the man has to take the lead if they are to enjoy any variations in their sex life, and many men are not up to doing so. In practice many more men seem to want women to beat them than the reverse and prostitutes flourish on fulfilling this need. However, women may tease men or provoke them to anger, perhaps in the hope that they will end up being treated in a rough way and then 'forced' into intercourse.

Possibly the best way of thinking of true sado-masochism is to think of sadists as being afraid of retaliation by the opposite sex so that they feel that their partners have to be controlled and punished. The masochist is afraid of his or her own sexuality and so hands over the control of it to someone else. In most cases, for the sadist really to enjoy the act, the masochist must enjoy it too. Some masochistic men have their hardest erections and most satisfying orgasms when they are being beaten by a woman; a few like a woman to 'force' them to lick up the semen afterwards; a few even want the woman to castrate them; and so on.

Sadism may have its origin in the anal stage of development but it may also be due to a fusion of sexual and aggressive forces. Symbolic aggression expressed in a sexual form can impart a degree of ardour to a man's love-making. Nobody thinks badly of an aggressive man in bed, provided he does not harm his lover. Masochism is thought to be, amongst other things, the reversal of sadism or the eroticisation of submission. Sado-masochistic desires are frequently combined in the same person, and couples who practise sado-masochism frequently change roles. The ability to do this is not present in the true pervert.

Much pornography is based on sado-masochism and sadists can ejaculate simply by looking at photographs of such scenes. Although very few couples are sado-masochistic in the gross way that many people imagine when looking at pornographic representations of the subject, many use some force, restraint or pain during love-making and intercourse in a perfectly harmless way. Many men enjoy having their testes squeezed, especially as they come off, and lots of women like hard nipple and breast stimulation but again often only near their climax. Many couples bite each other playfully quite hard, but the

Few sado-masochistic couples.

rule should always be that nothing you do should continue to hurt after you have both had your orgasms. It is easy to inflict too much pain during the run-up to and during orgasm, so be careful.

Putting objects in the vagina

Many women when they masturbate or couples when making love put objects other than their fingers or penis into the vagina, and many wonder if this is safe. Probably the best advice is *not* to put anything into the vagina that is not meant for it—and especially never to put in any sharp or breakable object. An ice cube, if it is small and melts quickly, can produce a pleasant sensation, and a few women use penis-shaped fruits and vegetables when they are masturbating. The most dangerous things are round objects that can be pushed in during the excitement phase just before orgasm but which will not come out again once the vagina returns to its normal state. These can be really difficult even for a doctor to remove.

When it comes to vibrators obviously things are different because they do not break and hurt the vagina. Because the vagina is a closed-off passage there is no danger of losing a vibrator and it is perfectly safe to put it in as far as you want it to go. If it hurts, of course, don't push it in any further. Any persistent pain either with a vibrator or on intercourse should be reported to your doctor.

Finally never blow into the vagina. Several women have died as a result of air being forced into their abdominal cavities up their fallopian tubes.

Sex aids

These have been used for thousands of years and are now widely available through marital-aid and sex shops, either directly or by mail order. Almost all sex aids are sold to couples to enhance their foreplay and to increase the pleasure they get from intercourse. The biggest-selling sex aid by far is the vibrator, which comes in many sizes. Vibrators are mostly penis-shaped, made of plastic and designed to be used on the clitoris or to be put into the vagina while the clitoris is being stimulated by hand or with a gadget on a vibrator. Many women who cannot have orgasms in any other way can learn to have them using a vibrator but few women who have orgasms alone or with their partner prefer a vibrator for long. So they are probably a good learning tool for women with orgasm difficulties and are fun to play with from time to time otherwise. A word of caution about using vibrators in the back passage (anus). Quite a lot of people enjoy having a vibrator in the anus when masturbating or even during intercourse and this is fine provided it does not then get put into the vagina where it could cause a troublesome infection. Anything that has been in the anus should be washed thoroughly before being put into the vagina. The second problem is that by putting the vibrator too deeply into the anus it can get lost, and this is very dangerous because it may have to be removed surgically.

Sexy underwear and various types of condoms (sheaths) are

probably the next-best-selling lines in a sex shop but both are, of course, available elsewhere too. These are purely for fun and can do no harm but we should give one word of warning about putting rings and other things around the penis. When the penis is limp it will obviously be easy to put a ring around it, but when it is erect the ring will be impossible to remove. Some erection enhancers are ring-like structures but none is safe that is not made of something that can instantly be released or cut in an emergency. A ring in place on an erect penis stops the blood from leaving, so the erection cannot subside until the constricting band is released. This may well have to be done in hospital, and because there is a danger of damaging the penis permanently it is best never to do it.

Whilst on this subject it should be said that some people put things inside the urethra, but this is foolish because they can get stuck or cause an infection.

Anal sex

Anal (rectal) sex has always been a difficult subject because so many people associate the rectum with dirt and/or homosexuality. Quite a large number of people find that they enjoy stimulation of the anal area as part of foreplay, and many men enjoy having a finger inserted into their anus just before orgasm and whilst they are ejaculating. Some women like this too.

Technically, anal sex is illegal between a man and a woman but not between two men of the required age and by mutual consent in private. Until 1861 anal sex was punishable by death in England and it is still illegal in most states in the US.

Still illegal in certain places.

About one in five married couples admit to having tried anal sex (although the actual figure is undoubtedly higher than this) and historically it has been widely used as a form of contraception and at times when the woman was menstruating or had a vaginal infection.

Anal intercourse is perfectly acceptable medically with a few provisos. First, the man will have to take things gently if he is not to hurt the woman. A couple who are keen to have anal sex should spend some days preparing for it. Start by gently inserting a well-lubricated finger tip into the woman's anus while she masturbates or while you are having intercourse. Over the next few days insert another finger or two, never causing pain, and then eventually—with plenty of lubrication—try to use the penis. Never thrust the penis quickly or you will be sure to hurt the woman.

The only real problem with anal sex is that it is easy to transfer bowel germs from the anus to the vagina and this can cause troublesome infections. If a penis has been in the anus it should be thoroughly washed before being put into the vagina, or indeed anywhere else.

Exhibitionism and voyeurism

The accepted generalisation is that women are more exhibitionist (like to show their bodies) than men but less voyeuristic, with men being more voyeuristic (wanting to look at women) and less exhibitionist. This seems to make biological sense given that our notion of beauty is based, at least to some extent, on the female body. So, in general, women enjoy displaying themselves and men like looking at them. The female body in itself is quite capable of producing an erection in many men, especially if it is scantily clad or naked. In the West women are allowed to show off their bodies (albeit not entirely naked) whereas the law intervenes if a man puts his genitals, called his 'person' on public display.

Small girls are fascinated with the penis but soon learn that 'nice' girls faint or send for a policeman if they see one! Older women speak of the intense erotic pleasure they get from seeing an erect penis and the nude male body generally. Because men are not allowed to show off their sexuality as overtly as women they are more likely to show off in athletic prowess and demonstrations of power generally, with smart, fast cars and so on.

Exhibitionism becomes a perversion when it is a person's preferred sexual activity, leading to his greatest sexual pleasure. It is most common in timid young men who frequently best enjoy the activity if the selected victims, usually pubescent girls, look at them just as their masturbation has reached the point of ejaculation. Such acts are not intended to be seductive, and if the man has a partner of his own, (some are married) he does not usually want intercourse. Such men are basically harmless but other types of exhibitionists certainly are not. Some alcoholics, psychotics, criminally sadistic paedophiles and brain-damaged people may exhibit themselves occasionally but this may not be the limit of their activities. Similarly, disturbed women may also exhibit their genitals and perhaps masturbate in public. Some mentally deficient people exhibit themselves too, probably to attract attention rather than for any overt sexual pleasure.

Survey evidence suggests that nearly a half of all girls and women can expect to be the victim of male exhibitionism or, as it is called, indecent exposure. A third or so of these tell no one, but if they are under the age of sixteen or so they can be very upset by the episode. The young girls who are subsequently most disturbed are those who tell their parents who then over-react, perhaps involving the police, as happens in a fifth of cases.

In its most usual form, exhibitionism is thought to be caused by the man wanting to show his penis to young and startled girls. Treatment includes punishment by the courts but the relapse rate is high. Other techniques revolve round giving the man insight into his condition or training him out of it, perhaps using masturbation fantasies as we explained earlier. One technique is to make him undress totally in front of a mixed audience and then to get him to describe his activities. This makes him so anxious that change becomes possible. He never gets an erection under such circumstances. Masturbation in front of a willing 'victim', such as a prostitute, does not appeal to exhibitionists and anyway is no good as a form of therapy.

Few members of either sex would fail to watch nude members of the opposite sex or a couple having intercourse if the opportunity presented itself, especially if there were little chance of detection. Inhibited people of either sex who have been fitted with an eye-camera, and who therefore know that the experimenter knows what they are looking at, will look anywhere except at the nude body of a member of the opposite sex with whom they are confronted. When looking is allowed, as at strip shows, which are now available for both sexes, or on nude beaches, the inhibition recedes. Probably we are all reared, by others if not by our parents, to believe it is 'dirty' to look at the genitals or sexual behaviour of others, and indeed almost all

The sultan/sultana game: The male 'voyeur' responds to the exhibitionist behaviour of his partner—usually as a prelude to intercourse. Such games enable the woman to take control in foreplay as she teases her man and confirms the power she has to arouse his passion.

societies in the world cover their genitals and have sex in private. As long as this is so there will be a curiosity drive to see the unwatchable, but in most people this does not come anywhere near to being a perversion or a deviation; they simply find it a sexual turn-on.

Whilst this is voyeuristic behaviour it is not really voyeurism in the true sense of the word. Voyeurism is a condition in which the person usually, but not invariably, takes deliberate steps to watch others undressing or copulating and so gets his or her kicks from witnessing 'realistic pornography'. Some conceal themselves in bushes, creep on knee pads, drill holes in walls, or climb ladders in pursuit of their peeping-Tom activities. Some homosexuals spy on their own sex and some specialist voyeurs concentrate on watching women urinate. An occasional voyeur such as a psychopath may assault the woman he is watching but the vast majority of peeping Toms are harmless.

Fetishism

Fetishism is usually, but wrongly, said to apply only to men. It can take many forms and can merge into transvestism or even sadism. Usually the affected person becomes 'hooked' on a particular object and cannot have a successful orgasm unless the conditions are just right. Some men have fetishes about women's shoes or underwear, for example, and others are equally affected by fur, leather or other fabrics and textures.

In a book of family love and sex the subject is worth discussing because some fairly convincing but controversial evidence suggests that an individual's mother may be the cause of such fetishes. Treatment of the adult fetishist is difficult, although effective, so prevention is obviously very important. A few words of explanation are necessary before proceeding, because they will help explain in general how a person's rearing can deeply affect his sexual functioning as an adult.

As it grows, a baby passes from a totally self-centred stage (see chapter 1) to a stage at which he or she relates to others around him or her and most of all to the mother. At the stage when the child moves from self-centredness to the development of an object-relationship with the mother, he or she may fix on an inanimate object, such as a doll or a piece of cloth which the child treats as a comforter. The main difference from the mother is that the comforter does not have to be shown the same consideration as a love object. Such articles are called 'transitional objects' and quite a lot of insecure and lonely children get considerable solace and comfort from them. In certain cases an attachment to such things can become pathological, and far from helping the child to form object-relations they hinder the process. Some unfortunate children have no human relationships (for example those in the care of institutions and who have numerous care-takers) they can rely on. They can only form relations with their transitional objects.

Whatever the contributory factors which go into making a fetishist, the affected person responds erotically only to the fetish object, usually stockings, gloves, shoes or underclothes, all preferably permeated with a body odour. Newly purchased objects are of little interest but stolen ones are especially valued. The fetishist handles and kisses the object, perhaps ejaculating or masturbating during the process. Even the thought of the object can lead to sexual arousal. In the infinitely more common form the fetish object may not be inanimate but can be a part of the body such as the buttocks or the feet. Whatever the object the fetishist homes in on, it stands for the whole person and the individual relates to the partner through the object. The object has to be present for maximum sexual satisfaction. In a sense, it is like a talisman which has to be present in order to ensure a good performance, although this type of fetishist is usually able to undertake less than satisfactory sexual activity in its absence. Some such men are impotent.

Transvestism and transsexualism

These are rare forms of sexual perversion but ones which can and do often affect otherwise happily married, family men, so they are worth looking at here. Transvestites get sexual pleasure from wearing the clothes of the opposite sex. They usually look at themselves in a mirror and are excited by the signs of sexual arousal in themselves. Masturbation is usually the result. Sometimes a woman partner will be involved, some being willing to provide female attire and make-up. Either intercourse or masturbation may then be the outcome.

Some cross-dressers do not become sexually aroused but describe a sense of peace and contentment which comes over them. These are probably not true transvestites because there is no arousal. Both, however, no doubt reflect some disturbance in the early relationships with their mothers. Around four years of age many boys go through a stage of putting on their mother's clothes, presumably because their softness symbolically represents the mother's skin. However, there is evidence that more mothers of transvestites would have preferred a girl than other mothers, and some even treat their little boys like girls for some years.

Where a transvestite responds to only one article of clothing, such as panties, the distinction between him and the fetishist is difficult to make. More commonly, the transvestite will put on his wife's, or his own, female attire when she is out. His general interest in other sexual activities, including intercourse, is usually low. How common transvestism is in women is an open question and some experts believe it does not occur at all. This is improbable and some causes of orgasm problems in women may be due to its presence. Psychotherapy can be an effective treatment. One woman therapist gets transvestites to dress up and then films them. On seeing the film they feel ridiculous and so often abandon the practice.

Most transvestites indulge their interest only occasionally, although some need to expand their activities so that they are dressed as the opposite sex most of the time. They do not usually want to change sex: as one said, 'I'm just a cock in a frock,' but he nevertheless had a female name for himself in the role.

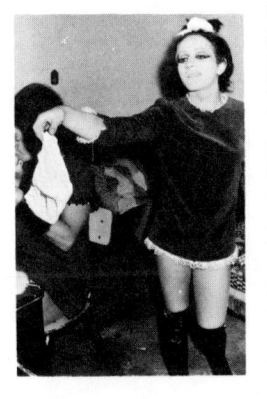

Transvestism—a male preserve? Our culture allows women to wear male-style clothes if they want but the reverse is still considered peculiar.

Where there is a desire to change sex (the individual believing he or she is a member of the opposite sex trapped in the wrong body), the condition is known as transsexualism. As well as wearing the clothes of the opposite sex, these people want to be rid of the body they have and replace it with one which resembles that of the opposite sex. As a result they seek hormone therapy and surgery. Women want testosterone so as to grow a beard, break their voice and, perhaps, to enlarge the clitoris, and surgery to have their breasts and their uterus removed. Men want oestrogen to create breasts, reduce beard growth and make their contours more rounded, and surgery to remove their genitals and construct a vagina. Most seem to be more sexually inhibited than sexually expressive and their preoccupation with their sex-change is obsessional. However they can subsequently regret and resent the change. If frustrated in this quest, however, the transsexual can become depressed and suicidal. Although transsexuals may be homosexual, the problem is not basically one of which sex they are orientated towards sexually but rather one of gender-identity. They have identified their gender incorrectly. Mothers of male transsexuals (like those of transvestites) also more commonly wanted a girl than other mothers, and it is said that they feminise the boy from childhood onwards. The father does not rescue the child and is usually distant. These mothers are said to be unfeminine and disappointed tomboys themselves.

Transsexuals say they have always known that they were of the wrong sex and need to belong to and be accepted by everyone as a member of the opposite sex. At school such boys usually relate only to girls, and girls become their reference or peer group. They put on female clothing and continue to do so in spite of any rebuke or punishment. They may even say they want babies. Successful attempts have been made to rescue boys from a future of transvestism or transsexualism by therapy administered before puberty. The justification is that gender-role disturbance (an incomplete or unsatisfactory acceptance of the masculine role in boys or the feminine role in girls) or cross-gender identification (the belief that one belongs to the opposite sex) leads to so much disorganisation and unhappiness that it should be prevented if at all possible. Girl transsexuals can be treated successfully even in adolescence. In their case it is the mother who has been neglectful and the father who has taken care of them and encouraged masculine tendencies. The father perhaps wanted a boy, or wanted to exclude the mother from his relationship with the girl.

Again, as with all these perversions and deviations, often the child's rearing has so scarred his or her development that he or she is trapped into believing and feeling the way he or she does. For the families of the individual involved things can be very difficult and professional assistance is almost always needed. Self-help groups can be a great help.

Incest

There is probably an erotic component to all forms of love but when it comes to close relations it is suppressed. When they are in the Oedipal stage of development (see page 26) young children, other things being equal, love their opposite-sex parent and in some child-like way want a physical relationship with him or her. These wishes are dealt with, as a rule, in later psychosexual development as the child grows, but they come to light again at puberty, when the old repressed wish is updated with the knowledge about sex gained since childhood.

Girls and women often, and boys almost never, report that opposite-sex relations (usually fathers, brothers and uncles) have made sexual advances or undertaken sexual acts with them. An intelligent and truthful young woman, for example, may claim that her father had intercourse with her when she was three years old. When asked, she will say it did not hurt, nor did she bleed. Obviously this represents an old wish updated. Incest dreams and fantasies, though usually repressed or turned into symbolic form, are quite common, especially in young teenage girls. Parents themselves may be affected. A daughter may remind her father of his young wife and a son may appear as an idealised young lover to an emotionally unhappy mother. Grandparents, aunts and uncles, brothers and sisters may all be involved.

Although tales of incest need to be treated with caution, if only because incest fantasies are so common, it does, of course, occur. The commonest form is that between brothers and sisters with father–daughter incest second. Incest is prohibited in most cultures and rightly so since the mixing of two very similar sets of genes, which is what occurs if a pregnancy results, exposes the offspring to a greater chance of recessive gene disorders. Incest technically means having intercourse with a close blood relation, and though this is more common than the statistics suggest, sexual contacts short of intercourse are even more common.

Clearly, sexual forces do exist within families, especially those with young children. It is all a part of love, but the control that children have to learn to impose on themselves, and the frustrations they must accept are the starting-point for learning sexual restraint in general. Parents too have a responsibility not to encourage their children sexually, and in the last analysis the responsibility must lie with the adult because he or she is supposedly mature and responsible while the child is not. Incest can harm a child psychosexually for life, although it is often difficult to separate the actual incest and the abnormal general family environment from each other. Any father who is capable of having intercourse with his daughter is bound to be a rather odd father in all kinds of other ways.

Incest can harm a child for life.

Father–daughter incest tends to occur most where the father is ill-educated, unemployed and poorly-housed. Many mothers condone it and some are suspected of provoking it by denying their husbands sufficient sex within their relationship. In a few instances the child him- or herself may have initiated the activity.

The vast majority of incest is never reported to any outside body, let alone the police, for fear of the repercussions on the family if the father were to be imprisoned. Most men imprisoned for incest return to their old ways once out of prison and 'cures' for the condition are few and far between. Wives also keep quiet because they feel unconsciously that they would rather the husband had intercourse with someone in the family than with a woman outside it.

Why some fathers overstep the mark and go from normal and acceptable loving feelings to a frank sexual relationship is not known but many incestuous fathers are mentally unstable and large numbers are alcoholic or have aggressive and disordered personalities. No social class is excepted from incest—indeed in the past it has been very common among the landed gentry and upper classes.

Treatment is very unsatisfactory and anyway the damage has been done by the time the man sees a doctor. Some success has been obtained with psychotherapy, but supportive care, such as is provided by incest centres in the USA, is probably the only way of coping with this difficult problem.

In some surveys around 10 per cent of women report some form of incestuous activity in childhood. Most brothers and sisters play with each other genitally and may even become sexually aroused in the process but such play rarely ends up in intercourse. No harm comes from this sort of play except from guilt either at the time or later. True brother–sister incest usually produces few problems compared with adult–child incest, unless the brother is considerably older than the sister.

Paedophilia

No perversion, apart from rape, arouses such public outcry as does paedophilia, the name given to the condition in which an adult or older adolescent takes an erotic interest in children under the age of fourteen. Even hardened criminals cannot tolerate this crime and paedophiles often have to be isolated in prison for their own safety.

This indignation is justified in those cases of heterosexual paedophilia in which the victims, usually seven- to ten-year-old girls, are sometimes harshly treated or even killed. Usually a paedophiliac wants the girl to show her vulva, to look at pornography, or to handle his penis. He may fondle or smack her, or attempt to have intercourse with her. How parents can rear girls so as to avoid such individuals without encouraging them to fear all men or become discourteous to men who are being socially pleasant towards them is a real problem, and there are no easy answers. On balance it makes sense to teach children never to go anywhere with strangers without first asking permission from their parents, and children should never take sweets or anything else from people they do not know unless their parents are there. It is upsetting to think that we have to bring up our children fearing anyone they do not know but one has to be realistic and child molesters can be dangerous.

Oestrogen, anti-testosterone drugs and castration have been used in attempts to control paedophiles and rapists but the best course must be prevention. Usually men and women show a tendency to consort with individuals corresponding to their own stage in psychosexual development. Heterosexual paedophiles are immature, scared of women of their own age and often revengeful against them. They masturbate a lot to vivid fantasies of little girls, concentrating perhaps on their buttocks or even on things such as the ankle socks they wear. Whatever the precise cause, clearly the psychosexual development of the heterosexual paedophile has not prospered and he needs professional help.

The more common form of paedophilia is that in which men are attracted to young boys. To say they are homosexual may overstate the case since many, although not too attracted to it, do have heterosexual intercourse. Many are married. Their love of small boys is probably self-centred since what they really love is the image of themselves when young. They often shave off their pubic hair and watch themselves masturbate in front of a mirror. They are fascinated by boys, especially nude. Apart from the possible psychological harm they do, they are nearly all harmless.

A number of people who are mentally disordered also commit sexual offences against children.

Other perversions

There are many other perversions. For example, there are some people who get their best sexual pleasure from masturbation and prefer it to other activities. Rapists sometimes claim in their defence that pornography led to their condition, but as erotic and pornographic material is widespread and rapists are not, other factors must be involved, even if the original statement is true as far as it goes. The use of alcohol is probably a much more common precipitant factor in a rather inadequate individual who is basically afraid of women but hostile towards them. Some rapists find that the struggle and the power enhance their sexual drive, so perhaps they should really be considered perverted. Others can scarcely perform at all. Certain types of rapist are deterred if the woman fails to struggle or if she gives in. Psychopathic men may displace anger with one woman on to another and generally manage to convince themselves that the woman deserved what she received.

In general the conclusion which emerges from studying perversions is that there are components of them in most of us, but in most people they are integrated into the overall pattern of their sexuality and certainly do not dominate it. If they are to be at all useful, theories as to what causes them have to be sufficiently precise to allow parents to prevent their formation in the first place. Insufficient research has been carried out on this subject. The main dilemma such research would try to explain is why some individuals exposed to fairly similar situations in childhood and beyond as those experienced by deviants and perverts should develop normally or fairly normally. Some individuals are able to control their tendency towards a perversion, but may become neurotic and produce other physical and psychological symptoms.

On the whole psychiatry has been woefully inadequate in investigating these conditions and has very little to say about their prevention.

A more immediate solution may be to establish walk-in clinics where even the names of those attending need not be taken. In such clinics help, advice and treatment could be offered to those who suffer from, or think they might have, a problem. Many know something is wrong before they commit an offence and some would be sufficiently motivated to seek help if it were available.

Looking at the problem more generally, anything which promotes happy and fruitful man–woman relationships, better marriage and healthier, more rational attitudes towards sex would help. Parents and teachers need to be better informed about normal sexual development and, with increased knowledge about what is normal and what is not, should be able to get professional help for their children before things go too far.

Summary

Although many readers may be put off by the subject matter of this chapter, feeling that most of it is totally foreign to them, it must be seen as a part of human experience. Though we have tended to present the many facets of unusual sexual expression as simply as we can and in somewhat earthy ways, it should be realised that they also exist in lesser and less easily recognisable forms in most of us.

Rather than condemning the individuals whom this chapter describes, it perhaps behoves all parents to think critically about the impact of cultural restraints and excitations upon their children and to reflect on the long-term harm that can result from thoughtless actions.

Chapter 33

Sex and health

Good or bad for your health?

Intercourse undoubtedly makes most people feel better in themselves even though there is scant evidence that it has any long-term benefits physically. However, having said this, many people seem to be perfectly happy yet have no opportunity for having intercourse and others are very content with intercourse on very rare occasions.

Few people, even monks, priests and others who are normally thought of as celibate actually have *no* sexual outlet at all, of course. Most celibates masturbate, if only a few times a year when the pressure of their sex drive overwhelms their conscience. So the truly sexless are very rare indeed.

So it is difficult to argue that a lack of intercourse is detrimental to health. However, a good sex life does appear to confer some benefits as was mentioned on page 180.

If you are acutely ill you probably will not feel like sex, but many of the disabled and chronically ill can enjoy sex. You should not have sex if you have just had a vaginal operation, a hernia operation, or a hysterectomy, or if you have VD, and some doctors suggest that a woman who has a history of miscarriage should not have sex in early pregnancy (and especially on the anniversary of the first few periods). If ever your doctor suggests that you keep off sex, be sure to ask him or her why in some detail and make him or her justify it to you. A recent heart attack or operation, kidney or heart disease, and high blood pressure are all circumstances commonly thought to preclude sex but this is not necessarily so.

A doctor with insight will know that stopping sex for any length of time is difficult for most people and results in tension that is arguably more damaging than sex itself would have been. He or she may also realise on the other hand, that some people use their illnesses to escape from sex. Anyway, if you are unwell sexual activity does not have to take the form of sexual intercourse. You can be sexually intimate, cuddle a lot, indulge in oral sex, masturbate each other and so on and never have intercourse, if for some good reason it is inadvisable. Very few people indeed need be ordered to endure long periods entirely free of sex.

We covered in detail in chapter 32 certain things that are dangerous during sex play, but we'll summarise a few important things here.

1 During oral sex a woman should never blow down the penis—this could damage the penis and possibly cause a urinary infection.

2 Keep anal penetration and any form of anal or vaginal sex separate or you could cause an unpleasant infection.

3 Keep away from drugs and chemicals—it is very easy to overdo them and harm yourself.

4 Keep away from anything else that claims to be an aphrodisiac. At best you will be taken for a ride and will want your money back and at worst they can be really dangerous.

5 Never blow into the vagina. Air can be funnelled back up into the abdominal cavity and can cause sudden death because of an air embolus.

6 Never put a vacuum cleaner on the penis or a shower head up the vagina. Indeed anything under pressure in the vagina can damage the fallopian tubes.

Apart from fairly obvious items such as these sex is extremely safe and very few people ever come to any physical harm as a result of it.

Some things that can go wrong for women

Pain on intercourse

Most women experience some pain on first having intercourse, but this is usually shortlived. Pain after having a baby is usually only a problem if the woman has had an episiotomy but post-episiotomy pain can last for months. Some women have pain because they are insufficiently aroused before the insertion of the penis. A very few women have a condition called vaginismus in which the vaginal opening is shut off by an involuntary contraction of the muscles around the lower end of the vagina. This can be treated by an expert and involves simple psychotherapy and getting the woman confident enough to get used to having something (fingers first of all) inside her vagina. Other causes of superficial vaginal pain on intercourse are ageing (after the menopause the vagina becomes thinned and less well lubricated), infections of the vagina, and, rarely, conditions affecting the urinary passage. Deep pain on intercourse can be caused by conditions of the cervix, a backwards-tilted uterus, endometriosis, a uterine prolapse, a pregnancy in a fallopian tube, inflammation of a fallopian tube, constipation, or sexual dysfunctions of various kinds.

If any normal sexual activity hurts or if you have soreness of the genitals, tell your doctor. You may have an internal condition that is causing problems of which the pain is just a sign. Normal intercourse, no matter how deep the penetration, rarely hurts.

Retroverted womb

Usually the womb lies on top of the bladder at a 90° angle pointing forwards towards the front of the body. If the womb is tilted backwards instead of forwards it can produce pain on intercourse. This position of the womb is found in 15 per cent of women, though not all have pain on intercourse.

Prolapse

The womb can also fall down in the vagina and in some cases can appear at the opening of the vagina. There are several reasons for a prolapse. A few women have weak supports to the womb from birth. Others have their natural support mechanisms severely weakened by childbirth, lifting heavy weights, or by repeated straining to pass hard bowel motions. There is a swelling and a sense of fullness in the vagina and the woman feels as though something is coming down inside. There are often urinary symptoms, backache, heavy periods or a discharge. If you have any of these in combination see your doctor at once. Several studies have found that a woman's sexual functioning is reduced after a prolapse operation, with some 50 per cent of patients stopping intercourse completely or curtailing it. Sometimes this poor sexual functioning occurs because the surgeon has tightened the tissues too much, so making sex actually difficult. This is not the case for most couples, though, for whom psychosexual factors are at the heart of the trouble.

Sexual functioning can be poor.

Hysterectomy

This is an operation to remove the womb. Once the scars are healed, the operation does nothing to impair intercourse but many women say that it alters their orgasmic sensations, which is hardly surprising since the womb contracts during an orgasm. Because of this (amongst other reasons) some surgeons try to keep the cervix and lower part of the womb if possible and to remove the upper part only. Women's sexual responses to hysterectomy vary considerably. Some are so pleased to be rid of the heavy periods, or whatever caused them to have their womb removed, that they see the whole procedure as entirely welcome. Others mourn the loss of the organ and become depressed. All shades in between are seen and problems are common. Unfortunately hysterectomy is a very common procedure (about a quarter of a million women a year in the USA lose their uterus) and many operations are done unnecessarily. A great advantage to having a hysterectomy is that contraception is no longer a concern. Periods cease, of course, but ovulation continues as normal (if the ovaries have been saved) until the menopause.

Cystitis

This is a very common condition in which an infection of the bladder causes the woman to pass urine repeatedly, with pain or discomfort. About 90 per cent of sexually active women with cystitis relate it to intercourse. Such cystitis is of two types: infection or bruising. Soreness immediately following intercourse suggests bruising; pain and frequent passing of water after a gap of thirty-six hours after sex suggest infection. Washing beforehand and after with cool water, ensuring that the man's foreskin is perfectly clean underneath and careful washing after opening your bowels (wiping from front to back) are all ways of reducing the chances of infection. Bruising can be overcome by using plenty of KY jelly and avoiding positions in which intercourse is painful. If your cystitis begins with a change of contraception, think again about your choice. The bruising type of cystitis was very common on honeymoons but is less so now that most couples have a more gentle introduction to intercourse. Oral sex is not thought to cause cystitis.

For the vast majority of women with intercourse-related cystitis scrupulous attention to hygiene by them and their partners, passing water immediately after intercourse, and the use of plenty of lubrication usually solves the problem.

Hairiness

Women spend millions of dollars and hours in removing hair they believe to be unsightly. Hair on the upper lip, on the limbs, around the nipples and up the abdomen, and extensions of the pubic hair to the top of the thighs are all common but unwelcome. Men and women have about the same number of hairs—the real difference is in the type of hair at different locations and its visibility. Hairiness in women is occasionally the sign of the presence of disease but is mainly genetic in origin. Some men prefer hairy women and claim they are more sexy than others. Apart from electrolysis, periodic shaving is probably as good a solution as any, but many women find this objectionable.

Monthly check-up

Most women are understandably afraid of contracting breast cancer and it makes sense to detect a breast lump as early as possible so that it can be treated. It is best to feel your breasts for lumps regularly each month using the same routine a day or two after your period has stopped. Get to know how your breasts feel during other times of your menstrual cycle too and always report any suspicious lumps to your doctor. A delay could make treatment more difficult.

If you have an IUD pop a finger into your vagina each month the day your period stops to check that the tail of the device is still coming out of the cervix. If you can't feel it, take other contraceptive precautions and see your doctor at once to have a new one put in if necessary.

Some things that can go wrong for men

One testicle instead of two

Often a man who has two perfectly normal testes will appear to have only one. The other one will simply have popped into the canal above the scrotum and can be popped back down again just as easily. If a man has never had a testis down on one side he needs medical advice because experience shows that cancer is commoner in an undescended testis than in one which is down in the scrotum. If you can't feel two testes in your baby boy it is probably best to get an opinion from your doctor or baby clinic but most doctors do not worry about an

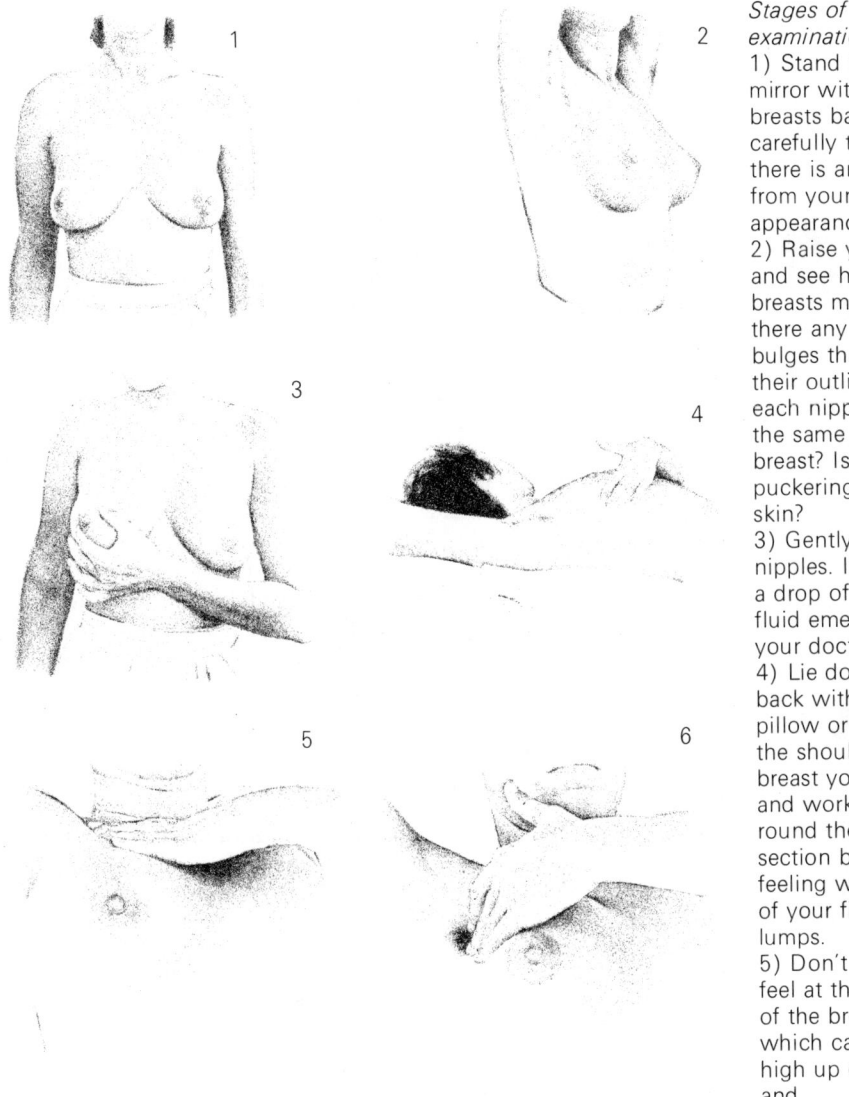

Stages of breast self-examination:
1) Stand in front of a mirror with your breasts bare. Look carefully to see if there is any change from your normal appearance.
2) Raise your arms and see how your breasts move. Are there any dimples or bulges that change their outline? Does each nipple point in the same axis as its breast? Is there any puckering of the skin?
3) Gently squeeze the nipples. If more than a drop of colourless fluid emerges see your doctor.
4) Lie down on your back with a small pillow or towel under the shoulder of the breast you are feeling and work slowly round the breast, section by section, feeling with the tips of your fingers for lumps.
5) Don't forget to feel at the very edge of the breast tissue which can extend high up on the chest and
6) under the arm

undescended testis much before the age of four or five.

Hydrocele

This is a fluid-filled swelling around a testis and epididymis. It can be present at birth but is much more commonly found in older men. A torch held behind the mass makes it glow red and a doctor can drain it with a special needle or operate on it to cure it permanently. It rarely causes any sexual problems—only discomfort during intercourse because of its size.

Priapism

This is the medical name given to an erection which is painful and will not subside. It is rare and needs medical attention urgently. More common (but not commonplace) is the man who is repeatedly woken at night by a painful erection even if he has already had intercourse or has masturbated. Repeated intercourse or masturbation does not seem to help. Time is the healer and no other cures are needed.

Phimosis

This is a condition in which the foreskin is very tight in an uncircumcised boy or man. It can be produced by parents forcibly retracting and tearing their baby's foreskin, which then rejoins, with the formation of scar tissue, so tightening up the whole area. Infection behind such a foreskin can cause troublesome *balanitis*. Anything other than a moderate degree of phimosis needs treating (by circumcision) because intercourse can be painful, balanitis increasingly troublesome and even masturbation difficult.

Peyronie's disease

This is a distressing condition the cause of which is unknown. It comes about as a result of a layer of fibrous tissue being laid down in the penis. This abnormal tissue can be felt as a firm plaque on the top surface of the penis. The man has painful erections with angulation of the erect penis itself. Intercourse is difficult and painful for the man though he can ejaculate normally. Various treatments have been tried but none is really successful.

The effects of illness, disease and surgery on sexual function

In our society we tend to equate sex with health and youth and assume that the ill and the handicapped are sexless. This simply is not true. Only during the most acute of illnesses do people go off sex, and increasingly doctors are realising that couples continue their sex lives wherever possible even if they have chronic illnesses.

Heart disease and high blood pressure

During intercourse the heart rate may double, as may the breathing rate, and the blood pressure rises too. There is considerable public concern that sexual activity with heart disease or high blood pressure is dangerous or even possibly fatal. Such deaths are in fact very rare and when they do occur they do so more commonly during extra-marital intercourse.

Advice about sex after a heart attack varies enormously but it is probably safe to resume sexual activities five to ten weeks after the heart attack unless the attack was exceptionally severe. One way to tell if you are ready is to see how you feel after a quick walk or after going up a couple of flights of stairs.

People with angina should take a tablet before intercourse and should ideally avoid sex immediately after a meal.

Even if one of these conditions makes one wary of returning to or carrying on with intercourse there are several half-way houses that can be tried which stop short of actual intercourse and its exertions.

Drugs that alter sexual performance

Many drugs are now known to alter the sex drive of both men and women but the most dramatic and well-proven effects are usually seen in men because a woman can have satisfactory intercourse even if she is not highly aroused.

Alcohol in moderation is said to enhance sexual responses, but is in fact a common cause for a temporary loss of potency.

These lists summarise some of the known sexual side-effects of drugs:

Drugs interfering with ejaculation

Antipsychotic drugs
Thioridazine (Melleril)
Trifluoperazine (Stelazine)

Antidepressant drugs
Pargyline (Eutonyl)
Imipramine (Tofranil)
Amitriptyline (Elavil)

Antihypertensive drugs
Reserpine (Serpasil)

Guanethidine (Ismelin)
Methyldopa (Aldomet)
Phenoxybenzamine hydrochloride (Debenzyline)

Other Drugs
Heroin
Methadone

Drugs interfering with erection

Antipsychotic drugs
Fluphenazine (Stelazine)
Thioridazine (Melleril)

Mood-modifying drugs
Lithium
Imipramine (Tofranil)
Tranylcypromine (Parnate)
Desipramine (Pertofran)
Phenelzine (Nardil)
Amitriptyline (Elavil)

Antihypertensive drugs
Methyldopa (Aldomet)
Guanethidine (Ismelin)
Clonidine (Catapres)
Reserpine (Serpasil)
Spironolactone (Aldactone)

Other drugs
Clofibrate (Atromid-S)
Heroin

Drugs that interfere with female orgasm

Antidepressant drugs
Phenelzine (Nardil)

Few drugs are known to affect female orgasm but common sense dictates that many that affect men could well affect women too.

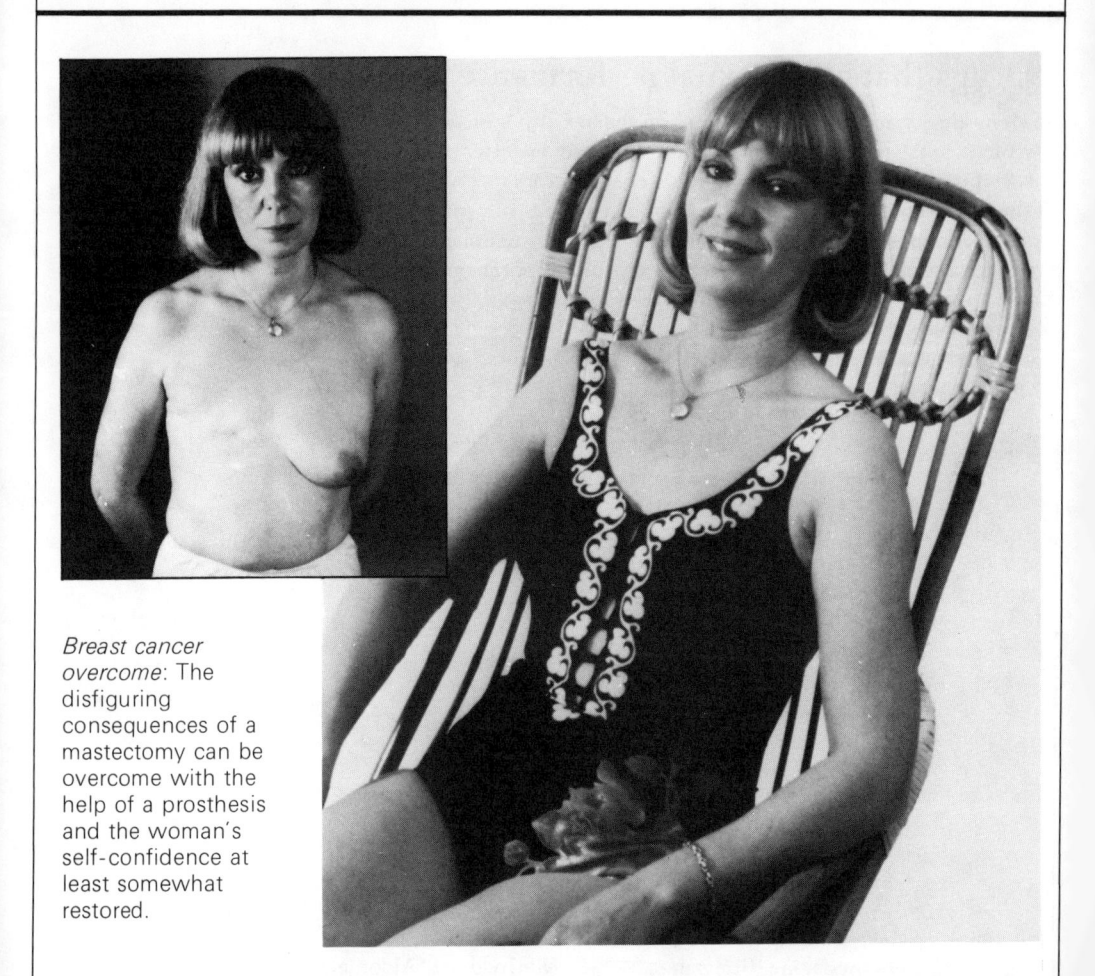

Breast cancer overcome: The disfiguring consequences of a mastectomy can be overcome with the help of a prosthesis and the woman's self-confidence at least somewhat restored.

Mutual masturbation relieves sexual tensions but is less strenuous. The next stage can include woman-on-top positions—when it is the man who is recovering—in which the woman makes most of the physical effort. Slowly a couple affected by heart disease can wean themselves back to a normal sex life.

Diabetes

About half of all diabetic men eventually become impotent but this may not happen until their seventies or eighties. However, for the unlucky few, impotence is the first sign of diabetes. A middle-aged man who suddenly becomes impotent for no apparent reason should have his urine checked for sugar in case he has become a diabetic. A diabetic's sex drive is usually normal: it is only the ability to erect that is the problem. When caught early, careful management of the diabetes can improve things but in more serious cases a mechanical prosthesis may be needed. Diabetic women also experience sexual dysfunction and, as with men, there is no link between the severity of the disease and the onset of their sexual dysfunction.

Vaginal thrush is more common in diabetic women and this can cause uncomfortable sex or even an avoidance of sex altogether.

Some diabetic women find that their insulin requirements are raised when they become sexually active.

Mastectomy

A mastectomy (removal of one or both breasts) is a major blow to most women's sexuality but the negative psychosexual effects can be greatly reduced by careful psychological preparation before the operation.

Once the operation and its immediate after-effects are over, worries about sex and sexuality often dominate a woman's emotions about mastectomy. Many women say that they feel less of a woman and the natural reaction in the early days is to feel totally unsexy and undesirable. Some women even feel strongly enough to say that they would rather have kept their breast and lived a few years less.

The one key factor to emerge from the large amount of research into this subject is that the role of the woman's partner is absolutely crucial. This is true of women of all personalities and of all levels of intelligence and education. Ideally, the woman's husband should be actively involved throughout the whole process right from the time when the lump is discovered. In this way the woman feels she has the support she needs and she fares much better.

There is no reason why sexual intercourse should not be resumed the day the woman gets home. There is no such thing as too much sex after a mastectomy and as long as the wound area is not hurt there are no problems. It is a matter of trial and error to find a position that suits the couple and then to use it until healing is complete.

Some women are afraid that their partners will leave them—the underlying fear being that a woman with one breast is not able to attract and keep a man. The facts are that men are no more likely to leave their partner after a mastectomy than otherwise and that most worry a lot about how to be supportive and helpful. Although most women try to hide their chests from their partners (especially in the early days), most men are not as upset by the loss of the breast as their women think they will be.

Some couples approach mastectomy with considerable existing psychosexual and relationship problems, and for them the mastectomy may be the last straw. That this is unusual can be seen from one study which found that two-thirds of post-mastectomy women judged their emotional state to be excellent or very good. Women who fared best had been married longer, had found their partners (and doctors) more supportive and were pleased with the response from their children and the hospital staff.

Mastectomy may be the last straw.

Strange though it may seem, most women say that the worst time emotionally is immediately after the lump is discovered. Only one in seven women in one study found the immediate post-operative period the most difficult. Although most women have thoughts about mutilation, loss of femininity and death, several studies have found that the good news outweighs the bad. One study, for example, found that 71 per cent of women rated their husband's reaction to the mastectomy as extremely or very understanding; 76 per cent felt that the loss of the breast made no difference or had a positive effect on their sexual satisfaction or their ability to be orgasmic; and 60 per cent rated their overall post-mastectomy adjustment as 'very good'.

Many women have married after a mastectomy. If you are still having periods, you may find you will get the same sort of discomfort on your mastectomy side as you previously had at this time of the month.

Remember that talking about it with your husband, family and friends is bound to help. Slowly they will all come to terms with your new condition.

Gynaecological surgery

Now that hysterectomy is such a common operation, its sexual aftermath is a source of considerable concern to millions of middle-aged couples. As one famous gynaecologist so succinctly put it, 'Only the baby carriage has been removed—I've left the play-pen completely alone.' Most women are ready to resume intercourse about six weeks after the operation but there can be a sensation of bruising for a further month or two. Provided there is nothing wrong, post-operative intercourse, gently at first, will if anything help the vagina to stretch again and get back to normal.

A D and C and other simple gynaecological operations call for only a few days off intercourse.

Brain damage

Certain specific kinds of brain damage affect the sexual functioning of the brain and certain tumours can alter a person's sexual behaviour but this is rare.

Blindness

This is, of course, no bar to sexual expression but it can be difficult for the blind to learn about their bodies and sex generally.

Arthritis

As we grow older our chances of suffering from some kind of arthritis increase and osteoarthritis of the hip can severely impair a person's ability to have pain-free intercourse. About two-thirds of sufferers have intercourse difficulties. A hip replacement, of course, remedies the situation all round. It is interesting to point out here that many couples find that regular intercourse actually lessens their arthritic symptoms, though no one knows why. If you have a problem in this area talk to your doctor and see if he can get the pain better controlled with drugs if you cannot have an operation or while you are waiting for one.

Arthritis affecting other parts of the body (except the knees) usually has no effect on sex.

Colostomy, ileostomy and bowel surgery

Having major bowel surgery and ending up with a colostomy or an ileostomy can have major psychological effects on the sex life of the individual and his or her partner. As well as this there are often very real neurological problems caused by the removal of key nerves along the bowel. Impotence and sexual dysfunction are very common after the removal of lower bowel cancers but surgery for non-malignant conditions produces far fewer problems.

An American study found that men were more supportive of their wives after such surgery than the other way round, but that women are more afraid of being unacceptable to their husbands. There are now 'ostomy' ('stoma') nurses in most large hospitals who can advise those about to undergo such surgery about the problems and how to overcome them right from the beginning. There are also 'ostomy' clubs in most Western countries whose members have seen and heard it all before and can be very helpful and encouraging.

The role of stoma nurses.

Sex and the handicapped

The handicapped need love, affection and a chance to express their sexuality just like the rest of us. Sex education in the special schools that deal with various handicaps is at last beginning to take the sexuality of the handicapped seriously. Until recently it was a subject ignored even by those involved with the handicapped. Unfortunately, a lot of handicapped people live in situations or institutions where privacy is in short supply and this makes life even more difficult for them.

Girls who are handicapped (and especially the completely paralysed) start to menstruate very young (often as early as eight). Men with multiple sclerosis may become partially or completely impotent (60 per cent have an erection problem). Women with the condition often have problems with orgasms because they feel tired, and they may be advised against pregnancy because relapses are so common shortly after having a baby.

The mentally handicapped also have rights in this area and some are keen to be sexually active. With the trend towards community-based living (rather than hospital care) for the less severely handicapped, this demand will undoubtedly rise over the years. IUDs are the best method of contraception for mentally handicapped women whose intelligence level or unsatisfactory motivation would make other methods too risky.

The mentally handicapped.

Chronic diseases

Any long-term (chronic) disease can exhaust the individual, as can long-term drug therapy, hospital visits, treatment and so on. All of these can adversely affect the most sex-centred person, as well as those who were content with very infrequent sex before his or her trouble began. Many diseases actually cause a loss of libido (sex drive), as do many drugs; so if you think your sex life should be better, and you are suffering from a long-standing illness, discuss it with your doctor in case the two could be linked.

Strokes

Far too little is known about the sexual problems of stroke patients. The trouble is that a stroke is a very complex business and results not only in physical weakness and loss of sensation but in mental and

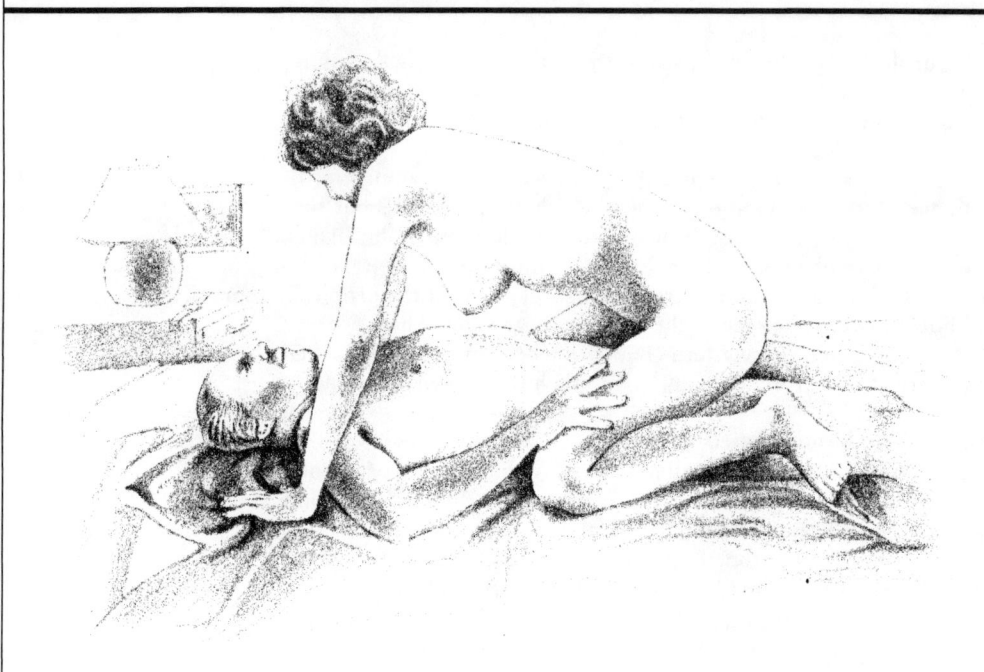

Intercourse after a serious illness: This man is recovering from a heart attack. His wife is taking most of the initiative and is playing the active role.

psychological changes too. This raises all kinds of anxieties about sexual performance, and the physical problems often make physical sexual expression difficult even if the 'heart is willing'. All of this can alter the way a couple relate to each other after a stroke, but physical closeness, other manifestations of love and sexual activities which are not genital-to-genital can often work well. Loss of bladder and anal control is very upsetting, but many couples who really want to can find ways around these practical problems. Sex therapy can greatly help stroke sufferers and it can be useful to experiment with sex until the couple finds a way of living with the disability.

Summary

There are many connections between sex and health, and the sex drive can be buried under anxieties, chronic sickness and ill health. It can also be adversely affected by inhibitions, with medical conditions being used as excuses to avoid sex. Some people unconsciously use work in the same way.

Under normal circumstances one's sex drive is at its best when one is well, comfortable and relatively untroubled, but the excessive quest for physical fitness is also used by some to avoid sex.

Chapter 34

Sex in old age

Any account of ageing is bound to seem like a catalogue of physical decline but, as at all ages, a person's psychological state, flexibility and previous experience all affect the situation. Every age has its opportunities and there are people of both sexes who do not reach their full potential until their fifties, sixties or, in some cases, even later.

Again, as at all ages, ill health can dominate the picture and is more common, though by no means inevitable, as age increases. The notion of remaining healthy and active, perhaps with medical assistance, as age advances is increasingly accepted as the norm. A continuing sex life is also seen as a part of this healthy and active life.

Although we could hardly claim that the services and money provided by the community for the care of its ageing population are over-abundant, poverty and a lack of suitable accommodation are not problems any longer for the majority of old people. Because of early rearing influences, some pensioners voluntarily enforce poverty on themselves by unnecessarily trying to economise and save but this is a manifestation of their personality rather than a social or economic necessity. Others, because of misguided pride, will not accept state help to which they are entitled and so are worse off financially than they need be. Some fail to take adequate care of themselves, which could be a late expression of hidden rebellion against over-strict training during childhood or an expression of emotional despair.

Men who have lived for work or women who have lived their lives only in terms of their emotional relationships may begin to feel that there is nothing left to live for when these come to an end.

Preparation for old age starts in childhood with the development of the capacity to accept and enjoy life. This involves keeping interested and interesting. Boredom kills. Productivity can continue, but perhaps in forms other than paid work. Some ageing people take up entirely new pursuits in fulfilment of long-held wishes—pursuits that the pressure of other work and family commitments prevented earlier in life. Many say they are busier in their sixties and seventies than ever before and that they enjoy life more as a result.

However, there are problems. One is our cultural attitude towards old age. At some point society sets the ageing individual aside from its main stream and a lifetime of experience, knowledge and wisdom can count for nothing or even be regarded as foolishness. The older generation is now an untapped and unrecognised national resource of great potential value to society although at the level of the family this may not be quite so true. Grandparents often make an essential contribution to child rearing, but because the world is changing so fast many feel out of touch with current views and practices in this field and this reduces their own feelings of value.

Another of our cultural attitudes that may cause problems is that towards sex. Many older people retain an interest in sex but fail to indulge it because they feel ashamed. Sex belongs to life, and its harmless expression, in appropriate forms, at all ages should be welcomed and accepted as normal.

One problem in this sphere is that even if ageing people escape the cultural pressures against sex and retain an interest in it which they want to express, they may not have a partner who is available, willing or able to indulge. As a result of higher death rates among men than among women at all ages, there is an increasing surplus of women as age advances, and the suggestion has been made that for those who want, bigamy should be legalised from a certain age, say fifty or sixty. It is easy to see the difficulties and moral or emotional objections to this, but if everyone involved were happy about it then it could be a solution, at least for some people. For some people, the friendship component could be of greater value than the sexual one. Masturbation is another solution, though somewhat unsatisfactory because not everyone is well adjusted about it, even by the time they reach old age, and some men refrain from masturbation for fear of possible harm.

Old people with no opportunity.

It is all very well talking positively about sex in old age, but very substantial numbers of people (many more women than men) simply do not have the opportunity for any kind of sex life—and this can go on for twenty years or more. No other age group would tolerate it, so why should the elderly?

A part of sex education should be devoted to encouraging the younger generation to accept that the older generation are sexual, if only to prepare the young themselves for old age. The retention of sexual prowess and pleasure in old age helps to maintain a person's self-respect and morale and it should be encouraged by all. In a society with sensible attitudes towards sex it would not be necessary to say any of this—it would be taken for granted.

The presence of all these complicating issues makes it difficult to disentangle psychological from physical effects influencing sex in the elderly, especially as the two interact anyway.

As at all ages, among the elderly it is the man who mainly controls the level of sexual intercourse, if only for the obvious reason that if he does not have an erection intercourse cannot occur. Information about the sexual behaviour of older men is somewhat sparse. If Kinsey is to be relied on, and in the main his findings in the US have been found to be fairly accurate, and to apply to the UK as well, the incidence of impotence by age was as on page 411.

Although this curve looks a little gloomy, it has to be remembered that the figures are averages and there is a considerable variation either side of the mean. For example, one man of seventy was experiencing over seven orgasms a week. Also, there are signs

Male sex drive through the years

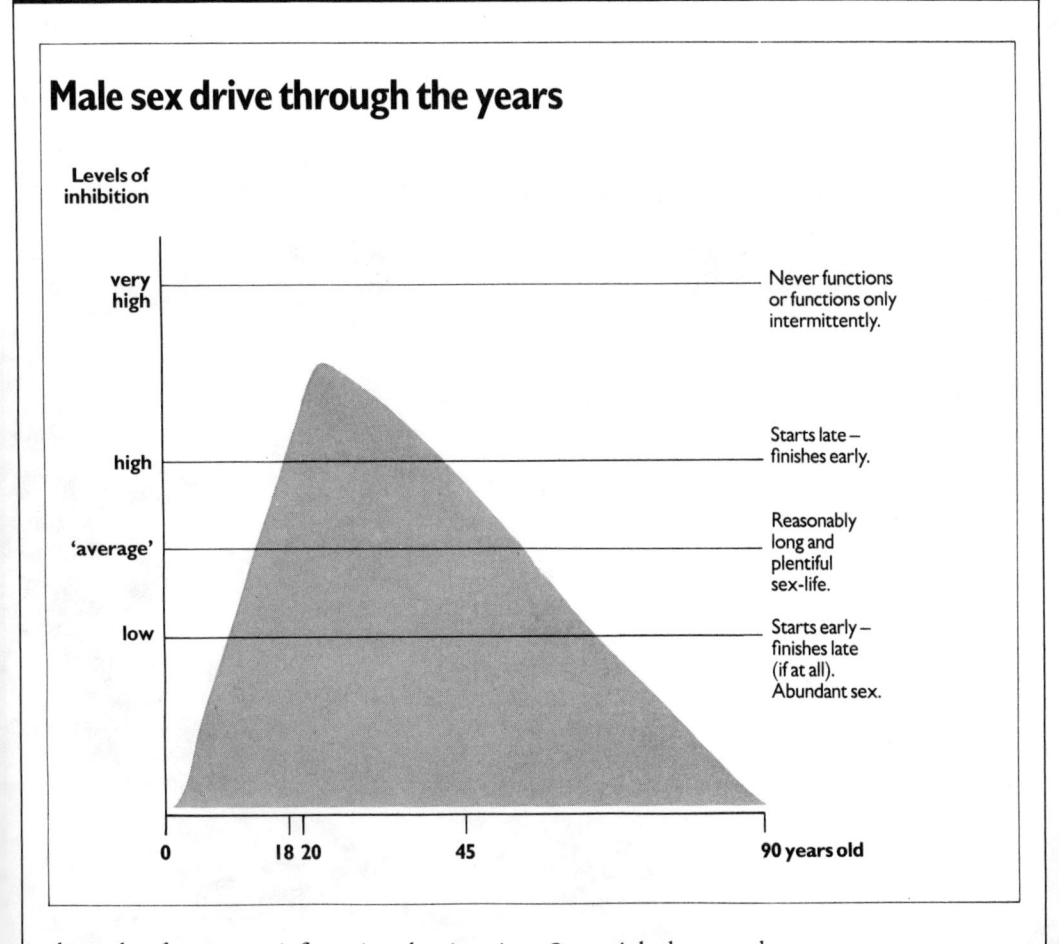

Levels of inhibition

- very high — Never functions or functions only intermittently.
- high — Starts late – finishes early.
- 'average' — Reasonably long and plentiful sex-life.
- low — Starts early – finishes late (if at all). Abundant sex.

0   18 20   45   90 years old

that other factors are influencing the situation. One might be sexual boredom with the partner. A new partner or a new technique usually results in increased sexual activity, at least for some months. Of Kinsey's sample of over 6000 men almost 70 per cent had had experience with prostitutes. For the older men as a group, prostitutes were important in replacing other sources of sexual satisfaction. This may be a bit misleading because prostitution, at least in the USA, was as much a social as a sexual activity in the earlier years of this century. Morning erections tend to continue, although with decreasing frequency, for years after the onset of impotence and this suggests that the man could have intercourse if his perceptions or circumstances were different. A further sign that elements of frustration may be involved is the fact that a third of fifty-year-olds were still experiencing occasional 'wet dreams' as was one man of eighty-six!

A more recent survey of over 1000 Danish men, who may not be representative of men in other countries, found that although a third of those in their nineties said they had an interest in sex and a third said they had morning erections, only 3 per cent had had intercourse in the previous year. The investigators found a considerable degree of reluctance to answer questions about masturbation, from which they

(overleaf) *The sunbathers*: This older couple are keeping fit which will in turn enhance their interest in sex. Both of these pursuits may prolong their lives.

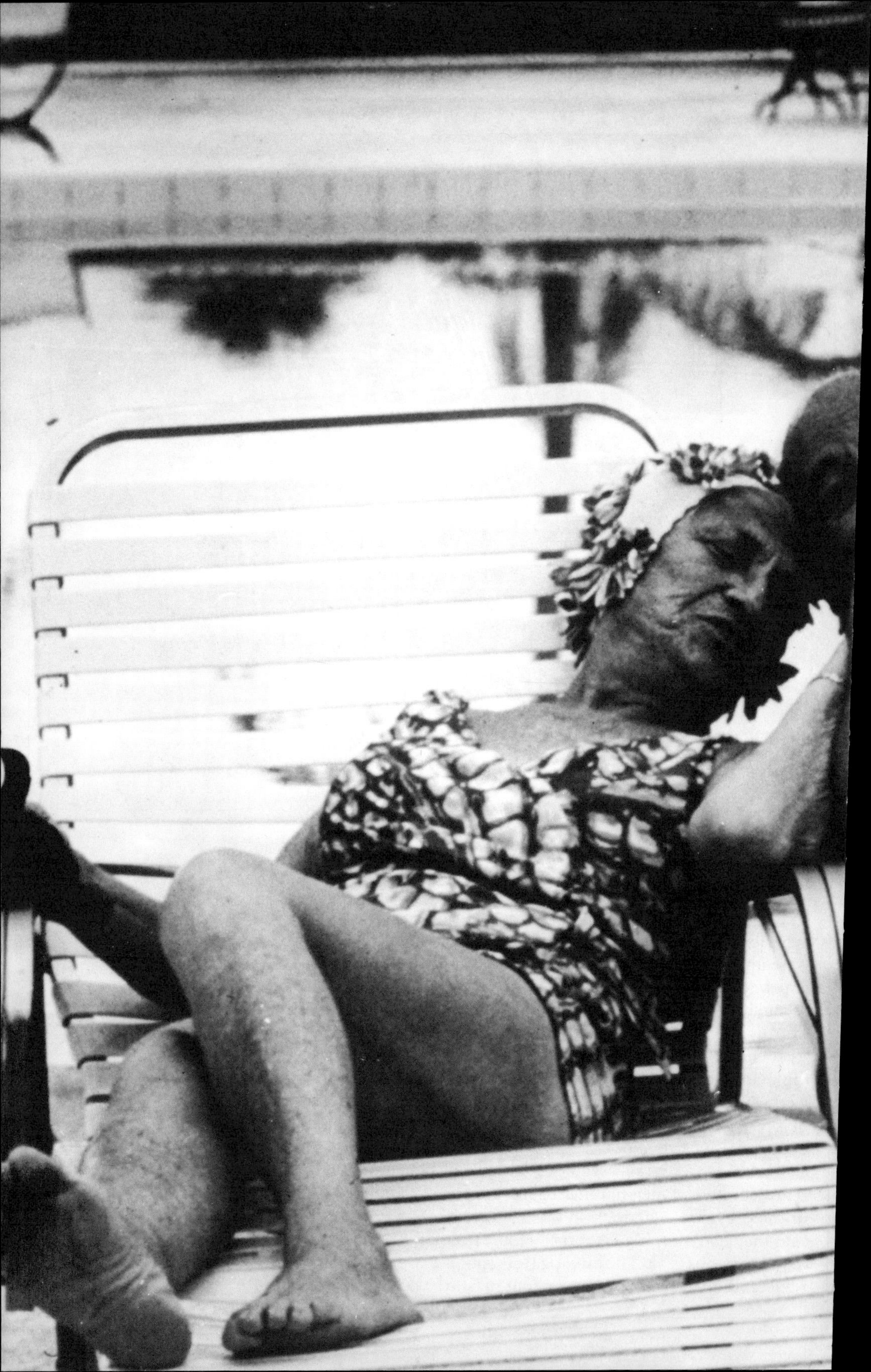

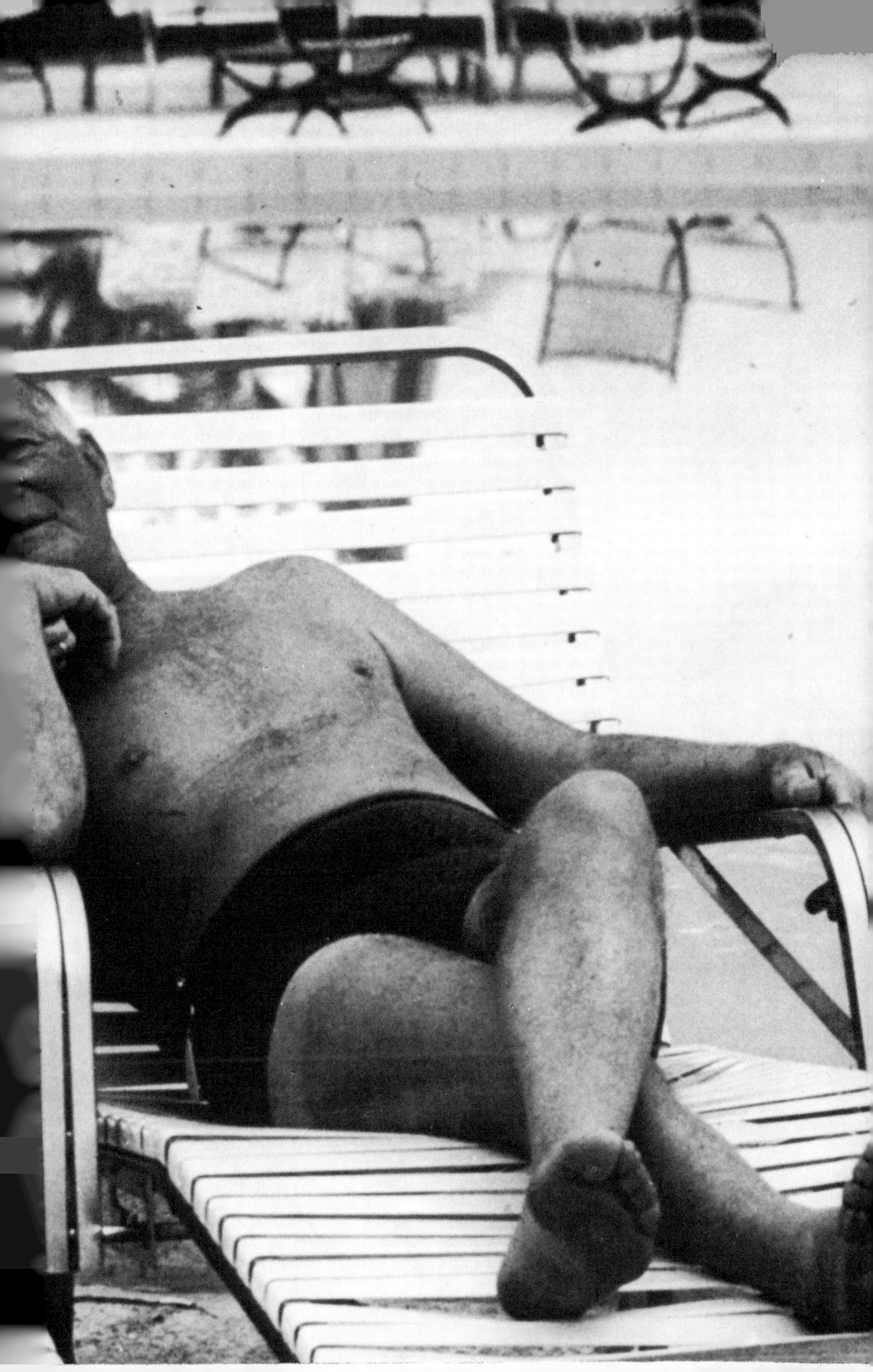

deduced that guilt about it is widespread but about a quarter of men seventy-five to ninety-five years old did admit to it. So this survey again demonstrated that intercourse rates decrease faster than those of other sexual activities.

A recent in-depth investigation of nearly 200 men aged sixty to seventy-nine in the USA more or less confirmed these findings. It also confirmed the great differences between individuals. As a measure of sexual behaviour in the past it is interesting to note that for the whole group, the average age at first intercourse was around twenty-two years, with marriage at around twenty-seven years, and the number of sexual partners before the age of forty, three or four. Only a small percentage of the men regarded their partner as being sexually unattractive and the great majority regarded their marriage as being highly successful. Of the men who were least active sexually, some reported difficulties with erection and premature ejaculation, and this could be taken to prove that they wanted, no matter how unconsciously, to avoid intercourse. This could have led to lack of interest on the part of their wives but, on the other hand, lack of interest in sex on the part of the woman could have been the cause of the man's sexual problem in the first place.

What emerged from the findings was that those men who had been most sexually active in their early years remained the most active in their later ones. The most sexually active men still responded to the sight of nude women and were the least tolerant of prolonged sexual frustration. However, if men are not in contact with women their interest in sex slowly declines. A further interesting finding was that many men in the least sexually active group who had problems did not report much in the way of reduced self-esteem. A comparison of the most sexually active men with a group of men aged fifty to fifty-nine showed that many older men are as sexually vigorous as those fourteen to twenty years their junior.

It is worth commenting in passing that the sex life of older couples can be assisted or enhanced by the use of sex aids. Some devices have a physical benefit, while others have more of a psychological one, but either way they are worth considering as a means of overcoming declining interest, decreasing pleasure and some minor sex problems. Vibrators and devices to help with erections may be particularly useful. Sex shops could do more to encourage the older generation to patronise them.

From about the age of forty, the hormone-producing cells in the testes decrease in number, so less of the male sex hormone testosterone is produced. Although there is a considerable variation between individuals, even in extreme old age, the amount of testosterone actively available in the body is around a third to a half of that in young men. The testes themselves become somewhat smaller and fewer sperms are produced. Nevertheless, men of almost any age can father a child if they can perform sexually. As age advances, the angle the erect penis makes with the trunk increases and erection is slower and needs more help from the partner. Pre-ejaculatory secretion decreases and ejaculatory spurts have less force.

For women, the sexual situation can be complicated by the

menopause. This is another area in which physical and psychological factors interact. Some women welcome the menopause because it liberates them from the fear of pregnancy but its approach is viewed by many as the end of their sex life. Those who really believe that sex is only for babies often suffer badly, as do self-centred women who measure their personal worth by their sexual attractiveness.

Because the menopause often coincides with the departure of children from home, a woman who has invested all her energies in loving and caring for her children loses her role at the same time as her sex life (in her view). As her husband, who on average is three or four years older than she is, may be becoming sexually uninterested, or seeking new sex partners, additional stresses are added. If her husband is successful in his career, he may be even more involved in his work than in previous years and will be less available just when she needs him most. Understandably some women become anxious, critical and unhappy, which tends to alienate their partners and perhaps discourage them from sex.

Any social, personality and temperamental differences between the couple become more pronounced and some such couples divorce once their children have left home. Unless a woman takes steps to counteract it even her circle of women friends diminishes as they lose the common experience of rearing children. In such a state of mind her preoccupations are more likely to turn inwards and menopausal symptoms assume an importance greater than would otherwise have been the case. She may also be overtaken by anxiety and depression along with feelings that she is worthless or that everyone else thinks she is.

As a man ages, his testes continue to function, but a woman's ovaries begin to 'shut down' from her mid to late thirties. The supply of available eggs gradually becomes exhausted and their quality declines. The pituitary gland increases its secretion of sex hormones in an effort to stimulate the ovaries but, when the egg production finally stops supplies of oestrogen and progesterone fall. The menopause is treated as a bit of a catch-all and any problems a woman encounters at around this time of life are likely to be attributed to it, often wrongly. Although some women continue to produce fairly large quantities of oestrogen, its lack is thought to be the cause of vaginal dryness, of a loss of calcium from the bones—at a rate of 15 per cent every ten years—resulting in a vulnerability to fractures, and of, by some indirect mechanism, hot flushes. This last symptom is a bit of a mystery. Women who suffer from them have, on average, the same blood levels of oestrogen as those who do not.

Some women report a loss of sex drive after the menopause. In some of them this can be explained by the modest fall, of around 25 per cent, in testosterone (the sex-drive hormone of both sexes), but in others depression, a deteriorating relationship with her partner, sex-avoidance by him, or the belief that her sex life should have ended may also be involved. There may be pain on intercourse, resulting from vaginal dryness and thinning of its lining, and this too can put a woman off sex.

As the menopause approaches, some women experience an

increase in sexual interest and pubescent fantasies of the rape and prostitution type may occur. Extra-marital intercourse is not at all uncommon at this stage if a woman sees it as her last chance. Many women say that they have less intercourse than they want at this period of their lives. Masturbation rates often peak as the inhibitions taught in early life recede, but in general, as with men, women tend to continue the habits of earlier years. However, although the intensity of sexual arousal may decrease around the time of the menopause, orgasmic capacity in intercourse certainly does not. In fact, some women first experience orgasms in intercourse at this time of life.

Around the time of the menopause and afterwards women become more likely to suffer from heart attacks. This is probably due, in the main, to the reduction in oestrogen levels which previously protected them. But there are certainly other factors too. In a survey comparing 100 women who had suffered a heart attack (and survived—those who died obviously were not available for questioning), between the ages of forty and sixty with a similar group of women who had not, it was revealed that 60 per cent of the heart-attack group had either not been able to have orgasms during intercourse or no longer had intercourse because of their husband's incapacity, compared with only 24 per cent of the second group.

Similar evidence is available from studies of men suffering from heart attacks. Around two-thirds have been found to have had significant sexual problems before the onset of the attack. From this and other research it seems reasonable to conclude that to the established practices for the avoidance of heart attacks—such as taking exercise, reducing animal fat intake, keeping slim and not smoking—we should add, for both sexes, the establishment of a successful sex life. Some investigators have also concluded that a good sex life in later years wards off mental deterioration. Some older people with arthritis, which is increasingly common with age, find that their condition improves after intercourse. There is also some evidence to suggest that people who continue to practise and enjoy sex tend to live longer, but it is not possible to claim that sex itself makes for a longer life because it is equally possible that whatever factors promote a full sex life also promote a long life.

The average age for the menopause is now around fifty. Those who start menstruating late tend to finish early; around 4 per cent do so in their early forties. Women of fifty-two and fifty-three have given birth to live babies—sometimes after a year or two without periods. Because of this, it is advisable to use some form of contraception for a year after the periods stop. The menopause lasts for six months to three years. Although it is a controversial topic, menopausal symptoms can be relieved by giving the woman oestrogen, perhaps combined with a progestogen. There may be some dangers in this but informed opinion now claims that the possible dangers have been exaggerated. This hormone replacement therapy (HRT), as it is called, is slowly becoming more acceptable to the medical profession. HRT can reduce the chances of coronary heart disease occurring. Vaginal difficulties can usually be relieved by the use of oestrogen cream in the vagina, and a loss of sex drive is sometimes treated by giving the woman testosterone.

Although the topic is the subject of considerable debate and controversy, it is now widely agreed that men can also have a menopause. It is thought to affect around 15 per cent of men. A few even have hot flushes. Psychological factors can also afflict men in their fifties and sixties as they realise that they are not going to live for ever, that they have not fulfilled their earlier ambitions and dreams and that younger men can beat them in many ways. Obviously if both partners are suffering from bruised egos at this stage of their lives they can either mutually support each other or blame each other.

The best sexual advice for ageing couples is as follows.

1 Try to get a good sex life going before the effects of ageing set in.

2 Try to avoid losing the habit of intercourse as can happen so easily, for example after a period of enforced abstinence because of illness.

3 Be resourceful and imaginative in finding ways round problems as they arise, for example, with arthritis.

4 Continue having lots of physical contact even if you do not want to have intercourse as often as before.

5 Indulge in mutual genital stimulation.

6 Do not expect the man always to have an orgasm in self- or mutual stimulation or in intercourse.

7 Overcome any shame about the possible use of erotica and sex aids, which can add a new dimension at this time of life.

8 Expect some failures and do not be demoralised by them.

9 Get medical advice for any condition that makes intercourse difficult or painful.

10 Ignore what people say about sex being only for the young.

Summary

Increasing research indicates that a good and continuing sex life is beneficial for the older citizen. As at all ages the most serious detrimental factors are inhibitions instilled in childhood. They affect the sexual behaviour of the elderly more than age itself.

Sex in old age has received very little attention—or indeed encouragement. Obviously much more could be done in this direction, especially as there are now many millions of elderly people with increasing expectations in the Western world. The problems are heightened and made more poignant because of the numerical imbalance of the sexes over the age of sixty. Anything that could be done to help the growing numbers of elderly to enjoy their lives and fulfil themselves better in this area would probably be welcomed by most people of all ages.

Chapter 35

Love

Although love and loving behaviour are common themes throughout this book, nowhere have we isolated them from their surroundings and looked at them separately. In a sense this fragmentary approach is inevitable because love is indefinable, means different things to different people (and even to the same people at different times of their lives) and subtly affects many of the areas of life we have covered.

Because there are such difficulties with words when discussing love, scientists have used the term attachment for a particular type of love—especially that between a baby and its mother. Whether love and attachment are exactly the same is difficult to decide but attachment is a good starting-point in a subject that is very difficult to define.

By attachment we mean a need which is independent of feeding and sexuality by which a young animal forms social and emotional bonds with its mother. The need for attachment has become clear from animal experiments which have clearly separated the young's need for food and their need for attachment, and numerous studies have shown that new-born animals removed from their mothers fare very badly and may even die because the mother subsequently rejects them even when they are returned to her after a few hours. Clearly, animals (and humans are no exception) have a crucial biological need to be kept with their mothers for a critical period after birth. The length of this period varies greatly from species to species.

As the young human infant grows up it engenders in its mother another kind of love—a feeling which is called bonding. The mother bonds to her baby and loves it. In our chapter on baby and childhood sexuality we showed how these two emotions are vital if a child is to grow up to be able to love and be loved, and the seeds of these loving feelings are sown in the very first few minutes after birth.

At this point it is probably valuable to have a look at what can go wrong with attachment, because in raising children such variations can dramatically alter the way a child turns out as an adult. There is no doubt that babies and young children who cannot, for whatever reason, form a loving bond with their mother (or a consistent mother substitute) and later their father and siblings, remain socially backward and isolated. They are joyless, anxious and extremely concerned when the person to whom they are attached disappears, even for a while. This must have harmful effects on them in later life, but we cannot as yet prove how.

An infant's need to receive attachment behaviour can, however, become fixed in some people, just as facets of one's psychosexual development can become fixed at various stages of development. Such a child (or even an adult) experiences 'anxious attachment', in which he has a tremendous need to receive, but cannot give in emotional terms. Such individuals are clinging and over-dependent, and if they become parents are unable to answer their children's need for attachment because they have none of their own to give.

Mother and child love

Clearly there is a bond of vital importance between a young mammal and its mother, especially in the earliest days and weeks. This is true of human infants, though research into the subject is very difficult to carry out in an ethically acceptable way. But enough work has been done with babies who have been separated from their mothers in non-experimental situations for us to gauge the effects.

A baby must be cared for in order to survive and, like other animals, human mothers are genetically programmed to respond to their new-born offspring's behaviour. A baby continually tries to attract the mother's (and, later, the father's) attention to make sure that she is aware of his or her needs. As she cares for him or her in response to these needs, she'll talk to him or her, smile, cuddle and play. In return the baby will stop crying, listen intently, gaze at her face (and eyes in particular), keep quite still or sometimes kick in a certain way, and smile or coo at her.

At around three months, it is clear that the baby recognises his mother. He or she has an extra special smile for her and within a few months will cry when she leaves him or her, or if a stranger approaches. The baby is said at this stage to be 'attached' to his mother and treats her in a special way, clearly liking her more than anyone else. He is now in love with her and responds very badly to losing her as his love object. If his mother does not look after him or her, the baby becomes attached to whoever does. Whoever brings them up, babies form an attachment to one person in particular (if given the opportunity to) by between six and twelve months. Babies brought up in institutions by many caretakers can become confused and even emotionally deprived. This is why it is always best for one particular person to be responsible for a baby for much of the time.

It is well known that a baby can become attached to people other than his mother. Babies can, in fact, form multiple attachments. This is obvious, but can be forgotten when one talks in psychological jargon. However many people a baby is attached to, there is always a favourite (usually the mother). If she is not there, someone else will do and the baby will turn to the person next on the list in his own personal hierarchy—it may be his father, sister, granny or nanny, for example. Although they are 'second best' in his or her attachment league they are still very important to him or her. When babies or young children are with several people to whom they are attached, they automatically choose to be with the one they are most attached to. For instance, if a baby is tired or falls over and both his or her

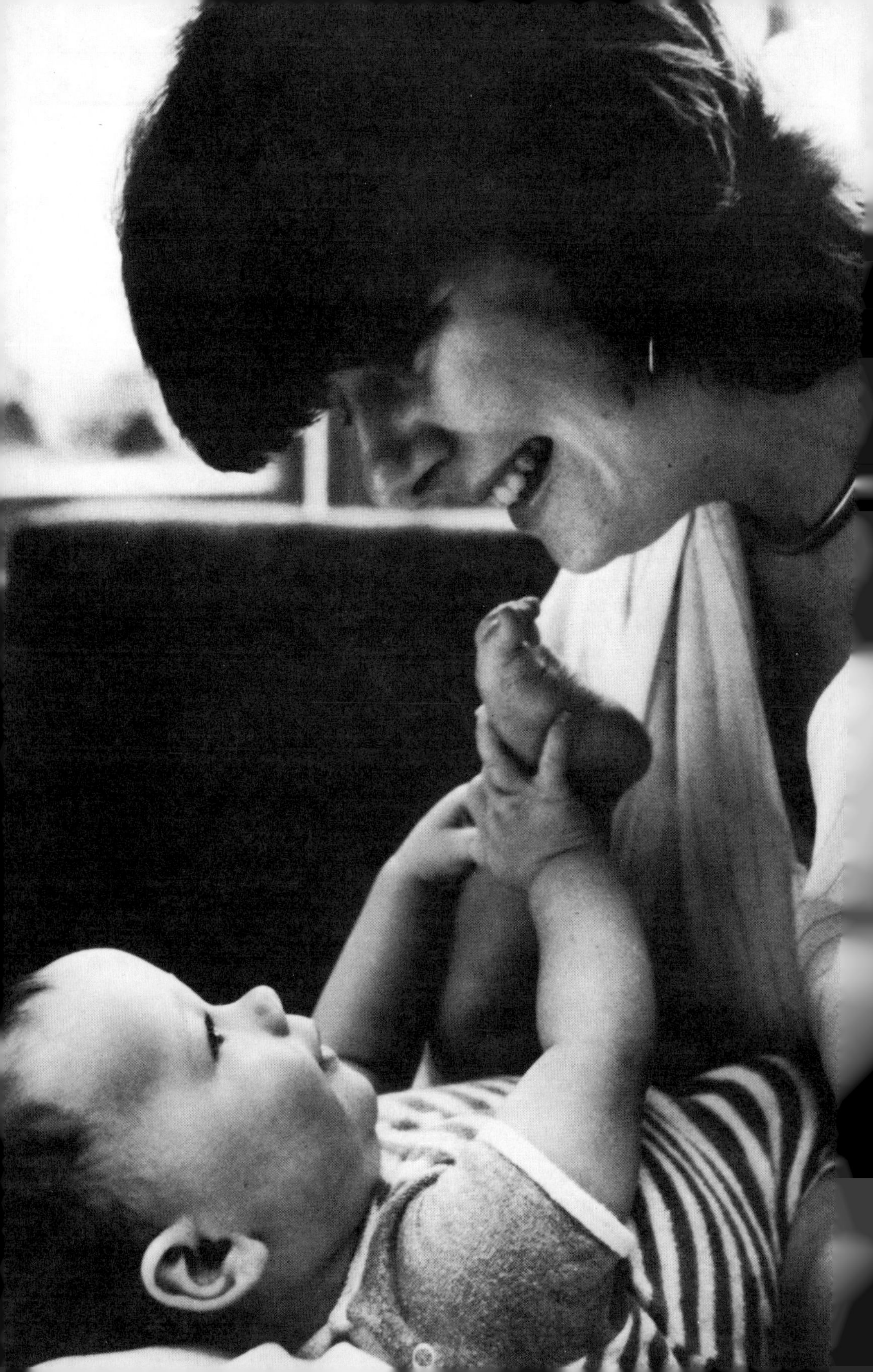

mother and nanny are there, he or she will want to be comforted by the mother if he or she is most attached to her. One thing is certain and that is that a stranger will not do. A baby does not become instantly attached to someone new but takes time to get to know them.

It is the emotional aspects of the baby's attachment experience that are most important and this is true of all love-bonds. One person may take physical care of him or her—feeding, washing and keeping him or her warm, for example—but if another person is the one who mainly reacts to him or her in a loving way (even if only for a short time each way), he or she will become attached to that person. Active and responsive interaction with a baby is what counts, and sensitive responsiveness is the one quality most likely to foster attachment. Usually, of course, the person who gives a baby this also meets his or her physical needs, besides comforting him through anxiety, fear, illness and tiredness.

It is through a baby's first love with the person to whom he or she is attached that he or she learns to love other people. The more adequately the emotional needs are met, the better able he or she will be to respond to others in turn.

A child can become attached (or remain attached) to someone even though he or she may treat him or her very inconsistently or even harshly. This explains why a baby or young child who is sometimes physically or emotionally hurt by his or her mother will still cling to her when in the company of others. It seems that it is better for children to have someone to be attached to, however he or she treats them, than to have no one special to call their own.

Almost all of this attachment form of love arises because young babies rely totally on their mothers (or other close people) to answer their needs and cravings. This makes it very important, in our view, that such needs are met lovingly, unconditionally and promptly by the attached adult figure, so that the baby thinks well of the world from day one of life. Although it is extremely difficult to prove what the effects of poor mother–baby love are in later life, and there is little doubt that even quite severe harm in this area can be repaired in later childhood, we feel safe in stating that a really close, loving relationship must be the best way of starting off life.

It is fairly obvious that babies can either grow up knowing they are loved and loving someone else or they can grow up with feelings of anger, resentment, frustration and sadness because they have not experienced such love. This is a totally dependent form of love and one which most people can easily understand. It also raises another important concept when discussing love and that is *caring*.

One way in which we can recognise love (even if we cannot define it) is to watch people's behaviour. This shows that whatever they love, they care for. It matters to them what happens to it. They are prepared to make sacrifices for it. They jealously guard it in the face of threats and they want the best for it. So it is with mother-love. A mother knows all these feelings and recognises them as a part of the complex emotion we call love. The baby cannot, of course, realise such things but knows, even before he can express himself, what love means to him.

The growth of love: Mother-baby love.

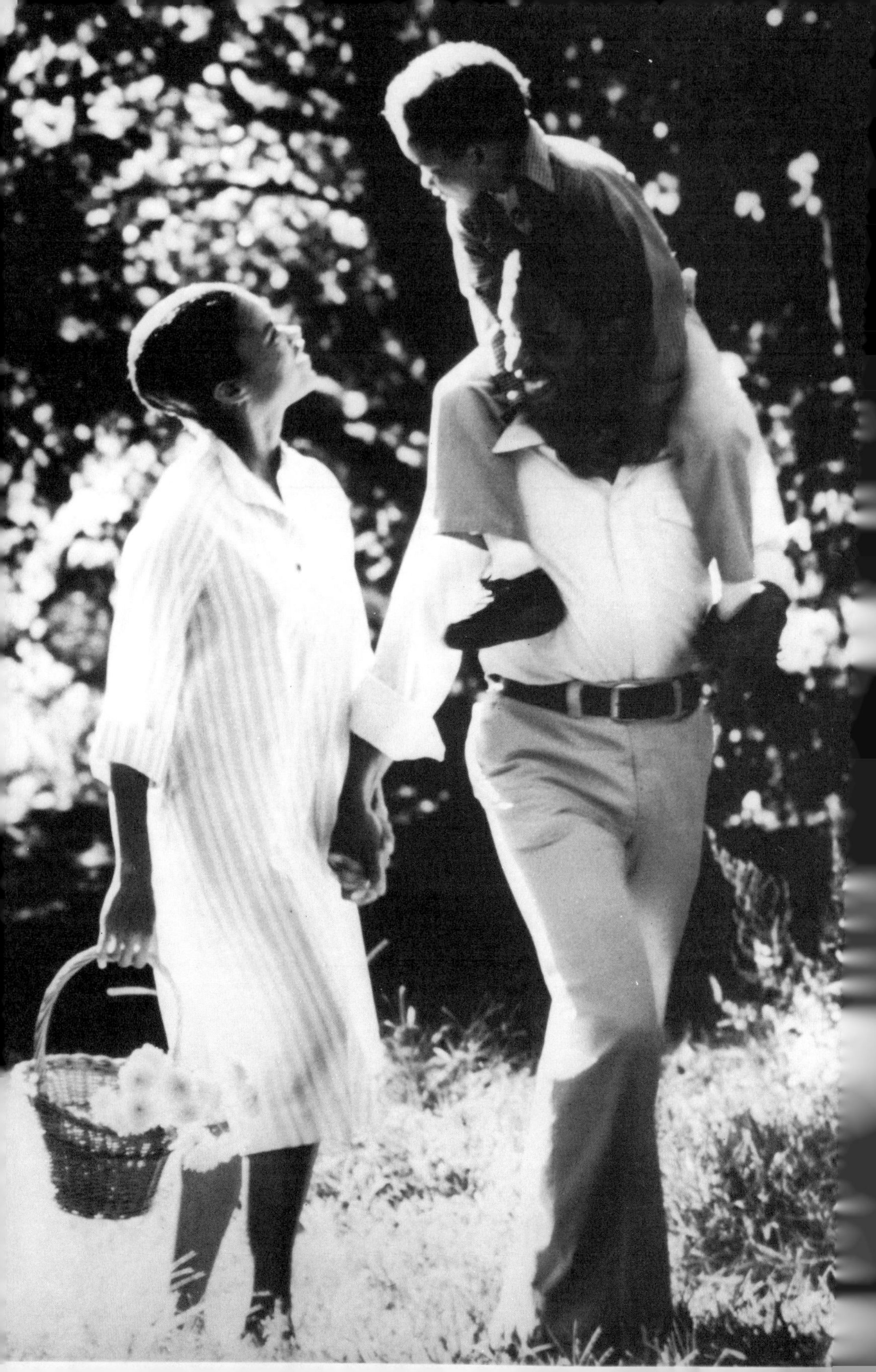

Every love experience in life to some extent takes us back to our first childhood experience. Indeed, it is this very aspect of love that many people find so difficult. In every adult loving relationship there are seeds of child-like love, yet many adults fight them, thinking that adult love, linked as it so often is to genitality, is something apart.

The evolution of love

Most people are quite happy with concepts of mother–baby love and have no difficulty accepting such notions. However, love clearly does not stand still—it changes and matures. In the mother–baby relationship love is both given and received by both parties, to their mutual satisfaction. This clearly has to happen biologically or mothers would not feel sufficiently motivated to put up with the real and provable problems of rearing a totally dependent little baby or young child. Babies are at first totally self-centred—all they want is to satisfy their needs. This changes, though, over the first few weeks and months, so that the mother and baby become a mutually rewarding love unit.

In the Oedipal phase of young childhood this love is vested in the opposite-sex parent, at least to some extent, until eventually in early adolescence the opposite-sex parent is de-loved as teenagers invest their loving feelings in themselves. There is abundant clinical experience to show that if the teenager does not negotiate this stage successfully he or she can never truly love another person of the opposite sex and this can lead to the disturbed man–woman relationships we have described elsewhere (such as the mistress–madonna syndrome).

In late adolescence teenagers seek an emotional object to love and in our society combine this with a sex-object. So it is that love and genital sex start to grow together. Now the masturbating, self-centred kind of love is giving way to a more mature type of love. Around this time many adolescents experience a generalised kind of love.

Generalised love

This is an immature, late-adolescent phenomenon but one (like the others) which can last throughout life in certain people. Some never get beyond it at all. Such love is almost totally idealistic (not romantic) and is sometimes centred around good causes, concepts of freedom, political ideologies and similar concerns. At this stage a youngster will throw a brick through an embassy window to protest at a country's treatment of whales or whatever. His or her sense of outrage on behalf of the underprivileged knows no bounds, and in the name of love all kinds of unloving acts are possible.

The late adolescent loves everybody—this is probably why there is such an interest in socialism at this age. Social wrongs are seen as totally unacceptable and the young person sets out to put the world to rights.

One way of looking at this not-altogether-amicable phenomenon is to see late adolescents as groping to find a way to express their love and need for love in relation to others. Because they are still

(opposite) *The growth of love;* Family love.
(overleaf) Lover love.

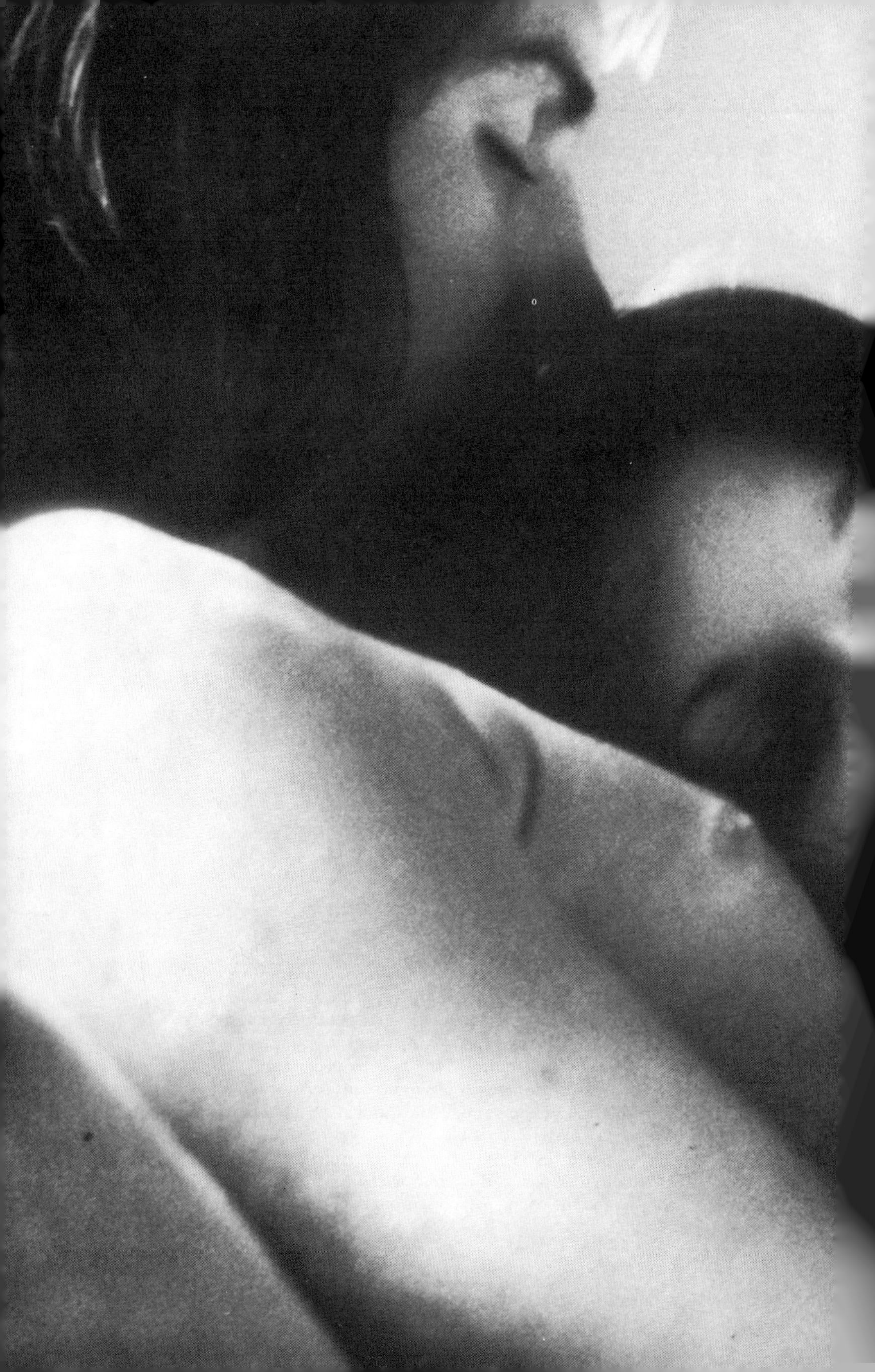

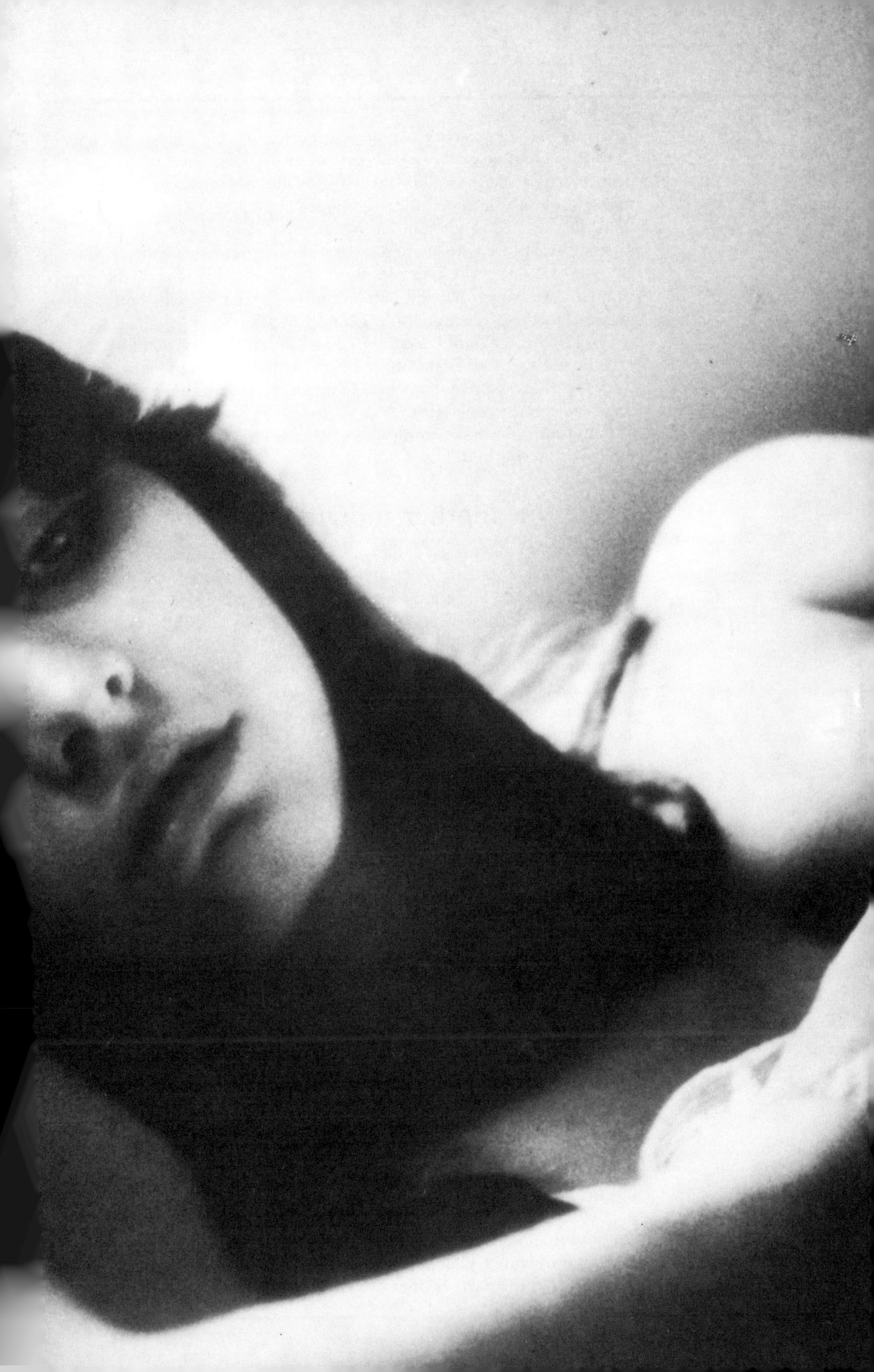

insecure in their capacity to give and receive love they generalise it to any individual or group who seems oppressed. Because such love is not inter-personal (as adult love is) the adolescent is freed from the dangers of rejection, yet able to convince him- or herself that he or she is a decent, loving person. Unfortunately, elements of hatred also intrude and those who are perceived as the oppressors are attacked to show how loving the late adolescent really is. This is probably the stage in life when love and hate are most poignantly felt, but by no means are these reactions solely found in adolescents.

Love is an ambivalent business and most psychiatrists and psychoanalysts find that hate is never far from loving feelings. The very fact that we protest our love so much often underlines feelings of hate we cannot cope with.

Out of all these complex emotions of late adolescence grows a love for another individual.

Love for another individual

It is this that most people call love in everyday speech but clearly true love is much more complex. Love at this adult stage brings together, probably for the first time ever, a love-object and a sex-object. This needs a little explanation. An 'object' in psychological jargon is a thing with which an individual is able to indulge his instinctual needs. A mother can therefore be a love-object to a baby and a wife a sex-object to a husband. When adults are in love, if they are mature, their love-object and their sex-object is one and the same person. This makes for a happy and meaningful marriage.

However, for many these two are separate. Some men, for example, cannot have a meaningful sexual relationship with someone they love (their wife, for instance) because they see her as untouchable. Such men (and there are many of them) will be able to have perfectly enjoyable sex outside marriage but not within it. Most, if not all, of this attitude is, of course, in the man's unconscious—he does not realise that it is all happening unless it is pointed out to him. Others see their partners purely as sex-objects and have little or no love-object relationship with them. Such a couple can be happy loving their children, their home, their possessions or whatever and enjoy each other purely as sex-objects.

The ideal marriage blends the two in perfect harmony to satisfy both the childhood craving for love and the adult craving for sex.

The thing to remember is that, whatever sex books may suggest, sex alone is never enough. We all need loving 'rewards' in life from one source or another. Psychologists call such rewards 'strokes' and say, quite rightly, that we all need 'stroking' throughout our lives.

Adults who love each other stroke each other (physically or metaphorically) as much as they need and a good relationship is built up of physical and psychological strokes that demonstrate the partners' love for each other. This begins to explain why people have such different ideas of what loving someone means. Many people with marital problems say, 'If he(she) *really* loved me they would/wouldn't do . . . .' But the partner does not realise that this is the definition of love to which they are supposed to be adhering.

Communication is vital within any loving relationship because each of us is unique and we all need to get our strokes in different ways. Some want all their strokes to be physical and require an active sex life as a proof of the other's love. Others want praise, outward signs of affection, practical signs of love, and so on, as their sources of strokes. In a short chapter such as this we cannot possibly do anything more than scratch the surface of this subject, but interested readers should examine their lives to see what they like best in the form of strokes and then discuss with their partners why they are not getting them—if they are not. The giving and receiving of strokes is the hallmark of mature adult love. The final stage of love expands one's love for an individual to a love of all mankind.

Love of all humankind and the whole world

The Ancient Greeks saw this as the highest plane of love. From the security of having been loved as a baby and child, from loving oneself and being confident that one is lovable, and from having a mature love for another adult comes the ultimate—the maturity of love that enables an individual to extend all these feelings to mankind in general. This is no longer an adolescent 'change the world' form of love but one forged from the experience that life cannot and will not go the way you want it to, that everyone else has their rights and points of view, and that yours have to fit in with those around you. At this stage you can love those that persecute you; you can turn the other cheek and no longer retire hurt or angry when the world refuses to go your way. Such love is the Christian love of the New Testament in which one loves one's neighbour as oneself. People in this stage of love really *do* change the world and contribute to it. The mature adult at this stage expresses his or her general love in specific ways—often with powerful effects.

Displacement of love

As we grow through our teens and early twenties we may think at various times that we are in love with or even 'love' several members of the opposite sex. Sooner or later we realise that this particular person is not right for one reason or another, and we part. This causes real grieving on occasions and certainly most of us feel unhappy or depressed, at least temporarily. It is a vital part of growing up and maturing psychosexually that we *do not* marry our first love object after puberty—it would usually be disastrous if we were to do so. This then implies that we have to be able to accept the loss of a loved one and live to fight another day. This, of course, applies not only to love-sex objects but also to the loss of relatives, parents, or even pets. Throughout life people's love-objects are withdrawn from them (by death or divorce for example) and most grieve this loss. At this time the affected person says to him- or herself, 'I'll never have another

(overleaf) *The growth of love*: Love of all humankind.

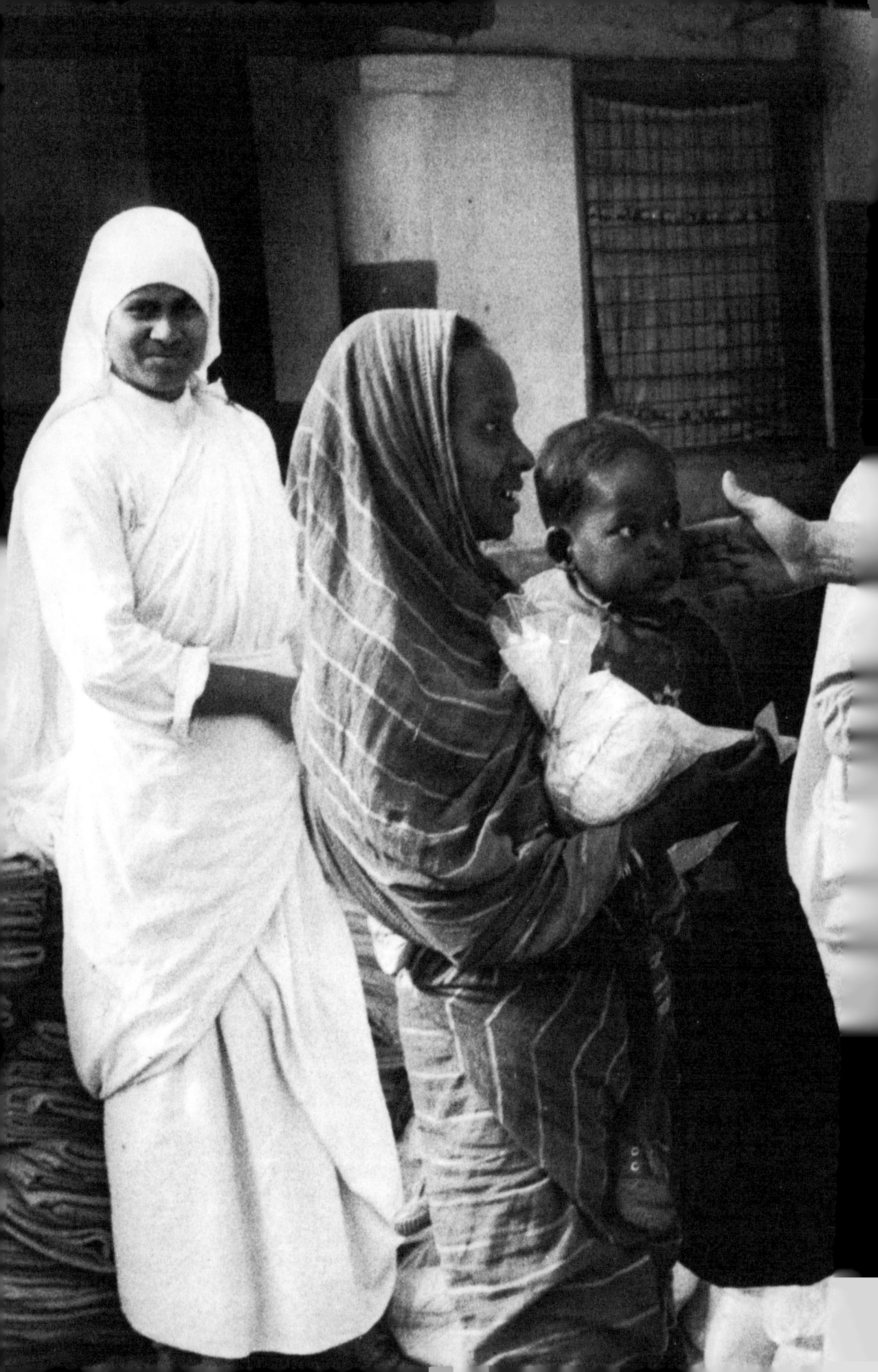

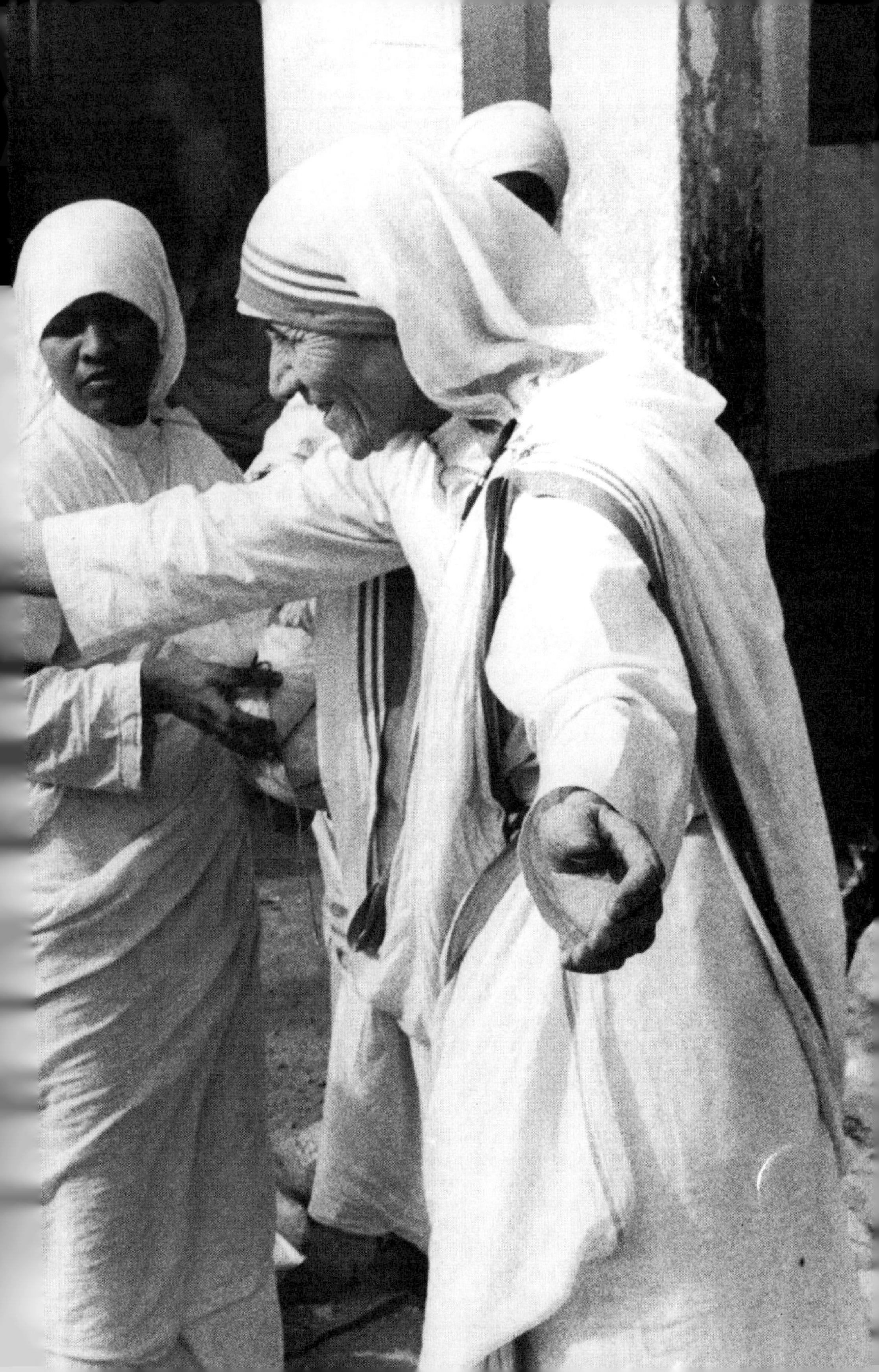

husband/dog/daughter/mother like that again,' and of course they are right because all people and animals are unique. However, Nature heals this wound over about two years (sooner for some)—depending on their personality and the nature of the relationship involved—and they are soon on the way to investing their love in someone else.

In a sense the original love for the love-object is displaced on to the new one, because, as we have seen, we all need to love and be loved. This primitive, instinctual drive, leads many people to rush into the search for new love-objects after the loss of their original one and such people often choose someone very similar to the last one. In this way the lost love-object never dies (or disappears, in the case of divorce)—they live on in the remaining person's memory, yet may be related to through the 'new' love-object. Those who have invested an enormous amount of love in a person who subsequently dies or leaves often tell how they never really get over the loss but simply put on a brave face for the world and even to a new partner. Such a reaction can become troublesome to some people because they hanker after one *perfect* love-object (even if during the object's time with them things were far from perfect), idealise the past and cannot step into the future because they fear that no one will ever match up to the lost love-object.

But where does all this leave the kind of love that story books talk about? We have looked at romantic love in chapter 9. Let us look here at 'being in love'.

Being in love

'Falling in love' or 'being in love' are strange experiences with which most of us have at least a passing acquaintance, and they do not necessarily have anything to do with the types of love we have already been discussing.

The person who is 'in love' has a fairly well recognised collection of signs and symptoms—in fact, some people have likened the condition to an illness and speak of people being 'sick with love'. The signs of the 'illness' are restlessness, agitation, an irregular heartbeat, a raised blood pressure and pulse rate, clammy palms, sudden flushes, a loss of appetite, poor sleep, an inability to think straight, extreme mood swings and even hallucinations.

Is it any wonder that the newly in-love feel so strange and confused? Such feelings are commonplace, especially in the young whom we condition to expect them.

Although women tend to fall in love earlier and to have more 'attacks' before the age of twenty; once past this age men continue to fall in love while women seem relatively immune. In one survey women were found to consider it quite reasonable to marry an otherwise suitable partner without being love-sick. Another study found that women are much tougher than men when it comes to breaking up (they 'de-love' men quicker than men 'de-love' them); that they were much more likely to take the initiative in ending things; and were less likely to report nostalgia, depression and loneliness afterwards. Also see Chapter 12.

The most vulnerable time for falling in love is during adolescence, and teenagers whose parents are divorced, those at odds with their parents or authority in general and those with poor self-esteem are most at risk. In later life wars and other socially stressful events tend to make people profess love for each other, perhaps as a bid for reassurance or biological survival.

Falling in love is more common in men during the mid-life crisis, in women just before the menopause, and in those facing retirement or redundancy. In fact research has found that situations that increase the body's adrenalin make people more inclined to attach themselves to each other.

Unfortunately, in our Judaeo-Christian culture, 'being in love' has become a cultural essential for intercourse. We would certainly be happy to go along with any argument that linked intercourse to real love, but not necessarily to 'being in love'. Unfortunately, for the young, the three are almost indistinguishable. They think true love is what they are feeling and, whatever their parents say, by way of guidance, love-sickness clouds their judgement and hampers rational decisions. If only we could separate falling in love from copulation and intercourse the world would be a happier and more stable place but several hundred years of cultural conditioning cannot be undone overnight.

Jealousy

It is impossible to think of love without jealousy—a wholly negative emotional state in which the sufferer becomes anxious, suspicious and angry in response to real or imagined threats to the love-bond between him or her and another. Some degree of sexual jealousy is probably normal and it has been extensively studied and copiously represented in literature over the centuries. Such normal jealousy probably plays a part in holding couples (and their families) together and probably stops errant partners from indulging their sexual whims more than they otherwise would. It can, of course, work the other way and turn homes, in the words of one expert, 'into hells of discord and hate'. Marital sexual jealousy can be very dangerous indeed and men are more dangerous than women because of their greater physical strength and aggressiveness. Sexual jealousy affects both homosexual and heterosexual couples and can drive people to commit crimes of violence and even murder.

Jealousy is a strange emotion because it has a large component of self-pity and selfishness to it. In jealousy there is often more self-love than love. Any situation that makes one of the partners feel at a disadvantage in the struggle to obtain or keep a mate predisposes the handicapped person to sexual jealousy. Impotence on the part of the husband and frigidity on the part of the wife and a marked disparity between the sexual appetites of the couple are often predisposing factors. There are perfectly well-recognised psychological and medical causes for sexual jealousy too. For example, mental subnormality and certain sorts of brain damage are known to cause it. Drunkenness makes people jealous; as do cocaine and amphetamines. During pregnancy, in the post-natal period and around the menopause women often feel jealous even when there is no reason for them to do so. This could be hormonal in origin but is more likely to come about because at these times women feel disadvantaged in the sex market in comparison with other women.

Often jealousy is a sign of inferiority in the complaining (jealous) partner. He or she is threatened because of the possible loss of his or her spouse's love. This often means he or she has no confidence and sees every man or woman as a threat to the relationship.

Love and commitment

Although we can love many things and many people, most of us put our one-to-one love relationship on a rather special pedestal and try to preserve it. This is important because it is probably the most powerful emotion in our adult lives and is the glue that holds the family unit together. We see all around us what happens when this glue gets weak—families fall apart in fragments. Although most of us would like to see our one-to-one relationship as the perfect blending of love-object and sex-object, for all but a minority this simply is not a reality. In our society we are 'allowed' lots of love-objects but only one sex-object within marriage. This creates problems for millions of people who do not want to threaten their love-bond for their spouse yet are not content with only one sex-object. So what can they do?

There are no simple answers but discreet adultery has always been an answer. There are, needless to say, considerable dangers to this approach and many people prefer to relate to their sex-objects in fantasy during masturbation rather than in reality. Clinical experience shows that people who have multiple fantasies of different members of the opposite sex are more likely really to enjoy the opposite sex than are the bedroom cowboys who misuse the opposite sex in reality. Everyone wants to be happy, to love and to be loved, but every deal in life has a price and marriage is no exception. Other men and women exist in the world around the loving, married couple and they have to be dealt with. Each individual will have to find his or her own way of coping with this problem and we have given several hints and tips in the book. Most women want and need clear lines of commitment and are very sensitive to any signs of withdrawal of love. Women appear to be much more love-dependent than are men—even little girls demonstrate this—and this makes them vulnerable to losing this love. True, they can build up the 'strokes' they need from other sources, including their children, but deep down most women want a loving, secure relationship at the heart of it all.

Many marriages get to the stage in which the couples are separately counting the cost of their loving commitment to one another and the one who receives too few strokes is vulnerable to an extra-marital affair.

Unfortunately, many people look for unattainable and unrealistic perfection within their marriage, demanding perfection of their spouse when they are not themselves perfect and forgetting the simple fact that everybody is a package deal. You cannot buy life in units of perfection—life is really only a heap of things that have fallen together in a particular way that you are trying to make the best of.

Summary

From the point of view of attachment, a mature adult is one who can both give and receive love. Life, to be successful, depends on maintaining a balance of dependence on and independence from others.

A mature person can ask for love when he or she needs it and, knowing he or she will get it, feels confident to give love to others. It is difficult and probably impossible to extend love to others in a mature way if one has not received it or is receiving none oneself. To this giving and receiving of attachment love genitality is added in adulthood and this further deepens and strengthens the loving bonds.

There is no more an 'ideal love' than there is an ideal marriage. We are all complex, ever changing beings whose ability to give and receive love varies from day to day and from year to year. What a shame it is that more couples do not realise this as they cast around the sexual arena, or go for professional help in an effort to improve their lot when in reality what they already have is pretty good.

Perhaps the final thought should be along these lines.

In matters of love, don't commit the grievous error of making the best the enemy of the good. Always remember that the ideal doesn't exist in this world.

INDEX

abortion 123, 247, 249, 250, 254, 280–3, 283–93 *passim*, 307, 308
abstinence 180, 247
adolescence 22, 28–9, 30–48, 60–70, 98–9, 104, 105, 292, 316, 328, 333, 337, 338, 423, 426, 431 *see also* boys; girls
adoption 308–11, 340, 342, 438
adrenogenital syndrome 172
adultery 340, 342, 432
affairs 104, 122–5, 128, 129, 278, 294, 374, 432
age gap 73
AIDS 373
aids, sex 241, 245, 386–7, 414, 417 *see also* vibrators
alcoholism 17, 121, 166, 353
amniocentesis 283, 289
anorexia nervosa 35
antibodies 267, 373
anal intercourse/sex 21, 215, 247, 362, 370, 376, 387, 398
  stage 12, 20–1, 28, 367, 382, 385
  stimulation 21, 195–6, 198, 333, 362, 386, 387
anus 21, 154, 155, 158, 195, 198, 213, 227, 238, 367, 386
anxiety 45, 60, 70, 84, 89, 99, 141, 203, 233, 235, 237, 240–2, 289, 294, 304–5, 330–3, 337, 354,

357–8, 373, 383, 408, 415
apathy, sexual 231
aphrodisiacs 398
areola 30, 183
arousal 49, 67, 85, 98, 180–201, 382, 391
  female 35, 36, 59, 165, 183–5, 187–96, 235, 236, 240, 244, 266, 269, 301, 329, 330, 332, 333, 416
  male 154, 181–3, 196–9, 329
arthritis 406, 416, 417
attachment 433
  in marriage 130, 135
  mother-child 19, 119, 418–21
  opposite-sex parent 29, 42, 44, 48, 72, 132, 352, 393, 423
attraction 32, 43, 49–59, 123, 129, 201, 241

babies 14, 15–20, 85, 118, 119, 128, 166, 170, 176, 231, 244, 249, 289, 301, 303, 305–7, 358, 418–21
battering 305–6
reasons for having 284–7, 358
test-tube 271, 279
balanitis 402
beating 21, 217, 377, 385
bedwetting 20, 148
bereavement 221, 427
Bible 288, 343, 344

bigamy 410
birth *see* childbirth
bisexuality 359, 375
biting 189, 385
'bleeding, withdrawal' 251–2, 264
boredom 123, 218, 231, 411
Bossard 71
bowels 21, 22; surgery 406–7
boys, adolescent 38–40, 41–8, 61–70, 338
  and fathers 26–7, 38, 48
  and girls 27, 38–9, 41, 44
  and homosexuality 359–60, 362, 364
  and intercourse 39, 45, 56, 64, 68–70, 84, 337
  and masturbation 24, 28, 38, 43, 49, 81, 329
  and mothers 26, 27, 28, 38, 40, 53, 81, 94, 106, 108
  and parents 42, 44
  and puberty 24, 28, 30, 38–40, 167
  and virginity 57
brain 167, 172; damage 406, 431
breastfeeding 12, 17, 19, 119, 120, 161, 164–5, 247, 263, 300–4 *passim*, 320
breasts 30, 35, 40, 49–50, 128, 155–7, 183, 189, 198, 206, 212, 213, 224, 227, 246, 252, 301–3, 320, 330, 392, 400–1
  fondling 37, 43, 67, 68,

69, 84, 189, 288, 294, 303, 385
  size 150, 155, 250
Britain/UK 142, 143, 147, 235, 257, 280, 282, 292, 311, 371, 410
brothers and sisters 106
  sex play between 27, 394
buttocks 21, 49–50, 189, 213, 215

Caesarian section 254, 300
Canada 56
cancer 154, 157, 166, 252, 259, 367, 372, 400, 435
caressing 189, 197, 224
caring 12, 118, 119, 421
celibacy 178, 397
cervix 151, 153, 154, 157, 159, 160, 190, 250, 257, 258, 266, 267, 269, 270, 271, 273, 282, 283, 300, 367, 369, 372, 398, 399
chancre 371
childbirth 12, 119, 120, 231, 241, 254, 288–9, 297–301, 307, 315, 437
  sex after 304
childhood 20–9, 230
  repression in 15, 28, 36, 177–8
childlessness 132, 277–9
children 308–28, 345–55
  – Act (1975) 311
  and divorce 143, 147, 148
  and marriage 111, 127–9, 136, 221, 287–8, 352–3
  and sex 312–28, 345–55
choice, of partner 9, 49–59, 71–81, 95
Christianity 61, 340–5, 427
chromosomes 168–71, 270
churches 137
circumcision 24, 153–4, 321, 402
class 73, 76, 143
clitoris 16, 21, 119, 157, 158, 165, 172, 183, 185, 190, 191, 193, 195, 196, 205, 206, 212, 213, 215, 227, 237, 294, 301, 335, 362, 386
clothes 50, 53–4
clubs 148, 407
commitment 79, 85, 88, 95, 104, 121, 122, 136, 432
communication 52, 56, 67, 80, 85, 94, 106, 107, 113, 126, 127, 201, 204, 227, 231, 240, 243, 316, 427
conception 264–79
condom/sheath 238, 255, 258, 259, 260, 263, 370, 386
confessing/telling 81, 125
contraception 84, 123, 137, 193, 219, 220, 247–64, 290, 291–2, 294, 304, 308, 312, 314, 316, 340, 342, 387, 399, 407, 416, *see also individual headings*
copulation 13, 68, 85, 136, 177–85, 201, 220, 227, 232, 373, 382, 431
counselling 108, 127, 139–42, 144, 233, 235, 282, 288, 306, 307, 363
courtship 76, 77, 79–87, 92, 95, 97, 233, 240, 382
couvade 305
Cowper's glands 153
crushes 37, 364
cuddling 19, 187, 197, 211, 220, 224, 300, 303–4, 397
culture 8, 11, 15, 17, 19, 22, 27, 50, 61, 62, 64, 81, 120, 122, 128, 136, 137, 155, 164, 165, 178, 180, 203, 215, 220, 230, 248, 249, 264, 277, 284, 286–7, 289, 305, 306, 307, 326, 339, 340, 342, 348–9, 357, 374, 375, 376, 380, 383, 385, 393, 396, 409, 410, 431
cunnilingus 191, 194, 215, 362, 381, 382
cystitis 399–406

D and C 257, 406
'daddy' figure 127
dating 53, 65, 69, 79, 148
daughters and fathers, 26, 27, 32, 35, 36, 40, 94, 375, 393–4
  and mothers 26, 31, 32, 35, 36, 41, 48, 231, 243, 288, 375
delinquency 44, 70, 148
Denmark 142, 411
deodorants 50, 165, 368
depression 17, 29, 35, 45, 89, 95, 99, 128, 240, 252, 283, 290, 304, 399, 415
  post-natal 231, 305
deviations 15, 337, 376, 377, 380–96
diabetes 239, 242, 245, 269, 368, 404–5
diaphragm 193, 259, 264
differences, sex 166–76
dildo *see* vibrator
dirty jokes 39, 326
discussion 139
  in marriage 104, 106, 110–11, 139, 233
diseases 367–73 *see also individual headings*
displacement 19, 427, 430
divorce 11, 85, 122–8
  passim, 130, 136–8, 142–9, 221, 310, 311, 380, 415, 427, 430
dominance
  female 56, 76, 106
  male 54, 119, 243
  in marriage 135
Dominica 171
douches 368
dreams, wet 40, 193, 321, 332, 411
dressing up 199, 212, 216, 376
drinking 53, 56, 111, 431
drugs 230, 239, 242, 251, 252, 258, 269, 293, 333, 403, 407, 431

dysfunction 201, 229, 383, 398, 404, 407

education 14, 70
  for marriage 137
  sex 8, 13, 36, 44, 45, 70, 80, 149, 230, 235, 240, 243, 244, 249, 250, 264, 292, 312–28, 407, 410
eggs 31, 161–2, 168, 247, 253, 254, 261, 265, 266, 267, 269, 270, 271
Egypt 20, 142
ejaculation 21, 38, 56, 67, 85, 151, 153, 182–3, 197, 202, 220, 232, 235, 236, 260, 261, 266, 268, 269, 330, 331, 364, 376, 385, 387, 391, 403
  control 202, 206, 211, 237
  female 193
  premature 141, 202, 204, 231, 236–8, 414
  retarded 202
engagement 69, 71, 87–97, 142
England 56, 71, 142, 387, 393
engyesis 89, 91
epididymis 152, 153, 401
episiotomy 231, 245, 300, 304, 398
erection 20, 26, 38, 66, 85, 151, 177, 181, 197, 201, 206, 220, 231, 235–42 *passim*, 269, 401–2, 403
  maintenance of 215, 236, 239, 269
erotic zones, female 188–9, 331
  male 188, 196
excretion 20–1, 28, 242
exhibitionism 382, 387–90
experimentation 43, 95, 123, 127, 128, 189, 201, 205, 214, 220, 362, 366, 382, 408

face 51–2
faithfulness 78, 340
fallopian tubes 160–1, 253, 259, 265–6, 269–71, 370, 386, 398
family 11, 12, 14, 16, 310–11, 340
  one-parent 11, 147, 148, 438–9
  planning 246, 264–6
fantasies 21, 28, 35, 36, 38, 39, 43, 48, 49, 81, 84, 98, 102, 122, 123, 203, 215–18, 232, 237, 242, 245, 289–90, 307, 316, 326, 331–7 *passim*, 366, 376, 382, 384, 393, 416, 432
fathers 24, 305, 392
  and daughters 26, 27, 32, 35, 36, 40, 94, 118–19, 375, 393–4
  and sons 26–7, 38, 48
fellatio 121, 198, 215, 241, 337, 362, 381, 382
femininity 26
fertility 31, 153, 248, 250, 252, 286, 291
fetishism 390–1
fiction, romantic 98, 103
Finland 71
flirting 79, 119, 122, 217, 332
flush, hot 415, 417
  sex 183
foetus 17, 166, 172, 280
foreplay 154–5, 165, 185–202, 215, 218, 219, 235, 237, 238, 239, 241, 245, 260, 273, 337, 380, 382, 387
foreskin 24, 152, 153, 154, 183, 321, 402
fostering 310
France 71, 79
French West Africa 71
friendship 60, 71
  in marriage 108, 119, 121, 135, 228, 410
Freud, Sigmund 15–16
frigidity 56, 179, 431

G-spot 158, 191–4, 205

games, sex 28, 245, 327
gender identity 24–7, 170–6, 392
  role 170, 172–6, 392
genes 168
genitals 12, 20–4, 27, 50, 120, 142, 196, 224, 227, 325, 389, 390, *see also individual headings*
  playing with 22, 84, 154, 165
Germany 56
girls, adolescent 30–7, 41–8, 61–70, 171, 337
  and boys 37, 41
  and contraception 248–9
  and fathers 26, 27, 32, 35, 36, 40, 393
  and homosexuality 359, 363–4
  and intercourse 32, 37, 45, 56, 57, 58, 64, 68–70, 81
  and masturbation 28, 35, 36, 43, 48, 49, 81, 329
  and mothers 26–7, 31, 32, 35, 36, 41, 48
  and parents 32, 41–2, 44
  and puberty 12, 28, 30–5, 167, 172
  and virginity 57
glans 151, 181, 197
glue-sniffing 333
gonorrhea 259, 268, 270, 271, 369–71
Gräfenberg, Ernst 191
grandchildren 129
growth 30, 31, 166
guilt 28, 30, 36, 38, 44, 45, 56, 59, 120, 124, 180, 203, 215, 223, 233, 234, 237, 242, 245, 248, 249, 283, 288, 291, 292, 316, 325, 330, 331, 333, 337, 344, 346, 357, 358, 375, 383–5

hair, facial 38, 152, 400
  body 31–2, 38, 59, 152, 400
  pubic 30–1, 157, 189, 400

hand-washing 36
handicapped 269, 407
health 180, 397–408, 416
heart disease 402, 404, 416
height 52
hepatitis 373
hermaphrodites 170–1
herpes 371–2
hobbies 104, 110
homogamy 73–4
homoxesuality 14, 21, 28, 38, 172, 247, 337; 340–2, 350, 359–66, 370, 373, 375
hormones, female 161–2, 172, 250, HRT 416
  male 150, 152, 171, 172
  sex 171–2
Hungary 142
hydrocele 401
hygiene 165, 367, 400
hymen 158, 163, 219, 220
hypospadias 269
hypothalamus 161, 171, 172, 239, 360
hysterectomy 334, 397, 399, 406

identity, sexual 170–6, 290
illegitimate children 60, 308
illness 89, 91, 108, 127, 128, 129, 143–4, 162, 166, 179, 229, 245, 397, 402–9
  mental 35, 56, 76, 108, 140, 143–4, 179, 233, 380, 407
  sex in 129, 397, 402–9
immaturity 88, 96–7, 122, 132, 355, 358, 378
impotence 56, 141, 229, 231, 232, 237, 239–40, 256, 269, 391, 404, 407, 411, 431
incest 392–4
India 71
infatuation 59
infection 190, 196, 259, 268, 272, 283, 367–73
  passim, 386, 387, 398, 399
infertility 265, 267–79

female 160, 265, 267, 270–1, 273–5
  male 153, 267–9, 275–7
inhibitions 60, 120, 125, 127, 201, 203–4, 215, 217, 232, 233, 243, 354, 358, 385, 408, 416, 417
insemination, artificial 269
intelligence 76, 167;
  tests 167, 168
interests 73–4, 80–1
intercourse 15, 21, 24, 27, 29, 31, 32, 41, 43, 45, 57, 58, 74, 113, 124, 128, 129, 137, 158, 177, 186, 199, 200–21, 224, 227, 228, 231, 237, 240–2, 245, 261, 262, 265, 294–7, 321, 324, 332, 333, 339, 344, 345, 382–4, 397, 402, 410, 411, 414, 417, 431
  difficulties in 229–46
  early 37, 64, 236, 416
  extramarital 122–5, 129, 180, 290, 332, 416, 426
    see also affairs
  pre- 56, 60, 61–70, 81, 84, 85
  frequency of 74, 76, 127–9, 178–9, 203, 218–19, 229, 272
  location of 215, 216, 218
  movement in 211–13, 218
  non-intercourse sex 383
  pain in 219, 245–6, 398–9
  positions in 205–13, 218, 245, 272–3, 294, 303, 400
  role reversal in 203
  time of 215–16
IVD 247, 257–9, 262, 264, 271, 283, 286, 400, 407

jealousy 96, 111, 124, 125, 130, 242, 431–2
Johnson, Virginia 180, 235, 272

Kinsey 56, 410, 411
kissing 37, 54, 60, 65–8, 81, 84, 187, 189, 196,

198–9, 213, 215, 220, 227
KY jelly 163, 190, 220, 237, 400

labia 157, 183, 334
language 204, 212, 218, 221, 227, 240
  body 54, 230
laparoscopy 253, 254, 259
latency stage 16, 27, 81, 313, 317
legs 49
lesbianism 37, 124, 246, 362, 376
lice, pubic 373
love 8, 13, 14, 19, 44, 52, 59, 60, 67, 79, 98–9, 102–5 *passim*, 124, 201, 221–8, 418–33
  at first sight 52–4
  being in 59, 99, 102, 430–1
  calf/puppy 102
lover role 104, 119–20

maintenance, of wife 123, 147
  of children 147
marriage 11, 12, 58, 71, 79, 80, 87, 96–7, 106–49, 340, 342, 344, 359, 414, 426, 432, 433
  bureaux 148
  children in 111, 127–9, 136, 221, 287–8, 321, 324, 352–3
  exclusivity of 121–3
  failure of 100, 137–49
  friendship in 108, 119, 121, 135, 228
  homosexuality in 366
  in name only 126–7
  non-consummation of 383
  phases of 127–30
  problems in 88, 96–7, 107–13; sexual 12, 84, 110, 123, 126, 127, 137–42, 229–46, 278, 426

roles in 118–20, 132,
134–5, 342
  romance in 103–5
  second 147, 310
  trial 94, 97
  types of 130–3
Marriage counsellors 108,
  140, 306, 363, 366
masculinity 84, 96, 106, 123,
  240, 294, 375
masochism 217, 382, 384–5
massage, sensual 113–17,
  223, 224, 227, 240
  parlours 377
mastectomy 404, 405–6
Mastero, William 180, 235,
  272
masturbation 19, 21, 22, 42,
  49, 98, 178, 201, 216,
  218, 227, 316, 328,
  329–38, 340, 342, 346,
  350, 380, 386, 391, 395,
  397, 410, 432
  female 20, 27, 28, 30,
    35–7, 48, 85, 165, 185,
    190–2, 196, 203, 215,
    220, 223, 243, 245, 267,
    329–33, 333–34, 366,
    384, 386, 388, 416
  male 24, 27, 28, 38, 81,
    154, 179, 180, 181, 197,
    202, 206, 212, 237, 241,
    268, 269, 326, 329–33,
    364, 376, 377, 384, 395,
    402, 411
  mutual 43, 84, 179, 224,
    234, 240, 247, 279, 297,
    362, 383
maturity 167, 344, 351–8
magazines 378; girlie 38–9,
  98, 326–7, 332
Mead, Margaret 15
men, and babies 118, 128,
  303, 306–7
  and foreplay 196–9,
    201–2
  and intercourse 56, 58–9,
    84, 180–3, 202, 203,
    218, 229, 231–2, 237
  and masturbation 179,
    329–38 passim, 384

and romance 104
and sex drive 48, 178,
  375, 411; problems
  236–42
and virginity 57
menarche 31
menopause 129, 157, 161,
  162, 164, 245, 249, 264,
  341, 368, 398, 399,
  415–16, 431, 432
  male 417
menstruation 31, 32, 35, 51,
  161–5, 227, 261, 282,
  334, 372, 387, 407
  premenstrual symptoms
    31, 108, 164, 251
miscarriage 259, 269, 280,
  293, 297, 397
mismatching 74, 76
mittelschmerz 161, 265
mongolism 283
monogamy, serial 123
morals 11, 52, 53, 61–2, 64,
  84, 339–50
mortality rates 166
mothers 288, 314, 352, 390,
  418
  and babies 17, 19–21,
    119, 305–6, 309, 418–21
  and daughters 26, 27, 31,
    32, 35, 36, 41, 48, 231,
    243, 288, 375
  and sons 24, 26–7, 40, 94,
    106, 108, 118, 126, 132,
    231, 242, 391, 392
  unmarried 308
mothering 118, 119, 120,
  127, 132
mucus method 247, 262
mumps orchitis 249

nagging 106, 108, 111
narcissism 360–1
neuroses 35, 36, 76, 395
nipples 30, 156–7, 183, 185,
  189, 192, 196, 213, 227,
  300, 303, 320, 371, 385
'no-go areas' 108, 110, 111,
  228, 325

Norway 56
NSU 371
nudity 24, 26, 28, 84, 337,
  388

odour, body 50–1
oedipal stage 26, 38, 48,
  321, 393, 423
offenders, sexual 395–6
old age 12, 185, 409–17
'one-night stands' 56, 79
oral sex 17, 84, 121, 157,
  198–9, 217, 227, 228,
  247, 272, 279, 297, 300,
  350, 370, 376, 381–3,
  397, 400
  stage 15–20, 382
  stimulation 191, 193–5,
    198–9
orgasm 20, 21, 200, 227,
  229, 231, 384, 386
  duration of 202–3
  female 24, 36, 37, 56,
    126, 141, 159, 164, 185,
    186, 190, 192–3, 196,
    202–5, 212, 215, 235,
    236, 243–5, 249, 252,
    261, 267, 273, 288, 294,
    300, 301, 303, 304, 324,
    328, 329, 330, 331, 333,
    334, 358, 386, 399, 403,
    407, 416
  male 38, 182–3, 197, 206,
    211, 333, 362, 382, 383;
    retarded 241–2
  simultaneous 228
overeating 17, 252
ovulation 31, 51, 157, 160,
  161, 164, 172, 247, 261,
  262, 265, 267, 269, 270,
  272, 304, 399
oxytocin 301

paedophilia 394–5
parenthood, preparation for
  287–8
parents 11, 12, 13, 14, 19,

22, 29, 32, 41–4, 64, 65, 69, 73, 78, 80, 86, 91–2, 94, 97, 102, 106, 119, 136, 147, 176, 178, 228, 236, 290, 292, 313, 346, 351–4, 363, 394, 396
  and morals 313, 345–50, 354
  and sex education 313, 317–28
  opposite-sex attachment 26, 29, 42, 44, 48, 72, 132, 352, 393, 423
  step- 148, 310–11
Parents Anonymous 306
peer groups 40, 42, 324
penetration 185, 201, 202, 205, 206, 212, 213, 236, 238, 239, 246, 272, 337
penis 16, 20, 21, 24, 38, 43, 150–4, 156–8, 165, 171, 177, 181–2, 186, 192, 197–9, 202–5 *passim*, 211, 219, 227, 232, 237–9, 241, 242, 246, 256, 260, 261, 268, 269, 272, 294, 318, 320, 321, 333, 362, 367, 368, 370, 371, 380, 387, 388, 398, 402
  blowing down 398
  size 39, 150–1, 155, 205, 215, 246, 249, 364, 377
perfume 50, 157, 165, 187
periods 31, 157, 162–5, 172, 261, 272, 279, 282, 293, 321, 399, 416
permissiveness 56, 347
perversions 15, 126, 328, 337, 380, 382–96
pets 325–6
petting 67, 187, 220
Peyronie's disease 402
phallic stage 16, 21–4, 382
pheromones 50–1, 230
phimosis 402
pill 248, 249, 250–2, 257, 262, 264, 271, 286, 293, 373
  male 252
  and health 250, 264

pituitary gland 161, 239, 250, 265, 270, 415
placenta 300
pornography 38–9, 98, 324, 377, 385, 395
possessiveness 130
post-coital contraception 262
pregnancy 31, 161, 162, 164–5, 205, 232, 249, 259, 284–307, 328, 339, 398, 407, 432
  fear of 59, 60, 129, 171, 231, 232, 242, 246, 249
  phantom (pseudo-cyesis) 292
  premarital/unwanted 11, 44, 61, 96, 125, 180, 249, 290–2
  preparation for 287–90, 305
  sex in 128, 294–7, 397
  positions 207–11
  test 293
priapism 401–2
professional help 64, 108, 111, 126, 137, 139–40, 228, 230, 234–5, 292, 327, 363, 366, 382, 392, 396, 433
prolapse 399
promiscuity 52, 56, 81, 95, 123, 292
prostaglandins 282, 297
prostate gland 150, 152–4, 182, 193
prostitution 14, 21, 35, 126, 199, 203, 217, 236, 342, 374–9, 385, 411
psychosexual medicine/ therapy 140, 234, 236, 239, 245, 297, 334, 366, 391
  'neutrality' 170, 171
  problems 64, 230, 291–2, 383
puberty 12, 16, 24, 28, 30–40, 167, 171, 172, 393

'quickie' 186, 216

race 14
rape 35, 43, 244, 246, 262, 394, 395, 439
rebellion 32, 37, 40, 41, 42, 44, 64, 65, 70, 78, 316, 362
rejection 44, 45, 95–6, 102, 179, 231
religion 8, 14, 54, 61, 62, 64, 69, 84, 230, 233, 242, 309, 340, 342, 347, 379, 380
remarriage 122, 145, 147–9
repression 15, 28, 36, 70, 178, 336
rhythm method 247, 261
rings 387
romance 79, 80, 85, 88, 98–105, 187, 221
rows 107–13, 227

sadism 24, 382, 385
sado-masochism 199, 381, 384–6
saliva 190, 220, 273
saunas 377
scabies 373
schizophrenia 35, 353
Schofield, Michael 65–70
scrotum 38, 150, 152, 154, 181–2, 212, 241, 255, 256, 333, 400
seduction, child 230
self-criticism/doubt 17, 29, 42, 45, 95
self-esteem 17, 95–6, 107, 123, 125, 149, 222, 414, 431
self-help 222, 233, 236–46, 392
self-image 222–7
self-love 8, 48, 98, 353, 423, 424, 431
semen 151, 153, 157, 182–3, 198, 227, 256, 260, 266–9 *passim*, 273, 297, 300, 321
separation 123, 130, 143
  temporary 94–5
sex drive 13, 42, 60, 74, 76,

INDEX

144, 149, 177, 178, 332, 397, 403, 407
   female 17, 177, 178, 231, 243, 249, 252, 291, 415
   male 48, 176, 411
sex organs 150–62 *see also individual headings*
sexlessness, female 27, 203, 218, 232
shame 20, 22, 31, 36, 59, 85, 145, 205, 230, 245, 291, 337, 357, 380, 410, 417
'shaping-up' 111–13
sheath *see* condom
shyness 43, 78, 85, 201, 232, 243
smacking 189, 381, 384
smoking 17, 53, 56–7, 239, 269
sons, and fathers 26–7, 38, 48
   and mothers 24, 26, 27, 40, 94, 106, 108, 118, 126, 132, 231, 242, 391, 392
spermicides 258, 259, 260
sperms 152, 153, 160, 161, 168, 169, 182, 250, 254, 256, 257, 261, 265–71 *passim*, 273, 321, 414
spots 36
sterilisation 232, 247, 249, 252–7
stillbirth 269
stripping 35, 43, 84
strokes 407–8
'stroking' 426–7, 432
sucking 17, 19, 67, 189, 198–9, 382
suicide 38, 44, 95, 125, 143, 363
sulking 108
suppressions 22, 28, 29, 35, 48, 98, 120, 230, 232, 236, 243, 245, 329, 375, 380
Sweden 71
'swinging' *see* wife-swapping
syphilis 370–1

taboos 60, 62, 164
talk 204, 227, 233 *see also* discussion; therapy
tampons 43, 158, 163, 220, 369
teenagers 8, 11, 12, 14, 40, 64, 65, 100, 423, 431 *see also* adolescence; boys; girls
temperature method 262
testes 38, 150, 152, 170, 171, 172, 181, 198, 212, 227, 249, 253, 255, 256, 268, 385, 400, 414, 415
testicular feminisation 172
testosterone 38, 150, 152, 171, 172, 245, 392, 414
therapy 108, 392
   psychosexual 140, 230, 234, 236, 239, 245, 297, 334, 366, 391
   sex 141–2, 234–6, 239, 244–6, 380, 434, 435
thrush/monilia 367–9, 404
togetherness 12, 129–30
   lack of 111, 125
toilet training 20–1
transsexualism 171, 392
transvestism 217, 333, 390, 391
trichomoniasis 369
troilism 124
Turner's syndrome 171
twins 270
tying up 217, 377

underwear 386
undressing 84, 187
upbringing 8, 13, 29, 80, 177–8, 200, 231, 233, 243, 345–52, 354–5, 357 *see also* education; parents
urethra 151–2, 165, 192, 205, 369, 370, 387, 398
urination 20, 192, 371, 372, 376, 400
   problems 20, 193, 371, 372
USA 56, 74, 142, 143, 148, 155, 180, 235, 289, 345, 371, 372, 387, 394, 399, 410, 411, 414
USSR 142
uterus 159–62, 183, 185, 192, 247, 250, 253, 257–9, 266, 267, 269, 270, 273, 282, 283, 304, 320, 392, 398–9

vacuum aspiration 282
vagina 31, 43, 128, 151, 155, 158–9, 160, 163, 165, 177, 183, 188, 190–3, 195, 196, 203, 205, 206, 211, 215, 220, 227, 232, 241, 242, 246, 257, 266, 267, 269, 272, 273, 288, 318, 320, 334, 358, 371, 380, 386, 392, 398, 415
   blowing into 386
   discharge 245, 367–70 *passim*
   jellies 289
   lubrication 20, 183, 190, 220, 231, 245, 246, 266, 273, 368, 398, 400
   objects in 386
vaginismus 158, 232, 246, 269, 398
varicocoele 268
vasectomy 253–7 *passim*, 267, 268, 435
VD 11, 60, 61, 67, 125, 180, 199, 242, 260, 271, 286, 315, 316, 328, 345, 366, 367, 369–73, 397
vibrators 196, 244, 246, 334, 376, 386, 414
virginity 45, 57, 60, 138, 220, 292
voice-breaking 38, 40, 392
voyeurism 39, 337, 382, 387–90
vulva 20, 35, 36, 43, 155, 157, 183, 190, 195, 329, 331, 334, 367, 369, 381

wife battering 106–7
wife-swapping 124–5
withdrawal method 247, 249, 260, 261

women *see also* mothers
   and babies 286–7, 300–1, 304–6
   and contraception 249–50
   and foreplay 187–96, 201, 202
   and intercourse 56, 58–9, 81, 137, 183–5, 202–3, 211–12, 218, 219, 229–31 *passim*, 374, 398–400, 416
   and masturbation 27, 30, 35–7, 165, 245, 329–31, 333, 334
   and perversions 384, 385
   and romance 103–5
   and sex drive 17, 178, 231, 249, 252, 291, 415; problems 236, 242–6
   unmarried 138
work 104, 110, 129
   women at 124